Lecture Notes in Computer Science 14026

Founding Editors

Gerhard Goos
Juris Hartmanis

The series Lecture Notes in Computer Science (LNCS), including its subseries Lecture Notes in Artificial Intelligence (LNAI) and Lecture Notes in Bioinformatics (LNBI), has established itself as a medium for the publication of new developments in computer science and information technology research, teaching, and education.

LNCS enjoys close cooperation with the computer science R & D community, the series counts many renowned academics among its volume editors and paper authors, and collaborates with prestigious societies. Its mission is to serve this international community by providing an invaluable service, mainly focused on the publication of conference and workshop proceedings and postproceedings. LNCS commenced publication in 1973.

Adela Coman · Simona Vasilache
Editors

Social Computing and Social Media

15th International Conference, SCSM 2023
Held as Part of the 25th HCI International Conference, HCII 2023
Copenhagen, Denmark, July 23–28, 2023
Proceedings, Part II

 Springer

Editors
Adela Coman
University of Bucharest
Bucharest, Romania

Simona Vasilache
University of Tsukuba
Tsukuba, Japan

ISSN 0302-9743   ISSN 1611-3349 (electronic)
Lecture Notes in Computer Science
ISBN 978-3-031-35926-2   ISBN 978-3-031-35927-9 (eBook)
https://doi.org/10.1007/978-3-031-35927-9

This Springer imprint is published by the registered company Springer Nature Switzerland AG
The registered company address is: Gewerbestrasse 11, 6330 Cham, Switzerland

Foreword

Human-computer interaction (HCI) is acquiring an ever-increasing scientific and industrial importance, as well as having more impact on people's everyday lives, as an ever-growing number of human activities are progressively moving from the physical to the digital world. This process, which has been ongoing for some time now, was further accelerated during the acute period of the COVID-19 pandemic. The HCI International (HCII) conference series, held annually, aims to respond to the compelling need to advance the exchange of knowledge and research and development efforts on the human aspects of design and use of computing systems.

The 25th International Conference on Human-Computer Interaction, HCI International 2023 (HCII 2023), was held in the emerging post-pandemic era as a 'hybrid' event at the AC Bella Sky Hotel and Bella Center, Copenhagen, Denmark, during July 23–28, 2023. It incorporated the 21 thematic areas and affiliated conferences listed below.

A total of 7472 individuals from academia, research institutes, industry, and government agencies from 85 countries submitted contributions, and 1578 papers and 396 posters were included in the volumes of the proceedings that were published just before the start of the conference, these are listed below. The contributions thoroughly cover the entire field of human-computer interaction, addressing major advances in knowledge and effective use of computers in a variety of application areas. These papers provide academics, researchers, engineers, scientists, practitioners and students with state-of-the-art information on the most recent advances in HCI.

The HCI International (HCII) conference also offers the option of presenting 'Late Breaking Work', and this applies both for papers and posters, with corresponding volumes of proceedings that will be published after the conference. Full papers will be included in the 'HCII 2023 - Late Breaking Work - Papers' volumes of the proceedings to be published in the Springer LNCS series, while 'Poster Extended Abstracts' will be included as short research papers in the 'HCII 2023 - Late Breaking Work - Posters' volumes to be published in the Springer CCIS series.

I would like to thank the Program Board Chairs and the members of the Program Boards of all thematic areas and affiliated conferences for their contribution towards the high scientific quality and overall success of the HCI International 2023 conference. Their manifold support in terms of paper reviewing (single-blind review process, with a minimum of two reviews per submission), session organization and their willingness to act as goodwill ambassadors for the conference is most highly appreciated.

This conference would not have been possible without the continuous and unwavering support and advice of Gavriel Salvendy, founder, General Chair Emeritus, and Scientific Advisor. For his outstanding efforts, I would like to express my sincere appreciation to Abbas Moallem, Communications Chair and Editor of HCI International News.

July 2023   Constantine Stephanidis

HCI International 2023 Thematic Areas and Affiliated Conferences

Thematic Areas

- HCI: Human-Computer Interaction
- HIMI: Human Interface and the Management of Information

Affiliated Conferences

- EPCE: 20th International Conference on Engineering Psychology and Cognitive Ergonomics
- AC: 17th International Conference on Augmented Cognition
- UAHCI: 17th International Conference on Universal Access in Human-Computer Interaction
- CCD: 15th International Conference on Cross-Cultural Design
- SCSM: 15th International Conference on Social Computing and Social Media
- VAMR: 15th International Conference on Virtual, Augmented and Mixed Reality
- DHM: 14th International Conference on Digital Human Modeling and Applications in Health, Safety, Ergonomics and Risk Management
- DUXU: 12th International Conference on Design, User Experience and Usability
- C&C: 11th International Conference on Culture and Computing
- DAPI: 11th International Conference on Distributed, Ambient and Pervasive Interactions
- HCIBGO: 10th International Conference on HCI in Business, Government and Organizations
- LCT: 10th International Conference on Learning and Collaboration Technologies
- ITAP: 9th International Conference on Human Aspects of IT for the Aged Population
- AIS: 5th International Conference on Adaptive Instructional Systems
- HCI-CPT: 5th International Conference on HCI for Cybersecurity, Privacy and Trust
- HCI-Games: 5th International Conference on HCI in Games
- MobiTAS: 5th International Conference on HCI in Mobility, Transport and Automotive Systems
- AI-HCI: 4th International Conference on Artificial Intelligence in HCI
- MOBILE: 4th International Conference on Design, Operation and Evaluation of Mobile Communications

List of Conference Proceedings Volumes Appearing Before the Conference

47. CCIS 1836, HCI International 2023 Posters - Part V, edited by Constantine Stephanidis, Margherita Antona, Stavroula Ntoa and Gavriel Salvendy

https://2023.hci.international/proceedings

Preface

The 15th International Conference on Social Computing and Social Media (SCSM 2023) was an affiliated conference of the HCI International (HCII) conference. The conference provided an established international forum for the exchange and dissemination of scientific information related to social computing and social media, addressing a broad spectrum of issues expanding our understanding of current and future issues in these areas. The conference welcomed qualitative and quantitative research papers on a diverse range of topics related to the design, development, assessment, use, and impact of social media.

A considerable number of papers focused on presenting advancements and recent developments in online communities and social media, discussing machine learning, artificial intelligence and algorithmic approaches for understanding social interactions, user behavior, as well as language and communication. Acknowledging and embracing cultural diversity in the field, several works focused on exploring cultural diversity and cultural influences in the design of social computing, fostering the design of technologies that are culturally sensitive and inclusive. Furthermore, a theme that emerged pertains to digital transformation in business and industry 4.0, highlighting the role and the importance of social computing to facilitate connectivity, communication, and collaboration, allowing organizations to adapt and remain competitive in the rapidly evolving digital landscape of Industry 4.0. An additional topic that is addressed this year is the prominence of SCSM in understanding consumer behavior, allowing businesses to tailor their marketing strategies, product and service development, and customer experience to address the needs and preferences of their target audience. Another field that can be revolutionized by social computing is that of learning and education, with contributions discussing new avenues for collaboration, knowledge sharing, and interactive learning experiences. Moreover, many papers targeted the topic of social computing for well-being and inclusion, presenting advancements that promote mental health, support individuals with developmental and learning disorders, and enhance rehabilitation efforts. In the health domain, discussions focused on the role of social computing during the pandemic and post-pandemic era. Finally, a significant number of papers elaborated on innovations in the design and evaluation of social computing platforms to create user-centric and socially meaningful digital spaces that enhance communication, collaboration, and information sharing.

Two volumes of the HCII 2023 proceedings are dedicated to this year's edition of the SCSM conference. The first volume focuses on topics related to developments in Online Communities and Social Media, SCSM in multi-cultural contexts, digital transformation in business and Industry 4.0 through Social Computing, as well as consumer behavior in SCSM. The second volume focuses on topics related to Social Computing in learning and education, Social Computing for well-being and inclusion, Social Computing in the pandemic and post-pandemic era, as well as advancements in the design and evaluation of Social Computing platforms.

The papers in these volumes were included for publication after a minimum of two single-blind reviews from the members of the SCSM Program Board or, in some cases, from members of the Program Boards of other affiliated conferences. We would like to thank all of them for their invaluable contribution, support, and efforts.

July 2023   Adela Coman
                                                            Simona Vasilache

15th International Conference on Social Computing and Social Media (SCSM 2023)

Program Board Chairs: **Adela Coman,** *University of Bucharest, Romania,* and **Simona Vasilache,** *University of Tsukuba, Japan*

Program Board:

- Francisco Alvarez-Rodríguez, *Universidad Autónoma de Aguascalientes, Mexico*
- Andria Andriuzzi, *Université Jean Monnet, France*
- Karine Berthelot-Guiet, *Sorbonne University, France*
- James Braman, *Community College of Baltimore County, USA*
- Adheesh Budree, *University of Cape Town, South Africa*
- Tina Gruber-Mücke, *Anton Bruckner Private University, Austria*
- Hung-Hsuan Huang, *University of Fukuchiyama, Japan*
- Ajrina Hysaj, *University of Wollongong in Dubai, United Arab Emirates*
- Ayaka Ito, *Reitaku University, Japan*
- Carsten Kleiner, *University of Applied Sciences & Arts Hannover, Germany*
- Jeannie S. Lee, *Singapore Institute of Technology (SIT), Singapore*
- Gabriele Meiselwitz, *Towson University, USA*
- Ana Isabel Molina Díaz, *University of Castilla-La Mancha, Spain*
- Takashi Namatame, *Chuo University, Japan*
- Hoang D. Nguyen, *University College Cork, Ireland*
- Kohei Otake, *Tokai University, Japan*
- Daniela Quiñones, *Pontificia Universidad Católica de Valparaíso, Chile*
- Jürgen Rösch, *Bauhaus University, Weimar, Germany*
- Margarida Romero, *Université Côte d'Azur, France*
- Virginica Rusu, *Universidad de Playa Ancha, Chile*
- Cristian Rusu, *Pontificia Universidad Católica de Valparaíso, Chile*
- Christian W. Scheiner, *Universität zu Lübeck, Germany*
- Tomislav Stipancic, *University of Zagreb, Croatia*
- Yuanqiong Wang, *Towson University, USA*

The full list with the Program Board Chairs and the members of the Program Boards of all thematic areas and affiliated conferences of HCII2023 is available online at:

http://www.hci.international/board-members-2023.php

HCI International 2024 Conference

The 26th International Conference on Human-Computer Interaction, HCI International 2024, will be held jointly with the affiliated conferences at the Washington Hilton Hotel, Washington, DC, USA, June 29 – July 4, 2024. It will cover a broad spectrum of themes related to Human-Computer Interaction, including theoretical issues, methods, tools, processes, and case studies in HCI design, as well as novel interaction techniques, interfaces, and applications. The proceedings will be published by Springer. More information will be made available on the conference website: http://2024.hci.international/.

General Chair
Prof. Constantine Stephanidis
University of Crete and ICS-FORTH
Heraklion, Crete, Greece
Email: general_chair@hcii2024.org

https://2024.hci.international/

Contents – Part II

Social Computing for Well-Being and Inclusion

Contents – Part I

Social Computing and Social Media in Multi-cultural Contexts

**Digital Transformation in Business and Industry 4.0 Through Social
Computing**

Consumer Behavior in Social Computing and Social Media

Social Computing in Learning
in Education

Spinning (Digital) Stories in STEM

Pranit Anand[✉]

University of New South Wales, Sydney, NSW, Australia
pranit.anand@unsw.edu.au

Abstract. Stories are inherently part of human nature. Its one of the most natural ways in which we communicate and continue to used it in various informal settings. Unfortunately the use of storytelling does not seem to have made the transition to contemporary learning and teaching settings, likely due to the massification of education and familiarity or lack of on the part of the educators.

A novel storytelling assessment was implemented with two higher education STEM courses at two different universities in Australia. A mix methods case approach using current and former students' perceptions about their experiences was used to evaluate its appropriateness through its influence on student engage, transferable skills and academic integrity. Teaching staff were also interviewed about their experiences with this mode of assessment.

Results indicate storytelling implemented through digital technologies is relevant for contemporary education settings and has a positive influence of students learning experiences. Students indicated that they felt more engaged with their learning and the teaching staff felt a lot less concerned about academic integrity issues.

This paper will discuss details about the 'Digital Storybook' assessment including the evaluation methodology and results. It will be of interest to other educators interested in diversifying their assessment approaches in higher education STEM disciplines.

Keywords: Student Engagement · STEM Assessment · Stories

1 Narratives and Storytelling

Stories are inherently part of human nature. For most people it's how we started out in our learning journeys as young people. Stories allow shared experiences to be passed on from generations to generations and therefore is contextualised by the storyteller as well as the receiver of the stories [1]. While storytelling is recognised as an appropriate knowledge sharing methodology within informal settings, it has lost its appeal within more formal settings such as education environments [2]. Questions around validity and objectivity are often associated with objections towards the use of storytelling within educational environments [3]. Massification of education, especially higher education may also attribute towards the use of more standardised and inflexible methodologies of assessment. This tends to be particularly the case within various Science, Technology, Engineering and Mathematical (STEM) disciplines, where some of the more identifiable

A. Coman and S. Vasilache (Eds.): HCII 2023, LNCS 14026, pp. 3–11, 2023.
https://doi.org/10.1007/978-3-031-35927-9_1

forms of assessments such as examinations, reports and presentations are common. Arguments such as 'anybody can spin a story' is frequently used to justify not using it to assess students' knowledge, skills and attitudes.

Historical and commonly used assessment practices often continue to be accepted without much validation. Most assessment practices using by higher education academics are based in the types of assessments they themselves have experienced themselves [4]. Noting that, for good or bad, many of these assessments were experienced by many academics 20 to 30 years prior, and even though many thinking and research around effective assessment approaches and validity has improved, the assessment practices tend to persist [5]. Unfortunately when new forms of assessments are introduced, there is an expectation for these to meet the standards of the old forms of assessments, even though those may not have gone through relevant validations in the first instance [6].

While there are pockets of innovations around assessments approaches, these sadly are few and far between [7, 8]. As an innovative solution, storytelling would be one of the easiest to implement due to the inherent tendency for most humans towards storytelling [2, 9, 10]. However, the lack of ability of the educators in using storytelling for both knowledge sharing as well as assessment approaches may also explain its relative underuse [11].

When used appropriately, storytelling can be a very powerful methodology for knowledge sharing, and due to the 'stories' being contextualised for the storyteller and the receiver, is much more meaningful and authentic. Storytelling therefore can help achieve a lot more than just help students construct knowledge within their disciplines [7, 9, 10]. Attitudes towards work and life more generally, confidence to persevere, and resilience can often develop effectively through engaging 'stories'.

2   Digital Storytelling in STEM

A novel assessment using 'Digital Storybook' was implement at two different universities' programs. Both implementations however were within STEM disciplines, primarily around information technologies and computer sciences, disciplines often least likely to embed storytelling [7]. Both implementations aimed to improve student engagement, influence short and long term attuites towards students' studies and work, and ensure longer term student success.

In the first instance students studying a first-year general introduction to computer science course were required to create a digital storybook to explain the area of work they wish to pursue, types of technologies and skills needed within that area, and how they will go about acquiring all those skills. Students were encouraged and allowed to use any technology tools they wished to use for this this and were also allowed to structure their digital storybook according to their own inclinations. They were also required to explore emerging technologies likely to impact their future work and provide arguments about how they would incorporate these into their work. While many of these were speculative, students often engaged with this aspect in a very reflexive way.

Similarly for an advanced Master in Robotics course, students were required to create a 'Digital Storybook' to document their reflections on various coding experiments they conducted to control their allocated robots. Each student was provided with a programable robot, and they were required to document ion their 'Digital Storybook' their various experiments with different algorithms with these robots. Students also were able to use any available tools, approaches and methods freely available on the Internet for their experiments and include these in their 'Digital Storybooks'. Once again, students were allowed to apply their own flare to these 'storybooks'.

3   Methodology

As higher educations institutions come out of the various COVID-19 related emergency teaching and learning response, there is rightly a renewed focus of student engagement [12]. While it can be difficult to gain objective data about students engagement and learning outcomes from learning interventions, students' perceptions about their learning can be used to get a good idea about the impact of learning interventions on their learning [12–15]. Similarly teaching staff who are at the forefront of implementing these learning interventions can also provide their own experiences and how they felt the students responded to them, especially in comparisons with any other forms of assessments used previously. Even though teaching staff, especially the tutors, are at the forefront for the teaching experiences, they are often ignored in many student engagement and learning experience studies.

A case study methodology [16], involving mixed method data collection was used to explore the students and staff experiences with 'digital storytelling', as well as short- and long-term influence on students' study behaviours and their motivations to learn within the courses, and beyond. Anonymous online surveys were used while the students were 'in-flight' undertaking this assessment task, and again once they had completed the task. The tutoring staff involved in marking this task provided feedback about their experiences through a semi-structured focus group interview that explored some of the themes emerging from the student survey responses. Another anonymous online survey was again conducted once the students had completed their studies and progressed towards their careers and/or further studies. The teaching staff involved in teaching these cohorts of students were also interviewed about their experiences with the 'digital storybook'.

4   Results/Discussions

The results from the various data collected were framed within three themes. While many of these themes may well be further categorised, we felt that for the purposes of understanding the impact of storytelling on students learning these three themes for sufficient.

4.1   Student Engagement

Although students engagement can be difficult to define, and then measure, often if students feel that they enjoyed a learning activities and if they are prepared to recommend that to other students it is more likely than not that they felt engaged with their learning.

Despite most students not being familiar with making videos (Fig. 1), majority of the students that completed the survey indicated that they were satisfied with the final product (Fig. 2).

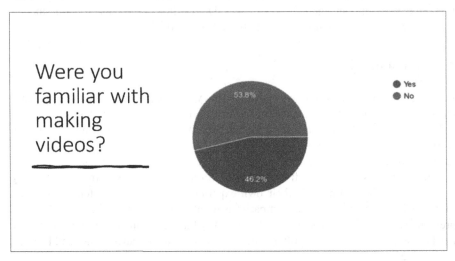

Fig. 1. Familiarity with making videos

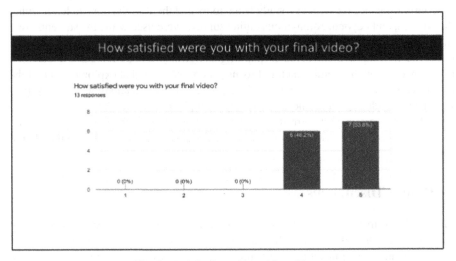

Fig. 2. Satisfaction with making videos

Similarly, majority of the students indicated that they had an enjoyable experience creating the videos (Fig. 3) and they were happy with the final mark that they received for their videos (Fig. 4).

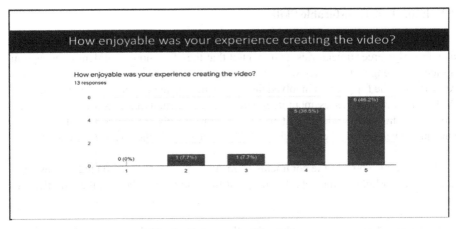

Fig. 3. Enjoyment making videos

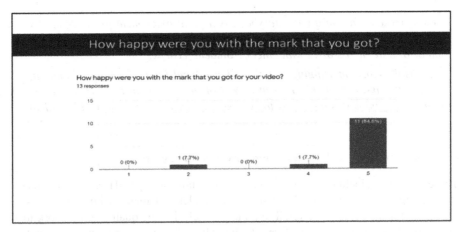

Fig. 4. Happy with the grading

While some students were skeptical about 'Digital Storybook' as assessment, almost all students who participated in the study indicated that they preferred this form of assessment over others they did as part of their studies. Most students preferred doing a digital storybook than doing more traditional reports, as indicated in the following chart:

Similarly, the tutoring staff also indicated that they felt that the quality of the work that was submitted was better than other, particularly written forms, of assessments.

4.2   Impact on Transferable Skills

Longer term, students who had progressed through their studies, and many who were now in early career trajectories, commented that they felt more confident to engage in difficult challenges while they were at university as they could see that all assessments, regardless of the form, often involved them reflecting on their own learning experiences. As for this individual assessment item they also commented that they felt this approach would benefit more students if it was used more widely in higher education. Many students indicated that they tend to use storytelling approaches within their workplace settings.

For example some of the comments from students who had completed this task and are now in workplaces indicate that they felt this had helped them in their studies can careers.

"It made me think of different aspects of my study field and what digital skills i require earlier. Later on, i focused to enhance and develop these skills." Student feedback

"I still reckon that the digital storybook is a great assessment for students. By doing this assessment, students can not only treasure their memories in a video, but also share their stories with others." Student feedback

"It was the most entertaining task that I have done! I actually enjoyed doing it, most of the assessments given us at UoW College were reports to write and the digital story book was a fun way to express what we know and learned." Student feedback

4.3   Concerns Around Academic Integrity and Plagiarism

The teaching staff, including the tutors and marking staff participated in a semi-structured focus group interview conducted after they had completed all their teaching and finalised the marks for the semester. Overall, the markers felt that the quality of the work that the students had submitted was of very high quality. They were very impressed by the diversity of responses that they received and because of this they found it easier to remain focused on the task of marking, and further they felt each assessment received their full attention as opposed to some marker feeling bored marking exactly the same type of assessment over and over again.

The tutors further noted that they had far less concerns around unethical behaviour such as plagiarism from students, likely because, as students had commented, it was an assessment that they "wanted to do" [17, 18] (Fig. 5).

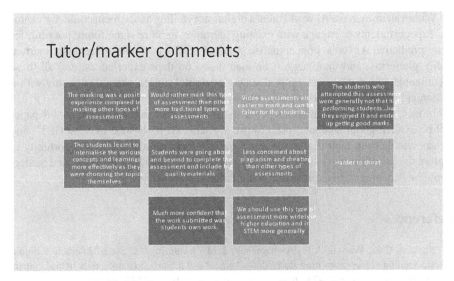

Fig. 5. Comments from tutors regarding plagiarism

5 Conclusion

Measuring student engagement and motivations to learning can be difficult to measure objectively [14]. Using students' perceptions [19] about their learning are a powerful way to understand the impact of learning interventions on their learning and learning behaviours. While discussions about how to improve student engagement in higher education continues, especially since the downturn of it due to COVID-19 related responses, storytelling can be a provide the tools for educators to re-engage students in meaningful ways. Storytelling and digital storytelling are knowledge sharing tools that has existed for a long time, and as this paper has indicated it is possible to apply them in more contemporary settings. Since each student composes their 'stories' in their own way and presents it in a way that is authentic to them individually, they tend to be more engaged with this form of assessment than many other types of assessments [12].

While this study was done prior to the various discussions about the impact of AI tools such as ChatGPT on higher education and especially assessments, the approaches used in digital storytelling assessments and the results of this study indicate that this form of assessment would enable students to continue to use these AI tools within their learning and get help with their assessment in an ethical way. Many assessment in higher education often focus on expecting students to write significant pieces of text the is based on existing ideas and knowledge domains [6]. As we move out of the various COVID-19 related emergency teaching and learning responses, it is clear that there much more of an appetite to explore more appropriate assessment regimes that prepares students for the jobs of the future [20]. This will require a shift of expecting students to produce /versions' of what is already known, towards suggesting ideas that will be useful in an evolving world of work.

Within an immersive AI world then, a digital storytelling assessment could, for example, expect students to engage with existing literature, explore some future possibilities using predictive AI tools, conceptualise some of these ideas within immersive virtual reality platforms, and then suggest an idea based on their experiences, and all these documented within their personalised, engaging digital stories, sharable not only within academia but with potential employers as well.

In fact, future implementations of the assessment approach discussed in this paper will be explicit about students' need to use available AI tools such as 'ChatGPT', and incorporate them in their digital stories. Similarly there now also exists opportunity to explore the use of immersive virtual reality platforms for 'meta' storytelling, and readers would be encouraged to explore that within their own settings.

References

1. Shelton, C.C., Warren, A.E., Archambault, L.M.: Exploring the use of interactive digital storytelling video: promoting student engagement and learning in a university hybrid course. TechTrends **60**(5), 465–474 (2016). https://doi.org/10.1007/s11528-016-0082-z
2. Cardiff, S.: Critical and creative reflective inquiry: surfacing narratives to enable learning and inform action. Educ. Action Res. **20**(4), 605–622 (2012)
3. Wood, L.: Values-based self-reflective action research for promoting gender equality: some unexpected lessons. Perspect. Educ. **32**(2), 37–53 (2014)
4. Dawson, P., et al.: Assessment might dictate the curriculum, but what dictates assessment? Teach. Learn. Inquiry ISSOTL J. **1**(1), 107–111 (2013)
5. Boud, D.: Reframing Assessment as If Learning were Important, pp. 14–26. Routledge, Taylor & Francis Group (2007)
6. Bearman, M., et al.: How university teachers design assessments: a cross-disciplinary study. High. Educ. **74**(1), 49–64 (2016). https://doi.org/10.1007/s10734-016-0027-7
7. Anand, P.: Using a digital storybook as assessment for learning to motivate students in an enabling and pathways to university program. Int. J. Innov. Res. Educ. Sci. **7**(5), 2319–5219 (2020)
8. Bryan, C., Clegg, K.: Innovative Assessment in Higher Education. Routledge, London (2006)
9. Price, K.: Aboriginal and Torres Strait Islander Education: An Introduction for the Teaching Profession, (Ed. by, K. Price). Cambridge University Press, Port Melbourne (2012)
10. McDrury, J.: Learning Through Storytelling in Higher Education: Using Reflection & Experience to Improve Learning (Ed. by, M. Alterio). Kogan Page, London (2003)
11. Richardson, D., et al.: Measuring narrative engagement: the heart tells the story. BioRxiv (2018)
12. Arsenis, P., Flores, M., Petropoulou, D.: Enhancing graduate employability skills and student engagement through group video assessment. Assess. Eval. High. Educ. **47**(2), 245–258 (2022)
13. Bonafini, F.C., et al.: How much does student engagement with videos and forums in a MOOC affect their achievement? Online Learn. (Newburyport, Mass.) **21**(4), 223 (2017)
14. Deslauriers, L., et al.: Measuring actual learning versus feeling of learning in response to being actively engaged in the classroom, 201821936 (2019)
15. du Rocher, A.R.: Active learning strategies and academic self-efficacy relate to both attentional control and attitudes towards plagiarism. Act. Learn. High. Educ. **21**(3), 203–216 (2020)
16. Yin, R.K., Campbell, D.T.: Case Study Research and Applications: Design and Methods, 6th edn. SAGE Publications, Inc., Thousand Oaks (2018)

17. Bretag, T.: A Research Agenda for Academic Integrity. Elgar Research Agendas. Edward Elgar Publishing, Cheltenham (2020)
18. Ellery, K.: Undergraduate plagiarism: a pedagogical perspective. Assess. Eval. High. Educ. **33**(5), 507–516 (2008)
19. Campbell, J., et al.: Students' perceptions of teaching and learning: the influence of students' approaches to learning and teachers' approaches to teaching. Teach. Teach. **7**(2), 173–187 (2001)
20. OECD: The Future of Education and Skills: Education 2030, Paris (2018)

Flexible Formal Specifications to Design Robust Technology-Enhanced Learning Applications

Juan Felipe Calderon[1]([⊠]) [iD] and Luis A. Rojas[2] [iD]

[1] Facultad de Ingeniería, Universidad Andrés Bello, Quillota, 980 Viña del Mar, Chile
juan.calderon@unab.cl
[2] Facultad de Ciencias Empresariales, Departamento de Ciencias de la Computación y
Tecnologías de la Información, Universidad del Bío-Bío, Chillán, Chile
lurojas@ubiobio.cl

Abstract. In real-time systems with changes in specifications, resources status, and ambient conditions, the computational support requires adapting to new conditions to satisfy the goals defined for those applications. Technology-enhanced learning applications (TEL) can be formalized by Educational Modelling Languages (EML), which provides a mechanism to design, deploy, and execute learning activities providing pedagogical flexibility. However, this flexibility is focused on design time and not in execution. Consequently, compliance satisfaction is a challenge when flexibility in workflows is provided. In addition, deadlock-freeness and reachability are critical properties in learning design execution of applications because learning objectives must be achieved by students without avoidable impediments provided by the execution of learning applications and their corresponding technical infrastructure. Currently, to provide flexibility to learning design scenarios, real-time flexibility and real-time compliance cannot be balanced since the improvement of flexibility mechanism affects compliance assessment, and vice-versa. The aim of this work is to explore real-time flexibility features in a workflow specification, supporting deadlock-freeness and reachability as compliance parameters during application in learning design scenarios. An extension of Petri-Net formalism was developed as a workflow specification. To validate this approach, a learning scenario with a set of test cases were formulated to define pedagogical and validation constraints. Results show that a learning scenario involving changes to the run-time can be successfully created, deployed, and executed. These changes can be based on properties that are intrinsic to the learning scenario, as well as on others that are related to the proposed workflow specification base Petri-net.

Keywords: flexible workflow · learning design · petri-net · model-checking

Supplementary Information The online version contains supplementary material available at https://doi.org/10.1007/978-3-031-35927-9_2.

1 Introduction

Real-time systems and applications are conditioned to heterogeneous hardware stake-holders, ambient factors, and subjacent processes. Consequently, these systems may require adapting to the new working conditions to satisfy, complete or partially, pre-defined goals [1]. In this line, Technology-enhanced learning (TEL) applications are real-time applications: they are deployed on portable and interoperable devices; they are designed for a wide technology-level range of users; they are ambient-pervasive accord-ing to indoor and/or outdoor settings; and their aim is to facilitate how people learn, according to pre-defined learning results. This complexity must be tackled by an ade-quate heterogeneity management to a fulfilment of the expected learning results by the targeted users, avoiding overloading them. In this line, heterogeneity management can be supported by formalisms to provide mechanisms of runtime verification and validation. In TEL field, a relevant and current concept is Learning Design, as an approach to provide learning technological applications with a correct pedagogical design [2–4].Currently, there are several learning design tools focused on content delivery, students' assessment, pedagogical planning, and authoring [5, 6] Particularly regarding to pedagogical plan-ning and authoring, heterogeneity management must be aligned to how Learning Design is formally represented [7, 8]. Educational Modelling Languages (EML) [9] provides for-malisms to Learning Design approach. Any EML implementation must provide not only formalization, but pedagogical flexibility, personalization, interoperability, sustainabil-ity, and reusability. Most-known EML implementation is IMS-LD [10], an XML-based language for TEL applications formalization providing a domain-specific metamodel with three complexity levels:

- Level A – definition of core entities: pedagogical method, plays, acts, roles, learning activities, environment setting and status, etc.
- Level B – monitoring over level A status.
- Level C – notifications over level B, related to monitoring process in that level.

As seen, IMS-LD level B This level provides mechanisms to create more heteroge-nous and complex TEL applications using state variables, pre-defined properties, and flexibility conditions [11]. Then, TEL applications can be created with a flexible learning flow, i.e., with a sequence of activities and tasks to achieve learning results, introduc-ing new tasks, rules, or pedagogical resources. Therefore, all possible modifications in learning flow must be defined as a pool, before runtime execution with students, with-out real-time interaction by a user (e.g., lecturer or teacher). To solve these issues, [12] propose an architecture to orchestrate external software components into an IMS-LD implementation using human or automatic agents (i.e., a virtual teacher), as media-tors. Other approaches to solve flexibility issues are related to how provide an adequate learning flow to improve learning [13], how flexibility can be implemented in constraints and variable geolocations and places (e.g., [14]) and flexibility in authoring when task of learning flow is designed (e.g., [15]). These approaches extend IMS-LD, providing events and exception support, creation and insertion of new tasks and distributed data exchange, but all of them pre-defined. Therefore, an unexplored issue is how an EML formalism (e.g., IMS-LD) can specify flexible Learning Designs, considering hetero-geneity management and real-time supporting on pedagogical planning changes [7]. As seen, TEL applications are limited to solve issues in a design stage, because flexibility is provided by a pool of rules described by the corresponding EML implementation.

Related to heterogeneity management, an issue is how variated and spare components and data resources support a right learning results achievement by learners. As seen, [12] focuses on flexible orchestration to satisfying complex requirements in collaborative learning, using some distributed components and resources to satisfy pedagogical requirements. This approach uses IMS-LD as specification formalism, extending it using service choreography with external resources to provide adaptation in content presentation to learners. Its aim is to provide robustness features related to group formation and external resources, but there is not flexibility in task descriptions or exception handling.

1.1 Workflows and EML

The EML formalisms may be considered as an instance of workflow concept. A workflow is composed by a sequence of steps, where certain tasks are carried out using specific resources, to satisfy pre-defined goals [16] in a wide range of business domains [17]. Workflow executions are supported by its specification (i.e., a formal language), and an operative infrastructure over workflow management systems (WfMS). Previous research has looked at introducing changes without having to restart the entire system. These approaches are called flexible workflows [18]. Flexibility in this type of workflow can operate in three ways. First, the decision making is delayed when faced with an event (e.g., specifying a spot in the workflow definition to be filled, marked by a language sentence). Second, new tasks can be added or changed to build the workflow sequence immediately, both for current and future executions. Finally, the current model is ignored by skipping tasks and/or violating restrictions that were in place with the previous tasks and running sequence [19].

As aforementioned, TEL applications may need flexibility and heterogeneity management in their operation. Regarding heterogeneity, a TEL application can be deployed over various kind of systems: cloud servers, mobile devices, and recently, IoT devices [20]. Another method is to make nodes available for playing the role of both data and control servers, as well as executors of the workflow. This allows distributed control of the process, in addition to the migration of the execution of processes between nodes, enabling runtime flexibility [21]. The advantage of these systems is the autonomy they can provide each node for decision making. However, this autonomy can result in potential problems with syncing, reachability of all possible states in workflow, possible locks in tasks and resources access given the way they are set up as a distributed system, and temporal availability of resources [22].

1.2 Execution Control and Rules

In any TEL application specification, the mechanism of execution control needs to be defined. First, transition between tasks must be defined, generally embedded into a sequence of tasks. Then, traceability between technical requirements and expected learning results must be defined. This traceability is specified by rules, statements that define or constrain some aspects of a certain problem. Precisely, it is intended to assert domain structure to control the behavior of the learning flow. Examples of this kind of rules are: "each student must achieve a minimum score in a task to develop a next task"; "every student must work in a group". Rules-based approach distinguishes between definitions, facts, and formal rules, such as constraints, derivation, or reaction rules [23]. These rules must be associated to expected learning results, because a traceability between pedagogical and technical requirements it is needed to get success in any TEL application. An issue in this traceability is how rules are formally described in a workflow specification language. If the rules are explicit, then the way the rules are incorporated in the definition will depend on the language, in which the learning design is defined if this is modelled by a workflow specification, and how is this specification is adopted by designers and instructors [5].On the other hand, when rules are implicit, these can be deduced from other elements in the specification, and it is not explicitly coded in the specification. This fact can be illustrated using the analogy with the process of putting on shoes and socks: a first step is to put on the socks, followed by the shoes; then, based on this sequence, the deduced rule is that the socks must be covered by the shoe. However, a rules deduction is not useful because it inhibits verification and validation processes with not clear sequence reference parameters.

1.3   Verification and Validation of Flexibility in Learning Designs

Flexibility enables to add new tasks to workflows, according to the state of resources, ambient, and other factors. Nonetheless, flexibility may add other issue: every change within the workflows should be validated against a set of goals and requirements [24]. Regarding TEL applications, compliance in flexibility and goals satisfaction are balanced depending on the context where the application is deployed and executed. This is needed to determine whether the learning results can be still fulfilled before making any kind of modification to guarantee the robustness of the TEL application. Then, specification flexibility and its verification in real time may not be trivial, depending on how the learning flow is represented. An issue is how to verify if changes in its specification are internally consistent with their other element in the same specification [22]. If these changes are only in the sequence of tasks, this process can be automated. On the other hand, this activity is manual, if there is a redefinition of tasks which requires time and effort. Therefore, a manual redefinition decreases performance of workflow execution [24]. From a technical point of view, for TEL applications verification process is critical with respect to how non-functional requirements are defined. A right definition has an impact in the whole performance in execution time and processing when a TEL application is executed in a real-time context, such as a presential classroom or remote synchronous activities. On the other hand, from a pedagogical point of view, verification and validation can be subordinated to how the learning design adapts its specifications (parameters, resources, state variable), as a medium to satisfy learning results.

Some examples in the literature attempt to incorporate the change within the workflow itself. One of the main attempts has been to integrate rules into workflows that explicitly represent the restrictions of the domain. This is a critical issue in learning design, because the definition of constraints is important to design flexible systems supporting unexpected events of the enactment of learning design scripts [14]. A first approach is to directly incorporate blocks of code that represent the rules in the code where the workflow is defined. However, this makes changes to the workflow difficult and therefore makes it difficult to maintain or to become inflexible [21]. The rules that can be defined using this approach must be simple (i.e., without using variables that represent the state of the workflow). These rules must also be local without including workflows with distributed elements [21]. One way of solving these problems is to take full advantage of using service-oriented architecture by explicitly decoupling the sequence of tasks in the workflow from the rules. For example, the rules are stored and performed in external rule engines, which are requested by the workflow using web services [23].This approach allows a posteriori flexibility as it defines spots, where the rules that are contained in a web service and remain decoupled from the workflow can be modified. A limitation of this approach is that as it does not allow changes to the running order when the workflow is being performed because such changes could affect the rules or require new rules.

Creating a workflow with the characteristics indicated above makes the process of verifying properties after changes more complex. According to the literature, the verification of properties in imperative workflows can be achieved independently using Petri-nets [25]. Petri-nets come from a language for mathematical modelling, which allows distributed systems to be described using a bipartite graph. Additionally, the elements of a Petri-net represent the semantics of the modelled process and allow properties, which are expected to be met during the execution of a workflow to be checked, such as deadlock-freeness, reachability of workflows expected states, safety, and liveness [16]. One disadvantage of separately verifying the properties of workflows and rules is that the compliance to these properties cannot be directly assessed. This issue emerges because there is dependency between workflow tasks and the rules that define the transition between workflow tasks. This assessment is required when making changes to the workflow that affect the running order or the definition of the set of rules because inconsistencies may appear due to the changes.

1.4 Modelling Workflows and Rules Using Petri-Nets

In the literature, an approach for modelling and formally defining workflows has been performed explicitly using Petri-nets. Nevertheless, there are approaches that consider the problem of flexible rules, although they do not consider the definition of a workflow. This problem is partially covered using ontology-based Petri-nets [26], defining an extra semantic layer, to provide knowledge over the specified Petri-net. In this case, new rules and axioms can be integrated to the system, with no reprogramming, such as the OPENET LD approach [26]. However, this leads to the following problems: (1) Complex rules (i.e., rules that are made up of other rules through disjunction and conjunction) can return different results for the same input; and (2) Given that Petri-nets use decision thresholds to make decisions, calibrating this type of system leads to a high overhead for incorporating flexibility.

Consequently, following research questions emerge: (1) Is it possible to incorporate complex rules into an imperative workflow so as to allow dynamic changes (during runtime), both to the properties that govern it as well as the order in which the tasks are defined and performed, guaranteeing the integrity of the rules that govern the problem's domain?, and (2) Is it possible to define a methodology for automatic property verification based on Petri-nets for the workflow proposed in the first research question?. To answer these research questions, this paper is structured as following: Sect. 2 presents Petri-nets as a modeling tool; Sect. 3 presents the proposed integration of workflow specification and rules, Sect. 4 presents the validation of this proposal, and Sect. 5 presents the conclusions about this work.

2 Petri-Nets as a Formalism for Modelling Workflows and Rules

In the literature, an approach for modelling and formally defining workflows has been performed explicitly using Petri-nets [25]. Using this concept, the definition of a workflow can be directly translated to a representation in Petri-net. The flexibility is incorporated by inserting snippets or blocks of code into a workflow specification, such as BPEL. These snippets can be directly translated to a certain pattern in Petri-net. Although this allows for some flexibility, it is only to a certain extent. The changes are limited to adding and modifying tasks, but do not allow rules that establish a transition from one task to another to be incorporated. Therefore, the validation of the changes is based on how these matches with the patterns in Petri-net. While the creation of these is well defined according to the methodology, this is not the case for a change in the rules that govern the workflow.

Nevertheless, there are approaches that consider the problem of flexible rules, although they do not consider the definition of a workflow. These allow a world to be represented where changes can be made to the context of the problem. However, this leads to the following problems:

- Complex rules (i.e., rules that are made up of other rules through disjunction and conjunction) can return different results for the same input.
- Given that Petri-nets use decision thresholds to make decisions, calibrating this type of system leads to a high overhead for incorporating flexibility.

3 Integration of Workflows and Rules

This study proposes the definition of a framework for integrating workflow and rules, with a methodology for verifying properties. An approach like that described in [27] is used to develop the integration between workflow and rules. With this approach, the following elements must be defined separately:

- The definition of the rules that govern the application's domain. These rules are defined as they are logic propositions, programed in a certain language. With this, two types of rules must be distinguished: those which are invariant to the application's state (i.e., that must always be met), and those which regulate the change from one state to another (i.e., those that are used to control the flow of the sequence of tasks).
- The definition of the workflow that represents the temporal sequence of the tasks to be performed.

3.1 Formalization

This section gives a formal account of workflows integrated with rule. Before defining our workflows, we define formally what we mean by a variable. We assume that a *variable* v is a mathematical object with an associated domain Dom(v). An *assignment* is a set of tuples(v,k), where v is a variable and k is a value in Dom(v). Given a set of variables, a *rule* is defined inductively as:

- v OP K is a rule when OP is in, v is in V and K is a value in v's domain.
- OR(R) where R is a finite set of rules. Intuitively OR is the Boolean OR operation.
- AND(R) where R is a finite set of rules. Intuitively AND is the Boolean OR operation.

The truth value of a rule r can be determined given an assignment *a* that assigns a value to every variable in V. We say that r evaluates to true in A if r reduces to true given the assignment A, and we say that r evaluates to false in A if r reduces to false given A. An inductive definition is straightforward, and we omit it here. For example rule AND $(v = k, u > m)$ evaluates to true if A assigns k to v and A assigns a value to u that is greater than m.

A workflow integrated with rules W is defined as a tuple, where:

- is a finite set of variables.
- is an (initial) assignment of values to all of the variables in V.
- is a set of sentences. There are two classes of sentences: (a) assignment of values to variables, denoted by, where is in the domain of variable and (b), where is a value and is a distinguished constant which intuitively denotes a procedure call.
- is a set of tuples where are sentences and is a rule.

Intuitively, tuples model transitions of the workflow. Tuple represents the fact that after finishing the execution of the control will transfer to if takes the value True, and to otherwise. To model unconditional transitions, which do not involve a rule (i.e., go from one task to another regardless of the state), we can use an expression that is always true (e.g.) for, and

- is the initial sentence.
- is the final sentence.

3.2 Execution

Given a workflow integrated with variables, we now define the semantics of an execution. To this end, we start off by defining *instant descriptions* which are mathematical representations of snapshots of the state of execution. Then we define how execution can move from one instant description to another.

Formally, an instant description is a tuple, where is a sentence and is an assignment to all variables in *V*. In addition, we define the binary relation between two instant descriptions, such that intuitively means that is reachable from in one step of computation. Formally, if and only if:

1. When then a′ is like a, but with the assignment of variable v replaced with value b. Thus, a' assigns all the variables in, in the same way as a, and assigns b as a value of v.
2. If then is like, with v assigned to some value of the domain of
3. for some and some, belongs to and evaluates to true in or belongs to and evaluates to false in.

   An execution of is a sequence, where, and for all in.
   An execution is successful if.

3.3 Formalization of Petri-Nets

A Petri-net P is defined as a tuple where:

- corresponds to the set of places
- corresponds to the set of transitions
- corresponds to a set of tuples of the form, where are places, while corresponds to a transition, which directly relates two places to each other, from to.
- :initial place.
- :set of final places of the Petri-net

3.4 Translation

Given a workflow integrated with rules, *W*, we define below a procedure for generating a Petri-Net

1. For each variable v, we define one place for each value in.
2. For each sentence, we define a place.
3. For each transition
   a. If is or, we define two places, and.
   b. If it corresponds to the assignment of a value to the variable, a transition, is defined, where corresponds to the index of the sentence.

4. Following this, a transformation pattern to Petri-net is applied to each sentence, resulting in a sub-Petri-net.
5. After this, each resulting sub-Petri-net is added iteratively, depending on the function of the associated transition. With this and depending on whether or not can be true or false, the place represented by each value of the evaluated variables is added to the corresponding entries to the sub-Petri-net that must be executed if is true or false.

An example of some of the transformation patterns are included below.:

- AND: a pattern that represents an AND conjunction is represented as a Petri-net with as many entry places as there are rules in the conjunction. Each of these points to a transition, which in turn is directed to an exit place. This also makes it possible to add other conjunctions and disjunctions as they are also established as rules.
- OR: a pattern that represents an OR disjunction is represented as a Petri-net with as many entry places and transitions as there are rules in the disjunction. Each entry place points to a transition, and each transition points to the same exit place. This also makes it possible to add other conjunctions and disjunctions as they are also established as rules.
- Comparison = (equality): is represented as a Petri-net that has several entry places: one that corresponds to the value of the variable that is being evaluated in the comparison (i.e., the answer to the rule is True), others that correspond to the values that do not correspond to those that were evaluated (i.e., the answer to the rule is False), as well as another place that corresponds to the previous task that comes before the evaluation of the comparison. There are two exit places. The first is one that connects the place corresponding to the value of the variable that returns True with the place of the previous task using an AND. The other connects the places corresponding to the values of the variable that return False with the place of the previous task using an AND. Both have an exit place that connects with the sub-Petri-net that represents the relevant task to be performed once the condition has been evaluated, regardless of whether it is True or False.

Consequently, this work proposes the definition of a specification for flexible workflows, integrating domain rules with a technique for automated compliance assessment, to satisfy performance, deadlock-freeness, and reachability in workflow execution. In the field of learning design, rules specify corresponding pedagogical constraints; also, workflow defines the learning flow proposed by a TEL application as an instance of a learning design specification. Therefore, these elements must be defined independently and consequently must be integrated in a common specification:

The definition of the rules that govern the learning design instance. Two types of rules must be distinguished: those which are invariant to the application's state (i.e., that must always be met), and those which regulate the change from one state to another (i.e., that are used to control the flow of the sequence of tasks).

The definition of the workflow that represents the temporal sequence of the tasks in the pedagogical plan.

In Fig. 1 is presented an example of this idea. Using Petri-net notation, a small learning scenario is presented: an application for English pronunciation learning needs to evaluate the correction in pronunciation in a certain word and the rightness in the word choosing process. These events in learning process, signed as "validatePronunciation", and "comparison", correspond to the combinate use of a consume of an external service of pronunciation evaluation, called in transition between OR and Comparison stages, and an internal decision process implementation (OR, Comparison, & AND stages). In the first case, a "Decision as-a-service" approach is followed, similar to Hasić, et al. (2020) work. In the second case, the Petri-net design uses well-known patterns to represent corresponding explicit and implicit pedagogical constraints. In this example, the changes are limited to adding and modifying tasks, but do not allow pedagogical constraints to be incorporated in the workflow as a mechanism to establish a transition from one task to another. Therefore, the validation of the changes is based on how these constraints match with the patterns in Petri-net.

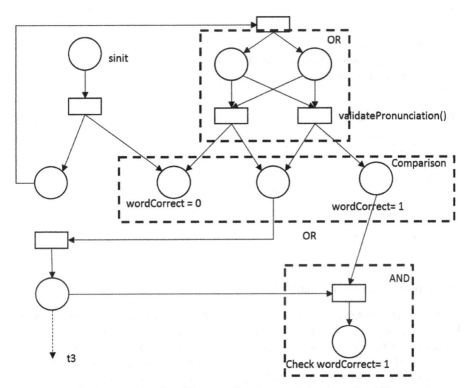

Fig. 1. Example of workflow specification translation into a Petri Net.

Context: A student must correctly pronounce a word. They have three opportunities to do so.

Rules (in natural language)

R1: The word must be correct to advance to the next activity

R2: There are three opportunities to correctly pronounce a word

Variables (V) and their initial configuration ()

correctWord = 0, attempts = 0;

Formalized rules

: correctWord = 1

: OR(attempts = 0, attempts = 1, attempts =2)

Tasks

t0: sinit

t1: isCorrect := 0;

t2: isCorrect := validatePronunciation()

t3: attempts = attempts + 1

t4: send

Transition function (T)

<t0, {1=1},t1,t1>

<t1,{1=1}t2,t2>

<t2,r1,t4,t3>

<t3,r2,t2,t4>

Goals (G)

<isCorrect = 1, t4>

3.5   Implementing the Formalization

BPEL is used to define the workflow to implement the methodology. BPEL was chosen as the language for representing the workflows because it is considered the industry standard and because it fully integrates into a service architecture. Furthermore, there are standardized methodologies for BPEL, as well as automatic translations to representations in Petri-nets. More specifically, the following tasks must be carried out:

- Define a WSDL file that represents the rules as a service. In this file, each rule is used through an entry-point. With this, the coding of the rule remains independent from the BPEL.
- Define synchronous calls to service in the BPEL that represents the workflow. This service represents the rules using the invoke and receive BPEL commands. The invoke command will reference the corresponding rule (using the name of the corresponding

entry-point) and the receive command will save the result of the request (true or false) for use controlling the flow of the application.

The BPEL2oWFN tool is used to translate the workflow to Petri-nets (Lohmann, 2007). This allows the translation to multiple representations of Petri-nets, to which the formalization presented above adjusts. To integrate the resulting Petri-nets, of both the workflow and the rules, a semi-automatic methodology was used to recognize the places and transitions in Petri-nets, based on the patterns used in the translation of BPEL2oWFN.

With this it is possible to find the points where the requests are made to the service representing the rules. Here, the initial and final points of the Petri-nets that represent each rule are inserted.

3.6 Validation and Correction

A model-checker for Petri-nets must be used for verifying the properties. The chosen model-checker is LoLA2 [28], which allows properties that are intrinsic to the Petri-nets to be examined, as well as ad-hoc properties that are expected of the domain (i.e., adherence to the proposed rules). These properties must be analyzed every time there is a change to the application, whether it be to the workflow or the rules. The properties that were analyzed are the following:

- Deadlock-freeness analysis: checks whether there are any possible configurations of the Petri-net that led to deadlock. It does not require parameterization.
- Reachability analysis: checks that each of the expected states is reached (i.e., the goals defined in the workflow). It requires the specification of the test input sets.
- Safety-Liveness analysis: Determines the temporal logics according to the sequence of the workflow. To be evaluated, the valid sequence of steps in the workflow is deter-mined, before determining whether the rules are adhered to. To follow the indicated flow, the proposed rules must also be followed. Therefore, the introduction of valid inputs (i.e., the evaluation of reachability) must be analyzed together. The input model consists of the following elements:

  o Petri-net with model to be tested
  o Valid and invalid inputs for each rule
  o Expected states (post-conditions or goals)
  o Valid sequences within the context, written in Linear Temporal Logic – LTL –. The model-checker generates a combination of possible sequences (not necessarily feasible and/or consistent with the rules), with the aim of testing the Petri-net against boundary conditions.

Given that the Safety-liveness evaluation includes the other properties, the resulting output from the verification is the following:

- Safety-liveness evaluation indicates points in the Petri-net where all of the possible combinations of sequences fail.
- Reachability evaluation: indicates whether all the expected states were reached.
- Deadlock-freeness evaluation: indicating the points in the Petri-net where deadlocks occur.

4 Validating the Proposal

An extension of the scenario presented by [29] was used to validate the proposal presented in this study. This scenario consists of an application for learning a foreign language, based on single-display groupware and collaborative learning. In the original application, three students work in front of a shared screen, interacting with the application using headsets. The application allows the students to carry out activities which develop their grammar, vocabulary, listening skills and pronunciation. Automatic feedback is given by the system using a speech recognition engine and speech synthesizer. Both the use of multimedia in this scenario (such as the speech engines), as well as the collaborative learning dynamic, are of interest to this study because, based on these, new requirements can be developed. With these new requirements it is possible to formulate new task definitions and make changes to those that already exist. This enables the definition of a new scenario using a flexible workflow. With this, the original scenario is extended to include the following features:

- Interconnection between the computers where the activity takes place.
- Unbalanced distribution of resources. E.g., not all the computers necessarily have a speech-recognition engine available all the time.
- Possibility for the teacher to change the sequence that is followed during an activity: adding new tasks, modifying tasks, changing certain rules etc.

4.1 Instance for the Integrated Framework for Workflows and Rules

The methodology proposed in this study was followed to develop this scenario. First, the pedagogical rules that govern the system were clearly defined. In parallel to this, the sequence of tasks was also defined. Each rule is specified by an ID, with the aim of categorizing the purpose of each rule and detecting possible dependency between rules. There are two types of rules: rules that must be followed for there to be a specific transition between tasks in the workflow (IR), and rules that must always be followed for there to be any transition between tasks in the workflow (RR). The repetition of a figure in the ID indicates that there is dependency between rules. For example, rule 05IR depends on rule 055IR.

4.2 Instance of the Validation Model

To validate the implementation of the proposed methodology, it is necessary to validate the fulfilment of all the elements that comprise the pedagogical context. In this case, this corresponds to the pedagogical rules and respective sequence of tasks. The evaluation criteria used will correspond to properties that can be evaluated in a Petri-nets model (Table 1).

Table 1. Elements to evaluate and properties evaluated in the respective elements.

Element to be evaluated	Properties of the element evaluated
Adherence to pedagogical rules	Reachability, Deadlock-freeness
Adherence to expected sequence	Safety-liveness (using LTL), Deadlock-freeness and Reachability (derived from the adherence to the pedagogical rules)

4.3 Defining Alternative Situations

One aspect to evaluate is the robustness of the proposal presented in this study when faced with the incorporation of new tasks and changes to existing tasks. With this, a set of alternative situations to the existing sequence determined by the workflow and rules is defined. These are then incorporated into the modelling of the problem. When incorporating these situations, it must be verified that there are no inconsistencies with the pre-defined rules. Adherence to the pedagogical rules and expected sequence must also be evaluated, based on the properties included in Table 1. The definition of the alternative situations can be found in Appendix I, with the respective rule that triggers each one. A nomenclature like that used for rules was adopted to identify the alternative situations, using the keyword RP.

4.4 Test Cases

To carry out the validation, simulations are performed using the Petri-nets that were generated based on the transformation methodology proposed in Sect. 3.4. Different models were created based on the definition of the proposed pedagogical scenario: one that considers the original sequence of tasks, and three others that each separately incorporate an alternative situation. With this, the robustness of the modelling can be analyzed separately for each of the proposed alternative situations.

The use of 1, 2, 3, 4 and 5 nodes were considered for evaluating each of these models. A limited number of nodes were used as it measures the robustness of the modelling without considering requirements of scalability. According to the definition of the scenario, each node corresponds to a computer shared by 3 students. Each configuration is tested using both valid and invalid input sets with regards to the specifications of the scenario. The respective models were coded using LTL to evaluate adherence to both the expected execution sequence, as well as the execution sequences deriving from the alternative situations. This code is used by the model-checker to evaluate the validity of the Petri-net in following the tested sequence. Furthermore, the model-checker also generates the entire set of combinations for the order of tasks for each of the test cases.

4.5 Results

As described in Sect. 3, the analysis of the results is focused on the behavior of the Petri-net with regards to the properties that it must fulfil. In the proposed scenario, this analysis is performed for the aspects detailed below. Together, these aspects allow the validity of the modelling to be checked in terms of its translation to Petri-net, as well as in terms of the properties that must be fulfilled when incorporating changes into the original formulation, as described in Table 1. The aspects are as follows:

- Appearance of inaccuracies (i.e., violations of the rules) in the model for all the test cases. This is implicit in the reachability analysis and LTL.
- Detection of deadlock-freeness problems when expected.
- Detection of reachability (i.e., fulfilment of the expected states).
- Detection of problems in LTL (i.e., if an expected sequence is not adhered to).

4.6   Detection of Deadlocks

The appearance and detection of deadlocks was observed when there was no alternative to the use of the speech recognition engine. No other deadlocks appeared (Table 2).

Table 2. Results of the deadlock-freeness analysis.

Scenario	Scenario	Scenario	Scenario	Scenario	Scenario
1 node	1 node	1 node	1 node	1 node	1 node
2 nodes	2 nodes	2 nodes	2 nodes	2 nodes	2 nodes
3 nodes	3 nodes	3 nodes	3 nodes	3 nodes	3 nodes
4 nodes	4 nodes	4 nodes	4 nodes	4 nodes	4 nodes

4.7   Reachability Analysis and LTL

Reachability analysis is performed implicitly when evaluating the expected sequence order using LTL. This is because not adhering to the sequences ensures that not all the expected states are reached in the Petri-nets. In particular, the following situations are observed as causing problems with reachability:

- When the order of the tasks in the original sequence is automatically altered by the model-checker (i.e., models generated by the model-checker vs. expected sequences).
- When there is incorrect input. With this, not all the expected states are reached.

In the reachability analysis for the cases that were used to test the proposed modelling it can be observed that all the expected states are achieved when inserting alternative situations (Table 3).

Table 3. Results of reachability and LTL analysis.

Scenario	1 node	2 nodes	3 nodes	4 nodes	5 nodes
Change in order of tasks	Fail	Fail	Fail	Fail	Fail
Incorrect input	Fail	Fail	Fail	Fail	Fail
Original	Ok	Ok	Ok	Ok	Ok
Original + 10RP	Ok	Ok	Ok	Ok	Ok
Original + 11RP	Ok	Ok	Ok	Ok	Ok
Original + 12RP	Ok	Ok	Ok	Ok	Ok

5   Conclusions

The research question "Is it possible to incorporate complex rules into an imperative workflow so as to allow dynamic changes (during run-time), both to the properties that govern it as well as the order in which the tasks are defined and performed, guaranteeing the integrity of the rules that govern the problem's domain?", was answered by creating an integrated framework when developing an imperative workflow. This framework allows rules to be explicitly incorporated, as well as offering great flexibility in a distributed setting. This was achieved by proposing a definition of the workflow using BPEL and integrating rules using service orientation approach. The changes that were introduced can be introduced at any point of the workflow and rules. These changes include adding and eliminating tasks, changing a rule, and changing the order of the tasks, and must be programed in the same language as the language used to program the workflow and rules. Both the workflow and rules are translated to Petri-nets to check that these changes are consistent. This answers the research question "Is it possible to define a methodology for automatic property verification based on Petri-nets for the workflow proposed in the first research question?" To do so, a methodology was proposed in which the workflow and rules are translated to Petri-nets and then integrated into a single network. This allows the validity of the changes that were introduced to be evaluated jointly, verifying intrinsic properties of the Petri-nets and Linear Temporal Logic.

Based on the execution of the example presented in this study, it was seen that the proposal is robust when incorporating alternative situations into the original sequence of tasks. Alternative situations were formulated based on the requirements of the problem, with the observation that the expected results were achieved in terms of the properties of deadlock-freeness, reachability, and safety-liveness. The latter of these is a critical property as it considers the adherence to an expected order of the tasks, meaning that the other properties depend on safety-liveness. In the context of the application presented in this study, the use of collaborative learning allowed for more complex dynamics to be developed, including sequences with interdependency between the activity's participants. With this, any change to the order of the tasks has a high incidence in the non-fulfilment of safety-liveness. This is contrasted with the incorporation of new tasks within the sequence. In that case, the original sequence is maintained but new possibilities are added to the activity. These can bring with them possible pedagogical requirements, or indeed they can correct certain problems that could have otherwise hindered the fulfilment of the pre-defined requirements.

As shown in Sects. 3 and 4, certain steps of the methodology were done semi-automatically. This made it difficult to use the methodology transparently in a real setting. It remains as future work to build a workflow engine that automatically carries out all the stages in the methodology. Another limitation is related to the reach of the requirements of the problem that was presented in this study, as is a scalability analysis. With this, the growing incorporation of more multimedia resources and a larger number of nodes remains as future work. Finally, another limitation has to do with the generic nature of the scenario that was presented. Although a pedagogical setting was chosen as the basis for this study, the reach of the proposed methodology is not restricted just to this context. However, the chosen scenario must have characteristics, which allow the requirements relating to flexibility to be formed, as well as the definition of the rules that govern the domain of the problem, with the aim of satisfying the model presented in this study.

References

1. Hofmann, M.,Betke, H., Sackmann, S.: Automated Analysis and Adaptation of DRP 266 Long Paper-Decision Support Systems (2004)
2. Macfadyen, L.P., Lockyer, L., Rienties, B.: Learning design and learning analytics: Snapshot 2020. J. Learn. Anal. 7(3), 6–12 (2020). https://doi.org/10.18608/JLA.2020.73.2
3. Online, R., Agostinho, S., Bennett, S., Lockyer, L., Jones, J., Harper, B.: Learning designs as a stimulus and support for teachers' design practices. http://ro.uow.edu.au/sspapers/422
4. Educational Technology & Society. http://www.ifets.info/
5. Asensio-Pérez, J.I., et al.: Towards teaching as design: exploring the interplay between full-lifecycle learning design tooling and Teacher Professional Development. Comput. Educ. 114, 92–116 (2017). https://doi.org/10.1016/j.compedu.2017.06.011
6. Celik, D., Magoulas, G.D.: A review, timeline, and categorization of learning design tools. In: Chiu, D.K.W., Marenzi, I., Nanni, U., Spaniol, M., Temperini, M. (eds.) ICWL 2016. LNCS, vol. 10013, pp. 3–13. Springer, Cham (2016). https://doi.org/10.1007/978-3-319-47440-3_1
7. Pozzi, F., Asensio-Perez, J.I., Ceregini, A., Dagnino, F.M., Dimitriadis, Y., Earp, J.: Supporting and representing learning design with digital tools: in between guidance and flexibility. Technol. Pedagog. Educ. 29(1), 109–128 (2020). https://doi.org/10.1080/1475939X.2020.1714708
8. Persico, D., Pozzi, F.: Informing learning design with learning analytics to improve teacher inquiry. Br. J. Educ. Technol. 46(2), 230–248 (2015). https://doi.org/10.1111/bjet.12207
9. Torres, J., Cárdenas, C., Dodero, J.M., Juárez, E., Rosson, M.B.: Educational modelling languages and service-oriented learning process engines. Adv. Learn. Process. 17–38 (2010)
10. Koper, R., Miao, Y.: Using the IMS LD standard to describe learning designs. In: Handbook of Research on Learning Design and Learning Objects. IGI Global (2011). https://doi.org/10.4018/9781599048611.ch003
11. Vesin, B., Mangaroska, K., Giannakos, M.: Learning in smart environments: user-centered design and analytics of an adaptive learning system. Smart Learn. Environ. 5(1), 1–21 (2018). https://doi.org/10.1186/s40561-018-0071-0
12. Magnisalis, I., Demetriadis, S.: Extending IMS-LD capabilities: a review, a proposed framework and implementation cases. Intell. Adapt. Personal. Tech. Comput.-Support. Collab. Learn. 85–108 (2012)

13. Hermans, H., Janssen, J., Koper, R.: Flexible authoring and delivery of online courses using IMS learning design. Interact. Learn. Environ. **24**(6), 1265–1279 (2016). https://doi.org/10.1080/10494820.2014.994220

14. Pérez-Sanagustín, M., Santos, P., Hernández-Leo, D., Blat, J.: 4SPPIces: a case study of factors in a scripted collaborative-learning blended course across spatial locations. Int. J. Comput. Support. Collab. Learn. **7**(3), 443–465 (2012). https://doi.org/10.1007/s11412-011-9139-3

15. Garreta-Domingo, M., Hernández-Leo, D., Sloep, P.B.: Education, technology and design: a much needed interdisciplinary collaboration. In: Kapros, E., Koutsombogera, M. (eds.) Designing for the User Experience in Learning Systems. HIS, pp. 17–39. Springer, Cham (2018). https://doi.org/10.1007/978-3-319-94794-5_2

16. van der Aalst, W.M.P., Pesic, M., Schonenberg, H.: Declarative workflows: balancing between flexibility and support. Comput. Sci. Res. Dev. **23**(2), 99–113 (2009). https://doi.org/10.1007/s00450-009-0057-9

17. Baiyere, A., Salmela, H., Tapanainen, T.: Digital transformation and the new logics of business process management. Eur. J. Inf. Syst. **29**(3), 238–259 (2020). https://doi.org/10.1080/0960085X.2020.1718007

18. la Rosa, M., van der Aalst, W.M.P., Dumas, M., Milani, F.P.: Business process variability modeling: a survey. ACM Comput. Surv. **50**(1) (2017). Association for Computing Machinery. https://doi.org/10.1145/3041957

19. Murguzur, A., Intxausti, K., Urbieta, A., Trujillo, S., Sagardui, G.: Process flexibility in service orchestration: a systematic literature review. Int. J. Coop. Inf. Syst. **23**(3) (2014). https://doi.org/10.1142/S0218843014300010

20. Kloos, C.D., et al.: SmartLet: learning analytics to enhance the design and orchestration in scalable, IoT-enriched, and ubiquitous smart learning environments. In: ACM International Conference Proceeding Series, October 2018, pp. 648–653 (2018). https://doi.org/10.1145/3284179.3284291

21. Andrews, K., Steinau, S., Reichert, M.: Enabling runtime flexibility in data-centric and data-driven process execution engines. Inf. Syst. 101 (2021). https://doi.org/10.1016/j.is.2019.101447

22. Seyffarth, T., Kuehnel, S.: Maintaining business process compliance despite changes: a decision support approach based on process adaptations. J. Decis. Syst **31**(3), 305–335 (2022). https://doi.org/10.1080/12460125.2020.1861920

23. Hasic, F., de Smedt, J., vanden Broucke, S., Serral, E.: Decision as a Service (DaaS): a service-oriented architecture approach for decisions in processes. IEEE Trans. Serv. Comput. **15**(2), 904–917 (2022). https://doi.org/10.1109/TSC.2020.2965516

24. Kittel, K., Sackmann, S., Betke, H., Hofmann, M.: Achieving flexible and compliant processes in disaster management. In: Proceedings of the Annual Hawaii International Conference on System Sciences, pp. 4687–4696 (2013). https://doi.org/10.1109/HICSS.2013.71

25. Aalst, W.M.P.: Everything you always wanted to know about petri nets, but were afraid to ask. In: Hildebrandt, T., van Dongen, B.F., Röglinger, M., Mendling, J. (eds.) BPM 2019. LNCS, vol. 11675, pp. 3–9. Springer, Cham (2019). https://doi.org/10.1007/978-3-030-26619-6_1

26. Vidal, J.C., Lama, M., Bugarín, A.: OPENET: ontology-based engine for high-level Petri nets. Expert Syst. Appl. **37**(9), 6493–6509 (2010). https://doi.org/10.1016/j.eswa.2010.02.136

27. Nagl, C., Rosenberg, F., Vitalab, D.: VIDRE-A Distributed Service-Oriented Business Rule Engine based on RuleML. http://www.vitalab.tuwien.ac

28. Wolf, K.: Petri net model checking with LoLA 2. In: Khomenko, V., Roux, O.H. (eds.) PETRI NETS 2018. LNCS, vol. 10877, pp. 351–362. Springer, Cham (2018). https://doi.org/10.1007/978-3-319-91268-4_18

29. Calderón, J.F., Nussbaum, M., Carmach, I., Díaz, J.J., Villalta, M.: A single-display groupware collaborative language laboratory. Interact. Learn. Environ. **24**(4), 758–783 (2016). https://doi.org/10.1080/10494820.2014.917111

From Internet Celebrity to Teacher – The Evolutionary Challenge of Design Courses

Yueh Hsiu Giffen Cheng[(✉)] [iD] and Kuan Ting Fur

National Yunlin University of Science and Technology, 123 University Road, Section 3, Douliou, Yunlin 64002, Taiwan R.O.C.
Giffen.cheng@gmail.com, m10836006@gemail.yuntech.edu.tw

Abstract. The use of the YouTube platform as a medium for knowledge transfer is a phenomenon that has become increasingly popular in recent years with the advent of new online media. The core idea of this study is to convert knowledge content into motivation for learning, and effectively enhancing learning effectiveness, so as to nurture innovative and creative design professionals. According to the results of examining the content and characteristics of knowledge-based YouTube videos and knowledge transformation techniques, it is clear that the application and process of the Basic Design course must take into account the following points on the teaching side. 1)Explicit knowledge transformation which are the information content, structure and practicality are the key points that teachers must consider when preparing lessons. 2)Conversion of tacit knowledge starts with inspiration and motivation to boost learning achievement.3) Personality affects the ambience of the classroom and the viewership. 4)Knowledge summation is a requisite training for the instructor. 5) The ability to narrate is a source of brilliance.

Keywords: YouTube · Tacit knowledge · Explicit knowledge · SECI model of knowledge dimensions

1 Introduction

The use of the YouTube platform as a medium for knowledge transfer is a phenomenon that has become increasingly popular in recent years with the advent of new online media. In the past, conventional methods of teaching confined to the dissemination of information in classrooms were not conducive to student learning. It is an innovative teaching model for students' self-directed learning that incorporates design concepts into new forms of learning, transforming the role of the teacher into that of an Internet personality, who imparts knowledge through the charm of the YouTube platform and the multiple presentation methods of moving images, and advocates the translation of knowledge, notions or techniques in the field of design into knowledge content with different expressions, and integrates them into the subject curriculum. The core idea of this study is to successfully convert knowledge content into motivation for learning. Through the multi-faceted presentation of moving images and an unconventional style that suits the learners' mindset, it aims to create a relaxed and fun learning atmosphere,

© The Author(s), under exclusive license to Springer Nature Switzerland AG 2023
A. Coman and S. Vasilache (Eds.): HCII 2023, LNCS 14026, pp. 31–48, 2023.
https://doi.org/10.1007/978-3-031-35927-9_3

and combine it with the planning of the curriculum, with a view to increasing learning autonomy and motivation, and effectively enhancing learning effectiveness, so as to nurture innovative and creative design professionals. The aim of education is to inspire students to learn. Through a variety of innovative teaching techniques, students are further prompted to think in different ways and are more likely to be motivated for learning and to take pleasure in gaining knowledge. Motivating learners is often a major challenge for teachers in the classroom, and a key to nurturing their independence. With the evolution of the Internet and the rise of self-media platforms in recent years, teaching practices need to be constantly updated. Only by keeping pace with the times and catering to students' varied learning needs can teachers create a positive interactive relationship with students and enhance their enjoyment of learning.

By adopting a qualitative action research approach, this study was conducted throughout a six-week visual-graphic dimension teaching process in the course "Basic Design" offered in the first year of study by the Department of Creative Design at National Yunlin University of Science and Technology (NYUST) to put into practice the learning process and results of applying the "YouTube influencers teaching method" to motivation and inspiration at the teaching site. According to the results of the researcher's on-site teaching and observation, the traditional classroom instruction is no longer able to satisfy the students' desire and motivation to learn. The transmission of knowledge is far-reaching and has led to a shift in learning styles. Previously, the acquisition of knowledge relied on the face-to-face transfer of information from others. In recent years, the rise of online platforms has allowed learning to break through the constraints of time and space, and as long as one has access to the Internet, one can open a platform for information exchange and learning, no matter where one is. YouTube is one of the most popular online platforms among the students enrolled in the course interviewed by this research. According to the "Taiwan YouTube User Profiling" conducted by Google and Ipsos in Taiwan, 49 percent of users in Taiwan learn new knowledge via video and audio content on the platform, and the total number of views of knowledge-related content in a single day worldwide can reach 500 million (Google blog 2017), a trend that shows that YouTube is an emerging medium for learning. YouTube The variety of video genres and styles on YouTube attracts many viewers, and there is no shortage of knowledge-based videos. The fun delivery and successful translation of knowledge content allows viewers to learn independently, acquire knowledge in a short period of time and have fun during the process.

"Basic Design" is an alternative to the traditional rules of thumb that designers are accustomed to, using a scientific and rational approach, so that novice designers can learn the aesthetics of design expression in an effective way. The pedagogy at this stage is neither innovative nor interesting in terms of teaching techniques, despite its scientific and rational approach. The traditional mode of instruction leaves students somewhat drained and unmotivated and uninterested in learning. The course is designed to transform the knowledge content into a fresh and entertaining new media format by incorporating the current knowledge transfer mode in the new media and integrating it with the subject curriculum, which will benefit the students with a different learning experience and pleasure. It is hoped that the new generation learning approach will boost the learning effectiveness for "Basic Design" and inspire learning autonomy.

Through literature review and observation and application on the teaching site, this study attempts to convert the knowledge content into an Internet influencers format in order to enhance students' stickiness to the curriculum, thereby creating a relaxed and enjoyable learning ambience, which in turn stimulates self-learning and boosts learning effectiveness. As such, the research topics are set out below:

i. Understanding the learning habits and characteristics of design students
ii. The gap between knowledge transfer in physical courses and on YouTube
iii. Feedback on the application of the knowledge delivery model of YouTube influencers to design courses.

2   Literature Review

2.1   YouTube for Knowledge Acquisition

With the rise of knowledge-based video and audio content, more and more people are looking to YouTube as a conduit for knowledge. In 2017, Google released a survey on "Taiwan YouTube User Profiling" conducted with Ipsos, which found that Taiwanese users who visited YouTube more than once a month spent 14.6 h a week on the platform. In particular, apart from killing time, half of the Taiwanese users browse YouTube for the purpose of "learning," indicating that YouTube is not only an entertainment for people's lives, but also a practical tool for transmitting knowledge (SmartM 2017). Previously, knowledge could only be acquired in the classroom or through books. If one was interested in painting, one could only learn through art classes, tutors or art departments. Nevertheless, with the advent of the YouTube platform, this situation has been reversed. Anyone with an interest in any field can find videos on YouTube, making learning resources readily available. In addition, the nature of online video platform YouTube allows viewers to interact directly with the creators through comments, and questions from viewers can echo each other's need for knowledge, so that more people can benefit from the creators' responses to their inquiries. According to Alias et al. (2013), YouTube draws billions of subscribers, including educators and academics, who use the sharing services on YouTube videos. Ahmad (2016) also suggested that using YouTube as a "visualized" tool can improve teachers' teaching efficacy.

In the past, knowledge was mostly gained in the classroom or from books. If one was interested in painting, one would usually have to sign up for art classes, art schools or employ tutors, but the emergence of the YouTube platform has changed this situation. Anyone with an interest in any field can find videos on YouTube, with all the learning resources at your fingertips. Moreover, the traditional classroom approach to learning, which restricts the delivery of the same knowledge to the same group of students in the same classroom, disregarding the differences in backgrounds and learning speeds of students in the same classes, and limits the instruction to the same venue, the same time, and the same pace, can pose challenges at the teaching site. However, if teaching is offered through the YouTube platform, these constraints can be overcome, allowing for a more diverse range of learning styles to be adapted to individual learning efficiency (Table 1).

Table 1. YouTube platform features vs. challenges in the classroom.

Challenges in the Classroom	Corresponding Solutions Offered by YouTube
One-way oral instruction tends to wear out students	YouTube, as a self-media platform, not only adds to the fun with its moving images, but can easily incorporates a number of knowledge transfer techniques to suit the learning habits of students as the video content can be self-produced, so that the teaching content can be adapted to fit the students' needs. The platform also enables users to leave comments and feedback to increase interactivity, and even has a live streaming service that allows for real-time interaction and response online
Differences in the background of students in the same class	Students can skip or re-watch parts of the content at their own pace, and can preview or review after class
Differences in the learning speed of students in the same class	
Lessons are restricted to the same location	Students can study not only in the classroom, but also on the Internet whenever they have access to it, and learning is not confined to the classroom, but can be done before or after class
Lessons are restricted to the same time frame	There is no time limit on the platform, so students can watch the content anytime and anywhere
Lessons are restricted to the same pace	The speed of learning can be adjusted to suit your own learning and absorption capacity by speeding up or slowing down the video

Source: Compiled by this study

2.2 Knowledge Classification and Sharing

Knowledge can be categorized into tacit knowledge and explicit knowledge. Explicit knowledge is clearly visible, objective, can be coded through spoken language or behavior, or presented in other ways, is derived from tacit knowledge, and ultimately has its origins in an individual's mental models and abilities, is static, does not change over time or due to changes in the external environment, is shareable, and can be transmitted and shared through spoken language, text, diagrams, etc. (Nonaka and Takeuchi 1995). Tacit knowledge is knowledge that has not been systematized or expressed in other forms, such as words (Shen 2006), and is an experience or practice that emerges from a mental process, often transferred through learning by doing and learning by seeing. Since tacit knowledge is not easily mobile, cannot be fully imitated and is irreplaceable, it is often seen as an essential basis for a company's competitive advantage (Zack 1999; Barney 1991; Grant 1996). Knowledge sharing is an interaction between tacit knowledge and explicit knowledge (Nonaka and Takeuchi, 1995). The teacher passes on explicit knowledge in a variety of ways so that the learner can transform the explicit knowledge into tacit knowledge, which in turn lays the foundation of his or her own scholarship; and the learner can translate the tacit knowledge into explicit knowledge and share what he or she has learned with others. Therefore, the role of the teacher and the learner is the result of the constant interaction, transformation and dialogue between the tacit knowledge and the explicit knowledge.

Drawing on the arguments made by different academics, it is clear that tacit knowledge is quite distinct from explicit knowledge, both in terms of its characteristics and the way in which it is transmitted, and it is thus important to understand and categorize the types of knowledge in the process of transmission. By analyzing the different characteristics of tacit and explicit knowledge, it is possible to develop appropriate ways of passing on and sharing knowledge for effective knowledge transfer.

The sharing of tacit knowledge is not as easy as the sharing of explicit knowledge. Therefore, in the process of knowledge transfer, should the methods of transforming and sharing tacit knowledge be acquired, knowledge in various fields can be disseminated more extensively and conveniently, making it more widely available and enhancing the effectiveness of teaching and learning. Table 2 below is a consolidation of the ways of sharing tacit knowledge proposed by academics, in the hope of pooling their approaches and getting to grips with the techniques of sharing tacit knowledge, so as to achieve efficient and effective knowledge exchange. Based on the table, eight main approaches to transferring tacit knowledge are identified in this study: observation, reflection, dialogue, communication, interaction, practice, storytelling, and direct contact (Table 3).

2.3   The SECI Model of Knowledge Transfer

For knowledge to be transferred without a hitch, there must be a venue and a target audience for knowledge sharing, as well as a suitable means of knowledge transformation. The theory of knowledge creation developed by Nonaka is suited for application to learners' learning processes, and this theory can help foster learners' learning to be spread across both tacit and explicit knowledge, and through the alternation of tacit and explicit knowledge, knowledge can be effectively transformed to enable learners to possess new knowledge. The transformation of knowledge can be divided into four dimensions, namely socialization, which enhances dialogue and interaction between people and facilitates the acquisition of knowledge through observation, practice and communication; externalization, which stimulates individuals to visualize their insights and experiences so that they can share them; internalization, which accumulates experience and skills by translating external knowledge into one's own; and combination, which combines external knowledge gained to build systematic knowledge or even to create new knowledge with others. The learning of knowledge hinges on knowledge sharing, which is a process of communication and an act of transfer. As knowledge is not material and cannot be directly traded, bought, sold or exchanged, the sharing of knowledge relies on reconstructed methods and modes of transformation. Hendriks (1999) suggested that knowledge needs to be shared between two subjects: the first is the knowledge owner, who needs to voluntarily transform the knowledge and pass it on

Table 2. Characteristics of explicit and tacit knowledge.

Author	Explicit Knowledge	Tacit Knowledge
Polanyi (1967)	Explicit knowledge is clearly visible and can be expressed in written text, diagrams, etc.	Subjective, not expressed in explicit words and unarticulated knowledge
Hedlund (1994)	Knowledge that can be described in detail or represented by text, computer programs, patents or graphics	Knowledge that is non-verbal, intuitive and unarticulated and cannot be expressed explicitly
Nonaka & Takeuchi (1995)	Can be coded by spoken words or deeds, or rendered in other ways Derived from tacit knowledge that does not change over time or in response to changes in external circumstances Can be communicated and shared in the form of spoken words, texts, diagrams, etc.	Subjective knowledge that cannot be expressed in words. Extremely personal, difficult to systematize or formalize, e.g. intuition and experience, and therefore not easily shared with others. Includes both cognitive and technical aspects. The technical side includes skills or expertise that are difficult to convey in writing or in speech; the cognitive side includes perceptions, mental models, beliefs, etc.
Edvinsson and Sullivan (1996)	Can be recorded, transferred and shared, and protected by intellectual property rights	Difficult to describe concretely or to codify; experience and skills that have been accumulated over time by an individual, team, department or organization and that are difficult to articulate may also appear in ways of working, such as problem solving, process improvement techniques, a craft or a specialized skill

Source: Compiled by this study

to others in different ways; and the other is the knowledge receiver, who internalizes or recombines the knowledge received, thereby accruing experience and skills.

Knowledge sharing is an interaction between tacit knowledge and explicit knowledge. Through various means, educators can pass on explicit knowledge so that learners can turn what they have learned into tacit knowledge, which forms the foundation of their scholarship; and learners can also share what they have learned with others by converting tacit knowledge into explicit knowledge. Thus, the role of the educator and the learner is the outcome of the ongoing interplay, transformation and dialogue between tacit knowledge and explicit knowledge.

Table 3. Tacit knowledge transfer methods.

Author	Tacit Knowledge Transfer Methods	Approaches
Nonaka and Takeuchi (1995)	Through dialogue and collective thinking processes, tacit knowledge and concepts can be clarified so that knowledge can be shared and utilized	Dialogue
Holtshouse (1998)	The exchange and sharing of tacit knowledge take place through direct first-hand observation, as well as through interaction with others and body language	Observation
Davenport and Prusak (1998)	The transfer of tacit knowledge can be achieved through interpersonal communication and interaction, especially through face-to-face contact, such as teamwork, mentoring, partnership, mentorship, chat rooms, in-person conversations, and the use of information technology as a tool for knowledge sharing	Communication Interaction Direct contact
Zack (1999)	Tacit knowledge is embedded in the subconscious and is difficult to express in written form, but must be acquired by direct experience and action, often through storytelling, interaction, dialogue, or sharing of experiences	Storytelling Interaction Dialogue
Martensson (2000)	Transfer of tacit knowledge is developed through practice and interpersonal interaction	Interaction
Nonaka (1995)	Tacit knowledge can be gained by observers directly watching how experienced educators teach, or how educators solve problems in teaching, thereby enhancing their ability to cope with similar problems	Observation
Hargreaves (2000)	In teacher training, special emphasis is placed on teachers' professionalism and reflective skills. Apart from learning systematic knowledge and pedagogy, teachers are required to explore the tacit nature of their experience and knowledge, so that the tacit knowledge can be made visible and imparted to students and the professional growth of teachers can be realized	Reflection

(*continued*)

Table 3. (*continued*)

Author	Tacit Knowledge Transfer Methods	Approaches
Hashweb (2003)	Reflection is one of the learning values that educators can realize when they become aware of the significance of tacit knowledge and bring it to light through methods	Reflection
Gertler (2003)	1. Observation: Pay attention to the behavior and practices of others 2. Field of Trust: Create an environment of mutual trust and respect for each other 3. Learning by doing: Acquire knowledge naturally through behavior and movement 4. Feedback mechanism: Allow sufficient time for interaction and response during any exercise	Observation Practice Interaction

Source: Compiled by this study

3   Methodology

The first-year undergraduate program in basic design in the Department of Creative Design at NYUST consists of 7 h per week, divided into a 4-h theme day and a 3-h practice day. The theme day is devoted to design discussion and creative execution, while the practice day is dedicated to the impartation of specialist knowledge required for the main topic. The creative design department offers a 7-h program each semester from freshman to senior year, collectively known as thematic courses, to consolidate design-oriented education and training sessions. The department concerned is geared towards the development of creativity and the integration of the three disciplines of spatial, product and visual design as its main curriculum structure, with the aim of nurturing creative design talents with integrated skills. As such, subject teachers are drawn from the spatial, product and visual disciplines. This study introduced the basic design program in the second semester of 2020 in YunTech, Taiwan. The number of students enrolled was about 80, classified into three groups, and the 18-week period was split into three phases, featuring 6 weeks of basic visual graphic design, 6 weeks of product design and 6 weeks of spatial field as curriculum planning. In this way, the teacher of each subject area only taught 6 weeks of the theme days and then rotated through the three groups of students. The program was structured as a 6-week course with a 4-h theme day as the researcher is an instructor of visual graphics and rotated through the three groups of students, which was precisely in alignment with the revised reflective cycle of teaching action research.

The six-week visual dimension course is divided into three sequential stages: Stage 1 Corporate CIS System, Stage 2 Logo and Standard Characters, Stage 3 Color Schemes and Symbols, and Stage 4 Text Styling and Composition. This four-stage plan was structured around the theme of visualization supporting corporate image building as the teaching content of the YouTube moving images, and then based on the knowledge content, reference cases, design concepts, and related symbols and other axial elements of each stage, the subject knowledge was transformed into motion picture content and applied to the four phases of teaching and course interaction, so that students could recognize the process and notions of CIS corporate identity and image building in the design field by watching knowledge-based YouTube channels. Drawing on the deconstruction of design knowledge and its corresponding contextual demonstrations, as well as the translation of knowledge into symbolic imagery, the "YouTube influencer teaching technique" was integrated into the curriculum planning, providing students with a dual visual and auditory stimulation mode of learning. The interesting nature of this approach enables students to internalize the learning by watching videos that are linked to imagination, memory or experiential evocations. In the case of the "Basic Design" program in the first year of the Department of Creative Design at NYUST, after internalizing the design knowledge acquired through the "YouTube influencer teaching method," the first exercise on the application of the CIS corporate identity system design began, followed by recognizing the criteria and standards for the application of logos and standard characters, text and styling, and finally integrating the design of the complete identity system into the complete graphic design product.

4 Research Results

4.1 Learning Habits and Characteristics of Design Students

In this study, classroom observations, questionnaires and interviews were administered to understand the learning habits and characteristics of the students in the class. It was found that students' attentiveness in class was influenced by external conditions such as the teacher's reminders and questions, the teacher's dress, the learning atmosphere and the excellence in the work of their peers, and internal factors such as "wanting to listen" and "wanting to solve their own problems." Students' inattention in class was caused by external factors such as the time slot of the lesson, their connection to the lesson, the teacher's PowerPoint presentation, the amount of text in the slides, the number of cases cited, the duration of the presentation, the speed of the teacher's speech, the volume of homework and the pressure of the midterm, etc., and internal causes such as poor sleep the previous day, feeling that the course was off focus, short attention span, and wanting to play with their cell phones. This study further outlines the following factors that affected students' attention: (1) poorly made slides and too much text by the teacher; (2) the teacher speaking too slow when explaining; (3) the teacher's redundant words and unnecessary sharing; (4) the teacher taking too long in giving explanations; (5) the teacher citing an excessive number of cases; (6) the content of the lesson irrelevant to the students; (7) the lesson slot set too early in the day; (8) the teacher not dressed well; (9) the teacher being slack in giving reminders of salient points and posing questions; (10) the learning atmosphere; and (11) the peers' performance.

Classroom observations and interviews also revealed that students felt that systematic teaching was important, that the practice days on Thursday helped with the assignments in the basic design course, and that the teacher's presentations on practice days were now clear and to the point. And students suggested the following for the basic design course: (1) videos or animations should be included in the course; (2) the teacher should slow down the speed of speech when making key points; (3) the teacher may speak faster when talking about easy-to-understand parts; (4) the teacher could give interesting examples and lead the students in small exercises; (5) the teacher could make a summary of the salient points in the middle or at the end of the lesson; (6) the teacher could tie in what he/she has said with the current events or punch lines; (7) the jokes and stories told by the teacher should be relevant to the theme of the course; and (8) several teachers in charge of the course should coordinate on and communicate over the teaching progress. In addition, students prefer short, intensive learning sessions, indulgence, seeing great pieces of work being shared, teachers not interrupting or interfering when showing videos, videos not running too long or being boring, teachers putting leading questions before playing videos, and a variety of course content. In terms of teacher attributes, students prefer teachers who are distinctive in their personalities, speak logically and coherently, manage their time well, create a learning atmosphere, and do not dismiss students' answers. To sum up, students' learning preferences are as follows: (1) the lessons are tightly timed without delays; (2) the teacher does not interrupt or interfere when screening a film; (3) the teacher putting leading questions in advance will make students more attentive when watching a video; (4) the choice of films should be entertaining and not too long; (5) the teacher's distinctive personality will attract the students' attention; (6) it is important that the teacher speaks logically and coherently; (7) the teacher contributing to the learning atmosphere will make the students more willing to share and be involved in the class; and (8) negating the students' responses to questions put by the teacher will be offensive to them.

4.2   Differences in Knowledge Transfer Between Physical Courses and YouTube

This study, by drawing on the pedagogical practices of knowledge transformation by teachers in the delivery of basic design courses, further probes the knowledge transformation practices in the videos of channel "Ray Du English," which has over a million subscribers in Taiwan. It is hoped that by consulting the knowledge teaching practices on site and the knowledge translation modes on the popular YouTube channel "Ray Du English," a "YouTube influencer knowledge transfer model" can be constructed to attract students to watch and to convey the form of aesthetic principles of basic design knowledge smoothly.

Knowledge Conversion Techniques by Teachers in Delivering the Basic Design Courses on Site

At present, teachers put questions, cite cases and use visualized images and text, and utilized PowerPoint slides as the main teaching aids for the externalization of knowledge in the Basic Design course; regarding the combination of knowledge, teachers ask open-ended questions, give oral presentations and engage in discussions and dialogues; in respect of the internalization of knowledge, teachers give assignments to students to reflect on and internalize knowledge through practical exercises; and in terms of the socialization of knowledge, teachers share personal experiences and stories, and students discover the connections between knowledge and life through observation. Thus, if this study is to construct a "YouTube influencer delivery model" for designing basic knowledge to be transmitted after class to aid student learning, it will make reference to the knowledge conversion model used by teachers on site and improve on the inadequacies of the tools used in their instruction (Table 4).

Table 4. Knowledge conversion practices of teachers in delivering basic design courses on site

The SECI model of knowledge conversion	Teaching methods	Aids
Externalization	1.Teacher puts questions to students 2.Teacher asks students to work in groups and communicate with teams 3.Teacher cites examples, metaphors, hypotheses or analogies to illustrate knowledge content 4.Teacher uses visualized text, images or diagrams to teach	1.PowerPoint slides (with text, diagrams, pictures, etc.) 2. Pictures of cases or other graphics 3. Video clips
Combination	1. Open questions put by teacher 2. Teacher conveys knowledge by oral presentation 3. Teacher discusses with students	Nil (primarily delivered orally)
Internalization	Teacher asks students to do exercises for homework (e.g. bionics)	Nil (mainly based on students' hands-on work)
Socialization	1. Teacher shares their personal experiences and stories with students 2. Students discover the connection between knowledge and life through observation	Nil (mainly based on teachers' experience sharing and students' observations)

Source: Compiled by this study

YouTube Influencers' Video Content Features

Based on the analysis and collation of literature, this study has identified the content, management, interaction and marketing dimensions as the key factors influencing the viewing of YouTube videos. Among which, the content aspect includes topic setting, presentation style, information conversion, and character traits; the management aspect covers video releasing frequency, video quality, channel optimization, user satisfaction, and optimal search; the interaction aspect contains dialogue with viewers, rating mechanism, and message interaction; and the marketing aspect comprises website promotion, charity marketing, and mutually beneficial cooperation. In this study, three educational YouTube channels with more than one million subscribers each were selected for examination, and the case study method and content analysis were applied to summarize the success factors of these educational channels in terms of video content. Table 5 below gives the list of study subjects (data as of December 14, 2021), as well as individual information and introductions.

Table 5. List of study subjects

Informative YouTube channel	Ray Du English	Mr. & Mrs. Gao	ChuChuShoe
Created by	Ray Du	Mr. Gao	Jen-chieh Hsieh
Date of creation	2015.01.11	2014.11.17	2013.07.31
Content	English language teaching	Science fiction, suspense, technology, history	Technology, chemistry, trivia, book reviews
Subscriptions	2,690,000	3,910,000	1,500,000
No. of videos uploaded	546	213	573
Total channel views	276 million	1,063 million	232 million

Source: NoxInfluencer data analysis report. https://reurl.cc/L1vEgX. Compiled by this study

Case study Findings of Three Informative YouTube Channels

These three channels - Ray Du English, Mr. & Mrs. Gao and ChuChuShoe - have their own characteristics in topic setting, presentation style, information conversion and personality traits on the "content" side. The following is a compilation of the characteristics of the three channels (Tables 6, 7 and 8):

Table 6. Ray Du English

Topic Setting	Topicality	Moderate-This channel is centered on English teaching, sometimes combined with current events, songs, or other interesting topics
	Relevance	High-for channel viewers
	Value	High-for the acquisition of knowledge in the field
Presentation Style	Open Caption	Large, clear, lovely font types, multiple colors
	Background	Simple graphics, lovely style, colorful
	Background	Bright and clean study
Information Conversion	Information Content	Medium-by the length of episodes

(*continued*)

Table 6. (*continued*)

	Delivery	Mainly oral, with small graphics and enlarged text. Backgrounds change according to the subject matter, or another person showing up for a dialogue or a skit
Personality Traits	Speaking Characteristics	Clear and articulate, appropriate speed of speech, with marked fluctuations in tone
	Body Movements	Speech often accompanied by hand gestures, and key words emphasized by hand movements when mentioned
	Narrative Style	Coherent, focused, sincere and steady

Table 7. Mr. & Mrs. Gao

Topic Setting	Topicality	Very high-The choice of topics is highly interesting, including science fiction and suspense stories, knowledge about the universe, or unexplained mysteries that have not been solved in the past, arousing the audience's curiosity and desire to know more
	Relevance	Low-for channel viewers
	Value	High - for the acquisition of knowledge in the field
Presentation Style	Open Caption	Large, clear, mainly white on black
	Background	Multiple images appear with high frequency and clarity
	Background	Bright and clean living room
Information Conversion	Information Content	High (judged by the length of episodes)
	Delivery	Oral narrative accompanied by high-definition animations and clear photographs, with a good mix of illustrations and text, just like watching a story
Personality Traits	Speaking Characteristics	Clear and articulate, soft-spoken, appropriate speed of speech, steady volume of speech
	Body Movements	Not many body movements
	Narrative Style	Coherent, sincere, honest and steady

Table 8. ChuChuShoe

Topic Setting	Topicality	Moderate The topics are primarily science-related, and sometimes integrated with current events or the background of the times to share knowledge or marvelous tales that are not well known to the public, so as to resonate with the audience and make it more entertaining
	Relevance	Low (for channel viewers)
	Value	High (for the acquisition of knowledge in the field)
Presentation Style	Open Caption	Large, clear, mainly white on black
	Background	Multiple images appear with high frequency and clarity
	Background	White backdrop
Information Conversion	Information Content	Medium (by the length of episodes)
	Delivery	Oral narrative accompanied by high-definition animations and clear images, with a good mix of illustrations and text
Personality Traits	Speaking Characteristics	Clear and articulate, appropriate speed of speech, steady volume of speech
	Body Movements	Hand gestures in conjunction with spoken words, but not many body movements
	Narrative Style	Coherent, relaxed, natural, sincere and steady

Based on the results of the above analysis, this study further summarizes the common features of the three channels with regard to their content, including the setting of topics: high value in the field and rich knowledge content. Presentation style: The open caption font size is large, clear and highly visible. Images, graphics or high-resolution photographs are used frequently in conjunction with the video content. The background is bright and clean. Information conversion: The films are medium or high in information content and range in length from six to 15 min on average. Information conveyance: mainly verbal, with images, photos and animations depending on the subject matter and narrative text. Personal traits: They are articulate and speak at an appropriate speed. Their body movements are kept to a reasonable level, accompanying the spoken narration at the right time. They are well-organized, sincere and steady in their narrative.

These three channels -Ray Du English, Mr. & Mrs. Gao and ChuChuShoe - share a common characteristic in terms of "content." Compared to other types of channels, theses knowledge-based channels are more prominent with respect to the value of the topics set, the associative approach to knowledge transfer, and the well-structured narrative, which makes viewers willing to watch informative content without feeling rejected or bored by the dissemination of knowledge.

4.3 Feedback on the Application of the Knowledge Transfer Model of YouTube Influencers to Design Courses

The form of aesthetic principles constitutes the most crucial training method for basic design courses. As such, this study adopted the results of literature review and the analysis of Internet celebrities' informative channels as a way to design the curriculum on the transfer of the form of aesthetic principles and run the courses. The table below shows the types of knowledge and the corresponding contents summarized for the form of aesthetic principles. By means of knowledge simplification and clarification, the knowledge content conveyed by instructors is optimized and the complex information transmission by the recipient is thus alleviated (Table 9).

Table 9. Types of knowledge and corresponding content for the form of aesthetic principles

Form of Aesthetic Principles	Type of Knowledge	Content
Repetition	Explicit	A regular or irregular arrangement of the same or similar shapes, colors, notes, etc. in a repetitive manner
	Tacit	A visually vibrant or fresh look
Gradation	Explicit	The arrangement of identical shapes, colors and other unit forms in order of size or strength, resulting in a gradual change by order
	Tacit	An aesthetic sense of order
Symmetry	Explicit	One or more hypothetical axes, with opposing form elements arranged on either side of the axis to achieve a symmetrical expression of lines and points
	Tacit	A sense of calmness, poise and solemnity
Balance	Explicit	A symmetrical form on the left and right of one or more axes, where the visual senses do not favor one side over the other
	Tacit	A sense of mental stability and beauty
Harmony	Explicit	The placement of unit forms of the same or similar nature together in an orderly or non-orderly manner in the picture, with elements varying

(*continued*)

Table 9. (*continued*)

Form of Aesthetic Principles	Type of Knowledge	Content
	Tacit	A harmonious sense of integration and visual beauty
Proportion	Explicit	The numerical variation in the size or form of a unit form, which was applied to ancient Greek architecture and sculpture
	Tacit	Aesthetically pleasing visual proportions
Contrast	Explicit	The juxtaposition of two or two sets of opposing unit forms, in contrast to each other, bringing out their individuality
	Tacit	A strong visual impression
Rhythm	Explicit	The composition of the layers of the unit forms of shape, sound and color, and repetition, overlap and intricate arrangement, which can produce a continuous dynamic visual aesthetic without losing a sense of unity
	Tacit	A sense of lightness, slowness, exhilaration, and depression
Unity	Explicit	An orderly and non-fragmented organization of similar or identical forms, colors and other elements, which are linked by their common characteristics
	Tacit	A sense of visual calmness and harmony
Order	Explicit	The orderly and regular arrangement of elements such as shapes, forms and colors
	Tacit	A sense of visual stability or comfort

Based on literature review, design curriculum observation, and analysis of knowledge conversion techniques in Internet celebrities' informative videos to be transformed into a module on the "form of aesthetic principles" in the basic design curriculum for recording, with cognition, discovery, practice and reflection forming the pedagogical process, each episode invited a guest to join the host in a dialogue to transfer knowledge in an interactive and sharing mode. The primary approaches to knowledge transformation in the three videos were externalization and combination. Externalization was achieved through text captions, graphic insertions, hands-on demonstrations of AI software by guests, and examples of real-life situations. Combination was based on interaction and spoken conversations between guests and the host, open-ended questions posed to guests by the host, and the sharing of documents and personal design pieces by guests. Following the course, questionnaires, post-class focus groups and presentations were administered to analyze the YouTube influencer knowledge transfer model in terms of its appeal and knowledge reception benefits for design students, which is described as follows:

- Knowledge transfer is more readily accepted when done primarily with pictures. Whether delivered live or in a post-class video, students' reactions to the use of images instead of texts indicate that they comprehend the former better.
- "Form of Aesthetic Principles - Repetition and Rhythm" is a transfer of tacit knowledge, but the externalization, combination and socialization strategies in the film are effective in enhancing the receptivity of learners.
- The host at the beginning of the film gives a separate outline of the form of aesthetic principles, which helps in making sense of what is to follow.
- Examples from everyday life can easily lead to contextual applications and are effective in increasing stickiness.
- The film "AI Demonstration: Creating Beauty in Small Materials" provides a hands-on demonstration that facilitates comprehension of the aesthetic and practical applications.

5   Results and Discussion

From examining the content and characteristics of knowledge-based YouTube videos and knowledge transformation techniques, it is clear that the application and process of the Basic Design course must take into account the following points on the teaching side:

- Explicit knowledge transformation - the information content, structure and practicality are the key points that teachers must consider when preparing lessons.
- Conversion of tacit knowledge starts with inspiration and motivation to boost learning achievement.
- Personality affects the ambience of the classroom and the viewership.
- Knowledge summation is a requisite training for the instructor.
- The ability to narrate is a source of brilliance.
- Each class is preceded by a recap of the prior lesson and followed by a mini-review to enhance the learner's personal knowledge base.
- The teacher is not an Internet celebrity, but he/she can imitate their traits.
- The topics introduced in each lesson, if so well handled in terms of their topicality, relevance and value, can really catch the students' eyes.
- It is better to try to share the context in which information is transformed into knowledge than to forcefully promote the content of that knowledge.

References

Ahmad, J.: Technology assisted language learning is a silver bullet for enhancing language competence and performance: a case study. Int. J. Appl. Linguist. English Lit. 5(7), 118–131 (2016)

Alias, N., Razak, S.H.A., elHadad, G., Kunjambu, N.R.M.N.K., Muniandy, P.: A content analysis in the studies of YouTube in selected journals. Procedia Soc. Behav. Sci. 103, 10–18 (2013)

Barney, J.: Firm resources and sustained competitive advantage. J. Manag. 17(1), 99–120 (1991)

Davenport, T.H., Prusak, L.: Learn how valuable knowledge is acquired, created, bought and bartered. Aust. Libr. J. 47, 268–272 (1998)

Edvinsson, L., Sullivan, P.: Developing a model for managing intellectual capital. Eur. Manag. J. 14, 356–364 (1996)

Gertler, M.S.: Tacit knowledge and the economic geography of context, or the undefinable tacitness of being (there). J. Econ. Geogr. 3, 75–99 (2003)

Grant, R.M.: Toward a knowledge-based theory of the firm. Strateg. Manag. J. 17, 109–122 (1996)

Google blog: Taiwan's "YouTube User Behavior Survey" reveals the latest audio-visual trends. https://taiwan.googleblog.com/2017/10/youtube.html. Accessed 20 Dec 2019

Holtshouse, D.: Knowledge research issues. Calif. Manag. Rev. 40(3), 277–280 (1998)

Hedlund, G.: A model of knowledge management and the N-form corporation. Strateg. Manag. J. 15, 73–90 (1994)

Hargreaves, D.: The production, mediation and use ofprofessional knowledge among teachers and doctors: a comparative analysis. In: OECD (ed.) Knowledge Management in the Learning Society, pp. 219–238. OECD, Paris (2000)

Hashweb, M. Z.: Teacher accommodative change. Teach. Teach. Educ. 19(4), 421–434 (2003)

Hendriks, P.: Why share knowledge? The influence of ICT on motivation for knowledge sharing. Knowl. Process. Manag. 6(2), 91–100 (1999)

Mårtensson, M.: A critical review of knowledge management as a management tool. J. Knowl. Manag. 4(3), 204–216 (2000)

Nonaka, I.,Takeuchi, H.: The Knowledge Creating Company. Oxford University Press, Oxford (1995)

Polanyi, M.: The Tacit Dimension. Garden City, N.Y. (1967)

SmartM New Web Technology: Knowledge-based video content dominates; half of the population watches YouTube for "learning." (2017). https://www.smartm.com.tw/article/34333235cea3

Shen, H.-M.: A study on the acquisition of knowledge in knowledge management. Tamkang University, Department of Information Engineering (2006)

Zack, M.H.: Developing a knowledge strategy. Calif. Manag. Rev. 41(3), 125–145 (1999)

What Does It Take to Develop Critical Thinking? The Case of Multicultural Students in a Digital Learning Platform

Ajrina Hysaj[1] and Doaa Hamam[2](✉)

[1] UOWD College, University of Wollongong in Dubai, Dubai, United Arab Emirates
Ajrinahysaj@uowdubai.ac.ae
[2] Higher Colleges of Technology, Dubai, United Arab Emirates
dhamam@hct.ac.ae

Abstract. The focus of this study was to explore ways of developing critical thinking in multicultural undergraduate students in the digital learning platform (DLP). Two different classes participated in the study, and they were both taught by the same lecturer. The lecturer utilised topics related to culture and identity to encourage students' active involvement in online forums and breakout sessions. Students were placed in groups of four and were asked to research their own culture and the culture of another group member. Students researched cultures and discussed their viewpoints during the breakout sessions and discussion forums. The process aimed to stimulate the multicultural students' desire to explore, research, challenge their worldviews, and most importantly, reflect on their accumulated information about their group members, and describe the academic and social experience. A sample size of 30 multicultural undergraduate students was selected during the spring semester to collect data. The progression of ideas, vocabulary, and negotiation of thoughts was analysed at the start and the end of the semester. The purpose was to analyse the development of critical thinking. Finally, the findings were described and recommendations for future research were presented.

Keywords: DLP · Critical Thinking · Online Learning · Reflective Learning · Multiculturalism

1 Introduction

Our traditional or virtual classrooms create natural teaching and learning contexts on a daily basis. These contexts vary based on the topics being taught, the demographics of the cohorts of students, the multiculturalism they present, and of course, the educators' desire and hard work to explain concepts appropriately and enable students' understanding [30, 37]. Many factors are involved in the students' desire to learn, understand, and, more importantly, connect with the material taught in person or in the digital learning platform (DLP) [6, 42]. These aspects are unique to each individual based on their personal and social environments. Although it seems extremely challenging to create an appropriate context of learning in a class of students from a multicultural and multilingual corpus, it is always worth trying. This should be done while considering the possible variations that multiculturalism brings along and looking to create an inclusive environment for all students, irrespective of their culture, race, or mother tongue [17]. According to references [12, 28], critical thinking as a metacognitive process is developed through purpose-driven activities, self-reflective perceptions, creation of inferences, evaluation of facts, and, most importantly, a genuine disposition to utilise thinking, aiming at understanding problems to find solutions. From this array of processes involved in the critical thinking process, the majority are individual self-driven [9, 10], and if they are not present in all students, they need to be created by the utilisation of external sources that educators' involvement provides [40]. The development of critical thinking in our classrooms serves the purpose of students' academic and individual satisfaction, improvement of inclusiveness, and creates citizens who aim for a logical purpose when approaching issues and challenges [41, 44]. The presence of critical thinking in the curriculums allows the prevalence of critical thinkers, which adds to educational institutes' cultural perspectives and creates open-minded citizens who tend to include analytical and critical thinking in their decision process [38]. This opens the path to superior maturity levels of judgment and improved confidence in reasoning that result in mature and well-thought decisions taken in complex and challenging circumstances [10] require social and interpersonal levels daily [12].

2 Literature Review

2.1 Defining Critical Thinking in Academic Writing Classes

Critical thinking is one of the factors that influences our decisions in how we see the world and the people around us [18, 31]. We are always required to make well-informed decisions on a daily basis, these decisions may impact our lives and the lives of others [43]. While considering the purpose and the consequences of our choices, we unknowingly connect our present to our past, create inferences between circumstances and situations that help us connect with our new present, and create mental maps of our past and future. The variations of our thoughts facilitate the diversity developed within us [10], and this display of variety is highly vulnerable and considerate of our emotions. In other words, we are trying to understand our present and connect it to our past, so we do not get disappointed by the outcome of our decisions, their implementation, and subsequent consequences [38]. In creating a bond with the matter we are analysing, we utilise our critical thinking ability and diversify it depending on the circumstances [16]. Critical thinking allows us not only to connect to what we need to, but it also enables us to think about the solutions in various ways, which, most of the time, are different from those of others [43]. Diversification of ideas comes from implementing critical thinking and is valuable to us as individuals and others around us in private, social or business environments [16, 38].

According to references [8, 15, 50], critical thinking is a combination of our desire to achieve something or find a solution to a problem. Usually, the self-confidence that what we are trying to reach is worth of our attention and it becomes achievable under our circumstances. Understandably, external sources such as family, work, and society impact our individual belief that something is manageable and worth trying. Furthermore, as curious creatures, humans need to have the desire to find solutions to problems and, as brave creatures, have the courage to voice our opinions despite the antagonism they might employ [51]. Noticeably, critical thinking allows the people who aim to develop it, to understand concepts and try to find solutions which are not necessarily understood by everyone [34]. In other words, critical thinking separates people's thoughts and the ways they see the world [49], and it offers people and the society as a whole endless possibilities for diversification, innovation and, most importantly, growth.

2.2 Exploring the Diversity of Worldviews Through the Use of Online Discussion Boards

Critical thinking is not considered an inner characteristic of humans; therefore, it requires nourishment through thoughtful enrichment and continuous development of its components [37]. Academic settings have to nurture the development of critical thinking by creating adequate conditions for students to develop this indispensable higher-order thinking skill [9]. Since critical thinking requires constant challenges, academic settings can offer this through a continuous and purposeful approach to develop it, and allow students to progress in their chosen fields and careers [27]. According to reference [12], critical thinking can be developed once educators are aware of developing critical thinking as a higher-order thinking skill while creating curriculums, activities and assessments that encourage, but not challenge it. It is valuable to mention that aspects of developing critical thinking should take into consideration our globalised world and globalised education systems. Reflective learning is now used by an increasing number of educators as a very practical approach to teaching, contemplating learning and events and most constantly on individual challenges, disadvantages and growth [21, 30]. A very important factor of reflective learning is the possibility of being individualised and internalised. According to reference [39], subjects and assessments that encourage internalisation and personalisation allow students to explore their beings from academic, personal and social perspectives [2, 50]. Such personalisation will enable students to consider the rapport they may or may not have with a piece of writing, an assessment, a group they are working with, the subject they are studying and most importantly, themselves [49]. Generally, students' academic growth is associated with individual self-satisfaction and higher retention rates [36, 46]. This empowers higher education with individuals who are ambitious to succeed and yet brave enough to accept their failures and look for ways to overcome their challenges [33].

2.3 Development of Critical Thinking Through Discussion Forums

Opponents of debates believe that participation in a debate neither challenges students' existing beliefs nor promotes an objective analysis of an issue [29]. Nevertheless, reference [48] asserts that such development can occur as a result of participating in role-playing or debate. Another common issue prevalent in class debates is the limited number of students who participate actively throughout the debate or even those who do not even participate at all. This leaves the rest of the class in an atmosphere of passive learning. Very often, the most fluent students tend to be the most persuasive [22, 53]. However, this does not account for their self-organisation, the proper flow of thoughts, backed up by adequate and recent research sources and eventually presentation of argument through a series of verbally appropriate actions, e.g., appropriate eye contact with the audience, adequate responses to all of the opponent's points with reasonable and thought-provoking arguments [22, 53]. Moreover, as debates are held in real-time, the possibility for errors in the delivery or the evaluation methods is relatively high; and it could only be tackled by fostering active learning, understanding of the topic, and proper application of skills learned in class [47].

Another platform for developing critical and analytical thinking in undergraduate students is online discussion forums. Some of the instructional design techniques commonly used in online discussions are based on triangulation, they do not only support the development of critical and analytical thinking, but they also encourage undergraduates to actively engage in the discussion forums since the methods of getting involved are inclusive of their preferred styles of argumentation. Another crucial component of learning through discussion forums is inquiry-based learning, which applies to almost all learners, age groups, and education systems. The adaptation of technological advances, tools [20], and inquiry skills are inextricably intertwined [13] and hence encourage an integrated understanding of concepts and solutions. Therefore, if they are used actively during the discussion sessions, they may encourage the development of critical thinking. Furthermore, critical thinking as a metacognitive process involves purposeful and reflective judgment, which has the potential to develop the ability to find logical solutions to problems [11]. Therefore, according to reference [32], the instructional design of online discussions requires a combination of inquiry-based-learning and integration of online tools, e.g., asynchronous and synchronous discussion forums, resource sharing, and web search engines to name a few.

Moreover, the exceeding importance of critical thinking correlates with the utilisation of the latter in understanding information, advancement in sound decision-making, and problem-solving of real-world applications [13, 14, 21]. For instance, online discussions allow students to negotiate inquiry-based learning if they offer practical solutions to existing problems. Also, students should be informed about the expectations of inquiry-based learning and instructed to respond to a minimum of three of their friends' posts. In this case, naturally, they will try to use their judgment in inquiring about the topic and responding to their peers' posts in a formal and academic way. When inquiring about a topic and responding to the peers' comments, students will develop a sense of curiosity, raise awareness of their critical thinking, engage actively in reflection, and develop higher-order thinking skills [5, 22]. Reference [19] emphasises that the development of critical thinking through the online format differs from the face-to-face counterpart in many aspects. Finally, the importance of discussions over its development remains the same. Therefore, the provision of various methods and applications that encourage the utilisation of undergraduates' intellectual capacity while setting continuous higher standards of critical and analysis not only allows students to recognise their true potentials, but also empowers them with the skills of understanding and appreciating other students' potentials. Therefore, this creates an atmosphere of improved and purposeful engagement in the DLP, which allows the prevalence of effective critical thinking development through the digital learning platform [23, 24].

3 Methodology

The present study contributes to the research on developing critical thinking in multicultural undergraduate students in the DLP during the COVID-19 pandemic. The researchers used Bloom's taxonomy of the hierarchy of educational goals categories to analyse the work of undergraduates. According to Bloom's taxonomy, the ways of measuring the outcomes of students' goals start from lower-order learning goals of "remembering" and "understanding", to the mid-level uses of knowledge as evidenced in "applying" and "analysing", with "evaluation" and "creation" that indicate the achievement of deeper understanding [7]. The target population for the study were multicultural undergraduate students enrolled in different majors in an international university in the United Arab Emirates. Two different classes participated in the study and were taught by the same lecturer. The lecturer utilised topics related to culture and identity to encourage students' active involvement in online forums and breakout sessions. A sample size of 30 multicultural undergraduate students enrolled in the spring semester was used to collect data. Students were enrolled in two different classes and were taught by the same instructor. As for the procedures, students were placed in groups of four, and asked to research their own culture and the culture of another group member. The study involved designing and structuring questions to cover various aspects of culture and identity. Students conducted the research process as homework while the discussions were done in breakout sessions and in the discussion forums. The DLP was used in the study, and students used applications like miro-map for brainstorming ideas on cultures and breakout sessions to discuss cultures. The students were encouraged to explore, research, present, challenge their worldviews and, most importantly, reflect on their accumulated information about the cutlures of their peers. Discussion forums were analysed using Bloom's Taxonomy of educational goals outcomes, aiming to develop critical thinking skills through the time spent in higher-order thinking activities like oral and written discussion forums.

4 Results

Data was collected from students' written tasks in the discussion forums and then organised and tabulated within the contingency tables. The data was analysed using descriptive methods where necessary, and the undergraduates differed based on the development of critical thinking and content description. The progression of ideas, the vocabulary used, and the negotiation of thoughts was analysed at the start of the semester and at the end to analyse the development of critical thinking. The overall results of undergraduates' experience of working in groups and discussing about cultures and identities were highly positive. 70% of multicultural students expressed that they enjoyed spending time being actively engaged in group discussions. Around 68% of students enjoyed being involved in higher-order thinking activities that required problem-solving skills. Over 80% of students were satisfied with increased opportunities for interacting with other students. Moreover, 75% of students saw an improvement in their level of thought negotiation, and 60% of students witnessed an increased interest in researching cultures and identity. The majority of students with over 80% enjoyed collaborating with their classmates and felt comfortable discussing concepts of culture and identity in the DLP. Furthermore,

76% of students presented their findings efficiently during the breakout sessions and 66% clearly negotiated their worldviews in discussion forums. 70% of students enjoyed collaborating in the DLP, and over 78% did not find it difficult to communicate with their group members despite not being physically present with them. Although most students felt that the thoughts of culture and identity challenged them, over 67% of them believed that their communication with their group members was efficiently done through the breakout sessions and discussion forums. Two of the most challenging items for most students were the need to explore cultures to understand other students' viewpoints and the development of open-mindedness through challenging biased opinions. Respectively, over 67% of students saw the need to collaborate continuously with students of other cultures in group work, and more than 63% found it easy to find similarities and differences among cultures. 82% of students believed that their desire to explore cultures and individual identity was increased due to group work. Furthermore, 67% expressed an interest in presenting their findings to the group members and answering their questions about culture and identity. Around 76% of students expressed interest in reflecting on their accumulated information and academic and social experience. Finally, over 70% of students expressed the development of ideas through a progressive curve and used improved vocabulary and grammatical forms.

5 Discussion

The study led to certain significant findings. The first finding is that the undergraduates found the online group discussion experience very positive. This finding is similar to the previous findings of [25, 35, 52]. The students enjoyed interacting with others, and they also liked the involvement in higher-order thinking activities and the development of problem-solving skills, and this finding also concurs with the findings of references [22, 26]. The students also showed a lot of interest in conducting research and collaborating with their peers, which agrees with the findings of reference [45]. Moreover, the students described the communication process as easy and smooth despite the fact it was done online and not face-to-face. This finding disagrees with the findings of reference [3] who mentioned that there was no significant difference between the level of communication skills in the live classes and the face-to-face classes. Another interesting finding was that the majority of students were challenged by two aspects, the first was the need to explore cultures to understand others' points of view and they also found the need to collaborate with students from other cultures in group work. The students reported that their desire to explore culture and identity was increased after doing the group work which agrees with the findings of references [1] and [4].

6 Conclusion and Recommendations

The study concludes that online discussions on culture and identity positively impacted the students' critical thinking abilities. Most students reported that they enjoyed working in the DLP and researching topics related to culture and identity. Furthermore, students preferred discussion forums as an alternative form of assessment. Furthermore, online discussions also made it possible for multicultural students to interact with each other and learn about cultures and identities. Therefore, based on empirical evidence from the existing literature and the findings of this study, it is recommended to incorporate online discussions into the curriculum to ensure the development of the students' critical thinking skills, their active engagement in the learning process as well as the degree of interaction with their peers. In conclusion, group work increases the interest of multicultural undergraduate students to research culture and negotiate the thought with their group members. However, it is worth considering exploring the growth of critical thinking in other discipline-related subjects aiming to improve students' cognitive and analytical skills. To sum up, the students accepted and enjoyed the online discussions and described a positive experience learning through the DLP.

References

1. Abrams, Z.I.: Surfing to cross-cultural awareness: using internet-mediated projects to explore cultural stereotypes. Foreign Lang. Ann. **35**(2), 141–160 (2002)
2. Akpur, U.: Critical, reflective, creative thinking and their reflections on academic achievement. Think. Skills Creat. **37** (2020)
3. Aslan, A.: Problem-based learning in live online classes: learning achievement, problem-solving skill, communication skill, and interaction. Comput. Educ. **171**, 104237 (2021)
4. Baker, W., Fang, F.: 'So maybe I'm a global citizen': developing intercultural citizenship in English medium education. Lang. Cult. Curric. **34**(1), 1–17 (2021)
5. Bai, H.: Facilitating students' critical thinking in online discussion: an instructor's experience. J. Interact. Online Learn. **8**(2) (2009)
6. Benzie, H.J., Harper, R.: Developing student writing in higher education: digital third-party products in distributed learning environments. Teach. High. Educ. **25**(5), 633–647 (2020)
7. Bloom, B.: Bloom's taxonomy (1956)
8. Bowman, R.F.: A new story about teaching and learning. Clearing House **92**(3), 112–117 (2019)
9. Chaisuwan, C., Kelly, K., Kelman, G.B., Continelli, T.: Relationship between cultural value and critical thinking dispositions and their difference among nursing students in Thailand and United States. Pac. Rim Int. J. Nurs. Res. **25**(2), 199–212 (2021)
10. Cleary, M., Lees, D., Sayers, J.: Leadership, thought diversity, and the influence of groupthink. Issues Ment. Health Nurs. **40**(8), 731–733 (2019)
11. Dwyer, C.P., Hogan, M.J., Stewart, I.: An integrated critical thinking framework for the 21st century. Think. Skills Create. **12**, 43–52 (2014)
12. Dwyer, C.P., Walsh, A.: An exploratory quantitative case study of critical thinking development through adult distance learning. Educ. Tech. Res. Dev. **68**(1), 17–35 (2019). https://doi.org/10.1007/s11423-019-09659-2
13. Edelson, D.C., Gordin, D.N., Pea, R.D.: Addressing the challenges of inquiry-based learning through technology and curriculum design. J. Learn. Sci. **8**(3–4), 391–450 (1999)
14. Farouqa, G., Hysaj, A.: Active learning in the lenses of faculty: a qualitative study in universities in the United Arab Emirates. In: Meiselwitz, G. (ed.) HCII 2022. LNCS, vol. 13316, pp. 77–90. Springer, Cham (2022). https://doi.org/10.1007/978-3-031-05064-0_6
15. Genç, G.: The relationship between academic achievement, reading habits and critical thinking dispositions of Turkish tertiary level EFL learners. Educ. Res. Q. **41**(2), 43–73 (2017)
16. Giannouli, V., Giannoulis, K.: Critical thinking and leadership: can we escape modern Circe's spells in nursing? Nurs. Leadersh. (1910–622X) **34**(1), 38–44 (2021)

17. Grice, K.M., Rebellino, R.L.R., Stamper, C.N.: Connecting across borders by reading without walls: using non-prose narratives to multiply multicultural class content. Engl. J. **107**(1), 48–53 (2017)
18. Halpern, D.F.: Whither psychology. Perspect. Psychol. Sci. **12**(4), 665–668 (2017)
19. Hall, R.A.: Critical thinking in online discussion boards: transforming an anomaly. Delta Kappa Gamma Bull. **81**(3) (2015)
20. Hamam, D., Hysaj, A.: Technological pedagogical and content knowledge (TPACK): higher education teachers' perspectives on the use of TPACK in online academic writing classes. In: Stephanidis, C., Antona, M., Ntoa, S. (eds.) HCII 2021. CCIS, vol. 1421, pp. 51–58. Springer, Cham (2021). https://doi.org/10.1007/978-3-030-78645-8_7
21. Hoffmann, M.H.G.: Stimulating reflection and self-correcting reasoning through argument mapping: three approaches. Int. Rev. Philos. **37**(1), 185–199 (2018)
22. Hysaj, A., Hamam, D.: Understanding the development of critical thinking through classroom debates and online discussion forums: a case of higher education in the UAE. J. Asia TEFL **18**(1), 373–379 (2021)
23. Hysaj, A., Hamam, D.: Academic writing skills in the online platform-a success, a failure or something in between? A study on perceptions of higher education students and teachers in the UAE. In: 2020 IEEE International Conference on Teaching, Assessment, and Learning for Engineering (TALE), pp. 668–673. IEEE (2020)
24. Hysaj, A., Suleymanova, S.: The analysis of developing the application of critical thinking in oral and written discussions: the case of Emirati students in the United Arab Emirates. In: 2020 IEEE International Conference on Teaching, Assessment, and Learning for Engineering (TALE), pp. 819–824. IEEE (2020)
25. Hysaj, A., Hamam, D., Baroudi, S.: Efficacy of group work in the online platform: an exploration of multicultural undergraduates' attitudes in online academic writing classes. In: Meiselwitz, G. (ed.) HCII 2021. LNCS, vol. 12775, pp. 246–256. Springer, Cham (2021). https://doi.org/10.1007/978-3-030-77685-5_20
26. Jaenudin, R., Chotimah, U., Farida, F., Syarifuddin, S.: Student development zone: higher order thinking skills (hots) in critical thinking orientation. Int. J. Multicult. Multireligious Underst. **7**(9), 11–19 (2020)
27. Kabwete, C.M., Kambanda, S., Kagwesage, A.M., Murenzi, J.: Fighting intellectual marginalisation through critical thinking: a glimpse at mature women's tertiary education in Rwanda. Res. Post-Compulsory Educ. **25**(1), 68–90 (2020)
28. Kalelioğlu, F., Gülbahar, Y.: The effect of instructional techniques on critical thinking and critical thinking dispositions in online discussion. J. Educ. Technol. Soc. **17**(1), 248–258 (2014)
29. Kennedy, R.: In-class debates: fertile ground for active learning and the cultivation of critical thinking and oral communication skills. Int. J. Teach. Learn. High. Educ. **19**(2) (2007)
30. Kmieciak, R.: Critical reflection and innovative work behavior: the mediating role of individual unlearning. Pers. Rev. **50**(2), 439–459 (2021)
31. Kyung-Ae, O.: Developing critical thinking skills through a mandatory English course in Korean higher education. English Teach. **72**(4), 53–80 (2017)
32. Lau, J.Y.: An Introduction to Critical Thinking and Creativity: Think More, Think Better. Wiley, Hoboken (2011)
33. Lewis, C.L., Wanzy, D.M., Lynch, C.M., Dearmon, V.A.: GROWTH: a strategy for nursing student retention. J. Nurs. Educ. **58**(3), 173–177 (2019)
34. Matthee, M., Turpin, M.: Teaching critical thinking, problem solving, and design thinking: preparing IS students for the future. J. Inf. Syst. Educ. **30**(4), 242–252 (2019)
35. Maqableh, M., Alia, M.: Evaluation online learning of undergraduate students under lockdown amidst COVID-19 Pandemic: the online learning experience and students' satisfaction. Child. Youth Serv. Rev. **128** (2021)

36. Neolaka, F., Corebima, A.D.: Comparison between correlation of creative thinking skills and learning results, and correlation of creative thinking skills and retention in the implementation of predict observe explain (POE) learning model in senior high schools in Malang, Indonesia. Educ. Process Int. J. **7**(4), 237–245 (2018)

37. Nippold, M.A., LaFavre, S., Shinham, K.: How adolescents interpret the moral messages of fables: examining the development of critical thinking. J. Speech Lang. Hear. Res. **63**(4), 1212–1226 (2020)

38. Norman, M., Chang, P., Prieto, L.: Stimulating critical thinking in U.S business students through the inclusion of international students. J. Bus. Divers. **17**(1), 122–130 (2017)

39. Novakovich, J.: Fostering critical thinking and reflection through blog-mediated peer feedback. J. Comput. Assist. Learn. **32**(1), 16–30 (2016)

40. Núñez, Q.Á.: Systemic pedagogy and interculturalism: keys to creating and inclusive classroom. RevistaLusofona de Educacao **37**(37), 165–179 (2017)

41. Olson, C.B., et al.: The pathway to academic success: scaling up a text-based analytical writing intervention for Latinos and English learners in secondary school. J. Educ. Psychol. **112**(4), 701–717 (2020)

42. Org, A.: The process of essay writing in a literature course: the student's views and the tutor's feedback. Estonian J. Educ. /EestiHaridusteadusteAjakiri**7**(2), 124–127 (2019)

43. Pagani, C.: Empathy, complex thinking and their interconnections. Interface/Probing Bound. **92**, 41–60 (2017)

44. Pereg, M., Meiran, N.: Power of instructions for task implementation: superiority of explicitly instructed over inferred rules. Psychol. Res. **85**(3), 1047–1065 (2020). https://doi.org/10.1007/s00426-020-01293-5

45. Read, D., Barnes, S.M., Hughes, O., Ivanova, I., Sessions, A., Wilson, P.J.: Supporting student collaboration in online breakout rooms through interactive group activities. New Dir. Teach. Phys. Sci. **17**(1) (2022)

46. Roohr, K., Olivera-Aguilar, M., Ling, G., Rikoon, S.: A multi-level modeling approach to investigating students' critical thinking at higher education institutions. Assess. Eval. High. Educ. **44**(6), 946–960 (2019)

47. Scannapieco, F.A.: Formal debate: an active learning strategy. J. Dent. Educ. **61**, 955–961 (1997)

48. Simonneaux, L.: Analysis of classroom debating strategies in the field of biotechnology. J. Biol. Educ. **37**(1), 9–12 (2002)

49. Vero, E., Puka, E.: The effectiveness of critical thinking in higher education. Online J. Model. New Europe **26**, 217–233 (2018)

50. Wallis, A.K., Westerveld, M.F., Waters, A.M., Snow, P.C.: Investigating adolescent discourse in critical thinking: monologic responses to stories containing a moral dilemma. Lang. Speech Hear. Serv. Sch. **52w**, 630–643 (2021)

51. Young, A.S.: Effects of integrative simulation practice on nursing knowledge, critical thinking, problem-solving ability, and immersion in problem-based learning among nursing students. Korean J. Women Health Nurs. **26**(1), 61–71 (2020)

52. Yu, Z.: The effects of gender, educational level, and personality on online learning outcomes during the COVID-19 pandemic. Int. J. Educ. Technol. High. Educ. **18**(1), 1–17 (2021). https://doi.org/10.1186/s41239-021-00252-3

53. Zare, P., Othman, M.: Students' perceptions toward using classroom debate to develop critical thinking and oral communication ability. Asian Soc. Sci. **11**(9), 158 (2015)

Theory of Planned Behaviour in Higher Education: Exploring the Perceptions of Multicultural ESL Students About Cheating

Ajrina Hysaj[1]([✉]) [iD], Mark Freeman[2] [iD], and Zeenath Reza Khan[1] [iD]

[1] University of Wollongong in Dubai, Dubai, United Arab Emirates
{ajrinahysaj,zeenathkhan}@uowdubai.ac.ae
[2] University of Wollongong, Wollongong, Australia
mfreeman@uow.edu.au

Abstract. The theory of planned behaviour (TPB) is explored in relation to the different aspect of education. However, little work has been undertaken to explore the impact of TPB in the field of English language teaching. The aim of this paper is to understand the possible ways of utilising TPB in English as second language (ESL) classes. This study took place in a variety of private and federal universities in the United Arab Emirates, Malaysia and Japan and it evaluated the perceptions of undergraduate students about concepts related to TPB like intention, attitude, subjective norms, social desirability bias, academic writing and the tendency to plagiarise. The study was concerned with the concept of cheating amongst undergraduate students. The approach used for this study was a survey that contained questions about plagiarism, academic writing and the notions of TPB. The sample size was 336 multicultural undergraduate students enrolled in a variety of majors belonging to a variety of ethnic and linguistic background. The quantitative findings of this study indicate that there is a correlation between the intention to cheat and plagiarism instances. Nevertheless, this study highlights the need to further explore TPB in the context of English teaching to ESL students. Finally, this study discusses the necessity to consider the continuous adaptations of teaching and learning environments to create inclusiveness for students and teachers based on the concepts of TPB.

Keywords: TPB · Academic Writing · ESL Students · Plagiarism · Active Participation

1 Introduction

The theory of planned behaviour (TPB) first introduced by Ajzen [1] and later extended by Ajzen [2], Ajzen, Brown and Carvajal [3–5], Ajzen and Fishbein [6] and finally Ajzen [7]. In the field of education TPB can be utilized to explore, understand and predict behaviour which could involve any of the stakeholders of the education field. Furthermore, TPB can be utilized to assess the system of ideas present in learners, peers, families and other significant ones to ensure inclusive and proactive education [34]. The

A. Coman and S. Vasilache (Eds.): HCII 2023, LNCS 14026, pp. 58–71, 2023.
https://doi.org/10.1007/978-3-031-35927-9_5

system of ideas and moral values present in students and exhibited under specific circumstances can be utilized to predict the desired behaviour and the possible outcomes in relation to all aspects of teaching and learning [10, 13, 34], including classroom participation, teacher-student interaction, student-student interaction, as well as instructional design that includes stages involved in teaching, learning, assessing and reflecting on teaching and learning [3–5]. Teaching and learning processes are highly correlated and require equal and appropriate attention for the benefit of all the stakeholders. Since TPB encourages us to look into the behaviour of all parties involved, it as well facilitates our consideration for the respective needs, aiming to achieve the common goal of education which is teaching and learning.

The widespread use of technology has facilitated learning in all corners of the world and has created the possibility of a more inclusive education arena. Due to the extensive use of ICT, the humanity has seen a continuous increase in the degree, width and spread of theories and practices involving education in general and more specifically higher education. Furthermore, since TPB considers the psychological aspects of human behaviour as the driving force behind their actions, it makes it valuable to correlate it with the use of technological advances utilized in higher education. The perceptions of undergraduate students about technology have changed through the years based on the advancement of technology and its spread worldwide. For instance, a study by Siragusa and Dixon [37] that analysed the likelihood of undergraduate students to use ICT through a quantitative and qualitative approach found that although students considered ICT as helpful and easy to manage, they tended to experience anxiety and intimidation when using it. This experience then guided their decision to use ICT with caution and understandably opens the path for investigating the relationship between TPB and the many uses of ICT in a teaching and learning environment [16, 24, 27, 31, 37].

Exploration of ways that facilitate students learning and support their academic achievement require adequate consideration and represent the focal point of a successful education system [24, 27, 31]. Furthermore, it is valuable to explore the underlying processes that may have an impact on a successful university experience for the university students. Moreover, TPB allows the exploration of educators' behaviour and their perception with regard to teaching and learning processes while bridging the gap between students and educators' measures of past behaviour and actual behaviour in the context of higher education [33, 34]. A very interesting and valuable aspect of TPB is its consideration for the development of cognitive skills in both students and educators, as well the prediction of current behaviour of both parties based on previous exhibited behaviour [31, 34]. Understanding previous displayed behaviour can influence current realization of possible actions and guide an expected behaviour which is recognized and acknowledged by teachers and students. Likewise, this can be influencing the perceived behavioural control (PBC) as well as subjective norms(SN) resulting in being significant predictors of yet to be explored students' future actions and most importantly the prediction of their academic success[42, 40]. TPB can be utilized to explore teachers' behaviour with respect to the prediction of future actions addressing issues pertaining the design of curriculum, classroom management and most importantly creation of an inclusive environment for all students [22].

2 Literature Review

2.1 Exploring ESL Learning and Teaching Based on the Theory of Planned Behaviour (TPB)

The valuable individual beliefs like attitudes, intentions, subjective norms and perceived behavioural control, are acknowledged to act as guided influencers of people' s future actions [15]. Therefore, it is worth to consider the application of TPB to all aspects of teaching and learning process aiming to predict students and teachers' intentions towards an improved teaching and learning environment [31]. Since TPB guides many aspects of human activity, it influences teachers and students' intentions to perform a given behaviour and can simultaneously be adopted as a given framework that encourages the implementation of an inclusive education [32, 33]. Such initiatives require careful consideration of previous research that has tapped into the explored trends of TPB and its research gaps [33]. Furthermore, according to a study by Gatfield and Chen [16], the differences in motivations in undergraduates guide their academic perspectives and subsequent choices starting from the choice of the study degree to the choice of elective subjects, and finally the choice of internships and consideration of suitable job opportunities [16, 21].

Despite being widely explored and utilized in many aspects of education, the theory of planned behaviour is yet to experience a deeper utilization in the field of English language teaching and specifically with regard to curriculum design and student- teacher interaction [36–39]). One way that TPB can be utilized in English language classrooms is by analyzing the different ways that support students learning of grammar and vocabulary. For instance, a study by Tight [39] found that students who are concerned about high-stake examinations may opt in unfavourable attitudes towards studying for those tests and fail therefore to meet expectations of parents, teachers and more importantly themselves [17, 21]). The attitudes of learners of English language may support of hinder their learning process by means belonging to any of the constructs of TPB or its extended models explored by many researchers. Study by Girardelli, Patel and Martins-Shannon [18], that aimed at exploring the in-class participation of a group of Chinese students in an English class, found that the core TPB constructs such as intention, subjective norms and perceived behavioural control or in other words self-efficacy were seen by students equally important to other additional constructs, unique to Chinese students and their culture, which were face-saving and anxiety induced due to foreign language learning. Constructs of face-saving and foreign language anxiety in Chinese students are commonly discussed in English as a foreign language with the aim of supporting the learning process of Chinese students [17, 18, 43].

Another aspect of English teaching worth exploring is the use of Information and Communication Technology (ICT) and the tendency of EFL students to adopt it in their learning. According to a study by Wang, Zhao and Cheng [40] that surveyed 409 Chinese students indicated that individuals who are genuinely interested in utilization of technology tend to not suffer from the stress induced as a result of the use of technology. Based on TPB, the determinants of ESL learners' technology adaptation require exploration since they are used in combination with the other aspects of foreign language learning [40]. Furthermore, the influences of 'techno stress' and the desire to adopt technology implies the tendency of students to engage in English learning online and offline more often and for longer period of time. Understandably the effects of adoption intention in the context of English language learning resulted in increased frequency of studying English and improved duration of the study period [21]. Additionally, the successful integration of ICT enables flexible teaching and learning approaches and creates an inclusive environment that permits educators and learners to continuously progress in ESL teaching and learning. Consequently, it is important for the educators to consider the positive and drawback aspects of using ICT in relation the TPB so they can match students' expectations and their patterns of behaviour towards learning and more specifically learning with ICT. The careful consideration of students' needs should be regarded as substantial to improve students' learning environment, their retention and subsequently improve their academic outcomes.

2.2 Exploring Angles of ESL Student Active Participation Based on the Theory of Planned Behaviour (TPB)

Teaching and learning processes are highly correlated; hence, the alignment of curriculum design is as important to the learning and teaching process as it is the active participation of students. The attitude of students towards ESL learning with regard to perceived behavioural control and subjective norms influences their levels of active participation in learning activities online and offline [41–43]. Compatibility of these aspects of TPB can be a strong predictor of their active participation in the learning process [9, 11]. Research on students' retention first appeared into radar screen back in the 1960s [36] and continued with the works of Dewberry and Jackson [12] and Tight [39] and many others, who looked at the retention process of undergraduate students from the perspective of TPB. The underlying assumptions of what translates into higher students' retention degrees has changed continuously during the years. Nevertheless, back then and now, a considerable number of researchers view the issue using lens of psychology since it is closely related to the individual attributes of learners as well as their unique sets of skills, motivation and importantly intention as much as it is related to the society and the environment where education takes place [12, 39].

One of aspects seen as crucial in improving students' retention levels is students' engagement [14, 25]. Expected active students' participation seen during the classroom activities is often interpreted in improved students' academic satisfaction and subsequently greater students' retention. According to the works by Call [9] and Girardelli and Patel [17] the predictors of students' self- efficacy and self-esteem were correlated with the intention of students to participate in classroom activities and to complete assessment tasks on-time. These findings agree with the findings of Wolf-Wendel, Ward and Kinzie [41] which connected the notions of engagement with the learning process with those of involvement and integration. Nonetheless, it is quite important to point out that students' engagement cannot and it is not expected to occur without the efforts made by the teachers. Therefore, it can be said that the engagement levels of undergraduate students in the ESL classrooms, present multifaceted issues that are related to the many aspects of teaching and learning [12, 39, 41].

Individual involvement of undergraduate students in classroom activities in ESL classrooms depends on factors that are related to students and teachers' individual behaviours, choices, perceptions and beliefs [40, 42, 43]. For example, when ESL teachers integrate teaching of communication of English language in the many aspects of classroom teaching because they believe that students' intention to learn the spoken English exceeds their desire to study grammatical forms in isolation, students tend to focus for an extended period of time and with higher degree of concentration [8, 13, 32]. Furthermore, when ESL students consider academic writing as boring but do not view as such debates used to brainstorm ideas and generate thoughts, hence, their subjective norms and the tendency to plagiarise decrease because their intellectual being is seen as valuable and students' self- esteem and self-efficacy is improved [10, 34]. Another important factor of ESL teaching and learning is the level of difficulty and application of the assessment tasks [24, 28]. According to Conner and Armitage [11], Li [32], Benesch [8, 13] and Scales et al. [35] with respect to the prediction of actual received grades based on genuine work and not plagiarized work, it was found that active classroom engagement tends to instil in students the sense of responsibility and improve their set of moral obligation. Furthermore, as highlighted in the works of Dörnyei [13], Girardelli and Patel [16]; Girardelli, Patel and Martins-Shannon [17] and Hysaj [26, 27] active participation in a face-to-face classroom or in the online platform supports learners' development of critical thinking and it encourages them to explore the different aspects of learning process.

3   Research Methodology

3.1   Description of the Instrument

The research instrument used for this study was a survey questionnaire consisting of eleven questions. The first three questions sought to ascertain demographical information like gender, faculty and first language used in prior schooling system. The second section of the questionnaire, adapted from Ajzen [3], aimed at gauging undergraduate students' perception of cheating as a phenomenon. These questions were a set of five and they were divided in pairs. Each pair had opposing beliefs about cheating such as: I believe cheating is good, I believe cheating is bad, I believe cheating is pleasant, I believe cheating is unpleasant, I believe cheating is wise, I believe cheating is foolish, I believe cheating if useful, I believe cheating is useless, I believe cheating is profitable, I believe cheating is unprofitable, I believe cheating is useful, I believe cheating is useless.

The study employed a mixed approach; a descriptive approach on explaining the sample and a quantitative approach with the intention of exploring the understanding of undergraduate **students' attitudes towards subjective norms, moral obligation, and intention to cheat.** Furthermore, the study aimed at exploring the perceptions of undergraduate students pertaining to issues like the difficulty to write academically. Finally, the study aimed at exploring the perceptions of undergraduates about cheating with questions related to concepts of good and bad, useful and useless, profitable and unprofitable, pleasant and unpleasant, foolish and wise. The sample for this study was comprised of **336** students enrolled in a variety of majors within the spectrum of computer science, engineering, humanities and health sciences. Students were all undergraduates enrolled in academic study skills classes at the time when this study took place.

3.2 Measures

The questionnaire was constructed to assess the components of the modified theory of planned behaviour (attitudes, subjective norms, perceived behavioural control, moral obligation, intentions) with regards to academic dishonesty, as adapted from Beck and Ajzen [1–3]. The components were chosen to assess negatively and positively assigned variables aiming to assess the perceptions of undergraduate students about plagiarism. All constructs were measured using a 5-point Likert type scale. The scale that measured attitudes towards cheating utilized the scale created by Ajzen [3] and utilised five evaluative semantic differential: good-bad, wise-foolish, useful-useless, pleasant-unpleasant and attractive-unattractive. High scores indicate unfavourable attitudes towards academic misconduct while low scores indicate favourable attitudes towards academic misconduct. All items for each scale were summed using SPSS software to form composite scores for attitudes, subjective norms, perceived behavioural control, moral obligation and intentions.

3.3 Data Collection Procedures

The data collection process spanned over three months and it was administered to undergraduate students enrolled in academic writing classes at the time of the study. Individual items on this scale were summed to form a composite measure for measuring students' attitudes towards cheating. The survey was administered online and all the students were informed of the purpose and nature of the study. The study was anonymous to ensure confidentiality and students were informed that their participation was voluntary and they could withdraw from the study at any time they felt uncomfortable, without any prejudice. The study was first pilot tested with two randomly selected undergraduate students whose first language was not English to ensure that adjustments were made accordingly in case students had any concerns with regards to the grasp of English language. Another purpose of the pilot study was to explore participants willingness to disclose information regarding to cheating. Students were a male and a female. They were both from the Faculty of Computer and Information Sciences. The questionnaires were completed manually and returned within 20 min. This helped the researchers to establish a level of confidence in proceeding with the main questionnaire as the participants showed a good grasp of the questionnaire and had no major issues in completing it.

4 Results

4.1 Characteristics of the Sample

Table 1 shows that slightly over 51% of the participants were females while 48.7% were males. Since all the students were enrolled in undergraduate classes, it is fair to assume that they were a relatively young age sample. Furthermore, the distribution of the participants shows that a considerably higher number of students were enrolled in Computer and Information Sciences and Engineering majors compared to the students that were enrolled in Social Sciences and Humanities degrees.

Table 1. Demographics of the sample

Characteristics of the	Frequency (N)	Percent (%)
Gender:		
Male	167	48.7
Female	169	51.3
Total	336	100.0
Faculty:		
Social Sciences	60	16.5
Humanities	48	13.2
Computer and Information Sciences	155	42.6
Engineering	100	27.5
Total	336	100.0

4.2 Descriptive Statistics

Table 1 presents the descriptive statistics (means and standard deviations) regarding the key variables in the current study. It was found that students to a larger extent held unfavourable the desire to cheat and considered it unfair. Nevertheless, their intention to indulge in cheating behaviour was on the opposite spectrum of their moral values. This table also shows the Pearson's bivariate correlations among the key variables in the study.

The results reveal that modest to strong correlations exist between the independent variables (attitudes, subjective norms, perceived behavioural control and moral obligation) and the dependent variables (intentions to cheat and lie).

Table 2. Correlations among positively and negatively assigned variables

Correlations		Attitude	Intention	Social Desirability Bias	Subjective Norms	Moral Obligation
Pearson Correlation	Attitude	1.000	.071	.245	−.029	.074
	Intention	.071	1.000	.038	.498	.739
	Social Desirability Bias	.245	.038	1.000	−.041	.039
	Subjective Norms	−.029	.498	−.041	1.000	.651
	Moral Obligation	.074	.739	.039	.651	1.000
Sig. (1-tailed)	Attitude		.097	.000	.296	.088

(continued)

Table 2. (*continued*)

Correlations

		Attitude	Intention	Social Desirability Bias	Subjective Norms	Moral Obligation
	Intention	.097		.243	.000	.000
	Social Desirability Bias	.000	.243		.227	.237
	Subjective Norms	.296	.000	.227		.000
	Moral Obligation	.088	.000	.237	.000	
N	Attitude	337	337	337	337	337
	Intention	337	337	337	337	337
	Social Desirability Bias	337	337	337	337	337
	Subjective Norms	337	337	337	337	337
	Moral Obligation	337	337	337	337	337

Table 2 shows the 10 Likert scale items and the percentage of each response. The options for the Likert-scale items were: 1- Strongly Agree, 2 = Agree, 3 = Neither agree nor disagree, 4 = Disagree, and 5 = Strongly disagree. For this study, the coding used for the quantitative analysis was: Strongly Agree/ Agree = 1, Strongly Disagree/ Disagree = 2 and Neither Agree nor Disagree = 3. The descriptive analysis of each Table 3 follows the same order to ensure consistency and credibility.

Table 3. Correlation between approved and disapproved behavioral beliefs on cheating

Correlations

		BAD.CHEAT	GOOD.CHEAT
BAD.CHEAT	Pearson Correlation	1	−.063
	Sig. (2-tailed)		.255
	Sum of Squares and Cross-products	256.943	−32.423
	Covariance	.769	−.098
	N	335	333
GOOD.CHEAT	Pearson Correlation	−.063	1
	Sig. (2-tailed)	.255	
	Sum of Squares and Cross-products	-32.423	1047.833
	Covariance	-.098	3.137
	N	333	335

**. Correlation is significant at the 0.01 level (2-tailed)

The value −0.063 shows that the correlation between good cheat and bad cheat is negative, which means that if one of them changes, the other one inversely changes. However, this is too close to 0 which makes it less reliable to be used for future predictions or for other populations.

Table 4. Correlation between pleasant and unpleasant behavioral beliefs

		Pleasant	Unpleasant
Pleasant	Pearson Correlation	1	−.386[**]
	Sig. (2-tailed)		.000
	Sum of Squares and Cross-products	223.426	−78.119
	Covariance	.667	−.234
	N	336	335
Unpleasant	Pearson Correlation	−.386[**]	1
	Sig. (2-tailed)	.000	
	Sum of Squares and Cross-products	−78.119	183.988
	Covariance	−.234	.549
	N	335	336

[**]. Correlation is significant at the 0.01 level (2-tailed)

The value −0.386 shows that the correlation between pleasant cheat and unpleasant cheat is negative, which means that if one of them changes, the other one inversely changes too. The Table 4 shows that the correlation is significant at 0.01 level of significance, and the value is big enough to be considered as a reliable prediction value to be used for future or for other populations.

Table 5. Correlation between wise and foolish behavioral beliefs on cheating

Correlations			
		Wise	Foolish
Wise	Pearson Correlation	1	−.513[**]
	Sig. (2-tailed)		.000
	Sum of Squares and Cross-products	193.214	−109.976
	Covariance	.584	−.336
	N	332	328
Foolish	Pearson Correlation	−.513[**]	1
	Sig. (2-tailed)	.000	
	Sum of Squares and Cross-products	−109.976	244.703
	Covariance	−.336	.737
	N	328	333

[**]. Correlation is significant at the 0.01 level (2-tailed)

The value -0.513 shows that the correlation between wise cheat and foolish cheat is negative, which means that if one of them changes even the other one inversely changes.

The Table 5 shows that the correlation is significant at 0.01 level of significance, and the value is big enough to be considered as a reliable prediction value to be used for future or for other populations.

Table 6. Correlation between useful and useless behavioral beliefs on cheating

Correlations

		Useful	Useless
Useful	Pearson Correlation	1	−.574**
	Sig. (2-tailed)		.000
	Sum of Squares and Cross-products	227.234	−140.158
	Covariance	.682	−.427
	N	334	329
Useless	Pearson Correlation	−.574**	1
	Sig. (2-tailed)	.000	
	Sum of Squares and Cross-products	−140.158	267.952
	Covariance	−.427	.810
	N	329	332

The value −0.513 shows that the correlation between useful cheat and useless cheat is negative, which means that if one of them changes, the other one inversely changes. The Table 6 shows that the correlation is significant at 0.01 level of significance, and the value is big enough to be considered as a reliable prediction value to be used for future or for other populations.

Table 7. Correlation between useful and useless behavioral beliefs on cheating

Correlations

		Useful	Useless
Useful	Pearson Correlation	1	−.574**
	Sig. (2-tailed)		.000
	Sum of Squares and Cross-products	227.234	−140.158
	Covariance	.682	−.427
	N	334	329
Useless	Pearson Correlation	−.574**	1
	Sig. (2-tailed)	.000	
	Sum of Squares and Cross-products	−140.158	267.952
	Covariance	−.427	.810
	N	329	332

**. Correlation is significant at the 0.01 level (2-tailed)

The value −0.513 shows that the correlation between profitable cheat and unprofitable cheat is negative, which means that if one of them changes, the other one inversely changes. The Table 7 shows that the correlation is significant at 0.01 level of significance, and the value is big enough to be considered as a reliable prediction value to be used for future or for other populations. Finally, the correlation analysis, ascertain that positively and negatively correlated values were significant for the case of profitable and unprofitable, useful and useless, wise and foolish, pleasant and unpleasant. The only two variables that did not display a significant correlation were the good and bad cheat. Therefore, the result from correlating these two variables cannot be considered as a reliable prediction value to be utilized for future or for other populations.

5   Discussion

This study revealed that while it should be notified that while a vast majority of participants in the study were against the notion of cheating, yet they responded that would possibly cheat if necessarily. Moreover, the respondents considered the correlated values as significant for the case of profitable and unprofitable, useful and useless, wise and foolish, pleasant and unpleasant. The only two variables that did not display a significant correlation were the good and bad cheat. Therefore, the result from correlating these two variables is interconnected with the ethical values that undergraduates hold. Therefore, emphasis should be given to ways of tackling the issue of plagiarism in higher education and most importantly understanding reasons why undergraduate students may exhibit behavioural intentions to engage in such practices. Undergraduate students are the next batch of professionals, therefore the values that they hold and exhibit are highly likely to be carried forward and guide their work life [8, 14, 19]. Furthermore, exploration of perceptions about cheating may stimulate undergraduates to discuss the issue among the relevant parties and eventually facilitate the creation of an improved ethical climate in higher education [30, 37, 38]. Another valuable fact that need to be taken into consideration is the consideration of cheating and the negative effects that it carries for learners beginning from primary school level [23, 34, 37]. Procedures and policies that may act as preventive measures against academic dishonestly may start from an early age and be intensified in higher education, however, it is equally valuable to understand that great emphasis should be also placed on the skills sets of students since it was seen that ethical conduct was not necessarily related to the moral values of undergraduates. This study recognized the need to improve undergraduates academic writing skills especially when considering that English is not their mother tongue. This finding concurs with the findings of Huisman et al. [23] and Khan et al. [29] who found that undergraduates benefit from understanding their errors and supporting their learning through proactive measures which can potentially make editing of pieces of academic writing simpler and subsequently having a positive impact on reducing instances of plagiarism. Finally, as this study has shown as students were opposed to the idea of cheating their intentions to act in opposition with their beliefs can potentially be reduced. To conclude the findings of this study, provide empirical support to the study by beck and Ajzen [3] that concluded that planned behaviour theory is very effective in predicting cheating behaviour.

6 Concluding Remarks

To conclude, this study stressed the importance of exploring the perceptions of undergraduate students with regards to planned behaviour theory and academic misconduct. Furthermore, it highlighted the need to have more courses that address the ethical content of plagiarism so students can be actively, creatively and critically involved in issues pertaining ethical conduct. Moreover, this study has opened the path to exploring ESL undergraduates' behaviour in academic writing skills classes and it has highlighted the need to have open discussions about the tendency of cheating and ethical aspects of it. Adding new strategies to teaching academic writing skills in a proactive way is not an innovation but instead a necessity guided by the need to support our students learning process. The thorough analysis of the descriptive and quantitative data showed that the theory of planned behaviour proved to support the exploration of undergraduates' attitudes about cheating. In conclusion, the theory of planned behaviour provides a wealth of possibilities of exploring human behaviour and understanding the factors that influence ethical and unethical behaviour. Future research could include exploration of ways of determining whether undergraduates are aware of how their academic experience can impact their employment prospects and work experience, especially for students who seek to be employed in positions that require higher levels of integrity like accounting, finance, computer sciences and engineering.

References

1. Ajzen, I.: Attitudes, traits and actions: dispositional prediction of behaviour in personality and social psychology. In: Berkowitz, L. (ed.) Advances in Experimental Social Psychology, vol. 20, pp. 1–64. Academic Press, New York (1987)
2. Ajzen, I.: Attitudes, Personality and Behaviour. Open University Press, Milton Keynes (1988)
3. Ajzen, I.: The theory of planned behaviour. Organizational Behaviour and Human Decision Processes **50**, 179–211 (1991)
4. Ajzen, I.: Residual effects of past on later behaviour: habituation and reasoned action perspectives. Pers. Soc. Psychol. Rev. **6**, 107–122 (2002)
5. Ajzen, I., Brown, T.C., Carvajal, F.: Explaining the discrepancy between intentions and actions: the case of hypothetical bias in contingent evaluation. Pers. Soc. Psychol. Bull. **30**, 431–434 (2004)
6. Ajzen, I., Fishbein, M.: Questions raised by a reasoned action approach: reply on Ogden (2003). Health Psychol. **23**, 431–434 (2004)
7. Ajzen, I.: The theory of planned behaviour: Reactions and reflections. Psychol. Health **26**(9), 1113–1127 (2011)
8. Benesch, S.: Critical English for academic purposes: Theory, politics, and practice. Routledge (2001)
9. Call, A.: Participation in Dual Language Immersion Programs: Using Theory of Planned Behaviour to Explore Enrolment Factors (2015)
10. Chamot, A.U., O'malley, J.M.: The cognitive academic language learning approach: A bridge to the mainstream. TESOL quarterly **21**(2), 227–249 (1987)
11. Conner, M., Armitage, C.J.: Extending the theory of planned behaviour: a review and avenues for further research. J. Appl. Soc. Psychol. **28**(15), 1429–1464 (1998)
12. Dewberry, C., Jackson, D.: An application of the theory of planned behaviour to student retention. J. Vocational Behav. **107**, 100–110 (2018)

13. Dörnyei, Z.: Attitudes, orientations, and motivations in language learning: advances in theory, research, and applications. Lang. Learn. **53**(S1), 3–32 (2003)

14. Farouqa, G., Hysaj, A.: Active Learning in the Lenses of Faculty: A Qualitative Study in Universities in the United Arab Emirates. In: International Conference on Human-Computer Interaction, pp. 77–90. Springer, Cham (2022). https://doi.org/10.1007/978-3-031-05064-0_6

15. Freitag, S., Dunsmuir, S.: The inclusion of children with ASD: Using the theory of planned behaviour as a theoretical framework to explore peer attitudes. Int. J. Disability Dev. Educ. **62**(4), 405–421 (2015)

16. Gatfield, T., Chen, C.H.: Measuring student choice criteria using the theory of planned behaviour: the case of Taiwan, Australia, UK, and USA. J. Mark. High. Educ. **16**(1), 77–95 (2006)

17. Girardelli, D., Patel, V.K.: The theory of planned behaviour and Chinese ESL students' in-class participation. J. Lang. Teach. Res. **7**(1) (2016)

18. Girardelli, D., Patel, V.K. and Martins-Shannon, J.: "Crossing the Rubicon": Understanding Chinese EFL students' volitional process underlying in-class participation with the theory of planned behaviour. Educ. Res. Eval. **23**(3-4), 119–137 (2017)

19. Hamam, D., Hysaj, A.: Technological pedagogical and content knowledge (TPACK): Higher education teachers' perspectives on the use of TPACK in online academic writing classes. In: International Conference on Human-Computer Interaction, pp. 51–58. Springer, Cham (2021). https://doi.org/10.1007/978-3-030-78645-8_7

20. Harding, T.S., Mayhew, M.J., Finelli, C.J., Carpenter, D.D.: The theory of planned behaviour as a model of academic dishonesty in engineering and humanities undergraduates. Ethics Behav. **17**(3), 255–279 (2007)

21. Hasegawa, H.: Theoretical Investigation into Students'' Study Behaviour Patterns: Learning through ICT and Policy Making/Administrative Management. Int. J. Lang. Literat. Linguist. **1**(4), 290–295 (2015)

22. Hellmich, F., Löper, M.F., Görel, G.: The role of primary school teachers' attitudes and self-efficacy beliefs for everyday practices in inclusive classrooms–a study on the verification of the 'Theory of Planned Behaviour.' J. Res. Spec. Educ. Needs **19**, 36–48 (2019)

23. Huisman, B., Saab, N., Van Driel, J., Van Den Broek, P.: Peer feedback on academic writing: undergraduate students' peer feedback role, peer feedback perceptions and essay performance. Assess. Eval. High. Educ. **43**(6), 955–968 (2018)

24. Hysaj, A., Hamam, D.: Academic Writing skills in the online platform-A success, a failure or something in between? A study on perceptions of higher education students and teachers in the UAE. In: 2020 IEEE International Conference on Teaching, Assessment, and Learning for Engineering (TALE), pp. 668–673. IEEE, December 2020

25. Hysaj, A., Elkhouly, A.: Why do students plagiarize? The case of multicultural students in an Australian University in the United Arab Emirates. In: ENAI Conference

26. Hysaj, A.: December. COVID-19 pandemic and Online Teaching from the Lenses of K-12 STEM Teachers in Albania. In: 2021 IEEE International Conference on Engineering, Technology & Education (TALE), pp. 01–07. IEEE (2021)

27. Hysaj, A., Haroon, H.A.: Online formative assessment and feedback: a focus group discussion among language teachers. In: International Conference on Human-Computer Interaction, pp. 115–126. Springer, Cham (2022). Doi: https://doi.org/10.1007/978-3-031-05064-0_9

28. Hysaj, A., Freeman, M., Khan, Z.R.: Teaching academic writing skills: a narrative literature review of unifying academic values through academic integrity. Concurrent Sessions **12**, 157 (2022)

29. Khan, Z.R., Hysaj, A., John, S.R., Khan, S.: Gateway to preparing K-12 students for higher education–reflections on organizing an academic integrity camp. In: European Conference on Academic Integrity and Plagiarism 2021, p. 65 (2021)

30. Khan, Z.R., Hysaj, A., John, S.R. and Khan, S.A.: Transitional Module on Academic Integrity to Help K-12 Students in the UAE Prepare for Next Stage of Education. In Academic Integrity: Broadening Practices, Technologies, and the Role of Students, pp. 263–287. Springer, Cham (2022). https://doi.org/10.1007/978-3-031-16976-2_15

31. Kovac, V.B., Cameron, D.L., Høigaard, R.: The extended theory of planned behaviour and college grades: The role of cognition and past behaviour in the prediction of students' academic intentions and achievements. Educ. Psychol. **36**(4), 792–811 (2016)

32. Li, D.: "It's always more difficult than you plan and imagine": Teachers' perceived difficulties in introducing the communicative approach in South Korea. TESOL Q. **32**(4), 677–703 (1998)

33. Opoku, M.P., Cuskelly, M., Pedersen, S.J., Rayner, C.S.: Applying the theory of planned behaviour in assessments of teachers' intentions towards practicing inclusive education: a scoping review. Eur. J. Spec. Needs Educ. **36**(4), 577–592 (2021)

34. Rothman, P.: Ethics in Higher Education: A study of the perceived ethical climate of administrators and faculty at a higher education institution (2017)

35. Scales, E.: A study of college student retention and withdrawal. J. Negro Educ. **29**(4), 438–444 (1960)

36. Schwab, S., Sharma, U., Hoffmann, L.: How inclusive are the teaching practices of my German, Maths and English teachers?–psychometric properties of a newly developed scale to assess personalisation and differentiation in teaching practices. Int. J. Incl. Educ. **26**(1), 61–76 (2022)

37. Siragusa, L., Dixon, K.: Planned behaviour: Student attitudes towards the use of ICT interactions in higher education. Hello! Where are you in the landscape of educational technology? Proceedings ascilite Melbourne 2008, pp. 942–953 (2008)

38. Susilowati, N., Kusmuriyanto, K., Abiprayu, K.B.: Encouraging student ethical behaviour through ethical climate in higher education. J. Educ. Learn. (EduLearn) **15**(2), 213–222 (2021)

39. Tight, M.: Student retention and engagement in higher education. J. Furth. High. Educ. **44**(5), 689–704 (2020)

40. Wang, Q., Zhao, G. and Cheng, Z.: Examining the Moderating Role of Technostress and Compatibility in EFL Learners' Mobile Learning Adoption: A Perspective from the Theory of Planned Behaviour (TPB) (2022)

41. Wolf-Wendel, L., Ward, K., Kinzie, J.: A tangled web of terms: the overlap and unique contribution of involvement, engagement, and integration to understanding college student success. J. Coll. Stud. Dev. **50**(4), 407–428 (2009)

42. Yan, Z., Sin, K.F.: Inclusive education: teachers' intentions and behaviouranalysed from the viewpoint of the theory of planned behaviour. Int. J. Incl. Educ. **18**(1), 72–85 (2014)

43. Zhong, Q.M.: Understanding Chinese learners' willingness to communicate in a New Zealand ESL classroom: a multiple case study drawing on the theory of planned behaviour. System **41**(3), 740–751 (2013)

Exploring the User Experience and Effectiveness of Mobile Game-Based Learning in Higher Education

Nicos Kasenides[iD], Andriani Piki[(⊠)][iD], and Nearchos Paspallis[iD]

University of Central Lancashire – Cyprus, Larnaca, Cyprus
{nkasenides,apiki,npaspallis}@uclan.ac.uk

Abstract. Recent technological and societal changes have heightened the uptake of mobile educational games across all subjects and levels of education. Nevertheless, developing mobile games with a set of design guidelines in mind, does not necessarily imply they will naturally engage learners and improve the learning experience. Building on this tenet, this study aims to explore how higher education students experience learning programming principles by playing a maze-solving mobile educational game; evaluate how effective the game's features are in terms of engaging students; and inquire how effective mobile devices are as a learning platform for teaching programming and algorithmic thinking. The overarching theme that emerged by analysing the gathered data is the need to promote 'engagement by design', indicating that subtle synergies are required between the technological qualities and design features of a mobile educational game, the pedagogical context, and human factors, towards achieving the desired level of learner engagement.

Keywords: Educational Games · Mobile Learning · Mobile Game-Based Learning · Learner Engagement · Higher Education

1 Introduction

The ongoing advances in mobile digital technology and the widespread availability and flexibility of mobile devices have increased the application of mobile learning [5,58] and educational games [7,27] across all levels of education. The utilisation of mobile devices for teaching and learning was further accelerated during Covid-19 pandemic, revealing their wide-ranging capabilities as learning devices [48]. Mobile learning and Game-Based Learning (GBL) approaches have the potential to provoke learner autonomy [3], positive learning outcomes, and experiential learning [7,26]. Nevertheless, the exploitation and evaluation of mobile educational games for learning programming and algorithmic thinking is limited. The importance of developing problem-solving, critical thinking, and coding skills in higher education is well documented in the literature [6,63]. Several initiatives are launched towards promoting coding skills, such as hackathons and coding competitions (e.g., Code Week [39] and Hour of Code [62]), and using computer games as learning activities [7,11,18,26,33]. Computer games, including Massively Multiplayer Online Games (MMOGs), are increasingly employed as agents of motivation in higher education [7]. Even though GBL and educational gamification approaches are popular in the context of STEAM (Science, Technology, Engineering, Arts, and Mathematics) subjects, including programming and algorithmic thinking [23,30,37], such endeavors focus predominantly on desktop and laptop computer games (such as the Code Combat educational game [30]), while only a few games target mobile devices (like the Lightbot [23] and Run Marco [37] mobile games). Furthermore, there is a limited number of studies evaluating the user experience and effectiveness of mobile games for learning programming in higher education. In this paper, we aim to fill these gaps by conducting an empirical study to explore the learner experience with a mobile educational game, namely aMazeChallenge, and evaluate how effective it is in terms of learning and engagement. aMazeChallenge [27,43] is an interactive, multiplayer, mobile educational game developed to introduce learners to the fundamental principles of programming and algorithmic thinking. The following research questions are addressed:

1. How do higher education students experience learning programming through a mobile game-based educational activity?
2. Which aspects and game features affect engagement with mobile game-based learning?
3. How effective are mobile devices as a platform for learning programming and algorithmic thinking?

2 Related Work

2.1 Game-Based Learning

Amongst prevalent innovating pedagogies, playful learning emerges first in terms of immediacy and timescale to widespread implementation, compared to other technology-mediated pedagogical methods, such as learning with robots, drone-based learning, and virtual environments [18]. Educational or serious games, game thinking, and GBL approaches are widely employed in learning and skills development initiatives [8,11,20,34,59]. GBL is commonly associated with positive outcomes including increased learner engagement with learning content; active participation in educational activities; enhanced understanding, knowledge acquisition, skills development [52]; and improved emotional and motivational outcomes [7,11,20,26,33]. GBL triggers learners' interest and leverages curiosity-driven learning [1,7,18,20,59], hence offering an alternative to the conventional focus on memorisation, assessment, and performance traits in education, which often counteract active exploration, collaboration, and understanding [18]. Through GBL activities, learners are engaged in playful quests which present genuine opportunities for developing critical thinking, problem-solving, analytical and communication skills [18]. By blending entertainment and learning elements, serious games constitute a powerful educational medium. Games like virtual environments and educational escape rooms [31,34,51] activate learning, intensify learner involvement and blend formal and informal learning experiences through dynamic, seamless, and multimodal interactions [56].

2.2   Mobile Game-Based Learning

Mobile Game-Based Learning (mGBL) fuses the unique and distinguishing features of mobile devices (such as portability, social interactivity, context sensitivity, ubiquity, autonomy, and flexibility) [3,58] with the captivating and engaging nature of games [7,11,20,59] transforming mobile devices into an appealing learning medium. Contemporary research has shown that the ubiquity of mobile devices and the seamless integration of mobile technology in both formal and informal learning contexts is conducive to learner engagement [3,24,53]. Nevertheless, formulating an effective mGBL approach is not straightforward. Introducing 'any' mobile game or gamified application as a supplementary tool for enriching the instructional process will not automatically engage students [49]. Even if the game initially captures students' attention, there are several factors which need to be considered for the successful design, development, and deployment of mobile educational games [50]. These are discussed next.

2.3   Challenges and Gaps in Game-Based Learning

While the benefits associated with educational games are evident, recent research findings highlight several challenges in designing, developing, evaluating, and using educational games [18,20,27]. The following paragraphs discuss key pedagogical and technological considerations.

Pedagogical Considerations. Firstly, although GBL is entwined with increased motivation and engagement, very few studies have examined the influence of gamification on the varied dimensions of engagement [1]. Learner engagement is a complex concept that dynamically transpires through the interactions of the learner with a technology-mediated learning activity [45,46]. Recent literature suggests that despite innovative applications and technological advancements, situations like student disengagement, rising levels of dropouts [8], course withdrawals, surface learning, and students' decreasing motivation to learn are still present and peaked following the intricate effects of Covid-19 pandemic [36,47].

Secondly, educational games need to establish a symbiotic relationship between educational and entertainment requirements [35] which are not always aligned [27]. Furthermore, entertainment is not always prioritised in traditional instructional approaches which are guided by strict curricula, fixed timelines, and formal teaching and assessment methods, which constitutes some of the key reasons why the use of games has not yet had a profound influence on education [18]. Therefore, new modes of assessment and delivery need to be developed which are more relevant and aligned to today's needs [44].

Another challenge lies in the fact that, despite the increasing utilisation of GBL approaches and the rising number of educational games available, no comprehensive policy exists for the use of games in education [60]. Furthermore, the connection between gamification and actual learning still appears to be vague [20]. This can be attributed to the complexity inherent in measuring the benefits of GBL compared to traditional learning approaches [18], and the increased time and effort required for assessing learners' performance, which may inevitably affect educators' willingness to incorporate technology in education [44]. Moreover, educators may need to be trained in devising efficient monitoring, feedback, and assessment strategies appropriate for mGBL [18,28,31,44,49,60], while also contemplating the mobile technologies at hand and their inherent constraints [50]. Thus, beyond the pedagogical challenges, manifold technological considerations emerge for the successful deployment of mGBL.

Technological Considerations. Students tend to find mobile learning less convenient and more frustrating [21], compared to learning using a personal computer [15], for several technology-oriented reasons, including: small screen size constraining the text and controls that can be displayed [2,4,55]; poor user interface (UI) design hindering information transfer and making learning more cognitively demanding [2]; operating system compatibility [41]; variability in Internet speed [34,50]; and short battery life affecting resource-demanding games, all of which are crucial for the successful deployment of mGBL. Ensuring high UI design quality [2,16] and creating mobile-friendly content [28] are important aspects to consider when promoting mobile learning. These aspects also bring forward various human factors. The effects of mobile learning on lowering the learners' cognitive load and increasing their achievement depend heavily on the quality of the mobile learning design [2,9,57]. The design itself can influence user acceptance, adoption, and use of a mobile learning application. Hence, usability and user experience (UX) goals must be thoughtfully considered along with pedagogical objectives [42,49]. Despite recent developments, and the fact that most higher education students describe themselves as technologically savvy and active on social media mobile apps, many students still lack essential digital literacy skills to embark on playing a new game [41] or participate online [21]. Developing digital skills can reduce negative experiences, such as frustration while trying to understand how the game works [27], or disappointment while attempting to complete advanced tasks through the game [29].

There is also a paradox regarding whether mobile learning enables or hinders learning and engagement. On one hand, the literature shows that well-designed mobile apps featuring multimedia or gamified elements can increase learner participation, contextualise learning, promote inquiry-based learning, and improve learners' achievements compared to traditional, formal learning approaches [17,32,57]. On the other hand, when mobile apps are not developed with learning objectives and learner engagement in mind, this may act as a barrier to learning [49]. For certain learning tasks, presenting dense information with small fonts on a single screen [2,13], or displaying redundant information and animations [32], may be perceived as a distraction by students, hence inhibiting their concentration and learning [28], increasing their cognitive load [2,13,32] and creating mental overheads, which may negatively impact learners' affective and cognitive involvement [16] and the learning outcomes altogether [8]. These findings suggest that further research is needed on the learning benefits of mobile apps, including competitive and collaborative games for learning programming [38,43].

3   Mobile Game-Based Learning with aMazeChallenge

To address the research questions, we utilise aMazeChallenge[1] - an interactive, multiplayer, mobile game developed for teaching programming and algorithmic thinking to higher education students. This section describes the key learning objectives, features, game rules and components of aMazeChallenge.

3.1   Learning Objectives

The learning objectives of aMazeChallenge focus on the skills that higher education students must acquire on their journey to become successful programmers.

(i) **Read and understand existing code.** Before writing their own code, students need to understand the concept of programming statements and be capable of reading and interpreting code. This objective is achieved via a tutorial environment in aMazeChallenge, which links the actions of an avatar (such as moving and turning) to programming commands or statements.

(ii) **Improve or fix existing code.** Students must be able to identify syntactic and semantic errors in pre-written code and fix them. To achieve this, aMazeChallenge provides players with a set of incrementally harder challenges for training, enabling them to develop their skills and confidence.

(iii) **Write code from scratch.** When students feel confident in reading, understanding, and improving the existing code, aMazeChallenge reinforces code writing by allowing students to easily form their code by dragging blocks in the workspace while minimising syntactic errors by accepting only valid connections between the blocks.

(iv) **Write clean and efficient code.** This slightly more advanced programming skill is a significant aspect of software development. aMazeChallenge rewards players who create more efficient code, as these players may generally exit the maze faster and thus score more points than other players.

The above skills enable students to develop problem-solving, algorithmic, and critical thinking skills, which are not limited to Computer Science, but are transferable to multiple domains. Through the use of graphics, sound effects, interactive gameplay, learn by try-and-fail, playful learning, unlimited attempts, competition, and other game-like elements, aMazeChallenge aims to engage students with the learning process and achieve these objectives.

---

[1] aMazeChallenge can be downloaded from the Google Play Store: https://play.google.com/store/apps/details?id=org.inspirecenter.amazechallenge.

3.2   Features

aMazeChallenge is introduced to the players through the *Learning* section (Fig. 1(a)) featuring a text-based tutorial enhanced with screenshots of each game feature along with explanations on how it works. Players can optionally personalise their character by selecting an avatar icon and color. To play online, players must also set their name and email address, through the *Personalization* screen, which serves as an engagement medium. They are then directed to create the first version of their code by using the workspace found in the *Code Editor* screen (Fig. 1(b)). In this screen, players drag blocks to create their code, or load pre-defined samples of maze-solving algorithms. When ready, players can see how their code affects the behavior of an in-game avatar by visiting the *Training* section. This section includes a set of challenges that are initially very simple but get progressively more difficult, aiming to challenge players to produce more complex code by making incremental changes to adjust to the requirements of each challenge. When the players advance sufficiently through the tutorials, they may opt to compete against others in the *Online* mode. This mode makes a set of challenges available online, which players can join in and play against each other in real-time. Alternatively, players can also form teams and cooperate to create code for an online challenge, competing against other teams. Finally, aMazeChallenge also includes a *Maze Designer*, which allows players to create their own mazes choosing from a diverse set of settings such as the maze type, size, background image and audio, and wall color. These custom mazes can be added to the training mode, allowing players to practice in their own mazes to improve their code, while also aiming to increase learner engagement.

3.3   Game Rules and Components

aMazeChallenge features highly dynamic maze arenas (Fig. 2), presenting a grid that is divided into cells representing the valid positions within the maze. Player avatars are positioned in these cells and can move to adjacent cells using commands issued by the players before the start of the game, using Google's block-based graphical language Blockly [22,54]. Players program their avatar to escape the maze by moving from the start to the finish cell. These cells are often located at opposite ends of the grid to allow for more challenging gameplay and are colour-coded to distinguish them from the rest (red for start and green for finish). The cells also have walls that prohibit the players from arbitrarily moving from one cell to another. The gameplay is based on commands the players have previously specified in their code for their avatar to execute. Once their code is compiled, each player can either choose to train solo or participate in an online challenge. In either case, players joining a challenge will play in turns with the game executing a single iteration of their instructions in each turn. The outcome of the player's code in each turn needs to result in a valid move (i.e., moving forward or turning toward a specified direction).

Moving through and interacting with the maze can be achieved by using game-specific functions such as `moveForward`, `turnClockwise`, `look`, and so on.

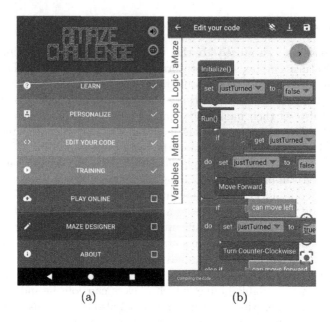

Fig. 1. (a) aMazeChallenge Main menu (b) Code Editor (Color figure online)

The maze includes objects that are randomly spawned inside the game arena, allowing a more dynamic and interactive experience, and also complicating the task of exiting the maze. For instance, objects like coins and fruits are beneficial to the players allowing them to gather points and increase their health when collected. On the other hand, objects such as traps and bombs have a negative effect, slowing players down or causing them to lose health. Players lose when their health falls to 0, but they can always start over. Such objects add an element of randomness and luck, aiming to make the game more interesting by allowing the players to find ways to either pursue or avoid objects. From an educational perspective, they encourage the use of decision-making programming constructs which can be used to decide whether an encountered object is beneficial or not. The winner of a challenge is the player who manages to exit the maze in the shortest time. Various maze-solving algorithms may have similar performance, and players may also utilise identical algorithms causing them to exit the maze within the same turn. To differentiate among the players who have exited the maze within the same turn, points are used as a secondary criterion, with those having more points being ranked higher [19].

3.4 Programming and Code Execution

The players can program their avatars using specific block-based instructions. Block-based languages have been successfully utilised in many educational games, especially at an introductory level [10]. To leverage Blockly assets, we created a specialised Blockly library that contains specific commands related to

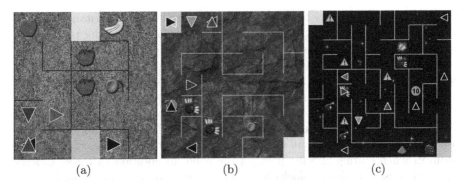

Fig. 2. Three different aMazeChallenge arenas, containing player avatars (colored triangles) and various types of interactive objects, during a multiplayer competition. (Color figure online)

aMazeChallenge. Coupled with existing Blockly commands for basic programming constructs like expressions, variables, math, and logic, this enables players to create a diverse set of programs. The custom-defined library includes blocks for moving, turning, navigation and directionality, and logical functions to retrieve the state of adjacent cells. For instance, the `Direction` class enumerates the possible directions an avatar could be facing. Similarly, the `Item` type enumerates the possible types of items a player's avatar could be facing (i.e., a penalty item, a reward item, or no item). This is typically utilised in the `look` command, which allows players to determine if one of such items is in their way and decide if they want to avoid or attempt to retrieve it.

The code structure is guided by the need to first initialise several values and then run a set of commands continuously at each turn until the exit is reached. To allow players to define these two distinct parts in their programs, we introduce two special functions: `Initialize` and `Run`. These functions are then called at specific points during the game to implement the functionality defined by the players. The `Initialize` function is executed only once, right before the gameplay starts. Conversely, the `Run` function is executed at each turn of the game by their avatar. This code is executed continuously until the player either loses, exits the maze, or the game is stopped. This function must return a single valid move to be performed at each turn by the player's avatar. If players place any blocks outside these two functions those blocks are ignored.

Players can create their code using Blockly's workspace, which provides an environment to edit code blocks by dragging them on the screen and joining them to form meaningful programming instructions. To make it easier for users to interact with this workspace, Blockly organises blocks into different panels containing sets of blocks based on their functionality. This also enables users to view only a certain number of blocks at a time, which is useful, especially when working with the limited screen size of a mobile device. In addition, blocks are colour-coded and have a specific shape based on their functionality, which makes it easier for players to choose an appropriate block. For instance, expression blocks only fit within the context of an expression (e.g., using them as the condition in an if statement). Using the metaphor of puzzle pieces, this limits the scope in which they can be used, and therefore prevents a wide set of errors that would occur during the code writing process. Hence, this satisfies the principle of error prevention. Furthermore, Blockly's workspace allows users to adjust the zoom level to accommodate different screen sizes and orientations. This makes the process of editing code significantly easier and more flexible as users can select to zoom out when reading code. On the contrary, users can zoom in when editing specific parts of the code. In addition to these, Blockly also allows users to delete blocks by dragging them toward a delete icon.

The default Blockly workspace is enhanced with additional features adding the capability of saving and loading code, as well as loading several sample algorithms (i.e., pre-written pieces of code that can be loaded by players, allowing them to see full solutions of specific maze problems, and inspiring them to write their own code). The aMazeChallenge code editor (Fig. 1), includes the default Blockly workspace coupled with customised navigation and buttons that enable players to use these functionalities. Additionally, it includes options that allow the players to go back to the main menu or proceed through in-app controls.

When players finish their code, the next step is to convert it into a high-level language that can be executed by an interpreter. This process triggers a static checker which analyses statements in the program, detects errors (i.e., empty statements, run function returning an invalid move, cases where the code may execute indefinitely, etc.), and warns players to fix them before the code can be compiled. When such issues are detected, the code editor's interface displays colour-coded dialogs (red for errors and gold for warnings) containing relevant information and potential solutions. This approach improves the user experience by catching problematic circumstances and handling them, before causing any catastrophic situations such as the entire server crashing. Most importantly, code checking is part of the learning process, helping novice programmers understand different types of errors, how these are communicated, and how to fix them, all of which are crucial skills in the field of software development. Once the static checks have passed, a confirmation message is shown indicating that the code has been successfully compiled. The player is then automatically transferred back to the main menu and can opt to either train or play online.

4   Research Methodology

To explore the students' experiences with learning programming through a mobile educational game, and evaluate its effectiveness, we conducted an empirical study utilising mixed methods.

4.1   Study Context and Participants

The study involved the planning and execution of two data gathering phases during the first semester of the academic years 2021–22 and 2022–23. A total of

112 first-year undergraduate students were involved in the study, including both female and male students studying Computing, Electrical engineering, and Computer engineering. The students had varying backgrounds and prior experiences with programming, but they were all enrolled on the same introductory programming module and hence exposed to basic programming constructs in Java before participating in the study. User feedback was gathered through observation of live play sessions during which students competed online using their personal mobile devices, as well as through two questionnaires. Both phases were performed during the same period (respective teaching weeks) in each academic year, following an identical process to ensure that the study design remained as consistent as possible and that the presented results are comparable. The UI and features of aMazeChallenge, the content presented during the demonstrations, the difficulty of the maze challenges, and the conditions under which students engaged with the game also remained unchanged.

4.2   Data Gathering

Prior to their participation in the study, students were asked to provide their consent by carefully reading and signing an informed consent form. In both phases of the study, data collection took place during class time. The first part of the study involved asking students to provide their responses to a background questionnaire including basic demographics, academic background, familiarity with programming, and opinion about programming. A 20-min session was then delivered introducing aMazeChallenge to students in which the game's objectives and mechanics were discussed, and the students were encouraged to download the game during their own time to try it out. Predictably, only a small number of students downloaded the app and interacted with it outside class time.

A second session took place a week later as a physical event and involved a live demo of aMazeChallenge, during which the game was presented to the students, illustrating how to use the various features of the game, including the code editing workspace, personalisation options, executing code in training mode, and joining and playing in online challenges. Students were then given time to interact and familiarise themselves with the game UI and engage with various game features (e.g., read the tutorial, personalise their avatar, create code, load code samples, and test them in training mode). After letting students become acquainted with the game, the first online challenge was published and students were asked to join in. Students participated in a total of three online challenges with varying difficulty (easy, moderate, difficult). To further motivate students to participate in this event, multiple winners (such as the first to exit the maze, or the one to exit with the most points) were rewarded with coupons for the university's cafeteria. While the students interacted with the online challenges, we took screenshots during the live online gameplay (through the app), photographs in the classroom space (with participants' consent), and field notes based on observed behaviour. Participant observations took place in a real-life classroom setting placing emphasis on students' feelings and mood (such as frustration, boredom, joy, or excitement), level of involvement in the activity, performance in the game (through the shared leaderboard displayed on the projector screen), winners' responses after successfully exiting the maze, and other noteworthy facts. This data highlighted key issues pertinent to learning and engagement which constitute the focus of inquiry, and further contributed to our understanding of user experience, feelings, and actions during data collection and analysis [12,25].

Following the experimental session, participants were asked to fill out a post-event questionnaire, focusing on their experience with aMazeChallenge in both training and online modes, their opinion about programming following this experience, their perception regarding the game's effectiveness, and the features they liked and disliked the most. Furthermore, the questionnaire included two open-ended questions, the first asking students to indicate any problems they faced, and the second inviting students to provide their recommendations for potential improvements. The background and post-event questionnaires included the name of the students in order to relate their responses to their academic performance. After the data was collected and linked to overall academic performance, responses were anonymised. Following a data cleaning process, out of 112 registered students, a total of 81 background and 68 post-event questionnaires (across both phases) were used for further data analysis.

4.3   Study Results

Background Questionnaire. The majority of participating students were male (79%). While this confirms that Computer Science constitutes a male-dominated field [61], the results appear promising as the female students increased from only 4 in 2021, to 12 in 2022. The overwhelming majority (94%) of participants use a smartphone, with the most popular being Android (51%) and iOS devices (44%). This was a barrier for our study since aMazeChallenge is available only for Android-enabled devices. To circumvent this, and in an effort to engage all students, we asked students with iOS devices to pair with one of their peers so they could participate as a team.

In terms of their prior experience in programming, approximately half of the students (52%) responded that they had previously attended a programming course, while the rest (48%) had no programming experience before joining the University. Amongst those with previous experience, the results show that C++ is by far the most popular language, followed by Python and Java. Furthermore, students were asked to self-assess their programming level. Data from both groups yielded similar results. The majority of students considered themselves to be Beginners (57%), followed by Intermediate (20%) and Confident (11%), while some students reported that they were not sure (12%). The latter is not surprising given that almost half of the students were just starting to familiarise with core programming concepts as part of their degree. When asked to report on their perception of programming, the vast majority of students (83%) reported they consider it an 'Interesting' or 'Very interesting' activity, with the remaining students (17%) were neutral. None of the participants reported finding programming either 'Boring' or 'Very boring'.

Regarding their favourite methods for learning programming, the most popular responses were 'Learning and practicing on my own' (89%), 'Watching instructional videos' (72%), and 'Attending lectures' (65%). Alternative learning methods, including 'Playing educational games on the web' or 'Playing educational games on a mobile device' were less frequent, but still relatively popular (37% and 31%, respectively). When asked whether they have previously used an app to learn a new skill, only 32% of students responded 'Yes', 53% responded 'No', and 15% were 'Not sure'. When asked to rate how good a competitive environment is for learning programming, most students responded either 'Definitely good' or 'Good' (56%), many responded they are 'Neutral' (41%), and a few found it either 'Bad' or 'Definitely bad'. In addition, participants were asked to indicate their opinion on how helpful games are for learning programming. As shown in Fig. 3, the majority of participants believe that games are either 'Very helpful' or 'Helpful' for learning programming (79%), while only a few believe that they are either 'Not helpful' or 'Completely ineffective' (5%). 16% of students indicated that they are 'Not sure'.

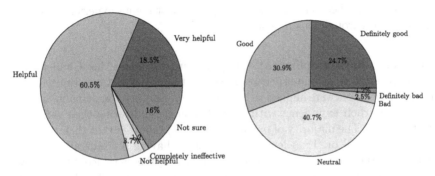

Fig. 3. Perceived usefulness of games (left) and competitive environments (right) toward learning programming.

Students were also asked to report which features of an educational game they consider as important. According to the responses, Performance is the most important feature in an educational game (72%), followed by User Interface (68%), Graphics (61%), and Multiplayer mode (58%). Other features, like Rewards and Battery-friendliness, were also recorded. These results are aligned with key considerations reported in recent literature, in relation to mobile learning [2,28] and mGBL [50]. The background questionnaire also included an open-ended question asking students to report the expectations from playing the aMazeChallenge mobile educational game. Students responses related to gaining experience in programming (58%), entertainment (18%), and improving critical thinking (10%), while 14% reported that they did not have any expectations.

Observation in the Field. Observing students provided additional insights into their experiences with aMazeChallenge. Common observations across both phases included frustration, especially at the beginning when they were trying to figure out how to play the game, and a positive response to the competitions and the prizes for winners. Typical questions posed by students focused on whether their participation counts towards their marks for the module and whether it is compulsory to participate (neither of which was the case). Overall, students spent less time than expected on the learning and training mode, and were more eager to proceed to the live online competitions. Although overall the findings were similar across the two phases of the study, in the second phase students demonstrated more enthusiasm, their actions and reactions were more energetic, and they appeared to be more engaged during gameplay. These observations provided evidence that they also exerted themselves to try and win the challenges; they appeared more concentrated, they were asking more specific questions or requested hints more often compared to students in the first phase, indicating their eagerness to play 'for the win' and their willingness towards making a mental effort. A parallel observation is the fact that in the second group most students participated as teams rather than individually, which made competitive play more thrilling and fun. In addition to questionnaire data, these observations enriched our understanding of how students experienced learning programming through this mGBL activity.

Post-event Questionnaire. After their experience with aMazeChallenge, students were asked to provide their responses to the post-event questionnaire. The questionnaire items were aligned to our research questions. Participants were first asked to rate their experience with aMazeChallenge indicating their satisfaction with the game. The majority of participants (64%) reported that their experience was either 'Good' or 'Excellent', 29% reported having a 'Neutral' experience, while 6% of the participants reported having a 'Bad' experience. Students were also asked to rate their experience in the single-player and multi-player modes of the game, which yielded analogous results. When asked to rate their perceived level of programming experience after engaging with aMazeChallenge, 41% of participants reported feeling 'Confident', 32% ranked themselves as 'Intermediate', and 12% as 'Beginner'. Furthermore, the vast majority of students (79%) responded that programming is either 'Very interesting' or 'Interesting', with 19% responding with 'Neutral', and 1% finding this activity 'Very boring'.

The post-event questionnaire also asked students to report how difficult they found aMazeChallenge to be. As shown in Fig. 4, 43% of participants found aMazeChallenge either 'Very easy' or 'Easy', and 40% found it either 'Very difficult' or 'Difficult'. The remaining 18% reported that they were not sure. In addition, when asked about how helpful aMazeChallenge is when learning programming, most participants responded with 'Neutral' (49%), while 37% found it 'Helpful', and 15% found it either 'Not helpful' or 'Completely ineffective'. None of the participants found aMazeChallenge 'Extremely helpful'. Similarly, most participants (62%) indicated that their skills were unchanged after playing aMazeChallenge, 34% reported an improvement, and 5% reported a reduction.

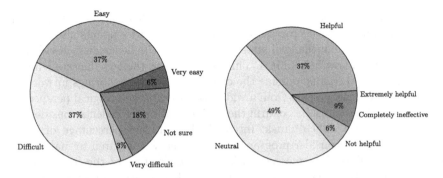

Fig. 4. Perceived difficulty when playing aMazeChallenge (left) and its helpfulness in terms of learning programming (right).

When asked to rate the usefulness of a competitive environment, 66% of students reported that such environments are conducive toward learning programming, 30% were neutral, and 5% said that they did not help the learning process. Asked whether they are likely to play aMazeChallenge again in the future, most participants (48%) responded with either 'Very likely' or 'Likely', 31% responded with 'Unlikely' and 'Very unlikely', whereas 22% were not sure. Finally, the most liked feature of aMazeChallenge was Personalization, followed by Code editing and Multiplayer mode. Paradoxically, the code editor was both a liked and disliked feature for different student groups. In total, 7 participants reported several issues involving app crashes, among other features that were disliked.

5   Discussion of the Findings

The analysis of questionnaire responses, observational data, and field notes were used to extract useful insights about user experience with aMazeChallenge, explore how and whether students' perceptions about programming were affected after their experience, as well as to evaluate the effectiveness and usability of aMazeChallenge (and to an extent of mGBL), in terms of engaging learners.

5.1   User Experience with mGBL

The first objective of this study is to explore learners' experiences and perceptions on learning programming through a mGBL activity. Prior to interacting with aMazeChallenge, the majority of the students (56%) considered themselves as beginners in programming, while after the intervention only 11% of the students considered themselves beginners, and the proportion of students who felt confident or at an intermediate level increased to 74%. There was also a slight increase (+3%) in the number of participants who found programming to be an interesting activity after their mGBL experience. A controversial finding was that while most students' satisfaction was 'Good' or 'Excellent' and their self-perceived confidence levels increased, the majority of the students also reported that their skills were unchanged after playing aMazeChallenge and provided low rating in terms of how helpful it is. This may relate to the fact that students did not engage with the game outside the class time, which also brings forward the need to consider engagement from a wider socio-techno-pedagogical perspective.

Additionally, the results confirm the notion that most students consider programming to be a difficult task. Interestingly, a higher percentage of female participants (29%) consider programming to be easy, compared to male participants (21%). This also emerged during the observation of the live gameplay session, especially in the second phase, where female students appeared more intrigued and involved. In contrast with their responses about programming in general, a significantly lower percentage found aMazeChallenge to be difficult. Based on these results, it is evident that the learners' perspectives on learning programming were affected by introducing the game-based learning activity with aMazeChallenge. The vast majority of participants (79%) consider games to be helpful toward learning programming, which provides additional motivation for exploring GBL. The results indicate that students felt more confident in their abilities as programmers, which may suggest that aMazeChallenge, and to a certain extent mGBL, can serve as an alternative method to engage students with programming concepts in higher education.

5.2   Engagement Effectiveness

The second objective of the study was to explore which aspects affect learner engagement with mGBL and how effective the game's features are in terms of engaging students. Even though more students found programming with aMazeChallenge easier than those who found it difficult, conversely, only 41% found aMazeChallenge to be helpful, and many students (46%) reported feeling neutral. The latter finding potentially uncovers limitations in terms of engagement effectiveness. Observational data also highlight the multiplicity of aspects that affect learner engagement in mGBL, many of which go beyond the inherent technical or design characteristics of the game. Aspects such as the overall user experience, intrinsic and extrinsic motivation, assessment methods, and feedback strategies highly impact learning experiences and learner engagement. Although further research is needed to explore this in the context of learning programming, the findings confirm that learning engagement is a complex construct that may be affected by a multitude of factors [45, 46]

The results of the final questionnaire also revealed that the most liked features of aMazeChallenge among the participants were personalisation, code editor, and multiplayer gameplay. However, the code editor appears to be both disliked and loved by different groups of participants. During observation it was evident that some students were frustrated with the drag-and-drop mode used in the Blockly workspace. Such languages may appear to be less direct, with more advanced students considering them as less powerful tools of expression. Notably, several participants also reported app crashes during the online gameplay. Such issues must be avoided altogether so that user experience and learner engagement are not negatively impacted.

Another aspect related to engagement has to do with collaborative and competitive game elements. Most students (56%) seem to believe that competitive game environments can be beneficial to the learning process. The responses of the students to the same question after playing aMazeChallenge reveal an increase (+14%) in the number of students who considered competitive environments advantageous toward the learning process. Therefore, incorporating such environments in interactive multiplayer games may intrigue and engage students to get involved in the learning process. Finally, the game also seems to have relatively high long-term engagement, as about half of the students said that they are likely to play aMazeChallenge again in the future. Other studies also support the claim that MMOGs can be employed as agents of motivation enhancing the learning experience due to the manifestation of collaborative and competitive gameplay, rendering them a promising game genre for university students [7].

5.3   Technological Readiness

The results also provide insights into the technological effectiveness of aMazeChallenge and can help explore how effective mobile devices are as a learning platform specifically for learning programming and algorithmic thinking. Firstly, mobile operating system usage trends indicate that future mobile educational games may benefit by being developed as cross-platform apps that can be deployed on a variety of operating systems [40]. This may increase their uptake and effectiveness alike, as more students will be able to interact with the game on their own mobile devices. Secondly, technological features (namely, game performance, UI, and quality of graphics) prevail in what students consider as the most important features when playing an educational game. These results highlight the importance of human-factors, game design, usability and UX goals, as all of the top features selected by the participants relate to UX. Performance and UI design are widely regarded are the most critical factors affecting the user's experience in an online game [14]. Similarly, graphics and game mechanics play a significant role in player immersion and contribute to the player's overall experience in games [54]. These results are also supported by relevant literature [4,34,41,50,55] and therefore indicate the potential areas where developers may need to focus on in the future to create an enhanced user experience and more effective mobile educational games.

6   Conclusion

The outcomes of the evaluation illustrate that aMazeChallenge has the engagement efficacy and technological capability to induce university students into basic programming concepts, yet highlight the multiplicity of aspects that affect learning and learner engagement in game-based learning, many of which go beyond the inherent technical characteristics of the game. Students felt significantly more confident with their programming skills after playing aMazeChallenge; enjoyed the competitive gameplay; but also voiced their frustrations, and assessment-related concerns, and indicated aspects they considered significant, such as performance, user interface, graphics, online gameplay, and personalisation. The findings re-emphasise that aspects such as the overall user experience, intrinsic and extrinsic motivation, assessment methods, and feedback strategies employed, highly impact learning experiences and learner engagement, in addition to the design features of the game. The overarching theme that emerged by collectively addressing the research objectives is what we refer to as 'engagement by design', that is, engagement must be treated as the fusion of pedagogical design, technological design, and game design rather than an external student trait. This theme emphasises the genuine need to achieve a constructive alignment between the inherent technological qualities and design features of a mobile educational game, the broader pedagogical context, and human-centered factors, in order to achieve the desired learner engagement and learning outcomes. The study findings can inform the development of heuristic or theoretical frameworks that can guide the design, development, and evaluation of interactive education mobile games in higher education.

References

1. Adams, S.: The role of gamification in the facilitation of student engagement: an exploratory industrial psychology application. Ph.D. thesis, Stellenbosch: Stellenbosch University (2019)
2. Ahmad Faudzi, M., Che Cob, Z., Omar, R., Sharudin, S.A., Ghazali, M.: Investigating the user interface design frameworks of current mobile learning applications: a systematic review. Educ. Sci. **13**(1), 94 (2023)
3. Al Zieni, H.: The effect of mobile learning on learner autonomy: a suggested measurement tool to assess the development of learner autonomy. J. Asia TEFL **16**(3), 1020 (2019)
4. Alasmari, T.: The effect of screen size on students' cognitive load in mobile learning. J. Educ. Teach. Learn. **5**(2), 280–295 (2020)
5. Ally, M.: Mobile learning: from research to practice to impact education. Learn. Teach. High. Educ. Gulf Perspect. **10**(2), 3–12 (2013)
6. Barr, V., Stephenson, C.: Bringing computational thinking to k-12: what is involved and what is the role of the computer science education community? ACM Inroads **2**(1), 48–54 (2011)
7. Bawa, P., Watson, S.L., Watson, W.: Motivation is a game: massively multiplayer online games as agents of motivation in higher education. Comput. Educ. **123**, 174–194 (2018)
8. Carrión12, M., Santorum12, M., Aguilar, J., Peréz, M.: iPlus methodology for requirements elicitation for serious games (2019)
9. Chu, H.C.: Potential negative effects of mobile learning on students' learning achievement and cognitive load-a format assessment perspective. J. Educ. Technol. Soc. **17**(1), 332–344 (2014)
10. CodeMonkey: Coding for kids - game-based programming (2019). http://www.codemonkey.com/. Accessed 19 Dec 2019

11. Connolly, T.M., Boyle, E.A., MacArthur, E., Hainey, T., Boyle, J.M.: A systematic literature review of empirical evidence on computer games and serious games. Comput. Educ. **59**(2), 661–686 (2012)
12. Creswell, J.W.: Research Design: Qualitative, Quantitative, and Mixed Methods Approaches. Sage, Thousand Oaks (2003)
13. Curum, B., Khedo, K.K.: Cognitive load management in mobile learning systems: principles and theories. J. Comput. Educ. **8**(1), 109–136 (2021)
14. Einfeldt, L., Degbelo, A.: User interface factors of mobile UX: a study with an incident reporting application. arXiv preprint arXiv:2102.02510 (2021)
15. Elkhair, Z., Abdul Mutalib, A.: Mobile learning applications: characteristics, perspectives, and future trends. Int. J. Interact. Digit. Media (IJIDM) **5**(1), 18–21 (2019)
16. Faisal, C.M.N., Fernandez-Lanvin, D., De Andrés, J., Gonzalez-Rodriguez, M.: Design quality in building behavioral intention through affective and cognitive involvement for e-learning on smartphones. Internet Research (2020)
17. Feng, Y., Liao, Y., Ren, Y.: Effects of m-learning on students' learning outcome: a meta-analysis. In: Deng, L., Ma, W.W.K., Fong, C.W.R. (eds.) New Media for Educational Change. ECTY, pp. 115–123. Springer, Singapore (2018). https://doi.org/10.1007/978-981-10-8896-4_10
18. Ferguson, R., et al.: Innovating pedagogy 2019: Open university innovation report 7 (2019)
19. Fotaris, P., Mastoras, T., Leinfellner, R., Rosunally, Y.: Climbing up the leaderboard: An empirical study of applying gamification techniques to a computer programming class. Electronic Journal of e-learning **14**(2), 94–110 (2016)
20. Giannakoulopoulos, A., Limniati, L., Konstantinou, N.: Examining the contemporary status of gamification in education. In: INTED2020 Proceedings, pp. 6467–6473. IATED (2020)
21. Gikas, J., Grant, M.M.: Mobile computing devices in higher education: Student perspectives on learning with cellphones, smartphones & social media. Internet High. Educ **19**, 18–26 (2013)
22. Google: Blockly - google developers (2019). https://developers.google.com/blockly. Accessed 08 Jan 2020
23. Gouws, L.A., Bradshaw, K., Wentworth, P.: Computational thinking in educational activities: an evaluation of the educational game light-bot. In: Proceedings of the 18th ACM Conference on Innovation and Technology in Computer Science Education, pp. 10–15 (2013)
24. Hambrock, H., De Villiers, F., Rusman, E., MacCallum, K., Arrifin, S.: Seamless learning in higher education: Perspectives of international educators on its curriculum and implementation potential: Global research project 2020. International Association for Mobile Learning (2020)
25. Hammersley, M., Atkinson, P.: Ethnography: Principles in practice. Routledge, New York (2007)
26. Kanellopoulou, C., Giannakoulopoulos, A., et al.: Engage and conquer: an online empirical approach into whether intrinsic or extrinsic motivation leads to more enhanced students' engagement. Creat. Educ. **11**(02), 143 (2020)
27. Kasenides, N., Paspallis, N.: amazechallenge: An interactive multiplayer game for learning to code (2021)
28. Kim, J., Choi, Y., Xia, M., Kim, J.: Mobile-friendly content design for MOOCS: challenges, requirements, and design opportunities. In: CHI Conference on Human Factors in Computing Systems, pp. 1–16 (2022)

29. Krajcsi, A., Csapodi, C., Stettner, E.: Algotaurus: an educational computer programming game for beginners. Interact. Learn. Environ. **29**(4), 634–647 (2021)

30. Kroustalli, C., Xinogalos, S.: Studying the effects of teaching programming to lower secondary school students with a serious game: a case study with python and codecombat. Educ. Inf. Technol. **26**(5), 6069–6095 (2021)

31. Lathwesen, C., Belova, N.: Escape rooms in stem teaching and learning-prospective field or declining trend? a literature review. Educ. Sci. **11**(6), 308 (2021)

32. Li, X., Heng, Q.: Design of mobile learning resources based on new blended learning: a case study of superstar learning app. In: 2021 IEEE 3rd International Conference on Computer Science and Educational Informatization (CSEI), pp. 333–338. IEEE (2021)

33. Liu, M.: Motivating students to learn using a game-based learning approach gaming and education issue. Texas Educ. Rev. **2**(1), 117–128 (2014)

34. Manzano-León, A., et al.: Online escape room during COVID-19: a qualitative study of social education degree students' experiences. Educ. Sci. **11**(8), 426 (2021)

35. Marfisi-Schottman, I., George, S., Tarpin-Bernard, F.: Evaluating learning games during their conception. In: European Conference on Games Based Learning, vol. 1, p. 364. Academic Conferences International Limited (2014)

36. Marinoni, G., van't Land, H.: The impact of COVID-19 on global higher education. Int. Higher Educ. (102), 7–9 (2020)

37. Meftah, C., Retbi, A., Bennani, S., Idrissi, M.K.: Evaluation of user experience in the context of mobile serious game. In: 2019 International Conference on Intelligent Systems and Advanced Computing Sciences (ISACS), pp. 1–5. IEEE (2019)

38. Miljanovic, M.A., Bradbury, J.S.: A review of serious games for programming. In: Göbel, S., Garcia-Agundez, A., Tregel, T., Ma, M., Baalsrud Hauge, J., Oliveira, M., Marsh, T., Caserman, P. (eds.) JCSG 2018. LNCS, vol. 11243, pp. 204–216. Springer, Cham (2018). https://doi.org/10.1007/978-3-030-02762-9_21

39. Moreno-León, J., Robles, G.: The Europe code week (CODEEU) initiative shaping the skills of future engineers. In: 2015 IEEE Global Engineering Education Conference (EDUCON), pp. 561–566. IEEE (2015)

40. Nawrocki, P., Wrona, K., Marczak, M., Sniezynski, B.: A comparison of native and cross-platform frameworks for mobile applications. Computer **54**(3), 18–27 (2021)

41. Ng'ambi, D., Brown, C., Bozalek, V., Gachago, D., Wood, D.: Technology enhanced teaching and learning in South African higher education-a rearview of a 20 year journey. Br. J. Edu. Technol. **47**(5), 843–858 (2016)

42. Papadakis, S.: Advances in mobile learning educational research (AMLER): mobile learning as an educational reform. Adv. Mob. Learn. Educ. Res. **1**(1), 1–4 (2021)

43. Paspallis, N., Kasenides, N., Piki, A.: A software architecture for developing distributed games that teach coding and algorithmic thinking. In: 2022 IEEE 46th Annual Computers, Software, and Applications Conference (COMPSAC), pp. 101–110. IEEE (2022)

44. Pauli, M., Ferrell, G.: The future of assessment: five principles, five targets for 2025 (2020)

45. Piki, A.: Learner engagement in computer-supported collaborative learning activities: natural or nurtured? In: Zaphiris, P., Ioannou, A. (eds.) LCT 2014. LNCS, vol. 8523, pp. 107–118. Springer, Cham (2014). https://doi.org/10.1007/978-3-319-07482-5_11

46. Piki, A.: Learner engagement in mobile computer-supported collaborative learning contexts: an integrative framework. In: Proceedings of the 16th World Conference on Mobile and Contextual Learning, pp. 1–7 (2017)

47. Piki, A.: An exploration of student experiences with social media and mobile technologies during emergency transition to remote education. In: World Conference on Mobile and Contextual Learning, pp. 10–17 (2020)

48. Piki, A.: Re-imagining the distributed nature of learner engagement in computer-supported collaborative learning contexts in the post-pandemic era. In: In: Meiselwitz, G. (eds.) HCII 2022. LNCS, pp. 161–179. Springer, Cham (2022). https://doi.org/10.1007/978-3-031-05064-0_13

49. Piki, A., Markou, M., Vasiliou, A.: Learning through play: the role of learning and engagement theory in the development of educational games for intellectually challenged children. In: 2016 International Conference on Interactive Technologies and Games (ITAG), pp. 1–6. IEEE (2016)

50. Piki, A., tefan, I.A., Stefan, A., Gheorghe, A.F.: Mitigating the challenges of mobile games-based learning through gamified lesson paths. In: World Conference on Mobile and Contextual Learning, pp. 73–80 (2020)

51. Piñero Charlo, J.C.: Educational escape rooms as a tool for horizontal mathematization: learning process evidence. Educ. Sci. **10**(9), 213 (2020)

52. Schell, J.: The Art of Game Design: A book of lenses. CRC Press (2008)

53. Schindler, L.A., Burkholder, G.J., Morad, O.A., Marsh, C.: Computer-based technology and student engagement: a critical review of the literature. Int. J. Educ. Technol. High. Educ. **14**(1), 1–28 (2017). https://doi.org/10.1186/s41239-017-0063-0

54. Shih, W.C.: Mining learners' behavioral sequential patterns in a blockly visual programming educational game. In: 2017 International Conference on Industrial Engineering, Management Science and Application (ICIMSA), pp. 1–2. IEEE (2017)

55. Sophonhiranrak, S.: Features, barriers, and influencing factors of mobile learning in higher education: a systematic review. Heliyon **7**(4), e06696 (2021)

56. Stefan, I.A., Gheorghe, A.F., Stefan, A., Piki, A., Tsalapata, H., Heidmann, O.: Constructing seamless learning through game-based learning experiences. Int. J. Mob. Blended Learn. (IJMBL) **14**(4), 1–12 (2022)

57. Suartama, I.K., Setyosari, P., Ulfa, S., et al.: Development of an instructional design model for mobile blended learning in higher education. Int. J. Emerging Technol. Learn. **14**(16) (2019)

58. Sung, Y.T., Yang, J.M., Lee, H.Y.: The effects of mobile-computer-supported collaborative learning: meta-analysis and critical synthesis. Rev. Educ. Res. **87**(4), 768–805 (2017)

59. Swacha, J.: State of research on gamification in education: a bibliometric survey. Educ. Sci. **11**(2), 69 (2021)

60. Tsekleves, E., Cosmas, J., Aggoun, A.: Benefits, barriers and guideline recommendations for the implementation of serious games in education for stakeholders and policymakers. Br. J. Edu. Technol. **47**(1), 164–183 (2016). https://doi.org/10.1111/bjet.12223

61. Vitores, A., Gil-Juárez, A.: The trouble with 'women in computing': a critical examination of the deployment of research on the gender gap in computer science. J. Gend. Stud. **25**(6), 666–680 (2016)

62. Wilson, C.: Hour of code–a record year for computer science. ACM Inroads **6**(1), 22–22 (2015)

63. Wing, J.M.: Computational thinking. Commun. ACM **49**(3), 33–35 (2006)

Strategy Based on Agile Methodology to Improve Communication on Digital Platforms (Social Networks) of Higher Education Institutions

Andrea Martinez-Duran$^{(\boxtimes)}$, Jhony Garcia-Tirado, Victor Villamizar,
and Viviana Alejandra Álvarez

Corporación Universitaria Taller Cinco, 58 North Highway Kilometer 19, Chia, Colombia
andrea.martinez@taller5.edu.co

Abstract. The present study consists of monitoring the creation of a photographic game plan as an approach to further strengthen the brand strategies for social networks of the Universidad Tecnológica del Usumacinta (UTU) in Mexico. As a framework for action, the vision of Taller Cinco was applied, which consists of connecting the areas of knowledge in the applied arts through the Agile Design Thinking methodology, which allows the visual communicator to recognize that an important part of the communication that uses in social networks obeys a visual language; granting at the same time the tools for the creation of a photographic strategy thatevokes the meaning of a product of ideological knowledge and technique that allows to adequately express the identities of the brand, in this case the exhibition scenario of the UTU. This approach acknowledges the development of visual concepts as a way of projecting the university philosophy to its community and society in general. It is intended that the photographs achieve three main objectives for UTU: visual identity, a sense of belonging among the student community and a brand communication strategy that influences the decision-making of the applicants and their family context. Applying the agile methodology Design Thinking process has nurtured the design of a visual concept, allowing the creation of an empathic and decisive visual communication strategy that centers the user experience enabling optimal brand development in UTU's social networks. These methodologies opened new paths and ideas in the development of projects through creativity, building innovative solutions that positively impacted UTU's brand development. It is important to recognize that this project would not have been possible without the application of new technologies and trends that arise every day in social networks.

Keywords: Agile methodology · Digital platforms · social networks · Higher Education Institutions

1 Introduction

Social networks have transformed the world and the way we interact [1]. Through them, it is possible to communicate with other people in a matter of seconds; share experiences, ways of thinking and perceptions. Social networks allow us to learn about places, cultures

© The Author(s), under exclusive license to Springer Nature Switzerland AG 2023
A. Coman and S. Vasilache (Eds.): HCII 2023, LNCS 14026, pp. 92–102, 2023.
https://doi.org/10.1007/978-3-031-35927-9_7

and traditions from anywhere in the world [2], making it possible to promote, buy or sell a variety of products and services from any corner of our planet [3].

This is the main reason why more organizations and institutions are making use of social networks as a means to strengthen their strategy and brand development. In fact, using social networks as a means of attracting potential customers is an increasingly common practice within new business structures. Both individuals and companies are aware of the value that social networks bring to the market [4].

In this sense, Higher Education Institutions (HEIs) are no strangers to the boom in social networks; They have recognized its impact on their communication and the role in their corporate interests such as attracting students, transmitting their values in virtual ecosystems, key factors that affect their viability and sustainability [5]. However, the challenge faced by many HEIs is to guarantee that what they share on social networks is effectively what is best for them, that is, to ensure that the published content generates positive interaction in the internal and external community of the institution [6].

To answer this question and achieve the best results, it is necessary to implement strategies and methods to set a course to follow that ensures competitiveness and innovation while creating brand value. This is where a methodology that has been successful in the global business environment, but has not been widely explored in the Latin American educational environment, comes into play: the agile methodology Design Thinking [7, 8]. The following figure shows the Design Thinking process (Fig. 1):

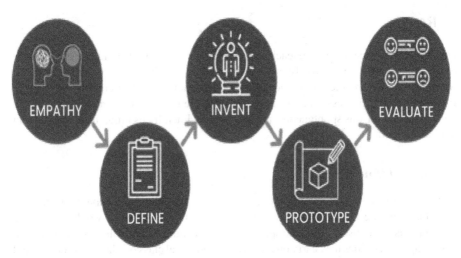

Fig. 1. Design Thinking phases.

To test the usefulness of this method in the educational field, each of the phases of the agile methodology Design Thinking are applied at the Technological University of Usumacinta (UTU), in order to design a photographic strategy on social networks headed to solve the problems from the UTU, valuing the needs of the brand and creating a greater impact and interaction within its community.

2 Materials and Methods

The project is developed through a qualitative approach using field experimentation and a descriptive research design. For this, interviews were applied to students and teachers who are active in the research institution. The guidelines of each of the interviews were marked by the six phases of the design thinking methodology: Empathize, Define, Ideate, Prototype, Test and Implement [9].

For the focus group carried out with the students, 3 sessions were applied. Each session had the participation of 15 to 20 students from different careers, posing pre-questions related to the content that has been previously shared on social networks: Do you currently use social networks? How do you like the content that is shared through the networks? What would you like to see on social media? How do you rate the photographic content that is shared on social networks?

On the other hand, the second focus group was held with the professional community. Three meetings were held with an attendance of five to seven participants. The following questions were asked: What are the sciences preferred by the students? What are the most requested equipment by students? What do you hear from students about content shared on social media? What content do you think could create a sense of belonging in students? The complete methodology allows a 360° study resulting in successful solutions.

3 Results

Focus groups with students and teachers were held behind closed doors to create a circle of trust and allow them to freely express their ideas. The intention of the focus group was made known and the importance of its transparency when participating was raised. Initially, it was a process that required a lot of patience; However, after about 15–20 min, participation was spontaneous and unanimous. Each focus group took place for an hour and a half.

3.1 Student Outcome Stage

The students stated that they did not feel identified with the photographic content that was shared on the UTU social networks; They mentioned that they would like to see photographs of themselves and the spaces of their institution, while they showed interest in sharing the activities they carry out during their practical classes. They also commented that they do not get involved in the digital language they use through social networks. This is observed in the following figures related to the collection of information with students (Fig. 2).

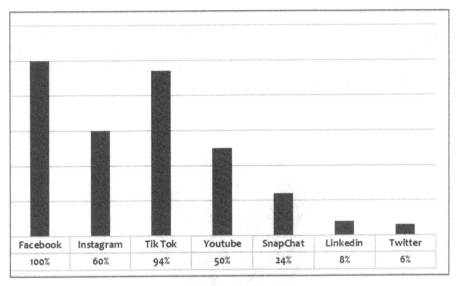

Fig. 2. Use of social networks.

The previous figure represents the networks used by the students who participated in this case study. The results showed the following interaction: Facebook with 100%, being the most used by the sample; followed by TikTok with 94%, Instagram with 60%, YouTube with 50%, Snapchat with 24% and LinkedIn and Twitter with 8% and 6%, consecutively (Fig. 3).

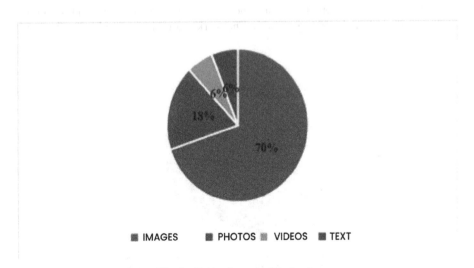

Fig. 3. Type of post on Facebook.

The figure above shows that the most common type of use within the social network Facebook contains interdisciplinary visual communication between the areas of photography and graphic design, with a participation of 70%; followed by photographic images, with 18% and videos, with 6%. This demonstrates the impact that visual communication causes in the interaction between the user and social networks (Fig. 4).

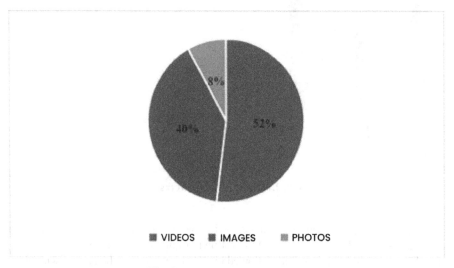

Fig. 4. Type of post on Instagram

What is shown in the previous figure shows the most common type of publications by those surveyed on the Instagram social network, observing the videos as the most

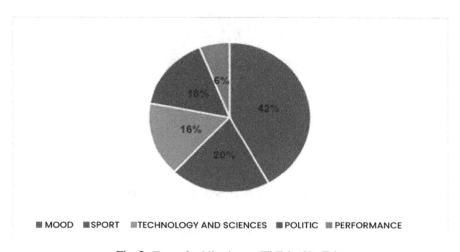

Fig. 5. Type of publication on TikTok - YouTube

representative with 52%, images with 40% and photos with 8% of the whole sample value (Fig. 5).

Regarding the type of content generated on the social networks TikTok and YouTube, humor was the best positioned with 42%, followed by Sports with 20%, Science and Technology and Politics with 16% each, and Entertainment with 6%. This demonstrates how humor and sports are the type of advertising most valued by the group of students at the institution.

3.2 Professors Results Phase

This focus group showed the professional interest and projection that students have shown during their training through social networks. In addition, the professors mentioned that most of the students are distant from the institution's social networks, because there is no spontaneity, the visual language is not youthful at all, and they do not feel listened to.

3.3 Strategy Development

Following the process of creating the strategy through agile methodologies, the Empathy phase allowed the institution not only to listen to the students, but also to put themselves in their place, see what they see and speak as they do, bringing an understanding of their perspective.

This phase allowed the team and its process to be brought closer to the students, this approach provided a better understanding of their behaviors, tastes and thoughts in relation to the content of social networks. It should be noted that in this phase, students and teachers were interviewed so that they could express their opinions freely and honestly, providing a more complete detail of their opinion towards the brand. Subsequently, with the UTU communication team applying an empathy mapping process with the aim of helping the creative team gain a real understanding of their potential audience, recognizing where they came from and what they want, and therefore, creating key information to work towards a 360° strategy to impact students, graduates and applicants, while allowing the creative team to deliver a more effective solution in its communication strategy that focused its focus on client expectations (Fig. 6).

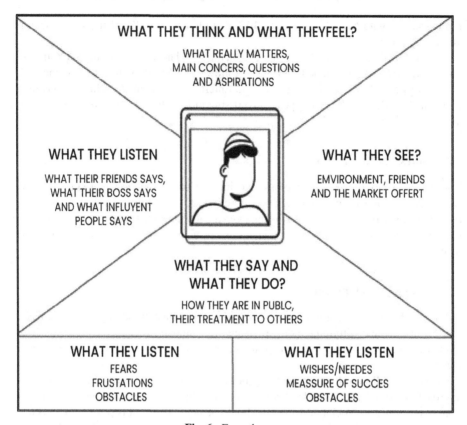

Fig. 6. Empathy map

In the definition phase, joint work was carried out with the communication team of the UTU. In this coworking, the data collected in the Empathy phase was analyzed and the team started working on creating a strategy, using Simon Siner's Golden Circle methodology, defining the problem and focusing ideas to build a clear and focused insight. of the existing problem. The purpose of this phase was to communicate attractively to young applicants, active students, and graduates, making them feel an important part of the institution and, finally, making them fall in love to create brand loyalty.

Therefore, when a creative team is required to solve problems/opportunities, it is important to show the greatness and solutions that creative thinking can bring to the business world, especially by properly communicating brand value. Subsequently, once the team defines how to define the client, it can structure the strategy to work on the brand from a cultural aspect, then develop strategies in each of the areas that we deem appropriate and, in the end, offer each of the actions that we deem opportune to solve each of the interests that they have towards the products (Fig. 7).

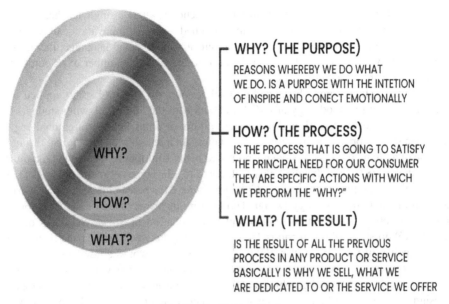

Fig. 7. The Golden Circle

Taking these facts, the strategy takes into account the Definition and Ideation phases; attending to each suggestion by students and professors. From this information arose several ideas that involve the institutional identity and the economic context of the institution. Among this ideas, came the realization of showing the students in different activities on social networks, promoting the programs showcasing the students' academic work and not so much from a formal perspective; In addition, showing the facilities and equipment of the UTU, publicizing what the graduates do, illustrated the educational method taught by the UTU (70% practical and 30% theoretical), present the scholarships that offer by the institution to further its social protection, among others. Most of the ideas that came out of this phase were of high interest to the community.

Before finalizing the plan of actions, it was imperative to create a prototype (Phase 3) that can be tested (Phase 4) to validate or foresee further problems to allow for adjustments to ensure that the implementation results will enhance communicational innovation to the brand and its value.

4   Conclusions and Discussions

The use of agile methodologies such as Design Thinking has attracted the attention of researchers around the world to provide solutions to various problems, especially those that aim to address problems associated with communication and innovation at different levels. Certainly, technologies show important powers for the generation of solutions within the educational field [10].

For example, Montserrat Magro Gutierrez and Silvia Carrascal Dominguez used the Design Thinking tool as a resource and methodology for visual literacy and learning in preschools in multi-grade schools in Mexico (schools where a single teacher teaches students from different grades). The results obtained were that innovation can be introduced in these classrooms through co-communication and visual language, increasing the probability of success and without the need to increase the number of resources or improve their infrastructures [11].

In Spain, Alicia Jordán-Fisas and Graciela Esperanza Diestra-Espino applied the Design Thinking methodology at UIC Barcelona with the aim of allowing students to approach the world of work and the current affairs of companies through challenges and case studies presented by various companies. As a result, they found that, through the use of agile methodology, students proposed better solutions to challenges and more efficient, innovative and dynamic ideas compared to other types of methodologies [12].

Another example is presented in Colombia, where the researcher Jonathan Velasco applied the agile methodology Design Thinking in his project Design and Creation of Graphic Captions for Communication and Dissemination in Social Networks of the Creation Workshops of the Territory Dialogues Project between Boyacá and Santander. The objective of the project was to devise a strategy that would allow them to design graphic pieces to effectively communicate the outcome of the workshops, avoiding monotony and repetition of graphic pieces. Through the application of the five phases of Design Thinking, the objective of designing and creating effective graphic pieces, with adequate and accurate information to convey key concepts of the creative workshops, was achieved [13].

In turn, continuing in the Colombian context, Alvarez and Varela developed the Sinergy Flow methodology for the optimization of business agility as part of a strategy of brand intervention and sales at fairs; seeking and achieving the generation of value and increased profits of the actors involved in the research process [14].

This process map articulates the constructivist and constructionist fundamentals of Taller Cinco's university base essence and pedagogical model which adopts the agile and disruptive methodologies that empower endogenous and exogenous teams to adapt to collaborative and co-crehation environments that achieve the necessary competitiveness. Based on the humanistic environment that puts the end user at the center. This is achieved by creating an iterative circuit of research, trial and error that helps to formulate and test these business models and the visual and communication strategies in advance for their target markets, creating an environment of competitiveness and assertiveness where user needs take precedence.

The success of Sinergy Flow T5 is based on permanent feedback aimed at oriented learning that consolidates a culture based on results, continuous and systemic improvements that incorporate tactical and strategic exercises that result in productivity as a permanent policy propelling innovation.

As it has become evident, the agile Design Thinking methodology is extremely useful for the resolution of current problems that require innovative solutions. In this sense, it was considered that, for the realization of this project, given its characteristics, the use of the Design Thinking methodology was the most pertinent, taking into account that the aim was to create visual material for UTU that would influence the student community and the social environment.

Thus, from the information obtained, it is possible to conclude some important things. First, it is essential to have a profile of the audience you want to reach, through a deep and empathetic knowledge that includes their social, economic, cultural, aspirational context, tastes, skills, weaknesses, opportunities, threats, among other things. Much of the failure in social networks is a consequence of the lack of knowledge of those you want to influence.

Second, to know and define which aspects of communication fail and need to be improved. In the particular case of UTU, one of the main problems is the lack of a sense of belonging to the university by both the student community and the social environment. Neither the students nor the general population feel totally part of the institution; there is no sense of ownership or institutional pride. This problem creates a separation between the operational side of UTU and its student enrollment, applicants and community. Therefore, the strategy in social networks implies the elimination of this barrier, creating a sense of belonging and institutional pride.

Third, to raise all possible ideas that provide a solution to the problem, approached from the collective, that is, including representatives from various areas of the institution.

The next step is prototyping, which implies the materialization of the ideas. In our specific case, it implies the presentation of photographic material made under the ideas and concepts proposed in the previous step. Last but not least, the validation of the prototypes where they are subjected to evaluation, in order to determine if the material is in line with the chosen strategy and if they are suitable for publication in the institution's social networks, or if they need to be improved, redesigned or discarded.

In this project, and under the application of the agile methodology Design Thinking, it was possible to publish photographic material according to the needs of the UTU and that empathizes with all the fields of influence of the institution, students, students, students, community.

References

1. Santos, Z.R., Cheung, C.M., Coelho, P.S., Rita, P.: Consumer engagement in social media brand communities: a literature review. Int. J. Inf. Manage. **63**, 102457 (2022)
2. Infante, A., Mardikaningsih, R.: The Potential of social media as a Means of Online Business Promotion. J. Soc. Sci. Stud. (JOS3) **2**(2), 45–49 (2022)
3. Kumar, B., Sharma, A.: Examining the research on social media in business-to-business marketing with a focus on sales and the selling process. Ind. Mark. Manage. **102**, 122–140 (2022)
4. Bonilla-Quijada, M., Perea, E., Corrons, A., Olmo-Arriaga, J. L.: Engaging students through social media. Findings for the top five universities in the world. J. Mark. High. Educ. **32**(2), 197–214 (2022)
5. Wong, L.W., Tan, G.W.H., Hew, J.J., Ooi, K.B., Leong, L.Y.: Mobile social media marketing: a new marketing channel among digital natives in higher education? J. Mark. High. Educ. **32**(1), 113–137 (2022)
6. Tkacová, H., Králik, R., Tvrdoň, M., Jenisová, Z., Martin, J.G.: Credibility and involvement of social media in education—recommendations for mitigating the negative effects of the pandemic among high school students. Int. J. Environ. Res. Public Health **19**(5) (2022)
7. Taimur, S., Onuki, M.: Design thinking as digital transformative pedagogy in higher sustainability education: Cases from Japan and Germany. Int. J. Educ. Res. **114**(1) (2022)

8. Rusmann, A., Ejsing-Duun, S.: When design thinking goes to school: a literature review of design competences for the K-12 level. Int. J. Technol. Des. Educ. **32**(4), 2063–2091 (2022)
9. Balakrishnan, B.: Exploring the impact of design thinking tool among design undergraduates: a study on creative skills and motivation to think creatively. Int. J. Technol. Design Educ. **32**(3), 1799–1812 (2022)
10. Moreno, M., Duran, S., Parra, M., Hernández-Sánchez, I., Ramírez, J.: Use of virtual resources as a tool for teaching language skills at the colombian caribbean region primary basic level. In: Stephanidis, C., Antona, M., Ntoa, S. (eds.) HCII 2021. CCIS, vol. 1499, pp. 286–293. Springer, Cham (2021). https://doi.org/10.1007/978-3-030-90179-0_37
11. Magro-Gutierrez, M., Carrascal-Domínguez, S.: El Design Thinking como recurso y metodología para la alfabetización visual y el aprendizaje en preescolares de escuelas multigrado de México. Vivat Academia. Revista de Comunicación **146**, 71–95 (2019)
12. Jordán-Fisas, A., Diestra-Espino, G.E.: La metodología design thinking y su implementación en las aulas universitarias: Análisis del proyecto B-SMART en UIC Barcelona durante el curso 2019/20. Revista Emprendimiento y Negocios Internacionales **5**, 18–23 (2020)
13. Velasco-Castellanos, J.M.: Diseño y Creación de Piezas Gráficas para la Comunicación y Divulgación en Redes Sociales de los Talleres de Creación del Proyecto Diálogos del Territorio Entre Boyacá y Santander. Universidad de Santander, Bucaramanga (2021)
14. Álvarez-Restrepo, V., Varela, C.: The competitive transformation of business based on agile innovation methods that engage visual creatives as business process leaders. In: The European Conference on Arts, Design & Education 2022 Official Conference Proceedings (2022) N

Towards Well-Being and Inclusion in the Educational System: A Preliminary Methodology for Evaluating Student eXperience Considering Cultural Factors

Nicolás Matus[1]([✉]) [iD], Cristian Rusu[1] [iD], and Federico Botella[2] [iD]

[1] Pontificia Universidad Católica de Valparaíso, Av. Brasil 2241, 2340000 Valparaíso, Chile
nicolas.matus.p@mail.pucv.cl
[2] Universidad Miguel Hernández de Elche, Avenida de la Universitat s/n, 03202 Elche, Spain
federico@umh.es

Abstract. Student eXperience (SX) is a particular case of Customer eXperience (CX). SX refers to experiences, interactions, and reactions of students of a Higher Education Institution (HEI) when interacting with services, products and systems that are provided to them. Proper SX management increases student satisfaction, which is directly related to the perceived quality of HEIs. Among the most notable attributes that influence SX are the cultural aspects of the student and his/her environment. Considering the importance of proper management of SX and cultural aspects to increase student satisfaction, we propose a preliminary methodology of SX evaluation, which considers cultural aspects of students and their environment. An evaluation methodology allows detecting weaknesses and strengths of a given HEI, generating a diagnosis that takes into account the opinion of its customers. The methodology is organized in a 5-stage process that involves a transversal work with the students and with the psycho-pedagogical and administrative staff of the HEIs. The process is interdisciplinary and flexible, allowing the methodology to be easily adopted by any HEI and adapted to its strategic objectives.

Keywords: Student eXperience · Evaluation Methodology · Customer eXperience · HCI · Culture · Cultural Aspects · Higher Education · Higher Education Quality

1 Introduction

Student eXperience (SX) concept is gaining relevance nowadays. SX, understood as a particular case of Customer eXperience (CX), allows studying the reactions and perceptions of students when interacting with products, systems and services provided by Higher Education Institutions (HEIs) throughout their total consumption cycle. Student interactions take place both inside and outside of strictly academic spaces. In addition, students' perceptions can be affected by environmental factors and determined by aspects of their private lives, such as sex, gender, socioeconomic level, culture, disabilities, medical conditions, personality, among others. In previous studies [1] we realized that cultural aspects have a special relevance regarding students' interactions and perceptions. For this reason, we think that it is necessary to include cultural factors in the development of tools that allow the SX to be analyzed and managed.

The subjectivity and diversity of student's experiences make SX analysis and administration a complex process, which requires a multidisciplinary approach and systemic work. The importance of proper SX management lies mainly in 2 key aspects. Firstly, this will make it possible to increase student satisfaction and well-being. Second, as with the CX, since the SX is a particular case of it, its effective administration can lead to differential advantages for service organizations [2], as can be the case of HEIs.

We propose as a solution to the SX management problems the development of an evaluation methodology. This will make it possible to detect the strengths and weaknesses of the products, systems, services, and environment provided by the HEIs to the students. Considering the relevance of cultural aspects in students' experiences, we have incorporated this element into our solution, guided by the six national culture dimensions proposed by Hofstede [3, 4]. The proposal consists of 5 stages that go from pre-planning data collection to a stage of modeling and interpretation of results.

This paper is organized as follows. Section 2 introduces the theoretical background and the key concepts of our proposal. Section 3 presents the proposal of the preliminary SX evaluation methodology, the limitations of our proposal, and the model and methods used for its development. Finally, in Sect. 4 conclusions and future work are presented.

2   Theoretical Background

2.1   Customer eXperience (CX)

CX is an important discipline to increase the satisfaction of a company's customers. Increasing customer satisfaction when using certain products and services is increasing the success of a brand. For this reason, companies are investing more and more in CX research. The CX concept is considered a theoretical extension of the UX concept because instead of analyzing the interaction with a single service or product, CX focuses on multiple products and services during the total consumption cycle. Hill et al. (2007) consider that CX refers to "the physical and emotional experiences occurring through the interactions with the product and/or service offering of a brand from the point of first direct, conscious contact, through the total journey to the post-consumption stage." [5]. Lemon and Verhoef (2016) consider CX to be "a multidimensional construct focusing on a customer's cognitive, emotional, behavioral, sensory, and social responses to a firm's offerings during the customer's entire purchase journey" [6].

Some authors consider that the CX consists of six dimensions: emotional, sensory, cognitive, pragmatic, lifestyle and relational [7]. Thus, regarding the impact, scope, and dimensionality of customer interaction with certain systems, products, or services. In the case of students this becomes evident. The interaction of students with the HEIs frequently occurs outside the classroom and in areas other than merely educational. To apply CX solutions and improve student satisfaction, it is necessary to understand their characteristics, needs, expectations and interactions. It is important to mention that all these elements are related to the student's cultural background, since it is in the people's cultural environment where group behaviors and society moral norms are manifested

[3]. To a large extent, what we consider good/desirable/acceptable can be transgressed, affecting our perception of a certain topic. This, along with expectations, is directly related to people's satisfaction [8].

2.2 Student eXperience (SX)

The Student eXperience or SX is a concept that has gained popularity in recent years. This is a particular case of CX where the students of an HEI are consumers of systems, products, or services in the field of their higher education. The SX was defined as "all the physical and emotional perceptions and reactions that a student or future student experiences in response to interaction with products, systems or services provided by a HEI, and interactions with people related to the academic field, both inside and outside of academic space" [1, 9]. As can be seen in Fig. 1, the SX consists of 3 clearly defined dimensions: i) Social Dimension, ii) Educational Dimension, and iii) Personal Dimension. The 3 dimensions are defined below.

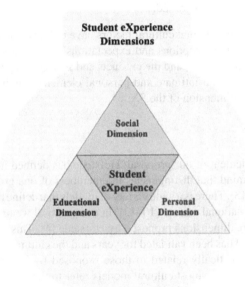

Fig. 1. Student eXperience Dimensions.

1. **Social Dimension**: This dimension is related to student's community relationship and institutional engagement. This dimension focuses on interpersonal relationships within HEIs (student-student) and especially with interactions with staff (e.g. student-administrative, student-psychologist or student-educator). Along with the interactions, this dimension analyzes the students' feeling of institutional belonging or engagement, due in part to activities organized in the university spaces or the inspiration of belonging feelings regarding ideological reasons or perceived quality. Factors

that make up this dimension include: i) Community Relationship, ii) Institutional Engagement.

2. **Educational Dimension**: This dimension encompasses any aspect that focuses on promoting an adequate educational environment, maximizing the educational outcomes of students, or increasing HEI perceived quality (teaching methodologies, technological infrastructure, educational support networks). These aspects directly affect the perceived satisfaction of students. Factors that make up this dimension include: i) Learning Engagement, ii) Higher Education Quality, iii) Learning Resources/Learning Environment, and iv) Educational/Support Services.

3. **Personal Dimension**: This dimension is related to students' life personal aspects that may influence interactions and perceptions with HEI services and products. This dimension encompasses a wide range of aspects related to culture, socioeconomic level, financial dynamics, physical or mental disabilities, personal aspirations, family structure, position towards leisure in society, student feelings, among others. Factors that make up this dimension include: i) Student Development and Outcomes, ii) Student Feelings and Emotions, iii) Environment Relationship, and iv) Student Thoughts, Identity and Background.

It is important to highlight that cultural factors have influence on all the dimensions of the SX in terms of the perceptions and expectations that the student has regarding their environment, their contacts, and the products and services they use. Even so, since the culture of a student is an intimate and personal element, it is included within the factors of the personal dimension of the SX.

2.3 Culture

Culture is the main element of our proposal. Hofstede has defined it as "the collective programming of the mind that distinguishes the members of one group or category of people from another" [3]. There is a wide variety of models that define the dimensions and factors that influence national culture [10–12]. In our proposal we have used as a guide the six national culture dimensions proposed by Hofstede [4]. This is not inconvenient, since Hofstede's model has been validated for years and the cultural dimensions of other models are usually statistically related to those proposed by Hofstede. This without mentioning that theoretically most cultural models refer to the same defining elements [13]. Table 1 indicates the six national culture dimensions proposed by Hofstede with their respective definitions.

Table 1. Hofstede's national culture dimensions.

Hofstede's National Culture Dimension	Description
Power Distance	Power Distance (PD) dimension refers to the level of acceptance shown by the subjects of a society in relation to a hierarchical structure. This applies in family, society, and institutions
Individualism vs. Collectivism	Individualism vs. Collectivism (IDV) dimension refers to the individuals' predisposition to integrate into primary groups in society. In this dimension problems such as group vs. individual thinking, competitiveness vs. cooperation, and sense of group identity are analyzed
Masculinity vs. Femininity	Masculinity vs. Femininity (MAS) dimension refers to aspects traditionally associated with men or women roles in society, institutions, and family. This element is related to individuals' assertiveness and caregiving, apart from his sexuality
Uncertainty Avoidance	Uncertainty Avoidance (UA) dimension refers to the stress perceived by individuals because of an uncertain future. This element determines the degree of risk that individuals are willing to accept in family, society, and institutions
Long-Term Orientation vs. Short-Term Orientation	Long-Term Orientation vs. Short-Term Orientation (LTO) dimension refers to people's efforts and goals. In LTO dimensions we observe if people are focused on the past, the present, or the future, and if they seek rewards in the short, medium, or long term. This in the family, society, and institutional context
Indulgence vs. Restraint	Indulgence vs. Restraint (IVR) dimension refers to the relationship between people's control-gratification and their desires. This element is related to enjoying life and the moral perception of leisure in family, society, and institutions

A previous study showed the relationship of communicative aspects regarding the individual's culture. This is relevant considering that communication is a common element in the 3 SX dimensions. Additionally, the relationship of cultural aspects regarding the use of technological devices was observed. The use of technological devices is today an important element for communication and support for learning and is mainly included in the SX educational dimension as "learning resources" [14].

3   Student eXperience Evaluation Methodology

3.1   Study Limitations

Our proposed methodology is preliminary. We plan that the methodology will be refined after each practical application. Thus, the main limitation of our proposal is that the number of test subjects selected to apply the evaluation methods must be varied. This implies that it must be tested on students from different cultures to corroborate the efficiency of the selected evaluation methods.

3.2   Student eXperience Model

Prior to proposing our SX evaluation methodology, it was necessary to develop an SX model that incorporates cultural aspects. In this way it is possible to analyze the various problems related to a specific SX dimension separately. In addition, by identifying which SX dimensions are affected by the students' opinions it is possible to know what cultural factors are involved and could cause discomfort or satisfaction in students (Fig. 2).

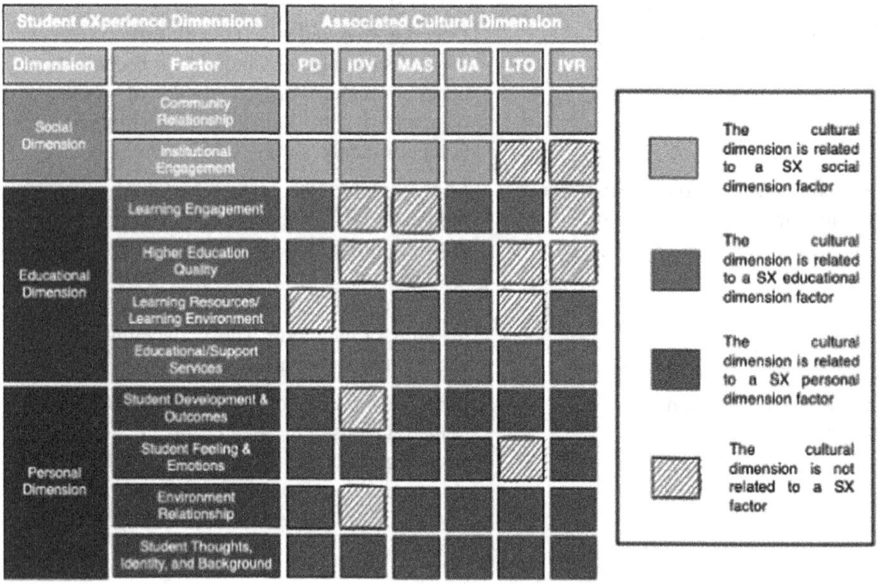

Fig. 2. SX-Culture Matrix.

The three SX dimensions indicate the factors that make up the holistic students experience throughout the cycles of pre-consumption, consumption, and post-consumption, both inside and outside the spaces provided by the HEIs [1]. Meanwhile, the national culture dimensions proposed by Hofstede [3, 4] indicate the elements that make up the cultural experiences of an individual within a society/nation. In this way, when detecting a problem in the students' experience, before proposing a solution from the SX perspective it is necessary to consider the cultural aspects that could be affected by these changes. For example, when proposing a solution that is related to the HEI perceived quality, it must be considered that this dimension is related to the PD dimension (Fig. 2). That is, the perceived quality by students can be affected by modifying the hierarchical structures within the classroom or the university depending on the students' culture.

3.3 Preliminary SX Evaluation Methodology

Our SX evaluation methodology proposal consists of a series of methods and techniques to be applied sequentially. The main objective is to detect the SX strengths and weaknesses from the students' perception considering cultural aspects of their experience. The first two stages (Fig. 3) focus on gathering information and planning the methods to be executed. Stages two and three respectively focus on the execution of the evaluation methods and on the analysis and integration of data. Finally, in stage five the results are modeled graphically to present them clearly and simply.

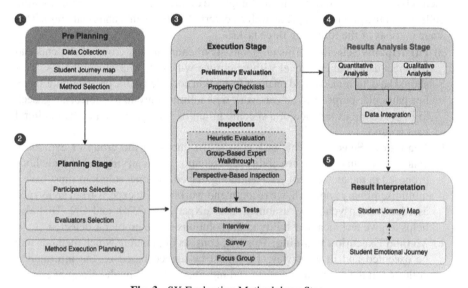

Fig. 3. SX Evaluation Methodology Stages.

The stages are detailed below:

1. **Pre-Panning:** In the pre-planning stage, the information that the HEI already has about the students is collected. This includes elements such as market studies, teacher evaluations, satisfaction surveys, among others. The objective of this stage is to have a starting point to contrast the information collected in later stages, in addition to ruling out possible evaluation methods that could provide information that is already available. This stage consists of the following three tasks:
   a) **Data Collection:** This task consists of collecting information that allows guiding the execution of evaluation methods and serving both as a starting point and to contrast the results obtained later. The previous information includes market studies,

teacher evaluations, satisfaction surveys, customer journey maps, financial studies on students, psycho-educational studies on students, and demographic studies on students.

b) **Student Journey Map** [15, 16]: The student journey map is a case of customer journey map (CJM) where the consumer is the student. In a CJM, the interactions (touchpoints) of a consumer with the services, products and systems provided by a brand are graphed throughout their consumption cycle (pre-consumer, consumption, and post-consumer). It is necessary to create a CJM per detected student profile (based on their own needs and characteristics) and incorporate the fluctuation of their emotions and channels used in each interaction.

c) **Method Selection:** In this task, the necessary methods are selected to evaluate the SX. The selection of methods must be made considering the time necessary to carry them out, the financial resources available, the personnel necessary to execute the methods, and the already available SX information.

2. **Planning:** In the planning stage, the participants, the evaluators/experts, and the methods to be executed of the methodology are defined according to the information collected in the previous stage, as well as external factors (time and financing). This stage consists of the following three tasks:

a) **Participants Selection:** This task consists of choosing the group of students and psychoeducational personnel with whom we will work to evaluate the SX. This should be determined based on the information collected in the pre-planning stage. For particular purposes, you can work with a limited group of subjects, e.g. seek to improve the experience of a specific group of students with a certain cultural background.

b) **Evaluators Selection:** This task consists of choosing the group of experts in charge of evaluating the feasibility of execution and carrying out the methods proposed in the methodology. Considering that educational solutions must have a multidisciplinary approach, we recommend working with experts from areas such as education, psychology, usability, User eXperience (UX), and CX. This also helps to give technical feasibility to the solutions of the problems detected.

c) **Method Execution Planning:** This task consists of planning which methods will be executed and in what way. This must be agreed based on the information collected in the pre-planning stage and must be validated by the group of experts from the previous task (b).

3. **Execution:** In the execution stage, the methods are applied to the subjects defined in the planning stage based on the requirements from the pre-planning stage. The methodology includes three methods to apply to psychoeducational and support staff to evaluate the usability not necessarily of software products, and three methods to mainly apply to students. The application of interviews with educational personnel is recommended to obtain second feedback on the problems reported by the students. Additionally, we included the heuristic evaluation method to evaluate the usability of educational platforms and applications provided by the HEI. The inclusion of methods for both staff and students is due to the need to include technical and procedural

feasibility in the solutions proposed to the students' suggested problems. The seven methods of our methodology are detailed below:

a) **Property Checklists** [17]: Property checklist method consists of applying a checklist associated with design properties. The objective is to see if the design objectives of a certain product are satisfied. In this method, an expert UX evaluator verifies that the elements associated with the checklist, such as low- and high-level properties, are met. The selection of this method lies in the possibility of associating certain items in the checklist with design objectives focused on student users with a specific cultural background. This considers design aspects whose interpretation varies from culture to culture such as colors, fonts, currency, number of people in the illustrations, among others.

b) **Heuristic Evaluation** [18]: Heuristic evaluation is a type of inspection method that allows evaluating software products through direct observation based on a series of usability principles called heuristics. It is done by groups of 3 to 5 evaluators who are supposed to detect, classify, and qualify usability problems. We find it important to utilize this method due to the existence of heuristics sets based on cultural factors which may yield results of interest [19]. It is important to mention that currently there are specialized heuristics sets for educational solutions related to the SX educational dimension [20].

c) **Group-Based Expert Walkthrough** [21]: Group-based expert walkthrough is a usability inspection method. This is done by expert evaluators in a specific domain area. In our proposal these experts must be related to the education sector (e.g., Teachers, psychologists, administrators). This inspection is supervised by one or more usability experts. The method consists of fulfilling predefined tasks assigned to evaluators who are under the usability experts' supervision. It is preferable that test subjects may not have previous experience performing usability inspections before. The obtained results in a primary phase of the walkthrough are noted down and subsequently discussed as a group. This method was included because it is important to have the opinions expressed in a group by people linked to the educational context.

d) **Perspective-Based Inspection** [22]: Perspective-based inspection method allows an evaluator to perform usability inspections from different perspectives. In this way, usability issues are addressed by grouping them into one of several usability perspectives. The perspectives addressed must be mutually exclusive of each other. This inspection is carried out in several sessions. We incorporate this method into our evaluation methodology proposal because of the large number of "student types" with different expectations and needs. Potential usability issues need to be addressed from the perspective of several types of students.

e) **Interviews** [23]: The interview is a conversation between 2 subjects (interviewer and interviewee) in which it is intended to obtain information on a specific topic. The interviews can be structured, non-structured, or semi-structured depending on the questions and the freedom to ask that the interviewee has. The structured interviews consist of concise questions, the non-structured interview is an almost not guided conversation, and the semi-structured interview addresses concise topics to be discussed but with a certain freedom degree for the interviewee. We recommend, as far as possible, the application of one (or more) semi-structured interviews, since the data analysis is not too complex or expensive, and the interviewee could provide valuable information. We find it prudent to apply interviews to educational personnel to corroborate the information provided by the students in the surveys.

f) **Surveys** [24]: Survey is a statistical method of data collecting from individuals. Surveys are made up of physical or digital forms with questions limited to a specific number of predefined answers (closed question survey), questions with answers to the free choice of the respondent (open question survey) or mixed-response questions (closed and open questions). Researchers perform statistical surveys in order to make statistical inferences about a population under analysis.

g) **Focus Group** [25, 26]: Focus group is a qualitative technique used to study the opinions and attitudes of a specific group of people regarding a product, system or service. This consists of organizing a discussion group session with a moderator in charge of guiding the correct course of the session. The sessions address topics related to the expectations, opinions and needs of the participants with respect to the topic of interest.

4. **Result Analysis:** In this stage, the results obtained from the methods executed in the previous stages are analyzed and the data obtained is contrasted with those consolidated in the pre-planning stage. The result analysis contemplates the integration of quantitative and qualitative data preceded by a separate analysis. This stage consists of the following three tasks:

a) **Quantitative Analysis:** The quantitative analysis includes the statistical analysis of the quantitative data of the heuristic evaluation, survey, and demographic data of the students under analysis.

b) **Qualitative Analysis:** The qualitative analysis includes the results of the property checklist, the qualitative data of the heuristic evaluation, the opinions and perceptions of the group-based expert walkthrough, perspective-based inspection, interviews, surveys, and focus group. Open-ended responses should be allowed only based on time and personnel available to process and interpret the data. We recommend analyzing the quantitative data with Natural Language Processing (NLP) techniques such as text emotion analysis and collecting the most common keywords. In this way trends can be observed, and it is easier to integrate the qualitative and quantitative data.

c) **Data Integration:** Data integration consists of associating and grouping the results of the statistical analysis of the quantitative data (e.g., correlations, covariances, mean, and mode) with the general opinions and perceptions coming from the qualitative data.

5. **Result Interpretation:** In the Result Interpretation stage, the results obtained in previous stages are graphically consolidated to present the information clearly and simply. This stage contemplates the execution of two graphic methods:

a) **Student Journey Map** [15, 16]: This method is a particular case of CJM where student interactions with the services, products and systems provided by HEIs are graphed. A CJM must be considered for each student profile detected. The profiling of the students must consider the national culture of the students.

b) **Student Emotional Journey** [15]: This graphic method allows to complement the CJM incorporating the mood and feelings of the students throughout their consumption cycle, when interacting with the different touchpoints. The emotional aspect is important not only for students, but also for all consumers since it influences the perceptions and expectations of a product or service [27].

As already mentioned, method execution may not be rigid. The application of the methodology is subject to the information available to the HEI, the time available to evaluate the SX, the availability of experts for evaluations, and financial resources. The methodology should ideally be adapted to the needs of each academic unit or HEI.

Considering the importance that we have given to cultural aspects in our proposal, we recommend the inclusion of sufficient cultural representatives in the test subjects. By contrasting quantitative and qualitative data, and national culture indices by country, significant differences due to cultural reasons can be detected [4]. The solutions proposed later should consider the three dimensions of the SX [1] and their relationship with the six national culture dimensions proposed by Hofstede (Fig. 2). Finally, we recommend the inclusion of professionals and experts from multiple disciplines to approach the proposed solutions in a holistic way and contemplate technically feasible solutions.

4 Conclusions and Future Work

Considering the importance of quality assurance in higher education and student welfare we have proposed a methodology for evaluating SX that includes cultural factors. Our methodology contemplates working with students, educators, and educational support personnel. We do this to have a holistic approach to the problems raised by students and not allow solutions without technical feasibility.

Our model consists of 5 stages which address i) the collection of prior information, ii) the planning of the methods to be executed, iii) the sequenced execution of the evaluation methods, iv) the analysis of the results, and v) the interpretation and modeling of the results. The execution of the methodology could not be strictly guided step-by-step by the proposed workflow and methods, which can be adapted to the specific needs of each HEI. The proposal is flexible in terms of its application, which allows it to be complemented with more models to diagnose and address the problems.

We plan to apply our evaluation methodology to the student and educational personnel of different nationalities and cultures. In this way we intend to obtain contrasted data on perceptions, expectations and procedures that may be influenced by cultural differences. The first implementation will be carried out with students and educational personnel from different careers in Chile and Spain. Among the validation mechanisms of our proposal, we contemplate the judgment of experts in the CX area corresponding to multiple nationalities and HEIs.

Acknowledgments. Nicolás Matus is a beneficiary of the PUCV PhD Scholarship 2022, in Chile.

References

1. Matus, N., Rusu, C., Cano, S.: Student eXperience: a systematic literature review. Appl. Sci. **11**(20), 9543 (2021)
2. Sujata, J.: Customer experience management: an exploratory study on the parameters affecting customer experience for cellular mobile services of a telecom company. Procedia Soc. Behav. Sci. **133**, 392–399 (2014)
3. Hofstede, G.: Culture's Consequences: comparing values, behaviours, institutions, and organizations across nations, 2nd edn. Sage, London (1980)
4. Hofstede, G.: Cultures and Organization: Software of the Mind, 3rd edn. McGraw-Hill, New York (2010)
5. Hill, N., Roche, G., Allen, L.: Customer Satisfaction. The Customer Experience Through the Customer's Eye, 1st ed. Cogent Publishing, Abingdon, United Kingdom (2007)
6. Lemon, K.N., Verhoef, P.C.: Understanding customer experience throughout the customer journey. J. Mark. **80**, 69–96 (2016)
7. Gentile, C., Spiller, N., Noci, G.: How to sustain the customer experience: an overview of experience components that co-create value with the customer. Eur. Manag. J. **25**, 395–410 (2007)
8. Parasuraman, A., Zeithaml, V.A., Berry, L.L.: A conceptual model of service quality and its implications for future research. J. Mark. **49**(4), 41–50 (1985)
9. Matus, N., Cano, S., Rusu, C.: Emotions and Student eXperience: A Literature Review. CEUR Workshop Proceedings, 3070 (2021)
10. Chinese Culture Connection.: Chinese values and the search for culture-free dimensions of culture. Journal of Cross-Cultural Psychology 18(2), 143–164 (1987)
11. Schwartz, S.H.: Beyond individualism-collectivism: new cultural dimensions of values. In: Kim, U., Triandis, H.C., Kagitcibasi, C., Choi, S.-C., Yoon, G. (eds.) Cross-Cultural Research and Methodology Series, vol. 18. Individualism and collectivism: Theory, method, and application, pp. 85–119. Sage, London, United Kingdom (1994)
12. Inglehart, R.: Modernization and postmodernization: Cultural, economic and political change in 43 societies. Princeton University Press, Princeton, New Jersey, United States (1997)
13. Taras, V., Rowney, J., Steel, P.: Half a century of measuring culture: review of approaches, challenges, and limitations based on the analysis of 121 instruments for quantifying culture. J. Int. Manage. **15**, 357–373 (2009)
14. Matus, N., Ito, A., Rusu, C.: Analyzing the impact of culture on students: towards a student eXperience holistic model. In: Meiselwitz, G. (eds.) Social Computing and Social Media: Applications in Education and Commerce. HCII 2022. LNCS, vol. 13316. Springer, Cham (2022). https://doi.org/10.1007/978-3-031-05064-0_10
15. Nielsen Norman Group: Journey Mapping 101. https://www.nngroup.com/articles/journey-mapping-101/. Accessed 02 Jan 2023
16. Nielsen Norman Group: Channels Devices Touchpoints. https://www.nngroup.com/articles/channels-devices-touchpoints/. Accessed 02 Jan 2023
17. Jordan, P.W.: Designing Pleasurable Products. An Introduction to the New Human Factors. Taylor & Francis, London, United Kingdom (2000)
18. Nielsen, J., Molich, R.: Heuristic evaluation of user interfaces. In: Proceedings of the SIGCHI Conference on Human Factors in Computing System, pp. 249–256. Association for Computing Machinery, Seattle (1990)
19. Diaz, J., Rusu, C., Pow-Sang, J., Roncagliolo, S.: A cultural-oriented usability heuristics proposal. In: Proceedings of the 2013 Chilean Conference on Human - Computer Interaction (ChileCHI '13). Association for Computing Machinery, New York, USA, 82–87 (2013)

20. Rajanen, D., Tornberg, A., Rajanen, M.: Heuristics for Course Workspace Design and Evaluation. Electronic Workshops in Computing (2021)
21. Følstad, A.: Group-based Expert Walkthrough. In: R3 UEMs: Review, Report and Refine Usability Evaluation Methods, 58–60 (2007)
22. Zhang, Z., Basili, V., Shneiderman, B.: Perspective-based usability inspection: an empirical validation of efficacy. Empir. Softw. Eng. **4**(1), 43–69 (1999)
23. Seidman, I.: Technique isn't everything, but it is a lot. In: Interviewing as qualitative research: a guide for researchers in education and the social sciences. Teachers College Press, New York, United States (1998)
24. Groves, R., Fowler, F., Couper, M., Lepkowski, J., Singer, E., Tourangeau, R.: An introduction to survey methodology. Survey Methodology. Wiley Series in Survey Methodology, vol. 561 (2 ed.). Wiley, Hoboken (2009)
25. Sierra, R.: Técnicas de investigación Social. Paraninfo S.A, Madrid, Spain (1994)
26. Callejo, J.: El Grupo de Discusión: Introducción a una Práctica de Investigación. Ariel, Barcelona, Spain (2001)
27. Nielsen Norman Group: Emotional Design Fail: I'm Divorcing My Nest Thermostat. https://www.nngroup.com/articles/emotional-design-fail/. Accessed 02 Jan 2023

Teaching and Learning in the New Normal: Responding to Students' and Academics' Multifaceted Needs

Andriani Piki[1] and Magdalena Brzezinska[2]

[1] University of Central Lancashire – Cyprus, Larnaca, Cyprus
apiki@uclan.ac.uk
[2] WSB University, Poznan, Poland
magdalena.brzezinska@wsb.poznan.pl

Abstract. Alongside the prolonged social and economic instability and the escalating demands for upskilling, Covid-19 pandemic had a detrimental impact on students' and academics' mental health and wellbeing. Social isolation and the emergency transition to remote education caused high levels of psychological distress, hindering students' self-efficacy and academic performance. The pandemic also induced sudden changes affecting academics' personal and professional lives, leading to mental disorders and risk of burnout. While recent research focuses on addressing the effects of the pandemic on either students or academics, this paper presents a collective analysis. The key themes that emerged by examining the experiences of both students and academics in higher education are framed in a multi-layered support system embracing qualities such as: self-efficacy, wellbeing, equality, diversity, and inclusion, social interactions, human-centred technologies, and authentic pedagogical methods. The findings are discussed with the aim to extract informed recommendations for enhancing teaching and learning experiences in the post-pandemic era.

Keywords: Higher Education · Emergency Remote Teaching · Wellbeing Education · Inclusive Education · Learner Engagement · Upskilling

1 Introduction

The unstable social situation and the unpredictable consequences of Covid-19 pandemic have challenged students, academics, and the broader higher education ecosystem (Al Miskry et al. 2021; Halabieh et al. 2022). Recent literature addresses academics' readiness (Yiapanas et al. 2022) and students' preparedness (Meletiou-Mavrotheris et al. 2022; Piki 2022) to respond to the emergency shift to online education. As the impact of the pandemic continues to unfold, governments, policymakers, and higher education institutions (HEIs) strive to reframe the education system and re-establish effective and engaging teaching and learning environments (Hodges et al. 2020; Marinoni and van't Land 2020; Piki et al. 2022; Piki 2022), while also attending to the increasing demands for reskilling and upskilling. Various initiatives have been recently launched leveraging digital and mobile technologies

© The Author(s), under exclusive license to Springer Nature Switzerland AG 2023
A. Coman and S. Vasilache (Eds.): HCII 2023, LNCS 14026, pp. 116–136, 2023.
https://doi.org/10.1007/978-3-031-35927-9_9

(Abu Elnasr et al. 2020; Engelbrecht et al. 2020; Marinoni and van't Land 2020; Muñoz-Carril et al. 2021; Piki 2020; Vlachopoulos 2020) and innovating pedagogies (Kukulska-Hulme et al. 2022) towards alleviating the consequences of the pandemic and responding to emerging needs. Despite these efforts, reimagining education in the new normal constitutes an ongoing challenge (Piki 2022; Brzezinska 2022), which needs to be addressed across institutional, technological, pedagogical, psychological, emotional, and social layers. Various problems have been identified in recent literature (Halabieh et al. 2022) including institutional challenges (such as low student retention, increased number of dropouts, inclusion issues, and inequitable access to higher education), technological limitations (including the need for upgrading the technological infrastructure and leveraging state-of-the-art systems in education), career-oriented and digital skills gaps and growing training needs, and inner and more severe consequences on students' and academics' mental health and wellbeing (Brzezinska and Cromarty 2022; Dinu et al. 2021; Halabieh et al. 2022; Kita et al. 2022; Urbina-Garcia 2020; Wray and Kinman 2021).

Recent research has explored the effects of the pandemic on students (Aucejo et al. 2020; Meletiou-Mavrotheris et al. 2022; Piki 2020; Piki et al. 2022; Piki 2022;) as well as academics (Al-Taweel et al. 2020; Brzezinska and Cromarty 2022; Dinu et al. 2021; McGaughey et al. 2021; Yiapanas et al. 2022; Watermeyer et al. 2021), although the former group has attracted more attention in the literature than the latter one (Dinu et al. 2021). On one hand, during emergency remote teaching (ERT) students have experienced high levels of psychological distress and mental disorders (Halabieh et al. 2022), hindering their self-efficacy and academic performance (Piki et al. 2022; Piki 2020), while the enduring social instability caused high levels of uncertainty, estranging and demotivating students (Piki 2022) and further increasing the number of dropouts (Halabieh et al. 2022). On the other hand, sudden and profound changes affected academics' personal and professional lives and resulted in escalating mental health disorders and risk of burnout, since many academics had to manage family obligations, teaching, and research duties alongside their increased workload (Dinu et al., 2021; Brzezinska and Cromarty 2022; Kita et al. 2022; McGaughey et al. 2021; Watermeyer et al. 2021).

Although the number of articles exploring the impact of Covid-19 pandemic on education has increased since its outbreak, most studies present either academics' or students' perspectives, with only a few addressing both (e.g., Al Miskry et al. 2021). To fill this gap, this paper takes a holistic and systemic approach, drawing on empirical insights, personal experiences, and recent literature, with a twofold aim: firstly, to collectively explore academics' and students' perspectives, and secondly, to extract informed recommendations highlighting the key qualities that forward-looking pedagogies should aspire to accommodate. The paper is structured as follows: Sect. 2 portrays the research background and a review of related studies exploring academics' and students' experiences and captures the juxtapositions between their views. Section 3 synthesises the findings and provides recommendations that can inform pedagogical approaches in higher education. Finally, conclusions are presented in Sect. 4.

2 Research Background and Related Work

Recent literature portrays abundant insights on the intricate impact of the pandemic, the impromptu coping strategies devised, and the role of social technologies. The paragraphs below discuss both academics' and students' perspectives, experiences, and visions indicating the inextricable connection among their worldviews.

2.1 Academics' Perspectives and Experiences

The negative effects of the pandemic were evident across various disciplines, career stages, and geographic locations (Al-Taweel et al., 2020; Brzezinska and Cromarty 2022; Dinu et al. 2021; McGaughey et al. 2021; Watermeyer et al. 2021; Yiapanas et al. 2022). These included the academics' technological (un)readiness, varying degrees (or lack) of support, increased workload and difficulty to maintain work-life balance, which altogether impacted academics' mental health and wellbeing. Some positive aspects attached to technology-mediated remote teaching were also identified, including flexible working hours, less commuting, and establishing stronger bonds with colleagues, helping each other to endure the challenges.

Techno-Pedagogical Challenges, Technological Readiness, and Skills Gaps. During the pandemic, various technological barriers hindered academics' experiences, including poor or unstable Internet connection; limited remote accessibility to software, hardware, and data resources; outdated personal computers; shortage of peripheral devices including headsets and web cameras; compatibility issues; and deficient home-working ergonomics (Dinu et al. 2021; Halabieh et al. 2022). Nevertheless, in a recent study, 91% of instructors reported that it was not technology that posed the biggest problem for them during ERT (Leone and Brzezinska 2021). Rather, key challenges included having to cope with poor student participation, low student engagement, ineffective interactions, increased distractions, and student interruptions (Bożykowski et al. 2021; Halabieh et al. 2022; McKenzie 2021; Piki 2020). Hence, most academics expressed their preference for traditional, classroom-based teaching where learning outcomes can be met more straightforwardly (Bożykowski et al. 2021). Besides techno-pedagogical factors, digital skills gaps, and the lack of familiarity with social technologies also affected academics' experiences. While some academics evaluated their technological readiness as relatively high (Bożykowski et al. 2021; Leone and Brzezinska 2021), for others, the demands to utilise new or unfamiliar technologies for teaching and interacting with students constituted a source of considerable anxiety (Dinu et al. 2021). Even in cases where the motivation to develop digital competencies was high, many academics reported insufficient time for adequate preparation and training (Killen et al. 2021).

Alongside the challenges, social benefits of technology were valued during remote education. A significant observation was that academics who were involved in collaborative activities, as well as those who had a strong social identity and high technological competencies, were more likely to report high mental wellbeing (Dinu et al. 2021). Online social interactions with colleagues were crucial for remaining connected with the academic community, reducing feelings of loneliness and isolation, and maintaining strong bonds amongst colleagues. These social aspects acted as key enablers contributing positively to academics' wellbeing. Flexible working hours and reduced commuting, online office hours and consultations with students (Bożykowski et al. 2021), fewer distractions (compared to working in a shared office at the University), increased attendance in research meetings, and widening access to conferences offering reduced fees for virtual participants were also some of the advantages reported during the pandemic. For some academics, homeworking was considered more flexible, effective, and efficient, hence contributing positively to professional development, productivity, and mental wellbeing (Dinu et al. 2021). Evidently, technology played a multifaceted role during the pandemic. On one hand, technical issues and prolonged exposure unfavourably impacted self-confidence and wellbeing, while on the other, social technologies played a crucial role in maintaining interactions and reactivating faculty motivation.

Disrupted Academic Responsibilities, Work-Life Balance, and Wellbeing. Unlike distance education, which is especially designed for remote delivery, ERT engendered many challenges due to rapid and unplanned changes (Brzezinska 2022; Brzezinska and Cromarty 2022; Halabieh, et al. 2022; Piki 2020). An eminent challenge was the additional time and effort required for managing remote interactions with students, redesigning educational activities, and adjusting learning content, assessments, and feedback strategies (Yiapanas et al. 2022). The unfolding economic and social consequences, the anxiety related to the negative health situation worldwide (Brzezinska and Cromarty 2022), the unmanageable workload and difficulty to find work-life balance (Dinu et al. 2021), the implicit assumption that academics should be available 24/7, limited resources and poor connectivity, digital skills gaps and the necessity to abruptly adapt to the new teaching environment constituted aspects which further hindered academics' experiences. Mental, physical, and emotional deficits academics had suffered were evidenced across continents (Brzezinska and Cromarty 2022; McGaughey et al. 2021; Kita et al. 2022). In certain contexts, more than half of the faculty members experienced mild psychiatric problems, high levels of worry, or work-related stress (Al Miskry et al. 2021), one in three academics admitted they neglected their personal needs due to the demands of their work (Wray and Kinman 2021), or considered leaving their jobs because of chronic pandemic stress (Flaherty 2020).

A key source of distress was the additional responsibilities academics had to assume, both towards the HEI and their students (e.g., offering additional feedback and support), while at the same time maintaining a research-active profile. As a result, poignant problems included work-related stress, 'digital fatigue', work-life imbalance, and significant concerns over potential longer-term changes to academia because of the pandemic (McGaughey et al. 2021). A common obstacle seemed to be unrealistic time pressures enforced to alleviate the eminent crisis (Wray and Kinman 2021). Senior academic staff members were more likely to be overburdened with increased time pressures and additional duties, such as academic and advisory support provision for students, dissemination, and administration of official policies to ensure they are properly applied by all faculty members. Although the number of teaching hours per academic semester was not generally affected during the pandemic, in many cases academics reported a substantial increase in their working hours and overall workload (Dinu et al. 2021; Wray and Kinman 2021). Migrating online engendered significant dysfunctionality and disturbance to academics' professional roles and personal lives (Watermeyer et al. 2021). Many felt that revising teaching material for online delivery, learning how to use new technologies, and devising new ways to keep students engaged at a distance required considerably more effort compared to face-to-face teaching (Wray and Kinman 2021). Almost every academic felt they devoted far more time for class preparation during ERT than had been the case for on-site classes (Czaja et al. 2020). On one hand, the increased workload made many academics more vulnerable to burnout, anxiety, and stress (Watchorn et al. 2020; Gewin 2021). On the other, some felt that it was not the increased workload or the lack of digital abilities and confidence in teaching online that negatively impacted their wellbeing; rather, factors such as rapid and enduring changes and the broader social instability were identified as deterrents to good mental health (Brzezinska and Cromarty 2022; Gewin, 2021; Watchorn et al. 2020). Furthermore, a lack of recreational activities, prolonged social isolation, and mobility restrictions inflicted several negative experiences including a sense of monotony (Dinu et al., 2021), overwhelming exposure to technology, lack of motivation, and fatigue, especially after spending long hours in front of a screen (Brzezinska and Cromarty 2022; McGaughey et al. 2021; Watermeyer et al. 2021).

The level of motivation and distractions fluctuated across different phases of the pandemic, affecting academics' performance and productivity in varying degrees. The reduction or loss of research funding, the interruption of research experiments and data-gathering activities, and the postponement of promotional procedures constituted additional factors which impacted academics' sense of belonging and, in turn, their mental health and wellbeing (Dinu et al. 2021). Many academics mentioned that they had to re-establish their work-life balance while working from home (McGaughey et al., 2021; Watermeyer et al. 2021). Distractions increased especially for academics with parental responsibilities, forcing them to balance full-time work and family caring responsibilities, which often negatively impacted their work performance and productivity (Dinu et al. 2021). Furthermore, during the lockdowns, many academics felt that teaching turned impersonal and distant (Dinu et al. 2021), both metaphorically and in practice.

It is also likely that students' anxiety and distress during ERT and subsequent lockdowns and social isolation periods may have had a knock-on effect on the workload and emotional strain of academic staff (Dinu et al. 2021). Students' increased demands for instructor time and assistance, which often meant one-to-one virtual meetings, further increased academics' already high levels of stress. Strong negative emotions and anxiety expressed by some students, who may have had no other vent, overburdened faculty, and often enhanced the feeling of helplessness (Wray and Kinman 2021). Thus, a significant downside to remote instruction, in addition to invading academics' privacy and blurring the borderline between professional and family life, was the prevalence of psychosocial hazards such as loneliness, alienation, isolation, and being overwhelmed (McGaughey et al. 2021).

Recent research re-emphasises the complex role that educators need to perform, not only in motivating and supporting their students during the lockdowns (Piki 2020; Piki et al. 2022; Piki 2022; Watermeyer et al. 2021), but also in responding to students' mental health concerns (Hughes and Byrom 2019; Dinu et al. 2021), which incurs an additional mental burden on academics. Moreover, the fact that the overheads incurred for adjusting materials for online teaching or the emotional investment and the time academics eagerly devoted to supporting their students were not adequately recognised by the University further impacted faculty's own mental health and wellbeing (Urbina-Garcia 2020). In many cases, academics felt that the time and effort spent in supporting students during ERT was unaccounted for, and often came at a cost to other academic and research responsibilities assessed in performance reviews and counting towards academic promotion (Dinu et al. 2021). These factors highlight the inextricable connection between students' and academics' wellbeing and put forward the need for adopting a systemic approach when formulating innovating educational practices. This observation emphasises the need to collectively explore and analyse their experiences, worldviews, and visions for the future – a need addressed in this paper.

Level, Type, and Source of Support.   The provision of technological and psychological support was not consistent across HEIs with regards to the level and type of support academics felt they received from their colleagues, the University, and governmental or policy making bodies (e.g., Higher Education Quality Assurance Agency or Ministry of Education).

Regarding psychological support from the University, academics reported fragmented connection with University services and felt that support was either unavailable or scarce. This increased academics' stress and spawned feelings of anxiety (Dinu et al. 2021; Wray and Kinman 2021). Many academics would have truly appreciated psychological support from their institution, yet most did not receive the expected caring response. Frequently, academics felt that their changing responsibilities were too demanding, making them feel anxious and lonely rather than supported, encouraged, and understood (Leone and Brzezinska 2021). Findings also revealed that communication with the leadership and professional support from the human resources department could have been improved (Dinu et al. 2021). A few HEIs attempted to respond to psychological needs by forming mentoring schemes and organising virtual drop-in sessions. These were positively received and helped involved academics navigate the abrupt changes (Dinu et al. 2021), yet the challenge was to get academics to participate in such endeavours (Wray and Kinman 2021).

Other actions of support included technological assistance, providing equipment such as tablets or laptops, and basic digital training. Nevertheless, the one-off and rapid nature of the training offered was often insufficient. Hence, many academics started looking for external resources, which further contributed to the information overload they were experiencing during the pandemic. Furthermore, the fact that ERT was implemented swiftly, with no transitional period, meant that training had to be prepared and delivered immediately. Thus, it was not feasible to tailor it to specific needs. Even in cases where academic faculty was provided with an in-depth, half-day training, this often addressed only the basic functionalities of a selected videoconferencing platform. Academics who wanted to further develop their skills had to pursue external training. Such training sessions covered a broad range of skills and knowledge areas including successful online teaching methodologies; effective strategies for transferring teaching skills and learning content from the classroom to the digital environment; converting classroom activities to engaging virtual activities; techniques for adjusting and personalising learning content; approaches for engaging students online; the use of specific applications for enhancing student-student and teacher-student connections; and methods for fostering student mental wellbeing, amongst other relevant topics. Drawing on the authors' experiences, while attending additional training was informative and instrumental for acquiring and further developing the desired skills and competencies, it required time-consuming online research, and often, the content was not relevant to the particular educational context. Thus, the invested time and effort did not always translate to substantial gains in personal or professional development. Such efforts often generated additional overheads and led to varied impromptu approaches. This, in turn, had an impact on students who found this diversity of approaches confusing (Piki, 2020).

During subsequent phases, the level of support and quality of training offered internally by HEIs were refined. In some cases, wellbeing questionnaires were administered amongst academics to gather their insights. Still, active psychological or wellbeing-oriented support was not always provided as a follow up. Many academics characterised their institution's approach as superficial and 'empty' gestures rather than an active response to the feedback from staff surveys, commenting that although HEIs had official policies on work-life balance, equality, and mental health awareness, the actual working culture was not aligned with them (Wray and Kinman 2021). Even in cases where the University employed strategies to address academics' mental health and wellbeing disorders, many academics emphasised that no intervention (including relaxation, mindfulness, or building resilience) could, in fact, substitute for a crucial reduction of workload, stating that the demands of the job absorbed their time, making it impossible even to make use of the solutions provided by the University (Wray and Kinman 2021).

In addition to the internal procedures adopted at each HEI, the respective governmental body (i.e., Ministry of Education or Higher Education Quality Assurance Agency) published official recommendations including the rights and responsibilities of academics while teaching remotely under lockdown, which were later revisited and adjusted for hybrid and blended teaching modes. These policies covered a range of guidelines and recommendations covering various aspects of teaching delivery, the compulsory recording of lectures, the provision of synchronous lectures and virtual office hours, as well as regulations regarding GDPR, for example ensuring that all learning materials are available on the University's Learning Management System (LMS) or communication platform, students' learning process is documented and monitored, and attendance records are kept to confirm the regularity of contact and interactions with students. Faculty may have been required to schedule online consultations for students and provide regular feedback on their learning progress. Evidently, the list of responsibilities was quite extensive, and in some contexts the only faculty rights were autonomy in the selection of tools to support distance learning and the right to receive support regarding distance learning methods, instruments, and techniques. Nevertheless, in many cases, the published policies were not accompanied by clear explanations of how the requirements were to be met nor by specific procedures to follow, which lead to diverse interpretations and ad hoc solutions.

A profound observation was that genuine support amongst colleagues was highly valued and appreciated at all stages of the pandemic. Social interactions amongst colleagues were crucial for reducing the consequences of isolation. The overall inference from published findings is that, in general, academics would have appreciated support at different levels: better technological assistance; improved access to necessary hardware, software and data resources; customisable resources and materials adapted for remote instruction; personalised training on online teaching and assessment methods; specific training and best practices on retaining students and reactivating learner engagement; and more time to adapt to the new teaching environment; psychological support from colleagues and the University; and wellbeing education to help faculty handle the complexities they were experiencing. All the above indicate the prominent need for teacher training, upskilling in technology-mediated teaching, and multi-layered support responding to multi-faceted needs.

2.2 Students' Perspectives and Experiences

Understanding what affects students' engagement and how they respond to various educational technologies and social interactions can make a valuable contribution and inform pedagogical design, theory, and practice (Aucejo et al. 2020; Muñoz-Carril et al. 2021; Meletiou-Mavrotheris et al. 2022; Piki 2020; Piki 2022). Prominent themes in recent literature include the impact of the pandemic on learning approaches and learner engagement, the ambivalent role of social technology and social media, and students' self-reports on how they envision the future of learning in the post pandemic era.

Learning and Learner Engagement Amidst the Pandemic. Learner engagement has become more fragmented and distributed than ever before due to the abrupt changes and enduring consequences of the pandemic (Piki 2020; Piki 2022). During ERT, students were compelled to continue their university studies at a distance. This brought several challenges to young adults' lives and degree of engagement (Kara 2021). First, for most students, remote education was an unfamiliar situation, and many had never attended classes online before, hence they lacked important digital skills. Naturally, the way students engage, learn, and interact in online education differs compared to attending a conventional classroom (Ma et al. 2020; Wang et al. 2022). Secondly, pedagogical procedures inevitably changed: lectures were often recorded impeding spontaneous student participation; assessments were an additional burden, even though the process for requesting extensions became more lenient; communications with lecturers became fragmented; while social, informal interactions during online lectures disappeared (Piki 2020). Thirdly, students were undergoing a fusion of swift and imposed changes beyond their control, including restricted mobility, social isolation, and reduced flexibility, which was contrary to their pre-pandemic lives. The severe health-related consequences of the pandemic globally further challenged students, similar to academics, and elevated student uncertainty and distress (Kara 2021; Vijayan 2021; Wang et al. 2022), especially for those in vulnerable groups of the population or whose family members were at risk (Brzezinska and Cromarty 2022). Due to the novelty of the situation, students frequently exhibited frustration and anxiety, which was sometimes manifested during ERT classes and one-to-one meetings with instructors.

Information overload or inadequate information further overwhelmed students. Learner engagement was more affected in practical modules, such as accounting and mathematics, where students found it more difficult to follow the lecturer's line of thought (Cassibba et al. 2020; Engelbrecht et al. 2020; Piki et al. 2022). Over time, these experiences made students feel detached from reality and disengaged from their normal routine, which inevitably had a negative impact on their learning, level of concentration and degree of participation (Piki 2020). This was evident during initial national lockdowns, which enforced ERT (Kara 2021), but also in subsequent lockdowns and self-isolation periods (Piki 2022).

Various technological adaptations (Veluvali and Surisetti 2022) and innovating pedagogies (Kukulska-Hulme et al. 2022) have been recently proposed emphasising the need to explore the role of individual learner characteristics (Kara 2021), to attend to diverse learners and learner abilities, and to promote learner engagement in higher education (Piki 2020; Piki 2022; Veluvali and Surisetti 2022). Despite efforts to understand the factors that impacted learner engagement during the pandemic, counter-engaging expressions such as boredom, fatigue, anxiety, stress, and poor mental health are commonly reported in the literature (Kara 2021; Vijayan 2021; Wang et al. 2022; Ma et al. 2020; Muñoz-Carril et al. 2021). This means that efforts need to be intensified to better understand the personal, pedagogical, technological, and social factors influencing student engagement (Piki 2022) and to move forward, towards actioning on these prominent findings and designing experiences, with engagement and wellbeing in mind (Peters et al. 2018).

Inequalities in access and accessibility were heightened during the pandemic, stressing the need for refocusing on human-centred design accounting for wellbeing needs (France 2020; McKenzie 2021) and on learning environments that afford quality and inclusive learning for all learners (Meletiou-Mavrotheris et al. 2022). On the contrary, during the pandemic, training and support offered to students was limited, inequitable, or completely non-existent. Hence, developing new learning strategies was largely opportunistic and most students had to become accustomed with new technological platforms on the fly. Furthermore, the variability in the approaches employed by different academics was confusing for students (Piki 2020). The unfolding crisis, coupled with the lack of appropriate training, and the unstable social situation inevitably affected students' engagement and motivation (Kara 2021; Piki 2022).

Multifaceted Role of Social Technology and Social Media. The multifaceted role of social technology and social media and the impact they have had on learner engagement and students' academic performance became evident during the ERT (Brzezinska and Cromarty 2022; Hodges et al. 2020; Kara 2021; Piki 2020). Familiarity with social and mobile applications led students to using various mobile applications intuitively, for learning, studying, and interacting with their peers and lecturers (Piki 2022). In fact, under lockdown, social media interaction was the only way students could stay connected with their peers, lectures, and the rest of the world (Piki et al. 2022). Unsurprisingly, the pandemic accelerated the uptake and utilisation of social, collaborative, and mobile game-based technologies (Abu Elnasr et al. 2020; Piki 2020; Piki 2022). In many cases, using those technologies was not merely an alternative or supplementary option for teaching and learning; rather, it became a necessity (Hodges et al. 2020). Still, the utilisation of those technologies has not been systematically considered in subsequent policies and official recommendations for teaching and learning in 'the new normal'. Furthermore, recent results underline that students' familiarity with social technologies (Piki, 2022), or students' self-efficacy in using e-learning tools does not directly equate to their preparedness to cope with the abrupt challenges brought by ERT (Meletiou-Mavrotheris et al. 2022).With the consequences of the pandemic still unfolding, it is imperative to leverage the unique characteristics and educational capabilities of mobile, collaborative, and social technologies towards reactivating learner engagement (Piki 2022), helping students to acquire the necessary skills, and improving the learning outcomes. Such technologies need to be seamlessly and systematically fused in the pedagogical process (Piki 2020).

Paradoxically, while students reported that social mobile technology was often the only channel for staying connected and supporting each other, they also admitted that the same technology constituted a major source of distraction and learning demotivation, both during live online lectures and while studying on their own (Piki, 2020; Piki, 2022). Coupled with technical problems, such as poor Internet connections and compatibility issues (McKenzie 2021), social media apps distracted students and negatively affected their engagement, concentration, and level of participation, which, in turn, impacted their overall academic performance (Piki 2020). A reason which elevated the adverse impact that social technology had on students' concentration was a lack of strict online participation requirements. In most cases, students preferred to keep their web cameras off, which also coincided with official recommendations in some countries. Therefore, it was impossible for lecturers to monitor how concentrated students were, whether they looked puzzled or had any questions, or even whether they were present at all (Piki et al. 2022). This made instructors feel like they were talking to the screen (Brzezinska and Cromarty 2022). Students could easily get away with joining the session simply to get their attendance recorded, yet without really engaging throughout the lecture (Piki 2020). Over time, this caused a cycle of negative emotions for both academics (who felt they could not connect with their students like they did in the classroom) and students (who felt they could not stay focused during online lectures and thus eventually lost interest).

Another intriguing finding was that students would behave differently in modules where they felt their lecturer was socially active, interacting with them and replying to their messages on social networking apps. This responsiveness and openness of some academics was highly appreciated by students; they considered it as a gesture of empathy and caring, which affected their decision to attend live online lectures. Many students admitted they consciously chose which lectures they would join based on their instructor's approach (Piki 2020; Piki 2022). All these observations re-emphasise the inextricable connection between the ways students and academics experienced ERT and how their actions affected each other.

Another important aspect from the technological point of view is the need to take a more human-centred approach in the utilisation of technologies. Technologies should not be seen merely as a tool for teaching and learning, but rather, as a means of establishing quality interactions. Such interactions need to be carefully designed, seamlessly incorporated in teaching and learning, and properly monitored to ensure they are ethical, inclusive, responsible, and sustainable, respect participants' privacy, and enhance human wellbeing (Darby and Lang 2019; France 2020).

Visions of Students for Learning in the New Normal. Recent studies show that most students are still in favour of traditional, face-to-face, classroom-based instruction over distance education (Gierdowski 2019; Piki 2022). The former is associated with an effortless and natural learning process, which students consider as ideal, particularly for practical subjects such as mathematics (Piki et al. 2022). This gives rise to several human-centred attributes of educational technology. Firstly, any online, virtual, or intelligent educational environment should offer a seamless fusion of multiple affordances, such as a simulation of the whiteboard to allow students to synchronously follow their lecturer's writing, natural representation of the lecturer's facial expressions and body gestures, and any additional learning materials, such as lecture slides. This portrays the need for multimodal and natural learning environments. Secondly, successful remote lectures are those that 'simply work', with no Internet connectivity hassles or compatibility issues. Thirdly, unsurprisingly, breaks are important. Both students and academics highlighted the need to recreate casual discussions, and 'social breaks' in online and virtual environments. This re-emphasises the notion that learning is inherently a social activity. Furthermore, many students stated they value aspects such as psychological support, empathy, and mutual understanding from their families, lecturers, and peers alike (Piki 2020). These findings indicate there is still a lot to explore about the affordances of emerging technologies for wellbeing-oriented, social and community-based learning. Such an exploration entails designing for motivation, engagement, and wellbeing in digital experiences (Peters et al. 2018).

2.3   Juxtapositions in Academics' and Students' Experiences and Perspectives

This paper undertakes to collectively investigate and analyse academics' and students' experiences and perspectives to inform pedagogical recommendations for teaching and learning in the new normal. Table 1 presents juxtapositions between key themes across multiple layers: self-efficacy, emotional and psychological, social, technological, pedagogical, institutional, and the broader educational ecosystem. We outline the key enablers (sources of support) and barriers (challenges) evident in each layer. The list is not intended to be exhaustive; rather, the goal is to highlight shared themes and constructs across academics' and students' experiences and perspectives.

Table 1. Barriers (challenges) and Enablers (sources of support) evident at different layers.

Layers	Academics' experiences & perspectives	Students' experiences & perspectives
Self-efficacy, personal capacity, level of confidence, readiness, preparedness, individual skills and competencies	*Barriers:* - Unfamiliar remote education - Gaps in social digital skills, impacting social identity - Insufficient time for upskilling - Extra time and effort for adjusting activities, teaching content, feedback, and assessments - Unmanageable workload and difficulty to maintain work-life balance *Enablers:* - Motivation to use technology for teaching and keeping in touch with students - Most academics were comfortable with technology	*Barriers:* - Unfamiliar remote education - Digital skills gaps, insufficient time for adjusting and upskilling - Practical modules challenging to follow online - Opportunistic, on-the-fly learning - Fragmented and distributed learner engagement and motivation - Rapid changes affecting self-efficacy, concentration, participation, and engagement and academic performance *Enablers:* - Familiarity with social media - Inner drive to show appreciation to lecturers
Psychological and emotional support, mental health, wellbeing	*Barriers:* - Health and social impact, unrealistic time pressures, digital fatigue, increased workload and distractions, work-life imbalance along with lack of recreational activities, prolonged social isolation and mobility restrictions causing work-related stress, anxiety, burnout, and poor mental health - Active psychological or wellbeing-oriented support unavailable or limited - Students' distress had a knock-on effect on workload and emotional strain *Enablers:* - Where available, mentoring schemes and virtual drop-in sessions - Inner drive to help and support students	*Barriers:* - Health and social impact, lack of concentration, reduced motivation, increased distractions, elevated anxiety, uncertainty, anger, distress, boredom, fatigue, poor mental health - Inconsistent or unavailable support from academics and University *Enablers:* - Emotional intelligence, empathy, caring approach of some academics - Ongoing feedback from some lecturers - Interactions with peers through social media - Family bonds and social interactions, playing a key role in maintaining motivation and hope
Social and peer-to-peer support	*Barriers:* - Difficulty in managing social breaks or encouraging informal discussions with students, particularly during online recorded lectures *Enablers:* - Support amongst colleagues - Social interactions, crucial for reducing the consequences of isolation	*Barriers:* - Social breaks (during lectures) and informal discussions were not recreated during remote education *Enablers:* - Peer groups contributing to stronger bonding and wellbeing - Social interactions with friends, family, and lecturers, which alleviated feelings of isolation

(continued)

Table 1. (*continued*)

Layers	Academics' experiences & perspectives	Students' experiences & perspectives
Technological support and effectiveness of technological interventions	**Barriers:** - More time-consuming and demanding remote teaching and assessment - Working from home, associated with increased interruptions - Deficient homeworking ergonomics - Limited access to hardware, software, and data resources, poor Internet connection, outdated systems, compatibility issues - Digital skills gaps in utilising the available technologies to engage learners - Prolonged online interactions resulting in digital fatigue - Utilising new or unfamiliar technologies for teaching, assessment, providing feedback, and interacting with students, which caused considerable stress and anxiety *Enablers:* - Technology allowing academics to continue providing education - Social technology enabled stronger bonds during lockdowns and remote teaching, facilitating mental wellbeing - Flexible working hours, reduced commuting, increased access to conferences conducted as virtual events - Technological support and occasional provision of hardware and software	*Barriers:* - Online lectures were cognitively demanding and negatively impacted concentration, motivation, participation, and academic performance - Social technology may have been a source of distraction that inhibited learning - Technological limitations, such as poor Internet connection and compatibility issues - Impromptu and inconsistent, confusing approaches adopted by academics - Digital skills gaps in knowledge management and utilising the affordances of the available technologies for learning *Enablers:* - Technology allowed students to continue their studies in Higher Education - Social media helped students remain connected with peers - Social media apps and mobile technologies enabled students interactions with academics as well as receiving feedback, support, and motivation to continue education
University-level support schemes	**Barriers:** - Lack of support, encouragement, and understanding towards academic - Increased workload, time, and effort - Fragmented connection with the University services and poor communication with leadership and the human resources department - Limited, inconsistent, or non-existent digital training and wellbeing support - Limited attention to academics' readiness and level of confidence with remote education - Increased demands for upskilling - Changing responsibilities, viewed as demanding, raising anxiety and loneliness **Enablers:** - Mentoring schemes, virtual drop-in sessions	*Barriers:* - Limited, inequitable, or non-existent technological training and wellbeing support offered to students - Limited attention to students' preparedness, level of confidence with remote education, and digital skills gaps - Inequalities in accessibility, diversity, and inclusivity - Information overload or insufficient information during ERT - Fragmented connection with University services *Enablers:* - More lenient procedures to request extensions to summative assessments

(*continued*)

Table 1. (*continued*)

Layers	Academics' experiences & perspectives	Students' experiences & perspectives
Broader educational ecosystem, government, policy makers	***Barriers:*** - An extensive list of responsibilities, while the rights, academic freedom, and flexibility were frequently constrained - Published policies and recommendations were often unclear, leading to diverse interpretations and ad hoc solutions ***Enablers:*** - Flexibility with remote work in higher education	***Barriers:*** - Students' indirect interaction with the broader educational ecosystem - Policies and recommendations communicated to students during lectures and through announcements published in the LMS ***Enablers:*** - Flexibility with remote attendance or recorded lectures

3   Synthesis of Findings and Recommendations

A collective analysis and exploration of how academics and students experienced teaching and learning during various phases of the pandemic illuminates certain gaps, eminent challenges, and complex needs that need to be attended to. These are discussed below, in the form of recommendation bands, with the aim to inform pedagogical design and educational decision making. Essentially, we argue that an 'onion structure of support' should be formulated (Fig. 1).

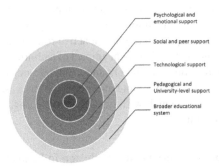

Fig. 1. Onion-structure capturing multifaced needs and respective layers of support.

3.1   Mental and Emotional Support and Wellbeing Education

In a world of crisis, educational efforts should focus on empathy (Rifkin, 2009), strive to restore humanity and equity and promote wellbeing (France 2020; France 2021; Raygoza et al. 2020). Put differently, educators ought to *"Maslow before Bloom"* (Berger, 2020). Wellbeing should be attended to, both in terms of provision of mental and emotional health support and in terms of wellbeing education. Regarding the provision of support, it is obvious that "*No education system is effective unless it promotes the health and well-being of its students, staff, and community. These strong links have never been more visible and compelling than in the context of the COVID-19 pandemic*" (WHO/UNESCO 2021). Therefore, this type of assistance should be abundant for students and academics alike. It needs to be emphasised that in crisis, when large numbers of people, including academics and students, experience sudden distress, fatigue, and depression, it is instrumental for HEIs to develop proactive mechanisms for recognising specific needs. It is vital that universities focus on truly customized, thought-out solutions fitting a particular context (Wray and Kinman 2021). This requires motivated and orchestrated efforts to identify what ought to be done at each level, how it should be done, and who should be involved in providing high quality specialist support (WHO/UNESCO 2021).

Educating students and academics about wellbeing and mindfulness is also a step forward. This can include alerting them about mental health conditions, how to recognise signs and symptoms of such conditions, and what the role of emotional intelligence is. Strategies for managing stress should also be provided. Wellbeing education can promote welfare across all aspects of teaching and learning and have a positive impact on academic attainment as well as such learning outcomes as self-efficacy, self-esteem, motivation, and decreased dropouts. Wellbeing education, which recently re-emerged as an innovating pedagogy, nurtures values like compassion and empathy in the learning process, supporting teachers' and learners' wellbeing (Dinu et al. 2021; France 2020; Kukulska-Hulme et al. 2022). While the concept or the need is not new, the vision of developing a sustainable wellbeing education system has not yet been met (Kukulska-Hulme et al. 2022). Such a system needs to be based on the premise that "*mental health [is] foundational to all aspects of university life, for all students and all staff*" (UUK 2021) – from curriculum design to university-level support services, promoting a healthy workplace culture attending to academics' workload demands (Wray and Kinman 2021), involving students and enabling them to play an active role in the development of interventions (Kukulska-Hulme et al. 2022), to the impact of technology on wellbeing. Hence, rather than focusing merely on assessments and academic performance, the emphasis in future pedagogical models, both remote and in person ones, should be on wellbeing support and coping strategies, which will, in turn, activate engagement and help attain the desirable learning outcomes.

3.2 Embracing Equality, Diversity, and Inclusion in Education

A university class, whether on-site or virtual, should be a safe, inclusive, culturally responsive space. All races, genders, ethnicities, cultural identities, and socioeconomic statuses should be embraced and cherished by the instructor, who also needs to scaffold such patterns among the students (France 2021). To foster equitable participation and personal connections, instructors ought to check in on student access, reduce/manage the length of online lectures and embed social breaks (Piki 2020; Piki 2022), share troubleshooting resources, enable a transcription service, make sure that the topics they discuss are not sensitive, invite students who have not yet spoken to share and contribute, allow students to alternate group roles, ask students what they learned or appreciated from a peer, or chat informally with the students a few minutes before the class (Raygoza et al. 2020). Other effective strategies of making teaching culturally responsive include using native languages and featuring traditions and customs in the class (Brzezinska and Cromarty 2022). To enable inclusivity, it is also important to closely attend to learning (dis)abilities and special needs and ensure that learning content is accessible, inclusive, engaging, and interactive, for the benefit of all learners.

3.3 Upskilling for Addressing Multifaceted Needs

The findings emerging from the preceding analysis provide support for the concept of 'systemic pedagogies,' which strategically follow a 'whole university approach,' focusing on increasing both academics' and students' motivation and resilience. Such a systemic or holistic approach needs to address a wide range of skillsets for both students and academics, including: (a) *social competences* (e.g., social resilience, empathy, social identity management, social presence, peer support and bonding strategies, collaboration and teamwork, and enhanced social interactions between students and academics), (b) *individual aptitudes* (e.g., self-efficacy, self-confidence, emotional intelligence, mental strength and wellbeing, and intrinsic motivation), (c) *digital and technological skills* (e.g., familiarity with computer-supported collaborative learning and work, computer-mediated interactions, social media, smart and intelligent emerging technologies), and (d) *digital literacy* (e.g., awareness of ethical, social, legal, privacy, and security considerations embedded in emerging technologies).

Given the inextricable connection between the ways students and academics experienced technology-enhanced education, a plausible way for motivating students while balancing the instructors' responsibilities and workload includes the promotion of peer learning, student autonomy (France, 2020), and agency (Darby and Lang 2019). Enabling students to feel responsible for their own learning and to develop a sense of control in a technology-rich society is amongst the responsibilities of every educator (Bates 2019). Promoting autonomy helps students become active agents and perceive their learning as a meaningful and fulfilling activity. Thus, assisting students in becoming more autonomous, instructors help them develop lifelong learning skills, which has powerful implications for students' future success.

Higher education should be relevant and closely connected to the real world and job market to prepare self-motivated graduates ready to join the workforce as autonomous agents (Bates 2019; Darby and Lang 2019) while, obviously, nurturing their engagement and providing them with direction, assistance, feedback, and high-quality education. This emphasises the important role educators play in creating a space for learners to develop the desirable global skills and become engaged and active citizens. At the same time, to better support students, academics should also develop self-care strategies (i.e., set clear boundaries between work and life, minimise exposure to technology to avoid feeling overwhelmed, embrace peer support, and celebrate goodwill), in addition to increasing their competences with technology-enhanced education and learning to use online tools skillfully and effectively. Strategic training and continuous professional development plans need to be established to cater for these needs.

An important step for preparing students better for a transition online would be to educate them on the technological capabilities of available educational platforms and technological tools; to familiarise them with netiquette, social rules, and online communication protocols; and to inform them about privacy, security, and data protection regulations. Such an approach, while initially possibly time and energy-consuming on the part of the instructor, brings significant benefits to academics, too. It is likely to result in greater student autonomy, which ultimately translates to the desired reduction in the overload experienced by faculty.

3.4 Microlearning, Actionable Feedback, and Authentic Assessment

The findings suggest that teaching and learning in the new normal requires re-establishing core pedagogical pillars. First, planning for a blended future requires setting clear learning objectives and reducing complexity. This can be achieved by chunking courses into manageable units with consistent organisation and temporal cadence (Joosten et al., 2021). Students should be aware of the what, why, and how of the course, the content should be released strategically, and complex tasks should be broken down (Darby and Lang 2019). The pedagogical approach which saw renewed focus as a means of maintaining student engagement and motivation during ERT and subsequent blended teaching and learning is microlearning or atomic learning (Leong et al. 2020; McKee and Ntokos, 2022; Stefan et al. 2022), founded on the philosophy of learning in small chunks (Kukulska-Hulme et al. 2022). Common features of such approaches include short duration, fast learning pace, and bite-sized chunks of learning content focusing on a single topic (Leong et al., 2020; McKee and Ntokos, 2022). Second, formative, actionable feedback should be frequently provided (Darby and Lang 2019) to enable reflection and revision. Comprehension is only achieved when students constantly reflect on what they study (Dewey 1933; Kumar et al. 2019). In addition to general feedback during the lecture or one posted on the LMS, social technology can be leveraged to provide timely and personalised feedback, guidance, and support (Piki 2022). Third, assessments and learning materials should be relevant and authentic. Learning content and assignments should have a practical relevance, feature real-life problems, and be authentic (Brzezinska 2022; Darby and Lang, 2019; Kumar et al. 2019; Shaw 2020). Virtual project-based learning can be employed to engage learners in authentic learning and foster student independence (Bates 2019; France 2021; Whitman and Kelleher 2020;). Finally, assessment should be forward-looking. Formative and summative assignments should evaluate the skills students will need in their future career and life-long learning (Shaw 2020).

3.5 Digital Transformation in Education

Besides techno-pedagogical considerations, several other aspects constitute vital drivers of digital transformation in education, such as strategic educational leadership, availability of resources to support staff to develop pedagogically informed digital practices, and further investment in improving the digital environment, technological platforms, and infrastructures (Killen et al. 2021). These upgrades are a necessity for providing a seamless integration of multiple affordances to support both students and academics. The role of social and mobile technologies should also be further explored, given the central role they played during the pandemic (Piki 2020; Piki 2022). These findings call for improvements of technological provisions in higher education (Halabieh et al. 2022), while also attending to academics' technological readiness (Yiapanas et al. 2022) and training needs to activate their engagement with social and emerging technologies – changes long overdue.

4 Conclusion

Within higher education, the persistence and extent of the consequences of the Covid-19 pandemic have compelled both students and academics to re-establish their discontinuous social interactions, fill the gaps caused by fragmented learning experiences, and reflect on personal and social values. Following a methodical examination of both sides, we extracted common threads and perspectives between academics and students, highlighting the key qualities that such novel pedagogies need to attend to as we enter a new normal in education.

Recent results demonstrate that students' familiarity with social technologies and students' self-efficacy in using e-learning tools do not directly equate to their preparedness to cope with the abrupt challenges brought by the pandemic. Upskilling-oriented pedagogical strategies, human-centred technologies, authentic assessments, and wellbeing support are indispensable for ensuring that students are promoted to competent digital learners equipped with the necessary skills and aptitudes, such as self-regulation and autonomy, to fully benefit from the application of emerging technologies in education.

The key themes emerging from synthesising both perspectives can inform forward-looking pedagogical approaches framed in a multi-layered support system focused on mental and emotional support; wellbeing education; upskilling for addressing multi-faceted needs; microlearning; actionable feedback and authentic assessment; equality, diversity, and inclusivity; and seamless integration of human-centred technology enabling enhanced interactions. These eminent qualities are discussed through the experiences, perspectives, and visions of both students and academics in higher education, with the view to extract useful recommendations for improving teaching and learning in the post-pandemic era.

Focusing equally on both perspectives, important findings emerged suggesting that HEIs and policymakers should carefully consider how to support academic staff post-pandemic. While many of these challenges are enduring, as we emerge out of the pandemic, it is imperative to reflect on the lessons learnt and on the social, emotional, psychological, technological, and training needs of both students and academics.

References

Abu Elnasr, E.S., Hasanein, A.M., Abu Elnasr, A.E.: Responses to COVID-19 in higher education: Social media usage for sustaining formal academic communication in developing countries. Sustainability **12**(16), 6520 (2020)

Al Miskry, A.S.A., Hamid, A.A.M., Darweesh, A.H.M.: The Impact of COVID-19 Pandemic on University Faculty, Staff, and Students and Coping Strategies Used During the Lockdown in the United Arab Emirates. Frontiers in Psychology 12 (2021)

Al-Taweel, D., et al.: Multidisciplinary academic perspectives during the COVID-19 pandemic. Int. J. Health Planning Manag. **35**(6), 1295–1301 (2020)

Aucejo, E.M., French, J., Araya, M.P.U., Zafar, B.: The impact of Covid-19 on student experiences and expectations: Evidence from a survey. Journal of public economics, 191 (2020)

Bates, A.W.: Teaching in a Digital Age, 2nd edn. Tony Bates Associates Ltd., Vancouver, B.C. (2019)

Berger, T.: How to Maslow Before Bloom, All Day Long. Edutopia (2020). https://www.edutopia.org/article/how-maslow-bloom-all-day-long/

Bożykowski, M., Izdebski, A., Jasiński, M., Konieczna-Sałamatin, J.: Nauczanie w dobie pandemii i perspektywa powrotu do normalności, Pracownia Ewaluacji Jakości Kształcenia Uniwersytetu Warszawskiego (University of Warsaw) (2021)

Brzezinska, M., Cromarty, E.: Emergency Remote Teaching in the University Context: Responding to Social and Emotional Needs During a Sudden Transition Online. In: Meiselwitz, G. (eds) Social Computing and Social Media: Applications in Education and Commerce. HCII 2022. LNCS, vol. 13316. Springer, Cham (2022). https://doi.org/10.1007/978-3-031-05064-0_3

Brzezinska, M.: Global skills in the global pandemic: how to create an effective bichronous learning experience during an emergency shift to remote instruction. In: Auer, M.E., Pester, A., May, D. (eds.) Learning with Technologies and Technologies in Learning. Lecture Notes in Networks and Systems, vol. 456. Springer, Cham (2022). https://doi.org/10.1007/978-3-031-04286-7_32

Cassibba, R., Ferrarello, D., Mammana, M.F., Musso, P., Pennisi, M., Taranto, E.: Teaching mathematics at distance: a challenge for universities. Educ. Sci. **11**(1), 1 (2020)

Czaja, K., et al.: Zdalne kształcenie na Wydziale Humanistycznym Uniwersytetu Śląskiego w Katowicach. Report (March-April 2020). (A Report. Remote Education at the Department of Humanities of the University of Silesia in Katowice), Uniwersytet Śląski w Katowicach 2020, https://us.edu.pl/wydzial/wh/wp-content/uploads/sites/15/Nieprzypisane/ZDALNE-KSZTAŁCENIE-NA-WYDZIALE-HUMANISTYCZNYM-RAPORT.pdf

Darby, F., Lang, J.M.: Small Teaching Online: Applying Learning Science in Online Classes (1st ed.). Jossey-Bass (2019)

Dewey, J.: How we think: A restatement of the relation of reflective thinking to the educative process. DC Heath (1933)

Dinu, L.M., et al.: A case study investigating mental wellbeing of university academics during the COVID-19 pandemic. Educ. Sci. **11**(11), 702 (2021)

Engelbrecht, J., Borba, M. C., Llinares, S., Kaiser, G.: Will 2020 be remembered as the year in which education was changed? ZDM – Math. Educ. **52**(5), 821–824 (2020)

Flaherty, C.: Faculty pandemic stress is now chronic. Inside Higher Ed, 19 (2020)

France, P.E.: Reclaiming Personalized Learning: A Pedagogy for Restoring Equity and Humanity in Our Classrooms (First). Corwin (2020)

France, P.E.: Humanizing Distance Learning: Centering Equity and Humanity in Times of Crisis (First). Corwin (2021)

Gewin, V.: Pandemic Burnout Is Rampant in Academia. Nature Publishing Group (2021). https://media.nature.com/original/magazine-assets/d41586-021-00663-2/d41586-021-00663-2.pdf

Gierdowski, D.C.: ECAR Study of Undergraduate Students and Information Technology (Research report). Louisville, CO: EDUCAUSE Center for Applied Research, October 2019 (2019). http://www.educause.edu/ecar

Halabieh, H., et al.: The future of higher education: identifying current educational problems and proposed solutions. Educ. Sci. **12**(12), 888 (2022)

Hodges, C., Moore, S., Lockee, B., Trust, T., Bond, A.: The difference between emergency remote teaching and online learning. EDUCAUSE Rev. **2020**, 3 (2020)

Hughes, G.J., Byrom, N.C.: Managing student mental health: the challenges faced by academics on professional healthcare courses. J. Adv. Nurs. **75**(7), 1539–1548 (2019)

Joosten, T., Weber, N., Baker, M., Schletzbaum, A.: Planning for a Blended Future: A Research-Driven Guide for Educators (2021). Available online: https://eduq.info/xmlui/handle/11515/38291

Kara, M.: Revisiting online learner engagement: exploring the role of learner characteristics in an emergency period. J. Res. Technol. Educ., 1–17 (2021)

Killen, C., Langer-Crame, M., Penrice, S.: Teaching Staff Digital Experience Insights Survey 2020: UK Higher Education Findings (2021). https://www.jisc.ac.uk/reports/teaching-staff-digital-experience-insights-survey-2020-uk-higher-education

Kita, Y., Yasuda, S., Gherghel, C.: Online education and the mental health of faculty during the COVID-19 pandemic in Japan. Sci. Rep. 12(1), 1–9 (2022)

Kukulska-Hulme, A., et al.: Innovating Pedagogy 2022: Open University Innovation Report 10. Milton Keynes: The Open University (2022)

Kumar, S., Martin, F., Budhrani, K., Ritzhaupt, A.: Award-winning faculty online teaching practices: Elements of award-winning courses. Online Learning 23(4) (2019)

Leone, V., Brzezinska, M.: Transatlantic Educators Dialogue (TED) Program for Global Citizenship. Idee in Form@Zione, 99–115 (2021)

Leong, K., Sung, A., Au, D., Blanchard, C.: A review of the trend of microlearning. J. Work-Appl. Manage. 13(1), 88–102 (2021). https://doi.org/10.1108/JWAM-10-2020-004

Ma, X., Liu, J., Liang, J., Fan, C.: An empirical study on the effect of group awareness in CSCL environments. Interactive Learning Environments, 1–16 (2020). https://doi.org/10.1080/10494820.2020.1758730

Marinoni, G., van't Land, H.: The Impact of COVID-19 on Global Higher Education. International Higher Education. Special Issue 102, pp. 7–9 (2020)

McGaughey, F., et al.: This can't be the new norm': academics' perspectives on the COVID-19 crisis for the Australian university sector. Higher education research & development, 1–16 (2021)

McKee, C., Ntokos, K.: Online microlearning and student engagement in computer games higher education. Res. Learn. Technol. 30 (2022). https://doi.org/10.25304/rlt.v30.2680

McKenzie, L.: Bridging the Digital Divide: Lessons From Covid-19. Inside Higher Ed (2021). https://www.insidehighered.com/content/bridging-digital-divide-lessons-covid-19

Meletiou-Mavrotheris, M., Eteokleous, N., Stylianou-Georgiou, A.: Emergency remote learning in higher education in Cyprus during COVID-19 lockdown: a zoom-out view of challenges and opportunities for quality online learning. Educ. Sci. 12(7), 477 (2022)

Muñoz-Carril, P.C., Hernández-Sellés, N., Fuentes-Abeledo, E.J., González-Sanmamed, M.: Factors influencing students' perceived impact of learning and satisfaction in Computer Supported Collaborative Learning. Comput. Educ. 174, 104310 (2021)

Peters, D., Calvo, R.A., Ryan, R.M.: Designing for motivation, engagement and wellbeing in digital experience. Front. Psychol. 9, 797 (2018)

Piki, A.: An exploration of student experiences with social media and mobile technologies during emergency transition to remote education. In: The Proceedings of the 19th World Conference on Mobile, Blended and Seamless Learning (mLearn 2020), November 2–4, 2020, Cairo, Egypt (2020)

Piki, A.: Re-imagining the distributed nature of learner engagement in computer-supported collaborative learning contexts in the post-pandemic era. In: Meiselwitz, G. (eds.) Social Computing and Social Media: Applications in Education and Commerce. HCII 2022 (June 26-July 1, 2022). LNCS, vol. 13316. Springer, Cham (2022). https://doi.org/10.1007/978-3-031-05064-0_13

Piki, A., Andreou, L., Markou, M.: Students' perspectives on the emergency transition to online education – a case study in mathematics education. In: 16th Annual International Technology, Education and Development Conference (INTED2022), March 7–2, 2022 (2022)

Raygoza, M., Leon, R. Norris, A.: Humanizing Online Teaching (2020). https://digitalcommons.stmarys-ca.edu/school-education-faculty-works/1805

Rifkin, J.: The Empathetic Civilization: The Race to Global Consciousness in a World of Crisis. Penguin, New York, NY (2009)

Shaw, A.: Authentic Assessment in the Online Classroom. Center for Teaching and Learning. Wiley Education Services (2020)

Stefan, I.A., Gheorghe, A.F., Stefan, A., Piki, A., Tsalapata, H., Heidmann, O.: Constructing seamless learning through game-based learning experiences. Int. J. Mob. Blended Learn. (IJMBL) **14**(4), 1–12 (2022)

UUK (Universities UK) (2021). Stepchange Mentally Healthy Universities. https://www.univer sitiesuk.ac.uk/what-we-do/policyand-research/publications/stepchange-mentally-healthy-uni versities

Urbina-Garcia, A.: What do we know about university academics' mental health? a systematic literature review. Stress. Health **36**(5), 563–585 (2020)

Veluvali, P., Surisetti, J.: Learning management system for greater learner engagement in higher education—a review. High. Educ. Future **9**(1), 107–121 (2022)

Vijayan, R.: Teaching and learning during the COVID-19 pandemic: a topic modeling study. Educ. Sci. **11**, 347 (2021)

Vlachopoulos, D.: COVID-19: threat or opportunity for online education? High. Learn. Res. Commun. **10**(1), 16–19 (2020)

Wang, Y., Cao, Y., Gong, S., Wang, Z., Li, N., Ai, L.: Interaction and learning engagement in online learning: the mediating roles of online learning self-efficacy and academic emotions. Learn. Individ. Differ. **94**, 102128 (2022)

Watchorn, D., Heckendorf, E., Smith, C.: Locked down, burned out: Publishing in a pandemic: The impact of Covid on academic authors. De Gruyter, Germany (2020)

Watermeyer, R., Crick, T., Knight, C., Goodall, J.: COVID-19 and digital disruption in UK universities: afflictions and affordances of emergency online migration. High. Educ. **81**(3), 623–641 (2021)

Whitman, G., Kelleher, I.: Your Checklist for Virtual Project-Based Learning. Edutopia (2020). https://www.edutopia.org/article/your-checklist-virtual-project-based-learning

WHO/UNESCO (2021). Making every school a health-promoting school: implementation guidance. Geneva: World Health Organization and the United Nations Educational, Scientific and Cultural Organization (2021). https://www.who.int/publications/i/item/9789240025073

Wray, S., Kinman, G.: Supporting Staff Wellbeing in Higher Education (ISBN 978-1-7399860-1-8). Education Support, London (2021)

Yiapanas, G., Constantinou, M., Marcoulli, E.: The readiness of higher education academic staff in cyprus for shifting the instructional delivery mode from face-to-face to emergency remote teaching. In: Handbook of Research on Digital Innovation and Networking in Post-COVID-19 Organizations, pp. 301–323. IGI Global (2022)

Virtual Clinic – AI Used in the Teaching of Medical Interviews, Diagnosis, and Treatment Planning

Marcin Szeliga(✉)

WSB University, ul. Sportowa 29, Chorzów, Poland
marcin.szeliga@chorzow.wsb.pl

Abstract. The Virtual Clinic is an artificial intelligence-based software that provides a safe environment for medical students and young doctors to simulate medical interviews and treatment. What sets the Virtual Clinic apart is its high degree of case realism. Users can ask patients any questions (including spoken language) and order various tests (objective and physical). The user trains their ability to think independently, combine facts, diagnose, and treat. After completing work with the case, the user receives detailed feedback, learning what they did well, and where they made mistakes or missed important information. The system tracks the user's (the person using the system) progress, informs them of the time and cost of the tests, offers suggestions, and finally informs the patient (the person receiving treatment) how they (the patient) feel after receiving treatment. This brings significant benefits and improvement of the quality of medical services.

Keywords: Artificial Intelligence · Machine Learning · Human-computer interfaces · Natural language processing · Chatbots · Chatbots in education · Benefits of chatbots · Challenges of chatbots

1 Introduction

Chatbots can be used to improve human-centered computing by making it easier for people to interact with technology. Chatbots are computer programs that use natural language processing (NLP) to understand and conversationally respond to user input [1, 2]. By using chatbots, people can interact with technology using simple and intuitive conversational commands, rather than having to navigate complex menus or learn specialized software [3, 4]. For example, a chatbot could be used to provide customer service on a website, allowing users to ask questions and get answers quickly and easily. Chatbots can also be used to provide information and support in a variety of other contexts, such as education, healthcare, and financial services [5–7]. Some of the key ways in which chatbots are being used in medicine include:

Virtual triage: Chatbots can be used to help patients determine their symptoms and provide guidance on the next steps, such as whether to visit a doctor or go to the emergency room.

© The Author(s), under exclusive license to Springer Nature Switzerland AG 2023
A. Coman and S. Vasilache (Eds.): HCII 2023, LNCS 14026, pp. 137–148, 2023.
https://doi.org/10.1007/978-3-031-35927-9_10

Medication reminders: Chatbots can remind patients to take their medication at the appropriate time, helping to improve adherence to treatment regimens.

Medical education: Chatbots can be used to teach medical students about different medical conditions and procedures, helping them to better understand the material and prepare for exams.

Communication with patients: Chatbots can be used to communicate with patients, providing them with information about their conditions, treatment plans, and upcoming appointments.

Remote monitoring of patients: Chatbots can be used to monitor patients remotely, helping to identify early signs of deterioration and prevent hospital readmissions.

Helping patients with mental health conditions: Chatbots can be used to help patients with mental health conditions such as depression and anxiety, providing them with support and guidance.

2 Virtual Clinic

The Virtual Clinic allows for a comprehensive simulation of a doctor-patient interaction (gathering medical history, physical examination, ordering diagnostic tests and consultations, medical procedures, and therapy).

The Virtual Clinic system is being built by BD Poland in collaboration with Polish medical universities, including the University of Warsaw, the Silesian University of Medicine, and the University of Medicine in Poznań. The National Center for Research and Development (NCBR) supports the project under the rapid track, project number POIR.01.01.01-00-0526/19.

In addition to its commercial aspect, the software brings significant social benefits. the main goal of the Virtual Clinic is to better prepare doctors to practice medicine. In the Virtual Clinic, users can ask patients questions (including spoken language) and order tests (objective and physical). The clinic visit forces the user to think independently, combine facts, and formulate a diagnosis and treatment proposal. After completing work with the case, the user receives detailed feedback, learning what they did well and where they made mistakes or missed important information. The system tracks the user's progress, informs them of the time and cost of the tests, offers suggestions, and finally informs the patient (the person receiving treatment) how (the patient) feels after receiving treatment. The virtual clinic fits into new trends in medical education: case-based teaching, problem-solving exercises, gamification, and evidence-based teaching.

There have been several studies that have provided research-based evidence of the effectiveness of chatbots in the field of medical education:

A study published in the Journal of Medical Internet Research found that a chatbot-based educational intervention was effective in improving medical students' knowledge and understanding of hypertension. The study showed that students who interacted with the chatbot scored significantly higher on a knowledge test than those who did not [8].

Another study published in the Journal of Medical Education and Curricular Development found that a chatbot-based virtual patient case simulation improved medical students' diagnostic reasoning skills. The study found that students who interacted with the chatbot performed better on a diagnostic reasoning test than those who did not[9].

The heart of the solution is a knowledge base containing over 12 million clinical case records. This allows the application to present realistic information, including the symptoms of the disease, test results, and treatment effects. The use of large data sets allows for realistic simulations of complex cases, such as multi-disease patients or scenarios of multiple meetings with the same patient.

The program has a modular architecture that clearly expresses and efficiently manages complex dependencies between classes and components:

Users interact with a chatbot (a client module) by initiating activities in turns, where activities refer to events such as a user joining a conversation or sending a message. The messages can take various forms, including text, speech, or visual interface elements like cards or buttons.

Each user message is analyzed by the natural language processor module, which provides the intelligence to understand the input text for the client module. The goal is to predict the overall intention of an incoming utterance and extract important information from it. The utterances and predictions are logged so the NLP module can actively learn from user input.

Based on predictions the query is sent to the knowledge base. The knowledge base contains detailed, multidimensional representations of patient cases, including symptoms, medical examination results, and treatment procedures. The query result is used to formulate a virtual patient response.

2.1 Patient Zone

In the patient zone, the user, a medical student or young doctor, can safely diagnose and treat patients in various locations, such as an ambulance, a health protection point, a specialist clinic, or a hospital ward.

- The medical interview carried out in the patient zone as realistically as possible reflects the nature of the visit. The user asks any questions, and the "patient" gives answers that potentially allow for a correct diagnosis to be made (see Fig. 1).

- In the "hint" mode, the system can guide the user to ask questions about certain characteristics and inform them of the need to order additional tests.
- After each completed "visit," the user has access to feedback with comments and recommendations regarding the scope and manner of conducting the interview and the correctness of the prescribed treatment.

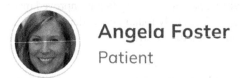

Angela Foster

Patient

What brings you to me?

I have a fever, my chest hurts, I am coughing and feeling unwell.

How long have you had these symptoms

The symptoms started 4 days ago

        Message...

Fig. 1. Talking with the virtual patients without an imposed scenario. It means that the chatbot or system is not limited to a specific set of responses or outcomes, and instead can adapt to the user's input and provide a more personalized or dynamic experience

- The patient zone includes the possibility of conducting an medical examination and automatically checking its results.

The exam not only allows for insight into the student's way of thinking but also enables the determination of learning outcomes that the student has achieved and those that require further work.

2.2 Disease Unit Wizard

The Disease Unit Wizard allows advanced users, such as medical university professors, to prepare any disease unit, which will then be available in the student module. The main features of the creator include (see Fig. 2):

- Determining the characteristics of the future patient, such as gender, place of patient admission, and others.
- Choosing characteristics for the subjective interview.
- Choosing characteristics for the objective interview.
- Choosing characteristics for laboratory, imaging, and additional tests.
- Labeling the created disease unit.
- Defining correct treatment protocols.

Fig. 2. Users can realistically simulate patients with internal or surgical problems, heart or lung diseases or infectious diseases, cancers at any stage, multi-diseases women in pregnancy (a separate category), and others.

2.3 Physical Examination Module

The student may examine different parts of the patient's body. Virtual Clinic supports different activities (see Fig. 3):

- Observation
- Percussion and tapping
- Auscultation
- Palpation
- Neurological examination

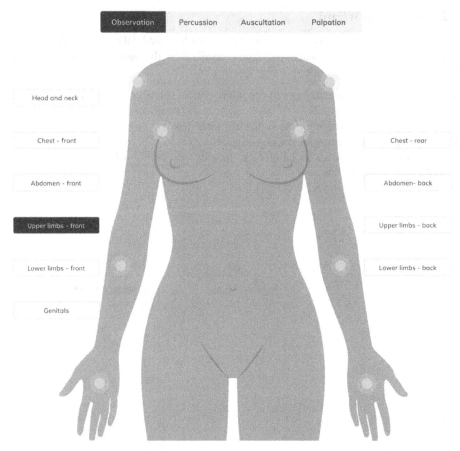

Fig. 3. Physical examinations are key to a proper patient assessment.

In addition, users can order any type of medical examination, including:

- Laboratory tests (blood, urine, stool, …),
- Microbiology,
- Diagnostic imaging (USG, EKG, XRAY, PET, MRI, TK, …) (See Fig. 4),

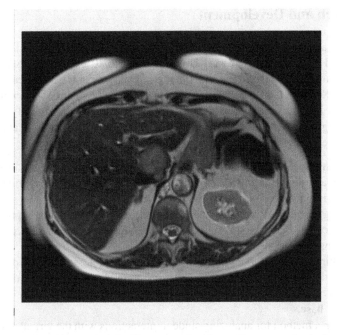

Fig. 4. Photographs, video, and audio files are a valuable supplement to physical examinations.

- Audio and video recordings,
- Specialist consultations.

Thanks to intelligent algorithms, the results of laboratory tests are always unique and realistic. Authors of medical cases can define any disease they want. Non-pathological features are drawn from the normative range.

2.4 Examination Module

In the Virtual Clinic you will quickly prepare and conduct a medical examination that allows checking both theoretical knowledge and practical skills:

- Assign unique patients to students according to the subject and level of difficulty of the exam,
- Evaluate the accuracy of interview and physical examinations, additional tests, and treatment,
- Verify students' skills in the following areas: medical documentation, diagnosis, and optimal treatment.

The system records all actions and provides feedback for users. That includes the student's progress, recording the history of student interaction with the patient, and verifying whether the student asked required questions or ordered an appropriate medical examination.

3   Research and Development

The research and development work are being carried out by BD Poland as part of a project funded by the NCBR. The work began in March 2020 and is ongoing. The work is being carried out by BD employees with the support of a subcontractor: Silesian Medical University in Katowice and in collaboration with the Warsaw Medical University. As part of the project, innovative functionality has been built that does not currently exist in the domestic and global markets. The main research problems and technological challenges being addressed in the project include:

- Building an effective natural language processing algorithm (spoken Polish),
- Designing a system that allows for conversational interaction with a virtual assistant (patient) without a predetermined script,
- Developing a self-learning mechanism that allows for continuous improvement in the precision of the dialogue, naturalness, and diverse nature of the conversations (medical interviews),
- Incorporating expert and domain knowledge into an ontological knowledge base that allows for the preparation of a universal description of many medical conditions,
- Building a creator that allows for the creation of any medical condition based on the knowledge base,
- Developing a method for analyzing student interactions with the virtual assistant and formulating suggestions and recommendations for users.

4   Novelty

The solution is innovative both from the perspective of the Polish market and the global market. The system is an intelligent assistant (patient) with whom the student has a conversation (in text or spoken language). The student can ask any questions and receive answers. Based on these answers, the student orders tests and then, based on the obtained information, makes a diagnosis and proposes treatment. In contrast to most existing solutions, the student communicates with the simulated patient using natural language, which increases the realism of the simulation. At the same time, the program does not require a specific order of questions, which allows for the development of a branching, complex narrative.

Virtual Clinic continuously analyzes and evaluates whether, while collecting information, the student asks about matters relevant to the diagnosis and orders the required tests, and whether the diagnosis allows for the exclusion of other, similar conditions. In this, the system analyzes the scope and amount of unnecessary or unnecessarily burdensome tests.

Similarly, in the therapeutic process, the system checks if the correct medical procedures and prescribed medications are ordered, according to the standard of care. This approach allows the student to optimize the diagnostic process and shorten the time needed to make a diagnosis, while at the same time forcing the execution of all necessary tests and procedures to confirm the suspected medical condition and exclude other diseases (i.e., differential diagnosis), which is important for ensuring the safety of the diagnosed patient.

5   Benefits

Virtual Clinic brings many benefits to users:

Cost reduction is one of the key benefits of using chatbots in medical education. The cost of learning is independent of the number of hours and is significantly lower than the cost of hiring professors, assistants, or actors. According to a study by SUM, the cost of teaching in the field of diagnostics per student will drop by 50%.

Increased flexibility is another key benefit of using chatbots in medical education. The system is more universal than a scenario prepared by lecturers, currently, it is difficult to go beyond the prepared scheme during classes.

The system allows for building new or modifying existing disease units. According to SUM, the cost of building disease units in a virtual clinic is 50% lower. This is a key benefit of using chatbots in medical education.

Providing constant access to cases is also a key benefit of using chatbots in medical education. A student can train at any time in 24/7/365 mode, not only at the university during classes but at any time and location.

Ensuring diversity is another key benefit of using chatbots in medical education. A specific simulation can be practiced multiple times, and artificial intelligence algorithms will ensure the variability of simulated cases, making them not perceived by the student as boring and stereotypical.

Introducing a wide range of functionality is also a key benefit of using chatbots in medical education. The software not only allows for learning how to ask the right questions and interpret the obtained answers but also how to carry out a correct diagnostic process, as well as a therapeutic one, while it is possible to test false hypotheses and methods of action.

Allowing for a personalized assessment of the student is also a key benefit of using chatbots in medical education. The system assesses the amount of time the student has spent on learning, the time and cost of the interview, and the relevance of questions (e.g., the assessment of the costs of commissioned tests in the context of the obtained results). According to SUM, the system will provide at least a 30% reduction in the costs associated with assessing the student's progress.

Provides automatic assessment of the student is also a key benefit of using chatbots in medical education. The system, based on the interaction with the patient, supports a selection of the appropriate educational path which is tailored to the needs of the virtual patient.

6   Summary

To summarize, Virtual Clinic has unique features that do not currently exist in the Polish and global markets.

The use of artificial intelligence algorithms to conduct a doctor-patient dialogue is one of the key features of the Virtual Clinic. The Virtual Clinic allows open communication with the patient, where the student can ask any questions to obtain the necessary information for further diagnostic steps. With the implemented "self-learning" mechanism, the algorithm increasingly simulates the student's interactions with the patient, which facilitates the elimination of the barrier between humans and bots.

The virtual patient responds to any question, even if the question is unclear or not covered by the simulation. The algorithm generalizes and provides a "sensible" answer based on the data from other conversations or cases in the database. This is a groundbreaking solution not found in other programs of this type. Simulation programs are unable to continue a logical narrative when they encounter the problem of creating a situation not covered by the case scenario. Typically, the program's reaction to such situations is to report the problem (e.g., "I do not understand the question"). The solution used in competing applications is to create a narrative based on a limited set of options, which prevents asking questions not covered by the case scenario. In this opinion, this is a significant limitation of existing simulation programs, and it introduces some unnaturalness. It is particularly difficult to predict all questions or situations in the diagnostic process, which requires the creation of very elaborate scenarios that require a lot of time and financial resources.

The system is open, meaning it does not require a predefined course of action. The student determines the path. Existing solutions usually require a specific order of procedures, imposed for example by a quizzing form of questions. A more natural and interesting form is one in which the learner, through the freedom of interaction with the virtual patient, creates their own diagnostic and therapeutic path. In this way, the student can acquire knowledge about the diagnostic process as a whole rather than just about the predefined steps. This feature of the Virtual Clinic allows for a more personalized and dynamic learning experience, which can be more engaging and effective.

The Virtual Clinic constantly analyzes and assesses whether the student is asking relevant questions for the diagnosis, whether the required tests are ordered, and whether the diagnosis allows for an exclusion of other, similar diseases. In this way, the system analyzes the range and amount of unnecessary or unnecessarily burdensome tests. Similarly, in the therapeutic process, the system checks whether the correct medical procedures, assigned drugs, and standard procedures have been ordered. This approach allows the student to optimize the diagnostic process and shorten the time needed to make a diagnosis, while at the same time forcing the completion of all necessary tests and procedures to confirm the suspected disease and exclude other diseases (differential diagnosis), which is essential for ensuring the safety of the diagnosed patient.

A wizard that allows for the automatic generation of new (random) patients is another feature of the Virtual Clinic. This feature allows for modification of test results within established norms for psychiatry and pathology, and selection of test results from a database to create a new case. The unique feature of the proposed solution is the ability to generate patients based on a knowledge base and descriptions of individual diseases. This allows the author to input information about the simulated disease, the variability of symptoms, and test results, while the specific simulated case is generated automatically each time. As a result, a set of cases matching the given description is created. The generated cases can vary in difficulty. Due to the automatic generation of the simulated patient's characteristics, a relatively small number of entered disease descriptions can correspond to hundreds of specific clinical cases that are equivalent to cases in other programs of this type. This feature of the solution increases the diversity and improves the attractiveness of the software – the learner can practice simulated cases multiple times.

Assessment of a student's empathy in a conversation with a patient, regardless of the assessment of their medical knowledge and problem-solving skills is another feature of the Virtual Clinic. The assessment of the form of questions asked is another innovative feature of the Virtual Clinic that is not available in other solutions. The assessment of form is adapted to the language in which communication with the program takes place. This function allows for the assessment of soft skills, in terms of interpersonal relationships and the form of conveying information. Modification of the difficulty of a given case (the occurrence of only some abnormalities and characteristics of the disease, availability of all or only part of the test results, co-occurring diseases) is also possible with the Virtual Clinic. Due to the algorithms used to build the knowledge base, unlike similar programs, the designed software will allow for easy modification of the difficulty of the simulated case. In competing applications, such a change in difficulty is not possible and requires a creation of a new, separate case.

The ability to define success criteria is an important feature of the Virtual Clinic. It allows for better evaluation of the student or provide them with hints, for example, for the diagnostic part or even for a selected set of tests. Since people with different educational experiences use the software, the system allows for the simulation to be narrowed down to selected aspects, such as ones related to the interview, physical examination, or ordering all or selected diagnostic tests; for example, narrowing down the simulation to laboratory or imaging tests.

Testing of false hypotheses and methods of action is another feature of the Virtual Clinic. Non-linear narration and access to a database of clinical cases and definitions of healthy people allow for learning through testing of false methods of action. The software does not limit the possibilities of simulation exclusively to the paths determined by the person who created a given simulation. The ability to assess the cost-effectiveness of a given diagnostic and therapeutic path is also possible with the Virtual Clinic. It allows for the assessment of cost-effectiveness of actions taken by the learner. This allows for the optimization of costs by finding alternative schemes of action or tests that are characterized by the same diagnostic usefulness in a specific case.

The ability to easily add new and modify the existing clinical cases by a person without technical education is another key feature of the Virtual Clinic. Most of the available software, with very few exceptions, does not allow for an easy addition of new cases or a modification of the existing ones. As a result, any modification requires contact with the software creators, who are also responsible for expanding the base of existing clinical cases. This is a significant limitation for the end user, who cannot create new scenarios independently. The result is the forced use of the existing database of diseases, which, due to limited representativeness, often does not include cases tailored to the needs or requirements of the user. With the Virtual Clinic, it allows for an easy creation of new cases or a modification of the existing ones by a medical expert who does not have specialist IT knowledge.

References

1. Ayanouz, S., Abdelhakim, B.A., Benhmed, M.: A smart chatbot architecture based NLP and machine learning for health care assistance. In: Proceedings of the 3rd International Conference on Networking, Information Systems & Security, Marrakech, Morocco, 31 March–2 April 2020, pp. 1–6. https://doi.org/10.1145/3386723.3387897
2. Kumar, R., Ali, M.M.: A review on chatbot design and implementation techniques. Int. J. Eng. Technol. **7**, 11 (2020)
3. Brandtzaeg, P.B., Følstad, A.: Why people use chatbots. In: Kompatsiaris, I., et al. (eds.) INSCI 2017. LNCS, vol. 10673, pp. 377–392. Springer, Cham (2017). https://doi.org/10.1007/978-3-319-70284-1_30
4. Go, E., Sundar, S.S.: Humanizing chatbots: the effects of visual, identity and conversational cues on humanness perceptions. Comput. Hum. Behav. **97**, 304–316 (2019). https://doi.org/10.1016/j.chb.2019.01.020
5. Dale, R.: The return of the chatbots. Nat. Lang. Eng. **22**(5), 811–817 (2016)
6. Følstad, A., Brandtzaeg, P.B.: (in press, 2017). Chatbots – the new world of HCI. ACM Interactions
7. Luo, X., Tong, S., Fang, Z., Qu, Z.: Frontiers: Machines vs. Humans: The Impact of Artificial Intelligence Chatbot Disclosure on Customer Purchases. Mark. Sci. (2019). https://doi.org/10.1287/mksc.2019.1192
8. Kaur, A., Singh, S., Chandan, J.S., Robbins, T., Patel, V.: Qualitative exploration of digital chatbot use in medical education: a pilot study. Digital Health **7** (2021). https://doi.org/10.1177/20552076211038151
9. Suárez, A., Adanero, A., Díaz-Flores García, V., Freire, Y., Algar, J.: Using a virtual patient via an artificial intelligence chatbot to develop dental students' diagnostic skills. Int. J. Environ. Res. Public Health. **19**(14), 8735 (2022). https://doi.org/10.3390/ijerph19148735.PMID:35886584;PMCID:PMC9319956

Embedding Brainstorming Tasks in Twitter

Yuki Wakatsuki[1] and Yusuke Yamamoto[2(✉)]

[1] Shizuoka University, Hamamatsu, Shizuoka, Japan
`wakatsuki@design.inf.shizuoka.ac.jp`
[2] Nagoya City University, Nagoya, Aichi, Japan
`yusuke_yamamoto@acm.org`

Abstract. In this study, we propose a system that encourages users to generate ideas using information about tweets they are reading as hints and creates opportunities for users to generate various ideas. By intervening during Twitter browsing, the proposed system aims to use time-consuming Twitter browsing as an opportunity for casual idea generation. To encourage users to come up with a variety of ideas, the proposed system presents a tweet with low similarity to existing ideas as a hint for generating ideas while the user is browsing Twitter. To evaluate the effectiveness of the proposed system, we asked participants to use it in our user study.

Keywords: UI/UX · User assistance · Creativity support

1 Introduction

The automation and streamlining of routine tasks have accelerated the commoditization of technologies and services. Moreover, technological progress and social environment changes are diversifying values. Under these circumstances, companies seek innovation to distinguish their technologies and products [6]. Therefore, exercising creativity, and generating various ideas at work is becoming increasingly important.

People use Brainstorming [16] and MindMap [3] to generate ideas. Brainstorming is an idea-generation method that emphasizes quantity rather than quality by generating ideas in a group, combining and improving them, and diverging ideas [16]. Brainstorming is demanding because it requires several people to gather at the same place and time. For this reason, only a few people frequently use Brainstorming in their daily lives.

In our daily lives, we have free time for traveling, waiting, and so on. However, only some people use such free time for productive activities; many spend it on unproductive activities such as social media browsing [13]. In recent years, studies have been conducted to embed microtasks, such as writing, into such free time to promote effective use of free times [5,10]. Nevertheless, to the best of our knowledge, there is no study on the implementation of creative tasks such as idea generation as microtasks.

© The Author(s), under exclusive license to Springer Nature Switzerland AG 2023
A. Coman and S. Vasilache (Eds.): HCII 2023, LNCS 14026, pp. 149–161, 2023.
https://doi.org/10.1007/978-3-031-35927-9_11

Effective ideation is to generate a large number of candidates with valuable ideas. For this purpose, it is practical to incorporate various concepts into idea generation [15,20]. Brainstorming is a method of diversifying ideas by sharing people's ideas as hints to come up with ideas. However, although other people's ideas can be a valuable source of inspiration for idea generation, constant Brainstorming on the same theme will make it difficult to generate ideas over time. It becomes challenging to keep coming up with various ideas because the perspectives become fixed on the theme of the idea-generation effort [15].

In this study, we propose a **Twitter excursion** system that encourages users to generate ideas daily by embedding opportunities for idea generation in their Twitter browsing. In Japan, 45 million people use Twitter monthly, with 68.9% of users in their teens to 40s using it for 20 min or more per day, citing "killing time/leisure" as the purpose of use[1].

The proposed system is designed as a Chrome extension and supports idea generation on multiple themes predefined by the user. Figure 1 shows an overview of the proposed system's operation. The system analyzes the user's Twitter timeline and the relationship between the predefined themes and the user's existing ideas related to them. When the system detects a tweet that may stimulate an idea, it prompts the user to generate an idea using the information in the tweet as a hint. When a user comes up with an idea, the user records the idea on the site, as shown in Figure 2. The proposed system will create opportunities for users to generate ideas effectively in their free time, such as when browsing Twitter.

2   Related Works

2.1   Idea-Generation Support

In cognitive psychology and human-computer interaction, there are studies on idea-generation methods and idea-generation support tools [7,8]. Paulus et al. found that mental ease and associations are essential for effective idea generation [14]. Wang et al. also stated that it is essential to incorporate various concepts for high-quality idea generation [20]. Hariharan et al. proposed affinity lens, which supports idea generation by analyzing and classifying information written on Post-its and visualizing the results in real-time using a computer [19]. A support for recommending a variety of images that contain concepts that are the basis of design ideas has been proposed to incorporate multiple concepts when generating ideas [15]. In this study, we support idea generation from various perspectives by making sentences computable using natural language processing as well as selecting and presenting tweets containing various concepts for users' existing ideas. Brainstorming is a typical idea-generation method aiming to efficiently generate diverse ideas by multiple people. Gallupe et al. proposed an online brainstorming system and solved interpersonal communication problems that inhibited idea generation [9]. As an advanced online method, crowdsourcing has

---

[1] https://service.aainc.co.jp/product/echoes/voices/0014#blogSec11.

Fig. 1. Example of a link embedded in Twitter by the system

been used to collaborate on ideas with an unspecified number of collaborators [18]. It is demanding to gather participants for these brainstorming methods, and the quality of the results varies because of the variation in participants' abilities and skills [17].

2.2 Support for Effective Use of Unproductive Time in Daily Life

There are several studies on the effective use of unproductive time in daily life. Belakova et al. proposed SonAmi, which creates an opportunity to reflect on writing by reading out the written text when the user lifts his/her mug while taking a break from writing a task that has been postponed [2]. Inie et al. proposed Aiki, which creates learning opportunities by redirecting users to a site where they can perform simple learning tasks, such as learning English words when they access a website where they are wasting time [12]. Hahn et al. proposed incorporating writing microtasks into Facebook timelines to leverage unproductive time in daily life to achieve meaningful goals [10]. The above systems all have one thing in common: they encourage productive activities by using time that has a low cognitive load in daily life and is available for use. Our proposed system focuses on Twitter browsing as an opportunity to embed an idea-generation task.

Fig. 2. Example of a web app for brainstorming tasks

3   Approach

In this study, we propose a system called Twitter Excursion. It creates valuable idea-generation opportunities by encouraging users browsing Twitter to generate ideas inspired by their read tweets. First, it creates informal idea-generation opportunities using the time spent on Twitter, which tends to be time-wasting. Second, it encourages diverse idea generation without being limited by existing ideas. We developed this system based on Hahn et al.'s [10] concept of casual microtasks. The proposed system comprises a Chrome extension that embeds an idea-generation task in Twitter and a web application (web app) that performs the idea-generation task. The Chrome extension selects tweets from the user's Twitter timeline that can be used as hints and embeds the theme and a link to the web app. The web app presents the tweet to be embedded as a hint and records the idea entered by the user. The details of each function and its implementation are as follows.

3.1 Embedding Ideation Tasks on Twitter

Figure 1.1 shows how the Chrome extension embeds a link to the ideation task in a tweet on a Twitter timeline. The light orange area is the embedded part. It contains a button with a user-defined idea-generation theme and a link to a web application for idea entry. When a user comes up with an idea, he/she presses the "Enter Idea" button to go to the web application. The Chrome extension sends the Tweet ID to the web app. The web app uses that ID to display the tweets. The tweets to be selected are those useful as hints for generating ideas. Section 3.2 describes the details of the tweet selection method. The proposed system selects one optimal tweet to embed for every ten tweets the user reads from the top timelines. As a specific scenario, assume that a user is thinking of an idea for a "new orientation to befriend newcomers." The user enters "new orientation to get along with newcomers" as the theme of the idea generation into the system and then enters as many ideas as he/she can think of, as shown in Fig. 1.2. When the user cannot generate more ideas, he/she stops idea generation and browses Twitter. The system selects tweets suitable for hints and inserts a theme and the "Enter Idea" button into a tweet with a picture of a person and a dog walking, as shown in Fig. 1.1. The user comes up with the idea of a "self-introduction walk" inspired by this tweet, goes to the web application shown in Fig. 1.2, enters the "self-introduction walk," and enters other ideas.

3.2 How to Select Tweets to Embed Tasks

The proposed system selects tweets that embed opportunities for idea generation by considering similarity with existing ideas. The proposed strategy aims to increase the diversity of users' ideas by encouraging them to generate ideas different from existing ideas. In this study, we focus on excursions. Excursions are used to increase the number of ideas and diversify perspectives in idea generation [1,11]. Word lists unrelated to the theme are used to generate new ideas. In this study, among the tweets on a user's Twitter timeline, the tweet with the lowest similarity to the user's previous idea is presented as an unexpected hint. We aim to achieve an excursion effect by doing so.

To calculate the similarity between tweets and existing ideas, the proposed system converts candidate tweets and existing ideas into a multidimensional vector. For vectorization, we use a pretrained universal sentence encoder (USE) [4]. A USE embeds a sentence into a multidimensional vector space. It calculates the vector of the entire sentence by vectorizing each word, considering its context. A USE can embed different languages, such as English and Japanese, into the same vector space. We adopted a USE for vectorization because many tweets are in Japanese and English and tweets are often sentences, so the semantic similarity can be calculated accurately by considering the context. Let $S = \{s_1, s_2, \ldots, s_l\}$ be the set of topics from which the user wants to get ideas, the set of tweets on the user's Twitter timeline $T = \{t_1, t_2, \ldots t_m\}$, the set of ideas previously generated by the user for theme s by $I_s = \{i_1, i_2, \ldots i_n\}$. Let $sim_{cos}(v_x, v_y)$ be the cosine similarity of the vectors v_x and v_y of x and y, respectively. The following equation defines the unexpectedness of a tweet $t \in T$ for a theme s.

$$U(t, I_s) = \frac{\sum_{i \in I_s} -sim_{cos}(\boldsymbol{v_t}, \boldsymbol{v_i})}{|I_s|}$$

Based on the above formula, the proposed system calculates the unexpectedness of each tweet on the timeline for all themes in the theme set S. Then, as shown in Fig. 1, the system embeds the most unexpected tweets for each theme as idea-generating opportunities (themes).

3.3   Web Application for Idea Input

As shown in Fig. 2, the user interface of the web app of the proposed system (referred to as "proposal UI") comprises a theme, an idea input form, tweets, and a list of ideas. This web app refers to tweets based on the tweet ID received from the Chrome extension and presents them to the user. The entered ideas are saved and added to the "List of Past Ideas" when the "Enter Idea" button is pressed.

4   Experiment

4.1   Participants

We asked college students who visit Twitter at least once a day daily to cooperate in the experiment. We recruited a total of 20 participants. We experimented over seven days and paid participants 2,500 yen at the end of the experiment. The data of three participants were excluded from the analysis because they did not complete the task or the data were not collected correctly.

4.2   Idea-Generation Task

On the first day of the experiment, we gathered the participants in the laboratory and explained the experiment to them. After the explanation, the participants performed a 15-minute time-limited idea-generation task. From the second day of the experiment, the participants were notified by email at noon each day. They performed the idea-generation task according to the instructions in the email. Section 4.3 provides details on the emails. From the second day, each user entered as many ideas as possible on the same theme as the first day on the website shown in Fig. 2. We instructed the participants to terminate their idea-generation task for the day if they ran out of ideas. We administered a daily questionnaire at the end of each day. The designated theme was "A new orientation to get along with newcomers." The theme was the same from the first day to the last day.

This theme has numerous possible ideas, and anyone can think about it regardless of knowledge.

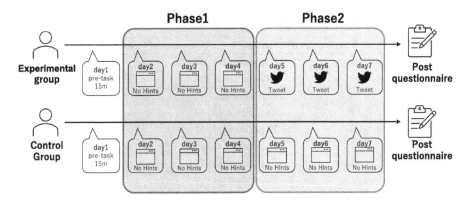

Fig. 3. Experimental Flow

4.3   Experimental Design

In this study, we employed a one-factor between-subjects design of experiment in which the presence or absence of a hint was a factor. The hint factor had the following two levels.

- Experimental Group: presenting users with tweets that have low cosine similarity to the user's existing ideas
- Control group: no hints displayed

Figure 3 shows the experimental flow. On the first day, after confirming the participants' consent to participate in the experiment, each participant was given a 15-minute pretask to generate ideas. After completing the pretask, we assigned participants to the experimental and control groups. To minimize differences in individual ability to generate ideas between groups, we assigned participants to groups based on the number of ideas they generated on the first day. The procedure is to arrange all participants in descending order of the number of ideas they entered in the pretask and assign them alternately to the experimental and control groups, starting with the one with the most ideas. For example, consider the case where the number of ideas entered by eight participants in the pretask is [1,1,3,3,3,3,5,5]. If we group the participants so that the number of ideas is [3,3,3,3] and [1,1,5,5], we would expect the mean number of ideas to be the same but with individual differences in results. Therefore, in this example, we divide the number of ideas into groups of [1,3,3,5] and [1,3,3,3,5]. Table 1 shows the assignment of participants.

The second through fourth days of the experiment is Phase 1. In Phase 1, all participants generated ideas with no hints. The three days following Phase 1 are Phase 2. In Phase 2, the experimental, and control groups generated ideas in different environments. Participants in the experimental group were presented with hints from the proposed system and performed the idea-generation task based on the hints. Participants in the control group performed the idea-generation task without hints, as in Phase 1. The purpose of the proposed system is to encourage

Table 1. Number of ideas and grouping of participants in the experiment

Participant ID	Group	Quantity of ideas
1	Experimental	47
3	Experimental	23
5	Experimental	17
7	Experimental	14
9	Experimental	11
11	Experimental	10
13	Experimental	10
15	Experimental	9
17	Experimental	7
19	Experimental	7
2	Control	27
4	Control	18
6	Control	15
8	Control	13
10	Control	10
12	Control	10
14	Control	10
16	Control	7
18	Control	7
20	Control	6

participants to come up with new perspectives by presenting ideas that are less similar to their existing ideas as hints. The effectiveness of the proposed system was verified by comparing the results with and without hints, with participants having generated all ideas they could generate. In Phase 1, both groups had no hints, so the experiment was designed to lose ideas gradually.

Participants completed questionnaires after each day's task and on the last day of the experiment. Each questionnaire includes items for all groups and the experimental group only. Tables 2 and 3 show the content of the daily questionnaire and the questionnaire given on the last day of the experiment, respectively. Response options for all questions are on a 5-point Likert scale (from 1: strongly disagree to 5: strongly agree). The daily questionnaire asked for a subjective evaluation of a day's task comprises two questions, as follows.

- Did you generate many ideas?
- Did you come up with different ideas compared with your existing ideas?

The last day's questionnaire investigated subjective resistance to and effectiveness of the proposed system's idea-generation method. This questionnaire assesses the extent to which users felt comfortable with the idea-generation opportunities created by the proposed system.

Table 2. Daily Questionnaire

	Target	Question
Q1	Experimental Group	Were the tweets presented helpful in generating a lot of ideas?
Q2	Experimental Group	Were the tweets you were presented with helpful in coming up with ideas for a different perspective?
Q3	All	Do you think you were able to come up with a lot of ideas?
Q4	All	Were you able to come up with a different point of view?

Table 3. Post Questionnaire

	Target	Question
$Q_{post}1$	Experimental Group	Do you think there is resistance to being interrupted with idea-generation tasks like this one when you are on Twitter in your free time?
$Q_{post}2$	Experimental Group	Do you think it is useful to be interrupted with an ideation task like this one when you are on Twitter in your free time?
$Q_{post}3$	All	How resistant do you think you would be to being forced to come up with ideas like this one at the appropriate time?
$Q_{post}4$	All	Do you think it is effective to be interrupted with an idea-generation task like this one at an appropriate time?

5   Result

We collected data on 544 ideas from 17 participants. We analyzed the data to determine the impact of the proposed system on the diversity of ideas generated by the participants. We also analyzed whether the proposed system creates opportunities for participants to generate new ideas by analyzing the questionnaire results. Because of the non-normality of the collected data, we performed the nonparametric Mann-Whitney U test. The significance level was set at $p < 0.05$. We used the SciPy statistical package[2] to analyze the results.

5.1   Daily Questionnaire

We analyzed the participants' responses to the questionnaires given after each day's task as subjective data. The purpose of the proposed system is to help users generate more ideas or consider ideas from different perspectives. The answer choices for $Q1$ and $Q2$, which are questions about tweets, are 1 to 5, with 1 and 2 indicating that the tweets were not helpful, 4 and 5 indicating that the tweets were helpful, and 3 indicating neither, so we expected the average value to be higher than 3. However, as shown in Table 4, the mean values of $Q1$ and $Q2$ are below 3. The proposed system aims to make the participants feel that they could generate more ideas and a variety of ideas by presenting tweets as hints. Therefore, we expected that participants would feel they could generate more diverse ideas in Phase 2 than in Phase 1. To verify this expectation, we analyzed

---

[2] https://scipy.org/.

Table 4. Result Daily questionnaire

	Control Group		Experimental Group		p-value
	Mean	Standard deviation	Mean	Standard deviation	
Q1	–	–	2.19	0.80	–
Q2	–	–	2.33	0.75	–
Q3	0.99	0.26	1.06	0.63	0.47
Q4	1.07	0.29	1.02	0.27	0.47

Table 5. Result Post Questionnaire

	Control Group		Experimental Group		p-value
	Mean	Standard deviation	Mean	Standard deviation	
$Q_{post}1$	–	–	3.44	1.30	–
$Q_{post}2$	–	–	3.00	1.41	–
$Q_{post}3$	3.50	1.20	2.88	1.05	0.29
$Q_{post}4$	2.87	0.99	3.33	1.12	0.56

the mean value of the sum of the responses in Phase 2 divided by the sum of the responses in Phase 1 for each of $Q3$ and $Q4$. If the mean value of $Q4$ is higher in the experimental group than in the control group, then the participants felt that the proposed system allowed them to generate more ideas. However, as Table 4 shows, there was no statistically significant difference between the experimental and control groups in both $Q3$ and $Q4$.

5.2 Post Questionnaire

We analyzed the responses to the questionnaire about the resistance and effectiveness of embedding idea-generation opportunities in Twitter timelines. $Q_{post}1$ and $Q_{post}2$ in Table 4 show the subjective evaluation values of the resistance and effectiveness of embedding idea-generation opportunities in Twitter timelines. We expected the mean value to be lower than 3 because 1 and 2 indicate no resistance, 4 and 5 indicate resistance, and 3 indicates neither. However, the result was that the mean value was not less than 3. Because the responses of $Q_{post}2$ were 1–5, 1 and 2 indicating inadequate, 4 and 5 indicating effective, and 3 indicating neither, we expected the mean value to be higher than 3. However, the results showed that the mean did not exceed 3. $Q_{post}3$ and $Q_{post}4$ in Table 4 show the resistance to being asked to perform the idea-generation task at the appropriate time and the subjective rating of the effectiveness of the idea generation. For $Q_{post}3$, the experimental group had a lower mean value, but the difference was not statistically significant (3.50 and 2.88 for the control and experimental groups, respectively; $p = 0.29$). For $Q_{post}4$, the experimental group had a higher mean, but the difference was not statistically significant (2.87 and 3.33 for the control and experimental groups, respectively) (Table 5).

6   Discussion

We analyzed the results of the daily post-task questionnaires and the questionnaire after completing all tasks. With the data from the daily post-task questionnaires, we analyzed the participants' subjective evaluation of idea generation. The analysis results indicated that the participants did not feel that the hints in the tweets helped them generate more or new ideas. There was no statistically significant difference between the experimental and control groups regarding whether the participants could generate more ideas or diverse perspectives. From the data of the questionnaire after completing all tasks, we analyzed the subjective evaluation of the resistance and effectiveness of the proposed idea-generation system. The analysis results did not support the predictions of the resistance and effectiveness felt by the participants to being interrupted in the idea-generation task while browsing Twitter. There was no statistically significant difference between the responses of the experimental and control groups concerning the resistance and effectiveness of idea generation. Therefore, the experimental results did not support that users would find it easy to generate ideas using the proposed system (Sects. 5.1, 5.2).

However, the hint tweet may have influenced the content of the idea. The free comments in the last questionnaire were as follows.

While the hints from Twitter helped me generate ideas I did not have, the hints bound me.

This response suggests that hints by the proposed system may encourage the development of ideas from new perspectives. However, it can be challenging to understand the perspectives of the hints; some participants felt that the perspectives of the hints restricted them, and this inhibited their free conception of ideas.

The last questionnaire evaluation results did not suggest that users found it easy to generate ideas when the proposed system created opportunities for idea generation. Moreover, the participants who did not feel much resistance to embedding idea-generation opportunities in their Twitter timeline and answered that it was highly effective responded as follows in the free-response section of the last questionnaire regarding the use of the proposed system: "It is hard to do it every day in a row." "It is not easy to keep coming up with ideas every day, but I found it very interesting if I did it in my spare time and thought it would be a good use of my time on Twitter."

7   Conclusion

In this study, we proposed a system that encourages users browsing Twitter to generate ideas using information from tweets they read as hints and creates opportunities for users to generate various ideas. The purpose of the proposed system is twofold: to make effective use of Twitter, which tends to be time-wasting, as an opportunity to generate ideas to encourage the creation of ideas dissimilar to existing ideas. The proposed system creates a vector of previously generated ideas and selects tweets with low similarity to them as hints from the user's timeline. This strategy increases the diversity of the set of user-initiated ideas by providing users with various hints for existing ideas. The experimental results did not show significant results that the proposed system effectively uses Twitter as an opportunity for idea generation or that it encourages diverse idea generation. However, we found that the tweets we presented as hints could induce ideas generated by users. In the future, it is necessary to perform long-term intervention experiments to verify the effectiveness of the proposed system.

Acknowledgment. The work was supported in part by the Grants-in-Aid for Scientific Research (18H03244, 18H03554, 18H03775, 22H03905) from the MEXT of Japan.

References

1. Barki, H., Pinsonneault, A.: Small group brainstorming and idea quality: is electronic brainstorming the most effective approach? Small Group Res. **32**(2), 158–205 (2001)
2. Belakova, J., Mackay, W.E.: Sonami: a tangible creativity support tool for productive procrastination. In: Creativity and Cognition. C&C '21. Association for Computing Machinery, New York, NY, USA (2021). https://doi.org/10.1145/3450741.3465250
3. Buzan, T.: The Mind Map Book: How to Use Radiant Thinking to Maximize Your Brain's Untapped Potential. Plume (1996)
4. Cer, D., et al.: Universal sentence encoder for English. In: Proceedings of the 2018 Conference on Empirical Methods in Natural Language Processing: System Demonstrations, pp. 169–174 (2018)
5. Cheng, J., Teevan, J., Iqbal, S.T., Bernstein, M.S.: Break it down: a comparison of macro- and microtasks. In: Proceedings of the 33rd Annual ACM Conference on Human Factors in Computing Systems. CHI '15, pp. 4061–4064. Association for Computing Machinery, New York, NY, USA (2015). https://doi.org/10.1145/2702123.2702146
6. Christensen, C., Raynor, M.: The Innovator's Solution: Creating and Sustaining Successful Growth. Harvard Business Review Press (2013)
7. Frich, J., MacDonald Vermeulen, L., Remy, C., Biskjaer, M.M., Dalsgaard, P.: Mapping the landscape of creativity support tools in HCI. In: Proceedings of the 2019 CHI Conference on Human Factors in Computing Systems, pp. 1–18 (2019)
8. Frich, J., Mose Biskjaer, M., Dalsgaard, P.: Twenty years of creativity research in human-computer interaction: current state and future directions. In: Proceedings of the 2018 Designing Interactive Systems Conference. DIS '18, pp. 1235–1257. Association for Computing Machinery, New York, NY, USA (2018). https://doi.org/10.1145/3196709.3196732
9. Gallupe, R.B., Cooper, W.H.: Brainstorming electronically. MIT Sloan Manag. Rev. **35**(1), 27 (1993)
10. Hahn, N., Iqbal, S.T., Teevan, J.: Casual microtasking: embedding microtasks in Facebook. In: Proceedings of the 2019 CHI Conference on Human Factors in Computing Systems. CHI '19, pp. 1–9. Association for Computing Machinery, New York, NY, USA (2019). https://doi.org/10.1145/3290605.3300249

11. Higgins, J.M.: Creative Problem Solving Techniques: The Handbook of New Ideas for Business. New Management Pub Co. (2005)
12. Inie, N., Lungu, M.F.: Aiki - turning online procrastination into microlearning. In: Proceedings of the 2021 CHI Conference on Human Factors in Computing Systems. CHI '21. Association for Computing Machinery, New York, NY, USA (2021). https://doi.org/10.1145/3411764.3445202
13. Mark, G., Iqbal, S.T., Czerwinski, M., Johns, P.: Bored Mondays and focused afternoons: the rhythm of attention and online activity in the workplace. In: Proceedings of the SIGCHI Conference on Human Factors in Computing Systems, pp. 3025–3034 (2014)
14. Paulus, P.B., Brown, V.R.: Toward more creative and innovative group idea generation: a cognitive-social-motivational perspective of brainstorming. Soc. Pers. Psychol. Compass **1**(1), 248–265 (2007)
15. Petridis, S., Shin, H.V., Chilton, L.B.: Symbolfinder: brainstorming diverse symbols using local semantic networks. In: The 34th Annual ACM Symposium on User Interface Software and Technology. UIST '21, pp. 385–399. Association for Computing Machinery, New York, NY, USA (2021). https://doi.org/10.1145/3472749.3474757
16. Putman, V.L., Paulus, P.B.: Brainstorming, brainstorming rules and decision making. J. Creat. Behav. **43**(1), 29–40 (2009)
17. Rhys Cox, S., Wang, Y., Abdul, A., von der Weth, C., Lim, B.Y.: Directed diversity: leveraging language embedding distances for collective creativity in crowd ideation. In: Proceedings of the 2021 CHI Conference on Human Factors in Computing Systems. CHI '21. Association for Computing Machinery, New York, NY, USA (2021). https://doi.org/10.1145/3411764.3445782
18. Siangliulue, P., Chan, J., Dow, S.P., Gajos, K.Z.: Ideahound: improving large-scale collaborative ideation with crowd-powered real-time semantic modeling. In: Proceedings of the 29th Annual Symposium on User Interface Software and Technology. UIST '16, pp. 609–624. Association for Computing Machinery, New York, NY, USA (2016). https://doi.org/10.1145/2984511.2984578
19. Subramonyam, H., Drucker, S.M., Adar, E.: Affinity lens: data-assisted affinity diagramming with augmented reality. In: Proceedings of the 2019 CHI Conference on Human Factors in Computing Systems. CHI '19, pp. 1–13. Association for Computing Machinery, New York, NY, USA (2019). https://doi.org/10.1145/3290605.3300628
20. Wang, H.C., Fussell, S.R., Cosley, D.: From diversity to creativity: Stimulating group brainstorming with cultural differences and conversationally-retrieved pictures. In: Proceedings of the ACM 2011 Conference on Computer Supported Cooperative Work, pp. 265–274 (2011)

Understanding Public Perceptions of K-12 Computational Thinking Education Through an Analysis of Quora

Stella Xin Yin[1], Dion Hoe-Lian Goh[1(✉)], Choon Lang Quek[2], and Zhengyuan Liu[3]

[1] Wee Kim Wee School of Communication and Information, Nanyang Technological University, Singapore, Singapore
xin013@e.ntu.edu.sg, ashlgoh@ntu.edu.sg
[2] National Institute of Education, Nanyang Technological University, Singapore, Singapore
choonlang.quek@nie.edu.sg
[3] Institute for Infocomm Research, A*STAR, Singapore, Singapore
zhengyua001@e.ntu.edu.sg

Abstract. As more education systems integrate mandatory computational thinking (CT) classes into their curricula, understanding how the public perceives this issue is an important step in making educational policies and implementing educational reform. In this paper, we retrieved all accessible texts related to K-12 CT education on the Quora platform. The textual data obtained ranged from June 2010 to September 2022. We then performed topic modeling analysis to identify major topics and uncover meaningful themes of the public responses to CT education initiatives. In general, people expressed positive comments about CT education. However, they were still concerned about the difficulties in learning and education equality for disadvantaged groups. In addition, since CT practices develop students' essential skills in the job market, people may overestimate the outcomes of CT education. Our findings provide insights into public perceptions of children's CT education. The results of this study can facilitate education policymaking, curriculum design, and further research directions.

Keywords: computational thinking · coding · education · topic modeling · Quora

1 Introduction

In the 1980s, Papert [1] introduced the term "computational thinking" (CT) with the Logo programming project. He demonstrated that children were able to develop procedural thinking through programming. This idea was then popularized by Wing [2], who elucidated CT as the thought processes of problem-solving, systems designing, and understanding human behaviors. The International Society for Technology in Education and the Computer Science Teachers Association [3] then expanded this idea by highlighting the importance of learning programming to develop problem-solving and critical thinking for K-12 students. Since then, an increasing number of K-12 schools have initiated curriculum revisions that integrated compulsory CT courses or combined them with mathematics and science classes.

© The Author(s), under exclusive license to Springer Nature Switzerland AG 2023
A. Coman and S. Vasilache (Eds.): HCII 2023, LNCS 14026, pp. 162–180, 2023.
https://doi.org/10.1007/978-3-031-35927-9_12

As more education systems integrate mandatory CT classes into their curricula, it is critical to understand how the public responds to such initiatives. Public discussions and opinions provide valuable information for researchers and policymakers to understand perceptions of CT education implementations. Although prior studies investigated stakeholders' perceptions of CT education, they primarily relied on questionnaires and interviews with none of them collecting data from social media platforms [4–6]. Social media plays an important role in empowering parents, students, and teachers to share information, exchange ideas, and build an educational community [7, 8]. Therefore, this is an important gap to address since social media is an alternative vehicle to reflect public responses to specific education policies, practices, and ideologies [9]. This will, in turn, shape future education policies [10].

In this paper, we aimed to answer the following question: How does the public perceive K-12 CT education on Quora platform? To address this question, we conducted a topic modeling analysis of user posts on Quora (www.quora.com). This helped us identify the major topics and meaningful themes of the public responses to CT education initiatives during the past decade. Through analysis, we gained a better understanding of the public perceptions, concerns, and attitudes toward K-12 CT education.

2 Related Work

2.1 CT, Computer Science, Coding, and Programming

Wing [2] defined CT as "thinking like a computer scientist," which indicated that CT is a characteristic of computer scientists. In contrast, several researchers argued that CT should not be only applied to the computer science discipline. They advanced the notion that "The ultimate goal should not be to teach everyone to think like a computer scientist, but rather to teach them to apply these common elements to solve problems and discover new questions that can be explored within and across all disciplines" [11]. Since then, a growing number of schools have modified their curricula to promote CT skills to all students, not just computer science majors [12]. Further, educators and professionals have made progress in teaching CT at the K-12 levels [13].

Coding and programming are sub-fields of computer science. These two terms are often used interchangeably. Coding is a part of programming that deals strictly with converting the language we understand into binary commands for the computing machine, while programming is more advanced knowledge that consists of a set of instructions that a computer can understand and execute, as well as debugging, organizing, and applying to solving problems [14]. CT, on the other hand, overlapping with computer science, coding and programming, is considered a much broader concept and an interrelated set of skills (i.e., creativity, algorithmic thinking, critical thinking, problem-solving, and cooperation) [15].

In the past decade, research has demonstrated that programming education was an ideal medium for the development of CT [13, 16, 17]. Empirical evidence has shown that the inclusion of coding or programming in the school curriculum provides a range of positive learning outcomes [17, 18]. Through the process of designing and debugging program artifacts, children are able to develop not only programming skills but also metacognitive approaches to problem-solving, critical thinking, and creative thinking [19].

2.2 Stakeholders' Perspectives on CT Education

In the last decade, numerous studies investigated stakeholders' perspectives on CT education in K-12. Generally, parents perceive the benefits of CT activities, and they hope children could have fun and enjoy the learning process [4]. For example, a survey result showed that parents identified a range of positive outcomes of CT practices, including creativity, problem-solving, planning, and collaboration skills [5, 20]. In addition, most parents expressed relatively high expectations of CT education. They anticipated that CT education can equip their children with essential skills for career success in the future [5, 6]. However, they were concerned about inadequate professional teaching and learning resources provided by schools [20].

Although academics and IT professionals believed that anybody could learn to code with sufficient resources, effort, and learning motivation [21], schools and teachers identified significant challenges in teaching activities, such as insufficient teacher training and no unified curriculum [22, 23]. For example, although teachers expected that integrating programming into mathematics classes would be fun and engaging, many teachers reported a lack of training and guidance in the teaching material. Particularly, they struggled with choosing tools or approaches to teaching CT skills [24]. Besides, while teachers perceived the value of introducing CT to primary students, they expected additional support in tool evaluation and CT assessment [25].

Given that most previous research relied on questionnaires and interviews as research methods, there are several limitations. First, the questionnaire is viewed as a cost-efficient approach to collecting quantitative data from a large-scale group on specific topics. However, this method is focused to test hypotheses and results in statistical generalizations. It is hard to generate in-depth data or "stories" from respondents [26]. Second, although the interview method allows for collecting a large amount of information about the behavior, attitude, and perception of the interviewees, it is considered time-consuming and labor-intensive with restricted numbers of participants [27]. Therefore, we propose a computational method to quantify public perceptions. As a means of triangulation, this approach can compensate for the limitations of questionnaire and interview methods undertaken in many prior studies.

2.3 Quora Analysis

There are two reasons for choosing Quora in our research. First, Quora is one of the largest and most popular community-driven Q&A sites with diverse user communities [28]. Second, its extensive, modern interactive interface and well-organized sections on the education sector enabled both depth and breadth of relevant data for collection. On this platform, individuals are able to post either questions or answers, as well as vote for preferences. The voting mechanism provides the potential to measure public preferences on particular opinions. Another important feature of Quora is that it requires users to provide personal identities in registration which increases the representativeness of Quora's data to reflect public opinions to some extent.

Prior research focused on a few topics, such as climate change [29], linguistic structure [30, 31], and autism-related questions [32]. In the education context, Le et al. [33] analyzed data from actual conversations on Quora and identified key factors attributed to students selecting a university. Nevertheless, the content analysis of educational issues on Quora is limited. Therefore, this study intends to uncover hidden patterns surrounding public discussions of recent education initiatives.

3   Methodology

3.1   Data Collection

We used Python to collect data from the Quora website. As shown in Fig. 1, several types of data were collected in this study: questions, answers, author information, and the number of upvotes.

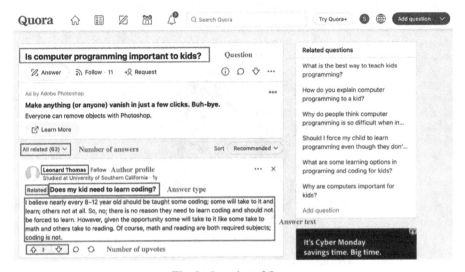

Fig. 1. Snapshot of Quora

The data collection process started with searching all questions associated with K-12 CT education, including but not limited to:

1. (children or kids) AND (code OR coding OR programming OR robotics OR "computer science") AND (study OR learn)
2. (children or kids) AND (code OR coding OR programming OR robotics OR "computer science") AND (teach OR instruct OR curriculum OR syllabus OR class)
3. (children or kids) AND "computational thinking"

The data ranged from June 2010 to September 2022 since Quora was first available to the public on June 21, 2010. A question may receive several answers, questions thus serve as guides to retrieve corresponding answers. In total, 2,269 questions and 43,839 answers related to K-12 CT education were collected.

3.2   Data Analysis

After eliminating duplications, 1,369 questions and 23,124 answers remained in the dataset. We then manually screened questions and deleted all irrelevant items which did not contain keywords such as "children," "kids," "coding" and "programming." Finally, 1,174 questions and their associated answers remained. We noticed that Quora categorized answers into three types and labeled them *normal, related, and promoted*. Specifically, *normal* answers are the replies posted for the given questions, *related* answers are similar posts recommended by the system, and *promoted* answers contain advertising content. As shown in Fig. 2, among 23,124 answers associated with the 1,174 questions, there were only 7,951(34%) answers are posted by users for the given questions, compared to over 60% of the system-recommended answers. To reduce algorithm bias and maximize the authenticity of public perceptions, we removed promoted answers and excluded answers without keywords such as "children," "kids," "coding" and "programming." Finally, 7,543 answers were prepared for topic modeling analysis (6,064 (80.39%) *normal* answers and 1,479 (19.61%) *related* answers).

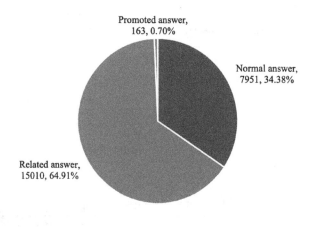

Fig. 2. Types of answers

Next, we preprocessed the answer data by removing emojis, URLs, punctuations, numbers, and special tokens (e.g., , &amp). We then converted the terms into single words and lowercase. Further, we removed standard stopwords and additional custom stopwords, including "don't," "'ll," and "'ve" in answer texts. Finally, we conducted a lemmatizing process to enhance interpretability. After preprocessing, 18,004 valid English terms were prepared for Latent Dirichlet allocation (LDA) analysis.

LDA is a popular and widely used machine learning method for text analysis. It is an unsupervised clustering technique to identify latent topics from a given corpus and then calculate topic distributions [34]. In our study, we aim to map all the documents to the classified topics and calculate the representatives of each topic. To make each document and each word as monochromatic as possible, we used the Gibbs sampling algorithm to increase the statistical inference [34]. Next, we apply Cao et al.'s [35] and Deveaud et al.'s [36] metrics to determine the optimal number of topics of collected data. Figure 3 illustrates the perplexity of the topic model. Since the best number of topics shows low values for Cao et al. [35] and high values for Deveaud et al. [36], we need to find the point that best fits the criteria.

According to Fig. 3, the optimal number of topics appeared at 10-topic model, 14-topic model, and 16-topic model. To compare the quality and interpretability of these three models, we calculated the coherence score of each model. A higher score indicates a better topic model. After calculation, the coherence scores are 0.46, 0.48, and 0.47, respectively. We thus decided to generate 14 topics in this study.

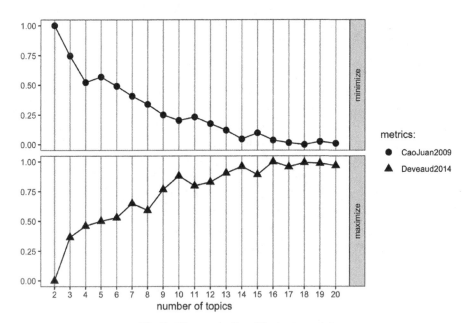

Fig. 3. The perplexity of the topic model

4 Findings

Among 1,174 questions, there are three types of questions that people are most concerned with. The first type is related to the benefits of learning CT skills. People were curious about "What are the benefits of learning programming?" The second type is surrounded with learning resources. For example, people ask "What are the resources you recommend learning to program at an early age?" and "Are there any recommended online platforms that help kids to learn to code?" The last type is focused on the school curriculum and CT framework. People ask for details about the CT curriculum. However, they also express feelings of uncertainty about the relation between CT education and children's future development. They question that "How important or unimportant do you think computer science is to your kids' education and their future careers?".

Intertopic Distance Map (via multidimensional scaling)

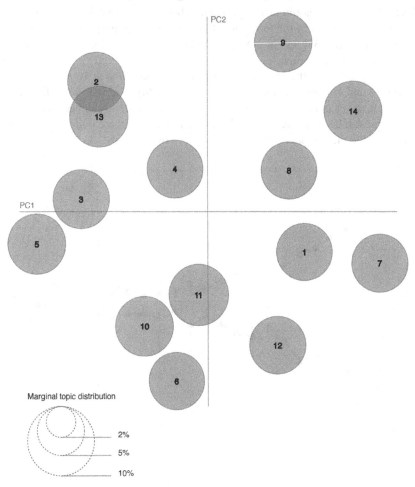

Fig. 4. The intertopic distance map of the answer dataset

Figure 4 shows an intertopic distance map of the answer dataset. We obtained this 2-D representations by computing the distance between topics and applying multidimensional scaling. Each bubble represents a topic whose size correlates to the prevalence of its topic within the text document. An ideal topic model is represented by large, non-overlapping bubbles that are scattered throughout the chart. However, we observed a slight overlap on edges between Topic 2 and Topic 13. It is because these two topics share a part of common words. If we looked at them closely, we found that Topic 2 and Topic 13 share common words on positive attitudes toward CT education. However, Topic 2 is focused on the education inequity of the poor while Topic 13 is concentrated on the general attitude toward CT education. Despite the minimum overlap, the majority of topics are of similar sizes and non-overlapping spread across the chart. This indicates that the 14-topic model is a good fit model. In addition, the topics are spread across the four quadrants and automatically filled into four themes.

The bar chart in Fig. 5 lists the top 30 most salient terms. The blue bars depict the total frequency of each term across the entire corpus. A higher saliency value indicates that a word is more useful for identifying a specific topic.

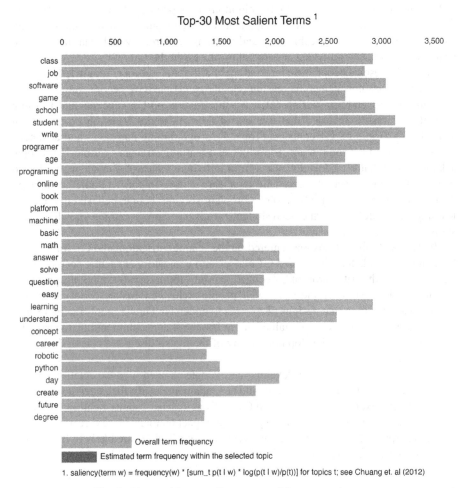

Fig. 5. The top 30 most salient terms of the answer dataset

As shown in Table 1, the 14 topics are classified into four themes according to the four quadrants.

Theme 1 consists of public attitudes and concerns with CT education. In general, people held positive views on CT learning, such as "happy," "interest," and "joy." (Topic 13). CT activities were considered valuable opportunities for children to develop friendships. Interestingly, although people expressed positive comments about CT education, they were still concerned about the difficulties in the learning process (Topic 3) (e.g., "A lot of the basic CS concepts can be very abstract and hence difficult to comprehend, even for grownups.") It is noteworthy that people also shared doubts and uncertainty with the implementation of CT education in different places. In Topic 2, people delivered their opinions on the pros and cons of CT education to disadvantaged groups. They believed that poor people equipped with CT skills can get out of poverty and live better lives with their families. However, others argued that even as technology becomes more affordable and internet access seems increasingly ubiquitous, poor people still faced a lot of barriers to learning. For example, one mentioned that "children from low-income families may have inadequate access to technology and teaching resources, which can hinder them from learning the CT skills that are crucial to success in the future."

Theme 2 presents people's understanding of different types of CT knowledge. Since CT education has now gained increasing popularity, people have become more familiar with this subject and are sharing extensive information on CT concepts and learning content. Our results revealed that five out of fourteen topics focus on programming and robotics (Topic 4), CT concepts (Topic 5), programming languages and advanced programming skills (Topic 6 and Topic 11), and learning strategies (Topic 10). People acknowledged that CT education starts from introducing basic CT concepts. Followed by variable hands-on activities, students then learn to use computers or other technology devices (i.e., robotics) as useful tools in problem-solving. People believed that the CT learning experience will further lead students to advanced programming knowledge and skills.

In Theme 3, discussions are centered on the school curriculum and CT framework. Since more schools have integrated CT classes into mandatory curricula, people gradually recognized the critical role of CT education in developing creative thinking, problem-solving, and logic skills (Topic 1). As well, people exchange ideas on school curriculum (Topic 7) and instructional designs (Topic 12) to understand how schools facilitate children's learning. People not only talked about in-school curriculum and extracurricular workshops for CT skills development, many of them also discussed course designs of online platforms.

Theme 4 focuses on career development. People showed high expectations on CT education and believed that CT skills would be fundamental skills for career development (Topic 14). For example, people valued CT skills as a "basic requirement for jobs in all fields." and "Coding skills can have a profound impact on their future career path." It is hence unsurprising that people naturally assume that CT skills are likely to bring more monetary rewards and help find a decent job in the future (Topic 8 and Topic 9).

5   Discussion

This study demonstrates the utility of the data collected from Quora for investigating public perceptions of children's CT education. Based on the answers posted by community users, we identified the major topics and meaningful themes of the public responses to CT education during the past decade. Several interesting findings were revealed through analysis.

First, the majority of people have positive attitude toward CT education (Theme 1: Topic 13). In line with previous studies [4–6], people perceived that CT classes provide

Table 1. 14 topics generated through LDA topic modeling.

Topic label	Top 10 words	Topic rate %	Document counts %	Example
Theme 1: Attitude and concerns with CT education				
Topic 2: Difficulties in implementation	reason; day; access; poor; country; demand; education; world; social; low	7.20%	523 (6.93%)	"Programming has a serious diversity problem, and the ceiling for poor people can be as hard as concrete. "
Topic 3: Difficulties in learning	understand; hard; difficult; question; find; answer; command; error; memory; age;	7.10%	186 (2.46%)	"…kids should not be oriented to learn the difficult concepts of coding from a very early age, as it will only increase the burden on their little shoulders."
Topic 13: Positive attitude	enjoy; pretty; friend; happy; age; thing; interest; love; joy; life	7.50%	639 (8.47%)	"It teaches a child's fundamental skills in coding and translates them into a real-world experience that is engaging, enjoyable, and fun! "
Theme 2: Types of CT knowledge				
Topic 4: Programming and robotics	robot; drive; function; line; step; object; move; sensor; command; control	6.90%	423 (5.61%)	"You can start with robotic classes… is a great way to concretize your basics and skills over time."
Topic 5: CT concepts	code; write; line; type; logic; number; memory; function; read; assemble	6.80%	495 (6.56%)	"Programming concepts such as data type and loops or some statements etc."
Topic 6: Programming languages	language; python; java; programming; basic; JavaScript; web; book; project; recommend	7.50%	558 (7.39%)	"…once your skills progress, work your way up to JavaScript, SQL, and other more complex coding languages."

(continued)

Table 1. (*continued*)

Topic label	Top 10 words	Topic rate %	Document counts %	Example
Topic 10: Learning strategies	book; solve; practice; logic; structure; base; follow; beginner; solution; web	7.30%	381 (5.05%)	"…follow a 2:1 ratio between conceptual learning and applied learning to practices…"
Topic 11: Advanced knowledge of programming	machine; learning; data; human; algorithm; model; intelligence; process; deep; train	7.80%	346 (4.58%)	"Your kids will start with core programming concepts, and they will have an excellent understanding of artificial intelligence, machine learning…"
Theme 3: School curriculum and CT education framework				
Topic 1: Future skills (e.g., creative thinking, problem solving, etc.)	skill; technology; future; develop; world; creative; think; solve; math; logic;	6.70%	837 (11.09%)	"Learning to code will improve a child's abstract thinking, logic, problem-solving skills but also increases creativity and concentration."
Topic 7: CT curriculum	class, online, platform, teacher, provide, offer, curriculum, age, live, session	7.00%	821 (10.88%)	"…as a part of the existing classroom curriculum or as an extracurricular assignment…parents are also increasingly turning to online coding programs for their kids."
Topic 12: Game-based learning	game; basic; create; interest; fun; play; easy; scratch; tutorial; block	6.90%	675 (8.94%)	"Your kids can use code to build their own games, animation, and apps, fundamentally changing their relationship to technology from consumer to creator."

(*continued*)

Table 1. (*continued*)

Topic label	Top 10 words	Topic rate %	Document counts %	Example
Theme 4: Career development				
Topic 8: Major choices	math; engineering; degree; field; job; college; school; education; major; university	6.70%	559 (7.41%)	"I want to be an engineer and I was one of the top programmers in high school, I chose CS for my university major, and it helps a lot."
Topic 9: Money reward	company; job; money; competition; market; google; pay; top; hire; industry;	7.20%	446 (5.91%)	"Working in IT is usually paid pretty well."
Topic 14: Job requirement	developer; software; career; engineer; application; system; database; industry; field; programmer	7.40%	658 (8.72%)	"This has become a basic requirement for jobs in all fields."

children with fun and engaging learning experiences through hands-on activities. Moreover, CT education supports children's problem-solving skills, creativity, and logical thinking. For example, people commented that "CT practices help kids to think logically and enhance their creativity." and "From designing games and apps to writing code and completing projects, it takes a child's fundamental skills in coding and translates them into a real-world experience that is engaging, enjoyable, and fun!" Surprisingly, there are 228 out of 639 answers (35.68%) in Topic 13 highlight the collaboration and communication skills in CT activities. There is little doubt that people supposed that CT education has effectively improved children's social and communication skills through collaborative learning activities. For instance, "As children create [projects] with Scratch, they learn to think creatively, work collaboratively, and reason systematically.", "Coding brings collaboration, communication, problem-solving, and other skills for kids." and "They make friends who share a common interest."

Second, people are concerned with the difficulties and challenges in teaching and learning CT skills (Theme 1: Topic 3). People expressed worries about challenges children might encounter in the learning process, such as difficulties in understanding CT concepts, lack of interest, and practice time. Some negative views on children's learning experience have been found in our analysis, such as "A lot of the basic CS concepts can be very abstract and hence difficult to comprehend, even for grown-ups." and "It is really difficult to retain their attention and interest in something like coding which can be a bit challenging in the beginning phase." Apart from that, our findings complement previous studies by presenting more insights into learning difficulties in CT learning. People identified several factors that contribute to learning difficulties. For example, one wrote, "There are many reasons [for difficulties in learning] such as financial conditions, lack of motivation and support from family/friends, etc., but most important is lack of interest." Since parents' perceptions play a pivotal role in children's learning, their positive attitude toward CT education considerably influences children's learning motivation. In contrast, parents' misconceptions and anxiety could become obstacles to children's engagement in learning [37]. Therefore, many researchers encourage parental involvement in children's learning [38–40]. Parental involvement could help gain a better understanding of their children and develop a closer parent-child relationship [41]. It could also improve children's engagement and academic performance [39, 40].

Third, the implementation of CT education is confronted with many doubts, particularly in less developed areas (Theme 1: Topic 2). Some people worried that the implementation would be delayed due to the fact that "not enough teachers are trained to teach coding in schools across the country, and resources are lacking as well (not all schools have a functional computer lab)." These comments are similar with previous findings that teachers perceived a lack of training and guidance when integrating CT activities into math classes [23, 25]. However, most previous research was conducted in schools with abundant educational resources, such as computer labs, ubiquitous networks, and qualified teachers. Teachers and students in these schools have advantages with internet access and computer use, compared with schools serving low-income households. These poor districts' schools usually have a greater number of students per class and less spending per student [42]. In a recent survey, among those with incomes below the federal poverty level, 65 percent of participants reported that lacking access to a computer or the internet had prevented their children from participating in class and completing their schoolwork [43]. We got similar results in our study, some people wrote, "In some countries access to computers is dramatically lower than the worst we find in America, such as 400 students per computer. I believe in most places where there is income disparity, there will also be a disparity in access to technology and computer education." and "Internet access, in many cases, is limited to their pay-as-you-go phones. No money this week? No phone, no Internet. There are no computers, laptops, or tablets in the classroom, nor are there any available for loan. These kids, living in the deepest poverty, don't have the basic education to learn to code." Therefore, we realized that the participants in previous studies did not cover the gamut of social groups, such as marginalized or underprivileged groups.

Fourth, the amount and complexity of information content bring a certain degree of confusion to identifying and extracting credible information (Theme 2). Community-driven platforms such as Quora create and maintain a space for productive discussion where users can freely share their thoughts, ideas, and concerns. However, the explosion of information may leave people feeling frustrated and confused. Eventually, the gap between the information that is presented and perceived can result in anxiety and stress which lead to poorer decision-making capacity and memory loss [44]. In this study, over 60% of answers labeled with *related* are system-recommended answers. These answers contribute part of the irrelevant content and advertising information that people may encounter. For example, when we looked through the answers to "How can parents learn to code with their kids?", we found 32 *related* answers. One of them devoted considerable space to describing the benefits of using one of the learning platforms and at the end of the answer, the author introduced a product as "The most dynamic and remarkable platform for the kids to learn coding is www.whitehatjr.com." Such information may mislead community participants in decision-making and judgment. Parents or teachers may be influenced by advertising information and choose inappropriate learning resources for children or even misunderstand the content and purpose of CT education. Therefore, people should be more diligent when they consume information online and be aware that not all information is accurate or genuine.

Besides, an array of choices of online resources was found to cause anxiety among parents. For example, some answers in Theme 2 wrote, "Among so many available options, choosing the right coding course for kids is challenging. There are multiple factors to consider before choosing a platform. An updated curriculum, expert teachers, hands-on-practice, and enjoyable learning." "If a kid is just starting out in coding then proper guidance will play a crucial role, because guidance can either build interest in coding or ruin it. Pre-recorded tutorials are great but they are not interactive." Even though some experts answered that "There is no one-size-fits-all answer to this question, as the best site to learn how to code will vary depending on your level of experience and expertise," they rarely gave specific guidance on how to select reliable resources for specific age groups.

Fifth, as more schools have initiated curriculum revisions to introduce K-12 students with CT skills [12], people shared divergent views on school curriculum and instructional design (Theme 3). Many people acknowledged that integrating CT classes into the mandatory curriculum is an inevitable trend. We found several positive comments that supported this argument, such as, "I support the initiative that students will be taught coding in the National Education Policy. It aligns with what these children will face in the future." and "Coding is a part of fundamental education. Moreover, with the launch of the National education policy, more and more parents have realized the importance of getting their young kids into coding." Nevertheless, people held controversial perspectives on the current school curriculum. A part of them had great expectations on the school curriculum. They looked forward "Schools have good faculties, great curriculum, and those faculties who would completely focus on kid's development." In addition, they hoped that "The curriculum is designed to make children learn real-world tech problems and tackle their solutions. The classes are interactive and interesting so that the child can learn in a fun way." In contrast, Pessimists argued that school curriculum is boring and outdated. For example, "Boring and tiring school curriculum are forcing kids and parents to look out for some better options which are practical, informative, interactive, full of fun and improve logical and critical thinking amongst kids.", "School Curriculum should now be customized according to the change." and "[online platforms'] course structure is the different-from-school curriculum. They are enough interesting for the kids to take up the coding concepts enjoyably." Further, some opponents doubted that the current school curriculum is incompetent and hardly covers creative and problem-solving skills. They thought "Creativity and problem-solving skills are tough to teach and learn, especially embedded with coding. It requires lots of planning, research, and engineering."

Lastly, the public seemed to overestimate expectations of CT skills. A large portion of answers revealed that people expect children who learn programming could find a decent job and get paid well (Theme 4). Furthermore, some even believed computer engineering jobs are much better than others. For example, "Professional programmers are in great demand, and they are generally paid well (relative to all other careers)." and "A computer science degree also lets you get into a field where (if you're either hard-working or extremely gifted) you are highly desired by many companies, paid well, and allowed to work with an exceptional amount of freedom." This overestimated expectation may become a burden for children if their parents place too much emphasis on outcome importance. Prior research indicated that when children are overstressed with expectations, they may become frustrated and feel depressed [45, 46]. As a result, children are less likely to enjoy learning for their own sake. In contrast, students who are less influenced by parents' over-expectations could enjoy and concentrate more on the learning process. Therefore, parents should be aware of the potential negative impact of high parental expectations on children's emotional well-being and learning.

6 Conclusion

This study analyzed posted answers on the Quora platform to gain a better understanding of public perceptions, concerns, and attitudes toward CT education. Through topic modeling, we identified 14 topics surrounding people's discussions of CT education. The findings have the following theoretical and practical implications.

Theoretical implications of this study are two-fold. First, the use of social media data and topic modeling could be applied as a complementary research method to investigate public perceptions of educational issues. The results of this study qualitatively and quantitatively reflect public responses to specific education policies, practices, and ideologies, which compensates for the limitations of the survey and interview methods undertaken in many prior studies. Future studies could attempt to combine the social media-based text analysis method with other research methods to gain a comprehensive understanding of stakeholders' views on particular educational issues.

Second, education inequality in the CT domain is an emerging issue. There thus should be further work done with disadvantaged and vulnerable groups to better understand CT education implementations in this context. For example, whether social-economic backgrounds impact students' CT education, and how the different social groups of people perceive CT education. What are the difficulties students face in CT learning, and what factors are attributed to the differences? We look forward to educators, policymakers, and developers aligning together to create diversity, equity, inclusion, and belonging CT education community for all children.

This study also provides practical implications for schools and instructors. First, schools provide adequate guidance and training for teachers. As more EdTech companies develop learning tools to facilitate CT education, teachers face an ever-increasing number of tools and resources on the internet to spice up their classes and keep their students engaged. However, a lack of professional training and guidance on integrating tools in CT classes may negatively impact effective teaching. This, in turn, will affect students' CT development. Therefore, schools should pay attention to providing pedagogical training for teachers. We expect more effective and high-quality teaching strategies and evaluation methods in CT education. On the other hand, teachers should upgrade themselves and be competent to deliver qualified CT education to students.

Second, another practical implication for schools is to provide collaborative learning opportunities to ease parents' anxiety, broaden their programming knowledge and gain first-hand experience in learning programming with their children. For example, we advocate schools to organize parent-child CT workshops and summer camps. Such events provide opportunities for developing a closer parent-child relationship. It could also improve children's engagement and CT performance. Further, technology companies could develop more interactive and user-friendly CT tools that parents could easily use to support their children in learning.

A few limitations should be noted. First, data collection was limited to a single Q&A site Quora. Other social media platforms may yield different sets of topics. Hence, it would be worthwhile to analyze other sources to ascertain the stability of our topics. Second, the geographical distribution of Quora users is mainly located in America and India. Therefore, our results may not be generalizable to all populations. Future studies could include other social media sources to validate our topics and gain a comprehensive understanding of public views on CT education.

References

1. Papert, S.: Mindstorms: children, computers, and powerful ideas. Basic Books, New York (1980)
2. Wing, J.M.: Computational thinking. Commun. ACM. **49**, 33–35 (2006). https://doi.org/10.1145/1118178.1118215
3. Computer Science Teachers Association (CSTA), International Society for Technology Education (ISTE): operational definition of computational thinking (2011)
4. Yu, J., Bai, C., Roque, R.: Considering parents in coding kit design. In: Proceedings of the 2020 CHI Conference on Human Factors in Computing Systems, pp. 1–14. ACM, New York (2020). https://doi.org/10.1145/3313831.3376130
5. Maruyama, Y.: Investigation into parents' impressions of computer programming with comparisons before and after a programming workshop. In: Uskov, V., Howlett, R., and Jain, L., (eds.) Smart Innovation, Systems and Technologies. pp. 421–431. Springer Nature Singapore (2019). https://doi.org/10.1007/978-981-13-8260-4_38/TABLES/5
6. Kong, S.-C., Wang, Y.-Q.: The influence of parental support and perceived usefulness on students' learning motivation and flow experience in visual programming: investigation from a parent perspective. Br. J. Educ. Technol. **52**, 1749–1770 (2021). https://doi.org/10.1111/bjet.13071
7. Davis III, C.H.F., Deil-Amen, R., Rios-Aguilar, C., González Canché, M.S.: Social media, higher education, and community colleges: a research synthesis and implications for the study of two-year institutions. Community Coll. J. Res. Pract. 39, 409–422 (2015). https://doi.org/10.1080/10668926.2013.828665
8. Goodyear, V.A., Casey, A., Kirk, D.: Tweet me, message me, like me: using social media to facilitate pedagogical change within an emerging community of practice. Sport. Educ. Soc. **19**, 927–943 (2014). https://doi.org/10.1080/13573322.2013.858624

9. Malin, J.R., Lubienski, C.: Educational expertise, advocacy, and media influence. Educ. Policy Anal. Arch. **23**, 6 (2015). https://doi.org/10.14507/epaa.v23.1706

10. Daly, A.J., Supovitz, J., Fresno, M.D.: The social side of educational policy: how social media is changing the politics of education. Teach. Coll. Rec. Voice Scholarsh. Educ. **121**, 1–26 (2019). https://doi.org/10.1177/016146811912101402

11. Barr, V., Stephenson, C.: Bringing computational thinking to K-12. ACM Inroads. **2**, 48–54 (2011). https://doi.org/10.1145/1929887.1929905

12. Bocconi, S., et al.: Reviewing computational thinking in compulsory education. Publications Office of the European Union, Luxembourg (2022). https://doi.org/10.2760/126955

13. Hsu, T.-C., Chang, S.-C., Hung, Y.-T.: How to learn and how to teach computational thinking: suggestions based on a review of the literature. Comput. Educ. **126**, 296–310 (2018). https://doi.org/10.1016/j.compedu.2018.07.004

14. Shute, V.J., Sun, C., Asbell-Clarke, J.: Demystifying computational thinking. Educ. Res. Rev. **22**, 142–158 (2017). https://doi.org/10.1016/j.edurev.2017.09.003

15. Bers, M.U.: Coding as a playground. Routledge, New York (2017). https://doi.org/10.4324/9781315398945

16. Buitrago Flórez, F., Casallas, R., Hernández, M., Reyes, A., Restrepo, S., Danies, G.: Changing a generation's way of thinking: teaching computational thinking through programming. Rev. Educ. Res. **87**, 834–860 (2017). https://doi.org/10.3102/0034654317710096

17. Zhang, L., Nouri, J.: A systematic review of learning computational thinking through scratch in K-9. Comput. Educ. **141**, 103607 (2019). https://doi.org/10.1016/j.compedu.2019.103607

18. Lye, S.Y., Koh, J.H.L.: Review on teaching and learning of computational thinking through programming: what is next for K-12? Comput. Human Behav. **41**, 51–61 (2014). https://doi.org/10.1016/j.chb.2014.09.012

19. Wong, G.K.-W., Cheung, H.-Y.: Exploring children's perceptions of developing twenty-first century skills through computational thinking and programming. Interact. Learn. Environ. **28**, 438–450 (2020). https://doi.org/10.1080/10494820.2018.1534245

20. Maruyama, Y., Kanoh, H., Adachi, K.: A preliminary investigation into parents' concerns about programming education in Japanese primary schools. In: Proceedings of the 14th International Conference on Cognition and Exploratory Learning in Digital Age, pp. 286–290. Springer, Vilamoura (2017)

21. Vivian, R., Falkner, K., Szabo, C.: Can everybody learn to code? In: Proceedings of the 14th Koli Calling International Conference on Computing Education Research, pp. 41–50. ACM, New York (2014). https://doi.org/10.1145/2674683.2674695

22. Kong, R., Wong, G.K.W.: Teachers' perception of professional development in coding education. In: 2017 IEEE 6th International Conference on Teaching, Assessment, and Learning for Engineering (TALE), pp. 377–380. IEEE, Hongkong (2017). https://doi.org/10.1109/TALE.2017.8252365

23. Wong, G.K.W., Cheung, H.Y., Ching, E.C.C., Huen, J.M.H.: School perceptions of coding education in K-12: A large scale quantitative study to inform innovative practices. In: 2015 IEEE International Conference on Teaching, Assessment, and Learning for Engineering (TALE), pp. 5–10. IEEE, Zhuhai (2015). https://doi.org/10.1109/TALE.2015.7386007

24. Humble, N., Mozelius, P., Sällvin, L.: Remaking and reinforcing mathematics and technology with programming – teacher perceptions of challenges, opportunities and tools in K-12 settings. Int. J. Inf. Learn. Technol. **37**, 309–321 (2020). https://doi.org/10.1108/IJILT-02-2020-0021

25. Greifenstein, L., Graßl, I., Fraser, G.: Challenging but full of opportunities: teachers' perspectives on programming in primary schools. 21st Koli Call. Int. Conf. Comput. Educ. Res. 1–10 (2021). https://doi.org/10.1145/3488042.3488048

26. Cohen, L., Manion, L., Morrison, K.: Research methods in education, 8th edn. Routledge, London (2017)

27. Blackstone, A.: Principles of sociological inquiry: qualitative and quantitative methods. Saylor Academy Open Textbooks (2018)
28. Aelieve: website rankings for the best question and answer sites. https://aelieve.com/rankings/websites/category/reference/best-question-and-answer-sites/. Accessed 25 Jan 2023
29. Jiang, H., Qiang, M., Zhang, D., Wen, Q., Xia, B., An, N.: Climate change communication in an online Q&A community: a case study of Quora. Sustainability. **10**, 1509 (2018). https://doi.org/10.3390/su10051509
30. Maity, S.K., Kharb, A., Mukherjee, A.: Language use matters: analysis of the linguistic structure of question texts can characterize answerability in Quora. In: Proceedings of the 11th International Conference on Web and Social Media, ICWSM 2017, pp. 612–615. AAAI, California (2017). https://doi.org/10.48550/arXiv.1703.04001
31. Maity, S.K., Kharb, A., Mukherjee, A.: Analyzing the linguistic structure of question texts to characterize answerability in Quora. IEEE Trans. Comput. Soc. Syst. **5**, 816–828 (2018). https://doi.org/10.1109/TCSS.2018.2859964
32. Zhao, Y., Min, C., Han, X., Deng, S., Wang, H., Li, J.: Listening to the user's voice: a temporal analysis of autism-related questions on Quora. Proc. Assoc. Inf. Sci. Technol. **56**, 513–516 (2019). https://doi.org/10.1002/pra2.57
33. Le, T.D., Dobele, A.R., Robinson, L.J.: Information sought by prospective students from social media electronic word-of-mouth during the university choice process. J. High. Educ. Policy Manag. **41**, 18–34 (2019). https://doi.org/10.1080/1360080X.2018.1538595
34. Blei, D.M.: Probabilistic topic models. Commun. ACM. **55**, 77–84 (2012). https://doi.org/10.1145/2133806.2133826
35. Cao, J., Xia, T., Li, J., Zhang, Y., Tang, S.: A density-based method for adaptive LDA model selection. Neurocomputing **72**, 1775–1781 (2009). https://doi.org/10.1016/J.NEUCOM.2008.06.011
36. Deveaud, R., SanJuan, E., Bellot, P.: accurate and effective latent concept modeling for ad hoc information retrieval. Doc. Numer. **17**, 61–84 (2014). https://doi.org/10.3166/DN.17.1.61-84
37. Pereira, A.I., Barros, L., Mendonça, D., Muris, P.: The relationships among parental anxiety, parenting, and children's anxiety: the mediating effects of children's cognitive vulnerabilities. J. Child Fam. Stud. **23**(2), 399–409 (2013). https://doi.org/10.1007/s10826-013-9767-5
38. Ma, X., Shen, J., Krenn, H.Y., Hu, S., Yuan, J.: A meta-analysis of the relationship between learning outcomes and parental involvement during early childhood education and early elementary education. Educ. Psychol. Rev. **28**(4), 771–801 (2015). https://doi.org/10.1007/s10648-015-9351-1
39. Park, S., Stone, S.I., Holloway, S.D.: School-based parental involvement as a predictor of achievement and school learning environment: an elementary school-level analysis. Child. Youth Serv. Rev. **82**, 195–206 (2017). https://doi.org/10.1016/j.childyouth.2017.09.012
40. Zellman, G.L., Waterman, J.M.: Understanding the impact of parent school involvement on children's educational outcomes. J. Educ. Res. **91**, 370–380 (1998). https://doi.org/10.1080/00220679809597566
41. Boonk, L., Gijselaers, H.J.M., Ritzen, H., Brand-Gruwel, S.: A review of the relationship between parental involvement indicators and academic achievement. Educ. Res. Rev. **24**, 10–30 (2018). https://doi.org/10.1016/j.edurev.2018.02.001
42. Biolsi, C., Craig, S.G., Dhar, A., Sørensen, B.E.: Inequality in public school spending across space and time. Rev. Econ. Dyn. **46**, 244–279 (2022). https://doi.org/10.1016/j.red.2021.09.004
43. Katz, V., Rideout, V.: Learning at home while under-connected (2021)
44. Phillips-Wren, G., Adya, M.: Decision making under stress: the role of information overload, time pressure, complexity, and uncertainty. J. Decis. Syst. **29**, 213–225 (2020). https://doi.org/10.1080/12460125.2020.1768680

45. Ma, Y., Siu, A., Tse, W.S.: The role of high parental expectations in adolescents' academic performance and depression in Hong Kong. J. Fam. Issues. **39**, 2505–2522 (2018). https://doi.org/10.1177/0192513X18755194

46. Kanter Agliata, A., Renk, K.: College students' affective distress: the role of expectation discrepancies and communication. J. Child Fam. Stud. **18**, 396–411 (2009). https://doi.org/10.1007/s10826-008-9244-8

Social Computing for Well-Being
and Inclusion

Model to Design Affective Conversational Interfaces to Support the Mental Health

Juan Apablaza and Sandra Cano(✉) [ID]

School of Informatics Engineering, Pontificia Universidad Católica de Valparaíso, Valparaíso, Chile
sandra.cano@pucv.cl

Abstract. In this study is presented a model to design affective conversation interfaces. Therefore, it is necessary to understand some concepts related with emotions and conversational interfaces. Studies reviewed are more related to UI recommendations for chatbots but not for mental health. In addition, that a conversational interface can be voice or text or both. Also, studies reviewed does not specify a structure of conversation that the dialogue should follow.

In this study is proposed a simple model following the approach of User-Centered Design to design an affective conversation interface for mental health. However, different mental health issues and types of therapy for anxiety and depression were not explored in depth in this study, as this involves a person's state of mind.

Keywords: Mental health · Affective computing · Emotions

1 Introduction

Nowadays, problems with mental health in Chile has increased. Studies show high a highest rate with anxiety and depression [1]. In 2022 World Health Organization (WHO) launched a report [2], which mentions that determinant of mental health are emotions. Negative emotions like anger, fear, disgust and sad can have an impact on the mental health, more when they become frequent and intense, can affect the quality of life of a person inducing depression and anxiety [3]. Therefore, negative emotions are regarded as one of the key risk factors in mental illness. Emotions as fear, anger, sad, disgust are considered as basic emotions.

Affective Computing (AC) studies the development of systems and devices that can recognize, interpret, and simulate emotions [4]. Emotions can be quantified; machines can understand it. Therefore, the recognition of negative emotions could help for the mental health care. AC is an interdisciplinary field spanning computer science, cognitive science, and psychology. Emotions can be manifested through physiological signals, gestures (facial and body) and verbal expressions (speech or voice).

Embodied conversational agents (ECAs) can be defined as "more or less autonomous and intelligent software entities with an embodiment used to communicate with the user" [5]. Therefore, theses interfaces can be to stablish a communication verbal or

© The Author(s), under exclusive license to Springer Nature Switzerland AG 2023
A. Coman and S. Vasilache (Eds.): HCII 2023, LNCS 14026, pp. 183–190, 2023.
https://doi.org/10.1007/978-3-031-35927-9_13

nonverbal, where embodiments can be virtual characters, robots, or bots (i.e. chatbots), and communication from text messages to human communication using modalities as speech, gestures, and facial expressions.

Conversational interfaces have increased due to advances in natural language processing and artificial intelligence. Designing an interaction through a conversation between the user and a bot requires interaction mechanisms through a visual interface. However, studies found are centered in how design conversational interfaces than affective conversational interfaces [6], which is the capacity to recognize, adapt to and render emotion. There are some questions: how could be expressed an emotion through a conversation or how could be adapted a conversation when the bot (agent) detects a negative emotion? Which could be the best option to recognize emotions in real-time?.

Studies reviewed, were not found recommendations or guidelines about how design affective conversational interfaces. From the covid pandemic, these affective conversational interfaces have become of interest to researchers related with mental health such as: Woebot [7], an automated conversational agent to support anxiety and depression. KokoBot [8], is a conversational agent designed to express empathy, which is a mobile application to promote emotional resilience [9]. Kokobot employs a text-based user interface and is available to be used on various messaging platforms (Facebook and Twitter), also employs an unsupervised learning method to automatically retrieve responses. Users can evaluate the quality of each response in a three-pint Likert scale (good, ok, bad). Some conversational interfaces are Wysa [10], an AI-based emotionally intelligent mobile chatbot to promote mental well-being using text-based conversational interface. Wysa responds to emotions that a user expresses through a conversation, which integrates some theories as CBT (Cognitive Behavioral Therapy), dialectical behavior therapy, motivational interviewing and positive behavior support, mindfulness and guided micro-actions and tools to encourage user to build emotional resilience skills. ViviBot [11], is a chatbot designed for young adult cancer than can improve the mental well-being of users. Finally, Tess [12], is an artificial intelligence chatbot for depression, which is based on coping strategies on the emotional needs of the users.

2   Background

2.1   Conversational UX Designing

From the field Human-Computer Interaction (HCI), User eXperience (UX) is used to measure conversational user experiences when interacting with conversational agents. Therefore, designing conversational interfaces require a user-centered design approach [13], which insure that be end product takes user's needs. From UX some studies presented as the book conversational design by Erika Hall [14], which mentions that a *conversation includes the selection of the medium of interaction, the visuals and interactions*. A study by [15] mention that individuals feel attraction in similarity for the design of conversational interfaces, where they found three issues (1) personification, where bot can express and mange different personas; (2) user modeling, or how to make that bot understand people and recognize their key human characteristics, and (3) personalization, how the bot can choose the right persona according to the user and task, for example extroverted people like more and react better to extroverted interfaces [16]. In addition, in the study presented by [15] mention that the design of conversational interfaces must be considered gender identify, therefore the bot should start with an unusual question in interface design such as: *should the computer agent be perceived as male or a female?* It is because in a conversational interface based on text men and women tend to write in different ways [17].

A book titled *Conversational UX design* wrote by Moore and Arar [19], which describes how to model natural conversation. Authors mention: *modeling simple question-answer interactions may be easy but modeling natural conversation activities is more challenging.* The book provides a conceptual framework for designing the UX with conversation user interfaces. Authors focused to understand the principles and patterns must be considered on conversational interfaces. They mention that conversational interfaces are different from graphical user interfaces (GUI), because on a conversational interface, the graphical elements are minimal, and the words are the main interaction with the user. However, questions and answers are simple, so how should the bot respond if the user says "okay" or "oh" or "what do you mean?" or include words culture-specific idioms.

Therefore, the UX designer is related in how design a dialogue between user- machine (computer, tablet, or smartphone) must be organized. A study presented by Gudmundsen et al.[20] explored how to design a mental health chatbot for youths. Therefore, authors applied a user-centered design process following the phases such as: (1) understand the context of use and to detail user needs and requirements, (2) chatbots concepts were explored through sketching and user feedback, (3) a simple prototype chatbot and (4) evaluation of the simple prototype. The UX methods applied were such as interviews with experts (nurses and youths), focus group and user testing. A study by [21] use the Wizard of Oz technique to identify conversation flow stoppers and recommendations for prototype design. This technique allows designers to test a concept on the user without needing to build a high fidelity, expensive prototype on focuses the test on the general idea.

Studies presented can help to design a conversational interface. However, a conversational interface centered for mental health should include emotions. A study presented by Fadhil and Schiavo [22] made a systematic literature review of research works designing for health chatbots. They categorized themes found in four main groups such as: bot-user interaction, bot response, bot development and user experience. The category user experience found features such as: empathy & emotional state, prediction & personalization, user engagement, security & privacy and user demographics. However, in this category studies are few. A study by [23] describe best practices for designing chatbots, where authors created iHelpr a guide self-assessment on the following topics: stress, anxiety & depression, trauma, sleep, and alcohol. Authors mention that there are psychometrically validated instruments used for each topic, which using a chatbot can reduce the amount of time spent answering these questions and the score can be calculated automatically. Authors stablished a list of usability best practices such as: analyze the complexity of language, appropriate delays and typing feedback/indicators need to be in place for each bot utterance, inclusion of humour, use of the user's name, include variance in content as multimedia text, use context awareness, finally it is important to be mindful of culture, are words and humour may mean different things to different cultures.

Therefore, a strong characteristic of conversational interface based on mental health is the ability to detect emotions, some ways could be (1) sentiment analysis (analysis of text), (2) biometric sensors (camera, microphone o physiologic responses).

2.2 Affective Conversational Interfaces (ACI)

In a conversational interface, the flow is not linear. Therefore, the conversation takes different courses according to the answers that influence dialogue. Affective conversational interfaces display behavior that are credible and expressive [6]. So, an ACI must recognize, adapt to, and render emotion. In [6] discuss how can be incorporated into conversational interfaces to make more believable and more expressive, where they mention a recommendation of the W3C for annotating features of emotion. The Emotion Markup Language (EmotionML) can be used to represent emotions, which may contain different < emotion > elements that represent the annotated emotions, and element may include attributes such as: dimension, category, or appraisal.

Emotion recognize includes a set of stages such as: data collection and annotation, learning and optimization. *Data collection* signals are recorded from the user and preprocessed to eliminate noise and other phenomena. These signals can be facial expression, voice and physiological or using a combination of them. However, facial expressions are expressions that a user can imitate without them occurring spontaneously. Jerrita et al. [24] mention that a person does not overtly express emotion through speech, gestures, or facial expression, but a change physiological pattern is inevitable and detectable. Patterns for each signal are different. The *annotation* procedure depends on how the data was collected. The *learning* are machine learning techniques applied to detect emotions. Finally, the optimization to keep only the relevant features.

In conversational interfaces, the user's input is text, where it is used to extract the semantics of the message conveyed and to compute the most adequate system response. The text can carry information about the user's emotional state. This is encoded in the words and grammatical structure. For example, saying "as you wish" is not the same "do what the hell you want". Therefore, there are techniques for extracting affective information form text and can be the process different to the speech and vision signals.

2.3 Emotions

An emotion can be represented as a dimensional model [25], such as: arousal, valence, and dominance. Arousal refers the level of activation. Valence defines whether it is a positive or negative emotion. Dominance is the degree of emotion control.

There are basic emotions which are considered universal in all cultures. Eckman et al. [26] identified six primary emotions in facial expressions such as: anger, fear, joy, sadness, surprise, and disgust. However, other authors consider that there are more than six primary emotions [27].

On another hand, emotions are related with problems of mental health as depression, anxiety. Negative emotions are a general factor of subjective distress, and subsumes a broad range of negative mood states, including fear, anxiety, hostility, scorn and disgust [28]. Therefore, depression is related with mood states such as sadness and loneliness.

A study presented by Zucco et al. [29] used sentiment analysis techniques and affective computing methodologies as tools to assess and monitor the depression. Normally, in affective computing is used hardware and software technology to detect emotional states of a person. Therefore, could refer on multimodal system, which includes measures and variables of physical aspects and physiological signals. Authors proposed an architecture based on multimodal data for depression monitoring. Authors used a architecture known as lambda architecture [30], which consists of three layers: batch layer, is designed to maximize accuracy with no regards of time and consists of a distributed processing system, and second layer called real-time layer, is design to minimize latency; when the batch data output for the same data available, and a third layer called serving layer can be joined with more accurate results.

Systems multimodal can receives several data from different sources, which it is issue typical of multimodal acquisition systems, how to integrate information extracted from different sources into the systems. Therefore, in multimodal systems is commonly used fusion techniques.

3   UX Model for Affective Conversational Interfaces

Studies reviewed were not found models that can support on how to design an affective conversational interface. Figure 1 shows a proposal of a model which follows an approach user-centered design (UCD). Designing a conversational interface, the dialogue established with the user is very important. Therefore, the inclusion of multimedia content, such as images, video, sound, and text, can favor a better understanding in the communication established between machine actors and a human (end user).

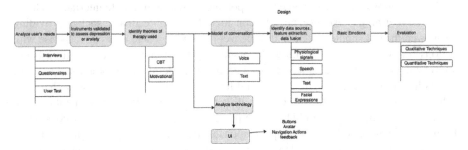

Fig. 1. UX Model for Affective Conversational Interfaces

User-centred design is a philosophy based on the needs and interests of the end user. Norman [13] has defined design principles, such as visibility, feedback, constraints, graphics, consistency, and affordance. Pricilla et al. [31] conducted a study for the design of chatbots for e-commerce systems, which mentioned some basic anatomies to be considered, such as: (1) brand, personality, human involvement, (2) Artificial Intelligence, (3) conversation, (4) rich interactions, (5) context and memory, (6) discovery and installation, (7) engagement methods, and (8) monetization. Therefore, for the design of an affective conversational interface following the user-centered design philosophy, it is important to consider the user's needs and the context of use. Accordingly, chatbot customization can be considered, such as: gender, avatar, conversation style, among others. The dialogue design for a conversational interface is one of the most relevant features, as it is through dialogue that the user will be able to interact with the end user. Therefore, a model of conversation for mental health is proposed (Fig. 2), which allows to recollect information about user, and to generate empathic responses that allow a diagnosis to be made and then apply a specific therapy according to the diagnosis detected.

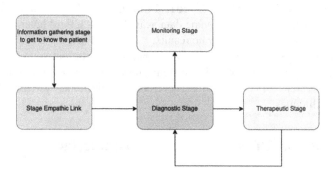

Fig. 2. Model of Conversation based on mental health

Also, on the conversational interface must be considered conversation navigation, where the user must learn how to navigate the space. Moore and Arar [19] proposed basic navigation actions such as capability check, repeat request, conversation close, sequence abort, sequence closer and paraphrase request.

Conversational interfaces can be incorporated on web and mobile interfaces. Therefore, after returning a response, must be considered the user feedback, such as providing an answer, the bot should ask "was this answer helpful?", where user can response with buttons for yes and no. In addition, understanding the user is key to designing better conversational interface, also it includes a group interdisciplinary professional such as: psychologist, programmers, designers, and linguistics. However, the biggest challenge is how to design a natural flow of conversation that does not differentiate that it is a bot.

Therefore, this model should be accompanied by recommendations to be considered for the user interface (UI), for example response types, avatar, rich text with multimedia content (emoticons, gifts, and videos), privacy and security. In a study present by Romero et al. [32] mention that it be necessary use advanced platforms that allow a fluid and rich interaction to have a certain level of intelligence. Therefore, to design the conversation is important three concepts that must be considered such as: intentions, entities, and dialogue [33]. Intentions are actions that the user requires as communicating a problem. Therefore, there are different ways to express the same intention and that the program must consider. Entities are as keywords. Finally, dialogue is programming according to the flow of questions-responses. Normally, the dialogue works like a decision tree that is according to the intentions and entities that it detect in the user's responses [32].

References

1. Salud mental en situación de pandemia. Documento para mesa Social Covid-19 (2020). https://cdn.digital.gob.cl/public_files/Campa%C3%B1as/Corona-Virus/documentos/Salud_Mental_V2.pdf
2. World mental health report: transforming mental health for all. https://www.who.int/publications/i/item/9789240049338
3. Menefee, D.S., Ledoux, T., Johnston, C.A.: The importance of emotional regulation in mental health. Am. J. Lifestyle Med. **16**(1), 28–31 (2022). https://doi.org/10.1177/15598276211049771
4. Picard, R.W.: Affective computing: challenges. Int. J. Hum.-Comput. Stud. **59**(1–2), 55–64 (2003)
5. Isbister, K., Doyle, P.: The blind men and the elephant revisited evaluating interdisciplinary ECA research. In: Ruttkay, Z., Pelachaud, C. (eds.) From brows to trust evaluating embodied conversational agents, pp. 3–26. Springer, Dordrecht, Netherlands (2004)
6. McTear, M., Callejas, Z., Griol, D.: Affective conversational interfaces. In: The Conversational Interface, pp. 329–357. Springer, Cham (2016). https://doi.org/10.1007/978-3-319-32967-3_15
7. Fitzpatrick, K.K., Darcy, A., Vierhile, M.: Delivering cognitive behavior therapy to young adults with symptoms of depression and anxiety using a fully automated conversational agent (WoeBot): a randomized controlled trial. JMIR Ment Health **4**(2), e19 (2017)
8. Morris, R.R., Kouddous, K., Kshirsagar, R., Schueller, S.M.: Towards an artificially empathic conversational agent for mental health applications: system design and user perceptions. J. Med. Internet Res. Jun 26, **20**(6) (2018)
9. Koko (2018). https://itskoko.com/. Accessed 06 Feb 2023
10. Inkster, B., Sarda, S., Subramanian, V.: An empathy-driven, conversational artificial intelligence agent (wysa) for digital mental well-being: real-world data evaluation mixed-methods study. JMIR Mhealth Uhealth **6**(11), e12106 (2018)
11. Moskowitz, J.T., Carrico, A.W., Duncan, L.G., Cohn, M.A., Cheung, E.O., Batchelder, A., et al.: Randomized controlled trial of a positive affect intervention for people newly diagnosed with HIV. J. Consult. Clin. Psychol. **85**(5), 409–423 (2017)
12. Dosovitsky, G., Pineda, B., Jacobson, N., Chang, C., Bunge, E.: Artificial intelligence chatbot for depression: descriptive study of usage. JMIR Form Res. **4**(11):e17065 (2020). https://formative.jmir.org/2020/11/e17065, https://doi.org/10.2196/17065
13. Norman, D.A.: The Design of Everyday Things. Doubleday, New York (1988)
14. Hall, E.: Conversational design. New York, NY USA: A book apart (2018)
15. Candello, H., Pinhanez, C.: Designing conversational interfaces. In: Tutorial XV SImpósio sobre factores humanos em sistemas computacionais. IHC (2016). BDBComp
16. Nass, C., Lee, K.M.: Does computer-synthesized speech manifest personality? Experimental tests of recognition, similarity-attraction, and consistency-attraction. J. Exp. Psychol. Appl. **7**(3), 171 (2001)
17. Newman, M.L. et al.: Gender differences in language use: an analysis of 14,000 text samples. Discourse Proces. 45, 3 (2008), 211–236 (2008)
18. Moore, R.J., Arar, R.: Conversational UX Design: a practitioner's guide to the natural conversation framework. Association for Computing Machinery, New York, NY, USA (2019)
19. Gudmundsen Høiland, C., Følstad, A., Karahasanovic, A.: Hi, can I help? Exploring how to design a mental health chatbot for youths. Hum. Technol. **16**(2), 139–169 (2020). https://ht.csr-pub.eu/index.php/ht/article/view/5
20. Høiland, G., Camilla Følstad, A., Karahasanovic, A.: Hi, can I help?: Exploring how to design a mental health chatbot for youths. Hum. Technol. **16**(2), 139–169 (2020). https://doi.org/10.17011/ht/urn.202008245640

21. Cameron, G., Cameron, D., Megaw, G., et al.: Best practices for designing chatbots in mental healthcare – a case study on iHelpr. https://doi.org/10.14236/ewic/HCI2018.129

22. Fadhil, A., Schiavo, G.: Designing for health chatbots. arXiv (2019). https://doi.org/10.48550/arxiv.1902.09022

23. Cameron, G., et al.: Best practices for designing chatbots in mental healthcare – a case study on iHelpr. In: Bond, R., Mulvenna, M., Wallace, J., Black, M., (Eds.), Proceedings of the 32nd International BCS Human Computer Interaction Conference (HCI-2018) BCS Learning & Development Ltd (2018). https://doi.org/10.14236/ewic/HCI2018.129

24. Jerritta, S., Murugappan, M., Nagarajan, R., Wan, K.: Physiological signals based human emotion recognition: a review. In: 2011 IEEE 7th International Colloquium on Signal Processing and its Applications (CSPA), Penang, Malaysia, 4–6 March 2011, pp 410–415 (2011). https://doi.org/10.1109/CSPA.2011.5759912

25. Russell, J.A.: A circumplex model of affect. J. Pers. Soc. Psychol. **39**, 1161–1178 (1980). https://doi.org/10.1037/h0077714

26. Ekman, P., et al.: Universals and cultural differences in the judgments of facial expressions of emotion. J. Pers. Soc. Psychol. **53**(4), 712–717 (1987). https://doi.org/10.1037/0022-3514.53.4.712

27. Calvo, R.A., D'Mello, S., Gratch, J., Kappas, A.: The Oxford handbook of affective computing. Oxford Library of Psychology (2015)

28. Deepika, V.: Relationship of positive and negative affect with depression in clinical and normal group. Psychol. Behav. Sci. Int. J. **2**(1), 555579 (2017). https://doi.org/10.19080/PBSIJ.2016.02.555579

29. Zucco, C., Calabrese, B., Cannataro, M.: Sentiment analysis and affective computing for depression monitoring. In: 2017 IEEE International Conference on Bioinformatics and Biomedicine (BIBM), Kansas City, MO, USA. pp. 1988–1995 (2017). https://doi.org/10.1109/BIBM.2017.8217966

30. Marz, Warren, J.: Big Data: principles and best practices of scalable realtime data systems. Manning Publications Co., (2015)

31. Pricilla, C., Lestari, D.P., Dharma, D.: Designing interaction for chatbot-based conversational commerce with user-centered design. In: 2018 5th International Conference on Advanced Informatics: Concept Theory and Applications (ICAICTA), Krabi, pp. 244–249 (2018). https://doi.org/10.1109/ICAICTA.2018.8541320

32. Romero, M., y Helena Montoro, C.C.: How to create a psychologist-chatbot. Papeles de psicólogo, vol. 41(1), pp. 27–34 (2020). https://doi.org/10.23923/pap.psicol2020.2920

33. Khan, R., Das, A.: Build Better Chatbots: A Complete Guide to Getting Started with Chatbots, 1st edn. Apress, New York (2017)

Online Dyslexia Intervention via Technology Support; Study in Greece

Ioanna Dimitriadou[✉]

Dyslexia and Learning Difficulties Specialist, PgD, Dimitriadou-Dyslexia Online Office,
Athens, Greece
idimitriadou@yahoo.gr

Abstract. Dyslexia is a learning disorder that affects reading, writing and spelling from the early school years and results from dysfunction of specific areas of the brain responsible for language processing. Children with dyslexia do not develop difficulties with their intelligence, hearing or vision, but experience a big gap between their learning ability and typical in-school standards. In Greece, it is estimated that 5% -10% of children suffer from dyslexia and that their reading and writing difficulties often influence their abilities to speak, listen, write, read and comprehend expression in native language. Therefore, teaching in-person or in class may not always be efficient for those children.

Internationally, distance learning for pupils with dyslexia and learning difficulties has already been developed, while in Greece it began during the period of COVID19, when students were forced to move towards the online education system. The purpose of this work is to analyze the advantages, disadvantages, benefits, and limitations of technological tools for online dyslexia learning. Moreover, the adaptation methods for efficient strategies in distance teaching, so that students with dyslexia can be trained remotely just as well as in face-to-face education, are discussed through different applications and models. Specifically, in this retrospective study, we evaluate 15 children with dyslexia who switched from in-person to online education during the pandemic, and we investigate the efficiency of two interventions. Based on the evidence, online intervention approved to have the same, and in some cases more advanced, results than in-person intervention, and it seems it is here to stay.

Keywords: Dyslexia · Online teaching · Distance learning

1 Introduction

The word dyslexia has Greek origins. It comes from the Greek 'dys', which means something difficult, and from 'lexia', which means words or language. Thus, the word dyslexia describes difficulties with words (1). Dyslexia is a learning disorder that affects reading, writing and spelling from the early school years and results from dysfunction of specific areas of the brain responsible for language processing (1,2). Children with dyslexia do not experience issues with their intelligence, hearing or vision (3,4), but rather a big gap between their learning ability and typical school standards. It is estimated that 5%-10% of Greek children suffer from some kind of dyslexia (5). Their reading and writing difficulties may influence their abilities to speak, listen, write, read and comprehend expression in their native language (6). Furthermore, their difficulties in organization, listening, taking notes, following multi-step directions, time management and making decisions often disorganize and frustrate them (7). Teaching in – person or in class may be a serious problem for those children.

Distance or online education is historically referred to as a way of communication and education between pupils, teachers, schools, mostly performed by exchanging emails (8). Specifically, distance learning is defined as a way of learning without the physical presence of pupils, who are not with their classmates and teachers, but in their own personal space, where they feel more comfortable (8,9). In the last 2 years, COVID-19 forced all students in Greece, including those with dyslexia and learning difficulties, to move to online education system. Since then, distance learning is advancing so that it includes any connected device and embraces a large group of systems and methods. However, because of the multifaceted and complex problems of students with dyslexia, distance education has been assumed to be a great challenge for them.

According to Leon & Diamond (10), when distance learning is carried out through targeted and recognized intervention programs, learning objectives can be achieved in the most meaningful way. Furthermore, according to the International Dyslexia Association (IDA), distance learning improves the way students learn, since they can pay more attention due to fewer distractions than in school classes, they receive more attention from the teacher and are more consistent in their obligations (11). In addition, due to technology, the lesson and the strategies to support students with dyslexia can be more interactive, so the students respond better. In a recent study, professors awarded in online education, claimed that if online teaching is done by experienced teachers and uses a wide range of reached- based strategies, distance education may have the same or even better results than in-person education (12). Even though there were different sources about the valuable help of technology in distance learning in children with dyslexia, a bigger research started by analyzing its advantages and disadvantages in the COVID-19 period. According to British Dyslexia Association (BDA), with the right online equipment and proper and robust organization and management during virtual learning, dyslexic students can be effectively taught online with long-term effects (13).

In addition, there are no existent studies whether distance learning is beneficial for Greek dyslexic students. So, during our retrospective study of over 2 years, we evaluated a number of 15 children with dyslexia who were being educated in–person, and because of covid, their education was transferred online to find out if the online intervention had the same results as in-person education.

We will describe the strategies used and adapted in distance teaching, through different applications and programs and will add arguments that students with dyslexia can be trained remotely just as well as in face-to-face education.

2 Materials–Methods

During this over two-year of Covid-19 period retrospective study, 15 children with dyslexia were evaluated. Those students had already been tested through Greek formal assessment from public institutions and diagnosed with dyslexia or learning difficulties.

For assessing students' reading, writing, and spelling, we have used reach-based programs, such as the Writing Revolution Program (14) for writing, the Assessing Reading: Multiple Measures (15) for reading, and the Curriculum-Based Measurement (CBM-16) for measuring spelling accuracy. Since we worked with Greek students in their native language, we used the basics elements of the assessing programs and the way to measure errors and improvement and quantify the efficiency of each method. Even though students were already tested, we used these kinds of assessments for preparing an innovative online intervention program according to dyslexic students' educational needs. Students were tested during the two years of COVID, at the beginning of intervention and at the end of the first and second year.

2.1 Methods of Writing

The Writing Revolution Program uses the Diagnostic Rubric applied mainly to writing sentences and paragraphs. For sentences, flash cards and lists with words were provided and students were asked to make sentences with them. Then, they got one sentence and have been asked to complete it with because, but and so. Furthermore, students were asked to expand sentences by following questions such as Who? Did what? When? Why? How? and writing a summary sentence. Students were measured on a scale of 0 to 2, where 0 = no response or significant errors, 1 = developing and 2 = proficient.

For a paragraph, based on our students' age, students were provided with a title, asked to complete an outline and then to write down the paragraph. The program uses the Single Paragraph Rubric (Expository), which handles the organization and writing of a paragraph and quantifies the efficiency with categories such as 5 (Exceptional), 4 (Skilled), 3 (Proficient), 2 (Developing) and 1 (Beginning). Finally, we assessed the topic sentence, the detail sentences and the concluding sentence.

2.2 Methods for Spelling

For monitoring dyslexic students' progress in spelling, the Curriculum-Based Measurement (CBM) was used, which is an important tool for measuring students' progress in academic fields such as reading, spelling, math, and writing. It helped to determine if there was a need for further exploration of students' educational needs in spelling or a need for different curriculum or intervention. An unknown paragraph was dictated, according to students' age. For the length of the paragraph, the graded scale from Zaner-Bloser was used (17). For example, for a fourth-grade student, the paragraph contained 45 words, whereas for a sixth-grade student -, the paragraph contained 67 words. The Total Words Written (TWW), the Total Letters Written (TLW), the Words Spelled Correctly (WSC), and the Correct Letter Sequences (CLS) were used as a brief summary for the whole paragraph. However, for spelling accuracy, we counted all the words (TWW-Total Words Written), even the misspelled words, and then the words spelled correctly (WSC). Then, the total number of words written were divided by one hundred and the result multiplied by the words spelled correctly (100: TWW x WSC) (16 -pg.228–229).

2.3   Methods for Reading

For reading assessment, the Assessing Reading: Multiple Measures was used, which is a collection of formal and informal reading assessments for students in Grades K (kindergarten) -12 that measures the strength or weakness of reading development. From the Multiple Measures, the MASI-R Oral Reading Fluency Measures (18) was used and depending on the Curriculum-Based Measurement (CBM), the reading rate and comprehension were measured. A passage was used to calculate the rate correct per minute (wcpm) for the words that were read correctly in 1 min, the rate incorrect per minute (wepm) for the words that were read incorrectly in 1 min, and accuracy, which is the correct words in the first 100 words, at which point we placed a slash in the passage. (15 -pg. 78).

At the end of one minute, the students were instructed to stop reading and the rate correct per minute (wcpm) was calculated by subtracting the number of words incorrect per minute (wepm). For example, if the student read 30 words in one minute and made 2 mistakes, then the result is 28. Then, the wcpm (28) was divided by the number of words in the passage (30) and the result multiplied with the number 100 (28:30x100 = 93% reading accuracy).

According to Brysbaert, M. (19), there are scales for reading speed from 80 words per minute (grade 1) until 195–250 words per minute (grade 12), hence, this scale was followed for quantifying the reading speed per minute. For the reading accuracy, the reading scales, such as Independent Level (95% word accuracy), Instructional Level (90% word accuracy) and Frustration Level (less than 90% word accuracy) (20), were used in order to see the students' reading level. For the first 100 words of the passage, the errors in the words read were subtracted to assess the difficulty of the text. In addition, after students read the passage, they had to answer reading comprehension questions.

2.4   Intervention Method

For the intervention program, assistive technology tools, developed for communication and online working due to Covid were used for teaching. Programs and techniques were enriched so that distance learning for students with difficulties was adequate and equally beneficial.

Fast internet was useful for online teaching to improve the quality of the lessons and for sharing material successfully. Furthermore, a UPS (Uninterruptible Power Supply) was used, in order for the computer to keep running for a short time in case of a power outage.

Greek students with dyslexia attended the intervention program through free and popular communications platforms, such as Skype. Skype is an advanced technology platform through which an online lesson can be successful (21). An external web camera was attached to the computer in order to provide more engagement and better communication with students. Headphones were used to reduce external stimuli and allow for more quiet during the lesson. A digital pen, an electronic writing pen, was used to store and transfer what was written onto the computer. It can be used instead of a mouse and have a USB or Bluetooth connection (22). The document camera was used in order to utilize materials that are normally used in in–person teaching, such as reading books or flashcards with letters or numbers (23).

With the PowerPoint on the PC, different kinds of presentations were created for grammar and spelling explanations, whereas video presentations were created for writing skills. Microsoft Word helped to create and edit/correct documents of dyslexic students with the use of a digital pen. Google Docs helped specialists and students to type together when teaching spelling or writing essays. At this point, spell checkers, specifically designed to help dyslexic students, were used to automatically make corrections of what the students write. Finally, Canva, an online design and publishing tool, was used as a graphic organizer for creating posters for the introduction to grammatical and syntactic rules as well as writing skills.

Globally recognized programs, such as handwriting without tears (24), Landmark School Outreach Program (25), Orton-Gillingham (26, 27), Nancy Bell (28,29), Hochman & Wexler (14), were used for our intervention.

Handwriting without Tears is a research-backed curriculum to evaluate, track and control students' handwriting. The Landmark School Outreach Program is a well-designed program for assessing and processing writing and for teaching basic writing skills for beginner writers. All these programs, well designed for online teaching, were adapted to teach Greek dyslexic students according to Greek educational data. The Orton – Gillingham is a structured, sequential, repetitive, diagnostic teaching approach which is designed to help dyslexic children with their reading, writing, and spelling (26). The OG approach is the gold standard for teaching students with learning difficulties (27, pg.34). The Lindamood-bell program from Nanci Bell is a helpful program which teaches students to build pictures in their minds during reading or listening, to comprehend and express oral language and to spell correctly through imagination (28, 29). The Writing Revolution by Hochman and Wexler, known as the Hochman Method, is a method for building sentences, paragraphs and essays by using the right vocabulary.

Furthermore, e-books were used, which were appropriate for students with dyslexia from different websites, such as upbility.gr, goodsensorylearning.com, tutor-success-academy.teachable.com and readtorewire.com. Upbility.gr is an international website with ready-to use resources fulfilling all the therapeutic and educational needs of children and adolescents with dyslexia and learning difficulties. Goodsensorylearning.com is Dr. Erica Warren's website with many instructional and remedial tools and resources, with digital downloads, for supporting students of all ages. Tutor-success-academy.teachable.com is another website with courses and resources for teachers. Finally, readtorewire.com is a website designed by Michelle Breitenbach, with tips and strategies to engage struggling readers and students with ADHD during online teaching. These programs were implemented because they all had effective elements useful in online teaching and were easy to use and understandable for the students.

3 Results

The 15 pupils examined were 9 boys and 6 girls aged between 7 and 13, where 10 of the pupils were at primary school and 5 at middle school. They were assessed in reading, spelling and writing during online lessons, at the beginning of intervention and at the end of the first and second year of intervention.

For writing, all the pupils were assessed in drafting and writing sentences and paragraphs. For sentences, students from primary school started at the developing stage and managed to reach the proficient stage during their two years of online teaching. Students from middle school also started at the developing stage and reached the proficient stage very quickly.

For paragraphs, all the students from primary school started from the developing stage, except for one student, who started from the proficient stage. 6 of them reached the skilled stage, 3 of them reached the proficient stage and one, the exceptional stage. For middle school students, 2 of them started from the developing stage and reached the skilled stage and the rest started from the skilled stage and reached the exceptional one (Fig. 1).

	AGE	CLASS	WRITING Sentences Baseline	1st year	2nd year	WRITING Paragraph Baseline	1st year	2nd year
1 M	7	PS	developing	developing	proficient	developing	developing	proficient
2 M	8	PS	developing	developing	proficient	developing	developing	proficient
3 M	8	PS	developing	developing	proficient	developing	proficient	skilled
4 M	9	PS	developing	developing	proficient	developing	proficient	skilled
5 M	9	PS	developing	developing	proficient	developing	proficient	skilled
6 M	9	PS	developing	developing	proficient	developing	proficient	skilled
7 F	10	PS	developing	developing	proficient	developing	developing	proficient
8 F	10	PS	developing	developing	proficient	developing	proficient	skilled
9 F	11	PS	developing	developing	proficient	developing	proficient	skilled
10 F	12	PS	developing	developing	proficient	proficient	skilled	exceptional
11 M	12	MS	developing	developing	proficient	developing	proficient	skilled
12 M	12	MS	developing	developing	proficient	developing	proficient	skilled
13 M	13	MS	developing	developing	proficient	skilled	skilled	exceptional
14 F	12	MS	developing	developing	proficient	skilled	skilled	exceptional
15 F	13	MS	developing	developing	proficient	skilled	skilled	exceptional

Fig. 1. The results in writing sentences and paragraphs, in percentage, where M is masculine, F is feminine, PS is primary school and MS is middle school in Baseline, 1st Year and 2nd Year.

In spelling, the primary school students at started from the average of 54,1%, and at the end of the second year, they reached the average of 78,5%. The middle school students started from the average of 71,2% and reached the average of 90,4%.

It is logical that there is a difference between primary and middle school students in spelling because middle school children are older and have worked on spelling more years. For the primary school students, the males started from 56, 16% and reached the average of 78, 83%. The female students started from 51% and reached the average of 78%. The results do not show a huge discrepancy between boys and girls. The girls started with lower percentages in spelling. However, they were more focused, worked systematically and managed to get closer to the boys at the end of the second year. Based on the results, both boys and girls showed a noticeable improvement in spelling during the two years of distance learning (Fig. 2).

	AGE	CLASS	SPELLING %		
			Baseline	1st year	2nd year
1 M		7 PS	53	63	78
2M		8 PS	66	71	85
3M		8 PS	65	70	84
4M		9 PS	50	68	80
5M		9 PS	46	54	71
6M		9 PS	57	62	75
7F		10 PS	52	68	82
8F		10 PS	40	58	72
9F		11 PS	65	76	88
10F		12 PS	47	59	70
11M		12 MS	75	81	90
12M		12 MS	66	72	90
13M		13 MS	74	80	92
14F		12 MS	71	82	90
15F		13 MS	70	82	90

Fig. 2. The results in spelling, in percentage, where M is masculine, F is feminine, PS is primary school and MS is middle school in Baseline, 1st Year and 2nd Year.

For reading, the primary school students started from 70, 3% and reached the average of 91,1% (Fig. 4). The middle school students started from 79, 6% and reached the average of 96%. These differences between the primary and middle school students in reading are normal, as although the high school students worked on more demanding texts, they had fewer difficulties because they had started the intervention program earlier. Although the students' reading intervention program continued remotely, their performance was not affected. Between the primary school boys and girls, there were some differences. The boys started at 63, 16% and reached the average of 92,73%. The girls started from 81% and reached the average of 95, 2%, which meant that girls didn't have any particular difficulties in reading. Results showed that when distance learning began, the boys found the way the intervention was done, interesting and thus, cooperated more, as they didn't feel like leaving the lesson or getting bored (Fig. 3).

	AGE	CLASS	READING %		
			Baseline	1st year	2nd year
1 M		7 PS	62	74	87
2M		8 PS	56	63	80
3M		8 PS	58	72	89
4M		9 PS	64	70	90
5M		9 PS	67	78	91
6M		9 PS	72	80	94
7F		10 PS	79	87	95
8F		10 PS	82	90	94
9F		11 PS	87	94	96
10F		12 PS	76	89	95
11M		12 MS	82	95	96
12M		12 MS	80	95	97
13M		13 MS	77	88	95
14F		12 MS	73	92	95
15F		13 MS	86	96	97

Fig. 3. The results in reading, in percentage, where M is masculine, F is feminine, PS is primary school and MS is middle school in Baseline, 1st Year and 2nd Year.

4 Discussion

Distance learning is defined as a way of learning which is done without the physical presence of students who are not physically with their classmates and teachers, but individually, in their own personal space. (30, 31).

During our retrospective study of over 2 years, despite the relatively small sample of students, we found out that distance education of students with difficulties had several advantages for their learning progress. The assessments were performed one time per year, giving encouraging results and proving that 15 pupils can work equally well in distance as in face-to-face learning.

4.1 The Advantages of Distance Learning

In the teaching process, boys in primary and middle school seemed to be attracted to the online lessons, because they were familiar with computers and thus were more cooperative. According to Growing Up Online-Connected Kids, which was carried out by Kaspersky Lab and the Institute "iconKids&Youth", boys seemed to be more attracted to computers for playing video games, so during the online lesson, they seemed to be familiar with computers, whereas girls seemed to use the computer for socializing and chatting with friends (32). On the other hand, girls seemed to work as well as in the face -to face intervention program, even if they sometimes preferred online lessons because they felt more free, independent, and less stressed (33). All the primary and middle school students had the freedom to follow their own pace, in their own stable and safe environment: something they badly needed. For many, working in the home environment was less stressful, resulting in better performance (33).

Many dyslexic students struggled with attention, time management, and task initiation so as to start and complete assignments independently (34, 35). Students were trained in proper time management, as they needed to be present at a specific time for the lesson. An alarm on their computer was used to remind them that the lesson starts in a few minutes. Then, in order to complete an assignment within a specific time frame, we educated our students to use electronic calendars with reminders about the deadlines. Moreover, online educational games gave the pupils the opportunity to optimize their tasks, to better manage their time and to be more focused. Most parents did not have the appropriate resources and/or information on how to deal with their kids' difficulties and support them successfully. If they so desired, parents had the opportunity to participate in their children's training during the lesson, watching the way the specialist works. Furthermore, for the students who felt unwell, the lesson was either in the morning, as they did not attend school, or some other time in the day, but it was never postponed. When the students had some obligation and could not be punctual, due to the flexibility that an online lesson had, the lesson began few minutes later. During the day, many dyslexic students had questions about their obligations or their work. Because of the online format of the lesson, they could send their questions in the chat, send a video showing what they had done so far and asking for help or make a call. Another major advantage of online teaching was that no one had to worry about commuting and any related delay.

4.2 The Advantages of Skype for Dyslexic Learners

Even though some students did not have computers, they used their tablets, and it turned out that they knew how to handle them very well. Skype was the free platform which was used for connecting with students. Two of them used Microsoft Teams, but during the lessons they found out that Skype was easier to use. With Skype, video and voice messages were recorded and messages were written in the chat for clarification during the lesson. We shared the screen in order to make all the learning materials available to the students, and different and colorful backgrounds engaged them in lively discussions. Also, the choice of color, the possibility to make the screen lighter or darker or to readjust the text and the font size during reading made learning more effective. In addition, online teaching proved to be suitable for many learner types. Auditory learners, for example, could listen to the recorded lesson again and again or go forward or backward until everything was clear. Visual learners could rewind the lesson to see all the interactive videos as many times as they needed (36). Moreover, most of the students learned to work independently, be more careful with their writing, spelling and reading, and be more organized because directions were remote, and they had to learn to work differently from in-person. Another significant advantage of online teaching was that the parents had the opportunity to choose the specialist they wanted for their child, even if specialists lived far away.

4.3 The Disadvantages of Distance Learning

However, there were also disadvantages to distance learning. As there was no personal interaction between the student and the specialist, deadlines were easy to miss. So, students were asked to use post-it notes or notes on their device, where they wrote down their to-do lists and discarded them when they had completed the activities. Another disadvantage was the over-reliance on technology, as sometimes students played computer games during the online classes. For this reason, students were reminded which tools were for learning and which ones for playing, and the games were a reward at the end of the lesson. Some students, especially those in primary school, did not have the appropriate skills for using a computer. They got confused by the keyboard and were slow to write or correct their mistakes, even though in Greek schools, computer lessons are among the basic ones.

According to Minero, (37), teachers should schedule sessions two or three times a week for the first lessons in order to give instructions and allow students to ask questions about online directions. Thus, the three first lessons were devoted to educating children how to use the computer and make lessons easier. Middle grade students did not encounter any issues with computers and had the flexibility to choose their preferred tools during our online lessons, as according to the British Dyslexia Association, it is the first step for learners to feel comfortable.

A lack of concentration or interest during the online course was a key disadvantage. For this reason, it was important that the lesson was designed so as to attract students to participate actively. For example, they took short breaks accompanied by movement exercises or various computer games (mazes, races, painting, collage with pictures), in order to make up stories (38).

Another disadvantage was our students' emotional and social well-being. According to Desautels, L. (39), moments of emotional connection with students are very important, especially during online teaching. Thus, when students were nervous or disappointed with their learning performance, time was given to them to express their feelings and they were advised them to have something familiar near them to relax or draw their feelings on a piece of paper. Finally, Skype sometimes developed technical issues, with sound quality being poor or with occasional dropped connections. In order for the online lesson to be more constructive, educators and students had to buy an extra microphone or web-camera and have a fast internet connection.

5   Conclusion

Many international schools, for example in Saudi Arabia, had established online learning platforms before the pandemic. Nowadays online teaching is starting to become a vision for the future (40). A study at the University of Zagreb, Croatia, confirmed that students with dyslexia and learning disabilities can adapt to any online course, regardless of age and preferences (41). Moreover, some studies in U.S.A suggested that students can experience learning online the same as face-to-face (42, 43). According to other studies, students with dyslexia who had access to technology used different applications to help them with reading, writing and reading comprehension and they performed well (44).

According to several studies, a large percentage of teachers had received less or no training for online teaching. Many of those teachers followed what they were doing in face-to-face lessons during online class, without considering that online teaching needs a different approach (45). Thus, when parents decided to use online teaching for their children, they were hesitant about the quality and effectiveness of lessons. It is proposed that educators teaching children with learning difficulties should have proper training, organization and preparation.

During the two-year Covid period, for the first time, Greek students with dyslexia had an opportunity to attend intervention programs through free platforms (e.g. Skype, Zoom Software, Microsoft Teams, Webex), have easy access to globally recognized programs, such as Orton-Gillingham, Nancy Bell, and Hochman & Wexler, and to use e-learning materials designed for students with dyslexia from different websites, such as upbility.gr and goodsensorylearning.com. In addition, special educators had to acquire computers, digital pens, document cameras and fast internet connections, such as 5G, in order for the distance learning to become interactive and more constructive. All these methods and online materials helped dyslexic students expand and improve their knowledge and enhance their skills. Through the teaching methods and online materials, online teaching proved to be particularly useful, as it was possible for students to process files and for the special educator to adapt the material in an interactive way to successfully cover all educational needs of each dyslexic student.

High quality of technology, innovative digital material adapted to the Greek language, and online training programs can support an online course in the most constructive way and make it no different from a face-to-face lesson. Although many are not yet familiar with new systems that support distance education or remain skeptical about the way teachers and students communicate remotely, there is no doubt that online tutoring has come to our country and is here to stay and evolve.

In Greece, the Covid pandemic was the main reason for distance learning to be implemented more quickly. This form of education clearly differs from its traditional form, but it does not mean that it cannot be made as effective. The necessary prerequisite is educational material which should be properly designed to address the goals of each lesson, the way each student learns, and the limitations that each communication platform has.

More studies, though, need to be done in order to answer questions such as which technological tools are the most appropriate ones and how they can be used efficiently in distance learning and be adjusted to the Greek educational system.

References

1. Reid, G.: Dyslexia: A Practitioner's Handbook, 4th Edition (2009)
2. Shaywitz, S.: Overcoming Dyslexia: a new and complete science-based program for reading problems at any level. 1st ed. First Vintage Books Edition (2003)
3. Brewster, D.C., Kellogg, J.: Dyslexia: Theory and Practice of Remedial Instruction, 2nd Edition. Jossey-Bass (1995)
4. Mattke, A.C.: Guide to Raising a Healthy Child, 1st Edition. Mayo Clinic (2022)
5. Mitsiou, G.L.: Neuropsychological approach and pedagogical intervention of the special learning disorders in all-day school. In the 4th Pan – Hellenic Paediatric Congress (23–10–2004)

6. Libera, S.D.: Dyslexia and learning English as a foreign language: the phonological/orthographic teaching through the multisensory method. Master's Degree programme – Second Cycle (D.M. 270/2004). In European, American and Postcolonial Language and Literature (2015)

7. Warren, E.: Developing Executive Functions & Study Strategies: A comprehensive Approach (2022)

8. University of the People: What is Distance Learning? The Benefits of Studying Remotely. uopeople.edu.gr (2020)

9. Knott, R.: What is Distance Learning? The complete Guide. TechSmith (2020)

10. Leon, A., Diamond, L.: Distance learning for students with word-reading difficulty or dyslexia. CORE: Consortium on Reaching Excellence in Education (2020)

11. International Dyslexia Association: a parent's guide to online virtual schools (2016)

12. Kumar, S., Martin, F., Ritzhaupt, A., Budhrani, K.: Online learning, teaching strategies of award-winning online instructors. Edutopia.org (2020)

13. British Dyslexia Association: dyslexia and virtual teaching and learning. British Dyslexia Association (2020)

14. Hochman, J.C., Wexler, N.: The Writing Revolution: a guide to advancing thinking through writing in all subjects and grades. Jossey-Bass A Wiley Brand (2017)

15. Core Phonological Segmentation Test, from Core Literacy Library: Assessing Reading Multiple Measures, p.78, 2nd Edition (2008)

16. Mather, N., Wendling, B.J., Roberts, R.: Writing assessments and instruction for students with learning disabilities, pp. 228–229. Jossey-Bass Teacher (2009)

17. Barbe, W.B., Wasylyk, T.M., Hackney, C.S., Braun, L.A.: Zaner-Bloser creative growth in handwriting (Grades K-8). Columbus, OH: Zaner-Bloser (1984)

18. Howell, K.W., Hosp, M.K., Hosp, J.L., Morehead, M.K.: MASI-R: multi-level academic skills inventory (2008)

19. Brysbaert, M.: How many words do we read per minute? A review and meta-analysis of reading rate. ResearchGate (2019)

20. Orton-Giullingham Online Academy: Developing Fluency. Orton-Gillingham Online Academy (2020)

21. Bridge.edu: how to teach English online with skype. Bridge.edu/tefl/blog (2020)

22. Techopedia: Digital Pen. Techopedia.com (2022)

23. Breitenbach, M.: Top 5 ways that a document camera can change lessons. Read to Rewire (2021)

24. Cook, M.A., Eisinger, J., Ross, S.M.: Efficacy study on the impact of handwriting without tears. Johns Hopkins (2022)

25. Jennings, T. M., Haynes, C.W.: From Talking to Writing: Strategies for Supporting Narrative and Expository Writing, 2nd Edition (2018)

26. Bishop, H., Katz, D., McHugh, Turner, L.: The Orton-Gillingham Educators' Guide. Whizzimo, LLC (2018)

27. Borkowsky, F.: Falling Students or Failing Schools? Cardboard Box Adventure Publishing, A Parent's Guide to Reading Instruction and Intervention (2018)

28. Bell, N.: Seeing Stars: symbol imagery for phonological and orthographic processing in reading and spelling. 2nd Edition (2013)

29. Bell, N., Bonetti, C.: Talkies/Visualizing and verbalizing for oral language comprehension and expression (2006)

30. University of the People: what is distance learning? The benefits of studying remotely, in uopeople.edu.gr (2020)

31. Webster, M.: What is Distance Learning? University of People, The Benefits of Studying Remotely (2022)

32. IconKids & Youth: Children's Dependency on the Internet Leads to Secrecy, Over-Sharing and Social Withdrawal. In a research for Kaspersky Lab (2016)
33. Fox, A.: What are the advantages and disadvantages that distance education can offer you? Elearning Trends (2020)
34. Gibbons, E.: Ways to support children with dyslexia during distance learning. The Literacy Nest (2020)
35. McIver, M.: Executive functioning: helping students with executive functioning deficits and maximizing learning. Orton-Gillingham Online Academy (2019)
36. Bajraktari, D.: A student's perspective online learning. Study in the USA (2021)
37. Minero, E.: Distance Learning FAQ: solving teachers' and students' common problems. Edutopia.org (2020)
38. Coy, K., Hirschmann, R.: Maximizing student success in online virtual schools in perspectives on language and literacy (2014)
39. Desautels, L.: 4 Strategies to help students feel calm during distance learning. Edutopia.org. (2020)
40. Slicher, A.: Identifying the right partner for K-12 school projects. Colliers: Project Leaders (2022)
41. Zak, D.: Introduction to Programming in C++. Microsoft Visual Studio. An introduction to Programming with C++, Diane Zak. 6th Edition (2012)
42. Johnson, C.C., Walton, J.B., Stricker, L., Elliott, J.B.: Online Teaching in K-12 education in the United States: a systemic review. North Carolina State University. Review of Educational Research (2022)
43. Carter, R.A., Jr., Rice, M., Yang, S., Jackson, H.A.: Self-regulated learning in online learning environments: strategies for remote learning. Inf. Learn. Sci. 121(5/6), 321–329 (2020)
44. Forteza-Forteza, D., Rodriguez-Martin, A., Alvarez-Arregui, E., Menendez Alvarez-Hevia, D.: Inclusion, dyslexia, emotional state and learning: Perceptions of Ibero-American children with dyslexia and their parents during COVID-19 lockdown. Sustainability 13 (5), 2739 (2021)
45. Delgado, P.: Teacher training, the great challenge of online education. Institute for the Future of Education (2020)

LexiaQuest: Exploring the Feasibility of a NLP-Based Screening Tool for Dyslexia Using Virtual Reality

Hoda ElSayed[1,2(✉)], Sara Aldegaither[1], Nashwa AlArifi[1], Aram Monawar[1,2], and Ahmed Hamidalddin[1,2]

[1] College of Engineering, Alfaisal University, Riyadh, Saudi Arabia
helsayed@alfaisal.edu
[2] Game Innovation Lab, Alfaisal University, Riyadh, Saudi Arabia

Abstract. Dyslexia is a specific learning difficulty that affects an individual's ability to process, store, and retrieve information. This learning disorder consequently affects the educational development of children with Dyslexia. Early screening for people with Dyslexia is essential to assist them in the critical stages of learning. This work thus fundamentally contributes toward designing and implementing screening tools for Dyslexia. It is specifically directed at Arabic-speaking children under 5 years of age who are being screened for Dyslexia. The goal is a virtual reality game that implements one or more screening activities engagingly and, at the same time, can indicate the level of the child's interaction in the activity. Our proposed project aims to create a screening for dyslexic preschoolers by creating a Virtual Reality game that is simple and exciting. A set of questions will be presented to the user. In this VR game, we use Natural Language Processing (NLP) to understand, analyze, manipulate, and interpret human languages. Clinicians can use our product, but it is recognized that parents and educators help in the early detection of Dyslexia. In conclusion, the proposed project aims to provide an objective tool for the screening process. Using VR, gamification, and NLP technology, LexiaQuest is designed to be an immersive experience that is fun, engaging, and empowering without the possible stigma of clinical or hospital settings.

Keywords: Dyslexia · Virtual Reality · Arduino Due · Game Development · 3D Unity · Machine Learning · Natural Processing Language

1 Introduction

Language, literacy, and technology are products of design. Language is a social and cognitive system that helps individuals create and express meanings, as rightly noted by Kern in [1]. In designing literacy screening instruments and literacy aids, the design process is aligned with the notion that language's meaning potential 'is only actualized in contexts of use such as in speech, writing thought or gesture' [1]. Many people with specific learning difficulties (SpLDs) depend on technology to augment their cognitive and sensory abilities [2–5]. In recent years, technologies have been designed for dyslexia screening in interventions for children with SpLDs to develop their reading and phonological processing skills [e.g., 2, 5]. The design process for innovative products in the context of SpLDs is often more effective when learners, practitioners, and educators are involved as co-designers, as noted in [6].

For decades, research indicated several reading predictors, including phonological awareness, naming speed, working memory, and morphological awareness [1]. These skills are crucial for the development of reading skills in young children. Struggling with fluent word recognition, spelling, and understanding written text may indicate a learning impairment related to reading, commonly known as *Dyslexia* [13, 16, 17].

Dyslexia is a language-based learning difficulty not associated with poor visual skills, cognitive skills, or intelligence. Besides having difficulty with decoding, fluency, and spelling, these children's vocabulary, reading comprehension, and background knowledge are usually compromised and therefore affect their school success [7].

Oral and written assessments have traditionally been conducted to screen, assess, and diagnose *Dyslexia*. Where this type of testing reveals language-related information, it fails to provide details related to physiological changes and cognitive skills underlying such difficulties, such as eye movement and arousal levels. However, recent research on language development and related disabilities utilized Magnetic Resonance Imaging (MRI), functional MRI, Electroencephalogram (EEG), and, most importantly, eye-tracking [8–10].

Previous findings in eye-tracking research confirm links between eye movement patterns and reading difficulties in Arabic and have demonstrated the invaluable information eye-tracking can offer therapists and educators in tailoring intervention programs to address a child's specific needs [5].

Similar to other languages, individuals with dyslexia in Arabic have poor phonological awareness skills and working memory compared to typical readers [11]. For this reason, this paper proposes LexiaQuest, a screening tool that incorporates these parameters and other information collected from the eye-tracking device.

2 Related Work

Although Dyslexia is a lifelong condition, remedial and adaptive therapy can help to manage it. Most of the existing traditional detection techniques for this learning disorder are mostly paper-and-pencil methods, which are often tedious and demanding, with high dropout rates. A high rate of dyslexic students who get traditional speech therapy withdraw because of how tedious it is.

It is critical to creating new intervention strategies that can support dyslexic students more easily and with greater cooperation from them. Since Virtual Reality (VR) technology incorporates immersion, presence, interaction, and conceptual transformation, it can effectively participate in building an interactive solution that detects this problem early. FORDYSVAR [15] is a Virtual Reality game that contributes to the social isolation of dyslexic students and improves their way of learning using Oculus VR headset with the Android Operating System and Arsoft [15] to create the VR application. Although the game was made in Spain, it wasn't specified whether they used Spanish or English.

Similar to this solution, other tools were developed to help in dyslexia detection [15], but the gap remains in finding a reliable solution designed to detect Arabic language defects to help the dyslexic Arabic audience. Another gap is that FORDYSVAR product is adapted for ages 13 to 16.

The best way to advance the adoption of new assistive technology platforms that support the Arabic language in content creation (such as Virtual reality applications) is to get these applications to individuals with disabilities, special educators, clinicians, caregivers, and other stakeholders. Assistive technology (AT) and Virtual Reality are diverse fields that could fulfill various needs and fits in this context. Our target population's strengths and needs are unique to each individual, and Virtual reality tools are another means of supporting people with SpLDs and the clinicians who serve them. Additionally, this work aims to target preschoolers in its ease-of-use level.

Screening is a medical test performed to detect a potential health disorder when no symptoms exist [2]. The screening and remediation of learning difficulties with augmented and virtual reality has been relatively under-researched. [1] The aim of this proposed project is to design and develop scalable, robust, and relatively low-cost screening system for Dyslexia in the Arabic language that uses mixed reality platforms for screening of young populations (e.g. preschoolers). Involving mixed reality allows for the gamification of screening and intervention, reproducibility, and automation. In addition, data collected from the screenings will provide therapists and educators with insight into the Arabic-speaking child's specific difficulties and, therefore, help them design a more individualized treatment plan. Moreover, this project aims to make the screening process less daunting. By using VR technology and gamification, this paper proposes an immersive experience that is fun, engaging, and empowering without the possible stigma of clinical or hospital settings.

LexiaQuest is a game project that targets Arab speaking children with Dyslexia for early detection of dyslexia symptoms unrelated to regular pronunciation issues. It is an entertaining VR-based experience, used in the screening process and can be used by clinicians, parents, and school faculty for remote monitoring.

The process starts when a teacher or caregiver escorts a child to a resource room or vacant classroom for the screening. The child will then be given a summary of the mission and a choice of a crown and cape to wear; These tangible items are designed to help the child's smooth transition to the immersive world. To ensure that the child is immersed and has passed the calibration stage, the child will be given a set of simple one-step instructions (i.e., pre-screening phase) such that if the child answers 10/15 or more of the questions correctly, the game progresses and moves on to the screening. On the other hand, if the child correctly answers 7/15 or less, the game ends and the dyslexia screening is conducted manually. During the user testing phase, the children's performance in the VR experience will be compared to their performance in the manual screening for validity and to ensure the experience is not distracting them from the assigned tasks. Once the experience is concluded, a simple Likert scale composed of 3 faces (i.e. happy, neutral, and sad) will be administered to indicate the level of entertainment and difficulty of the screening experience. The child will then be rewarded for the hard work related to the theme of the experience - a gold coin sticker or snack and finally, escorted back to the classroom or caregiver.

2.1 Objectives

Since a higher rate of Arabic people are diagnosed with Dyslexia in the past few years [18], creating a product that serves them became necessary. While most research work overlooks the solution to identifying and treating Dyslexia at an early age, it is undoubtedly under-searched to target Arabic language disability at preschool level for early detection and treatment.

The key goal of this work is to develop a Virtual Reality (VR) game that can identify whether a person has Dyslexia or not.

For the software part, the objective is to create the content for the screening regarding the Arabic words and make every aspect easy for the user at a young age. Our work aims to create three levels for the game to engage the user with a wonderfully magical storyline that ultimately captivates young children but also serves the medical purpose of early detecting dyslexic problems with the Arabic language.

In addition, our game design for the VR scene, including background, objects and word view should be attractive to users but not distracting. As part of this project, medical guidance was involved in designing components that fit into the medical context of Dyslexia. A Best practice approach focused on less distracting background colors that would ideally be a light creamy color (e.g., light yellow) and the text should be a dark color (e.g., black) for better view for dyslexic users.

Background Soundtrack: The background soundtrack must be very soft nature sound effects. The sound effects are planned to be in a soft tone to avoid distracting the users with Dyslexia. Using the sound of streaming water or the sound of chirping birds in the background can be utilized for a better immersive experience.

2.2 Storyline

The game's cut-scene story starts with a child being a prince or princess of a village with sick and starving people. He/she is assigned a mission to locate the cave of wonders and find the treasure chest. They are introduced to their companion- a talking bird- that helps give them instructions and guides them on their path. Following the pre-screening phase, the child proceeds to the first stage.

Level 1 (Color identification to screen working memory skills): The child is given rows of colored circles and is instructed to say as many as he/she can in order within a minute. Reading off the code unlocks the treasure map. This will give the child a preview of the remaining stages to overcome.

Level 2 (First X ~ Sound manipulation to screen phonological awareness): The child is given a list of hung pictures with birds or words and verbal instructions. He/she is instructed to manipulate the different sounds in words. Upon completion, the birds drop a key needed to open the treasure chest.

Level 3 (Second X ~ Sight word reading to screen early reading skills): The child is given real and nonsense words to read of different wooden signs. These signs will be used to make a wooden cart used to carry the treasure back to the village.

Finish line cave of wonders: Equipped with the treasure map, the key, and the cart, the child finds the cave and the treasure and returns to the village. He is praised and thanked by the villagers- adults and peers. Then he is instructed by the bird companion to remove the headset.

3 Methodology

A. Game Methodology

In several academic domains, including medical and military training, serious games (SGs) are increasingly often utilized as a technique to promote learning. SGs are said to make students feel empowered and entertained while studying. Additionally, they assist the growth of imagination, intelligence, emotional strength, and personality stability. [12]. The proposed project in this paper uses virtual reality to fully support medical objectives in an entertaining environment.

The game depends on the Unity engine that supports a variety of platforms, including mobiles and virtual reality. The programming languages used are C#, Blender and Spine2d may also be used for creating the design 2d/3d models of the game and animations,

Data storage and Machine learning part, it uses a ready audio dataset from an online digital library to feed our agent with data that identifies how a dyslexic person reads or views words and it will be connected to the unity project through the PhpMyAdmin portal.

B. Headset Methodology

VR headsets are designed to allow users to consume VR content by providing an immersive, three-dimensional experience using a head-mounted device that includes a display screen, stereo sound, sensors, and compatible controllers to deliver an immersive and interactive audiovisual experience. When users put on a VR headset, they can no longer see the real world around them, but instead only see VR content projected on the display screen such as 360-degree videos and VR games, workspaces, or meeting rooms for other activities. Some basic components of VR Headsets including the lenses and screen setup make up the bulk of the VR headset's hardware. There are stereoscopic lenses positioned between the screen and eyes that distort the image into appearing as three-dimensional objects [12] where two images are passed through the lens, one for each eye. Additionally, images in VR headsets appear to move side-to-side to recreate a 360-degree experience which is achieved by subtly moving the display content in response to head-tracking data and the game software is rendered by the Unity engine.

Sensors and modules (with extra electronic circuitry along with sensors) are electronic devices that detect and respond to some type of input from the physical environment [12].

3.1 Natural Language Processing

NLP stands for Natural Language Processing, a part of Computer Science, Human Language, and Artificial Intelligence. Computers use this technology to understand, analyze, manipulate, and interpret human languages. NLP helps machines interact with humans in their language and perform related tasks like reading text, understanding speech and interpreting it in a good format. Nowadays machines can analyze more data rather than humans efficiently. NLP is increasingly demanded as plenty of unstructured data is generated from various fields, such as the medical and pharma industry, and social media like Facebook, Instagram, etc., [14].

3.2 Speech Classification

The speech recognition software breaks the speech down into bits it can interpret, converts it into a digital format, and analyzes the pieces of content. It then makes determinations based on previous data and common speech patterns, hypothesizing what the user is saying [14].

Speech processing has emerged as one of the important application areas of digital signal processing using five key steps, as illustrated in Fig. 1. Various fields for research in speech processing are speech recognition, speaker recognition, speech synthesis, speech coding etc. Speech recognition is the process of automatically recognizing the spoken words of a person based on information contained in speech signals [14].

Speech recognition is used to recognize the word answers or the input that the user provides. Our dataset includes audio files of different voices of dyslexic and non-dyslexic children who provide all answers to each question in the game. These audio files are synthesized and slightly manipulated to get a larger set of data and to get accurate results. Our dataset should undergo preprocessing to ensure the quality and accuracy. The audio files are then inserted and added into our Unity project. Our Unity project will be able to detect each audio file and compare it to the appointed answer of the specified question. Detection is guaranteed to be accurate because our program (in the unity project) will check or detect the wavelength of each audio file and compare it to the chosen answer.

Fig. 1. Basic Model of the Speech recognition system

Matlab and machine learning can be used to classify sound for the purpose of screening dyslexia in children. By analyzing speech patterns and identifying potential indicators of dyslexia, machine learning models can identify children who may be at risk for the disorder. Using a CNN trained on a dataset of children's speech, the model can classify sound samples and detect patterns that may indicate dyslexia. This could be especially valuable in early childhood screening programs, where early detection and intervention can help improve outcomes for dyslexic children. However, as with any machine learning application, the accuracy of the model will depend on the quality and size of the training data, as well as the design of the network architecture and other hyperparameters. By using Matlab to develop and optimize the machine learning model, researchers and developers can help improve the accuracy and effectiveness of dyslexia screening programs for children.

4 Results

The results retrieved from this work are split into multiple stages, as illustrated in Fig. 2 below. This process gets refined and enhanced with every additional user and medical input according to the game requirements. The process starts by collecting audio data for letters, numbers, words, and color pronunciation for children below five years old who are native Arabic speakers. One of the challenges faced is finding audio data for children in the referred-to age group diagnosed with dyslexia and Arabic speakers. As a result, the data was collected for children not confirming any medical conditions that may affect their pronunciation and focus or cause any distraction or voice interruption. The data was then collected manually due to the lack of existing libraries that fit LexiaQuest's requirements. However, the data were modified to generate additional impactful data that may help in the analysis process and medical screening and to grow the existing samples' size. Accordingly, the data collected underwent some modifications, including speed changing, adding noise, and adding distracting factors to scale up for the machine learning stage. In the machine learning stage, speech recognition was used to distinguish spoken words with natural language processing techniques. During this stage, many features were considered including (1) *time period*, for how long the child needs to answer within one cycle of vibrations, (2) *amplitude*, for the sound intensity measured in decibels (dB) and (3) *frequency*, measured in Hertz (Hz) representing number of sound vibrations happening per second.

Fig. 2. LexiaQuest development lifecycle and Implementation stages

After extensive iteration on the framework for the machine learning-based solution that can help identify dyslexia at an early-stage, a comprehensive pipeline has been put forth. This allows for a plug-and-play and expandable solution. Furthermore, the results of each stage have been displayed. The pipeline for applying machine learning methods to develop the tool for dyslexia detection based on voice recording in Arabic-speaking children can be outlined as follows:

1. *Data Collection:* The first step is to collect voice recordings from a large number of Arabic-speaking children between the ages of 2 and 5 years who have been diagnosed with dyslexia and those who don't have dyslexia. The recordings should capture the child reading a list of standard Arabic words, which will serve as the basis for the model to identify dyslexia. To date, the initial data sample has been collected for pre-processing from children within the target range and imported into MATLAB as shown in Fig. 3.

2. *Data Pre-processing:* Once the voice recordings have been collected, they need to be pre-processed to remove background noise, normalize audio levels. In this experiment, we recorded 23 voice samples of children aged between 2 to 5 years old saying

30 pre-determined words. Afterwards, using MATLAB, spectrograms were generated for each sample as seen in Fig. 4. It is evident that the spectrograms exhibit considerable similarity to each other and can be used for feature extraction.

3. *Feature Extraction:* In this step, the features were extracted from the pre-processed audio data. The features may include frequency, intensity, duration, and other parameters that are relevant to speech processing as addressed in this paper earlier.

4. *Model Training:* After extracting the features, a machine learning model was trained to classify the voice recordings into two categories: dyslexic and non-dyslexic. This is done by feeding the model with pre-processed data and the corresponding labels and thereby training it to learn the patterns that distinguish the two groups.

5. *Model Evaluation:* an evaluation is conducted after training to ensure accuracy and reliability. The performance metrics vary and include sensitivity, specificity, and complexity.

6. *Deployment:* once the model is tested and validated, it's deployed as a tool for dyslexia screening in Arabic-speaking children. After the Model evaluation, the next step is to integrate it with the VR game.

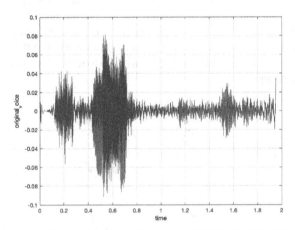

Fig. 3. Sample of the Voice Recording from a Child Saying "Red" in Arabic

The game is developed using unity to reflect the key requirements of testing letters, numbers, and words and examining a child's memory. The game was built with a connection to a VR Oculus Meta headset to help children with dyslexia get isolated from surrounding distractions while being in play mode. The game is then tested with dyslexic and non-dyslexic users to ensure accurate results.

The game was designed to reflect a cognitive and cultural storyline flow followed by the screening questions shown in Fig. 5. Figure 5 shows part of the game prototype built using unity on Oculus Meta Quest headset platform. In part (a), the child is asked to start the game and then pick a character that matches his/her gender from part (b) to increase the user experience and attachment to game characters. In part (c), the game level shows a letter or number and asks for the user's verbal input during a specific duration to check on the user's input accuracy and pronunciation. In part (d), the game level scales up by

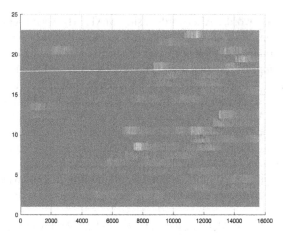

Fig. 4. Spectrogram of the Voice Sample of the Word "Red"

displaying words for the child to read and say aloud. In part (e), shapes are shown, and questions about colors are asked to increase the distraction level for a more accurate diagnosis. In parts (f) and (g), the child is given a picture for a few seconds then he/she is asked to color it after it disappears within a specific duration to test their memory skills. In later stages, game commands will be given in audio to test a child's mental perception and answer processing.

Fig. 5. LexiaQuest game interface and levels on Unity

The game introduces one of two main characters that assist the child throughout the journey to find the right answers and reach more goals. Given that the target age group for dyslexia screening was three to five years, the assistive characters were designed as birds to be more fun and interactive for the child. The gameplay relies on audio interactions, and time constraints add a layer of challenge to get the player's answer for dyslexic assessment. LexiaQuest uses instructing interaction mode for pressing buttons, selecting options from menus, and giving voice commands, in addition to a conversing

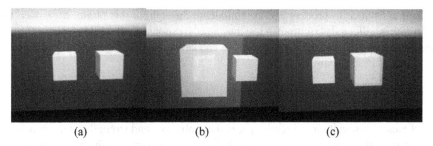

(a)   (b)   (c)

Fig. 6. Cubes size varies based on sound intensity of audio files or sound at run time on Unity

interaction mode for users' verbal inputs to the game. In addition, it uses controller interaction mode with Oculus Meta's arm controllers for in-game choices.

To capture and record the user's voice and store it in the Unity project, LexiaQuest used FMOD sound system engine tool for video games to play and mix various sounds. FMOD was used for many popular games like Fall guys, The walking dead, and Roblox. For our project, it's meant to use it for recording a player's voice. The most critical part in accomplishing this is to integrate both FMOD and Unity. After downloading both engines, our game tests its compatibility on the unity project by adding a cube, a GameObject for the script of the microphone. The player inputs a verbal command which is recorded and stored in the backend database for the machine learning analysis phase.

FMODUnity library facilitates controlling the audio file using different properties (e.g. playPause, latency, device Index, connectedDevices, sampleRate, numofDrivers and channelNum). In addition, FMOD objects could control sound, channel, channel-group, createsound index, and SpeakerMode. Moreover, the cube's size responds to both the recorded file's sound intensity and the player's sound at runtime, as seen in Fig. 6. In *part (a),* two cubes are shown. *Part (b)* shows how the left cube's size corresponds to the sound intensity of the recorded audio file saved in Unity's assets folder, whereas in *part (c)*, the cube size is sensitive to the real-time sound intensity received through the microphone. Therefore, the input can be extracted from the player at runtime and classified into valid or invalid input. This phase requires using a microphone, so the C# code checks the validity of the microphone connection then FMOD sound object is created to hold the player's voice and record it. Finally, it checks if the button is pressed to play or pause so we can play the sound object through the channel.

As the children answer more questions correctly, they can progress to the levels and finish more missions. The total score is then calculated and evaluated for dyslexia screening. The game will be accessible by physicians and parents for close monitoring in the coming implementation stage. Meanwhile, the data collection stage is limited due to the custom requirements for the game to function properly and the low amount of audio samples provided by Arab-speaking children. Another limitation resides in collecting data for children who are diagnosed with dyslexia instead of generating extended levels of audio data from intact children with distortions and interruptions. To resolve that and to test LexiaQuest more precisely, we intend to involve dyslexic and non-dyslexic children groups aged 3 to 5 years in the assessment and screening stages with the required medical assistance to process and communicate throughout this phase. Moreover, the audio data is collected at runtime to test the game's response to the child's voice intensity. However, the answer's audio file extraction and saving for machine learning analysis is still under implementation.

4.1 Social VR

LexiaQuest is a social virtual reality game that enhances and strengthens the way users interact with their assisting caregivers. Assisting caregivers are the people who may assist the young users throughout using our product. Users are very young children who will need help from their parents, guardians, clinicians, psychological clinicians, or medical physicians. Users will have improved their social skills by merely talking and connecting with their assisting caregiver. Although social skills may be limited to socializing only with the user's assisting caregiver, it is guaranteed to make the utmost difference, as children under five may not feel comfortable socializing with strangers. Future iterations of the game will consider embedding social VR in the context of assisting the users during the screening process.

5 Conclusion

The project aims to provide an immersive and objective screening process for Dyslexia in Arabic utilizing Virtual Reality (VR) technology. The child's experience will be the gamification of paper-based screening processes used manually in private practices, schools, and hospitals by educators and speech-language pathologists. This research develops a robust and engaging journey for children that could be implemented in schools and other public spaces with relatively low overhead and a VR headset using a gaming engine. Children will interact with prompts by reading words and playing with sound-based guidance, and their responses will be recorded, scored, and benchmarked to valid pronunciation using machine learning classifiers. The value added with VR lies in the possibilities- of reducing stigma & providing opportunities for capturing objective metrics in screening- visualizing words, numbers, and letters and testing the memory skills in an immersed and gamified experience. This paper discusses LexiaQuest implementation stages and the resulting interface, highlighting the significant role that machine learning, NLP, and game mechanics play in enhancing the medical and educational fields and young children developing dyslexia symptoms early.

Acknowledgement. We sincerely thank Dr. Mariam Ahmad Elsayed, MD, MSc, PhD, for providing the necessary medical guidance in the early design stage of our Virtual Reality game project. Her thorough feedback helped in improving the game interface taking into consideration the design principles that match the Dyslexic measures to help reduce the distraction level for young preschoolers who suffer from the developmental disorder for early detection purposes. This work has been done under CoE's game innovation lab and ORI and dimensions' game innovation center's support at Alfaisal university in collaboration with the CoCreate program for user research, winning Ithra's award in 2021. For that, we extend our thanks to the game center for granting us access to tools and resources and for helping our research to grow and we thank all other involved entities for the magnificent support. The authors acknowledge the support of Dr.

Mohamed A. Bahloul and Dr. Areej Al-Wabil in reviewing the draft of this manuscript and the contribution of speech pathologist, Rogaiyah M. Hamidaddin, in the co-design process for user research in the LexiaQuest project.

References

1. Kern, R.: Language, Literacy, and Technology. Cambridge University Press, United Kingdom (2015)
2. Alkhashrami, S., Alghamdi, H., Al-Wabil, A.: Human factors in the design of Arabic-language interfaces in assistive technologies for learning difficulties, Human-Computer Interaction. Advanced Interaction Modalities and Techniques, pp. 362–369 (2014)
3. Al-Edaily, A., Al-Wabil, A., Al-Ohali, Y.: Dyslexia explorer: a screening system for learning difficulties in the Arabic language using eye tracking. In: Holzinger, A., Ziefle, M., Hitz, M., Debevc, M. (eds.) SouthCHI 2013. LNCS, vol. 7946, pp. 831–834. Springer, Heidelberg (2013). https://doi.org/10.1007/978-3-642-39062-3_63
4. Al-Edaily, A., Al-Wabil, A., Al-Ohali, Y.: Interactive screening for learning difficulties: analyzing visual patterns of reading Arabic scripts with eye tracking. In: Stephanidis, C. (ed.) HCI 2013. CCIS, vol. 374, pp. 3–7. Springer, Heidelberg (2013). https://doi.org/10.1007/978-3-642-39476-8_1
5. Al-Wabil, A., Al-Sheaha, M.: Towards an interactive screening program for developmental Dyslexia: eye movement analysis in reading Arabic texts. In: Miesenberger, K., Klaus, J., Zagler, W., Karshmer, A. (eds.) ICCHP 2010. LNCS, vol. 6180, pp. 25–32. Springer, Heidelberg (2010). https://doi.org/10.1007/978-3-642-14100-3_5
6. AlSabban, M., Alorij, S., Alshamrani, G., Alharbi, O.: Humanistic co-design for specific learning difficulties using scenario-based personas: tangible Arabic alphabet blocks for Dyslexia. In: Stephanidis, C., Antona, M., Gao, Q., Zhou, J. (eds.) HCII 2020. LNCS, vol. 12426, pp. 24–33. Springer, Cham (2020). https://doi.org/10.1007/978-3-030-60149-2_3
7. Gamit, M.R., Dhameliya, K., Bhatt, N.S.: Classification techniques for speech recognition: a review. SemanticScholar (2015)
8. El-Baz, A., Casanova, M., Gimel'farb, G., Mott, M., Switala, A.: An MRI-based diagnostic framework for early diagnosis of dyslexia. Int. J. Comput. Assisted Radiol. Surg. 3, pp. 181–189 (2008)
9. Elnakib, A., Soliman, A., Nitzken, M., Casanova, M.F., Gimel'farb, G., El-Baz, A.: Magnetic resonance imaging findings for dyslexia: a review. J. Biomed. Nanotechnol. 10(10), 2778–2805 (2014)
10. Asvestopoulou, T., et al.: Dyslexml: screening tool for dyslexia using machine learning. arXiv preprint arXiv:1903.06274 (2019)
11. Abu-Rabia, S.: Dyslexia in Arabic. In: Smyth, I., Everatt, J. Salter, R., (Eds.), International Book of Dyslexia: A Cross-Language Comparison and Practice Guide, pp. 31–38. John Wiley & Sons, West Sussex (2004)
12. Al-Wabil, A., Meldah, E., Al-Suwaidan, A., AlZahrani, A.: Designing educational games for children with specific learning difficulties: insights from involving children and practitioners. In: Fifth International Multi-Conference on Computing in the Global Information Technology, pp. 195–198, IEEE (2010)
13. Global Entertainment & Media Outlook 2022–2026: TMT, PwC. https://www.pwc.com/gx/en/industries/tmt/media/outlook.html. Accessed 28 Nov 2022
14. Natural language processing step by step guide: NLP for data scientists. https://www.analyticsvidhya.com/blog/2021/05/natural-language-processing-step-by-step-guide/. Accessed 26 May 2021

15. Toma, R., Alcala, D.: FORDYSVAR EBOOK: Best practices and technological resources for students with Specific Learning Difficulties (SpLDs) (2022)
16. Proud to be an advocate for dyslexia. Arab News. https://www.arabnews.com/node/1852631/saudi-arabia. Accessed 04 Dec 2022
17. Alsswey, A., El-Qirem, F.A., Tarawneh, M.: Dyslexic Arabic students in the Arab Countries: a systematic review of assistive technology progress and recommendations. Int. J. Early Childhood Special Educ. 13(1) (2021)
18. Layes, S., Lalonde, R., Rebai, M.: Effects of an adaptive phonological training program on reading and phonological processing skills in Arabic-speaking children with dyslexia. Read. Writ. Q. 35(2), 103–117 (2019)

Immersion and Presence in Virtual Reality Applications for Physical Therapy and Upper Limb Rehabilitation

Mohamed Fayed[1], Faisal Almadi[1], Meteb Almadi[1], Rayan Taha Almudawah[1,2], Faisal Alotaibi[1,2], Abdullah Adam[1,2], Faisal Aldubaib[2], Alya Alshaikh[1], Layan Alhamad[1], and Hoda ElSayed[1,3(✉)]

[1] Software Engineering Department, Alfaisal University, Riyadh, Saudi Arabia
{mafayed,fmadi,malmadi,ralmudawah,fzalotaibi,aadam,alyalshaikh,
lalhamad,helsayed}@alfaisal.edu
[2] UpDown Game Studio, Riyadh, Saudi Arabia
faldubaib@alfaisal.edu
[3] Game Innovation Lab, College of Engineering, Riyadh, Saudi Arabia

Abstract. Human factors in the design of physical therapy virtual reality (VR) applications are important to consider in the creation of high-fidelity applications. The human factors contributing to the design concepts of immersion and presence in VR are inadequately understood. The aim of this study is to introduce a novel framework to design for immersion and presence in VR applications in the context of physical therapy in the virtual realm. The framework includes the dimension of self-embodiment for presence and realism for immersion. We present a use case of upper-limb therapy to demonstrate the framework's utility in the design process of a gamified VR physical rehabilitation application. Design implications are discussed.

Keywords: VR · Upper Limb Therapy · Occupational Therapy · Exergames · Virtual Environments (VE) · Virtual Rehabilitation · Immersive VR

1 Introduction

A proliferation of research in the design of virtual reality (VR) applications for rehabilitation has occurred during the past decade as noted in [1] and [2]. While applications range from immersive games to real-world simulations, little attention has been given to the human factors in the design for immersion and presence in virtual environments that focus on physical therapy (PT) and rehabilitation. The two concepts are particularly important in physical rehabilitation of upper-limbs or lower-limbs which require aligning the individual's attention with the limb involved in the rehabilitation session.

The notion of self-embodiment in VR brings forward design opportunities to support one's presence in the virtual environment as noted by recent studies in [3–11]. The concept of completeness has been explored to understand the tradeoffs in the design of the represented body segments, ranging from partial rendering (such as showing limbs only) to full body avatars in the virtual environment. The kinematic structures for limbs are essential for motion visualization and visual perception of objects within the visual field in the virtual realm.

In addition, the concept of realism has been extensively studied to help designers strike a balance between the degree of resemblance of the avatar (or the virtual segment being visualized in VR) to the real world and the constraints related to hardware, connectivity and/or computational complexity. The third concept of synchrony sheds light on the sensory feedback that needs to be considered to communicate the natural body behavior (e.g. when a person is grasping and twisting an object, the rotating motion of the object is displayed as "visual feedback" for the motion that is occurring in the virtual space, and the sound is audible in alignment with the actions "auditory feedback").

Although the importance of designing for optimal social presence in VR experiences has been well established in the literature as highlighted in [11, 12] and noted in [13], design guidelines for the context of PT and rehabilitation are inadequately understood. The question of how we might mimic realistic social presence in VR applications that are designed for PT and rehabilitation remains to be explored. In this paper, we address this gap in research by reviewing the concepts of social presence and immersion in the context of VR for physical and occupational therapy and rehabilitation, proposing a framework for social presence in such systems and reflecting on the framework in the context of a use case for upper-limb physical therapy in the VR game titled, "Mo3awen" which was collaboratively designed and developed by the co-authors of this publication[1].

The remainder of this paper is structured as follows: Sect. 2 presents an overview of the research and products that have been developed in the scope of VR for physical and occupational therapy (OT). Section 3 starts by presenting the framework and elaborates on the conceptual design of the VR for PT game, Mo3awen as a use case. Section 4 describes the design considerations for immersion and presence in VR applications for PT and OT. We conclude in Sect. 5 with a summary of findings and design implications, as well as an overview of areas for further exploratory research.

2   Related Work

This work is informed by prior work on interaction techniques in VR to attract and sustain users' attention with the aim to ensure that presence is established in immersive experiences. In this section, an overview of relevant work in discussing humanistic co-design methods is reflected, in addition to how prototyping in VR and the presentation of use cases in VR rehabilitation applications have been approached in the past.

2.1   Immersion and Presence in VR

Research in game design has leveraged VR to immerse users into fictional scenarios that are well-aligned with their existing abilities [3] and imagined abilities [4]. In recent years, researchers began exploring the human factors in the design of VR experiences that sustain the immersive experience and the sense of presence in the virtual realm

---

[1] mo3awen.com.

within a broad range of applied domains. Examples include [12] in consumer behavior and marketing and [13] in the context of training and education with a focus on the user experience (UX) design factors.

Immersion and presence can enhance the user's experience and create an engaging, enjoyable, and immersive experience for the user as noted in the systems described in [3] and [10]. Immersion can help to increase users' engagement, focus, and retention, while presence can provide a sense of realism that can make the UX more enjoyable and effective [5, 6]. Recent studies by Moinnereau et al. [14] and [5–8] have shown that immersion and presence can contribute towards providing a more realistic and engaging experience for interactions and activities in virtual environments, making it a viable tool for communication and overall engagement. Where the presence within the context of virtual reality is defined as one's sense of being in the virtual world [6], developers often focus on the visual perception and auditory perception as well as kinesthetic experiences (if applicable) as noted in the game described in [4] and in [9].

2.2 VR Design Considerations in Therapy

Being a computer simulation, many aspects of the user's activities in a serious VR game and behavior are customizable and measurable such as the VR systems reported in [8] for multiple sclerosis patients and in [16, 17] for post-stroke and post-surgery contexts. Performance metrics such as motion tracking via limb movement, stability and speed can be accurately measured and stored with timestamps that facilitate longitudinal progress monitoring.

Designers can also use VR to create an environment that is conducive to therapeutic goals as noted in [17, 18]. Environments in virtual spaces can be designed to be calming and relaxing, or they can be made to evoke certain emotions and feelings. Additionally, research has shown that designing environments to include certain elements, such as objects or characters, can help to create an immersive experience and facilitate the therapeutic process in PT and OT [16, 17] as well as mental health and psychology [19–21]. Additionally, the user's avatar can be designed to provide visual cues that can help to direct the user's attention to certain tasks, while also providing a sense of presence that can make the user feel as if they are actually in the environment. Collectively, these research studies have shed light on the role of affordance and alignment of interactive elements within the environment with the game mechanics that can help to engage the user and make the experience more immersive [22]. For example, puzzles and other interactive activities can be used to help the user focus on the therapeutic task at hand, while also providing a sense of progress and accomplishment. In the context of auditory perception, a growing body of literature has explored the use of sound and music in therapy contexts and its impact on creating a pleasant atmosphere that contributes toward relaxation and meditative contexts in the virtual realm [23]. Finally, the use of haptics, such as vibration and force feedback, can provide an additional level of immersion, allowing the user to interact with the environment in a more realistic way as noted in [24] and [25].

Additionally, research has shown various game mechanics in which VR serious games can provide adaptive feedback and guidance to the user based on their performance and goals in a treatment plan or remedial program [26]. For example, game designs can adjust the difficulty level, the amount of assistance, or the type of reward to suit the user's needs and preferences. VR games can also create immersive and engaging scenarios that motivate the user to practice and improve their skills. For instance, the game can simulate realistic environments, which are aligned with the users' familiar surroundings, that require the user to perform various tasks, such as picking up items or walking on uneven surfaces. VR games such as [26] and [16, 17] have also shown how embedding elements of fun, challenge, and social interaction can enhance the user's enjoyment and satisfaction.

However, designing serious VR games for therapy also poses some challenges and limitations. One of the challenges is to ensure the validity and reliability of the VR game as a therapeutic tool as noted in [18, 25, 26]. It is important to align game mechanics of the VR experience with scientifically sound theoretical and empirical foundations, and that it should be tested and evaluated with the target population and context. Another challenge is to balance the trade-off between realism and abstraction in the VR game [27]. Effective PT applications in the literature have shown that these games strike the balance between realism and abstraction within the technology limitations (i.e. the VR experience is realistic enough to elicit the desired responses and outcomes from the user, but also abstract enough to avoid triggering negative emotions or reactions). A third challenge is to ensure the accessibility and usability of the VR game for the target user populations. This means that the game should be compatible with different VR devices and platforms, and that it should be easy to use and understand for the user.

3 Conceptual Design of VR in Upper Limb Therapy

Conceptual design for VR for upper limb therapy is the process of envisioning a product or system that uses VR technology to provide a therapeutic environment for patients with upper limb impairments. This may involve the selection of hardware and software components, the development of virtual environments, the design of user interfaces, and the integration of various therapeutic protocols into the system.

3.1 Framework for VR Design Space in Therapy and Rehabilitation

The proposed framework for immersion and presence in VR for PT is an adaptation of the design space framework for VR that was introduced in [11] and is described in Table 1 for the applied context of PT.

Table 1. Framework for Immersion and Presence in VR for PT

Presence in VR for Rehabilitation (Self & Others)			
Presence in the PT Context		Interactive Presence	Shared Presence
Self Embodiment	Other's	Sensory	Association
Completeness	Proxemics	Gaze	Type of PT/OT
Realism → Visuals → Interaction Design Abstract → Perception → Concept Depiction	→ Co-located individuals in the PT session → Remote presence of users with therapist and/or caregivers	Gestures	Collaboration → Independent → Interdependent
		Acoustics → system feedback, → background audio, → notifications	
Synchrony	Interaction Type	Facial Expression	Affordance in PT/OT Activity

The hybrid psychological model of [11] facilitated the conceptualization of the framework for PT applications with a focus on human factors in the design of virtual spaces and objects in the virtual realm. In addition, the framework sheds light on the elements that need to be carefully articulated in the game mechanics as they pertain to interaction, perception and cognition in the VR experience.

3.2 Use Case: Upper-Limb Physical Therapy in Mo3awen

The goal of a conceptual design is to provide an overall plan for the development of a VR-based system that can be used to improve the functioning of the upper limbs for an individual. In this section, we describe the conceptual design for a VR application that was co-designed with physical therapists for upper-limb therapy, called "Mo3awen". The plan was co-created with subject-matter experts and users with the lived experience of PT for upper limbs, to ensure that the system is aligned with the needs of the individuals with upper limb impairments and the healthcare professionals involved in their treatment plans. An example is illustrated in Fig. 1 from the ongoing pre-production phase of

"Mo3awen" which is being conducted by the co-authors of this publication, which shows one example of the design design spaces being considered for the gamified approach in the virtual realm.

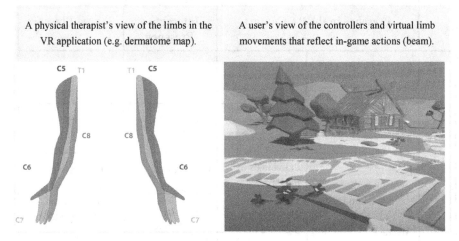

| A physical therapist's view of the limbs in the VR application (e.g. dermatome map). | A user's view of the controllers and virtual limb movements that reflect in-game actions (beam). |

Fig. 1. The self-embodiment dimension of Mo3awen considers the users' feeling of owning their virtual representation of their upper limbs in a virtual physical therapy session.

Debarba et al. have highlighted in [15] that the sense of ownership of a virtual body can be achieved in both first and third person perspectives under congruent visuo-motor-tactile conditions. Similarly, Borrego et al. reported in an experimental study [16] that "the sense of body-ownership, self-location, and presence were more vividly experienced in a first-person than in a third-person perspective" which was observed in both the healthy subjects and the stroke survivors who took part in that study [16]. Building on prior work, designers and developers align the game mechanics with what has been established as effective in supporting presence and immersion, and offer configurable settings for the design aspects that have not yet been established in the VR design space for therapy and rehabilitation.

This study focuses on upper limb therapy through the use of VR to simulate the same therapeutic exercises done in the clinical context. The VR game is dedicated to those who require exercise of a simple motion without the need for external guidance or specialized machines. It focuses on two types of exercises: Strengthening and range of motion. One of the activities in Mo3awen involve exercises that target the hands and wrists, elbows and shoulders (as shown in Fig. 2) through a predesigned set of guided movements in the VR experience which target these body parts in the remedial program.The realism aspect of design was considered to ensure alignment between visual perception, cognitive processing and virtual-physical mapping of limbs.

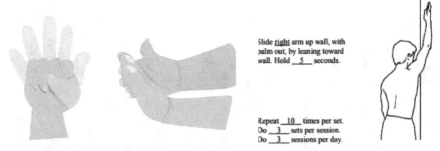

Fig. 2. The wrist and shoulder exercises can be imitated through a predesigned set of exercises in virtual reality physical therapy context. Designers considered realistic and abstract representations. of the limbs

The framework provides guidance on embedding elements in the virtual world along with their affordance as it pertains to manipulation and interaction in each exercise within the PT session. For example, research suggests that realistic renderings of the limbs in therapy contributes toward making the seemingly mundane, enduring rehabilitation therapies more engaging for the patients, when compared to the abstract representation as depicted in Fig. 3. While this has been reported in 2D game designs, the framework sheds light on the link between the design consideration and the elements of presence and immersion for the therapy context in the virtual realm.

Realism in Limb Visual Representations in PT   Abstract Visualization

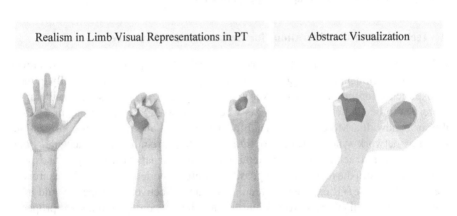

Fig. 3. Designing for self-embodiment and presence requires an in-depth understanding of the trade-offs between realism and abstract designs for the virtual objects and virtual scenes.

An example from Mo3awen is depicted in Fig. 4 which illustrates the representation of self, reflected as the limbs which are marked as the "steady hand" and the hand being targeted in that particular exercise in that particular phase of the game design. Aligned with the areas of focus, the remaining elements of the framework provide the team with clarity on the objective performance metrics to track and the sensory perception of space and the objects within the space. These design considerations include the visual, auditory, and visceral experiences.

Fig. 4. The hub of the VR PT game which establishes alignment between the virtual and physical worlds for the users prior to launching the PT exercise.

4 Design Considerations for Immersion and Presence in VR Applications for PT and OT

While VR immerses users in scenarios that are not necessarily bound by physical or technological constraints, it is important for VR in serious gaming designs to align with the objectives of physical therapy or occupational therapy.

4.1 Technological Considerations for Immersion and Presence

In PT contexts, it is evident that delivering 3D social VR experiences would require a great deal of alignment between gaze, gestures, and conversation to create a fully immersive experience for the patient, caregiver(s) and the therapists. This design consideration is foreseen to be challenging in contexts where there would be limitations in accessibility or bandwidth. Moreover, the need for performance and resolution optimization, as well as network synchronization optimization would require game mechanics that establish realism to achieve presence and immersion for a patient who might be experiencing fatigue from the repetitive and possibly painful experience of these PT exercises. To ensure that these VR experiences are realistic and effective, developers would need to optimize the available resources to ensure that the 3D content is rendered properly, that the user's movements and visual gaze is tracked accurately, and that the network synchronization is reliable as noted in [9].

Bandwidth and performance optimization are important considerations for virtual reality (VR) applications in PT. To ensure smooth and responsive experiences, developers must consider the bandwidth and latency of the network (e.g. reducing the size of the data being tracked for the PT session, compressing the data especially in homogeneous data tracking, using protocols that are optimized for VR, and using quality of service (QoS) techniques to prioritize latency-sensitive data). Resolution optimization is also an important factor to consider when developing for VR in PT. This involves using techniques such as anti-aliasing and supersampling to improve the quality of scenes in the virtual world as well as the visual representation of navigation elements, gestures and objects in the virtual realm. Also, techniques such as texture streaming can be considered to reduce the amount of memory needed to render the scene for PT exercise, while still providing an immersive experience for the user to focus on the limb being target for the exercise. Network synchronization optimization is also a challenge in developing for VR in PT contexts. This involves ensuring that the user's experience is consistent and lag-free across all sessions for the same patient as well as across all patients for the same exercise regardless of where the interaction was located. This can be achieved by using techniques such as client-side prediction and interpolation, and using server-side physics to ensure that all clients are in sync.

4.2 Methodological Design Considerations

One of the main methodological challenges in utilizing VR applications for physical therapy and occupational therapy is the lack of uniform standards for evaluation. Currently, the methods used to measure the effectiveness of VR applications vary greatly, making it difficult to compare results between different studies or across real-time data of the same patient across different points. Additionally, there is a lack of long-term studies looking at the effectiveness of VR applications in these areas, making it difficult to determine their long-term effectiveness. Another issue is the difficulty of replicating real-world exercises that involve touch and dexterity in VR. In order to accurately simulate physical therapy and occupational therapy scenarios, the VR environment needs to replicate the environment as closely as possible utilizing all sensory input channels of the user(s) and the therapists involved in the session. This remains a design challenge with the current limitations in the VR technology platforms, which may limit the effectiveness of VR applications in these areas. Finally, the use of VR applications in therapy can be cost-prohibitive if it is not recognized by healthcare systems as an alternative for in-clinic treatments, as the hardware and software required for the applications can hinder the accessibility of such setups for users that do not have the option of co-located VR sessions which could consequently limit their use in certain settings, such as in-home care. Overall, the use of virtual reality applications in physical therapy and occupational therapy presents some unique challenges that need to be addressed before they can be widely adopted in clinical settings.

5   Conclusion

This study reports our inquiry into the interaction dynamics among patients, therapists, and VR serious games during routine game-assisted therapy in the contexts beyond the clinical setting. Our study contributes to the field by presenting a framework for designing the VR experience with immersion and presence in mind for the individual and social VR contexts. The framework was applied to one use case as an example which demonstrated its applicability for designing user experiences that leverage immersion and presence as design features in the VR experience for PT. Finally, we also highlighted the design considerations and directions for future work in the design space of VR in rehabilitation.

Acknowledgment. The authors acknowledge the support of Alfaisal's Solve program in 2023 which is conducted in collaboration with MIT. The Mo3awen VR application was the recipient of an award at the Gamers8 Game Jam in 2022 (Gameathon) in the thematic track for exergames, and the authors acknowledge the support provided by the Saudi eSport Federation and Alfaisal University's Dimensions accelerator for the development phases of the Mo3awen game. The authors also extend their appreciation for the CoCreate program and the physical therapists who contributed towards the co-design phases of the application and to Dr. Areej Al-Wabil for supervising the capstone project for the VR application.

References

1. Felipe, F.A., et al.: Evaluation instruments for physical therapy using virtual reality in stroke patients: a systematic review. Physiotherapy **106**, 194–210 (2020)
2. August, K., Bleichenbacher, D., Adamovich, S.: Virtual reality physical therapy: a telerehabilitation tool for hand and finger movement exercise monitoring and motor skills analysis. In: Proceedings of the IEEE 31st Annual Northeast Bioengineering Conference, 2005. pp. 73–74. IEEE (2005)
3. Adalberto L., et al.: Immersive Speculative Enactments: Bringing Future Scenarios and Technology to Life Using Virtual Reality. In: Proceedings of the 2022 CHI Conference on Human Factors in Computing Systems (CHI 2022). Association for Computing Machinery, Article 17, pp. 1–20. New York, NY, USA (2022). https://doi.org/10.1145/3491102.3517492
4. Brown, J., Gerling, K., Dickinson, P., Kirman, B.: Dead fun: uncomfortable interactions in a virtual reality game for coffins. In: Proceedings of the 2015 Annual Symposium on Computer-Human Interaction in Play, pp. 475–480 (2015)
5. Kim, M., Jeon, C., Kim, J.: A study on immersion and presence of a portable hand haptic system for immersive virtual reality. Sensors **17**(5), 1141 (2017)
6. Servotte, J.C., et al.: Virtual reality experience: immersion, sense of presence, and cybersickness. Clin. Simul. Nurs. **38**, 35–43 (2020)
7. Postolache, O., Hemanth, D.J., Alexandre, R., Gupta, D., Geman, O., Khanna, A.: Remote monitoring of physical rehabilitation of stroke patients using IoT and virtual reality. IEEE J. Sel. Areas Commun. **39**(2), 562–573 (2020)
8. Hollywood, R.A., Poyade, M., Paul, L., Webster, A.: Proof of concept for the use of immersive virtual reality in upper limb rehabilitation of multiple sclerosis patients. In: Bio-medical Visualis., vol. 11, pp. 73–93. Springer International Publishing, Cham (2022)
9. Dongas, R., Grace, K.: Designing to leverage presence in VR rhythm games. Multimodal Technol. Interac. **7**(2), 18 (2023)
10. Slater, M.: Immersion and the illusion of presence in virtual reality. Br. J. Psychol. **109**(3), 431 (2018)
11. Yassien, A., ElAgroudy, P., Makled, E., Abdennadher, S.: A design space for social presence in VR. In: Proceedings of the 11th Nordic Conference on Human-Computer Interaction: Shaping Experiences, Shaping Society, pp. 1–12 (2020)
12. Cheng, L.-K., Chieng, M.-H., Chieng, W.-H.: Measuring virtual experience in a three-dimensional virtual reality interactive simulator environment: a structural equation modeling approach. Virtual Reality **18**(3), 173–188 (2014). https://doi.org/10.1007/s10055-014-0244-2
13. Tcha-Tokey, K., Christmann, O., Loup-Escande, E., Loup, G., Richir, S.: Towards a model of user experience in immersive virtual environments. Advances in Human-Computer Interaction. Hindawi (2018)

14. Moinnereau, M.A., de Oliveira Jr, A.A., Falk, T.H.: Immersive media experience: a survey of existing methods and tools for human influential factors assessment. Qual. User Experience **7**(1), 5 (2022)

15. Galvan Debarba, H., Bovet, S., Salomon, R., Blanke, O., Herbelin, B., Boulic, R.: Characterizing first and third person viewpoints and their alternation for embodied interaction in virtual reality. PLoS ONE **12**(12), e0190109 (2017)

16. Borrego, A., Latorre, J., Alcañiz, M., Llorens, R.: Embodiment and presence in virtual reality after stroke. A comparative study with healthy subjects. Front. Neurol. **10**, 1061 (2019)

17. Wolf, S., et al.: Immersive virtual reality fitness games for enhancement of recovery after colo-rectal surgery: study protocol for a randomised pilot trial. Pilot and Feasibility Stud. **8**(1), 1–8 (2022)

18. Wood, K., Uribe Quevedo, A. J., Penuela, L., Perera, S., Kapralos, B.: Virtual reality assessment and customization using physiological measures: a literature analysis. In: Symposium on Virtual and Augmented Reality, pp. 64–73 (2021)

19. Wilson, C.J., Soranzo, A.: The use of virtual reality in psychology: a case study in visual perception. Comput. Math. Methods Med. **2015**, 1–7 (2015). https://doi.org/10.1155/2015/151702

20. North, M.M., North, S.M.: A comparative study of sense of presence of virtual reality and immersive environments. Australas. J. Inf. Syst. **20**, 1168 (2016). https://doi.org/10.3127/ajis.v20i0.1168

21. Bell, I.H., Nicholas, J., Alvarez-Jimenez, M., Thompson, A., Valmaggia, L.: Virtual reality as a clinical tool in mental health research and practice. Dialogues Clin. Neurosci. **22**(2), 169–177 (2022)

22. Faric, N., et al.: What players of virtual reality exercise games want: thematic analysis of web-based reviews. J. Med. Internet Res. **21**(9), e13833 (2019)

23. Bosman, I.D.V., Buruk, O.O., Jørgensen, K., Hamari, J.: The effect of audio on the experience in virtual reality: a scoping review. Behav. Inf. Technol. 1–35 (2023). https://doi.org/10.1080/0144929X.2022.2158371

24. Kim, M., Kim, J., Jeong, K., Kim, C.: Grasping VR: presence of pseudo-haptic interface based portable hand grip system in immersive virtual reality. Int. J. Hum. Comput. Interac. **36**(7), 685–698 (2020). https://doi.org/10.1080/10447318.2019.1680920

25. Ziat, M.: Haptics for human-computer interaction: from the skin to the brain. Found. Trends® Hum. Comput. Interact. **17**(1–2), 1–194 (2023)

26. Kamkuimo K,S.A., Girard, B., Menelas, B.A.J.: Dynamic difficulty adjustment through real-time physiological feedback for a more adapted virtual reality exposure therapy. In: Marfisi-Schottman, I., Bellotti, F., Hamon, L., Klemke, R. (eds.) Games and Learning Alliance. GALA 2020. Lecture Notes in Computer Science, vol. 12517, pp. 102–111. Springer, Cham (2020). https://doi.org/10.1007/978-3-030-63464-3_10

27. Wenk, N., Penalver-Andres, J., Buetler, K.A., Nef, T., Müri, R.M., Marchal-Crespo, L.: Effect of immersive visualization technologies on cognitive load, motivation, usability, and embodiment. Virtual Reality **27**(1), 1–25 (2021). https://doi.org/10.1007/s10055-021-00565-8

Reflection: A Mirror Therapy VR Rehabilitation Prototype

Hanan Makki Zakari[1,2](✉) [iD], Atheer Alharbi[1], Omar Khashoggi[1], Leena Alotaibi[3], and Zain Aljandali[3]

[1] Qindeel Studio, Riyadh, Saudi Arabia
[2] Game Innovation Lab, Alfaisal University, Riyadh, Saudi Arabia
hzakari@alfaisal.edu
[3] Human-Computer Interaction (HCI) Lab, Alfaisal University, Riyadh, Saudi Arabia
zjandali@alfaisal.edu

Abstract. Mirror Therapy VR Rehabilitation (MTVRR) is an innovative form of rehabilitation therapy designed to help post-stroke patients regain motor and cognitive functions. The therapy uses virtual reality (VR) technology to provide a safe, comfortable and immersive environment for patients to practice their motor skills in a meaningful and engaging manner. MTVRR also incorporates elements of serious game design, allowing the patient to progress through levels of difficulty depending on their progress in the rehabilitation program. In this study, we will explore how MTVRR can be used by occupational therapists for post-stroke patients. We will examine how the use of VR technology, serious game design elements and cultural considerations can help occupational therapists tailor an effective rehabilitation program for each patient. We will also discuss potential challenges that may be encountered when using this type of therapy with post-stroke patients. The findings of this use study can provide occupational therapists with valuable insights into how they can incorporate MTVRR into their existing rehabilitation programs in order to provide effective and culturally appropriate treatment for post-stroke patients. By leveraging advances in VR technology and serious game design, occupational therapists can create personalized treatment plans that are tailored to the needs of their clients, helping them make more informed decisions about the best course of action for each individual patient.

Keywords: Virtual Therapy · Physical Therapy · Mirror Therapy · Game-Based Therapy · Serious Games · ExerGames · Head mounted displays (HMD) · Rehabilitation · Remote Therapy. Post-stroke

1 Introduction

Post-stroke rehabilitation for patients who experienced a cerebrovascular accident (CVA) often involves therapy sessions focused on building strength and endurance, upper-limb therapy, lower-limb therapy and/or cognitive and speech therapy [1]. Stroke recovery treatment (or rehabilitation) typically requires conventional therapy, which involves therapist-led training and patient education [2]. Post-stroke rehabilitation is a goal-oriented process that seeks to help patients reach their full potential.

© The Author(s), under exclusive license to Springer Nature Switzerland AG 2023
A. Coman and S. Vasilache (Eds.): HCII 2023, LNCS 14026, pp. 228–237, 2023.
https://doi.org/10.1007/978-3-031-35927-9_17

The growing landscape of VR rehabilitation for stroke survivors has been aligned with a proliferation in human-computer interaction (HCI) research in the design and development of such systems [3]. One approach for post-stroke rehabilitation is mirror therapy, which leverages the neuroplasticity characteristic of the human brain as described in [4] and [5]. VR technologies have been used in mirror therapy to replicate and enhance the efficacy of mirror therapy in the virtual realm, exploring the feasibility and viability [6].

In this paper, we describe the conceptual design of a novel Mirror Therapy VR Rehabilitation (MTVRR) system which was co-created with target user populations and subject matter experts. MTVRR is an innovative form of rehabilitation therapy designed to help post-stroke patients regain motor and cognitive functions. The therapy leverages VR technology features of capturing objective measures during sessions to provide a safe, comfortable and immersive environment for post-stroke patients to exercise their motor skills in a meaningful and engaging way. In Sect. 2, we present a brief overview of the literature in VR for stroke rehabilitation, followed by VR design considerations in Sect. 3. The paper concludes by considering how the VR design considerations can guide future design of VR applications for post-stroke rehabilitation therepy, and next steps for refining the MTVRR applications.

2 Related Work

Evidence from recent research has shown that patients with stroke benefit greatly from early, high-intensity therapy that involves technology as a tool [3–7]. Technology has been integrated in therapy programs to facilitate a broad range of interventions ranging from motor learning for balance and gait rehabilitation such as in [8] and [9] to occupational therapy programs as noted in [10]. In this section we highlight the technology utilization in the general applied health context of stroke rehabilitation, followed by the scope of research for mirror therapy in particular.

2.1 Technology in Post-stroke Rehabilitation

The integration of technological intervention toward conventional post-stroke therapies has shown a positive outcome to the patient's post-stroke recovery process as noted in the review reported in [3]. Technology is considered in rehabilitation for upper-limbs, lower-limbs (treatments focus on trunk and pelvis stability, positioning and control of the hips, knees and ankles, as well as stepping and propulsion) and speech and language therapy. In the scope of speech and cognitive abilities, assistive technologies have been developed to help stroke patients when they lose fundamental abilities that they need to reconnect with other such as being aware of their surroundings, communicating verbally and non-verbally, recognizing spoken dialogue and emotions, recalling words and expressing them verbally, and using gestures to convey meaning when speech is limited.

2.2 Virtual Reality (VR) in Post-stroke Rehabilitation

Recent research has demonstrated use cases for using VR in upper-limb therapy such as [10] and [11]. These studies have highlighted impact-driven research in VR applied to recovering and strengthening complex hand and reaching skills such as twisting, turning, pinching and grasping; all the many things we do with our hands, arms and fingers. Emerging research methods and approaches in this applied domain include experimental electromyography, kinetic analysis, movement analysis, biomechanics, sensor technologies, neuroimaging, brain physiology, musculoskeletal physiology, experimental biologics, experimental pharmacotherapeutics, and emerging technologies and use of smart devices [12–14].

In contrast to upper-limb therapy, the use of VR in lower-limb therapy focuses on advancing trunk, pelvic and leg function, movement and balance as noted in [15]. Typical upper-limb therapy focuses on body-weight support and large motor and rhythmic limb functions influenced by spinal cord and brain circuits which have been considered for modeling in the virtual realm with sensory and tactile modes of interaction. While therapeutic intervention makes use of anti-gravity support and weight-bearing assistive devices, which are used to support patients as they work on climbing and descending, the VR context remains exploratory in that the physical dynamics are not yet accurately represented in the virtual realm.

2.3   VR in Mirror Therapy for Stroke Rehabilitation

In this section, we describe the virtual depiction of mirror therapy in the context of post-stroke rehabilitation, as described in recent publications such as [15–20], with a specific focus on the features encapsulated by the established taxonomy of social VR applications, as noted in [21]. The features are listed in Tables 1 and 2, with highlights for relevant elements in mirror therapy.

Table 1. Taxonomy of Social VR Features in Mirror Therapy for Immersion and Presence

Category	Features	Variations in Mirror Therapy
"The Self" in Mirror Therapy	Avatar representation	- Visual cues of controls vs. limbs to reflect movement in the mirror therapy exercises - Partial body, full body, or no avatar. Limb visualization is essential
	Avatar customization	
	Avatar manipulation	
	Avatar Traversal	
Interacting with Others in Social VR settings for Mirror Therapy	Communication Privileges	Muting, blocking or adding others
	Communication Types	Ranked: Physical, bio-adaptive feedback, followed by voice, and text (language limitations)
	Activity to Scaffold Interaction	Event, Prototyping, Virtual Drawing or no activity in the scaffolding

(*continued*)

Table 1. (*continued*)

Category	Features	Variations in Mirror Therapy
	Openness of the environment	Public vs private settings

Table 2. Taxonomy of Social VR Features in Mirror Therapy Environments

Category	Features	Variations in Mirror Therapy
"The Environment" in Mirror Therapy	User Manipulation of the environment	Construct new elements vs alter existing elements
	Spawning area	Private vs. social spawning
	Openness of the environment	Public vs private settings

3 Human-Centered Design of VR Therapy

Despite an increasing awareness of user-centered design (UCD) in applied health applications, there is limited discussion of how such approaches can be translated into the constrained environments of virtual worlds for rehabilitation. The UCD method is often

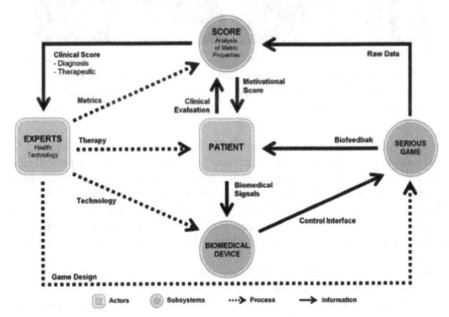

Fig. 1. Framework for the MTVRR game which highlights the roles of the actors (patients and therapists) in the virtual realm.

recognized as an effective means of bridging the gap between the differing mental models of a user (i.e., what users develop to make sense of the functional properties or the operation of any designed system) and a designer's conceptual model of the system. The framework in Fig. 1 illustrates the relationships between key players and concepts involved in the MTVRR game. The directed arrows depict the flow of information or the processes involved in the co-design.

A key design consideration that emerged in the ideation phase of the MTVRR game was to emphasize the sense of self, which encapsulates features that facilitate users' control of their virtual limb during the exercises.

The virtual limb representation, and the extent to which the physical human body is replicated in VR, had direct correlation to the design features which link visual attention to brain plasticity as noted in [22] and [23]. The screenshots of the virtual realm in Fig. 2 depict the visualization of the hands in which a mirrored image of the hand is visualized to create the illusion that both hands are moving in tandem.

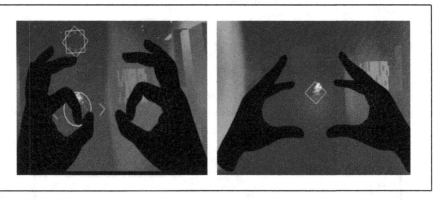

Fig. 2. Screenshots of Reflection prototype (2022), the sense of self is essential in physical rehabilitation and in mirror therapy, the visualization of both limbs is a core function of the therapy program to stimulate the brain.

The game mechanics in MTVRR also emerged from the contextual enquiry of mirror therapy sessions, in which repetitive exercise of limb movements are often prescribed in post-stroke rehabilitation. In using technological interventions as an alternative method to provide patients with remote therapy beyond the physical clinical settings, prompted VR exercises are designed to optimize long-term functional outcomes and promote stroke survivors' independence in carrying out the exercises [24–28]. This is particularly relevant for patients in rural regions who have difficulties traveling to the hospitals or rehabilitation facilities.

The game mechanics shown in Fig. 3 show the geometric shapes and their alignment with the gesture prompts that guide users through the exercise. The repetitive nature of exercises can be tracked and logged in the MTVRR system for progress monitoring in extended periods of time. The three main gestures were circles, triangles and hexagons visualized by the user as hand-gesture formations as depicted in the figure.

Fig. 3. Game mechanics involved gesture-based interaction with 3–5 min allocated for each exercise. Progression from level to level depends on completing the shape formations.

The VR environment encapsulates design choices of the virtual space through which post-stroke rehabilitation users (e.g. patients, therapists) interact and present themselves. Moreover, the game mechanics within the environment were aligned with personas and archetypes of post-stroke rehabilitation users, as described in [29] and the usability recommendations highlighted in [30] and [31].

The openness of virtual environments refers to the capability of users to freely traverse the virtual realm, and this was addressed by the design of the backdrop and the objects that are visualized within the MTVRR game. Figure 4 shows a screenshot of the in-game visualization of the limbs and the objects overlaid over the virtual world, and Fig. 5 depicts the design inspiration [32] of the backdrop that was considered to attract and sustain users' attention during the gameplay in the MTVRR application.

Fig. 4. Screenshot of Reflection prototype (2022), Iterative design considered different concepts for the mockup shown in the MTVRR virtual scenes.

Art Style

Inspired by Monument Valley (2014)
- Minimalist
- Colorful
- Usages of primitive shape

Fig. 5. Reflection's art style is inspired by Monument Valley[1] (2014) [32] visual designs for attracting and sustaining visual attention.

Playtesting was a key component for eliciting feedback on the game mechanics and the usability of the game by different target user groups. Initial playtesting was conducted in the game jam (Gameathon 2022) in the accelerated innovation context of a one-week competition, followed by several iterations of feature testing as shown in Fig. 6.

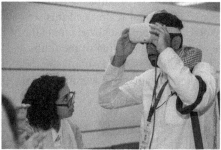

Fig. 6. Designers and developers evaluating Reflection prototype with Oculus head-mounted displays in the game jam.

4 Conclusion

This paper presents a research team's efforts to design considerations for post-stroke interventions that aim to engage patients in an extensive and continuous therapeutic exercise program for the stroke recovery process. Design implications for VR applications include the importance of features that facilitate immersion and presence of self and others in the context of the game as well as the visual representation of limbs within the game to ensure proper alignment for the neuroplasticity objective of the exercises.

---

[1] https://www.monumentvalleygame.com/mvpc.

Future research directions involve iterative testing of the co-designed application with therapists and users to assess the usability and efficacy of using the proposed VR exercises in the stroke recovery process. Usability and user experience (UX) evaluations will be conducted during the alpha and beta testing to identify areas of improvement in the VR design and to explore different modes of interaction for the physical rehabilitation exercises.

Acknowledgments. The authors acknowledge the support of Alfaisal's Solve program in 2023 which is conducted in collaboration with MIT. The Reflection VR application was the recipient of the grand award at the Gamers 8 Game Jam in 2022 (Gameathon), and the authors acknowledge the support provided by the Saudi eSport Federation and Alfaisal University's Dimensions accelerator for the development phases of the MTVRR game. The authors also extend their appreciation for the physical therapists and occupational therapists who contributed towards the co-design phases of the application.

References

1. Boukhennoufa, I., Zhai, X., Utti, V., Jackson, J., McDonald-Maier, K.D.: Wearable sensors and machine learning in post-stroke rehabilitation assessment: a systematic review. Biomed. Signal Process. Control **71**, 103197 (2022)
2. Edwards, D.F., Hahn, M.G., Baum, C.M., Perlmutter, M.S., Sheedy, C., Dromerick, A.W.: Screening patients with stroke for rehabilitation needs: validation of the post-stroke rehabilitation guidelines. Neurorehabil. Neural Repair **20**(1), 42–48 (2006)
3. Leong, S.C., Tang, Y.M., Toh, F.M., Fong, K.N.: Examining the effectiveness of virtual, augmented, and mixed reality (VAMR) therapy for upper limb recovery and activities of daily living in stroke patients: a systematic review and meta-analysis. J. Neuroeng. Rehabil. **19**(1), 1–20 (2022)
4. Ozen, S., Senlikci, H.B., Guzel, S., Yemisci, O.U.: Computer game assisted task specific exercises in the treatment of motor and cognitive function and quality of life in stroke: a randomized control study. J. Stroke Cerebrovasc. Dis. **30**(9), 105991 (2021)
5. Gandhi, D. B., Sterba, A., Khatter, H., Pandian, J. D.: Mirror therapy in stroke rehabilitation: current perspectives. Ther. Clin. Risk manag. **16**, 75–85 (2020)
6. Voinescu, A., Sui, J., Stanton Fraser, D.: Virtual reality in neurorehabilitation: an umbrella review of meta-analyses. J. Clin. Med. **10**(7), 1478 (2021)
7. Boian, R.F., Deutsch, J.E., Lee, C.S., Burdea, G.C., Lewis, J.: Haptic effects for virtual reality-based post-stroke rehabilitation. In: 11th Symposium on Haptic Interfaces for Virtual Environment and Teleoperator Systems, 2003. HAPTICS 2003. Proceedings, pp. 247–253. IEEE (2003)
8. Huber, S.K., Held, J.P., de Bruin, E.D., Knols, R.H.: Personalized motor-cognitive exergame training in chronic stroke patients—a feasibility study. Frontiers Aging Neurosci. **13**, 730801 (2021)
9. Manser, P., Adcock-Omlin, M., de Bruin, E.D.: Design considerations for an exergame-based training intervention for older adults with mild neurocognitive disorder: qualitative study including focus groups with experts and health care professionals and individual semi structured in-depth patient interviews. JMIR Serious Game. **11**, e37616 (2023)
10. Demain, S., et al.: Assistive technologies after stroke: self-management or fending for yourself? a focus group study. BMC Health Serv. Res. **13**, 1–12 (2013)

11. Choi, Y.H., Ku, J., Lim, H., Kim, Y.H., Paik, N.J.: Mobile game-based virtual reality rehabilitation program for upper limb dysfunction after ischemic stroke. Restor. Neurol. Neurosci. **34**(3), 455–463 (2016)

12. Laver, K.E., Lange, B., George, S., Deutsch, J.E., Saposnik, G., Crotty, M.: Virtual reality for stroke rehabilitation. Cochrane Database Syst. Rev. **11**, CD008349 (2017)

13. Choi, H.S., Shin, W.S., Bang, D.H.: Mirror therapy using gesture recognition for upper limb function, neck discomfort, and quality of life after chronic stroke: a single-blind randomized controlled trial. Med. Sci. Monit.: Int. Med. J. Exp. Clin. Res. **25**, 3271 (2019)

14. Bauer, A.C.M., Andringa, G.: The potential of immersive virtual reality for cognitive training in elderly. Gerontology **66**(6), 614–623 (2020)

15. Zhang, Y., et al.: Mirror therapy for unilateral neglect after stroke: a systematic review. Eur. J. Neurol. **29**(1), 358–371 (2022)

16. Jo, S., Kim, H., Song, C.: A novel approach to increase attention during mirror therapy among stroke patients: a video-based behavioral analysis. Brain Sci. **12**(3), 297 (2022)

17. Hartman, K., Altschuler, E.L.: Mirror therapy for hemiparesis following stroke: a review. Curr. Phys. Med. Rehabil. Rep. **4**, 237–248 (2016)

18. Miclaus, R.S., Roman, N., Henter, R., Caloian, S.: Lower extremity rehabilitation in patients with post-stroke sequelae through virtual reality associated with mirror therapy. Int. J. Environ. Res. Public Health **18**(5), 2654 (2021)

19. Hoermann, S., et al.: Computerized mirror therapy with augmented reflection technology for early stroke rehabilitation: clinical feasibility and integration as an adjunct therapy. Disabil. Rehabil. **39**(15), 1503–1514 (2017)

20. In, T., Lee, K., Song, C.: Virtual reality reflection therapy improves balance and gait in patients with chronic stroke: randomized controlled trials. Med. Sci. Monit.: Int. Med. J. Exp. Clin. Res. **22**, 4046 (2016)

21. Jonas, M., Said, S., Yu, D., Aiello, C., Furlo, N., Zytko, D.: Towards a taxonomy of social VR application design. In: Extended Abstracts of the Annual Symposium on Computer-Human Interaction in Play Companion Extended Abstracts, pp. 437–444 (2019)

22. Matamala-Gomez, M., Maselli, A., Malighetti, C., Realdon, O., Mantovani, F., Riva, G.: Virtual body ownership illusions for mental health: a narrative review. J. Clin. Med. **10**(1), 139 (2021)

23. Wiley, E., Khattab, S., Tang, A.: Examining the effect of virtual reality therapy on cognition post-stroke: a systematic review and meta-analysis. Disabil. Rehabil. Assist. Technol. **17**(1), 50–60 (2022)

24. Hao, J., Yao, Z., Harp, K., Gwon, D. Y., Chen, Z., Siu, K. C.: Effects of virtual reality in the early-stage stroke rehabilitation: a systematic review and meta-analysis of randomized controlled trials. Physiotherapy Theor. Pract. 1–20 (2022)

25. Lee, J.I., et.al. Effects of the home-based exercise program with an augmented reality system on balance in patients with stroke: a randomized controlled trial. Disabil. Rehabil. **45**, 1–8 (2022)

26. Dias, M.P.F., et al.: Is there a relation between brain and muscle activity after virtual reality training in individuals with stroke? A cross-sectional study. Int. J. Environ. Res. Public Health **19**(19), 12705 (2022)

27. Hilton, D., Cobb, S., Pridmore, T., Gladman, J., Edmans, J.: Development and evaluation of a mixed reality system for stroke rehabilitation : advanced Computational Intelligence Paradigms in Healthcare 6. Virtual Reality in Psychotherapy, Rehabilitation, and Assessment, pp. 193–228 (2011)

28. Aguilar Acevedo, F., Pacheco Bautista, D., Acevedo Gómez, M., Toledo Toledo, G., Nieva García, O.S.: User-centered virtual environment for poststroke motor rehabilitation. J. Med. Devices **16**(2), 021014 (2022)

29. Alkadhi, B., Al-Wabil, A.: Behavioral archetypes for stroke rehabilitation technologies. In: Stephanidis, C. (ed.) HCI International 2018 – Posters' Extended Abstracts. Communications in Computer and Information Science, vol. 851, pp. 10–16. Springer, Cham (2018). https://doi.org/10.1007/978-3-319-92279-9_2

30. Pyae, A.: Investigating the usability, user experiences, and usefulness of digital game-based exercises for elderly people: a case study of Finland. In: Proceedings of the 2018 Annual Symposium on Computer-Human Interaction in Play Companion Extended Abstracts, pp. 71–76 (2018)

31. Møller, J., Johansen, N.F., Khalid, M.S.: Trends within human-computer interaction on design for physical movement. In: The 14th European Conference on Game Based Learning, ECGBL 2020, pp. 305–313. Dechema eV (2020)

32. Monument Valley [Android]. Ustwo studio Ltd. (2022)

Development and Usability Evaluation of an Application for Language Literacy of Spanish-Speaking Children with Autism Spectrum Disorder

Luis A. Rojas[1]([✉]), Katrina Sorbello[2], John W. Castro[3], and Claudio Alvarez[4]

[1] Departamento de Ciencias de La Computación Y Tecnologías de La Información,
Universidad del Bío-Bío, Chillan, Chile
lurojas@ubiobio.cl
[2] The Stella Way, 17 Enford Street, Hillcrest, QLD, Australia
kat@thestellaway.com
[3] Departamento de Ingeniería Informática Y Ciencias de La Computación, Universidad de
Atacama, Copiapó, Chile
john.castro@uda.cl
[4] Facultad de Ingeniería Y Ciencias Aplicadas, Universidad de los Andes, Santiago, Chile
calvarez@uandes.cl

Abstract. Autism Spectrum Disorder (ASD) in children is characterized by persistent difficulties in their communication and social interaction abilities and recurring and restricted patterns of behavior. As a result, children with ASD require special assistance to practice the phonetics and semantics of words, phrases, and sentences. Applications to support teaching and learning of language literacy for children with ASD generally omit phonetic and semantic aspects of communication and offer limited pedagogical tailorability. This research presents Teleo, a web application that facilitates special education teachers creating learning activities for Spanish-speaking children with ASD, and that overcomes the limitations of other applications. With Teleo, activities can be tailored to different learning objectives and offer varying degrees of difficulty for learner tasks. To evaluate special education teachers' experience with the tool, a trial was conducted (N = 7), in which subjects conducted three different kinds of activity creation tasks. An evaluation was conducted using a usability questionnaire and interviews with each teacher. Results show that Teleo provides teachers with a coherent and consistent set of functionalities to support creating literacy activities for children with ASD, and that the application is easy to use. However, despite these positive results, overemphasis on simplicity in the design of the user interface was found to hinder teachers' comprehension of application processes and features. Thus, these remain aspects to improve.

Keywords: Autism Spectrum Disorder · Literacy Learning · Learning Tool · User Experience Evaluation

A. Coman and S. Vasilache (Eds.): HCII 2023, LNCS 14026, pp. 238–254, 2023.
https://doi.org/10.1007/978-3-031-35927-9_18

1   Introduction

Autism Spectrum Disorder (ASD) in children is characterized by persistent difficulties in their communication and social interaction abilities and recurring and restricted patterns of behavior [1]. Children with ASD present reading profiles characterized by higher decoding skills and lower reading comprehension. They are known to experience difficulties extracting words' meanings [2]. As a result, children with ASD require special assistance to practice the phonetics and semantics of words, phrases, and sentences. However, children with ASD possess superior visual abilities, due to which the global reading system appears to be the best for their literacy learning [3]. Therefore, there is a need to develop tailored activities to meet the learning needs of children with ASD, that can be dynamic and adaptable to the learning context. In doing so, the efficacy of technology in special education can provide many positive learning opportunities.

On the contrary, not improving technology can negatively impact the education of children with ASD. Currently, various learning technologies, i.e., so-called 'apps', support the global reading method, simplifying work with Spanish-speaking children with ASD in the classroom. For example, 'Leo con Grin' [4] and 'Leo con Lula' [5] provide reading tasks based on syllables and words, considering the discrimination and association aspects of learning.

Similarly, 'Yo También Leo' [6] and 'El Tren del Alfabeto de Lola' [7] focus on the memorization of vocabulary. While this may be successful for children with ASD who have higher decoding skills, the activity does not provide opportunities to practice vocabulary, phonetics, and semantics dynamically, which may cause further comprehension difficulties. The 'Prolexyco' app [8] supports language learning by focusing on expression and understanding. In general, these apps include a set of pre-established activities to support literacy learning. However, these apps fail to provide educators with tools for fostering phonetic and semantic communication skills in children with ASD. In addition, the abovementioned apps and the learning activities they enable are not tailorable to different learning goals and students' particular needs and learning context, all of which are sensitive aspects when considering the learning experiences of children with ASD.

This work aims to address the drawbacks of existing apps identified above by proposing a novel web application that supports literacy development in Spanish-speaking children with ASD, based on the global reading method. The proposed application allows Special Education Teachers (henceforth, SPED Teachers) to design and implement learning activities that adapt to the specific characteristics and needs of children with ASD. Furthermore, our proposal provides feedback to teachers based on data collection comprising of interactions and children's progress in the activities. Based on this feedback, teachers can improve their teaching and assessment.

The ISO 9241 [9] standard defines usability as the level at which a software product can be used by certain users to achieve specific objectives with effectiveness, efficiency and satisfaction in a defined context of use. In software development, this characteristic is considered a key quality attribute for user satisfaction [10], and therefore, it is a determining factor for the success of an application. Due to the characteristics of children with ASD, considering the usability of the proposed web application becomes more important.

In our attempt to maximize the usability of our application, a series of considerations were taken:

- Adoption of a development process that blends user-centered design and agile development [11].
- The user interface was designed following the graphic design guidelines identified by [12].
- The heuristics evaluation method was used to test and evaluate the usability of the app's initial version and improve its functionality.

The web application was evaluated with SPED Teachers, which included measurement of user experience, validity, and usefulness. The evaluation included: (i) individual interviews and (ii) usability questionnaires to quantitatively and qualitatively study the web application. User experiences indicate positive and acceptable evaluations regarding the usefulness, ease of use, ease of learning, and satisfaction.

This paper is organized as follows. Section 2 presents the proposed solution to support literacy in children with ASD. Section 3 formally evaluates the SPED Teachers' experience to study our proposal. Section 4 presents a discussion of the evaluation results of our proposal. Finally, Sect. 5 presents conclusions and future work.

2 Teleo: A Web Application to Support the Teaching of Literacy in Spanish-Speaking Children with ASD

The learning tool presented in this research consists of a web application called Teleo, which is aimed at dynamically generating literacy activities for Spanish-speaking children with ASD. Figure 1 presents the details of the proposed web application. As can be seen in Fig. 1, Teleo allows ASD specialists to create different types of activities, namely, (1) activities to create sentences and phrases, (2) activities to create words with syllables, and (3) activities to count syllables. The application includes a configuration module for dynamic activities to support literacy teaching. These activities allow different configurations by which they adapt to different levels of difficulty and learning objectives. Each type of activity allows the creation of an unlimited number of modules with literacy activities based on the global method. Likewise, these activities may contain different configurations related to a) Data Collection Settings: identification of the type of data to be collected during user interaction; b) Activity Assignment: determination of the groups or users associated with the activity; and c) Customization of Activities: establishing the level of difficulty and specific characteristics of the activities.

Each of the activities generated can be accessed dynamically by the different groups and users of the application, allowing dynamic and controlled access to the different activities. The interactions configured for recording through data collection settings can be reviewed by SPED teachers for analysis.

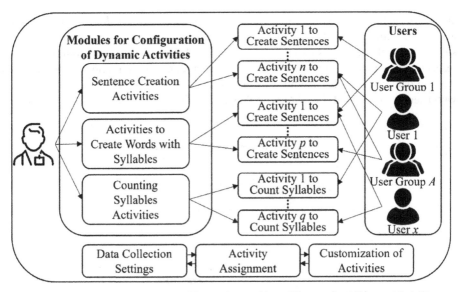

Fig. 1. The proposed solution to support the teaching of literacy in children with ASD.

2.1 Adoption of a User-Centered and Agile Development Process

A software process that blends user-centered design and agile development in the web application development [11] was adopted.

The development process began with a contextual investigation, in order to capture characteristics and acceptance criteria of end-users. Likewise, the relevant contents associated with the Web application were identified, that is, content and context mod-els, mockups, site maps, among others, were obtained. The information captured in this stage was used to improve requirements management, incorporating data related to end-user information criteria and priority content. The objective was to provide the team with a common understanding through a clear description of the needs of end-users.

Finally, following the guidelines in [11], the inspection and continuous improvement processes, including daily meetings, review of increments, and retrospectives, were used to encourage User-Centered Design and end-user involvement. For example, individual tasks were inspected to track compliance with end-user acceptance criteria; product increments were evaluated with the involvement of end-users; and retrospective meetings included reflections related to process improvements to efficiently integrate the needs of end-users.

2.2 Interfaces

Figure 2 presents the configuration module for creating sentence and phrase activities. This module permits customization of the title of the activity instruction (See "*Título de la Instrucción*" at the top of Fig. 2) and determines the number of words that the sentence or phrase will contain (See "*Número de Palabras*" on the upper part of Fig. 2). In this way, and according to the number of words indicated above, the options are dynamically enabled to indicate the words (See "*Palabras*") and images (See "*Imagen Asociada*") associated with each of them. Likewise, this module enables assigning activities to specific students or groups (See "*Asignar a*" and "*Asociar a*" at the bottom of Fig. 2, respectively). Finally, in the lower right part of Fig. 2, the configuration options of the types of data (time, clicks, attempts) to be collected and recorded during the interaction with users are presented (See "*Registrar*" option in Fig. 2).

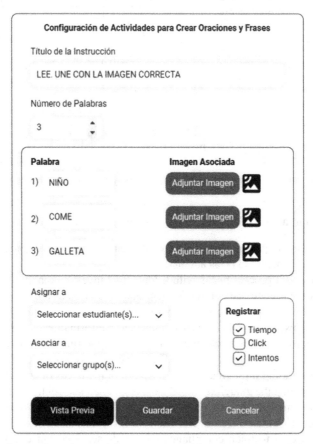

Fig. 2. Configuration module to create activities of sentences and phrases.

Figure 3 presents the configuration module that allows creating activities to establish and form words based on syllables that contain one consonant and a vowel. Like the previous module, this module also allows to describe of a specific title for the activity instruction (See "*Título de la Instrucción*" at the top of Fig. 3) and determine the number of words the activity will contain (See "*Número de Palabras*" at the top of Fig. 3). Unlike the previous module, this activity provides a section to enter the syllables on which the literacy activity will focus. For example, this module example focuses on syllables that start with B and contain one vowel (See "Sílabas" at the top of Fig. 3). There are five hidden syllable options that are used for students to practice the phonetics of a consonant with a vowel, such as RA, RE, RI, RO, RU. Subsequently, and according to the number of words established, the hidden syllable placeholders are dynamically enabled to indicate the images associated with each word. For example, the number of placeholders available for each word depends on the number of missing syllables entered next to the image (See "*Imagen Asociada*" in the central part of Fig. 3). The SPED Teacher can then define the correct answer for each hidden syllable placeholder along with the final syllable of the word; which is displayed to the student as a hint (See "*Palabra*" in the central part of Fig. 3). In the same way as the previous module, it is possible to assign the activities to particular students or groups (See "*Asignar a*" and "*Asociar a*" at the bottom of Fig. 3, respectively). Finally, in the lower right part of Fig. 3, the configuration options of the types of data (time, clicks, attempts) to be collected and recorded during the interaction with the users are presented (See "*Registrar*" option in Fig. 3).

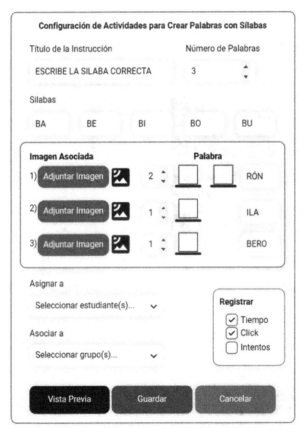

Fig. 3. Configuration module to create activities for the establishment and conformation of words based on syllables.

Figure 4 presents the configuration module to create activities requiring the learner to count word syllables. In this module, it is necessary to specify the text of the instruction for the learner and the number of words that the activity will contain (See "*Título de la Instrucción*" and "*Número de Palabras*" in Fig. 4, respectively). According to the number of words defined, the options to enter the images and the number of syllables associated with each word is dynamically enabled (See "*Imagen*" and "*Número de Sílabas*" in Fig. 4, respectively). This functionality enables SPED Teachers to tailor the activity to different learning goals, contextualized in a personalized way. Finally, and like the previous modules, there are the options to assign the activities to particular students or groups and the additional configurations of the types of data (time, clicks, attempts) to collect and record during the interaction with the users (See the options "*Asignar a*", "*Asociar a*" and "*Registrar*" in Fig. 4, respectively).

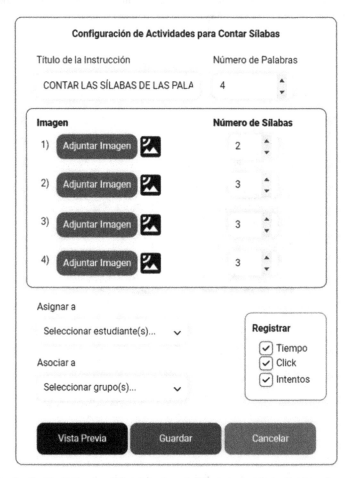

Fig. 4. Configuration module to create activities to count the syllables of words.

Finally, and as an example, Fig. 5 shows a specific activity generated based on the module for creating sentences and phrases (See Fig. 2). As can be seen, an activity with three words has been configured to create the sentence "*BOY EATS COOKIE*"

(See "*NIÑO COME GALLETA*" in Fig. 5), associating a specific image for each of the words. Likewise, a specific instruction has been established for the activity, that is, "*READ. MATCH WITH THE CORRECT IMAGE*" (See "*LEE. UNE CON LA IMAGEN CORRECTA*" in Fig. 5).

Fig. 5. Example of an activity generated with the module to create sentences and phrases.

3   Web Application User Experience Evaluation

This section describes the evaluation carried out to measure the user experience achieved with Teleo, both quantitatively and qualitatively. To measure the user experience achieved with this tool, a trial was conducted with a sample of potential users. Subjects were sampled by convenience from the environment close to the researcher.

3.1   Trial Participants

Trial participants were SPED teachers who are experienced in creating learning activities that meet the specific needs of children with ASD. All participants consented to participate in the study and willingly attended the interview. A total of seven SPED teachers (M_{age} = 32.85 years, SD_{age} = 5.81, ages 28 to 41; 57% males) participated in the study. Table 1 displays the participant attributes and demonstrates level of experience that each participant has in creating learning activities for children with ASD ($M_{experience}$ = 9.29 years, $SD_{experience}$ = 5.91).

Table 1. Participant Attributes

Participant	Age	Gender	Profession	Experience*
P1	30	M	Special Education Assistant	9
P2	41	F	SPED Coordinator	15
P3	25	M	SPED Teacher	2
P4	28	M	Special Ed Substitute teacher	6
P5	39	F	Special Education Coordinator	19
P6	35	F	Special Education Teacher	5
P7	32	M	ASD Teacher Aide	9

* Years of experience in creating learning activities for children with ASD

3.2 Tasks

In the trial, each participant was asked to perform three tasks to generate literacy activities using Teleo. Each task resulted in the creation of one of each of the activities presented in Sect. 2.2. Table 2 presents the three tasks performed by the participant users.

Table 2. Description of the proposed tasks to evaluate Teleo.

#	Task	Description
T1	Create an activity for the creation of sentences	The participant must enter a certain set of words and related images, in order to create an activity that allows users to create sentences
T2	Create an activity to complete words with syllables	The participant must enter a specific syllable and define a certain number of words, in order to create an activity that allows users to complete these words with their syllables
T3	Create an activity to count syllables	The participant must enter a certain set of words and indicate, for each of them, the number of syllables they contain

3.3 Procedure

The trial was conducted in person or remotely, depending on participant availability. In face-to-face mode, a physical place was agreed to hold the meeting, while in remote mode, a video conference was held using Zoom and Chrome's remote desktop so that users could share their screen and thus check the steps taken. In both cases (face-to-face and remote) the following steps were performed:

(1) First Stage: Initially, each participant in the evaluation was introduced to the general objective of the evaluation (note that this did not include instructions).

(2) Second Stage: Each of the participants was required to perform the above three tasks related to the creation of learning activities for children with ASD, using Teleo.

(3) Third Stage: In the last step of the experimentation, and once the session with the users was finished, each of the participants was invited to participate in a quantitative (See Sect. 3.4) and qualitative (See Sect. 3.5) evaluation to evaluate the user experience of Teleo.

3.4 Quantitative Evaluation

To study the SPED Teachers' user experience in using Teleo quantitatively, a questionnaire was designed based on [13], which was constructed based on some usability tests: Usability [14]; Usability checklist for computer-based testing programs [15, 16]; Usefulness, Satisfaction, and Ease of use [17]; Purdue usability [18]; Perceived usefulness and perceived ease of use [19].

Table 3 presents the analysis of the quantitative study responses. CQ1 and CQ6 are general questions that indicate if Teleo supported the SPED Teacher to create learning activities for children with ASD and if they would use Teleo again, respectively. Teleo supported SPED Teachers to create literacy learning activities for children with ASD ($M_{CQ1} = 4.71$ and $SD_{CQ1} = 0.49$) and all of participants will use Teleo again ($M_{CQ6} = 1$ and $SD_{CQ6} = 0$).

Table 3. Analysis of the Quantitative Study Responses.

No	Question	N	M	SD
CQ1	On a scale of 1 to 5, how did TELEO support you in creating learning activities for children with ASD??	7	4.71	0.49
CQ2	Did the functions of TELEO meet your ASD activity development needs?	7	1	0
CQ3	Was it easy for you to navigate through TELEO?	7	1	0
CQ4	Were you able to complete all three tasks assigned in TELEO to be able to create learning activities for children with ASD?	7	0.85	0.38
CQ5	Did all features work to create learning activities for children with ASD?	7	0.57	0.53
CQ6	Would you use TELEO again?	7	1	0

CQ1 has a Likert scale response between 1 and 5, whereas CQ2 to CQ6 are dichotomic (yes/no) items, in which yes $= 1$ and no $= 0$. Therefore, the mean and standard deviation of CQ1 differ from the remaining questions. Figure 6 compares the positive and negative responses for each question above.

CQ4 ($M_{CQ4} = 0.86$ and $SD_{CQ4} = 0.38$) and CQ5 ($M_{CQ5} = 0.57$ and $SD_{CQ5} = 0.53$) have the highest negative responses regarding the usability and validity of Teleo. M_{CQ4} indicates that one of the seven participants could not complete all three tasks assigned. This may be due to M_{CQ5} results demonstrating issues with features. However, this is only speculation from analyzing the quantitative study, which leaves space for ambiguity.

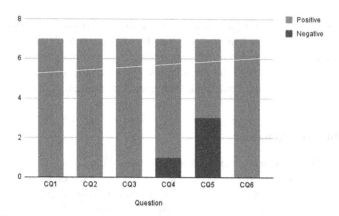

Fig. 6. Comparison between positive and negative responses per question.

For this reason, usability and validity, along with two other themes, are explored further in the qualitative study to identify opportunities for future work improvements.

3.5 Qualitative Evaluation

The objective of the qualitative evaluation was to obtain a deeper understanding of SPED teachers' user experience with Teleo and understand whether it facilitated them in creating literacy learning activities that met the specific needs of children with ASD. This was conducted via an interview with each of the participants. The instrument used was a questionnaire based on [20]. Each of the quantitative questions presented earlier (see Table 3) had a minimum of two qualitative follow-up questions to further understand the user experience of the SPED Teachers.

A total of four themes emerged from the interviews conducted with the seven participants. The themes are "Functionality," "Learnability," "Usability," and "Validity." Below is a description and analysis of the qualitative study results for each theme.

Functionality aims to identify if Teleo met the SPED teachers' needs to create literacy learning activities for children with ASD. The study further analyzed the functionality most beneficial to the SPED Teachers and those that were least beneficial.

All the participants indicated that all functions of Teleo were beneficial. However, they specified that the speed of building activities and the flexibility offered by the different activity types were most beneficial.

"Rapidly creating effective activities for students" [P1; positive].

"They were all equally beneficial - but I really liked the syllable activity. It is very thorough and more complex than some other simple activities on other apps" [P2; positive].

"Different activity types that are flexible" [P3; positive].

"All activities were very easy to build" [P4; positive].

"The flexibility and variety of activities" [P5; positive].

"The different activity types and that they were flexible - I could build them how I saw fit" [P6; positive].

"Different activity types" [P7; positive].

These comments demonstrate that Teleo achieves the goal of providing a Web application that tailors literacy activities to students' learning goals and unique needs and is adaptable to the learning context. However, there are opportunities for improvement in functionality, including providing stock images and ensuring that activities are not too complex to build.

"The syllabus activity took longer to build so wasn't that easy to build at the last minute" [P4; negative].

"Only being able to upload images. It would be nice to be able to use stock images or do a Google search" [P5; positive].

Learnability intends to determine the ease of use of Teleo by identifying if it is easy to navigate. It further explored what design elements the participants found most effective and which functionality was easier to learn. On the contrary, the study also explored what design elements the participants found least compelling and which functionality was more complicated to learn.

As seen earlier in the quantitative study, CQ3 displayed that only positive feedback was received (see Fig. 6). This shows that Teleo was easy to use and learn. When further discussed in the qualitative study, the positive responses fell into two categories of learnability: (1) how the information was displayed (layout) and (2) the design elements.

Layout

"All of them. Easy to navigate and create activities" [P1; positive].

"Quickly building a matching activity with words and images" [P4; positive].

"The building of the activities was very easy to learn. Simple and straight forward" [P7; positive].

Design

"Building the activities was very easy. It was always clear what I had to do on the screen" [P2; positive].

"The syllable activity was the most complicated to learn - but once I understood it I found it very effective" [P3; positive].

"Dragging and dropping an image would be easier for me" [P6; positive].

Usability seeks to determine if the SPED Teachers could complete all sections of Teleo and create literacy learning activities for children with ASD. It analyzed if the participants were able to complete all sections of Teleo. In addition to understanding, if the participants could follow the structure, the interviews aimed to discover if the participant successfully created literacy for each task outlined in Table 2. Furthermore, the interview explored if parts of Teleo became a distraction in achieving success.

Participants found that the structure of Teleo helped them to be able to create a literacy activity for their students.

"… it was easy and straight forward. Teleo allowed us to design activities that we have not been able to design on other platforms. It has saved us a lot of time …" [P1: positive].

"It allowed me to create activities that were more challenging for the children. It helped to engage students a little more rather than using the same monotonous activities repetitively" [P2: positive].

"It helped me to create activities at the last second. If I had to run a class for the day that I wasn't prepared for, I could quickly design an activity. I could even do it in class. If I wasn't quite sure of the students' needs, I could start the class, get an understanding of their needs and then quickly build an activity for them." [P4: positive].

"I was able to build activities that my students need without being heavily restricted by an application" [P5: positive].

"It was clear and concise. It helped me to build activities that were more robust" [P6: positive].

These comments further show that Teleo is a user-friendly web application that facilitates SPED Teachers to create literacy activities focusing on phonetics and communication skills semantics. However, designing a structure that could be flexible to meet the needs of all participants proved to be complicated.

"I didn't really know how to use the syllable activity and had to ask for instructions" [P3: negative].

"I didn't really understand the record options at first" [P7: negative].

However, these responses are constructive feedback indicating design element improvements to increase usability of Teleo; as opposed to negating the validity of the web application. The responses further imply that after instructions (or trial and error [P7]), the activities enabled SPED Teachers to create literacy activities for their stu-dents, but small improvements will facilitate easier adoption. Yet, the validity of Teleo is yet to be explored.

Validity addresses the error prevention capabilities of Teleo by analyzing the issues that participants experienced. The interview focused on the inconsistencies that the participant experienced to identify if these could be resolved in future work. Firstly, the interview identified if functionality worked as expected.

"Easy to navigate and smooth process. I like that everything was on one page and minimal" [P1; positive].

"The flexibility of what I wanted to add to an activity. The flexibility of the data I wanted to review" [P6; positive].

"Yes, [Teleo] worked perfectly" [P7; positive].

Secondly, the interview identified what inconsistencies were experienced across functionality, including navigation and design.

"Sometimes the title section was smaller than other activities" [P7; negative].

While the quantitative analysis shows negative responses, see Fig. 6 ($M_{CQ4} = 0.85$ and $SD_{CQ4} = 0.38$; $M_{CQ5} = 0.57$ and $SD_{CQ5} = 0.53$), on further investigation, in the interviews, the participants shared constructive feedback as opposed to negative user experiences.

"Initially, all of them [features worked well] apart from the syllabus activity. Maybe add instructions" [P3; constructive].

"I would have loved to see more flexibility in the 'create words with syllables' activity where we could move the syllable to different places (not just the end) – this way we could change the level of difficulty." [P5; constructive].

Generally, in addition to the above themes, when participants were asked if they would use Teleo again, see Table 3, (MCQ6 = 7 and SDCQ6 = 0), the interview further explored what functionality would be used again and which wouldn't.

"I really liked the ability to be able to choose what information we will track from the children so that we had a better understanding of how to improve our activities. This will definitely be used again." [P2; positive].

"all of them - especially now that I know how to use the syllable activity" [P3; positive].

"all of them but the syllable activity, unless I have more time" [P5; negative].

4 Discussion

The qualitative study explored the functionality, learnability, usability, and validity of Teleo, identifying that it is a successful tool for creating phonetic and semantic literacy skills; and will be implemented again by SPED Teachers. Teleo provided SPED Teachers with a dynamic web application that offers adaptability in creating tailored literacy activities focusing on different learning goals. Additionally, the participants provided valuable feedback to improve the usability and validity of Teleo.

For example, the ability to rapidly build literacy activities for children with ASD and the flexibility of different activity types were the most valuable to the SME. This was expected as this was the goal of this work; to provide educators with the tools they require to tailor activities to meet the learning needs of their students. However, consolidating more complex literacy activities into a web application brings complications when attempting to concisely layout information. This was identified from the difficulties experienced when learning how to configure the activity to establish and form words based on syllables. This was identified with feedback from P3 indicating that further instructions were required to complete Task 2 effectively. As this is the most complex activity, this feedback will support the refinement of building capabilities to create complex activities in Teleo for future versions. For example, help icons can provide the user with just-in-time instructions.

Constructive feedback on the functionality indicated that design elements could be enhanced to be more intuitive, thus improving the learnability of Teleo. Participant 7 indicated that it was difficult to understand using the record options. However, he understood the need for them after instructions were provided. This experiment specifically did not provide instructions to ascertain the usability of Teleo and identify its intuitiveness. Regardless, this feedback will help to improve and refine design elements.

Further suggestions were provided to allow for more flexibility in creating different difficulty levels within an activity, such as enabling the user to change the position of missing syllables and making questions more accessible or more difficult. Additionally, while there is a feature to upload images, additional features such as drag and drop for images or searching stock images online (via Teleo) will be considered for future versions.

Conclusively, no participant experienced errors or inconsistencies in Teleo, which is further illustrated by all participants indicating that they would use Teleo again.

5   Conclusion and Future Works

This research proposes Teleo, a web application to create literacy activities for Spanish-speaking children with ASD. The application was trialed with a cohort of special education teachers and evaluated quantitatively and qualitatively.

Teleo allows SPED Teachers to dynamically design different types of activities to support literacy instruction for children with ASD. These activities can be customized and adjusted according to the learning objectives defined by the SPED Teacher. Likewise, the different interfaces of Teleo have been introduced.

Results of the quantitative evaluation show that Teleo provides a coherent and consistent set of functionalities to support creating literacy activities for children with ASD. Even though positive results were obtained in the initial quantitative evaluation, it was also decided to conduct interviews with each participant to obtain more details about their experiences using Teleo.

Results of the qualitative evaluation based on interviews indicate that Teleo successfully supported SPED Teachers in creating literacy activities for children with ASD. However, improvements are required regarding the usability and validity of features. Furthermore, the qualitative evaluation raised challenges in consolidating user interface elements and processes to suit more complex learning activities. While Teleo is simple and easy to use, overemphasis on the simplicity of the user interface can ultimately hinder teachers' comprehension of application features. Overall, the application seems to lack sufficient guidance for teachers to follow the intended processes in creating learning activities tailored to learning goals. These are aspects that need improvement and further evaluation.

In future work, we hope to integrate more configuration modules, which allow the creation of different activities and simultaneously incorporate the improvements identified in the present study. In addition, we want to conduct a formal evaluation with children with ASD to study the usability of the Web application. Likewise, we hope to experiment to determine the learning gains of children with ASD by using Teleo. In addition, we want to formally study the priorities of the SPED Teacher through a formal method[21, 22] to adjust the modules proposed in Teleo. We also hope to create functionality for Teleo to capture more user interaction data. Finally, we also hope to use automated tools for usability evaluation [10], in order to obtain more information about the functionalities of our proposal.

References

1. Lord, C., Elsabbagh, M., Baird, G., Veenstra-Vanderweele, J.: Autism spectrum disorder. The lancet **392**(10146), 508–520 (2018)
2. Chandler-Olcott, K., Kluth, P.: Why everyone benefits from including students with autism in literacy classrooms. Read. Teach. **62**(7), 548–557 (2009)
3. Boyle, S.A., McNaughton, D., Chapin, S.E.: Effects of shared reading on the early language and literacy skills of children with autism spectrum disorders: A systematic review. Focus Autism Dev. Disabil. **34**(4), 205–214 (2019)
4. Educaplanet, S.L.: Leo con Grind: aprender a leer (2021). https://apps.apple.com/es/app/aprender-a-leer-1-con-grin/id932280561
5. Gomez, J., Jaccheri, L., Torrado, J.C., Montoro, G.: Leo con lula, introducing global reading methods to children with ASD, In: Proceedings of the 17th ACM Conference on Interaction Design and Children, pp. 420–426 (2018)
6. Diversity-Apps. Yo También Leo (2020). https://yotambienleo.com
7. BeiZ. El tren del alfabeto de Lola (2012). https://play.google.com/store/apps/details?id=com.beiz.lolaabclite&hl=es_CL&gl=US
8. Capel, F., Palazón, C.: Material de aula de Prolexyco. Programa de desarrollo del lenguaje expresivo y comprensivo, GEU (2016)
9. Din, E.: 9241–11. Ergonomic requirements for office work with visual display terminals (VDTs)–Part 11: Guidance on usability. International Organization for Standardization, Geneva (1998)
10. J. W. Castro, I. Garnica, L. A. Rojas: Automated Tools for Usability Evaluation: A Systematic Mapping Study. In: Social Computing and Social Media: Design, User Experience and Impact, pp. 28–46 (2022)
11. Rojas, L.A., Macías, J.A.: An agile information-architecture-driven approach for the development of user-centered interactive software. In: Proceedings of the XVI International Conference on Human Computer Interaction, pp. 1–8 (2015)
12. Ntalindwa, T., Nduwingoma, M., Karangwa, E., Soron, T.R., Uworwabayeho, A., Uwineza, A.: Development of a mobile app to improve numeracy skills of children with autism spectrum disorder: participatory design and usability study. JMIR Pediatr. Parent. **4**(3), e21471 (2021)
13. Chang, Y.K., Kuwata, J.: Learning experience design: challenges for novice designers. Learn User Experience Research (2020)
14. Pirnay-Dummer, P., Ifenthaler, D., Spector, J.M.: Highly integrated model assessment technology and tools. Educ. Technol. Res. Dev. **58**(1), 3–18 (2010)
15. Parshall, C.G., Harmes, J.C.: Improving the quality of innovative item types: four tasks for design and development. J. Appl. Test. Technol. **10**(1), 1–20 (2009)
16. Liu, J.: The Assessment agent system: design, development, and evaluation. Educ. Technol. Res. Dev. **61**(2), 197–215 (2013)
17. Lund, A.M.: Measuring usability with the use questionnaire12. Usability Interface **8**(2), 3–6 (2001)
18. Lin, H.X., Choong, Y.-Y., Salvendy, G.: A proposed index of usability: a method for comparing the relative usability of different software systems. Behav. Inf. Technol. **16**(4–5), 267–277 (1997)

19. Davis, F.D.: Perceived usefulness, perceived ease of use, and user acceptance of information technology. MIS Quart. **13**(3), 319 (1989). https://doi.org/10.2307/249008
20. Rojas, L., Sorbello, K., Contreras, P., Calderon, J.F.: Design, implementation and evaluation of a technical platform that supports spanish speaking children with intellectual disabilities learn english as a second language. In: Meiselwitz, G. (ed.) Social Computing and Social Media: Applications in Marketing, Learning, and Health: 13th International Conference, SCSM 2021, Held as Part of the 23rd HCI International Conference, HCII 2021, Virtual Event, July 24–29, 2021, Proceedings, Part II, pp. 257–269. Springer International Publishing, Cham (2021). https://doi.org/10.1007/978-3-030-77685-5_21
21. Rojas, L.A., Macías, J.A.: Toward collisions produced in requirements rankings: a qualitative approach and experimental study. J. Syst. Softw. **158**,(2019)
22. Rojas, L., Olivares-Rodriguez, C., Alvarez, C., Campos, P.G.: OurRank: a software requirements prioritization method based on qualitative assessment and cost-benefit prediction. IEEE Access **10**, 131772–131787 (2022). https://doi.org/10.1109/ACCESS.2022.3230152

A Mobile Application to Dynamically Design Activities to Promote Personal Autonomy in Children with Autism Spectrum Disorder: A Usability Evaluation

Katrina Sorbello[1], Luis A. Rojas[2(✉)], José Salas[2], and Enrique Chavarriaga[3]

[1] The Stella Way, 17 Enford Street, Hillcrest, QLD, Australia
kat@thestellaway.com
[2] Departamento de Ciencias de la Computación y Tecnologías de la Información, Universidad del Bío-Bío, Chillan, Chile
lurojas@ubiobio.cl, jose.salas1801@alumnos.ubiobio.cl
[3] Uground Gobal I+D+i, Madrid, Spain
echavarriaga@uground.com

Abstract. Autism Spectrum Disorder (ASD) is a neurodevelopmental disorder characterized by deficits in social communication, the presence of restricted interests, repetitive behaviors, and difficulty performing activities autonomously. Regarding children, personal autonomy is affected by having difficulties in carrying out activities appropriate to their age. ASD specialists use various activities during interactions with children with ASD to promote and encourage autonomy. Currently, there are different assistive technologies to support the development of autonomy in Spanish-speaking children with ASD. However, these proposals present a series of difficulties. In this paper, we propose a user-friendly mobile application that provides a set of activities designed by ASD specialists to foster the personal autonomy of Spanish-speaking children with ASD. Also, our proposal allows ASD specialists to dynamically create and adapt activities according to the specific characteristics and needs of children with ASD. Different evaluations were carried out with ASD specialists, children with ASD and their caregivers/relatives to study the usability of the proposal. User experiences indicate positive and acceptable evaluations in terms of usefulness, ease of use, ease of learning and satisfaction.

Keywords: Usability Evaluation · Autism Spectrum Disorder · Personal Autonomy · ASD

1 Introduction

Autism Spectrum Disorder (ASD) is a neurodevelopmental disorder characterized by deficits in social communication, the presence of restricted interests, repetitive behaviors, and difficulty performing activities autonomously [1, 2]. In regards to children, personal autonomy is affected by having difficulties in carrying out activities appropriate to their age [3]. In addition, as these children require special care, they will also need a caregiver, creating a mutual dependency [4] and generating, in the medium and long term, difficulties for their organization and general quality of life [5].

ASD specialists use various activities during interactions with children with ASD (such as puzzles, games with environmental interactions, pictograms, among others) to promote and encourage autonomy. However, this generates an environment that forces the child to interact with the specialist in addition to the activity, causing an overload of attention and discomfort in the child. The above difficulty can be addressed by using assistive technologies, which help to increase the autonomy and safety of people on the autism spectrum and thus decrease the burden of care. Currently, there are different assistive technologies to support the development of autonomy in Spanish-speaking children with ASD [6–8]. However, these proposals present a series of difficulties. For example, only paid applications offer a suite of activities, in contrast to free applications that offer a limited set of activities, with little content and are often outdated. In addition, some applications require a series of additional software installations to access the activities, generating entry barriers and difficulties for their use. Furthermore, most of the proposals do not provide information on their usefulness and acceptance [9], making it difficult to monitor and validate the details of the proposed activities.

In this paper, we propose a user-friendly mobile application that provides a set of activities designed by ASD specialists to foster the personal autonomy of Spanish-speaking children with ASD. Also, our proposal allows ASD specialists to dynamically create and adapt activities according to the specific characteristics and needs of children with ASD. This ensures to decrease interaction between specialist and children with ASD, to allow the child to focus on the activity designed to encourage autonomy. Different evaluations were carried out with ASD specialists, children with ASD and their caregivers/relatives to study the usability of the proposal. The techniques applied for usability evaluation were thinking aloud, audio and video recording, questionnaires, interviews, and heuristic evaluation.

This paper is organized as follows. Section 2 presents a technological platform to address autonomy in children with ASD. Section 3 describes the different evaluations carried out on ASD specialists, children with ASD, and their caregivers/relatives to study the usability of the proposal. Section 4 presents a discussion of the quantitative and qualitative results of our proposal. Finally, Sect. 5 presents conclusions and future work.

2 An Accessible and Easy-To-Use Technological Proposal to Promote Personal Autonomy in Children with Autism Spectrum Disorder

A mobile application, called TEAutonomía, is proposed to promote the personal autonomy of children with ASD. The proposal allows ASD specialists and caregivers/relatives of children with ASD to dynamically create activities aimed at supporting the teaching of autonomy. Figure 1 presents a summary of the proposed solution. As can be seen in Fig. 1, the mobile application allows ASD specialists and caregivers/relatives of children with ASD to create and configure different types of activities to promote the personal autonomy of children with ASD. Likewise, children with ASD can access activities configured specifically according to their characteristics and needs. Currently, the proposal consists mainly of three types of activities: sequence of pictograms, search for objects and musical instruments. In addition, it has a series of modules to configure end-user access and generate statistical reports on the use of TEAutonomía. The three main types of activities are described in detail below.

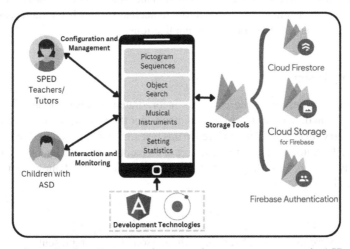

Fig. 1. Mobile application TEAutonomía proposed to promote autonomy in ASD children.

Pictogram Sequence: This type of activity consists of creating pictogram sequences with audio reading. The designed activities have a hearing aid in the pictograms and in the total sequence. The mobile application allows ASD specialists to create and adjust an unlimited number of sequence activities. Additionally, TEAutonomía includes 3 categories of activities: eating habits, personal hygiene, and dressing habits. For each of these categories, TEAutonomía has 8 pictogram sequence activities, which have been designed and created together with ASD specialists.

Object Search: This type of activity consists of creating lists of real objects relevant to children with ASD. The main objective of these activities is for children with ASD to search for objects presented in their immediate environment. These activities can be dynamically created by ASD specialists and caregivers/relatives of children with ASD.

Musical Instruments: This activity consists of incorporating musical instruments digitally, to simulate their use in real life and bring children with ASD closer to distinguishing the different types of incorporated instruments. The musical instruments represented correspond to an interactive xylophone, which, according to the key pressed, makes a note of the musical scale; and sounds of percussion instruments, which when pressed make a short sound according to the selected instrument. Each instrument was incorporated according to its ease of use and taking into account that they focus on children with ASD between 4–6 years [10].

It should be noted that each activity has functionalities to monitor the statistics associated with its use, so that ASD specialists and caregivers/relatives of children with ASD can view their records, the time of use, the activity carried out and the dates associates. TEAutonomía was developed using Ionic and Angular, in its version 13. This has facilitated the use of tools and languages focused on web development such as HTML, CSS and TypeScript. The Firebase platform was used to authenticate and store all the information. Also, the following modules were used: Cloud Firestore to manage NoSQL database; Cloud Storage to store heavy content in the cloud; and Firebase Authentication that provides an authentication service through mechanisms such as email, password, or third-party providers for integration into applications.

2.1 Activity Design

In the process of designing the activities incorporated in TEAutonomía, acceptance criteria are defined, in order to evaluate and consider their incorporation. These criteria are associated with key concepts covered in this research: autonomy, interface design and end users of TEAutonomía. In this way, a set of elements for the design of TEAutonomía are formally defined, according to what was explained in [11] and implemented in [12], using the following formulas:

$$U = \{S_n, C_g, M_p\} \tag{1}$$

where, S_n represents the set of senses of the person (U), C_g represents their cognitive functions and M_p represents the motor functions of the different parts of the body. Carrying out an action by the end user leads to a reaction to the stimulus (R_e) generated by the senses (S_n). This reaction to the stimulus is formally defined as:

$$R_e = \{C_g, M_p\} \tag{2}$$

where, a reaction to the stimulus (R_e) is formed by the mental representation of the information through cognitive functions (C_g). This, at the same time, is handled and a motor function (M_p) is given as a response to carry out the action that was taken as a resolution. Another key factor is age (Ed) since over the years people begin to show cognitive impairment. This worsening is due to the appearance of affections to both cognitive and motor functions. This allows us to reformulate the Eq. (1), such that:

$$U = \{\{S_n, R_e\}, Ed\} \tag{3}$$

where each user (U) through the senses (S_n) generates a stimulus, which has a reaction (R_e) through cognitive and motor functions according to the user's age (Ed).

Likewise, for the incorporation of activities, the concept of application (S) must be defined according to the specific case of the investigation, that is, the incorporation of activities that promote autonomy in children with ASD. A formal definition of the application is:

$$S = \{A_1, \ldots, A_n\} \in Au \tag{4}$$

where, S represents the software (TEAutonomía), A represents the finite set of activities that comprise it, and Au represents the concept of autonomy. In this way, it is possible to identify the personal, emotional, and behavioral categories and each activity (A) can be formally defined as:

$$A = \{\{I_1, \ldots, I_n\}, N\} \tag{5}$$

where, each activity (A) is made up of the different interactions (I) that the user can perform to interact with the application. These are mainly the reactions to the stimuli presented in formula (2). In addition, N represents the depth of the activity when browsing the application. That is, the number of nested screens for carrying out each activity.

In this way, it is possible to define the acceptance criteria to incorporate activities in the mobile application. On the one hand, the design principles presented in [13] are considered. These principles are associated with the dimensions of form, content, and behavior for the design of interfaces focused on ASD children. And furthermore, the objectives set out in the research (that is, promoting autonomy in children with ASD) allow formulas (3), (4), and (5) to be reformulated, and thus, establish the acceptance criteria (C_a) for the incorporation of activities. These criteria can be formally defined as:

$$C_a = \begin{cases} \forall A \exists \{\{I_1, \ldots, I_n\}, N \leq 3\} \\ \quad Au = personal \\ \quad U_{Ed} = \{3, \ldots, 6\} \end{cases} \tag{6}$$

where, for every activity to be considered suitable for the proposal, it is required that there is a set of interactions, such that the depth level of each activity is less than or equal to 3. Likewise, each activity must be focused mainly on promoting the concept of autonomy of the user (children with ASD). And each user (U) must be in the age range between 3 and 6 years.

2.2 Main Interfaces

In order to improve the usability of TEAutonomía, an agile and user-centered methodology was used [14] during software development. Figure 2 presents the interfaces related to pictogram sequence activities. In the upper left part of Fig. 2, there are the three categories with the pictogram sequence activities designed by ASD specialists, as mentioned above. In addition, there are options to add new activities (See "Crear Secuencia" button) and review the created activities (See "Mis Secuencias" option). In the upper right part of Fig. 2, there is the option to configure the details of the new pictogram sequences. TEAutonomía allows to automatically associate images according to the different words entered for the sequence (See input "Frase por crear"). Finally, in the lower part of Fig. 2, there is the interface to carry out the activities by children with ASD.

Fig. 2. Three interfaces related to pictogram sequence activities: categories (upper left), config-uration (upper right) and execution of pictogram sequence activities (lower).

Figure 3 presents the three interfaces associated with the object search activity. On the left side of Fig. 3, there is the interface that lists the activities created and presents the option to create new ones (See "Crear lista de objetos" button). In this interface, it is possible to select any of the activities created for execution. The central part of Fig. 3 corresponds to the interface to execute some of the created activities. In this way, a draw is made within the set of images of objects in the activity, to select an object at random to be searched for by the child with ASD. Finally, in the right part of Fig. 3, there is an interface to indicate the found object. In any situation, the object is eliminated from the list and another one is drawn.

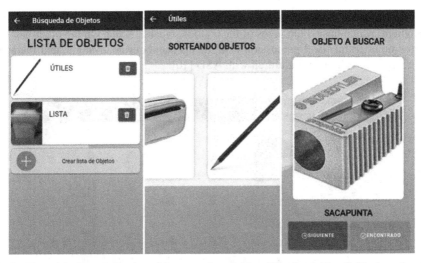

Fig. 3. Three interfaces related to object search activities: list of activities (left), draw (center) and selection of object to search (right).

Figure 4 presents the three interfaces for configuring new object search activities. On the left side of Fig. 4, the interface is presented to indicate the name of the list and the option to access to add the objects (See "Añadir Objetos" button). The central part of Fig. 4 presents the interface to add the objects to the activity. TEAutonomía allows to the addition of an unlimited number of objects per activity. For each object, it is necessary to associate an identifying name and an image. The latter may correspond to a photograph with the mobile device's camera or from the image gallery. Finally, on the right side of Fig. 4 is the object list configuration interface with the added images.

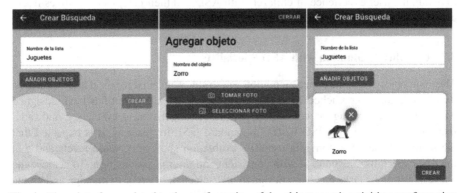

Fig. 4. Three interfaces related to the configuration of the object search activities: configuration (left), selection (middle) and list of objects (right).

Figure 5 presents the interface with the musical instruments activity options. Currently, the mobile application has two categories: xylophone and percussion instruments.

On the one hand, the xylophone corresponds to an interactive representation of the instrument, which has all the notes of the diatonic musical scale. On the other hand, in percussion instruments, 3 percussion instruments (tambourine, triangle, and maracas) are incorporated chords for children with ASD [10].

Fig. 5. Interface of the activities with musical instruments.

3   A Usability Evaluation of TEAutonomía

In this section, the experimentation carried out to measure the degree of usability achieved in TEAutonomía is described. Assessments have been conducted with ASD specialists, children with ASD, and their caregivers/relatives. On the one hand, an experiment has been carried out to quantitatively and qualitatively study the user experience of ASD specialists (see Sect. 3.1). And, on the other hand, an experiment has been designed to obtain the user experience of children with ASD and their caregivers/relatives freely using TEAutonomía for a certain period (See Sect. 3.2).

3.1   Usability Evaluation with ASD Specialists

The main objective of the experimentation was to study and analyze the degree of usability of TEAutonomía reached by ASD specialists. This experiment has been designed with the aim of meeting three usability conditions (effectiveness, efficiency, and satisfaction), described in the ISO-9241–11 standard [15]. In this way, it is expected that the results of the TEAutonomia usability evaluation show acceptable levels and that the ASD specialists perceive it with consistent and intuitive navigation. To achieve the above, a set of 10 tasks has been designed and selected, in order to manage and create activities to promote autonomy in children with ASD.

Participants. Specialists with studies related to the treatment of ASD children participated in the evaluation of TEAutonomia. Written informed consent was obtained from all participants. A total of 3 specialists (M_{age} = 36 years, SD_{age} = 9.64, ages 29 to 47;

33.33% male) participated in the case study. Specifically, a speech therapist, a teacher, and a psychologist with an average experience of 12.67 years (SD = 11.59) participated.

Tasks. To carry out the experiment, each user was asked to perform 10 tasks to set up activities to foster autonomy in children with ASD using TEAutonomía. Specifically, the 10 tasks performed by users correspond to:

Table 1. Description of tasks to be carried out by the participants during the experimentation.

# Task	Title	Description
T1	Sign up in the app	The participant must register in the application in order to make use of all the functionalities
T2	Log in	The participant must log in to access the specific data associated with their account
T3	Create Pictogram Sequence	The participant is asked to create a new pictogram sequence activity
T4	Reorder Sequence	The participant is asked to rearrange the pictogram sequence correctly
T5	Dictate Sequence	The participant is asked to dictate the phrase to order in a sequencing activity
T6	Add Objects	The participant is requested to add objects using the device's camera and the image gallery
T7	Create a list of objects	The participant is asked to create a list of objects, specifying the name and the objects it contains
T8	Create a child's profile	The participant is asked to create a profile of a child with ASD
T9	Select a child's profile	The participant is asked to select the profile of a child, in order to use the associated functionalities
T10	Exit of a child's profile	The participant is asked to exit the mode of use of a child profile, by solving a mathematical operation

Execution of the Experimentation. The execution of the experimentation was carried out in person or remotely depending on the availability of the participants. In the first case, a physical place is defined to hold the meeting, while a videoconference was held remotely using the device's camera. The experiment consisted of three stages:

- **First Stage:** The evaluation of TEAutonomía is carried out through the execution by the participants of the 10 tasks described above. In addition, each specialist is asked to indicate their thoughts aloud while performing each task, to apply the thinking aloud method and thus collect more information associated with the experience of the participants.
- **Second Stage:** Once all the requested tasks have been carried out, semi-structured interviews were carried out with the participants, to qualitatively study their user

experiences using TEAutonomía. This interview has been designed based on the work of [16] and includes questions that allow participants to reflect on all the functionalities of TEAutonomía.

- **Third Stage:** Finally, the participants were asked to complete a questionnaire to quantitatively evaluate the usability of the mobile application. The previous questionnaire was based on the USE questionnaire [17], with some modifications provided by two other questionnaires: Davis' Perceived Usefulness and Ease of Use [18] and Purdue's Usability [19].

Results Obtained. This section details and analyzes the results obtained from the experimental session with the specialists in each stage of the usability evaluation.

First Stage. This stage consisted of the results of carrying out the 10 tasks associated with TEAutonomía functionalities.

The first aspect to measure has been the effectiveness obtained in carrying out the tasks. This is calculated according to the degree of success that each participant had in completing each task presented in the evaluation. All participants have achieved 100% efficacy. Additionally, Fig. 6 has been enhanced to distinguish the cases in which the participants had doubts or queries in carrying out the task. The yellow bar indicates the percentage of completion in which the participants needed some help.

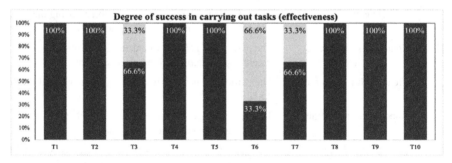

Fig. 6. Degree of success in carrying out the 10 tasks (effectiveness) achieved by the participants in the experimentation.

As can be seen in Fig. 6, only in tasks T3, T6 and T7 did the participants ask about the execution of the tasks (with a mean attendance of 33.3%, 66.6%, 33.6%, respectively). These tasks coincide in that they were associated with the creation of new content in the mobile application and required a greater number of actions to carry them out. For example, task T3 consists of creating a sequence of pictograms and a specialist had doubts as they were slightly confused about how the activity worked. This confusion was generated because when writing the phrase, the sequence of pictograms was automatically generated. Regarding task T6, which consists of adding 2 objects to a list, the participants made queries because when adding the first object they intuitively created the list and did not incorporate the second object. Finally, task T7 generated similar queries to those carried out in task T6, since they performed this task immediately after adding the object created in the previous task, this led to repeating the task to achieve the measurement properly.

The next measured point corresponds to the efficiency achieved in carrying out the tasks. This measurement is made based on the average time required by the specialists to carry out the 10 tasks. Table 2 shows the statistics associated with the times of each activity.

Table 2. Statistics of the time of execution of the tasks in the experiment (efficiency).

# Task	Media	Standard Deviation	Minimum	Maximum
T1	0:00:41	0:00:18	0:00:29	0:01:02
T2	0:00:14	0:00:02	0:00:12	0:00:15
T3	0:00:43	0:00:23	0:00:19	0:01:05
T4	0:01:00	0:00:34	0:00:24	0:01:32
T5	0:00:16	0:00:14	0:00:03	0:00:31
T6	0:02:08	0:00:35	0:01:43	0:02:48
T7	0:00:48	0:00:31	0:00:28	0:01:24
T8	0:00:35	0:00:15	0:00:19	0:00:47
T9	0:00:17	0:00:15	0:00:08	0:00:34
T10	0:00:21	0:00:14	0:00:07	0:00:35

As can be seen in Table 2, the participants took longer to perform tasks T6, T4 and T7 with an average time of 2 min and 8 s (SD = 35 s), 1 min (SD = 34 s) and 48 s (SD = 31 s), respectively. These tasks have in common the configuration of new content and interaction with more functionalities to create the activity, so that they require more time to complete. On the contrary, the tasks that require less time to complete are tasks T2, T5 and T9 with an average time of 14 s (SD = 2 s), 16 s (SD = 14 s) and 17 s (SD = 15 s). Seconds), respectively. These tasks corresponded to logging in, dictating a sequence, and selecting a child's profile, which have in common the performance of functionalities of a general nature between applications. Another common point of these tasks is that they did not require navigating between various interfaces, which made it easier to use their functionalities. The completion of the first stage of the evaluation had an average duration of 7 min and 3 s (SD = 38 s). The maximum and minimum time required by the participants were 7 min and 59 s and 5 min and 12 s, respectively. In general, the difference in time to perform the tasks is mainly due to the skills that each specialist has when using a technological tool. Prior to conducting the interview, two participants mentioned that they did not have in-depth knowledge of mobile devices, which may limit the benefits of the application. Finally, regarding the structure of the TEAutonomía design, the participants did not present major problems with navigation nor in the development of the requested tasks. In addition, the use of the Thinking Aloud protocol has been fundamental for the collection of qualitative data according to the interactions they had with TEAutonomía. For example, there were occasions in which the participants intuitively anticipated tasks or gave suggestions for the application. The data collected from the protocol is intended to improve the tool, seeking to incorporate the suggestions of all participants in future iterations in an optimal way.

Second Stage. This stage consisted of qualitatively studying the user experience from the tasks completed in the first stage. The study aims to identify if the mobile application allowed ASD specialists to create activities to promote autonomy in children with ASD. All participates indicated that it *"allows me to create things to promote autonomy."*

In addition to seeking the overall validity of the mobile application, the qualitative study provided an opportunity to conduct a deep analysis into the user experience through individual interviews. A total of five themes emerged from the interviews conducted with the three participants. The themes are "Suitability", "Feasibility", "Accessibility", "Practicality", and "Validity". Each theme is described below and a summary of the participants' responses is analyzed.

Suitability

Suitability explores if the mobile application supported the ASD specialists to create activities to promote autonomy in children with ASD. It further explores what functions of the mobile application met the needs of ASD specialists, and which were less suitable.

The three participants specified that the functions facilitated creating activities to promote autonomy in children with ASD.

"Yes, because actually throughout the game they are creating only new items. So that allows them autonomy." [Participant 1; positive].

However, not all functions promoted autonomy in all children with ASD.

"They do satisfy, but not all. Obviously it is a support, it depends on the level of performance of the child, for example: if they can manipulate technology or not, if they can follow instructions, if they have sustained attention." [Participant 2; constructive].

The most beneficial functions were the activities that required children to use emotions and included visual objects.

"The activity to order the sentences with feeling because they [children with ASD] have a hard time expressing feelings and emotions, so they identify with that." [Participant 1; positive].

"The search for objects activity, because it allows linking it with real life things to make visual to object matching of the child's daily life activities." [Participant 2; positive].

Yet, these are not always the most beneficial functions as it depends on the child's learning needs and their demographic.

"It depends on the point of view and the child with whom you are working. In the first instance, for autonomy, I believe that ordering sentences is the least

beneficial option, because when you work with people with autism and they have very compromised communication, sentence order or structure does not affect content as much." [Participant 2; constructive].

"It may be the musical instrument perhaps because it may seem simple to older children, although I consider all of them beneficial." [Participant 3; constructive].

While it is evident that the mobile application offers a suitable platform to create activities that promote autonomy in children with ASD, the participants illustrated that the level of autonomy facilitated differs depending on a diverse range of factors such as experience with technology, ability to follow instructions, attention spans, level of communication and age groups.

Feasibility
Feasibility identifies the ease of navigation of the mobile application. All participants stated its ease of use.

"Super easy, it's clear, it's super intuitive, it's simple, it has precise buttons, the interface is good." [Participant 2, positive].

This qualitative study additionally seeks to determine which design elements supported the ASD specialist to learn the mobile application by exploring the most effective feature. Musical Instruments and the Pictogram Sequence were the two most effective.

"Musical Instruments was the most intuitive of all." [Participant 2, positive].

"The main menu and the sequence of pictograms because the icons are representative in general." [Participant 3, positive].
Likewise, this qualitative study seeks to learn the least effective features of the mobile application that impacts feasibility. Two of the participants found the Object Search activity difficult to navigate due to *"the level of abstraction of the symbol is high" [Participant 3, negative]* and *"search object icon could be confused with other elements and within the search I had confusion to add objects" [Participant 3, negative].*
These difficulties in navigation were also identified in the first stage of the evaluation where 66.6% of participants required instructions to complete Task 6; which was the task that required most time to complete.

Accessibility
Accessibility determines the usability of the mobile application by identifying if all sections of the tasks were able to be completed. Each participate indicated that they successfully completed all tasks (see Table 1).

"Yes I could. In some more than others I had complications, but I could." [Participant 1, positive].

"Yes, I had no major problems creating and solving the activities." [Participant 3, positive].

On the contrary, distractions were also explored to identify if they affected the intuitiveness of the mobile application and therefore impact the usability.

"Yes, at some point I didn't know how to use the application because I didn't read, actually I didn't read everything that the application was giving me. For example, create, I did not read all my little tabs and that caused the time to increase when performing the tests." [Participant 1, constructive].

"One only, when adding an object to the list it is not intuited that they can continue to be added." [Participant 3, constructive].

While Participant 1 indicated that it is a necessity to read instructions before completing the activity, Participant 3 highlighted that it was not clear that more than one object could be added; both raise improvements for intuitiveness.

Practicality

Practicality ascertains inconsistencies in the mobile application across navigation, layout, calculations and automations. Participant 2 indicated *"When solving the sum it didn't come out immediately and I don't know whether to call it inconsistency. I would add the save password."*

Inconsistencies were further ascertained through deeper analysis in specific activities such as the Pictogram Sequence and Object Search activities. While no inconsistencies were found in either activity, the Pictogram Sequence can be improved to both be more diverse to children who do not have experience with technology, and to include more complex sentences.

"No, I did not find any inconsistencies, I think that for a child who uses phones and games it can be easier to guide. But as an adult who doesn't use games, it was difficult for me to guide myself. But nevertheless everything was fine, the activity was not incongruous." [Participant 1; constructive].

"No, it's easy to order. Of course, I got a script which could be interpreted as a type of juxtaposed sentence and that can be a distracting element. Although I don't know whether to call it inconsistency." [Participant 2; constructive].

Validity

Validity establishes if the participants will use the TEAutonomía again in the future. It identifies which activities will be used again and which wouldn't. All participants would use the mobile application again, specifically the Object Search and Musical Instruments.

"All of them would use the search for objects, the child mode and the audio-reading." [Participant 1; positive].

"I would use the xylophone and the search for objects again." [Participant 2; positive].

"To choose one it would only be the instruments because it is more casual compared to the others." [Participant 3; positive].

However, Participant 2 and 3 indicates that all three activities would be used again but *"it depends a lot on who you are working with"* and *"perhaps not all with one child since some activities may be difficult for them, but it could be better suited to another child. It all depends on the ease of the child to use the application";* respectively.

While the qualitative analysis exposes constructive feedback to make improvements in future work, the study demonstrates that the TEAutonomía successfully supports ASD specialists to create activities to promote autonomy in children with ASD.

"I think it is useful and helps autonomy, which is what is intended, and the other thing is that it helps self-concept because in sentences one identifies oneself." [Participant 1; positive].

"It seems to me a very good option, it is very simple and intuitive to use. It is a tool that can be easily held in hand." [Participant 2; positive].

"The activities are good and fulfil their function, but I would like new activities to be incorporated in the future." [Participant 3; constructive].

Third stage: This stage consisted in the completion of the usability questionnaire by the participants. The questionnaire has 31 closed questions and 2 open questions. The closed questions aim to measure the usability of the mobile application measured by utility, ease of use, ease of learning and satisfaction. While open questions are focused on obtaining feedback from the user. Each result is scored by the participants using a Likert scale between 1 and 5, with 1 being the lowest score (represented by Totally disagree) and 5 the highest score (represented by Totally agree).

Figure 7 shows the means obtained in the four variables to measure usability. High averages are obtained in all variables, with no significant differences between them. The variables ease of learning and utility obtain the highest and lowest means, respectively, with a value of 4.78 (SD = 0.43) and 4.46 (SD = 0.66). Regarding the variable with the highest score, the participants stand out with maximum scores in issues related to *"The order of the work areas is logical; It's easy to learn how to use the app; I easily remember how to use the app; and I learned to use the app quickly".* In general terms, a total mean of 4.46 (SD = 0.10) is obtained.

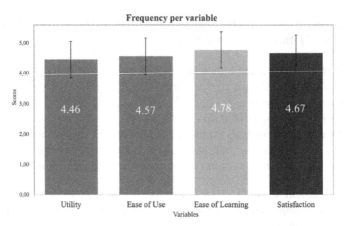

Fig. 7. Results of the usability questionnaire: average responses in the variables: utility, ease of use, ease of learning and satisfaction.

3.2 Usability Evaluation with Children with ASD and Their Caregivers/Relatives

The objective of this experimentation was to study the usability of TEAutonomía through the experience of children with ASD and their caregivers/relatives. To achieve this objective, user credentials have been enabled in TEAutonomía for children with ASD and their caregivers/relatives, so that they can use the application for one week. Both children with ASD and their caregivers/relatives could use the application freely, without any type of restrictions or specific associated tasks assigned in the previous evaluation.

Table 3. Participants of the TEAutonomía usability experimentation: Children with ASD and their caregivers/relatives.

# Tutor	Age	Gender	# Children	Age	Gender
T1	40	F	C1	4	M
T2	34	F	C2	5	F
T3	31	F	C3	5	M
T4	41	F	C4	4	F
T5	43	F	C5	6	M

Table 3 presents the participants in this experiment; children with ASD and their caregivers/relatives. The experiment involved 5 children with ASD (M_{age} = 4.8 years, SD_{age} = 0.84, ages 4 to 6; 60% male) and one tutor for each child (M_{age} = 37.8 years, SD_{age} = 5.07, ages 31 to 43; 100% female). On the one hand, the evaluation of caregivers/relatives of children with ASD consisted of completing the SUS usability questionnaire [20] after one week of using the application. On the other hand, the evaluation of the children with

ASD consisted of recording the interaction with the application for the entire period of use. Both results are presented below.

Results of the SUS Questionnaire of Caregivers/Relatives of Children with ASD. Caregivers/relatives of children with ASD obtained a final score of 77.5 on the SUS questionnaire. This result is in the acceptable range according to the usability scale system. That is, it is considered acceptable with a score greater than 68.

Interaction Results of Children with ASD Using TEAutonomía. Table 4 presents the data from the records of the ASD children's interactions with the TEAutonomía pictogram sequence activities. As can be seen, the C4 child registers the highest values in the time devoted to this activity, the number of clicks and movements. However, this child only did this activity twice. Conversely, the C5 child has the lowest total time, but the highest frequency number.

Table 4. Record of the interaction of children with ASD with the TEAutonomía pictogram sequence activities.

# Children	Usage Frequency	No. Clicks*	SD	No. of Movements*	SD	Average Time	SD	Total Time
C1	3	1.33	1.53	4.00	5.29	0:01:06	0:00:47	0:03:18
C2	1	3.00	3.00	10.00	10.00	0:02:03	0:02:03	0:02:03
C3	4	6.25	6.13	10.50	16.46	0:02:49	0:03:28	0:11:14
C4	2	46.50	57.28	53.00	57.98	0:07:55	0:10:22	0:15:51
C5	4	2.25	0.50	0.25	0.50	0:00:25	0:00:09	0:01:38

* Average values

Table 5 presents the data from the records of the ASD children's interactions with the TEAutonomía object search activities. As can be seen, the results do not show significant differences in terms of frequency of use, number of objects found, and time of use.

Table 5. Record of the interaction of children with ASD with the TEAutonomía object search activities.

# Children	Usage Frequency	Found Objects*	SD	Average Time	SD	Total Time
C1	3	1.00	1.00	0:01:45	0:01:17	0:05:15
C2	3	1.67	1.53	0:02:28	0:02:11	0:07:23
C3	4	1.25	1.26	0:01:24	0:01:02	0:05:36
C4	3	0.67	0.58	0:01:39	0:01:02	0:04:58
C5	3	1.67	0.58	0:01:33	0:00:38	0:04:38

* Average values

Finally, Table 6 presents the data from the records of the interactions of the ASD children with the TEAutonomía musical instrument activities. Notably, percussion music activities get more attention among children with ASD.

Table 6. Record of the interaction of children with ASD with the TEAutonomía musical instrument activities.

# Children	Percussion				Xylophone			
	Usage Frequency	Average Time	SD	Total Time	Usage Frequency	Average Time	SD	Total Time
C1	5	0:00:51	0:00:33	0:04:15	4	0:01:42	0:01:09	0:06:47
C2	3	0:00:15	0:00:19	0:00:46	-	-	-	-
C3	3	0:04:35	0:04:14	0:13:46	2	0:00:38	0:00:18	0:01:15
C4	1	0:00:06	0:00:06	0:00:06	5	0:00:13	0:00:05	0:01:07
C5	1	0:00:06	0:00:06	0:00:06	3	0:00:18	0:00:23	0:00:53

4 Discussion

The evaluation presented in this paper intended to identify the usability of the proposal. Focus groups, thinking aloud, audio and video recordings (over a week of usage), questionnaires, interviews and heuristic evaluations were conducted with ASD specialists, children with ASD and their caregivers/relatives to evaluate the usability of TEAutonomía. Both the quantitative and qualitative studies verified that the mobile application assists children with ASD to build autonomy. During the quantitative study, both the ASD Specialist and children's interaction with the mobile application were recorded and analyzed. User experiences demonstrated positive evaluations while the SUS questionnaire conducted with the children's caregivers/relatives achieved an acceptable score. The usability questionnaires conducted with the ASD specialists resulted in a mean of 4.46 in the areas of utility, ease of use, ease of learning and satisfaction. Overall, the ASD specialists were satisfied with TEAutonomía and would use it again in the future.

Using Thinking Aloud protocol during the interactions, significantly aided the collection of qualitative data when the ASD specialists were interacting with TEAutonomía. For example, during the interactions, two participants disclosed that their experience of mobile devices is limited. While this comment created expectations that the participants may have a reduced benefit in the mobile application, the qualitative analysis proves otherwise.

All tasks were completed with little to no instructions; however, there was confusion with some tasks. The ASD specialists had to seek instructions for Tasks 3, 6 and 7: Create Pictogram Sequence, Add Objects and Create a list of objects, respectively. Verily, 66.6% of participants required instructions to complete Task 6 which, correspondingly, was the task that required the most time and was the most difficult to complete. While these tasks are more complex than tasks such as Signing up in the application (T1) and Logging in (T2), the qualitative analysis identified that these were the least intuitive functions of the mobile application. With that being said, in the validity theme of the qualitative study, there was no specific mention that the Pictogram Sequence activity would be used again, indicating that this activity also requires improvements to enhance the intuitiveness and therefore impact the ease of learning.

Additionally, it was mentioned that deciding to use an activity is highly dependent on the children the ASD the specialist is working with and not all activities will be useful. This indicates that more variety of activities needs to be created with higher complexity to meet the diverse skillsets of the children. The ASD specialists indicated that some activities may be too difficult for children with little technical experience, while others may be too easy and require more complexity. This is evident in the qualitative analysis of the Pictogram sequence activity where C4 has a low usage frequency but a high total time and C5 has a high usage frequency but a low total time. That is, that C4 and C5 have opposite results; which is expected by the difference in their demographics. This supports the feedback from the ASD specialists that the activities chosen depend on the demographics and diversity of the children's needs.

However, with a range of activities to choose from, the ASD specialist can select the most appropriate activity to meet the children's learning needs. To provide a broader range of activities to meet these diversity challenges, more activities will be required to be built as future work.

The ASD specialists also indicated that the Music instruments activity may be too simple for some students. The quantitative study demonstrated that the percussion was preferred over the xylophone by the children as there were notable differences in the usage. However, looking at the ages groups of the children, it is apparent that, on average, the percussion was favored more by the older children whereas the xylophone was more suitable for the younger children. This verifies the ASD specialist concerns regarding the Musical instrument activity being too simple for some children.

Overall, the quantitative and qualitative studies indicate that TEAutonomía fosters autonomy, decreasing the level of interactions required from ASD specialists. However, the degree of autonomy differs depending on a range of factors including the children's technical experience, if they can follow instructions and their attention span.

"Perhaps not all [activities] with a child since some may be difficult for them, but it could be better suited to another child. It all depends on the ease of the child to use the application." [Participant 4, positive].

5 Conclusion and Future Works

In this paper, we proposed a mobile application (TEAutonomía) that promotes autonomy in children with ASD. TEAutonomía has a set of activities which can be dynamically created and adapted by an ASD specialist to meet the learning needs and specific characteristics of children with ASD. This intends to decrease the interactions between an ASD specialist and children with ASD, allowing the children to focus on the activity intended to foster autonomy. Quantitative and qualitative studies were conducted with

ASD specialists, children with ASD and their caregivers/relatives to evaluate the usability. Data was collected through focus groups, thinking aloud methods, audio and video recordings, questionnaires, interviews, and heuristic evaluations. The quantitative analysis demonstrated a positive and acceptable user experience in usefulness, ease of use, ease of learning and satisfaction. The qualitative analysis validated the data collected via the audio and video recordings, providing a further understanding of the user experience. All the participants indicated that they would use TEAutonomía again in the future. Their comments in the qualitative study provided invaluable feedback for future work. Overall, the results obtained demonstrate that TEAutonomía fosters autonomy in children with ASD while decreasing the interactions and interventions required from ASD specialists.

As future work, we will expand the evaluations to include quantitative results over an extended duration of time. We also will analyze that there is no negative impact on the child's autonomy when the specialist creates and adapts activities in accordance with the needs of the child. In addition, we want to analyze, prioritize and integrate new software requirements through a formal and qualitative requirements prioritization process [21, 22], in order to identify new functionalities. Finally, we also hope to improve the mobile application by building a DSL with JSON grammar [23], and with BPMN support for navigation [24].

References

1. Hodges, H., Fealko, C., Soares, N.: Autism spectrum disorder: definition, epidemiology, causes, and clinical evaluation. Transl. Pediatr. 9(Suppl 1), S55 (2020)
2. Shea, N.M., Millea, M.A., Diehl, J.J.: Perceived autonomy support in children with autism spectrum disorder. Autism-Open Access 3(1), 2 (2013)
3. Dieleman, L.M., Soenens, B., Vansteenkiste, M., Prinzie, P., Laporte, N., De Pauw, S.S.: Daily sources of autonomy-supportive and controlling parenting in mothers of children with ASD: the role of child behavior and mothers' psychological needs. J. Autism Dev. Disord. 49(2), 509–526 (2019)
4. Moreno, E.M.: Instrumentos de evaluación y variables de estrés en padres y madres de niños con autismo. Revisión y líneas futuras de investigación para la promoción de salud mental (2017)
5. Zamora, C.B.L.: Conceptualización de Trastornos del Espectro Autista (TEA) en madres cuidadoras y estrategias familiares de reducción de dependencia en Santiago de Chile. Latinoam. Estud. Fam. 12(2), 107–129 (2020)
6. Cárdenas, A., Segovia, E., Tobar, J., De la Cruz, D., Mejía, P., Paredes, N.: Pictoaprende: application that contributes to the personal autonomy of children and youth with Autism Spectrum disorder in Ecuador. In: 2015 Latin American Computing Conference (CLEI), pp. 1–8 (2015)
7. Larrea Vera, E.R.: Análisis y diseño e implementación de una aplicación movil para facilitar la comunicación alternativa de personas con TEA (transtorno con el espectro autista) (2016)
8. Sánchez González, A.: Aplicación móvil de cuentos personalizados para niños con TEA (2021)
9. Wohofsky, L., Scharf, P., Lattacher, S., Krainer, D.: Assistive technology to support people with autism spectrum disorder in their autonomy and safety: a scoping review. Technol. Disabil. 34(1), 1–11 (2022)

10. Ekholm, E., Petersson, A.: How interactive musical instruments influence children with intellectual disabilities?: a user study of the Rullen band (2021)
11. Mejía, A., Juárez-Ramírez, R., Inzunza, S., Valenzuela, R.: Implementing adaptive interfaces: a user model for the development of usability in interactive systems. In: Proceedings of the CUBE International Information Technology Conference, pp. 598–604 (2012)
12. Ntalindwa, T., Nduwingoma, M., Karangwa, E., Soron, T.R., Uworwabayeho, A., Uwineza, A.: Development of a mobile app to improve numeracy skills of children with autism spectrum disorder: participatory design and usability study. JMIR Pediatr. Parent. 4(3), e21471 (2021)
13. Hussain, A., Abdullah, A., Husni, H.: The design principles of edutainment system for autistic children with communication difficulties. AIP Conf. Proc. 1761(1), 020047 (2016)
14. Rojas, L.A., Macías, J.A.: An agile information-architecture-driven approach for the development of user-centered interactive software. In: Proceedings of the XVI International Conference on Human Computer Interaction, pp. 1–8 (2015)
15. Din, E.: 9241-11. Ergonomic requirements for office work with visual display terminals (VDTs)–part 11: guidance on usability. International Organization for Standardization (1998)
16. Luis, A., Rojas, P., Truyol, M.E., Maureira, J.F.C., Quiñones, M.O., Puente, A.: Qualitative evaluation of the usability of a web-based survey tool to assess reading comprehension and metacognitive strategies of university students. In: Meiselwitz, G. (ed.) Social Computing and Social Media. Design, Ethics, User Behavior, and Social Network Analysis. Lecture Notes in Computer Science, vol. 12194, pp. 110–129. Springer, Cham (2020). https://doi.org/10.1007/978-3-030-49570-1_9
17. Lund, A.M.: Measuring usability with the use questionnaire12. Usability Interface 8(2), 3–6 (2001)
18. Davis, F.D.: Perceived usefulness, perceived ease of use, and user acceptance of information technology. MIS Quart 13(3), 319–340 (1989)
19. Lin, H.X., Choong, Y.-Y., Salvendy, G.: A proposed index of usability: a method for comparing the relative usability of different software systems. Behav. Inf. Technol. 16(4–5), 267–277 (1997)
20. Sauro, J.: Measuring usability with the system usability scale (SUS) (2011). https://measuringu.com/sus/
21. Rojas, L., Olivares-Rodríguez, C., Alvarez, C., Campos, P.G.: OurRank: a software requirements prioritization method based on qualitative assessment and cost-benefit prediction. IEEE Access (2022)
22. Rojas, L.A., Macías, J.A.: Toward collisions produced in requirements rankings: a qualitative approach and experimental study. J. Syst. Softw. 158, 110417 (2019)
23. Rho Engine DSL-JSON. http://www.devrho.com/. Accessed 09 Feb 2023
24. Chavarriaga, E., Jurado, F., Dez, F.: An approach to build XML-based domain specific languages solutions for client-side web applications. Comput. Lang. Syst. Struct. 49, 133–151 (2017). https://doi.org/10.1016/j.cl.2017.04.002

Reality Pregnancy and the Online Recolonization of the Female Body

Alicia Julia Wilson Takaoka(✉) (iD)

Norwegian University of Science and Technology, Trondheim, Norway
alicia.j.w.takaoka@ntnu.no
https://www.ntnu.no

Abstract. This study defines and operationalizes reality pregnancy in the context of recolonization as an emerging composite construct. Using partial least squares, the concept of reality pregnancy is shown to have strong significance, 99.5%, on the total number of babies a YouTuber has at the time of analysis. The weights of each variable in reality pregnancy are: Gender of the content creator at -0.134, the image-making composite at 0.485, and the medical model at 0.627. Social media engagement was correlated with reality pregnancy but has no impact on the total number of babies a YouTuber has. While much work should be done to refine the reality pregnancy construct as an aspect of recolonization, this work shows the characteristics of reality pregnancy as depicted in videos on YouTube and can be used across social media sites for further validation.

Keywords: reality pregnancy · reality tv · birth journey · recolonization · social media engagement · image-making · medical model of birth · media representations · YouTube · partial least squares

1 Introduction

Every pregnancy and delivery is a personal experience. When a person shares their birth journey—an account of their pregnancy, labor, and delivery—in any medium to any audience size, they are sharing an experience associated with intimate knowledge that may challenge or reinforce ideas and norms about motherhood, womanhood, and the process of procreation. Any woman in the US cannot escape this connection to the birth journey. As Wilson states, "A woman cannot escape the connection to motherhood. Whether a woman is called infertile, involuntarily or voluntarily childless, a nonmother, or childfree, the available labels refer to something that is missing. She is not fertile or not the mother of a child...others see her as a woman who disrupts her prescribed role, who does not fit, who must be repaired, or, at least, explained" [46], (p. 13-14). This experience is gendered, and what information a pregnant person chooses to share about this process is an example of using one's own agency to articulate something unique and singular. In the patriarchy, the birth journey is gendered. It belongs only to

A. Coman and S. Vasilache (Eds.): HCII 2023, LNCS 14026, pp. 276–291, 2023.
https://doi.org/10.1007/978-3-031-35927-9_20

cis-gendered women, and only women can access or share this experience with outsiders. For most women who do not get to experience a live birth before their own pregnancy, many pregnant people turn to reality tv and vlogs for information about the labor, birth, and pregnancy process [15,25,29,31]. This study examines the characteristics of social media engagement [28,43], image-making [7], and the medical model of birth, labor, and delivery [9] as an act of recolonization as reality pregnancy.

Simulated birth experiences by male content creators and channels that feature men on YouTube have more viewers than first person birth narratives by their female counterparts. As seen in Table 1, the top two most viewed videos in this dataset are simulations of birth. Thomas Schwenke makes computer generated simulations, and the Buzzfeed video is the first of two pregnancy simulation videos produced by The Try Guys. Two channels, HonoreSquad and The Campbell Cloud, are family-focused, so men feature prominently. Only one channel in the Top 5, Colleen Ballinger, is a female content creator, sharing her birth journey.

Table 1. Top 5 Birth-Related Videos by Views

ChannelName	Subscribers	Date	Duration	Likes	Views	BabyNo.
Thomas Schwenke	1,390,000	April 2021	19:35	498,397	84,663,001	sim
BuzzFeedVideo	20,200,000	May 2015	8:02	404,928	35,722,680	sim
Colleen Ballinger	8,680,000	Dec 2018	14:10	1,400,000	33,606,673	1
HonoreSquad	74,700	Sept 2020	34:16	88,958	25,625,609	4
the campbell cloud	84,900	May 2021	13:56	254,000	17,279,996	3

Some famous birth journeys are told from the first person perspective with or without the aid of a large production company. As such, viewers get an intimate view of the birth journey which may break taboos even if the narrative reinforces ideals and norms about the construct "motherhood as womanhood" [37]. Brittani Louise Taylor, a YouTuber with nearly 1.4 million followers who shared her story of survivorship on Shane Dawson's channel, has 479,000 views on her video "My Labor and Delivery Story," and Emily Norris, a lifestyle YouTuber, has over 659,000 views for her birth narrative. Snooki televised both of her births on the MTV show Snooki and Jwoww in the episodes "Last Call at Club Uterus" in 2013 and "It's Like a Roller Coaster of Pain" in 2015. Jwoww also delivered her first baby on the same show in the episode "And Baby Makes Six." Although this show is now only viewable behind a paywall, news of these births garnered only 562,000 views at most on recap shows. Brie Bella of Total Divas, Total Bellas, and their YouTube channel The Bella Twins recounted her birth journey several times including a live update from the hospital when her baby was experiencing complications. This video received 458,000 views. The video of Brie's birth journey with the most views was "Welcome Birdie Joe! Looking Back at Brie's Journey to Motherhood" which has over 3,976,000 views. Still, the views of all of these videos in combination pale in comparison to The Try Guys' birth journey videos. This led to the question: *What is the landscape of birth videos and engagement on YouTube?*

2   Background

An understanding of select literature across disciplines is necessary to understand the emerging construct Reality Pregnancy. An overview of reality television will be presented. The process of colonization, decolonization, and recolonization will be discussed. This acts as a framework for exploring pregnancy on reality tv and the medical and social models of birth. Finally, social media engagement will be presented.

2.1   Reality TV

Many studies have evaluated reality television (tv) and its value in society. Reality tv can be defined by several characteristics. Reality tv developed as a genre that featured ordinary people instead of professional actors who are continuously filmed in a wide range of program types that attract audiences by promoting dramatic or taboo subjects presented in real, but often manufactured, situations [1,14,23,29,33,35]. Some formats include documentaries, game shows, and dramas. Now, reality tv is an area that actors can pursue, and these actors can be seen in shows like *Love is Blind* or *The Jersey Shore* and their cross-over universes. This growing genre of television has led to a robust area of research.

Most research takes a uses and gratifications approach to evaluate why reality tv is attractive [4,15,33]. Reiss and Wiltz [35] identify 16 types of joy that act as motivation under sensitivity theory that viewers may experience watching reality tv. Specific dimensions of human emotion have been evaluated as well. These include narcissism on *The Jersey Shore* [13], poor-blaming and poor-shaming [3], and the justification to air emotionally contagious content on television by broadcasters [24]. Some studies have also evaluated the structure of reality tv shows.

Reality TV shows may have both real and scripted elements. Shows are edited to tell a specific story or create an image of a character [1]. Ouellette and Hay [31] explain that subgenres of reality tv embed testing, judging, advising, and rewarding into content. Reality tv has several subgenres including dating, lifestyle, docusoaps, and sitcoms [44,45], and reality pregnancy can be seen in several of these subgenres as a plot or subplot. Reality pregnancy can then be defined as the documenting of any part of the birth journey for entertainment through story telling or character image creation. Several women have shared their birth journeys on tv programs or YouTube. While some may see this as a reclamation of the female body, others may argue that is a display of recolonization.

2.2   Colonization, Decolonization, and Recolonization

Even though areas of research in computing are dedicated to recognizing the effects of colonization and the process of decolonization [17,18], artifacts of colonization persist. Colonization is the act of assuming power and control over a people, land, resources, often through subjugation [36,38]. Controlling a people also often involves understanding that the creation and maintenance of narratives like the dichotomy of the sacred and profane [27], othering [32], gendering [8], and sexualizing [5] the female body are created as a part of the process. As Harb-Ranero [16] explains, female bodies are often colonized through violence and abuse and exploited under the patriarchy.

Throughout history, women's bodies have been a site of repeated colonization for the pleasure and entertainment of others, for profit, and for national endeavors. As Edgren [10] points out, Sweden, America, and France have all developed national policy to claim that having babies–whether for economic or political aims– is the most important work a woman can do. National financial systems were created for women, even unmarried ones, to focus on having babies for the good of the nation. A lack of agency and an internalization of values from the colonizer is necessary for the colonized to maintain the systems of oppression that keep them imprisoned.

Decolonization is a process of questioning, unlearning, and reclaiming a body, a history, and a culture. The decolonization of womxn thrived in the 1920s-1970s globally and is in a revitalized period of reclamation. Involved in this process is activism for social changes related to education, spirituality, and bodily autonomy as well as reconnection to the land and resources. Social programs and money are allocated for the intentional and specific purposes of gender balance and inclusion [6]. Specifically relating to the female body, decolonization includes stopping female genital mutilation, deciding what is ingested by the body, controlling the image of one's own body, and expressing how, when, and if the body is used for pleasure, work, or birth. There is some debate about if we are in a post-colonial or recolonial period.

Bourbonnais questions if we are in a period of post-colonialism, where the focus is on implementing indigenous cultural practices, genders, languages, and histories, or if we are in a period of recolonization in which the gaze and desires of colonialism and the patriarchy dominate cultural and societal norms. Bournnais writes, "Alexander has described this as a process of 'recolonisation', in which 'the neocolonial state continues the policing of sexualised bodies . . . as if the colonial masters were still looking on"' [6]. This can be seen in reality pregnancy videos on YouTube.

Buzzfeed is a lifestyle, food, and entertainment content creator, and their 14th most popular video is "The Try Guys Try Labor Pain Simulation, Motherhood: Part 4" with over 35,000,000 views to date. The Try Guys were a media production team at Buzzfeed from 2014 before they left to start 2nd Try LLC in 2018 when their existing content was put behind a paywall without their consent. Buzzfeed and The Try Guys were filming a show to exist solely behind the paywall [39]. Shortly after leaving Buzzfeed, one of the original owners of Second Try announced the birth of his wife's and his second child. The Try Guys created a video in which each of the members reenacted the labor and delivery process, and the video "The Try Guys Try 14 h of Labor Pain Simulation" has over 16,000,000 views to date. This video's views surpass the female birth journeys discussed previously, but this video's views are tiny when compared to their most popular video of all time, "The Try Guys Try Labor Pain Simulation, Motherhood: Part 4" with over 33,250,000 views to date. Upon evaluation, "The Try Guys Try 14 h of Labor Pain Simulation" is a recreation of Ariel Fulmer's birth journey. Ariel is the wife of one of The Try Guys, and her story is only told to enhance or explain the video's content.

Ariel not sharing her own birth journey is problematic for many reasons. First, her voice is minimized in the process of reality pregnancy as an act of recolonization of the female body. Recolonization is the act of colonizing an area previously colonized for a second or subsequent colonization [41]. During this process of recolonization, The Try Guys control the narrative about pregnancy, labor, and all aspects of the birth journey essentially taking away that experience to the person it happened to. Unwittingly, The Try Guys hijacked the birth journey in their retelling of Ariel's story and their Motherhood series to undermine the experiences of women in favor of likes, views, and monetization. They dictate expectations about interest in pregnancy and the birth journey for entertainment and reorient men to the focus of these processes. They use hegemonic vocabulary to create and share narratives about the pregnant body which reinforces the social and medical institution's narratives about birth in a pronatalist society.

2.3   Image-Making

Presenting a story in one's own words is a part of reclaiming the image-making process. Buckman explains that image-making is a process of domination, subordination, and control to maintain the hegemonic discourse of imperialism [7]. Image-making occurs in the four institutions that impact bodily autonomy for women: religion, politics, society, and medicine [37]. Examples of political [34], religious [30], and social [2,42] image-making research can be found. Image-making includes three elements: the producer, the process, and the content or composition.

The image-making process for colonization of the female body depicts domination and subordination. It maintains the institutionalization of imperialism. Among groups, it maintains difference or othering. For women's colonized bodies, image-making maintains gendered and sexual domination. Based on themes found in previous, research reality pregnancy may maintain the colonial values of the hegemonic culture. The indicators for image-making for reality pregnancy are:

- Women are incapable of giving birth without medical intervention (female body is inferior and other)
- Women are seen as a patient (dominant/subordinate relationship)
- Women deliver the baby in a silent birth because the baby deserves safe passage into world (not the object or focus, birth happens to her)
- Videos will be white dominated (lack diversity in representation)
- Women adhere to "good girl" standards about birth (doing hair and makeup, serenity, introspection, gratitude, and education about the process) [7,25]

2.4   Pregnancy on Reality TV

While reality TV has been a booming area for research, fewer studies have evaluated the value of birth narratives on reality [9,11,12,25,26,29,40]. Correlations between teen pregnancy and viewership have been examined. Kearney and Levine [21] have stated that changes in teen pregnancy by geographical area correlate to viewership of shows relating to teen pregnancy. they express that in areas of high viewership, there is a measured reduction in births. However, Jaeger, Joyce, and Kaestner [19] respond to this study, cautioning that there are issues with this type of point-in-time data and that other factors like race, gender, employment status, and level of education may also be contributing factors between a decrease in teen pregnancy in the US and the rise of popular reality tv shows about teen pregnancy. In response, Kearney and Levine thank Jaeger et al. for validating their results [22]. This cautionary tale of correlation and construct validity shaped the construction of the reality pregnancy model as a possible part of recolonization of the female body.

Themes that were identified in reality pregnancy align with the medical model of birth. As seen in Morris and McInerney [29], Luce [25], and Cummins [9], women look to reality prenancy for education, and the themes maintaining a reliance on the medicalization of the birth journey have impacted a lack of choice and agency and may also have contributed to the high maternal morbidity rate in the US [9]. Prior to the 20th century, midwives were the primary providers of childbirth in the US. Obstetricians categorized birth as either normal or abnormal, and women needed professionals with specific skills and training to deal with abnormal births. With this displacement, new narratives about birth and the role of women in the process began to develop. These include listening to authoritative sources about birthing and mothering, a timeline for the delivery process, and an increase in medical intervention during childbirth [25]. Along with fear and danger, these narratives construct the medical model of birth. In contrast, the social model of birth acknowledges that birth is a varied process and that women should be free agents to determine their delivery position, setting, and coping strategies that work best for their own bodies [9]. These models denote different focuses and priorities. For the purpose of this study, the medical model was selected for operationalization. The indicators for the medical model of reality pregnancy are:

- Video presents an innate fear and emphasis of risks
- Hospitals are described as the only rational place to give birth
- The body's ability to give birth is trivialized
- Video presents pregnant women as passive actors without agency in the process
- People in the video ignore or disparage midwifery [9].

2.5   Objectives

The objective of this exploration is identify characteristics of reality pregnancy as an example of recolonization of the female body in videos relating to birth journeys. This includes viewership of different reality pregnancy videos, simulated birth experiences, and delivering babies from the perspectives of male and female content creators. This study also seeks to define reality pregnancy using composite modeling.

3   Methods

Videos were scraped using Apify for YouTube and validated by repeating the search query on the YouTube API. This yielded a sample size of 50 videos, and the data gathered was the channel name, video title, description, total views, likes, channel, subscribers, and comments. A snowball sample of recommended videos was run to gather a larger, more representative sample of birth videos until all videos in the recommended videos were repeated. This process produced an additional 44 videos.

Data was manually cleaned. Videos were excluded if they were fictional birth stories or not about an actual birth experience (ex: birth and death of a minecraft character, a scene from a movie, or miscarriage) based on video title and description. Episodes about delivery and delivering the baby provided context cues for identifying correct episodes for analysis. This left a total of 74 videos by 51 unique channels. Of those, four were simulations of birth, eight were hosted on a parent channel like Buzzfeed, E! Entertainment, and World Wrestling Entertainment, and three were reclaiming ownership of the birth journey through retelling.

The latent variable constructs are the image-making process, gender of the content creator, the medical model, and social media engagement rates. Metadata discovery was performed to identify structural items that comprise social media engagement. Structural data includes viewership demographics of each video using the scraped data as well as capturing viewer statistics for the most rewatched or clipped segments of the videos. In addition, to further develop the items used for construct evaluation, data gathered from the content creators on YouTube were evaluated. The race of the channel owner, medical interventions used, marital status, and medical narratives persistent in birthing literature were identified. Partial least squares was used to establish the relationships among constructs in order to further define and operationalize the recolonization of the female body in reality pregnancy, birth narratives, and the reality birth journey.

The dataset was evaluated using Adanco, a software for structure equation modeling of composite and emerging constructs. Latent variable scores of the composite variables Image-Making, Medical Model (of birth and delivery), Gender of the YouTube channel owner, and Engagement Rate (by views and post) were obtained against the total babies of these YouTubers by December 2022. This depiction of babies was selected because some videos depicted one baby or twins being born, but the YouTuber could have between one and 8 babies at the time the data was captured and analyzed. An iterative effect on the body was considered because the effect of having one baby is not the same as having one baby for the eighth time, but it was difficult to standardize per video examined. The results of the evaluations will now be presented.

4   Results

As noted, a total of 74 videos were analyzed using thematic analysis for how the content contributes to the medical model of birth, the image-making process, and engagement rates in relation to the gender of the channel creator and YouTuber giving birth and the total number of babies these creators have at the time of analysis in December 2022.

4.1   Partial Least Squares Model

The Partial Least Squares (PLS) models were calculated and constructed using Adanco software for composite modeling. A two-step model was selected because of the nature of a combination of composite and latent constructs for recolonization. Latent variable scores (LVS) were calculated using goodness of fit and verified using bootstrapping. The variables calcuated in Step 1 were a composite score of the representation of Medical Model values (0–5), a composite score of the Image-Making Process (0–5) shown in the videos, gender of the YouTuber the channel belongs to AND the one delivering the baby (0 = female, 1 = male), and the composite of engagement rate by views and posts. The LVS used in Step 2 can be seen in Fig. 1.

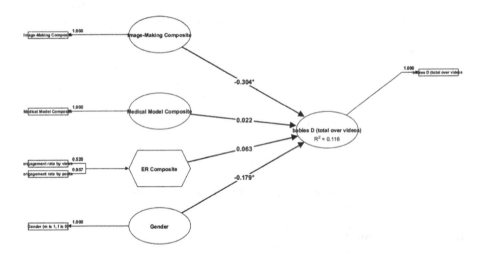

Fig. 1. Latent Variable Scores for Reality Pregnancy

The Goodness of Fit for Step 1 is within HI99 for SRMR, dULS, and dG. Fornell-Larcker Criterion and Indicator Reliability are in alignment with expected projections for calculating LVS. Indicator Multicolinearity and cross-loadings also showed no overlap. These variables were used in Step 2 of the Composite modeling as standard construct scores.

Table 2. Goodness of model fit (saturated model)

	Value	HI95	HI99
SRMR	0.0368	0.0676	0.0786
dULS	0.0284	0.0960	0.1296
dG	0.0053	0.0175	0.0258

Step 2 of the Construction of Recolonization involved using the latent variable scores calculated in Step 1 to construct the model for Recolonization (Table 2).

Reality Pregnancy Emerging Construct. The Reality Pregnancy Construct is comprised of the gender of the content creator, the image-making composite, and the medical model of birth. These have a high degree of impact on the total number of babies a YouTuber had at the time of analysis. As seen in Fig. 2, there is a correlation between engagement rate and reality pregnancy, and a high degree of significance is placed on the total number of babies a YouTuber has because of the reality pregnancy composite. Engagement rate has no significance on the number of babies a YouTuber has.

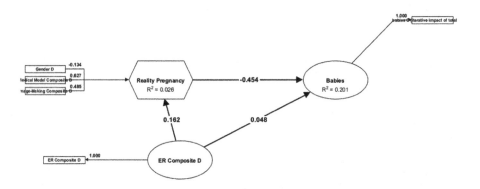

Fig. 2. Composite Model for Reality Pregnancy

4.2 Engagement Rate

Engagement rate was calculated by views and by post. These are two of the six most common ways to calculate engagement rate across social media and are particularly useful for video collections in context of this study. The engagement rate by views per video is calculated as

$$(comments + likes + downloads)/views \tag{1}$$

whereas the engagement rate by post is calculated as

$$(comments + likes + downloads)/subscribers \tag{2}$$

The averages for these totals were divided by the total number of videos in the dataset. The average engagement by post is 3.11% whereas the average engagement by views is 19.23%.

4.3   Image-Making Process

The predominant demographic composition of content producers in this dataset are white, American, cis-hetero women. Age was not captured. Race and nationality were compressed in this study to reflect the intersections in an aggregated state. Table 3 shows the total percentage of these intersections as American/International and White/Black, Brown, Asian, Pacific Islander as the YouTuber delivering the baby.

Table 3. Race and Nationality Intersections in Percents.

Race	American	International
White	54%	16%
BBAPI	26%	4%

Image-making is a process of power and dominance over a group or community through images of them. As such, women were depicted as a patient and incapable of giving birth in 79.7% of videos analyzed. Good girl messages were present in 94.6% of the videos. Of the videos analyzed, 69.8% expressed that a woman should do hair and makeup to feel pretty at least once, before heading to the hospital. Doctors told women expressly to quiet down, stop yelling, or be silent for the baby in 17.6% of videos, but women were silent or quiet in 87.8% of the videos. There was 100% of heterosexual couples presented, and only 1.3% of videos presented an unmarried couple.

4.4   Medical Model

The Medical Model of birth, pregnancy, and delivery has the highest impact on the Reality Pregnancy as a composite construct. An innate fear and danger of the birthing process was displayed in 81.1% of the videos. Hospitals were presented as the only logical place to give birth in 86.5% of the videos. Of these, one video expressed the choice to deliver at home or go to the hospital, and the couple decided to go to the hospital. One video depicted a delivery in the car on the way to the hospital. Only 12.2% of the videos depicted home births. Technology and interventions were depicted in 86.5% of the videos. Some videos tagged as raw and natural still used oxygen, gas, or fetal heart monitoring. Women were presented as passive agents in the delivery process in 75.7% of videos. This was demonstrated by the adherence to the anticipated timeline of delivery and being told what position to be in for the delivery. Finally, only 16.2% of videos expressly disparaged midwifery.

5   Discussion

Most rewatched segments of videos are where birthing moms are delivering the baby. These segments are clipped and are often downloaded. There are many reasons that may be attributed to this, and these should be investigated in future research.

As noted, the patriarchal, hegemonic views of marriage and family are still maintained in the videos in this dataset. The women are still married. The couples are all monogamous and heterosexual. The majority are white, whether from the US or other countries. The medical model is still maintained, with the exception of midwifery. Unfortunately, most home births are the polar opposite, constructing another set of institutionalized standards for birth.

Rewatched segments and clips appeared in videos that featured delivery. The most rewatched and clipped segments of these videos were the actual crowning and delivery of the baby or where that moment was expected, except in two videos. In the first, the most rewatched segment was when a mirror was brought in so the woman could watch herself and be inspired by her progress while pushing. The second video where the most rewatched segment was the mom holding her twins right after delivery. There are many possibilities about why these are the most rewatched segments, and this requires further investigation.

Two YouTubers in the dataset quit making videos within a year of their last reality pregnancy video. This is an interesting point to explore, especially since they were in two different stages of their careers at the time of quitting. One was very successful and quit so they could spend more time with their family while the other was at the beginning of their reality career. Both have above average engagement rates by view and by post, so this would be interesting to explore further.

5.1   Engagement Rate

It was expected that engagement rate would play a large role in reality pregnancy. However, this was not the case. In every model of partial least squares conducted, engagement rate as calculated by views, by posts, and as a composite were not significant. It was expected there would be a negative correlation between engagement rate and births given that simulations had higher views than most videos found with the initial and validating data scrape. While there is no correlation on the engagement rate and the number of babies a YouTuber has, there is some correlation between the engagement rate and the composite construct Reality Pregnancy.

5.2   Limitations

The initial data scraping did not produce results expected from such a broad query on YouTube. While the results were verified using Apify, a series of scheduled data wrangling scrapes at scheduled intervals may produce different results.

The reality pregnancy construct is emerging. With more data and testing, the construct's dimensions may become more refined. Engagement rate was expected to be a part of the construct, but it had greater correlation outside than as a part of the composite. This may be different with a larger dataset or if simulations or videos promoted by men or family channels are excluded from analysis.

As a critique of the algorithm, entire channels on YouTube feature births. Yet, they were not a part of the initial results. A question that arose from this is: why didn't these entire channels dedicated to home births show up in the initial search query run through Apify and through YouTube API?

5.3   Future Work

This work on reality pregnancy can expand beyond YouTube to other social media platforms. Instagram, Reddit, and other platforms can be analyzed for disparities in viewership and engagement, image-making, and institutional oppression for the maintenance of recolonization using this study as a guide. These points deserve further exploration across reality tv to see who is telling the stories of reality pregnancies and which stories subvert the roles of women in their own journey. In addition, this study can be used to evaluate other constructs and concepts relating to recolonization of the body. This can be done by replacing the medical model of birth for another institutional quality to be evaluated along with social media engagement and the image-making process.

Additionally, the framework of reality pregnancy must be evaluated in the context of recolonization and birth simulations. This model should also be applied to videos about the other parts of the birth journey. Since this study evaluates viewership in relation to the gender of the content creator, other gendered topics can be also evaluated. This can include marriage, hair, makeup, mental health, and fashion. These are "feminine" topics that can be evaluated from the perspective of recolonization [20].

Real and manufactured emotions in reality pregnancy should be further explored. The medical model encourages stories of pain, that a woman's body is inferior and needs medical intervention, and that complications are common, it is worth exploring what is real, what is manufactured, how audiences react to each, and why choices to produce real or manufactured emotions in reality pregnancy. As previously stated, it is well documented that women watch reality pregnancy and birth narratives for educational purposes, so these choices for real and manufactured emotions and experiences warrant their own evaluation.

How males are complicit in the perpetuation and maintenance of the recolonization of the female body in reality pregnancy should also be examined. Males represent the colonized and colonizer, and they play vital roles in the image-making process for the purposes of maintaining stereotypes related to gender and the birth journey. From a medical model of birth perspective, the male is usually complicit in acting out the support role. In the stories watched for this study, males serve as cheerleaders and sources of comfort. When the pregnant person is in distress, they are expected to take over. This role is maintained as a function of recolonization as an outside actor Males are also complicit in social media engagement practices on the viewer side, so evaluating their roles and habits in viewing, watching, pausing, and creating clips of reality pregnancy stories is important to understanding the exploitation of female bodies.

An examination of the use of ICT in reality pregnancy stories as well as an examination of how ICTs are used by pregnant people should be examined. ICTs are presented in reality pregnancy as communication devices, but they are also used to document the image-making process by acting as an intermediary between the pregnant person's body and what they *should* be doing at any stage in their own birth journey. This in turn facilitates the medical model of birth as well as social media engagement throughout reality pregnancy.

Finally, an area of important work is the reclamation of one's own body in the birth journey. When Doreen Fitt shared her thoughts, feelings, and reactions to her own reality pregnancy, the engagement was low. The reclamation of her experience no longer fit the medical model of birth, and it was relegated to other parts of the internet. These stories of reclamation need to be examined.

6   Conclusion

This study meant to evaluate reality pregnancy as recolonization, but reality pregnancy is only a part of recolonization of the female body. Reality pregnancy is comprised of the medical model of birth, the image-making process as it relates to birth, and the gender of the content creator. This construct has an impact on the total babies a YouTuber had by the time of analysis. Still, reality pregnancy ignores many other aspects of recolonization like education, whether the victims become the abusers, and finances. Reality pregnancy does give us one aspect of a larger picture, and it will be interesting to explore how recolonization of the female body changes as women try to reclaim the birthing process for themselves.

Acknowledgments. The composite construct model would not be possible without Jessica Braojos, PhD from University of Granada. Dr. Braojos taught a workshop on Adanco Partial Least Squares composite construct software as a Visiting Professor at Norwegian University of Science and Technology (NTNU), and assisted with the composite modeling process.

References

1. Akira, S.I., et al.: How television shapes our worldview: Media representations of social trends and change. Lexington Books (2014)
2. Alshawaf, E.: iphoneography as visual literacy: How image-making practices on social media encourage creative growth. TechTrends **65**(5), 896–906 (2021)
3. Barton, A., Davis, H.: From empowering the shameful to shaming the empowered: Shifting depictions of the poor in 'reality tv'. Crime, Media, Culture **14**(2), 191–211 (2018)

4. Barton, K.M.: Reality television programming and diverging gratifications: the influence of content on gratifications obtained. J. Broadcasting Electron. Media **53**(3), 460–476 (2009)
5. Benard, A.A.: Colonizing black female bodies within patriarchal capitalism: feminist and human rights perspectives. Sexualization Media Soc. **2**(4), 2374623816680622 (2016)
6. Bourbonnais, N.: Gender and decolonisation. Global Challenges: The Graduate Dossiers 10(Decolonisation: A Past That Keeps Questioning Us), 1 (2021)
7. Buckman, A.R.: The body as a site of colonization: alice walker's possessing the secret of joy. J. Am. Culture **18**(2), 89 (1995)
8. Chavez, L.: What a bitch: the complexities of gender in playwriting. University of New Mexico UNM Digital Repository (2012)
9. Cummins, M.W.: Miracles and home births: the importance of media representations of birth. Critical Stud. Media Commun. **37**(1), 85–96 (2020)
10. Edgren, M.: Colonizing women's bodies: population policies and nationhood in eighteenth-century Sweden. J. Women's History **22**(2), 108–132 (2010)
11. Feasey, R.: Good, bad or just good enough: representations of motherhood and the maternal role on the small screen. Studies in the Maternal 9(1) (2017)
12. Feasey, R.: Television and the absent mother: why girls and young women struggle to find the maternal role. The Absent Mother in the Cultural Imagination: Missing, Presumed Dead, pp. 225–240 (2017)
13. Gibson, B., Hawkins, I., Redker, C., Bushman, B.J.: Narcissism on the jersey shore: exposure to narcissistic reality tv characters can increase narcissism levels in viewers. Psychol. Popular Media Culture **7**(4), 399 (2018)
14. Greenwell, D.: How television shapes our worldview: media representations of social trends and change. Int. J. Commun. (Online), 1424–1427 (2017)
15. Hall, J.: As seen on tv: media influences of pregnancy and birth narratives. Essay. In: Ryan, K.M., Macey, D.A. (eds.) Television and the Self: Knowledge, Identity, and Media Representation, pp. 47–62 (2013)
16. Harb-Ranero, S.: Patriarchal colonization of the female body in machinal and clit notes. Graduate Rev. **7**(1), 69–80 (2022)
17. Jaccheri, L., Cutrupi, C.M., Diaconu, M.G., Szlavi, A., Takaoka, A.J.W., et al.: Where are the female professors in stem? Preprint on TechRxiv (2022)
18. Jaccheri, L., Pereira, C., Fast, S.: Gender issues in computer science: Lessons learnt and reflections for the future. In: 2020 22nd International Symposium on Symbolic and Numeric Algorithms for Scientific Computing (SYNASC), pp. 9–16. IEEE (2020)
19. Jaeger, D.A., Joyce, T.J., Kaestner, R.: A cautionary tale of evaluating identifying assumptions: did reality tv really cause a decline in teenage childbearing? J. Bus. Econ. Stat. **38**(2), 317–326 (2020)
20. Jung, C.G.: Aspects of the Feminine: (From Volumes 6, 7, 9i, 9ii, 10, 17, Collected Works), vol. 21. Princeton University Press (2020)
21. Kearney, M.S., Levine, P.B.: Media influences on social outcomes: the impact of mtv's 16 and pregnant on teen childbearing. Am. Econ. Rev. **105**(12), 3597–3632 (2015)
22. Kearney, M.S., Levine, P.B.: Does reality tv induce real effects? a response to jaeger, joyce, and kaestner (2016). Joyce, and Kaestner, A Response to Jaeger (2016)

23. Kowalczyk, C.M., Fox, A.K.: I don't think it's real: exploring the genres of reality programming: an abstract. In: Krey, N., Rossi, P. (eds.) AMSAC 2017. DMSPAMS, pp. 151–152. Springer, Cham (2018). https://doi.org/10.1007/978-3-319-66023-3_58

24. Lavie, N.: Justifying trash: regulating reality tv in Israel. Television New Media **20**(3), 219–240 (2019)

25. Luce, A., Cash, M., Hundley, V., Cheyne, H., Van Teijlingen, E., Angell, C.: "is it realistic?" the portrayal of pregnancy and childbirth in the media. BMC Pregnancy Childbirth **16**, 1–10 (2016)

26. McKelvin, G., Thomson, G., Downe, S.: The childbirth experience: a systematic review of predictors and outcomes. Women Birth **34**(5), 407–416 (2021)

27. McPhillips, K.: De-colonizing the sacred: feminist proposals for a post-christian, post-patriarchal sacred. In: Post-Christian Feminisms, pp. 129–146. Routledge (2016)

28. Moran, G., Muzellec, L., Johnson, D.: Message content features and social media engagement: evidence from the media industry. J. Product Brand Manage. **29**(5), 533–545 (2020)

29. Morris, T., McInerney, K.: Media representations of pregnancy and childbirth: an analysis of reality television programs in the united states. Birth **37**(2), 134–140 (2010)

30. Mukherjee, T.T.: Reporting two black and red ware sites at dantan: The cult of mother goddess, material culture and the chalcolithic imagination. Chitrolekha International Magazine on Art & Design 6(1) (2022)

31. Ouellette, L., Hay, J.: Better living through reality TV. Blackwell (2007)

32. Oyěwùmí, O.: Colonizing bodies and minds. Postcolonialisms an anthology of cultural theory and criticism, pp. 339–361 (2005)

33. Papacharissi, Z., Mendelson, A.L.: An exploratory study of reality appeal: uses and gratifications of reality TV shows. J. Broadcasting Electron. Media **51**(2), 355–370 (2007)

34. Raynauld, V., Lalancette, M.: Pictures, filters, and politics: Instagram's role in political image making and storytelling in Canada. Visual Commun. Quarterly **28**(4), 212–226 (2021)

35. Reiss, S., Wiltz, J.: Why people watch reality TV. Media Psychol. **6**(4), 363–378 (2004)

36. Saraceni, M., Jacob, C.: Revisiting borders: named languages and de-colonization. Lang. Sci. **76**, 101170 (2019)

37. Shapiro, G.: Voluntary childlessness: a critical review of the literature. Stud. Mater. **6**(1) (2014)

38. Smallwood, R., Woods, C., Power, T., Usher, K.: Understanding the impact of historical trauma due to colonization on the health and well-being of indigenous young peoples: a systematic scoping review. J. Transcultural Nursing **32**(1), 59–68 (2021)

39. Spangler, T.: Youtube picks up buzzfeed's try guys show comedy for subscription service. Variety, p. 49 (2014)

40. Takeshita, C.: Countering technocracy: "natural" birth in the business of being born and call the midwife. Feminist Media Stud. **17**(3), 332–346 (2017)

41. Tandon, Y.: Recolonization of subject peoples. Alternatives **19**(2), 173–183 (1994)

42. Tange, A.K.: Picturing the villain: Image-making and the Indian uprising. Victorian Stud. **63**(2), 193–223 (2021)

43. Trunfio, M., Rossi, S.: Conceptualising and measuring social media engagement: a systematic literature review. Italian J. Marketing **2021**(3), 267–292 (2021). https://doi.org/10.1007/s43039-021-00035-8

44. Tsay-Vogel, M., Krakowiak, K.M.: Inspirational reality TV: the prosocial effects of lifestyle transforming reality programs on elevation and altruism. J. Broadcasting Electron. Media **60**(4), 567–586 (2016)

45. Tsay-Vogel, M., Krakowiak, K.M.: Exploring viewers' responses to nine reality tv subgenres. Psychol. Popular Media Culture **6**(4), 348 (2017)

46. Wilson, K.J.: Not trying: Infertility, childlessness, and ambivalence. Vanderbilt University Press (2014)

Social Computing in the Pandemic and Post-pandemic Era

Leveraging Nodal and Topological Information for Studying the Interaction Between Two Opposite Ego Networks

Kossi Folly[1], Youssef Boughaba[2], and Maria Malek[3(✉)] (iD)

[1] Covéa Group, Paris, France
[2] ETIS Lab, CY Cergy Paris University, ENSEA, CNRS, UMR8051, Cergy, France
youssef.boughaba@ensea.fr
[3] ETIS Lab, CY Cergy Paris University, ENSEA, CNRS, UMR8051, CY Tech,
Cergy, France
maria.malek@cyu.fr

Abstract. The study of controversy in social media is not new, there are many previous studies aimed at identifying and characterizing controversial issues, mostly around political debates, but also for other topics. In this work, we aim to study the interaction between two ego networks around two influencers having opposite opinions on a given subject and its impact on opinion change and propagation within these two interconnected ego networks. We propose a method for detecting opinion modification in relation to several nodal and topological measures as the users centralities, the opinion of the community to witch belongs the users as well as textual information extracted from tweets. We firstly constructed a propagation network which is the union of 2-level opposite ego networks extracted from a set of collected tweets in relation to a given topic, where nodes are users and edges are tweets or replies. We then apply machine learning models to detect respectively: opinion change over time concerning users who are the authors of replies and opinion modification during the information propagation via an action of reply. The dataset contains nodal and topological information extracted from the propagation network.

Keywords: Social network analysis · Opinion dynamic · Influencers · Machine Learning

1 Introduction

Sentiment analysis is the study field that analyses people opinions, sentiments, attitude, emotions, evaluations, appraisals towards entities such as products, services, organisations, individuals, issues, events, topics [11].

We would like to warmly thank Charles-Philippe Frantz, Mohamed Sellami & Yvan Singuina students at CY Tech, speciality Data Science for helping us in the implementation.

The study of controversy in social media is not new [8,14] there are many previous studies aimed at identifying and characterizing controversial issues, mostly around political debates but also for other topics.

Polarisation, in which the network separates into two clusters the opposing opinions, has been also heavily studied [4]. Opinion formation is a complex process affected by the interplay of different elements, including the individual predisposition, the influence of positive and negative peer interaction (social networks playing a crucial role in this respect), the information each individual is exposed to, and many others. In this work, we aim to study the interaction between two ego networks around two influencers having opposite opinions on a given subject an its impact on opinion change and propagation within these two interconnected ego networks.

Given a complex network (and more particularly an online social network), the egocentric network defined around an ego node u is a sub-network containing the ego u and the alters (the neighbors up to certain level) as well as the set of links of the ego-network [1]. In the literature, two cases of online personal networks are identified depending on the distance of the alters from the ego: 1-level and k-level. Our goal is to explore the combination of sentiment analysis with complex networks analysis [7] in the context of two ego networks around influencers having opposite opinions on a given topic that interact.

In order to study the impact of influential users (influential nodes), we integrate several influencing factors extracted from the propagation network in the opinion study process. These factors are usually computed by using different centralities measures as degree, closeness, betweenness and page rank centralities, etc. [7]. We are interested in the notion of opinion stability inside the egocentric networks around influencers and inside the communities, opinion stability means the fact of sharing a majority of common preferences concerning a given topic in a group of users.

We propose in this paper a method for detecting opinion modification in relation to several nodal and topological measures as the users centralities, the opinion of the community to witch belongs the users, as well as textual information extracted from tweets. We firstly constructed a propagation network which is the union of 2-level opposite ego networks extracted from a set of collected tweets in relation to a given topic where nodes are users and edges are tweets or replies. We then apply machine learning models to detect respectively: opinion change over time concerning users which are the authors of replies and opinion modification during the information propagation via an action of reply. The dataset contains nodal and topological information extracted from the propagation network.

2   Related Work

Study of opinion dynamics is crucial in nowadays-ubiquitous on-line system context. Researchers with different background have presented several models to verify the development of the opinion formation, propagation and aggregation from different points of view [14,17]. For example in [6], authors introduce SLANT a probabilistic modeling framework of opinion dynamics, which represents users' opinion over time by means of marked jump diffusion stochastic differential equations.

Works based on social influence network theory have made remarkable progress in showing how networks of interpersonal influence contribute to the formation of interpersonal consensus in complex circumstances [5,9,12,13,15].

In [12], authors investigate on a consensus opinion model in social groups based on the input of influential user and aggregation methods.

In [16], authors propose the use of opinion-based graph whose vertices contain message objects and its reply-to edges label within opinion polarities.

In [5], authors consider the problem of modeling how users update opinions based on their neighbors' opinion and proposed new model and show preliminary results on the convergence and structure of opinions in the whole network.

In [13], authors propose an inference mechanism for fitting generative, agent like model of opinion dynamics to real-world social traces.

In [18], authors propose to use recurrent neural network (RNN) to model each user's posting behaviors on Twitter and incorporate their neighbors' topic-associated context as for user-level stance prediction.

3 Our Methodology

We aim to study the interaction between two ego networks around two influencers having opposite opinions on a given subject and its impact on opinion change and propagation within these two interconnected ego networks. We chose the Covid vaccination topic which was a trending subject presenting a controversy and that generates a lot of debate and, therefore, a lot of positive and negative opinions and reactions to it. This is a favorable ground for sentiment analysis that allows to see if people's opinions can change depending on several factors. We then realize the following steps on twitter (see Algorithm 1):

3.1 Data Collection and Influencers Selection

Collecting data in relations to two influencers with opposite opinions guarantees to have a significant number of opinions, the exchange between users of opposite opinions and the possibility of studying the stability or the modification of these opinions. To detect influencers, we studied different metrics as the popularity, the range, the propagation and the likeness scores and we explored also the profile of the personalities. We collected then data on the chosen topic (Covid vaccination): these data consist of tweets and retweets and replies to those tweets

---

Algorithm 1. Study of the interaction between two opposite ego networks

---

1: **Step1: Data collection from twitter**
2: retrieve tweets related the chosen topic
3: **Step 2: Find two opposite influencers**
4: metrics: popularity, range, the propagation, likeness scores and users profiles
5: **Step 3 Construction of the propagation directed network**
6: nodes: common repliers extracted from both influencers' egocentric networks at levels 1 and 2
7: edges: the actions of reply.
8: **Step 4: Study of the network characteristics**
9: Centralities
10: Community detection using Louvain algorithm
11: **Step 5: Sentiment Analysis**
12: polarity and subjectivity computing for users, ego networks, communities
13: **Step 6: Machine Learning for detecting opinion change of users**
14: Dataset: an entry is related to a link of the propagation network
15: nodal and topological features for both the **original tweet** and the **reply author** nodes
16: textual features are extracted with the TF-IDF method
17: **Step 6.1: Detecting opinion change over time**
18: the target variable indicates if the replier has changed his opinion polarity over time
19: **Step 6.2: Detecting opinion modification via the action of reply**
20: the target variable indicates if the opinion is modified via the action of reply
21: find the best ML method for both

---

until a certain level for both ego networks. This allows to consider the opinions of retrieved tweets, retweets and replies for common users of both influencers. We then focused particularly on users who reacted to both influencers at the same time.

3.2   Construction of the Propagation Directed Network

We constructed the propagation directed network by considering:

1. the set of nodes consisting of commune repliers extracted from both influencers' egocentric networks at levels 1 and 2,
2. the set of edges corresponding to the action of reply: the edge $A \rightarrow B$ means that user B has replied to user A.

Our aim is to study the opinion modification inside the egocentric networks around influencers and inside the communities, Different centralities measures were computed and disjointed communities were detected using the Louvain algorithm [3].

3.3 Machine Learning Models for Detecting Changes in User Opinion

We seek to find two machine learning models aimed at detecting (respectively) opinion change over time concerning users which are the authors of replies and opinion modification during the information propagation via an action of reply.

Detecting Changes in User Opinion over Time. We constructed a dataset in which an entry is related to a link (or edge) of the propagation network (see Table 1) with nodal and topological information related to both the **original tweet** and the **reply author** nodes, the target variable indicate if the replier has changed his opinion over time or not.

The target variable takes its values in the following set: {*static, increased, decreased*}. Static indicates that the polarity of the author node has not changed, increased means that the polarity has increased and decreased means that the polarity has decreased.

Table 1 shows a description of the dataset features apart from the textual content (tweet and reply texts).

We used the Python H2O AutoML (https://github.com/h2oai/h2o-3) packages which allow to test machine learning models automatically.

Detecting Opinion Modification via the Action of Reply. We used the same dataset described above but we take as a target variable a binary variable indicating if the opinion {positive, negative, neutral} is different between the original tweet user and the author of the reply.

Table 1. Dataset Features without textual content

Features nature	Features
Topological features	`Betweenness_centrality, Out_centrality, In_centrality, Pagerank, (for original tweet user) community_original_tweet_user, community_author, community_mean_subjectivity_original_tweet_user, community_mean_polarity_original_tweet_user, in_same_community`
Nodal features	`mean_polarity_original_tweet_user, mean_subjectivity_original_tweet_user, subjectivity_original_tweet_text`
Tweet features	`tweet_stopwords_ratio, reply_stopwords_ratio (low, medium, high, very high), length_reply_high (low, medium, high, very high), length_tweet (low, medium, high, very high)`

4   Experimental Results

4.1   Characteristics of the Propagation Network

The chosen topic was related to Covid vaccination, the period for retrieved tweets was defined as going from October 1, 2021 to December 14, 2021. The query returned approximately 65.000 tweets. The found influencers were *Florian Philippot*, politician against vaccination and *Olivier Véran,* for vaccination.

Table 2 shows some characteristics of the propagation network.

Table 2. The propagation network characteristics: intervals of the top ten values of centrality measures

Nodes#	edge#	Outdegree	Indegree	Betweenness	Pagerank	Communities#
21075	84441	[0.05,0.18]	[0.001,0.003]	[0.002,0.007]	[0.00004,0.0005]	36

The out-degree centrality have significant values, this can helps us to detect influencing users that contribute to the propagation of opinions.

4.2   Sentiment Analysis

To perform this step, we used the TextBlob library in Python (https:// github.com/sloria/TextBlob) and Vader sentiment analyser (https://github. com/cjhutto/vaderSentiment) that allowed to obtain both subjectivity and polarity indicators for the content of tweets. Subjective expressions are opinions that describe people's feelings toward a specific topic while objective expressions express facts. Subjectivity varies between 0 and 1. Polarity, taking values between -1 and 1, allows to quantify the general opinion expressed in the tweet using a numerical value. This helps to characterize positive, negative and neutral opinion.

Figure 1 shows the count of positive/negative and neutral reactions in both egocentric networks of the two opposite influencers. We notice that there are more positive reactions about COVID vaccination in both egocentric networks (even for that of the influencer who is against: Philippot). Figures in 2 show polarity scores obtained for communities. We notice that polarities are mixed and almost neutral within communities and do not exceed the value of 0.10. We see thus, that we can not reach polarisations of opinion within this configuration.

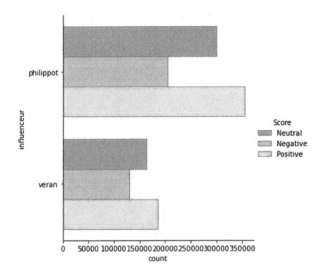

Fig. 1. Opinion propagation in both egocentric networks

4.3   Machine Learning Models for Detecting Changes in User Opinion

Detecting Changes in User Opinion over Time. As mentioned above, we constructed a dataset in which an entry is related to a link (or edge) of the propagation network (see Table 1) with nodal and topological information related to both the **original tweet** and the **reply author** nodes, the target variable indicates if the replier has changed his opinion over time or not.

The target variable takes its values in the following set: {*static, increased, decreased*}. Static indicates that the polarity of the author node has not changed, increased means that the polarity has increased and decreased means that the polarity has decreased.

In order to treat the textual content, we used the TF-IDF method.

The TF-IDF (Term Frequency - Inverse Document Frequency) method is based on the frequency of appearance of a word in a document but also on its rarescarcity within a corpus where this document is contained. This method generates values resulting from computing TF and IDF [10], the corresponding features are the words found in the documents of the corpus and their value is the value of the TF-IDF for each word.

We used the Python H2O AutoML (https://github.com/h2oai/h2o-3) [1] and PyCaret (https://pycaret.org/) packages which allow to test machine learning models automatically on a given training and test sets. We took the accuracy as metric to evaluate the models. We used a split training/stratified test on the

---

[1] H2O is an Open Source, Distributed, Fast & Scalable Machine Learning Platform.

Table 3. Polarity scores by community

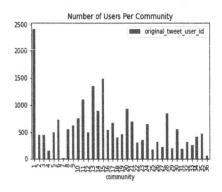

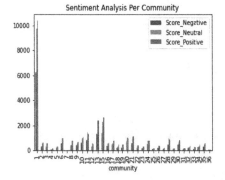

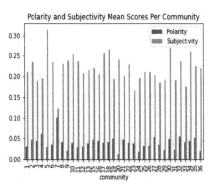

Table 4. Ridge model for detecting opinion change over time

	Performance for the 3 class values				
	Precision	*Recall*	*F1_score*	Accuracy	Support
TF-IDF				0.58	20062
Increased	0.67	0.64	0.65		8249
Decreased	0.56	0.63	0.59		8144
Static	0.44	0.36	0.38		3669

target variable with 33% of the dataset data for the test set. The best found model for detecting changes in user opinion over time was the ridge classifier.

We then use a RandomizedSearchCV as well as a stratified cross-validation in order to obtain the best ridge model among a selection of parameters (grid) and a number of maximal iterations (15 models were tested). Performances are shown in table 4.

Figures 2 and 3 and those in Table 3 show the ridge model coefficients for both class values *increased* and *decreased*, blue coefficients are retrieved from the TF-IDF results and green ones are extracted form the other features (topological and

Table 5. Ridge model coefficients for the increased and decreased class values: textual coefficients.

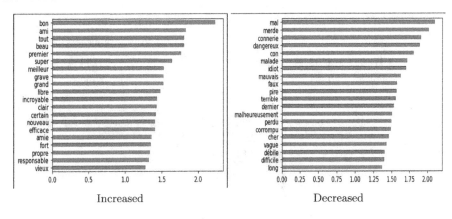

Increased   Decreased

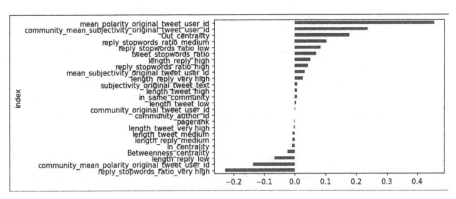

Fig. 2. Ridge model coefficients for the *increased* class value expect textual coefficients

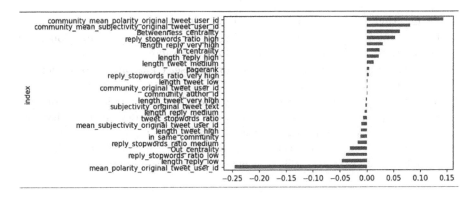

Fig. 3. Ridge model coefficients for the *decreased* class value expect textual coefficients

Table 6. Random Forest for detecting opinion modification via the action of reply

	Performances				
	Precision	Recall	F1_score	Accuracy	Support
				0.59	20062
True	0.62	0.68	0.65		11294
False	0.53	0.47	0.50		8768

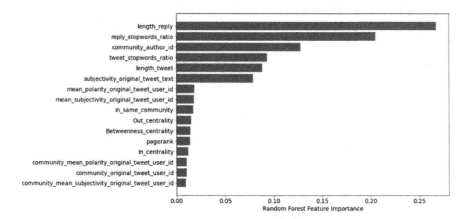

Fig. 4. Random Forest model: variable importances

tweet ones). These coefficients help us to explain the opinion change of users. The set of the top 20 words for users whose opinion polarity were increased (respectively decreased) is outlined. Likewise, other features related to tweet or topological information contribute to the opinion modification.

We can for example make the following observations concerning the increase or the decrease of the polarity of the replier (see Figs. 2 and 3):

- The fact that the origin user has a high polarity in comparison to the polarity of its community, a high out-degree centrality and a low betweenness one, will contribute to the increase of the polarity of the replier.
- The average of the subjectively of the origin user contribute also to increase the polarity of the replier.
- The fact that the community of the origin user has a high polarity in comparison to its polarity, a high betweenness and a low out-degree centrality one, will contribute to the decrease of the polarity of the replier.
- The average of the subjectively of the origin user still contribute to decrease the polarity of the replier (like the increase case) (Table 5).

Detecting Opinion Modification via the Action of Reply. As mentioned above, the same dataset described above is used but we take as a target variable a binary variable indicating if the opinion {positive, negative, neutral} is different between the original tweet user and the author of the reply. The best found model was a random forest one. Performances are shown in Table 6.

Figure 4 shows variable importances of the random forest model. We notice that some variables concerning the form of the reply text have an important role in the detection of the opinion modification of the replier compared to the original tweet user like the length of the reply text (and the original tweet) and the ratio of stop-words. The subjectivity of the original tweet has also an important role for detecting the opinion modification. Concerning the topological parameters, the different centralities have minor importances but the community of the author (replier) seems to have a significant importance.

5   Conclusion and Perspectives

As mentioned above, our main objective is to study the interaction between two ego networks around two influencers having opposite opinion on a given subject an its impact on opinion change and propagation within these two interconnected ego networks. The chosen topic was related to Covid vaccination and two influencers with opposite opinions were selected. We firstly constructed a propagation network extracted from a set of collected tweets and replies starting from both influencers, where nodes are users and edges are tweets or replies. The extracted propagation networks consists of a the common repliers at level 1 and 2 of both ego networks. We noticed that detected communities do not allow us to observe any polarisation. We then proposed two machine learning models in order to detect respectively: opinion change over time concerning users which are the authors of replies and opinion modification during the information propagation via an action of reply. We outlined different type of features related to textual, contextual or topological information that could help to explain the increase or decrease of opinion polarity as well as the opinion modification via the action of reply. We notice for example that the polarity of the origin user, its community, its out-centrality and betweenness centrality contribute to the increase and decrease of replier polarity. On the other hand, we notice that some variables concerning the form of the reply text as well as the community of the author (replier) have an important role in the detection of the opinion modification of the replier via an action of reply.

We are now studying the opinion formation [12] in the propagation network as well as the impact of the influencers ego networks' level (currently 2) on 1)the polarisation of detected communities and 2)the performances of opinion change detection models.

We also believe that applying overlapping community detection algorithms [2] could help use to detect users that have role of *moderators* when spreading the information in the network.

References

1. Arnaboldi, V., Conti, M., La Gala, M., Passarella, A., Pezzoni, F.: Ego network structure in online social networks and its impact on information diffusion. Comput. Commun. **76**, 26–41 (2016)
2. Attal, J.-P., Malek, M., Zolghadri, M.: Overlapping community detection using core label propagation algorithm and belonging functions. Appl. Intell. **51**(11), 8067–8087 (2021). https://doi.org/10.1007/s10489-021-02250-4
3. Blondel, V.D., Guillaume, J.-L., Lambiotte, R., Lefebvre, E.: Fast unfolding of communities in large networks. J. Stat. Mech. Theory Experiment **2008**(10), 10008 (2008)
4. Ye, M., Anderson, B.D.O.: Recent advances in the modelling and analysis of opinion dynamics on influence networks (2019)
5. Das, A., Gollapudi, S., Munagala, K.: Modeling opinion dynamics in social networks. In: Carterette, B., Diaz, F., Castillo, C., Metzler, D. (eds.) Seventh ACM International Conference on Web Search and Data Mining, WSDM 2014, New York, NY, USA, 24–28 February 2014, pp. 403–412. ACM (2014)
6. De, A., Bhattacharya, S., Ganguly, N.: Shaping opinion dynamics in social networks. In: André, E., Koenig, S., Dastani, M., Sukthankar, G. (eds.) Proceedings of the 17th International Conference on Autonomous Agents and MultiAgent Systems, AAMAS 2018, Stockholm, Sweden, 10–15 July 2018, pp. 1336–1344. International Foundation for Autonomous Agents and Multiagent Systems Richland, SC, USA/ACM (2018)
7. Folly, K., Malek, M., Kotzinos, D.: Social networks analysis for opinion model extraction. In: Networks 2021: first combined meeting of the International Network for Social Network Analysis (Sunbelt XLI), and the Network Science Society (NetSci 2021), Indiana, United States, July 2021
8. Garimella, K., De Francisci Morales, G., Gionis, A., Mathioudakis, M.: Quantifying controversy in social media. In: Bennett, P.N., Josifovski, V., Neville, J., Radlinski, F. (eds.) Proceedings of the Ninth ACM International Conference on Web Search and Data Mining, San Francisco, CA, USA, 22–25 February 2016, pp. 33–42. ACM (2016)
9. Gu, Q., Santos Jr., E., Santos, E.E.: Modeling opinion dynamics in a social network. In: 2013 IEEE/WIC/ACM International Conferences on Intelligent Agent Technology, IAT 2013, 17–20 November 2013, Atlanta, Georgia, USA, pp. 9–16. IEEE Computer Society (2013)
10. Jones, K.S.: A statistical interpretation of term specificity and its application in retrieval. J. Documentation **60**(5), 493–502 (2004)
11. Mathapati, S., Manjula, S.H., VenugopalK, R.: Sentiment analysis and opinion mining from social media: a review. Glob. J. Comput. Sci. Technol. (2017)
12. Mohammadinejad, A.: Consensus opinion model in online social networks based on the impact of influential users. (Modèle d'avis de consensus dans les réseaux sociaux en ligne basé sur l'impact des utilisateurs influents). Ph.D. thesis, Telecom & Management SudParis, Évry, France (2018)
13. Monti, C., De Francisci Morales, G., Bonchi, F.: Learning opinion dynamics from social traces. In: Proceedings of the 26th ACM SIGKDD International Conference on Knowledge Discovery and Data Mining. ACM, August 2020

14. Adi Prasetya, H., Murata, T.: Modeling the co-evolving polarization of opinion and news propagation structure in social media. In: Aiello, L.M., Cherifi, C., Cherifi, H., Lambiotte, R., Lió, P., Rocha, L.M. (eds.) COMPLEX NETWORKS 2018. SCI, vol. 813, pp. 314–326. Springer, Cham (2019). https://doi.org/10.1007/978-3-030-05414-4_25

15. Rao, B.: An approach to opinion mining in community graph using graph mining techniques. Int. J. Synth. Emot. **9**(2), 94–110 (2018)

16. Stavrianou, A., Velcin, J., Chauchat, J.-H.: A combination of opinion mining and social network techniques for discussion analysis. In: Poncelet, P., Roche, M. (eds.) Fouille de Données d'Opinions. RNTI, vol. E-17, pp. 25–44. Cépaduès-Éditions (2009)

17. Ureña, R., Kou, G., Dong, Y., Chiclana, F., Herrera-Viedma, E.: A review on trust propagation and opinion dynamics in social networks and group decision making frameworks. Inf. Sci. **478**, 461–475 (2019)

18. Zhu, L., He, Y., Zhou, D.: Neural opinion dynamics model for the prediction of user-level stance dynamics. Inf. Process. Manag. **57**(2), 102031 (2020)

Change in Social Media Use for Learning Among Japanese Internet Users During the COVID-19 Pandemic

Toshikazu Iitaka[✉]

Kumamoto Gakuen University, Oe 2-5-1 Chuo-Ku, Kumamoto, Japan
iitaka2@yahoo.co.jp

Abstract. This study examines how Japanese Internet users' use of social media for learning changed during the COVID-19 pandemic. The study in this paper is based on online research, demonstrating a major shift in learning among Japanese Internet users.

The research background is explained, research questions are offered, statistical analysis is given, and significance and limitations of the results are examined specifically in this work.

Keywords: COVID-19 · Social Media · Social Isolation

1 Introduction

As we know, the COVID-19 pandemic has influenced our life. Our learning conditions have also been under such an influence. Consequently, this research explores the change in social media use for learning among Japanese Internet users during the COVID-19 pandemic. We especially focus on the use of social media for learning.

This paper is based on studies on the utilization of social media for learning, including the literature [1–3]. The literature [1, 2] has shown statistical analysis of online research results. The literature [1, 2] is research on digital note-taking. According to the literature [1, 2], Japanese students tend to use social media, especially Twitter, for learning. The condition of learning, in general, has been altered by COVID-19 conditions because our life, including learning, has been restricted. So, the literature [3] has done almost the same online research. Furthermore, the research [3] has demonstrated the change under COVID-19 conditions.

However, the restriction was eased in April 2022 in Japan. This situation allows us to assess whether COVID-19 actually altered our learning condition permanently. So, we have done almost the same online research. Then, we compared the outcomes with those of the literature [1–3]. We have found that Japanese students tend to use social media for learning compared with other Japanese. However, the number of students who use social media for learning has decreased compared to before the pandemic of COVID-19.

Meanwhile, influential research maintains that social isolation is an important issue of research on online learning under COVID-19 conditions [4]. Consequently, this study

A. Coman and S. Vasilache (Eds.): HCII 2023, LNCS 14026, pp. 308–323, 2023.
https://doi.org/10.1007/978-3-031-35927-9_22

examined the connection between social media use for learning and social isolation. The analysis revealed the complicated influence of social isolation.

Specifically, in this work, the research background is explained, research questions are offered, statistical analysis is given, and the significance of the results and limitations is examined.

2 Background and Significance

This section discusses the research background and the significance of this research.

This paper has two crucial backgrounds. The first background is studies of social media use for learning. The second background is online learning under COVID-19 conditions.

As shown above, this paper refers to the literature [1–3] as significant previous studies of social media use for learning. The studies of digital note-taking are the contexts of these studies. The presentation of the literature [5] pointed out that digital note-taking allows us to share the data of studies. The inquiry into the nature of digital note-taking may give us useful information on using big data for learning. On the other hand, the literature [6] pointed out that young Japanese tend to use social media, especially Twitter, for learning.

Meanwhile, T. Seo, who is a journalist, revealed that users of the note-taking application Clear frequently connect through social media [6]. According to the literature [1], the design of the application Clear is similar to that of Twitter. As a result, the literature [1] estimates that Twitter can also be utilized for note-taking. So, online research on social media use has been done. Research [1] has shown that roughly 40% of Japanese students use Twitter for note-taking. The literature [2] has proven the result is reproductive and social media is also used for other learning activities. We must note that social media is a significant big data source.

The situation has been changed by the COVID-19 pandemic. The restriction because of the pandemic obliged us to learn online. The use of social media for learning may also have been changed. Therefore, online research whose design is nearly identical to the literature [2] has been conducted. More Japanese students still tend to use social media for learning. However, the number has decreased. However, the restriction was eased in April 2022. Repeating the same research and examining the change will be significant.

So, we must focus on the second background to check the change. The literature [4], which is a research about learning under the COVID-19 setting, pointed out that social isolation is a major issue of online learning. We have to note that social media can bind people and is designed to address the social isolation problem.

As mentioned above, social media is a crucial big data source. The analysis of social media use for learning is significant. Therefore, examining the change in social media use for learning is crucial.

3 Methods

This section shows the research design and statistical analysis. Firstly, we present the research questions and research methodology. Secondly, the variables which are used for the analysis are explained. Finally, statistical analysis is demonstrated.

3.1 Research Questions and Research Design

As we have shown above, the literature [3] confirmed the influence of the COVID-19 pandemic (the restriction because of the pandemic) on social media use for learning. However, the restriction was eased in April 2022 in Japan. So, we can examine the real effect of the pandemic on social media use for learning. Meanwhile, if we want to examine the impact of the COVID-19 pandemic and the use of social media for learning, we have to concentrate on the social isolation of users.

So, the following research questions are created.

RQ1 Do more Japanese students still use social media for learning?

RQ2 How does social isolation relate to social media use for learning?

We conducted a web search to verify these research questions. The research feature is almost the same as that of the literature [3] (Table 1).

Table 1. Research features

Type of Survey	Online Research
Period	2022.8.23-2022.8.25
Number of Samples	560

gender	
Female	50%
Male	50%

Age	%	Number of Samples
-19	25.2	141
20-29	31.8	178
30-39	10.4	58
40-49	10.2	57
50-59	10	56
60-	12.5	70

The research was conducted by the same research firm as the literature [3]. Half of the samples are students.

3.2 Description of the Variables

We need two variables to examine the research questions. The first is the use of social media for learning, and the second is social isolation. The first is the same as that of the literature [2, 3]. The UCLA loneliness scale (Japanese version), documented in the literature [7–9], is used to measure social isolation. Besides, there is a question that asks about social isolation directly.

There are a variety of social media uses for learning, "gathering information for learning," "asking concrete questions," "connecting with other users who have the same learning concern," "recoding daily learning experience," "taking notes," "uploading a photo of the note," "uploading a photo of blackboard or slide with comments," "uploading a movie for learning," "reading notes," "watching a photo of notes", and "watching a movie for learning." A variety of social media are also used for learning, including Twitter, Facebook, Instagram, YouTube, and others. We evaluated the frequency of social media use with four scale questions (never, seldom, sometimes, and often).

The questions in Table 2 are used to measure social isolation. We analyzed the situation prior to the COVID-19 pandemic (before March 2020), during the restriction (between April 2020 and March 2022), and after the restriction (after April 2022) by four scale questions (I never feel this way, I rarely feel this way, I sometimes feel this way, and I often feel this way).

Table 2. Questions of the Japanese version of the UCLA loneliness scale and the direct question

	text	abbreviation
Q1	I am happy doing so many things with friends. (reverse)	With Friends
Q2	I have nobody to talk to	nobody to talk to
Q3	There is no one I can turn to.	no one I can turn to.
Q4	I am not alone. (reverse)	not alone
Q5	I am a necessary person for my friends. (reverse)	necessary person
Q6	My friends and I have many things in common. (reverse)	in common
Q7	I am no longer close to anyone	no longer close
Q8	My interests and ideas are not shared by those around me	not shared
Q9	I prefer going out.(reverse)	prefer going out
Q10	There are people who are close to me.(reverse)	people close to me
Q11	I am ignored.	ignored
Q12	My social relationships are superficial.	superficial
Q13	No one really knows me well	No one knows me
Q14	I feel isolated from others	feel isolated
Q15	I can make friends anytime if I want. (reverse)	can make friends
Q16	There are people who know me well. (reverse)	knows me well
Q17	I am unhappy being so withdrawn	withdrawn
Q18	Though I have friends, their ideas are different from mine.	different idea
Q19	There are people to whom I can talk.(reverse)	people I can talk
Q20	There are people to whom I can turn.(reverse)	people I can turn
Q21	I am lonely (Original)	Direct isolation

The UCLA loneliness scale is composed of the answers to Q1 ~ Q20 in Table 2. Only Q21 is original. Q21 is a direct question of social isolation.

Then, we examine the distribution and reliabilities of the variables. We have to examine the reliability of variables that are created by summing up the answers or reversed answers to the questions (Table 3, 4, 5, 6, 7, 8 and 9).

Table 3. Description of variables(1)

	Text	Mean	Std. Deviation			Text	Mean	Std. Deviation
Q2-1	Gather Information by Facebook	1.44	.818		Q2-9	Ask concrete questions by other social media	1.55	.880
Q2-2	Gather Information by Twitter	1.65	.933		Q2-10	Connect with other people who have the same learning interest by Facebook	1.45	.801
Q2-3	Gather Information by Line	1.74	.987					
Q2-4	Gather Information by Instagram	1.80	1.047					
Q2-5	Gather Information by other social media	1.68	.963		Q2-11	Connect with other people who have the same learning interest by Twitter	1.53	.852
Q2-6	Ask concrete questions by Facebook	1.43	.813					
Q2-7	Ask concrete questions by Twitter	1.51	.842		Q2-12	Connect with other people who have the same learning interest by Line	1.67	.929
Q2-8	Ask concrete questions by Line	1.82	.997					

The reliability of all composed variables is greater than 0.5, and the distribution of all variables is normal enough.

Table 4. Description of variables(2)

	Text	Mean	Std. Deviation		Text	Mean	Std. Deviation
Q2-13	Connect with other people who have the same learning interest by Instagram	1.61	.879	Q2-19	Take note by Twitter	1.43	.786
				Q2-20	Take note by other social media	1.51	.869
Q2-14	Connect with other people who have the same learning interest by other social media	1.50	.820	Q2-21	Upload photos of notebooks on Facebook	1.38	.735
				Q2-22	Upload photos of notebooks on Twitter	1.45	.816
Q2-15	Record daily learning experiences by Facebook	1.42	.803	Q2-23	Upload photos of notebooks on Instagram	1.47	.809
Q2-16	Record daily learning experiences byTwitter	1.50	.858	Q2-24	Upload photos of notebooks on other social media	1.43	.795
Q2-17	Record daily learning experiences by other social media	1.52	.867	Q2-25	Upload photos of slides or blackboard with comments on Facebook	1.43	.847
Q2-18	Take note by Facebook	1.41	.776				

Table 5. Description of variables(3)

	Text	Mean	Std. Deviation		Text	Mean	Std. Deviation	Text
Q2-26	Upload photos of slides or blackboard with comments on Twitter	1.41	.804		Q2-33	Read notes on Facebook	1.40	.782
					Q2-34	Read notes on Twitter	1.46	.821
Q2-27	Upload photos of slides or blackboard with comments on other social media	1.45	.834		Q2-35	Read notes on other social media	1.48	.837
					Q2-36	Watch photos of notes on Facebook	1.43	.828
Q2-28	Upload movies for learning on Facebook	1.42	.832		Q2-37	Watch photos of notes on Twitter	1.50	.869
Q2-29	Upload movies for learning on Twitter	1.44	.838		Q2-38	Watch photos of notes on Instagram	1.56	.907
Q2-30	Upload movies for learning on Instagram	1.44	.807		Q2-39	Watch photos of notes on other social media	1.51	.856
Q2-31	Upload movies for learning on other social media	1.43	.820		Q2-40	Watch movies for learning on Facebook.	1.45	.827
Q2-32	Upload movies for learning on YouTube	1.43	.812		Q2-41	Watch movies for learning on Twitter.	1.49	.854

Table 6. Description of variables(4)

	Text	Mean	Std. Deviation
Q2–40	Watch movies for learning on Facebook.	1.45	.827
Q2–41	Watch movies for learning on Twitter.	1.49	.854
Q2–42	Watch movies for learning on Instagram	1.58	.905
Q2–43	Watch movies for learning on other social media	1.56	.903
Q2–44	Watch movies for learning on YouTube	1.80	.995

Table 7. Description of variables(5)

Variables	Mean	Std. Deviation	Skewness	Kurtosis	α
UCLA isolation scale (After Restriction)	62.8305	13.47815	-.423	.409	0.899
UCLA isolation scale (During Restriction)	63.6447	14.13903	-.427	.430	0.899
UCLA isolation scale (Before Restriction)	63.6447	14.13903	-.427	.430	0.944
Record Learning Experiences using Social Media	4.4411	2.23169	1.315	.482	0.858

Table 8. Description of variables(6)

Variables	Mean	Std. Deviation	Skewness	Kurtosis	α
Take Notes using Social Media	4.3464	2.18909	1.471	1.034	0.882
Upload Photos of Notes on Social Media	5.7214	2.83996	1.464	.904	0.921
Using Faceboo for Learning	15.6393	7.76755	1.514	1.046	0.97
Using Twitter for Learning	16.3839	7.74694	1.327	.718	0.956
Using Line for Learning	5.2250	2.48417	.795	-.462	0.812
Using Instagram for Learning	9.4554	4.36708	1.097	.205	0.897
Using YouTube for Learning	3.2286	1.52894	1.079	.401	0.589
Connecting using Social Media	8.3161	3.79932	.899	-.246	0.882
Gathering Information for Learning using Social Media	7.7429	3.53236	.999	-.171	0.857
Ask Questions using Social Media	6.3125	2.93712	1.094	.101	0.848

Table 9. Description of variables(7)

Variables	Mean	Std. Deviation	Skewness	Kurtosis	α
Upload Motives for Learning on Social Media	7.1679	3.74649	1.513	1.005	0.949
Reading Notes on Social Media	4.3375	2.17697	1.492	1.129	0.871
Watch Photo of Note on Social Media	5.9839	3.05608	1.340	.589	0.871
Watch Movies for Learning on Social Media	7.8839	3.71080	1.143	.277	0.883

3.3 Statistical Analysis

This part will show the statistical analysis which examines the two research questions. RQ1 is about the frequency of social media use for learning (Tables 10 and 11).

Table 10. Comparison of social media uses for learning(1)

	Q2–18 Take note by Facebook			
	Never	Seldom	Sometimes	Often
Not Student	227	33	14	6
	81.1%	11.8%	5.0%	2.1%
Student	190	43	36	11
	67.9%	15.4%	12.9%	3.9%
Total	417	76	50	17
	74.5%	13.6%	8.9%	3.0%

Table 11. Comparison of social media uses for learning((2)

	Q2–19 Take note by Twitter			
	Never	Seldom	Sometimes	Often
Not Student	224	32	18	6
	80.0%	11.4%	6.4%	2.1%
Student	182	48	41	9
	65.0%	17.1%	14.6%	3.2%
Total	406	80	59	15
	72.5%	14.3%	10.5%	2.7%

Evidently, more than 30% of students utilize social media for digital note-taking, which is comparable to that described in the literature [3].

Japanese students tend to use social media to learn more frequently than other Japanese. T-test has shown that the frequency difference in terms of note-taking is statistically significant (take note by Facebook: $t\ (521.38) = 3.8$, $p < 0.01$; take note by Twitter $t\ (532.68) = 3.86$, $p < 0.01$). Similar tendencies regarding other variables of social media use for learning can be found. Therefore, we can state that the literature [3] finding is reproducible. However, as we have shown above, the frequency of social media use for learning among students is decreased. So, ANOVA is used to compare the difference between three periods, i.e., before, during, and after the restriction. Data from the literature [2, 3] is used for checking the change (Table 12).

Table 12. The social media use change for learning among Japanese students

	Q2–18 Take note by Facebook	Q2–19 Take note by Twitter
2022	1.52	1.56
2020	1.53	1.64
2018	1.69	1.8

ANOVA on digital note-taking reveals a statistically significant variation. Only the difference in students before and during the restriction is statistically significant. The frequency in 2020 and 2022 has dropped in comparison with 2018. Students in 2018 tended to use Twitter for learning compared to 2020 and 2022. Moreover, the down is statistically significant (F $(2, 837) = 5.08, p < 0.01$). We cannot confirm any statistically significant difference between 2020 and 2022. A similar trend is seen in terms of other uses of social media for learning, though it is not so blatant as that of Twitter.

So, we can estimate that the number of Japanese students who use social media has decreased because of the COVID-19 pandemic. Additionally, the decline is not so temporal, though more students continue to use social media for learning than other Japanese.

Then, we examine RQ2. RQ2 concerns social isolation. We used the UCLA loneliness scale to ascertain social isolation. Additionally, a direct inquiry was prepared regarding social isolation. When we check the relationship between the UCLA loneliness scale and "direct isolation," we can confirm a statistically significant positive relation. Consequently, we can say the variables are valid (Table 13, 14 and 15).

The correlation between social isolation and social media use for learning is proven to be complicated. Although direct questions of social isolation related to social media use for learning relate positively, the UCLA loneliness scale related negatively to social media uses for learning. This tendency is remarkable in terms of "use of line," "gathering information for learning," and "connecting with other users who have the same learning concern."

Table 13. The correlation between social isolation and social media use(1)

	UCLA Loneliness During Restrictions	UCLA Loneliness After Restrictions	Direct isolation Before Restrictions	Direct isolation During Restrictions	Direct isolation After Restrictions
UCLA Loneliness Before Restrictions	.935***	.935***	.695***	.519***	.618***
UCLA Loneliness During Restrictions		1.000***	.672***	.690***	.736***
UCLA Loneliness After Restrictions			.672***	.690***	.736***
Direct Loneliness Before Restrictions				.612***	.622***
Direct Loneliness During Restrictions					.635***

The number is Pearson's Correlations Coefficient.
***. Correlation is significant at the 0.001 level (2-tailed).
**. Correlation is significant at the 0.01 level (2-tailed).
*. Correlation is significant at the 0.05 level (2-tailed).

Table 14. The correlation between social isolation and social media use(2)

	Note-Taking (Text)	Note-Taking(Photo)	Learning with Facebook	Learning with Twitter	Learning with Line
UCLA Loneliness Before Restrictions	-.061	.004	-.106	-.063	**-.563***
UCLA Loneliness During Restrictions	-.099	-.050	-.173	-.077	**-.465***
UCLA Loneliness After Restrictions	-.099	-.050	-.173	-.077	**-.465***
Direct isolation Before Restrictions	.256***	.238***	.247***	.258***	**.130**
Direct isolation During Restrictions	.259***	.284***	.285***	.283***	**.160***
Direct isolation After Restrictions	.257***	.273***	.248***	.298***	**.135**

The number is Pearson's Correlations Coefficient.
***. Correlation is significant at the 0.001 level (2-tailed).
**. Correlation is significant at the 0.01 level (2-tailed).
*. Correlation is significant at the 0.05 level (2-tailed).

Therefore, we have to analyze this complex relationship using several regression models.

Table 15. The correlation between social isolation and social media use(3)

	Leaning with Instagram	Uploading Movie for Learning	Watching Movie for Learning
UCLA Loneliness Before Restrictions	−.231	.029	−.092
UCLA Loneliness During Restrictions	−.149	−.041	−.102
UCLA Loneliness After Restrictions	−.149	−.041	−.102
Direct isolation Before Restrictions	.227***	.254***	.238***
Direct isolation During Restrictions	.238***	.289***	.226***
Direct isolation After Restrictions	.226***	.273***	.249***

The number is Pearson's Correlations Coefficient.
***. Correlation is significant at the 0.001 level (2-tailed).
**. Correlation is significant at the 0.01 level (2-tailed).
*. Correlation is significant at the 0.05 level (2-tailed).

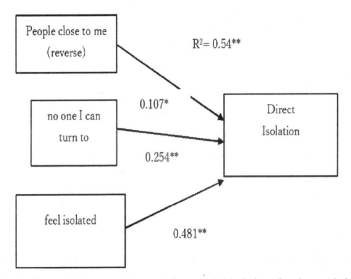

Fig. 1. The multiple regression analysis on social isolation after the restriction

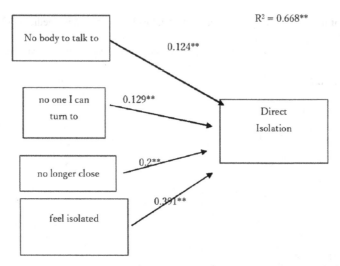

Fig. 2. The multiple regression analysis on social isolation during the restriction

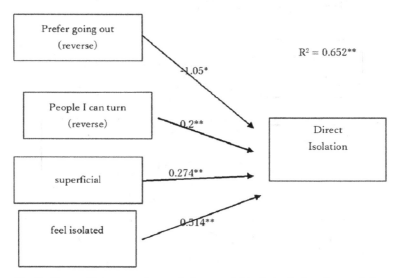

Fig. 3. The multiple regression analysis on social isolation before the restriction

Though there is a constant positive correlation between "direct isolation" and the UCLA loneliness scale, the analysis revealed that the background is different (Figs. 1, 2 and 3). "No one I can turn to" seems to impact "direct isolation." Meanwhile, "superficial" lose influences on "direct isolation" and "people close to me (reverse)" come to have influence.

Then, we have to investigate the background of complicated relationships between social isolation and social media uses for learning. Only the influence of the UCLA loneliness scale after the restriction is analyzed because the questions about social media use are about the present (Figs. 4 and 5).

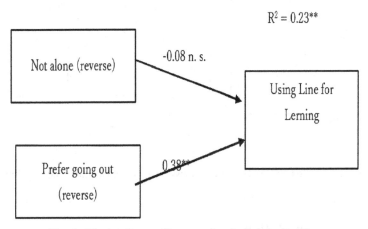

Fig. 4. The loneliness effect on using the line for learning

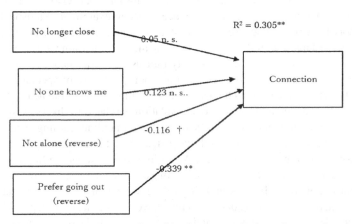

Fig. 5. The loneliness effect on connecting with other users who have the same learning concern

The first study revealed the effect of "no one knows me" in terms of "gathering information for learning," which is slightly significant. On the other hand, we can estimate that "prefer going out" affects "use line for learning" and "connecting with other users." The latter outcome is particularly acceptable.

We can estimate that the relationship in Fig. 6 exists after restriction.

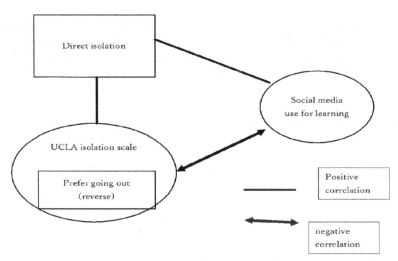

Fig. 6. The relationship between UCLA loneliness scale, direct isolation, and social media uses for learning

4 Result and Limitation

This paper focuses on social media use for learning and their change because of the COVID-19 pandemic. Online research has been done to examine it. Statistical analysis has been done based on online research. The statistical analysis results indicate a decrease in the number of Japanese students who use social media for learning during the COVID-19 pandemic. However, they did not simply quit using social media for learning. We might suppose that they instead discovered an appropriate use of special systems and social media. The analysis of such an assumption will be done in the near future.

Meanwhile, we can assume that social isolation is related to diverse ways of using social media for learning and is a significant problem in online learning. Therefore, this complicated relationship should be fully investigated in the future.

However, there are also restrictions. According to the "Japanese Society for Information and Media Studies" and "The Society of Socioinformatics," this research paper's design is unsuitable for online research. Therefore, we conducted offline research. But it takes too much time to input the data. As a result, we cannot meet this paper's deadline if we wait for it. However, we can present the result analysis of the offline (postal) research in the near future[1].

Acknowledgement. This work was supported by JSPS KAKENHI Grant Number JP15K12175 and 20K03196.

---

[1] The editors and reviewers of the journals of the "Japanese Society for Information and Media Studies" and "The Society of Socioinformatics" pointed out that this research should have been conducted offline. However, there are papers containing online research in the journals of both societies. Therefore, we requested a detailed explanation to describe the limitations of our paper for other journals. But they have not explained yet.

References

1. Iitaka, T.: A survey on use of social networking service for digital note taking. IEICE Tech. Rep. **117**(469), 223–228 (2018)
2. Iitaka, T.: An analysis on digital note-taking using social media in Japan. In: Stephanidis, C., Antona, M. (eds.) HCII 2020. CCIS, vol. 1226, pp. 177–184. Springer, Cham (2020). https://doi.org/10.1007/978-3-030-50732-9_24
3. Iitaka, T.: An analysis on social media use for learning under the COVID-19 condition in Japan. HCII 2022. Part of the Lecture Notes in Computer Science book series (LNCS,volume 13328). https://doi.org/10.1007/978-3-031-05657-4_18Author, F.: Contribution title. In: 9th International Proceedings on Proceedings, pp. 1–2. Publisher, Location (2010) (2022)
4. Kaplan-Rakowski, R.: Addressing students' emotional needs during the COVID-19 pandemic: a perspective on text versus video feedback in online environments. Educ. Tech. Res. Dev. **69**(1), 133–136 (2020). https://doi.org/10.1007/s11423-020-09897-9
5. Nakayama, M., Mituura, K., Yamamoto, H.: Relationship between factors of note-taking activity and student notes assessment in fully online learning environment. IEICE Tech. Rep. **111**(237), 13–18 (2011)
6. Seo, T.: 9wari ga SNS wo katduyou、Benkyouakade "Yuruku"tsunagaru shinzidaino Chukosei, My Navi News (2017). https://news.mynavi.jp/article/20170731-a269/). Accessed 11 Feb 2018
7. Moroi, K.: Loneliness and self-consciousness in high-school students. Jpn. Psychol. Res. **56**, 237–240 (1985)
8. Moroi, K.: Loneliness and self-consciousness in high-school students. Jpn. J. Exp. Soc. Psychol. **26**, 151–161 (1987)
9. Russell, D., Peplau, L.A., Cutrona, C.E.: The revised UCLA loneliness scale: concurrent and discriminant validity evedence. J. Pers. Soc. Psychol. **39**, 472–480 (1980)

Anonymous COVID-19 Channel on Jodel: A Quantitative Content Analysis

Karoline Jüttner[(⊠)], Philipp Nowak, Aylin Imeri, and Wolfgang G. Stock

Heinrich Heine University, Universitätsstr. 1, 40225 Düsseldorf, Germany
{Karoline.Juettner,Philipp.Nowak,Aylin.Imeri,
Wolfgang.Stock}@hhu.de

Abstract. This paper applied quantitative content analysis to investigate the conversations in the Corona channel of the anonymous social media app Jodel. Twenty thousand four hundred seventy-two postings from the German Corona channel have been published between March 3, 2020 and February 13, 2021. Those postings were classified into eleven content categories using an automated approach. The results show that, with an overall share of 41%, postings concerning the coronavirus itself and measures to contain the pandemic predominate. An evaluation of the 20 most frequent terms in the dataset underlines this and additionally shows that fellow humans, questions (#question), and temporal aspects are thematized. Interestingly, negative emotions such as fear, panic and worry are shared. At the same time, despite the more serious context of the Corona channel, humor and the search for entertainment seem to matter. The category denial & conspiracy theories comprises the fewest postings. This implies that Jodel, despite its anonymity, does not provide a breeding ground for conspiracy theories and points to a functioning self-regulation of the community.

Keywords: Content analysis · COVID-19 · Jodel · Social Media · Anonymity

1 Introduction

After almost three years, it is not a secret to say that COVID-19 and the measure of politics and administrations did affect our everyday life regarding social distancing, working remotely, and the channels we use to communicate. Until the beginning of 2022, hardly any topic seems more relevant in the media. In particular, the fact that many countries restricted private contact with other households by strict lockdowns suggests that people are increasingly using digital and social media to share information and communicate with each other. According to Kalman et al. (2021), digital and social media enables especially in crisis like this, to use online communication as compensation for social distancing.

Previous studies of computer-human mediated communication about COVID-19 on Twitter support this assumption (Ahmed et al., 2020; Chen et al., 2020; Prabhakar Kaila & Prasad, 2020; Stechemesser et al., 2020). Today's digital sources for human-computer mediated conversation, such as Twitter or Weibo (microblogging), Facebook (e.g., Facebook groups), WhatsApp, Signal and Telegram (messengers), Instagram (especially by using hashtags), TikTok, Reddit, and YouTube, can be reduced to a common denominator, namely, to need a unique and identifying user profile (Fischer et al., 2020). Knowing the person behind a post can have an impact on online communication. One topic, which is not solicited as widely in previous research, especially within the research community of digital mediated conversation, is the anonymity of users while communicating about crisis-related topics.

Jodel, an anonymous social network for sharing short postings, responded to the large number of COVID-19-related postings by creating a special Corona channel in February 2020. To gain further insights into the research area of anonymized online communication we conducted a quantitative analysis on the postings within the Corona channel.

It contributes to previous research in three ways:

First, the results of the anonymized Corona channels enable comparison with previous investigated non-anonymized digital and social media mediated conversations to highlight the differences and similarities. Due to the parallels of Jodel to the non-anonymous service Twitter, conclusions can be drawn about a possible influence of anonymity on online communication.

Secondly, while communication on Twitter has already been addressed in various studies related to COVID-19, few studies exist overall on Jodel and COVID-19 (Laaksonen & Rantasila, 2021; Seidenschnur, 2021; Vesterinen, 2021). As Jodel is described as a "high quality information service" (Nowak et al., 2018), the analysis of the anonymized postings can enable insights into thoughts, attitudes and topics that are raised by German users.

Thirdly, the automated analysis enables conclusion based on a rich dataset, which is not publicly available and was provided by The Jodel Venture GmbH specifically for the purpose of this study. To ensure scientificity, we published our research data.

Summarized, this investigation can provide valuable insights into the digital mediated conversation in which Jodel is used as an information service during a global pandemic and into the topics, that are of particular relevance to users of anonymous social media services in these times.

2 Background

Jodel was released in 2014 in Germany and its functionality strongly resembles the American app Yik Yak, which ceased operations in 2017. Jodel has already gained significant popularity beyond Germany, particularly in the Northern European countries (Nowak et al., 2018). Jodel allows users to connect with people in their vicinity through anonymous postings. These postings can be published in the form of short messages, photos, or videos. Published postings are displayed in a feed to other users within a radius of about ten kilometers, who in turn have the option of upvoting or downvoting these postings, commenting on it, sharing it outside the app, pinning it or even reporting it. By receiving upvotes for their own postings as well as for allocating votings, a user receives so-called karma points.

Users can subscribe to various channels concentrating mainly on one topic, such as the Corona channel. The postings in the feed can be sorted in three different ways: "newest", "most commented" and "loudest". The latter means a descending ranking of postings by votings. If a posting lands at a score of minus five due to the difference between upvotes and downvotes, it is automatically removed from the feed. Jodel also supports the use of hashtags. They can be searched for to display other postings that contain a specific hashtag, for example #corona or #question.

COVID-19 in the context of social media has already been subject of intensive, interdisciplinary research in the scientific community, but is seldom connected to Jodel.

Seidenschnur (2021) focused on social characters formed during the corona crisis and the approaches to controlling the pandemic that emerged from these social characters. Seidenschnur (2021) collected 156 Jodel postings to inductively extract the following social characters from the data: the social worker, the crisis entrepreneur, the worried and depressed loner, the crisis manager, the admonisher, and the health expert. According to the author, each of these characters also brings approaches to coping with the crisis, from economic to psychological to bureaucratic discourses.

This study aims to complement the rarely existing research by providing insights into crisis communication in anonymous social media services based on a content analysis of the Corona channel of Jodel. This enables a better understanding of human-computer mediated communication in crises, especially if users are anonymous.

3   Research Questions

The model that underlies the theoretical framework of this study is based on the Model for Information Behavior Research on Social Live Streaming Services (SLSSs) by Zimmer et al. (2018). The model combines approaches of communication science with research in human-computer interaction. The main core of the model consists of different roles of users, the content that is produced, consumed, and shared, as well as gratifications that were sought and obtained.

SLSSs offer many characteristics that can be applied to other social networks such as Jodel. Users are able to post their own content and share it with other users. In SLSSs, this is done through streams, whereas in Jodel it happens through postings. Other users can interact with the content creator as well as with other users, in the case of SLSSs via chat, in the case of Jodel by commenting on the corresponding posting. In addition, it is possible for other users to reward the content creator. With SLSSs this happens through points, badges, or money, with Jodel through votings, shares, and the resulting karma points. The biggest difference between Jodel and SLSSs is that communication in Jodel is asynchronous, while SLSSs enable synchronous exchange between streamers and viewers. In addition, there is the anonymity that distinguishes Jodel, which applies to both posting creators and all other users. In SLSSs, while it is possible for viewers to maintain anonymity, it is not usually possible for the streamer (Zimmer et al., 2018).

Due to the similarities of both systems, many aspects of the SLSS model can be transferred to Jodel. First of all, the different user roles can also be observed in Jodel (Jüttner et al., 2021). Jodel offers the possibility to publish postings (this corresponds to user X or the role of the producer), to vote, comment, and share postings (this corresponds to user Y or the role of the participant), and to scroll through the feed and merely read the postings (this corresponds to user Y' or the role of the consumer).

The building blocks of the Lasswell/Braddock formula (Lasswell, 1948; Braddock, 1958) can also be applied to Jodel. A user X (Who?) publishes a posting (What?) on Jodel (Which channel?) under certain motives (For what purpose?) and circumstances (What circumstances?) and reaches user Y and Y' (To whom?), which in turn leads to reactions (votings, comments and shares) to the original posting (With what effect?).

Since user roles can be transferred to Jodel, this is also possible for the gratifications sought and received. Jodel users use the app with the expectation of receiving gratifications for their motives. While a producer receives it through reactions (votings, comments and shares) to their posting, a participant receives it through reactions from the posting creator and other users (for example, through votings or replies to their own comment). Consumers, on the other hand, get their gratifications by reading postings.

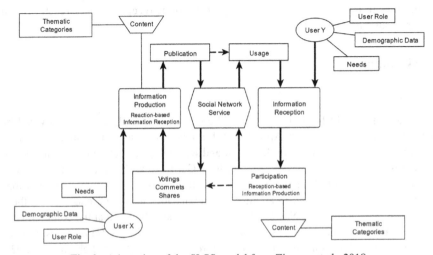

Fig. 1. Adaptation of the SLSS model from Zimmer et al., 2018.

As this study is specifically addressing the content of postings and the corona crisis, some adaptations of the SLSS model are necessary to fit the purposes of this study. The focus will be on the nature of the content, specifically the thematic categories into which the postings in Jodel's Corona channel can be classified.

Based on the adapted SLSS model from Fig. 1, the entire communication process in the Corona channel of Jodel is to be considered in an overreaching perspective. First, the information behavior of the user X with regard to information production, resulting in postings, as well as participation and reception-based information production in the form of votings, comments and shares on the part of user Y will be examined. In addition, frequently used terms and example postings are used to investigate which topics are essential in this communication process regarding COVID-19. For this purpose, the following research questions (RQs) are formulated:

RQ1a. In which way do Jodel users use the Corona channel?

RQ1b. What do Jodel users communicate about in the Corona channel?

The second block focuses more profoundly on the content of the postings published by user X in the Corona channel and thus with the producer's need of information. At the same time, the information need on the part of user Y is considered by analyzing the participant's reactions through votings, comments and shares. For this purpose, the topic categories into which the postings can be classified are examined more closely with regard to thematic differences. This results in the following research question:

RQ2. What are the thematic differences in the Corona channel?

Through the three formulated research questions, the communication process depicted in the adapted SLSS model is analyzed in relation to corona communication in the Corona channel of Jodel. Answering these research questions means valuable insights for information science, social science, and communication studies about information behavior, such as information production and communication on the part of user X and information acceptance on the part of user Y, and information needs in times of crisis in anonymous social media services. Particular attention is paid to thematic peculiarities in information production as well as to the reception-based reactions that the corresponding topics elicit.

4 Methods

4.1 Data

Since there is no API for Jodel that is publicly accessible, a dataset was provided by The Jodel Venture GmbH on April 8, 2021 for the purpose of this study. The four German cities of Munich, Bonn, Dresden, and Rostock were determined as locations. The cities were selected to cover the north of Germany with Rostock, the east with Dresden, the south with Munich and the west with Bonn in order to obtain impressions as representative as possible. In addition, university locations were chosen with these four cities, since a study by Nowak et al. (2018) already elicited that the community of Jodel consists to a large extent of students. The dataset contains 35,071 postings from the Corona channel of the four cities in the period from March 3, 2020 to February 13, 2021, thus covering the first pandemic year in Germany. Other data included in the dataset for each posting are location and time of publication, number of upvotes and downvotes, number of comments, and number of shares.

In preparation for the automated analysis of the dataset, the postings were extracted, and some modifications were applied. First, all posting texts were consistently converted to lowercase and cleaned of punctuation, special characters, numbers, and emojis using a self-written Python script. The result of this cleaning was later used as the base for filtering the postings according to identified categories. To generate a list of all relevant terms used in the dataset cleaning of stop words was necessary. This automated created word list provided the basis for deriving the categories and extracting the most frequent terms.

4.2 Content Categories

To perform the content analysis, the postings were sorted into content categories. Due to the high data volume of 35,071 postings, an automated approach was chosen.

For the deductive approach of deriving the categories, studies were analyzed that focus on content analyses at times of crisis on various platforms. Misinformation and conspiracy theories represent an important topic related to the corona pandemic, which has already been addressed in many studies (Islam et al., 2020; Rafi, 2020; Cinelli et al., 2020; Ahmed et al., 2020). Emotions have also been widely studied. Ahmad and Murad (2020) identified the occurrence of the emotions of fear and panic, as well as positive emotions such as hopefulness in the context of the corona pandemic on Twitter. Concern and hope at the same time could also be identified by Laaksonen and Rantasila (2021) on Jodel. Similarly, the sentiment analysis by Prabhakar Kaila and Prasad (2020) confirmed the prevalence of negative emotions such as fear along with positive emotions such as trust. Additionally, categories such as misinformation, questions, government and public health, and social networks were considered by Chew and Eysenbach (2010). Notably, current COVID-19 research looks more closely at reactions to various pandemic con- tainment measures. Both Li et al. (2020) and Laaksonen and Rantasila (2021) were able to identify content references in social networks to the measures undertaken. Li et al. (2020) also identified the pathogen itself and changes in the epidemiological charac- teristics of the virus as one of the main topics of discussion about COVID-19 on the Chinese platform Weibo. Rufai and Bunce (2020) examined the Twitter usage of world leaders in relation to the COVID-19 outbreak, suggesting that observing public figures can provide important value. Stechemesser et al. (2020) also found that the progression of the pandemic on Twitter led to increased discrimination and racist attacks against Chinese people. Accordingly, it is reasonable to also take a closer look at content that affects different countries and ethnicities.

For the inductive approach, the terms extracted from the postings were sorted by frequency, manually considered up to an occurrence of 25, and assigned to preliminary categories that resulted from these terms. Subsequently, the categories generated in this way were reviewed for relevance based on the word frequencies of their assigned terms and the accumulated findings of the deductive approach. The matching resulted in the eleven categories of (1) coronavirus, (2) measures, (3) positive emotions, (4) negative emotions, (5) public figures, (6) institutions, (7) healthcare, (8) countries & ethnicities, (9) media, (10) denial & conspiracy theories, and (11) Jodel.

Once the categories were established, the next step was to identify further relevant search terms for each category in order to cover all search terms relevant for the classifi- cation. During the derivation of the categories, each of the most frequent terms up to an occurrence of 25 was already checked for relevance and assigned to the corresponding category. Based on these, additional search terms were identified by searching for similar terms, synonyms, or partial occurrences of the already assigned search terms within the list of most frequent terms.

The classification of the postings into the categories was subsequently automated based on the identified search terms of the categories. If at least one of the terms appeared in a posting, it was assigned to the corresponding category. In this way, a posting could be assigned to several categories.

4.3   Analysis

Various methods were used to evaluate the obtained data. Descriptive statistics were used to derive statements on frequencies and percentage distributions. For each category, the number of postings, upvotes, downvotes, comments and shares was collected and used for the analysis. In addition, the 20 most frequent terms and top postings of the dataset were identified. The top postings include the posting with the most upvotes, downvotes, comments, and shares. They serve as specific examples of postings published on Jodel related to COVID-19 to provide qualitative insight into Jodel users' information behavior at the time of the corona pandemic, in addition to quantitative analysis of the dataset.

5   Results

5.1   RQ1a. In Which Way Do Jodel Users Use the Corona Channel?

The period of the dataset containing 35,071 postings spans 342 days with an average of 102.55 postings per day. Between March 11, 2020 and March 23, 2020, more than 300 postings were published per day. In this phase, the absolute high point of the entire dataset is found on March 16, 2020, with 723 postings. Other noticeable high points are present on October 28, 2020 (533 postings), February 10, 2021 (460 postings), and April 15, 2020 (443 postings). During an extended period in the summer, between June 17, 2020 and September 20, 2020, there were consistently under 100 postings per day on Jodel's Corona channel. Just before this period, the absolute low point is on June 2, 2020, with only 4 published postings. In the fall and winter, an increasing daily posting frequency can be observed, exemplified by the phase from December 6, 2020 to December 18, 2020, in which more than 100 postings per day were consistently published, with a high of 347 postings on December 13, 2020.

The postings in the dataset comprise a total of 432,741 comments. Therefore, each posting was commented on an average of 12.34 times. Jodel users shared postings from the Corona channel 1504 times, resulting in just 0.04 shares per posting. In total, the postings included in the dataset were voted on 766,517 times. On average, the postings comprise 17.10 upvotes and 4.75 downvotes.

5.2   RQ1b. What Do Jodel Users Communicate About in the Corona Channel?

In the following, the 20 most frequent terms of the Corona channel postings are examined, including their respective absolute frequencies. The English translation is given in parentheses for German expressions.

The word "corona" is used most frequently, 5173 times, more than twice as often as the second-placed term. There is also frequent use as a hashtag ("#corona"; 806 times). The broad paraphrase as "virus" results in 848 occurrences.

The Jodel users write repeatedly about their fellow humans in the Corona channel: "people" occurs 1991 times in the dataset, "humans" 1307 times. Christian Social Union (CSU) politician Markus Söder is the only public figure to appear in the list of the 20 most frequent terms ("söder"; 1111 times).

The various corona measures are broadly represented by the following terms: ("measures"; 1526 times), ("lockdown"; 1372 times), ("curfew"; 808 times), ("quarantine"; 785 times), and ("mask"; 769 times).

The fact that the Corona channel was used for numerous questions is shown by the occurrence of the hashtag ("#question;" 1366 times).

Terms related to time aspect appear three times: ("weeks"; 1009 times), ("day"; 708 times) and ("week"; 626 times).

Two places are mainly mentioned: ("germany"; 969 times) and ("munich"; 673 times), while the term "numbers" has an absolute frequency of 883 in the dataset.

The final item on the top 20 list is the term "live" (626 times).

The postings with the most upvotes, downvotes, comments, and shares of the entire dataset are presented next. The posting with the most upvotes is simultaneously the one with the most shares. It is posting 1 (see Table 1), which was posted on January 7, 2021, and has been upvoted 2084 times and shared 22 times.

This posting is part of a longer posting that is continued by the creator in the comments section. Without knowing the conclusion of the posting, it is initially unclear whether this is, for example, vaccine-skeptical fake news or a humorous, satirical posting. In the comments, the creator continues the posting as follows: "stood on end because so few people still have confidence in the absolutely safe vaccine ..." (translated into English). Thus, the most upvoted and shared posting of the Corona channel is a humorous, satirical posting.

Table 1. Top-postings of Jodel's Corona channel.

Posting ID	Posting (English translation)
1	Attention, disturbing news: 12 physicians at the Klinikum rechts der Isar have been vaccinated with the Pfizer/Biontech vaccine: one week later, suddenly everyone's hair (*continued in the comments section*)
2	I am honest, even though I have supported it so far, my solidarity is over. I now live my life and will circumvent the measures so that I don't get caught. Whoever wants to stone me, let them do it
3	Spahn recommends cancellation of events with more than 1000 visitors. Oh wow, let's actually do what others have been doing for months

Posting 2 is the posting with the most total downvotes (431 in total). It was published a few days later, on January 19, 2021, and announces the creator's solidarity with the corona measures. The posting was commented on frequently (384 times) and has a positive voting balance of 88 despite the most downvotes.

The posting in the Corona channel that has been commented on the most is posting 3 from March 8, 2020 and has 1016 comments. In this posting, a statement by Christian Democratic Union (CDU) politician and Federal Minister of Health Jens Spahn regarding recommended corona measures is commented on.

5.3   RQ2. What Are the Thematic Differences in the Corona Channel?

The coronavirus category comprises 26.04% of all postings in the dataset and is thus the most represented among the categories, as can be seen in Table 2. This is followed by postings of the measures category with 15.00%. All other categories comprise respectively less than 8% of the postings. In order, these categories are Jodel (7.28%), countries & ethnicities (5.80%), public Figs. (5.77%), institutions (4.35%), negative emotions (3.75%), healthcare (2.85%), positive emotions (2.11%), media (1.95%), and denial & conspiracy theories (1.77%).

Postings of the category public figures averaged the most upvotes (26.66) and the second most downvotes (6.37). The second most upvotes on average (24.52) occurred for postings of the positive emotions category. Both the third most upvotes (21.87) and downvotes (6.28) on average were received by postings of the institutions category. Postings of the denial & conspiracy theories category were voted down the most, with an average of 7.45 downvotes.

Table 2. Overview of postings, votings, comments and shares of all categories. N = 20,472.

Category	Postings		Ø Votings / Posting		Comments		Shares	
Coronavirus	Absolute	9134	Downvotes	5.08	Absolute	120,822	Absolute	464
	Relative	26.04%	Upvotes	17.41	Ø / Posting	13.23	Ø / Posting	0.05
Measures	Absolute	5262	Downvotes	5.14	Absolute	71,267	Absolute	238
	Relative	15.00%	Upvotes	19.41	Ø / Posting	13.54	Ø / Posting	0.05
Positive emotions	Absolute	740	Downvotes	5.70	Absolute	8721	Absolute	23
	Relative	2.11%	Upvotes	24.52	Ø / Posting	11.79	Ø / Posting	0.03
Negative emotions	Absolute	1314	Downvotes	5.96	Absolute	19,225	Absolute	52
	Relative	3.75%	Upvotes	20.74	Ø / Posting	14.63	Ø / Posting	0.04
Public figures	Absolute	2023	Downvotes	6.37	Absolute	24,084	Absolute	92
	Relative	5.77%	Upvotes	26.66	Ø / Posting	11.91	Ø / Posting	0.05
Institutions	Absolute	1527	Downvotes	6.28	Absolute	23,846	Absolute	73
	Relative	4.35%	Upvotes	21.87	Ø / Posting	15.62	Ø / Posting	0.05

(*continued*)

Table 2. (*continued*)

Category	Postings		Ø Votings / Posting		Comments		Shares	
Healthcare	Absolute	999	Downvotes	5.21	Absolute	15,653	Absolute	69
	Relative	2.85%	Upvotes	16.45	Ø / Posting	15.67	Ø / Posting	0.07
Countries & ethnicities	Absolute	2035	Downvotes	5.17	Absolute	29,362	Absolute	89
	Relative	5.80%	Upvotes	19.63	Ø / Posting	14.43	Ø / Posting	0.04
Media	Absolute	683	Downvotes	5.07	Absolute	9073	Absolute	30
	Relative	1.95%	Upvotes	17.82	Ø / Posting	13.28	Ø / Posting	0.04
Denial & conspiracy theories	Absolute	622	Downvotes	7.45	Absolute	9415	Absolute	18
	Relative	1.77%	Upvotes	18.09	Ø / Posting	15.14	Ø / Posting	0.03
Jodel	Absolute	2554	Downvotes	3.96	Absolute	31,345	Absolute	86
	Relative	7.28%	Upvotes	9.52	Ø / Posting	12.27	Ø / Posting	0.03

Postings of the healthcare category received the most comments, with an average of 15.67 comments per posting. The institutions category is close behind with 15.62 comments per posting. Postings of the category denial & conspiracy theories were also commented on more than 15 times on average (15.14 times).

These are followed by postings of the negative emotions category (14.63 times) and countries & ethnicities (14.43 times). On average, the fewest comments were published on postings of the categories public Figs. (11.91 times) and positive emotions (11.79 times).

In terms of average shares per posting, the values across categories range from 0.07 (healthcare) to 0.03 (positive emotions, denial & conspiracy theories, Jodel).

It stands out that postings of the healthcare category were both commented on and shared the most. Postings of the category people received the most upvotes in percentage terms, but were commented on little. Even if postings of the category positive emotions received more upvotes compared to postings of the category negative emotions, the category positive emotions got fewer comments.

6 Discussion

6.1 RQ1a. In Which Way Do Jodel Users Use the Corona Channel?

The total of 35,071 Jodel postings published between March 3, 2020 and February 13, 2021 show that the Corona channel created specifically for COVID-19-related content is accepted by users and used for exchange. The evaluation of the interactions also underlines this. Only the function to share postings is used very sporadically in the Corona channel. With regard to the distribution of votings among the total postings in the channel, it should be emphasized that the upvotes clearly predominate with a share of 78%. Computer-human mediated conversation is based not only on posting/writing textual content but also on making use of the algorithms, such as upvoting and downvoting. This kind of communication shows approval or disapproval by users.

With regard to the progression of postings written per day, it is striking that there are similarities to the COVID-19 case curve in Germany (Presse- und Informationsamt der Bundesregierung, 2022) in the same period.

The biggest difference between the COVID-19 case curve and the number of daily Jodel postings in the Corona channel is that the number of postings is particularly high during the first Corona wave. During the second wave, there are also a consistently higher number of postings, but by far not as many as during the first wave. One influencing factor here could be the novelty of the situation, which creates a greater need for exchange during the first wave and which would also align with Kalman et al. (2021) compensation for social distancing. That the number of postings show a coherence with the development of the infection event does not seem to be unusual. Li et al. (2020) found a positive correlation between the number of Weibo postings and the number of confirmed COVID-19 cases in a quantitative analysis of postings on the Chinese social media platform Weibo. Accordingly, this is not a Jodel-specific but a crisis phenomenon and how humans communicate and behave.

6.2 RQ1b. What Do Jodel Users Communicate About in the Corona Channel?

The 20 most frequent terms in the Corona channel demonstrate that the channel is used for the purpose for which it was created: For communicating about topics related to COVID-19. The term "corona" is by far the most common term in the cleaned dataset. The terms "virus" and "#corona" are also in the top-20. Terms such as "measures", "lockdown", "curfew", "quarantine", and "#question" suggest that the Corona channel is used by users to share questions regarding adopted measures, among other things.

The only reference to a person that occurs among the 20 most frequent terms is "söder". The reason for the frequent mention of the Bavarian Prime Minister Markus Söder is most likely the very high share of the evaluated postings from Munich (83%). This also explains the term "munich" in 18th place among the most frequent terms.

The most upvoted posting (see Table 1, posting 1) is interesting in several ways. The first part is intentionally worded to give the impression of a Fake News posting on effects of corona vaccination. That postings are split into multiple parts and continued in the comments is not uncommon on Jodel due to the limited characters. Such as in Twitter, the formal structure of the communication is forced through word limitation.

However, the fact that the length of the posting was not entirely used up suggests that the point of division was deliberately chosen to provide an unexpected twist in the comments. Accordingly, the posting parodies typical fake news about the corona vaccine, subliminally criticizes distrust of the corona vaccine, and demonstrates a positive attitude toward the vaccine. The numerous upvotes show on the one hand that this type of humor is appreciated by Jodel users, but also that many users agree with the position of the posting creator. The posting was at the same time shared the most outside the Jodel app with 22 shares.

In direct contrast, the posting with the most downvotes is viewed very controversially, 519 users seem to be able to identify with the posting and awarded an upvote, while 431 seem to reject the stance (see Table 1, posting 2).

Posting 3 contains ironically packaged criticism of delayed measures in Germany. 62 upvotes and 26 downvotes indicate that the majority of users feel similarly. However, the 1016 comments are particularly interesting, suggesting that the topic is highly controversial.

Complementary to the way the Corona channel is used, this research question considered the thematic aspect of Corona communication on Jodel. The most frequent terms, together with the top postings, show that the Corona channel is increasingly used for sharing one's own opinions and views regarding current measures as well as for clarifying COVID-19-related issues, in addition to the general exchange about COVID-19. The need to communicate one's own opinions and views suggests that a self-centered way of communicating occurs in the Corona channel of Jodel, for which users seek approval in the form of votings and comments. At the same time, the app is used as an information service for exchanging information and enriching knowledge.

6.3 RQ2. What Are the Thematic Differences in the Corona Channel?

The most frequently discussed topics in the Corona Channel are those related to the coronavirus. Almost every second posting belongs to this category. The measures category forms the second most frequent topic in the Corona channel of Jodel. Accordingly, the measures to contain the pandemic provide the highest need for communication next to the coronavirus itself. Among the postings in this category, there is some criticism of non-compliance with the measures, as the following posting shows: "These people who do not keep a distance" (translated in English). Postings of this type fall under the social character of the "Admonisher" identified by Seidenschnur (2021) in Corona communication on Jodel. This social character is particularly characterized by the acceptance of strict measures and criticism of non-compliance with them. In the analysis of Seidenschnur (2021), this social character occurred most frequently, suggesting that postings with similar content are particularly present in the Corona channel. The humorous posting "Subway ticket: 3.20 euros OP mask: 1.50 euros Being a pensioner licking your fingers under the mask during the ride to turn the page of the newspaper: priceless" (translated in English) received the most upvotes in the measures category. This shows that humor attracts upvotes even in the more serious context of the Corona channel. The user survey by Nowak et al. (2018) found that reading funny postings is the most important reason for using the app among Jodel users. The fact that such postings receive a lot of approval in the form of upvotes in the Corona channel suggests that this also plays a role in Corona communication on Jodel. Kasakowskij et al. (2018) also found in a comparison between usage motivations in anonymous and non-anonymous platforms, specifically Jodel and Instagram, that all three user roles (producer, participant, and consumer) seek entertainment in particular in the anonymous social media service.

The other categories are less frequently represented in the dataset. The category Jodel still comes to a share of 7.28% of the total postings. Accordingly, conversations take place in the Corona channel that directly deal with Corona communication on Jodel at a meta level, for example: "Interesting to see how this channel is becoming more and more radicalized" (translated in English).

Negative emotions such as fear and panic are slightly more prevalent in the Corona channel dataset than positive emotions such as joy and hope. Prabhakar Kaila and Prasad (2020) obtained similar results in a sentiment analysis of Corona communications on Twitter. Fear and panic are also strongly represented on Twitter when it comes to COVID-19. However, although negative emotions came out ahead, Twitter did not show much difference between the number of occurrences of negative and positive emotions. However, with regard to Jodel, negative emotions clearly predominated, with a total occurrence of 1314 compared to 740 mentions of positive emotions. Johann et al. (2016, June 9) noted that the anonymous environment of Jodel encourages self-disclosure among users, which may translate into a reduced inhibition to express negative emotions such as fear, panic, and anxiety in the context of Corona communication. However, positive emotions such as joy and hope occur in COVID-19 communication on Jodel as well. Laaksonen and Rantasila (2021) also found in content analysis of Jodel postings from the Corona channel from Helsinki that a mix of the emotions joy and fear can be observed in some of the communication. The authors describe this phenomenon as a possible mechanism of crisis management.

With regard to the categories of public figures and denial & conspiracy theories, the votings in particular stand out. Postings addressing public figures received the most upvotes, while postings on the topic of denial & conspiracy theories received the most downvotes. The votings reflect in particular the information needs of the participants and show that postings of the category public figures are positively received, while postings of the category denial & conspiracy theories rather meet with rejection. This and the fact that the category denial & conspiracy theories comprises the fewest postings of all categories implies that Jodel, despite its anonymity, is not a platform that provides a breeding ground for topics such as conspiracy theories and points to a functioning self-regulation of the community.

7 Conclusion

A quantitative-empirical content analysis of human-computer mediated communication in the Corona channel of the anonymous social media service Jodel was conducted. The results clearly show that there is a need among Jodel users to exchange information and to communicate with other users nearby about the topic of COVID-19.

It is noticeable that users frequently use both the voting function and the comment function, while postings are only occasionally shared outside the app via the share function. There also appears to be a correlation between the current occurrence of infection and the frequency of postings in the Corona channel.

Furthermore, in the adapted SLSS model, the published content was considered in detail with regard to deductively and inductively derived content categories, which resulted in the question of which thematic differences the communication in the Corona channel of Jodel presents. Based on the content analysis, it could be determined that emotions play a central role in anonymous Corona communication on Jodel. In particular, negative emotions such as fear and panic are the emotions that characterize the exchange in the Corona channel. Negative emotions predominate in Jodel's Corona channel, while positive and negative emotions were balanced in a study of Corona communication on Twitter (Prabhakar Kaila & Prasad, 2020).

However, the following limitations should be considered when using the results. First, the four locations included in the dataset result in different sized target groups. The fact that the proportion of postings from Munich predominates means that representative conclusions can only be drawn to a limited extent for the whole of Germany with regard to Corona communication. The same applies due to the consideration of four major cities, whereby influences of precisely this living situation on Corona communication in social networks cannot be ruled out. In addition, with regard to demographic data, it should be noted that the target group of Jodel comprises mostly students between the ages of 18 and 25 (Nowak et al., 2018). Second, due to the size of the dataset, the postings were essentially considered quantitatively, which meant that no statements could be semantically made about context as only frequency was considered?

For the scope of this study, the analysis was limited to eleven categories, based on the automated counting of words, leaving 14,599 postings (41.6%) of the dataset uncategorized. In addition, the study period is limited to March 2020 to February 2021, however, at the end of the data collection period there was no end to the corona pandemic in sight. Even at the current status (February 2023), the pandemic has not been completely overcome.

Since this study does not cover the entire period of the corona pandemic, it would be valuable to also examine the later stages of the pandemic and their influence on communication in an anonymous social media service such as Jodel. Related questions arising from this study would be, for example, how the relevance of each topic has shifted or even dissipated and what new topics may have gained importance as the pandemic progresses.

Data Availability.   The data of our study are publicly available in Zenodo at https://doi.org/10.5281/zenodo.7613095.

References

Ahmad, A.R., Murad, H.R.: The impact of social media on panic during the COVID-19 pandemic in Iraqi Kurdistan: Online Questionnaire Study. J. Med. Internet Res. **22**(5), 19556 (2020). https://doi.org/10.2196/19556

Ahmed, W., Vidal-Alaball, J., Downing, J., López Seguí, F.: COVID-19 and the 5G conspiracy theory: social network analysis of Twitter data. J. Med. Internet Res. **22**(5), 19458 (2020). https://doi.org/10.2196/19458

Braddock, R.: An extension of the 'Lasswell Formula.' J. Commun. **8**(2), 88–93 (1958). https://doi.org/10.1111/j.1460-2466.1958.tb01138.x

Chen, E., Lerman, K., Ferrara, E.: Tracking social media discourse about the COVID-19 pandemic: development of a public coronavirus Twitter data set. JMIR Public Health Surveill. **6**(2), 19273 (2020). https://doi.org/10.2196/19273

Chew, C., Eysenbach, G.: Pandemics in the age of Twitter: content analysis of Tweets during the 2009 H1N1 outbreak. PLoS One **5**(11), 14118 (2010). https://doi.org/10.1371/journal.pone.0014118

Cinelli, M.: The COVID-19 social media infodemic. Sci. Rep. **10,** 16598 (2020). https://doi.org/10.1038/s41598-020-73510-5

Fischer, J., et al.: Clustering social media and messengers by functionality. J. Inf. Sci. Theory Pract. **8**(4), 6–19 (2020). https://doi.org/10.1633/JISTaP.2020.8.4.1

Islam, M.S., et al.: COVID-19–related infodemic and its impact on public health: a global social media analysis. Am. J. Trop. Med. Hyg. **103**(4), 1621–1629 (2020). https://doi.org/10.4269/ajtmh.20-0812

Johann, M., Wiedel, F., Tonndorf, K., Windscheid, J.: Anonymous online communication between disinhibition, self-disclosure and social identity. A complementary mixed-method study [Conference contribution]. ICA Annual Conference, Fukuoka, Japan (2016)

Jüttner, K., Nowak, P., Scheibe, K., Zimmer, F., Fietkiewicz, K.J.: The Faceless Vicinity: Who Uses Location-Based Anonymous Social Networks Like Jodel and Why? In: Meiselwitz, G. (ed.) HCII 2021. LNCS, vol. 12774, pp. 54–73. Springer, Cham (2021). https://doi.org/10.1007/978-3-030-77626-8_4

Kalman, Y.M., Lewis, S.C., Rafaeli, S.: Social distancing meets mediated conversation. In Proceedings of the 54th Hawaii International Conference on System Sciences (2021). https://doi.org/10.24251/HICSS.2021.351

Kasakowskij, R., Friedrich, N., Fietkiewicz, K.J., Stock, W.G.: Anonymous and non-anonymous user behavior on social media: a case study of Jodel and Instagram. J. Inform. Sci. Theory Pract. **6**(3), 25–36 (2018). https://doi.org/10.1633/JISTaP.2018.6.3.3

Laaksonen, S.-M., Rantasila, A.: Rocketing sheep: affective discipline in anonymous mobile social media Jodel during the Covid-19 pandemic. AoIR Selected Papers Internet Res. (2021). https://doi.org/10.5210/spir.v2021i0.12198

Lasswell, H.D.: The structure and function of communication in society. In: L. Bryson (eds.) The Communication of Ideas, pp. 37–51. Harper & Brothers (1948)

Li, J., Xu, Q., Cuomo, R., Purushothaman, V., Mackey, T.: Data mining and content analysis of the chinese social media platform Weibo during the early COVID-19 outbreak: retrospective observational infoveillance study. JMIR Public Health Surveill. **6**(2), 18700 (2020). https://doi.org/10.2196/18700

Nowak, P., Jüttner, K., Baran, K.S.: Posting Content, Collecting Points, Staying Anonymous: An Evaluation of Jodel. In: Meiselwitz, G. (ed.) SCSM 2018. LNCS, vol. 10913, pp. 67–86. Springer, Cham (2018). https://doi.org/10.1007/978-3-319-91521-0_6

Prabhakar Kaila, R., Prasad, A. V. K.: Informational flow on Twitter – Corona virus outbreak – Topic modelling approach. Int. J. Adv. Res. Eng. Technol. **11**(3), 128–134 (2020). https://ssrn.com/abstract=3565169

Presse- und Informationsamt der Bundesregierung: Coronavirus: Die aktuellen Fallzahlen im Überblick (2022). https://www.bundesregierung.de/breg-de/themen/coronavirus

Rafi, M.S.: Dialogic content analysis of misinformation about COVID-19 on social media in Pakistan. Linguist. Lit. Rev. **6**(2), 131–143 (2020)

Rufai, S.R., Bunce, C.: World leaders' usage of Twitter in response to the COVID-19 pandemic: a content analysis. J. Public Health **42**(3), 510–516 (2020). https://doi.org/10.1093/pubmed/fdaa049

Seidenschnur, T.: A typology of social characters and various means of control: an analysis of communication during the early stages of the corona pandemic in Germany. Eur. Soc. **23**(1), 923–941 (2021). https://doi.org/10.1080/14616696.2020.1857422

Stechemesser, A., Wenz, L., Levermann, A.: Corona crisis fuels racially profiled hate in social media networks. EClinicalMedicine **23**, 100372 (2020). https://doi.org/10.1016/j.eclinm.2020.100372

Vesterinen, J.: The effects of information technology on student life during the COVID-19 pandemic [Master's thesis, University of Jyväskylä]. JYX Digital Repository (2021). http://urn.fi/URN:NBN:fi:jyu-202106093605

Zimmer, F., Scheibe, K., Stock, W.G.: A Model for Information Behavior Research on Social Live Streaming Services (SLSSs). In: Meiselwitz, G. (ed.) SCSM 2018. LNCS, vol. 10914, pp. 429–448. Springer, Cham (2018). https://doi.org/10.1007/978-3-319-91485-5_33

Analyzing User Communication on Mainstream and Alternative Social Media Platforms Using Natural Language Processing: A Case Study on the COVID-19 Pandemic

Matthew Morgan⬤ and Adita Kulkarni(⊠)⬤

SUNY Brockport, Brockport, NY 14420, USA
{mmorg9,akulkarni}@brockport.edu

Abstract. Social media platforms have gained massive popularity over the past decade as they enable users to express and share their opinions with millions of people. With the mainstream social media sites such as Twitter and Facebook performing content moderation, alternative or "free speech" platforms such as Parler and 4chan has seen increasing number of users. In this paper, we analyze and compare user communication on Twitter (mainstream platform) and Parler (alternative platform) using the case of the COVID-19 pandemic. Due to the severity of COVID-19, various prevention policies (e.g., lockdown, travel ban) were enforced by the governments of all countries. People widely used social media during this time to consume news and as an outlet to share their personal views. We analyze around half million posts related to COVID-19 on these platforms during the months of December 2020 and January 2021. We perform word collocation analysis and topic modeling and find that Twitter discussions focus only on topics related to COVID-19 while Parler discussions focus on politics along with COVID-19. We investigate the words interconnected to *'covid19'* and find that Parler contains words denoting misinformation and conspiracy theories. We perform shared links analysis and observe that Twitter users share content from external mainstream social media and news platforms whereas Parler users share external mainstream content as well as alternative content spreading fake news. We finally perform perspective and sentiment analysis and find that Parler content is more toxic, profane, and involves higher negative emotions than Twitter.

Keywords: Natural Language Processing · Social Media · User Communication Analysis

1 Introduction

Wuhan, China experienced an outbreak of the novel coronavirus 2019 (COVID-19) in December 2019 [34], and within months spread all over the world, after which it was declared a pandemic. Many countries undertook measures such as lockdown, travel ban, social distancing and wearing of face masks, to slowdown the spread of the virus. These measures changed the daily lives of people, and working from home became the new normal for most. People began spending more time on social media platforms such as

ⓒ The Author(s), under exclusive license to Springer Nature Switzerland AG 2023
A. Coman and S. Vasilache (Eds.): HCII 2023, LNCS 14026, pp. 340–354, 2023.
https://doi.org/10.1007/978-3-031-35927-9_24

Twitter, Facebook, Instagram, Parler, etc. for consuming news as well as sharing their opinions, feelings and struggles.

In December 2020, first set of vaccines for the prevention of COVID-19 started rolling out [1]. By this time, many countries relaxed some of the restrictions such as lockdown and travel ban while others such as wearing masks and social distancing still existed. Significant research has been published studying user behavior and response to COVID-19 during the initial days of the pandemic using social media data such as Twitter, Reddit, YouTube, etc. [15, 17]. Mainstream social media such as Twitter and Facebook place restrictions on the content being shared by users due to their moderation policies. Due to this, in the past few years, alternative platforms such as Parler and Gab have gained popularity as they allow uncensored content sharing. Unrestricted content sharing can potentially impact individuals and society significantly, making it important to understand communication on free speech platforms. Thus, in this paper, we study the user communication on a mainstream platform (Twitter) and compare it with the communication on an alternative platform (Parler) using COVID-19 as a case study. We analyze posts after a year into the COVID-19 pandemic during the months of December 2020 and January 2021.

We collect around 226K tweets related to COVID-19 from Twitter using the Twitter streaming API [4] from December 20, 2020, to January 16, 2021, and use around 298K Parler posts collected by [5] from December 01, 2020, to January 20, 2021. We classify the posts from both platforms based on hashtags and keywords into two groups — *General COVID-19* and *COVID-19 Vaccine*. We perform word collocation analysis on both the groups on both platforms to understand the main points being discussed. We then investigate the topics discussed by users on both platforms using the Latent Dirichlet Allocation (LDA) model [9] and analyze different words interconnected with *'covid19'* using the Word2vec model [25]. We next conduct shared link analysis to identify the most popular domains for sharing content in both groups. We finally assess how toxic the content is on both platforms using Google's Perspective API [2] and perform sentiment analysis using SentiStrength [3]. The main findings of our work are summarized below:

- Our results show that *'wear mask'* is the most frequent bigram and occurs in both *General COVID-19* and *COVID-19 Vaccine* groups on both platforms. We also observe that in addition to COVID-19 related terms, Parler bigrams demonstrate political issues like President Trump announcing covid relief for American people and small businesses as it includes terms such as *'president trump'*, *'relief bill'*, *'american people'* and *'small business'* while Twitter bigrams focus only on COVID-19 related terms such as *'social distance'* and *'vaccine rollout'*.
- We observe similar trends in the results generated by our LDA model where Parler discussion topics revolve around the 2020 US Presidential election, it's voting fraud controversy, and COVID-19 relief packages, whereas Twitter discussion topics are restricted to the virus and vaccines.
- Our results indicate that the words interlinked to *'covid19'* on Twitter include different strains (*'b117'*), vaccines (*'pfizerbiontech'*), and countries (*'brazil'*) facing surge in positive cases. On the other hand, the words on Parler include different illnesses

('*bronchitis*'), viruses ('*sars*', '*hiv*'), as well as words indicating misinformation and conspiracy theories related to COVID-19 ('*bioweapon*', '*engineered*', '*fabricated*').

- The shared links analysis indicates that Twitter users share content from other mainstream social media platforms such as YouTube and Instagram and mainstream news sites such as BBC, New York Times and Washington Post. Parler users share content from alternative entertainment and news platforms like Bitchute and Zero hedge besides mainstream content.
- We learn that Parler content is more toxic and profane as compared to Twitter and demonstrates more negative emotions. We observe these results due to high freedom of speech experienced by Parler users.

2   Related Work

In this section, we present existing literature analyzing social media data related to the COVID-19 pandemic. We also present existing work related to analyzing communication on mainstream and alternative social media platforms.

Authors in [28] examine tweets to understand the societal impact of COVID-19 in the United States during the early days of the pandemic. [22, 24, 29] present an analysis on helpful information vs misinformation related to COVID-19 being spread on Twitter. [11] studies vaccine opposition on Twitter during the pandemic. Authors use machine learning approaches on Twitter data in [30] for an infodemiology study. Authors in [20] study the human mobility dynamics from Twitter during the pandemic. In [31], authors propose a novel framework to analyze the topic and sentiment dynamics due to COVID-19 from large number of tweets. Work in [12, 16, 27] investigates COVID-19 tweets in politics. Sha *et al.* analyze the Twitter narratives around federal and state-level decision making by applying a dynamic topic model to COVID-19 related tweets by United States Governors and Presidential cabinet members in [27]. In [12], authors assess the prevalence and frequency of the phrase "Chinese virus" on Twitter after the US presidential reference of this term. Author in [16] study COVID-19 tweets to provide early evidence of the use of bots to promote political conspiracies in the United States.

[6, 8, 13, 23] investigate social media platforms to gain insights on communications related to the COVID-19 vaccine. Authors use machine learning techniques to monitor stance towards vaccination in Twitter messages in [23]. Authors in [13] conduct a sociolinguistic analysis of the two competing vaccination communities on Twitter: pro-vaxxers and anti-vaxxers. Bello-Orgaz *et al.* use data mining techniques to detect and analyze communities disseminating vaccination opinions on Twitter [8]. Authors in [6] analyze a small sample of Parler posts to understand online users' discussions on the COVID-19 vaccine. Research in [7, 15, 17, 26, 33] studies COVID-19 related content on different social media platforms such as Reddit, Gab, Instagram, and YouTube. Authors in [15] assess diffusion of information about the COVID-19 on Twitter, Instagram, YouTube, Reddit, and Gab platforms. [7] analyze structural variations in social posting behavior and emotional reactions to COVID-19 on Reddit and compare it with the data before COVID-19. Zhang *et al.* characterize user trajectories in two communities on Reddit, /r/China flu and /r/Coronavirus, from the beginning of COVID-19 to the end of September 2020 in [33]. In [26], authors quantify the change in discussions of COVID-19 throughout individuals' experiences for the first 14 days since symptom onset using topic modelling and sentiment analysis using posts to the Reddit forum r/COVID19Positive. [17] characterizes the media coverage and collective internet response to the COVID-19 pandemic using YouTube, Reddit, and Wikipedia data.

Authors in [18,19,32] analyze the content sharing on mainstream and alternative social media platforms. In [18], authors study content copying across the mainstream and alternative news ecosystem by collecting news data from 92 news sources. They create directed networks of news sources and find that despite many articles being copied verbatim, the headlines of the articles often change, where the alternative media change the emotional tone and the mainstream media change the structural features. Horne *et al.* also analyze content sharing between news sources in the alternative and mainstream media in [19] and find that content sharing happens in tightly formed communities, and these communities represent relatively homogeneous portions of the media landscape. Authors in [32] study mainstream and alternative news shared on Twitter, Reddit, and 4chan, and find that alt-right communities within 4chan and Reddit have a significant influence on Twitter, providing evidence that "fringe" communities often succeed in spreading alternative news to mainstream social networks and the greater Web.

3   Data and Problem Statement

3.1   Data

Twitter. We collect 226,009 tweets all over the world using the Twitter API [4] from December 20, 2020, to January 16, 2021. We keep a track of trending hashtags and keywords related to COVID-19 and collect the tweets containing those hashtags and keywords daily. We group the hashtags and keywords into two categories — *General COVID-19* and *COVID-19 Vaccine*. Hereon, we refer to these groups as *General* and *Vaccine*, respectively. From the original 226,009 tweets, we classify 120,207 tweets into the *General* group, and 105,802 tweets into the *Vaccine* group. A tweet can belong to both *General* and *Vaccine* groups if it contains hashtags from both groups. Table 1 shows the hashtags and keywords used for this classification.

Parler. Parler is as an "alternative" microblogging social networking site which promotes itself as a "free speech" service, without the fear of users being deplatformed for their posts. We use the publicly available Parler data [5] which contains 183M posts and comments made by 4M users between August 2018 and January 2021. From this data, we obtain 298,381 posts and comments containing the keyword *COVID* from December 01, 2020, to January 11, 2021, as that denotes the time frame of a year into the pandemic. We combine all the posts and comments to use in our analysis and hereby referred to them as just posts. We classify the posts into two groups similar to Twitter data — *General* and *Vaccine*. We use the same hashtags as mentioned in Table 1 to categorize the posts. The *Vaccine* group uses the following additional hashtags — *#nomandatoryvaccines, #notomandatoryvaccinations, #notovaccines, #pfizer, #moderna, #vaccines, #vaccinedamage,* and *#nomasksnovaccines*. Some posts that do not contain hashtags, are placed into the *General* group. The *General* group contains around 266,475 posts whereas the *Vaccine* group contains around 31,906 posts. Similar to Twitter, a Parler post can belong to both groups if it has the respective hashtags.

Table 1. Hashtags and Keywords by Category

Category	Terms
General	covid hoax, #covid19, #covid, #lockdown, #corona, #covid_19
	#coronavirus, #covididiots, #covidiots
Vaccine	covid vaccine, covid side effects, covid hydroxychloroquine,
	#Covid19Vaccine, #CovidVaccine, #ThisIsOurShot, #vaccine, #vaccination,
	#GetVaccinated, #antivaxxers, #AntiVaccine, #AntiVax, #NoVaccineForMe,
	#NoVaccine, #Pfizervaccine, #modernavaccine, #covidvaccine2020, #IGotTheShot,
	#vaccinated, #VaccinesWork, #CovidVaccinesideeffects, #COVIDvaccinated

3.2 Preprocessing

In this section, we describe the steps used to clean the data before using it in our analysis. Twitter and Parler undergo similar preprocessing. For Twitter, retweets do not provide any new information and so we filter out the retweets while collecting the data. Parler does not require this initial filtering step. We remove all the duplicate posts. We remove all URLs, hashtags, mentions, punctuation marks, emojis, and stop words in each post. This gives us some empty posts as they contain only URLs and hashtags. We remove these posts from our analysis. We finally lemmatize and stem the words in posts. After prepossessing, Twitter's *General* and *Vaccine* groups are reduced to around 109K and 93K posts, respectively, and Parler's *General* and *Vaccine* groups are reduced to around 223K and 25K posts, respectively.

3.3 Research Questions

We address the following research questions in our work:

RQ1 Which words and topics are most prevalent for COVID-19 on Twitter and Parler? What narratives are shared and discussed on both platforms?
RQ2 What are the sentiments related to COVID-19 and how toxic is the content on both platforms?
RQ3 How does the communication differ on mainstream platform and alternative platform?

4 Analysis and Discussion

In this section, we set out to answer the aforementioned research questions. Sections 4.1 to 4.4 address the first research question, Sects. 4.5 and 4.6 address the second research question and finally we summarize our findings and answer the third research question in Sect. 4.7.

Table 2. Top Bigrams

Twitter				Parler			
General	Score	Vaccine	Score	General	Score	Vaccine	Score
wear mask	46	first dose	41.7	wear mask	80.38	bill gate	28.91
new case	31.13	second dose	31.67	presid trump	71.09	presid trump	26.15
test posit	30.12	receiv first	31.18	relief bill	68.51	surviv rate	24.85
stay home	29.6	vaccin rollout	29.73	peopl die	62.37	immun system	24.11
peopl die	28.06	healthcar worker	28.12	small busi	60.31	wear mask	23.91
social distanc	25.45	got first	25.82	test posit	59.35	peopl die	20.67
stay safe	24.61	wear mask	25.56	american peopl	53.05	flu shot	20.37
public health	23.54	vaccin today	24.41	nurs home	52.21	big pharma	19.23
new year	22.03	long term	24.12	death rate	43.98	take covid	18.87
mani people	21.86	year old	24.1	heart attack	43.94	mrna vaccine	18.6

4.1 Word Collocation Analysis

In this section, we perform a word collocation analysis on both platforms by identifying bigrams that appear frequently in the posts. We use the Student's t-test to compute bigrams where each bigram is given a t-score and a higher t-score represents a bigram that occurs frequently and has more significance within the respective group. Table 2 illustrates the top 10 bigrams for each group. The bigram *'wear mask'* appears in every group, and it represents the highest score for the *General* category of Twitter and Parler. Twitter groups focus only on COVID-19 related terms whereas Parler groups focus on political discussions along with COVID-19. For instance, we see bigrams in Parler's *General* group such as *'presid trump'*, *'relief bill'*, *'american peopl'* and *'small busi'* (busi is the stemmed word for business) which indicate the president offering COVID-19 relief to the people in the US as well as small businesses. Furthermore, the Parler groups feature bigrams such as *'peopl die'*, *'death rate'*, *'heart attack'*, and *'surviv rate'*, which emphasizes the negative consequences of the pandemic in addition to negative beliefs surrounding the vaccine. On the contrary, the Twitter groups feature bigrams such as *'stay home'*, *'stay safe'*, *public health'*, and *vaccin rollout'*, and *'vaccin today'* all of which encourages Twitter's audience to practice precautionary measures while simultaneously engaging in the discussion of the vaccination procedure.

4.2 Topic Modeling

In this section, we assess the most prominent topics discussed on both platforms using the Latent Dirichlet Allocation (LDA) model [9]. For this, we put the posts into a term frequency-inverse document frequency (TF-IDF) vector, which is used to fit the LDA model. We get top 5 topics with 20 words each for *General* and *Vaccine* groups on both platforms. Table 3 shows topics for Twitter and Parler's *General* category. We observe that Twitter consists of discussions only surrounding COVID-19. We see that Topic 1 talks about precautionary measures such as lockdown, staying at home and staying safe. Topics 3 and 5 show discussions related to vaccines and Topic 4 talks about the new strain of the virus which was detected in the UK in the month of January. On the other hand, Parler users discuss politics along with COVID-19. We see that Topic 1 talks about bills related to COVID relief and stimulus checks, Topic 2 discusses the 2020 US Presidential election and the controversy with voting fraud (which indicates considerable Parler users being Trump supporters), while rest of the topics demonstrate COVID-19 discussions. We observe similar results for the *Vaccine* group on both platforms but do not include them in the paper due to limited space.

Table 3. LDA analysis for *General* group

Twitter	
Topic	Words per topic
1	lockdown, go, home, get, stay, mask, time, peopl, one, work, like, keep, day, need, back, look, safe, love, make, good
2	hoax, covid, peopl, think, trump, mask, like, die, believ, say, still, call, get, go, know, wear, lie, one, would, right
3	vaccin, get, first, receiv, covid19, dose, got, thank, effect, shot, today, patient, work, worker, covid, peopl, immun, care, take, one
4	case, new, death, test, uk, report, covid19, day, variant, posit, number, strain, coronaviru, record, total, rate, infect, januari, updat, today
5	vaccin, covid19, health, new, pandem, read, help, use, learn, get, inform, support, need, state, check, via, plan, avail, distribut, rollout

Parler	
Topic	Words per topic
1	bill, relief, american, money, trump, stimulu, congress, vote, countri, presid, get, need, veto, peopl, pelosi, give, foreign, busi, packag, million
2	trump, elect, peopl, biden, democrat, state, china, get, go, presid, fraud, covid19, vote, like, america, right, use, busi, need, countri
3	mask, get, peopl, wear, go, like, know, take, one, vaccin, got, work, covid19, flu, think, de, would, viru, make, die
4	covid19, vaccin, test, viru, new, posit, use, fauci, world, china, dr, news, hoax, peopl, doctor, say, get, take, pandem, video
5	death, die, flu, hospit, number, peopl, year, covid19, case, patient, caus, count, test, heart, nurs, kill, report, mani, rate, get

4.3   Text Analysis

In this section, we analyze different words interconnected to the word *'covid19'* on both platforms. We use the word2vec model [25] which is a two-layer neural network that generates word representations as embedded vectors from the given input. We train four word2vec models; one for each of the *General* and *Vaccine* categories on Twitter and Parler. The word2vec model uses the preprocessing steps as discussed in Sect. 3.2 except lemmatization and stemming. For the Twitter word2vec models, a context window of 5 is used, whereas the word2vec models for Parler use a context window of 7. Even though the size of the four datasets differs, we only consider words that appear 50 times in each corpus. We train our word2vec models for between 5 and 7 epochs, since that best fits our data.

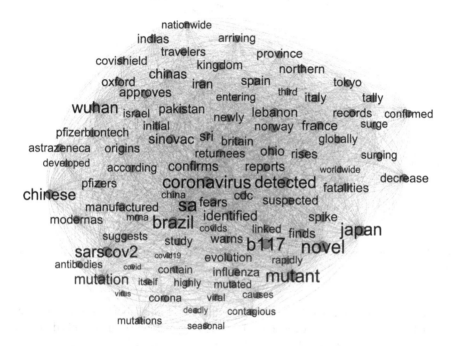

Fig. 1. Two-hop ego network around the word *'covid19'* in *General* group on Twitter (Color figure online)

We transform the word embeddings into a graph to visualize topics within the word embeddings. On the visualization, the nodes are words within the vocabulary, and the edges are weighted by the cosine similarity between the learned vectors of the nodes connected by the edge. We consider the edges with a cosine similarity above a specific threshold. We only present results for the *General* group on both platforms due to limited space. Figure 1 illustrates the two-hop ego network for the *General* category of Twitter, and Fig. 2 illustrates the two-hop ego network for the *General* category of Parler, both centered around the word *'covid19'*. We perform community detection [10] on the graphs, and each community is represented by a different color. Finally, we apply the ForceAtlas 2 algorithm [21], which creates a layout for the nodes depending on the weight of the edges.

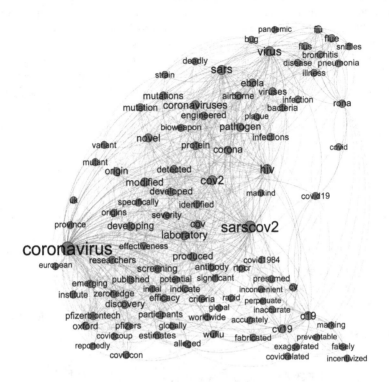

Fig. 2. Two-hop ego network around the word *'covid19'* in *General* group on Parler (Color figure online)

We observe that the purple community within Fig. 1 talks about COVID-19 spreading in different countries as it contains a large number of country names linked to words that represent the number of COVID-19 cases and deaths, such as *'surge,'* *'spike,'* and *'fatalities.'* We see that the green and orange communities are closely related; they represent words related to the virus and the companies that produce vaccinations. The orange community has more information related to different strains and mutations such as *'b117.'* In Fig. 2, we observe that the blue community links *'covid19'* to different illnesses and infections such as *'pneumonia,'* *'bronchitis,'* and *'flu.'* The orange community depicts links to different viruses such as *'ebola', 'sars'* and *'hiv'*. The orange, green and purple communities contain mixed ideas surrounding the credibility of the virus as well as the origin of the virus with words such as *'bioweapon', 'engineered'*, and *'fabricated,'* which indicate misinformation and conspiracy theories related to COVID-19 being spread on Parler.

Table 4. Top Domains

Twitter			
General	% tweets	Vaccine	% tweets
twitter.com	67.66%	twitter.com	56.15%
youtu.be	1.85%	youtu.be	1.35%
instagram.com	1.45%	theguardian.com	1.34%
bbc.co.uk	0.88%	nytimes.com	0.95%
theguardian.com	0.73%	instagram.com	0.71%
youtube.com	0.62%	cnbc.com	0.50%
nytimes.com	0.41%	washingtonpost.com	0.48%
lnkd.in	0.29%	nypost.com	0.42%
cbc.ca	0.27%	bloomberg.com	0.41%
washingtonpost.com	0.27%	bbc.co.uk	0.41%
Parler			
General	% posts	Vaccine	% posts
image-cdn.parler.com	24.54%	image-cdn.parler.com	20.06%
youtu.be	4.39%	thegatewaypundit.com	3.24%
thegatewaypundit.com	2.97%	youtu.be	2.88%
youtube.com	2.73%	bitchute.com	2.40%
twitter.com	1.82%	nypost.com	2.20%
rumble.com	1.51%	youtube.com	2.14%
nypost.com	1.44%	foxnews.com	1.67%
bitchute.com	1.36%	zerohedge.com	1.52%
breitbart.com	1.23%	rumble.com	1.48%
foxnews.com	1.20%	twitter.com	1.46%

4.4 Shared Links Analysis

Twitter and Parler users rely on pictures, videos, and external information to convey ideas and support claims. We observe the same in COVID-19 related posts. In this section, we analyze Unified Resource Locators (URLs) in the posts to determine the most popular domains in both groups. In our data, 67% tweets in *General* and *Vaccine* groups each contain at least one URL while 20% and 37% Parler posts contain at least one URL in *General* and *Vaccine* groups, respectively. Table 4 shows the top 10 domains on both platforms computed from the posts containing URLs. We observe that within each group, the most popular domain is the original social media platform (twitter.com and image-cdn.parler.com). We see that content from other social media platforms such as YouTube, Instagram and LinkedIn are shared on Twitter. We also notice multiple news platforms such as BBC, The Guardian, New York Times, Washington Post and New York Post on Twitter. We also observe business and market news domains such as CNBC and Bloomberg in Twitter's *Vaccine* group. Parler users share a mixture of mainstream and alternative content. For example, users share videos from mainstream platform YouTube as well as alternative platforms such as Bitchute and Rumble, known for hosting hate speech as well as accommodating far-right individuals and conspiracy theorists. Similarly, we observe news shared from mainstream platforms such as New York Post and Fox News as well as alternative platforms such as Brietbart, Zero Hedge, and The Gateway Pundit, known for publishing fake news.

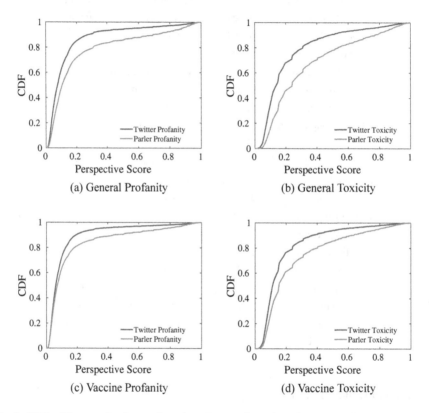

Fig. 3. CDF of Perspective Scores based on how toxic and profane a post is in *General* and *Vaccine* groups on Twitter and Parler

4.5   Perspective Analysis

We use Google's Perspective API [2] to investigate the toxicity and profanity in the posts. Using the API, a score between 0 and 1 is assigned to both the toxicity and profanity attributes for each post, where a score closer to 1 represents high toxicity or profanity. Figure 3 shows the cumulative distribution function (CDF) of the generated scores in the *General* and *Vaccine* groups on both platforms. We observe from the figure that Parler demonstrates a considerably higher score for both attributes when compared to Twitter in both groups. 22% of the posts in the *General* group on Parler have a toxicity value above 0.5, and 14.30% of the posts have a profanity value above 0.5,

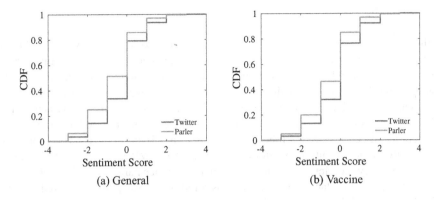

Fig. 4. CDF of Sentiment Scores for *General* and *Vaccine* groups on Twitter and Parler

whereas 9.24% of the tweets in the *General* group on Twitter have a toxicity value above 0.5, and 5.68% of the tweets have a profanity value above 0.5. Using the same criteria, 14.26% of the posts in the *Vaccine* group on Parler are toxic, and 9.35% of the posts have a high level of profanity, whereas 5.93% of the tweets in the *Vaccine* group on Twitter are toxic, and 3.59% of the tweets have a high level of profanity. As Parler has higher freedom of speech compared to Twitter, we observe more users are toxic and incorporate profanity into their vocabulary. Inferring from these results, the average post on Parler is more likely to contain hateful speech toward other users, individuals, and topics surrounding the COVID-19 pandemic.

4.6 Sentiment Analysis

We use the SentiStrength tool [3] to detect the extent of positive and negative emotions on both the platforms. We pick this tool as previous work shows that the tool gives 92% accuracy on social media data such as Twitter [14]. SentiStrength estimates sentiments on a scale of [−4, 4], where 0 denotes neutral, and negative and positive values denote negative and positive sentiments, respectively. Figure 4 shows the CDF of scaled sentiments in the *General* and *Vaccine* groups on both platforms. We observe from the figure that Parler shows a higher amount of negative sentiments as compared to Twitter. In the *General* group on Parler, we observe that 51.31% of the posts have negative sentiment compared to the 33.73% of tweets that have negative sentiment within the *General* group on Twitter. In the *Vaccine* group on Parler, we observe that 46.45% of the posts have negative sentiment compared to the 32.20% of tweets that have negative sentiment within the *Vaccine* group on Twitter. The sizable discrepancy between Twitter and Parler in both categories is once again rooted in Parler's higher freedom of speech. We observe that Parler features a higher quantity of swear words and negative terms such as *'lying'* and *'hate'*, which cause the posts to become more negative. As seen in the previous section, Perspective analysis demonstrates that there is a significantly higher amount of toxicity and profanity in Parler, which further adds to the negative scoring.

4.7 Discussion

In this section, we summarize the differences in the conversations on Twitter and Parler as seen from our analysis. The data analyzed in our work is during the time when Parler had no censorship and moderation, which results in a noticeable difference in the conversation that occurs on both platforms. We observe that Parler consists of a user base with far-right ideology and Trump supporters as we see discussions related to the 2020 US Presidential Election and its voting fraud allegations. Due to the difference in restrictions on censorship and moderation, we see that Twitter conversations focus on factual, useful, or precautionary information related to COVID-19, but Parler is home to many conspiracy theories and misinformation as we notice narratives such as 'COVID-19 is engineered in a laboratory and used as a biological weapon' are shared largely. We also notice high levels of toxic and profane content on Parler. Thus, our results demonstrate that freedom of speech leads to developing echo chambers and extremist groups on alternative platforms spreading misinformation. Spread of misinformation is detrimental to individuals and society. Hence, our preliminary analysis leads way for developing advanced models that are capable of timely detecting misinformation and preventing its spread.

5 Conclusion

In this paper, we analyzed communications related to COVID-19 on a mainstream social media platform, Twitter, and an alternative social media platform, Parler. We conducted word collocation analysis by identifying the most frequent bigrams on both platforms as analyzing co-occurring words give us the surrounding textual information. We then performed topic modeling to identify the main discussion points. We observed that the communication on Twitter focused only on topics related to COVID-19 while the communication on Parler focused on politics along with COVID-19. We analyzed the words interconnected with 'covid19' on both platforms and found that Parler contained words denoting misinformation and conspiracy theories. We performed a shared link analysis to understand the major sources of external content shared and observed that Twitter users shared content from external mainstream social media and news platforms whereas Parler users shared external mainstream content as well as alternative content spreading misinformation. We conducted perspective analysis to identify the extent of toxicity and profanity on both platforms, and finally performed sentiment analysis to study the amount of positive and negative emotions in the posts. We found that Parler content was more toxic, profane, and involved higher negative emotions than Twitter. Our results demonstrated that freedom of speech leads to developing echo chambers on alternative platforms spreading misinformation.

References

1. Cdc: Vaccine rollout. https://www.cdc.gov/coronavirus/2019-ncov/vaccines/recommendati ons-process.html
2. Perspective api. https://www.perspectiveapi.com/

3. Sentistrength. http://sentistrength.wlv.ac.uk/
4. Twitter api. https://developer.twitter.com/en/docs/twitter-api
5. Aliapoulios, M., et al.: A large open dataset from the parler social network. In: Proceedings of the International AAAI Conference on Web and Social Media, vol. 15, pp. 943–951 (2021)
6. Baines, A., Ittefaq, M., Abwao, M.: # scamdemic,# plandemic, or# scaredemic: What parler social media platform tells us about covid-19 vaccine. Vaccines **9**(5), 421 (2021)
7. Basile, V., Cauteruccio, F., Terracina, G.: How dramatic events can affect emotionality in social posting: the impact of covid-19 on reddit. Future Internet **13**(2), 29 (2021)
8. Bello-Orgaz, G., Hernandez-Castro, J., Camacho, D.: Detecting discussion communities on vaccination in twitter. Futur. Gener. Comput. Syst. **66**, 125–136 (2017)
9. Blei, D.M., Ng, A.Y., Jordan, M.I.: Latent Dirichlet allocation. J. Mach. Learn. Res. **3**, 993–1022 (2003)
10. Blondel, V.D., Guillaume, J.L., Lambiotte, R., Lefebvre, E.: Fast unfolding of communities in large networks. J. Stat. Mech. Theory Exp. **2008**(10), P10008 (2008)
11. Bonnevie, E., Gallegos-Jeffrey, A., Goldbarg, J., Byrd, B., Smyser, J.: Quantifying the rise of vaccine opposition on twitter during the covid-19 pandemic. J. Commun. Healthcare, 1–8 (2020)
12. Budhwani, H., Sun, R.: Creating covid-19 stigma by referencing the novel coronavirus as the "chinese virus" on Twitter: quantitative analysis of social media data. J. Med. Internet Res. **22**(5), e19301 (2020)
13. Carley, K.M.: Characterizing sociolinguistic variation in the competing vaccination communities. In: Social, Cultural, and Behavioral Modeling: 13th International Conference, SBP-BRiMS 2020, Washington, DC, USA, October 18–21, 2020, Proceedings. vol. 12268, p. 118. Springer Nature (2020)
14. Chatzakou, D., Kourtellis, N., Blackburn, J., De Cristofaro, E., Stringhini, G., Vakali, A.: Mean birds: detecting aggression and bullying on twitter. In: Proceedings of the 2017 ACM on Web Science Conference, pp. 13–22 (2017)
15. Cinelli, M., et al.: The covid-19 social media infodemic. Sci. Rep. **10**(1), 1–10 (2020)
16. Ferrara, E.: # covid-19 on Twitter: bots, conspiracies, and social media activism. arXiv preprint arXiv:2004.09531 (2020)
17. Gozzi, N., et al.: Collective response to media coverage of the covid-19 pandemic on reddit and Wikipedia: mixed-methods analysis. J. Med. Internet Res. **22**(10), e21597 (2020). https://doi.org/10.2196/21597, http://www.jmir.org/2020/10/e21597/
18. Horne, B.D., Adali, S.: An exploration of verbatim content republishing by news producers. arXiv preprint arXiv:1805.05939 (2018)
19. Horne, B.D., Nørregaard, J., Adalı, S.: Different spirals of sameness: a study of content sharing in mainstream and alternative media. In: Proceedings of the International AAAI Conference on Web and Social Media, vol. 13, pp. 257–266 (2019)
20. Huang, X., Li, Z., Jiang, Y., Li, X., Porter, D.: Twitter reveals human mobility dynamics during the covid-19 pandemic. PLoS ONE **15**(11), e0241957 (2020)
21. Jacomy, M., Venturini, T., Heymann, S., Bastian, M.: Forceatlas2, a continuous graph layout algorithm for handy network visualization designed for the gephi software. PLoS ONE **9**(6), e98679 (2014)
22. Kouzy, R., et al.: Coronavirus goes viral: quantifying the covid-19 misinformation epidemic on Twitter. Cureus **12**(3) (2020)
23. Kunneman, F., Lambooij, M., Wong, A., Van Den Bosch, A., Mollema, L.: Monitoring stance towards vaccination in twitter messages. BMC Med. Inform. Decis. Mak. **20**(1), 1–14 (2020)
24. Memon, S.A., Carley, K.M.: Characterizing covid-19 misinformation communities using a novel twitter dataset. arXiv preprint arXiv:2008.00791 (2020)
25. Mikolov, T., Chen, K., Corrado, G., Dean, J.: Efficient estimation of word representations in vector space. arXiv preprint arXiv:1301.3781 (2013)

26. Murray, C., Mitchell, L., Tuke, J., Mackay, M.: Symptom extraction from the narratives of personal experiences with COVID-19 on reddit. CoRR abs/2005.10454 (2020). https://arxiv.org/abs/2005.10454

27. Sha, H., Hasan, M.A., Mohler, G., Brantingham, P.J.: Dynamic topic modeling of the covid-19 Twitter narrative among us governors and cabinet executives. arXiv preprint arXiv:2004.11692 (2020)

28. Shanthakumar, S.G., Seetharam, A., Ramesh, A.: Analyzing societal impact of covid-19: a study during the early days of the pandemic. arXiv preprint arXiv:2010.15674 (2020)

29. Singh, L., et al.: A first look at covid-19 information and misinformation sharing on Twitter. arXiv preprint arXiv:2003.13907 (2020)

30. Xue, J., et al.: Twitter discussions and emotions about the covid-19 pandemic: Machine learning approach. J. Med. Internet Res. **22**(11), e20550 (2020)

31. Yin, H., Yang, S., Li, J.: Detecting topic and sentiment dynamics due to covid-19 pandemic using social media. In: International Conference on Advanced Data Mining and Applications, pp. 610–623. Springer (2020)

32. Zannettou, S., et al.: The web centipede: understanding how web communities influence each other through the lens of mainstream and alternative news sources. In: Proceedings of the 2017 Internet Measurement Conference, pp. 405–417 (2017)

33. Zhang, J.S., Keegan, B., Lv, Q., Tan, C.: Understanding the diverging user trajectories in highly-related online communities during the covid-19 pandemic. In: Proceedings of the International AAAI Conference on Web and Social Media, vol. 15, pp. 888–899 (2021)

34. Zhu, H., Wei, L., Niu, P.: The novel coronavirus outbreak in Wuhan, China. Global Health Res. Policy **5**(1), 1–3 (2020)

Adapting the "Networking During Infectious Diseases Model" (NIDM) for Science Communication Using Julia and Genie

Hendrik Nunner[(✉)][iD], Katinka Feltes, Pius Gutsche, Helen Kuswik, Erik Luda, Leonard Stellbrink[iD], and André Calero Valdez[iD]

University of Lübeck, Institute for Multimedia and Interactive Systems, Ratzeburger Allee 160, Lübeck, Germany
{hendrik.nunner,leonard.stellbrink,
andre.calerovaldez}@uni-luebeck.de,
{katinka.feltes,pius.gutsche,helen.kuswik,
erik.luda}@student.uni-luebeck.de
https://www.imis.uni-luebeck.de/en

Abstract. Scientific publications can be challenging for non-experts due to their complex concepts, technical terminology, and detailed descriptions of results. Interactive simulations can be used as a powerful way to communicate scientific progress to non-experts, providing a more engaging and hands-on experience that can help users understand complex processes. In this paper, we present a prototype of an interactive simulation for the "Networking during Infectious Diseases Model" (NIDM), which integrates theory from sociology, health psychology, and epidemiology to explore the interplay between social networks and the spread of infectious diseases. The prototype was developed using user-centered design and formatively evaluated. The goal of the contribution is to open the discussion on the evaluation of the prototype and to enhance the intuitive understanding of self-protective behavior and distancing measures following the outbreak of COVID-19. The results highlight the potential of interactive simulations as a tool for science communication and public engagement.

Keywords: Social Networks · Infectious Diseases · Risk Perception · Agent-based Models · Science Communication · Julia

1 Introduction

It can be challenging for non-experts to understand scientific publications for several reasons. That is, scientific publications tend to present intricate concepts and theories that necessitate in-depth knowledge of the underlying subject. In addition, scientists frequently employ specialized and technical terminology that may be unfamiliar to individuals outside the respective field. Furthermore, scientific

A. Coman and S. Vasilache (Eds.): HCII 2023, LNCS 14026, pp. 355–370, 2023.
https://doi.org/10.1007/978-3-031-35927-9_25

publications frequently describe results and discoveries in a highly detailed and technical manner, particularly when involving extensive statistical analysis and data.

A powerful way to communicate scientific progress to non-experts is by using interactive simulations, allowing users to manipulate variables and observe the resulting outcomes in real-time. This form of interaction provides a more hands-on and engaging experience compared to traditional forms of communication such as lectures or texts. Furthermore, interactive simulations can foster a sense of curiosity and encourage users to ask questions and form hypotheses about how different variables may affect the system. This can be especially useful when complex and dynamic processes are challenging to understand and visualize.

Take the interplay between social networks and infectious diseases, for example. It is known that social networks play a crucial role in the spread of infectious diseases. If, for example, a social network is highly connected, the disease is more likely to spread quickly through the network. Clusters within the network, on the other hand, highly connected areas with only a few connecting relations in between, tend to slow down disease spread [1,10,14]. Although this effect can be described with only a few words, true comprehension of the time-dependent interplay between social networks and the spread of infections is challenging.

This paper presents a prototype of an interactive simulation for the "Networking during Infectious Diseases Model" (NIDM) [16]. The NIDM is a previously developed individual-based mathematical model framework and agent-based simulation that integrates theory from sociology, health psychology, and epidemiology. Networking decisions in the NIDM are a trade-off between the benefits, costs, and potential harms of infections created by a social relationship. The degree to which agents avoid infectious others depends on individual risk perceptions regarding personal susceptibility to, and the severity of, an infectious disease. Simulations based on the NIDM give rise to complex interdependencies between individual behavior, network properties, and the spread of infections.

The goal of this contribution is two-fold. On the one hand, we aim to open the discussion on our method of evaluation and how to proceed in turning our prototype into a valuable tool for science communication. On the other hand, with the provision of our prototype, we aim to lay the foundation for enhancing the intuitive understanding of the efficacy of self-protective behavior and distancing measures following the outbreak of COVID-19. This way, we want to contribute to the discourse and arouse interest in the importance of science in the public domain.

2   Background

To fully understand the background of this paper, it is critical to understand the project's key purpose. For this, we discuss the aim of the prototype—science communication—and the content being communicated—the NIDM.

2.1 Science Communication

Classical methods of publishing scientific research, such as papers in peer-reviewed journals, chapters in textbooks, and presentations at scientific conferences remain arguably among the most popular channels to communicate and discuss scientific progress. A vast body of literature covers how to communicate scientific findings in the best possible way [4,6,9,15]. Over time, science communication has become a topic of increasing interest. Technological advances, especially the internet, have made it easier to gain access to even the most specialized information, whether in the form of open-access papers, science podcasts, social media, online lectures, or science slams. The success and ever-increasing number of such publications demonstrate the popularity both among the scientists presenting their results and among an audience that no longer necessarily consists only of experts.

From the scientists' perspective, communicating scientific research to a broader audience has not only promotional benefits. Including the general public in scientific discourse can be beneficial on various levels. For example, by making science more accessible to a broader audience, researchers can improve scientific literacy and promote a positive perception of science among the general public. In addition, the involvement of the general public can help to ensure that scientific research is conducted in an ethical and responsible manner. Including non-experts can help to identify potential risks and ethical concerns associated with research. Furthermore, this can provide valuable input on how to mitigate these risks and ensure that research is conducted in a socially responsible manner. Including the general public can also improve the relevance and impact of scientific research. By incorporating the perspectives and experiences of non-experts, scientists can identify research questions that are relevant to society and that address real-world problems. This can lead to the development of more impactful and relevant solutions.

Although there is no universal answer to how results should be communicated to a non-specialist audience, research has shown that different methods are effective in different contexts and for different goals. That is, visual elements, such as graphs, diagrams, and animations, can help to understand complex scientific relationships [11,13,18]. Incorporating storytelling into science communication can increase engagement and retention of information [7]. Interactive simulations, on the other hand, allow users to manipulate variables and see the effects of those changes in real-time. This can help users develop a more profound understanding of complex systems and their underlying mechanisms. A study among postgraduate science teachers by Zacharia [22], for example, showed that the use of computer simulations had a positive effect on the quality of explanations regarding physical phenomena in Mechanics, Waves/Optics, and Thermal Physics. Another study among elementary school students by Evagorou et al. [5] indicates that an interactive simulation of the ecosystem of a marsh can support the development of system thinking skills.

2.2 The Networking During Infectious Diseases Model (NIDM)

A complex system that is typically studied using computer simulations is the relationship between network structures and disease dynamics. A previously developed model framework to study the interdependencies between individual health behavior, social network properties, and spread of infections is the "Networking during Infectious Diseases Model" (NIDM) [16]. Realizations of the NIDM are individual-based models for infectious disease transmission [2, 19, 21], that assume an agent (i) to myopically optimize individual utility (U_i) composed of the benefits of social relationships (B_i), the costs to maintain these relationships (C_i), and the potential harm of infectious contacts (D_i):

$$U_i = B_i - C_i - D_i. \tag{1}$$

The realization of the NIDM used for this study is the "Small-worlds during Infectious Diseases Model" (SWIDM) [17]. The SWIDM allows studying the effect of small-world properties (i.e., clusters of densely connected areas within a network) on the spread of infections. To realize the incentive of clustering, the benefits of social relationships:

$$B_i = b_1 \cdot t_i + b_2 \cdot \left(1 - 2 \cdot \frac{|x_i - \alpha|}{\max(\alpha, 1 - \alpha)} \right) \tag{2}$$

are defined as the combination of the benefits (b_1)[1] for the number of social relationships (t_i) and the weighted (b_2) proportion of closed triads[2] (x_i) an agent i is part of. α defines the preferred proportion of closed triads and thus allows to control the degree of clustering in the network.

The costs of maintaining social relationships

$$C_i = c_1 \cdot t_i + c_2 \cdot t_i^2 \tag{3}$$

are defined as marginally increasing costs (c_1, c_2) dependent on the number of social relations an agent i has (t_i). These costs, in combination with the benefits for the number of social relationships $(b_1 \cdot t_i)$, allow controlling the actual number of social relationships an agent i has.

The potential harm of infectious contacts

$$D_i = p_i \cdot s_i. \tag{4}$$

is the combination of the *perceived* probability to acquire and infection (p_i) and the *perceived* severity of the disease (s_i). That means an agent i transforms the actual probability to get infected

$$\pi_i = 1 - (1 - \gamma)^{t_i I}, \tag{5}$$

---

[1] See Table 1 for an overview of all model parameters and state variables.

[2] A closed triad is a group of three nodes in a network where each pair of nodes (here: agents) is directly connected by an edge (here: social relation), forming a triangle shape.

with γ being the probability to get infected per single contact and t_{i_I} the number of infected social relations the agent has, into a subjective perception, depending on the agent's disease state:

$$p_i = \begin{cases} \pi_i^{2-r}, \text{ if } i \text{ is susceptible,} \\ 1, \text{ if } i \text{ is infected,} \\ 0, \text{ if } i \text{ is recovered.} \end{cases} \tag{6}$$

Finally, the actual severity of the disease (σ) is transformed into a subjective perception, depending on agent i's disease state:

$$s_i = \begin{cases} \sigma^r, \text{ if } i \text{ is susceptible,} \\ \sigma, \text{ if } i \text{ is infected,} \\ 0, \text{ if } i \text{ is recovered.} \end{cases} \tag{7}$$

As a result, risk perception values (r) above 1 cause agents to overestimate the probability of acquiring infections and disease severity. Consequently, these *risk averse* agents tend to dissolve infectious relationships quicker than agents with risk perception values (r) below 1.

In addition to the mathematical model, the NIDM defines an agent-based simulation. In the most basic form, the simulation consists of two processes that are computed consecutively for a number of discrete time steps, infectious disease dynamics, and ego-centered network formation:

```
% computation of discrete time steps
ts = 0
While ts < ts_max:
    Compute disease dynamics.
    Compute ego-centered network formation.
    ts++.
```

Table 1. Scales for model parameters and state variables.

	Scale
I. Model parameters	
I.I. Social benefits	
Benefit of neighbors	$b_1 \in \mathbb{R}_0^+$
Benefit of closed triads	$b_2 \in \mathbb{R}_0^+$
Preferred proportion of closed triads	$0 \leq \alpha \leq 1$
I.II. Social costs	
Cost per neighbor	$c_1 \in \mathbb{R}_0^+$
Marginal cost per neighbor	$c_2 \in \mathbb{R}_0^+$
I.III. Disease properties	
Disease severity	$\sigma > 1$
Infectivity[*]	$0 \leq \gamma \leq 1$
Recovery time in time steps	$\tau > 0$
I.IV. Individual level properties	
Risk perception	$0 \leq r \leq 2$
I.V. Simulation / network properties	
Number of agents	$N \in \mathbb{N}_0$
Number of offered agents per time step	$0 < \phi \leq N$
Proportion of ϕ as neighbors	$0 \leq \psi \leq 1$
Proportion of ϕ as neighbors' neighbors	$0 \leq \xi \leq 1$
II. State variables	
Number of neighbors of agent i	$0 \leq t_i \leq N$
Number of infected neighbors of agent i	$0 \leq t_{i_I} \leq t_i$
Proportion of closed triads of agent i	$0 \leq x_i \leq 1$
Time steps since infection of agent i	$ts_{i_I} \in \mathbb{R}_0^+$

[*]: Infectivity is operationalized as transmission probability per contact and time step.

Disease dynamics is realized as an update process of the agents' individual disease states (susceptible, infected, recovered):

```
% disease dynamics
Repeat until all agents have been processed:
    Randomly select an unprocessed agent i.
    If i is susceptible:
        If ~ U[0,1] ≤ πi :    % for πi, see Equation 5
            Infect i.
    If i is infected:
        If tsiI ≥ τ :
            Recover i.
```

Ego-centered network formation is realized as an update process of the agents' individual social relations. That is, agents myopically seek to maximize their individual utility based on the agents offered to them by the simulation.[3]:

```
% ego-centered network formation
Repeat until all agents have been processed:
    Randomly select an unprocessed agent i.
    Create an empty set of agents J⁴.
    Add to J until J consists of φ agents:
        With probability ψ:
            a random neighbor of i.
        With probability ψ + ξ:
            a random neighbor's neighbor of i.
        With probability 1 − (ψ + ξ):
            a random agent from the entire population.
    Repeat until all agents in J have been processed:
        If relation ij exists:
            If Uᵢ-ij > Uᵢ+ij:
                Dissolve relation ij.
        If relation ij not exists:
            If Uᵢ+ij ≥ Uᵢ-ij && Uⱼ+ij ≥ Uⱼ-ij:
                Create relation ij.
```

Simulation studies based on the SWIDM have shown that the co-evolution of social networks and infectious diseases produces outcomes that are hard to foresee, even for well-studied properties, such as clustering. In static networks, sparse connections between clusters can slow disease spread [1,10,14], while relations between clusters can facilitate disease spread through the entire network [20]. In networks with agents adapting their social behavior according to perceived risks of infection, the existence of only a few relations bridging two clusters, however, requires severing only a few relations for the disease to die out quickly [17].

3   Method

During the user-centered design approach, several user interface artifacts were developed at different levels of fidelity. These artifacts were used to formatively evaluate the ideas. We next present both artifacts and the processes to attain these artifacts.

---

[3] Offers can be considered the number of contacts an agent has on a given time step. This can be, for example, an individual meeting 12 other individuals throughout a single day.

[4] J allows prioritization of neighbors for selection.

3.1 Sketches

To determine the optimal initial user interface, we employed an iterative app-roach. As a first step, we created various sketches of user interfaces (see Fig. 1) using paper prototyping [8]. The advantage of hand-drawn sketches is that they can be produced quickly and in large numbers so that many ideas can be cap-tured and compared in a short time. The goal of creating these sketches was to identify the most important functions of the simulation and the UI elements best suited for them.

Our focus was on making the model as simple and understandable as possible. For this reason, the sketches were prepared by the members of our research group who had the least experience with the NIDM, as in-depth knowledge of the model could be a hindrance to identifying the minimal and essential elements.

To identify critical aspects of the design, the members of the sketch group evaluated the sketches and identified core elements of the user interface using a heuristic evaluation approach. Among these core elements of the user interface, we identified the following aspects in order of importance.

First, a visually delineated menu that includes all the elements for controlling the model. This should be conducive to the clarity of the controls. Second, the use of sliders, rather than number inputs, for setting parameter values. Third, parameter sliders should be supplemented with info tags with explanations that allow first-time users to operate them. Fourth, the selection of different diseases with preset parameter settings should be provided to allow for interesting and plausible scenarios to be observed. Fifth, nodes should be supplemented with hover effects, communicating status information such as disease states quickly and easily. Sixth, a click on a network node should infect it with the disease. Seventh, a static legend with color information, shall be used to explain health states. Eighth, users shall be able to switch between different representations of health states of nodes. Here, color codings, but also the use of emojis, are conceivable, promoting intuitive and accessible use. Ninth, a button should make it possible to add more nodes. Tenth, diagrams should provide information about the historical course of disease spread to make a better impression of the course of epidemics. Eleventh, it should be possible to speed up and slow down the simulation. Twelfth, it should be possible to switch between an expert and a lay mode, which differ in complexity and configuration options of the model.

3.2 Static Prototypes

After evaluating the sketches and identifying the most important elements, we started implementing a prototype. The backend logic, i.e., the implementation of the mathematical model, the simulation loop consisting of disease dynamics, and ego-centered network formation was implemented in Julia [3]. Julia is a pro-gramming language that was designed to address some of the shortcomings of existing languages, particularly in the domain of scientific and technical com-puting. Specifically, Julia's JIT (Just-In-Time) compiler is designed to generate highly optimized machine code on the fly, which makes it much faster than many

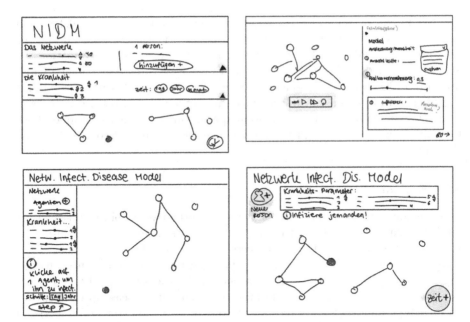

Fig. 1. Selected sketches of user interfaces. A common feature of all sketches is the visually delimited menu that includes all the elements for controlling the model. Furthermore, we quickly realized that sliders provide a more intuitive way to set the model parameters than numeric inputs. A large visual output of the network is also an element that appears in each of the sketches. However, it remained unclear where the menu should be placed and whether the elements to control simulation steps should be part of the model parameter menu. Since the user interface was designed for German-speaking users, the elements are labeled with German names: **Agenten+** = *agents+*, **Ansteckung** = *infection*, **Anzahl Leute** = *number of persons*, **das Netzwerk** = *the network*, **die Krankheit** = *the disease*, **einklappbar** = *collapsible*, **hinzufügen** = *add*, **Infiziere jemanden!** = *infect someone!*, **infizieren** = *infect*, **Klicke auf 1 Agent um ihn zu infect.** = *click on 1 agent to infect it*, **Krankheits-Parameter** = *disease parameter*, **Neue Person** = *new person*, **Person** = *person*, **Risikowahrnehmung** = *risk perception*, **Schritte: Tag Jahr** = *steps: day year*, **Zeit+** = *time+*, **Zeit: Tag Jahr Monat** = *time: day year month*.

other dynamic languages. This makes Julia a great choice for computationally intensive tasks, such as numerical simulations.

We used Genie for the technical implementation of the user interface. Genie is a web framework for the Julia programming language that allows developing high-performance web applications. One of the main advantages of using Genie with Julia is the performance benefits that Julia provides. Julia's JIT compiler and built-in support for parallelism and distributed computing make it well-suited for building high-performance web applications that can handle large amounts of data and high traffic loads, making it a suitable candidate for interactive simulations for a large audience through a web-based user interface.

Despite the benefits of Julia and Genie, we encountered some delays and setbacks, especially due to communication issues between the backend and the user interface. Consequently, we decided to perform a preliminary evaluation of a static prototype with limited functionality. That is, we created a detailed hand-drawn (see Fig. 2) and a web-based user interface (see Fig. 2) with sliders to set a minimal set of parameters, a legend to explain the different disease states, and a timeline for modifying the simulation speed. Furthermore, we dropped both the expert mode and the function of displaying the historical course of disease spread via a diagram.

3.3   Evaluation

The preliminary evaluation was conducted as formative usability testing using semi-structured interviews with three subjects. As a first step, the interview procedure was explained to the subjects. They were told that the goal of the study was to design a suitable and appealing user interface for a scientific model. Furthermore, it was explained that the goal of the scientific model is to explore how fast diseases can spread in a social network and that disease spread depends on various parameters both in terms of the disease (e.g., how contagious it is) and the people in the network (e.g., the strength of risk perception). Subjects were also asked to speak aloud any thoughts they had while viewing the prototypes (*Thinking Aloud* [12]) and to share both criticisms, ambiguities, and positive features.

Following these explanations, subjects were presented with our prototypes. After the subjects were given enough time to familiarize themselves with the prototypes and to verbalize their impressions, they were further asked to describe for each element whether it was clear without additional help what it was for, how to start a simulation, how to modify a simulation, and what conclusions could be drawn from the model. Finally, each respondent was asked which elements would be additionally necessary or should be modified to improve the user experience and understanding of the model.

4   Results

In the following, the impressions of the subjects are first discussed in detail. Subsequently, the combined findings are discussed, and how they influenced the design of our interactive prototype.

4.1   Insights from the Evaluation

With regard to the numeric inputs, subject 1 suggested omitting them or replacing them with other elements, since they bear no meaning for a layperson. Furthermore, subject 1 suggested that the sliders be colored so that setting such as severe and less severe are visually supported. In general, subject 1 found the terms described in a sufficient manner to acquire a general understanding of the

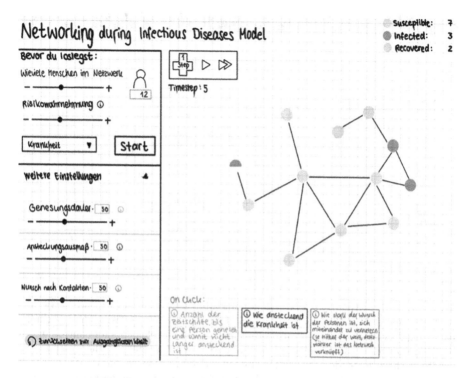

Fig. 2. Hand-drawn static prototype. The figure shows one of the two static user interfaces used for a preliminary evaluation of our designs. Both designs have a similar layout (e.g., a visually delimited menu that includes all the elements for controlling the model on the left, a panel to control the progression of time steps at the top, a legend describing the color codes for disease states). In comparison to the design in Fig. 3, this design is somewhat slimmed-down and uses a more playful language. Since the proto-type was designed for German-speaking users, the elements are labeled with German names: ***Bevor du loslegst:*** = *before you start:*, ***Wieviele Menschen im Netzw-erk*** = *how many individuals in the network*, ***Risikowahrnehmung*** = *risk perception*, ***Krankheit*** = *disease*, ***Start*** = *start*, ***weitere Einstellungen*** = *additional settings*, ***Genesungsdauer*** = *recovery time*, ***Ansteckungsausmaß*** = *infection level*, ***Wunsch nach Kontakten*** = *desire for contact*, ***Zurücksetzen zur Ausgangskrankheit*** = *Reset to initial disease*, ***Anzahl der Zeitschritte bis eine Person genesen und somit nicht länger ansteckend ist.*** = *Number of time steps until a person recov-ers and is therefore no longer contagious.*, ***Wie ansteckend die Krankheit ist.*** = *How contagious the disease is.*, ***Wie stark der Wunsch der Personen ist, sich miteinander zu vernetzen (je höher der Wert, desto stärker ist das Netzwerk verknüpft)*** = *How strong the desire of individuals is to connect with each other (the higher the value, the more connected the network)*.

model and the user interface. However, additional explanations were required regarding risk perception. Subject 1 also noted that information about how to

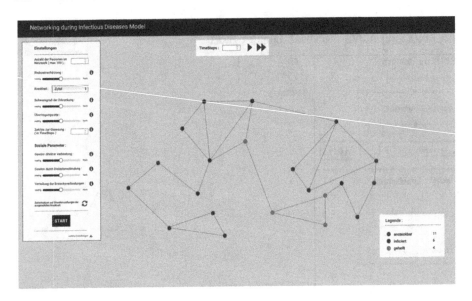

Fig. 3. Digital static prototype. The figure shows the other of the two static user interfaces used for a preliminary evaluation of our designs. Both designs have a similar layout (e.g., a visually delimited menu that includes all the elements for controlling the model on the left, a panel to control the progression of time steps at the top, a legend describing the color codes for disease states). In comparison to the design in Fig. 2, this design has a more technical/scientific approach in the way the parameters are presented and described. Since the prototype was designed for German-speaking users, the elements are labeled with German names: *Einstellungen* = settings, *Anzahl der Personen im Netzwerk* = number of individuals in the network, *Risikoeinschätzung* = risk assessment, *niedrig* = low, *hoch* = high, *Krankheit: Zufall* = disease: random, *Übertragungsrate* = transmission rate, *Zeit bis zur Genesung* = time to recover, *Soziale Parameter* = social parameters, *Gewinn direkter Verbindung* = benefit of direct connection, *Gewinn durch Dreiecksverbindung* = benefit of triadic connection, *Verteilung der Dreiecksverbindung* = distribution of the triadic connection, *Zurücksetzen auf Grundeinstellungen der ausgewählten Krankheit* = Reset to basic settings of the selected disease, *weitere Einstellungen* = additional settings, *Legende* = legend, *ansteckbar* = susceptible, *infiziert* = infected, *geheilt* = recovered.

infect a person and what happens during a single time step is missing. Finally, subject 1 suggested providing pre-defined diseases.

Subject 2 showed great problems in understanding the model and the individual parameters. According to subject 2, the parameters were not labeled clearly enough and required additional information for a sufficient understanding. Additionally, subject 2 did not understand what the model does, its background, how the model is started, and how a network node is infected. A suggestion to simplify the handling of the user interface was the use of colors to visually support sliders.

Subject 3 reported that the interfaces were confusing. In addition, subject 3 showed major problems in understanding the model, the parameters, and the influence of the model parameters on the model behavior. According to subject 3, a meaningful example could be helpful to promote understanding. Subject 3 liked the neutral design without many colors and preferred the design with fewer elements.

In summary, the preliminary evaluation shows that the user interface alone is not sufficient to understand the model and its parameters. It follows that an introduction with basic information about the functionality and operation is indispensable. In addition, subjects asked for formal guidelines specifying the sequence of operation. Such a sequence, however, could also be achieved implicitly by the arrangement of the menu and the controls. Furthermore, two subjects pointed out that colors can support the sliders in their expressiveness.

4.2   Interactive Prototype

Based on the findings from our preliminary evaluation, we created an interactive prototype (see Fig. 4). This prototype has a clear and simple structure that promotes focus on the essential elements of the user interface. The menu is now divided into two separate sections: network settings (top left) and disease settings (bottom left). Through this thematic division, we intend to create a structure that suggests an implicit sequence of actions.

Where appropriate, color coding is used. To indicate the risk of highly infectious diseases, we use red as a signal color. Diseases with a very low probability of transmission, on the other hand, are coded green. As the number of people in the network has no such positive or negative associations, it is presented in a neutral shade of gray.

To facilitate a better understanding, we have revised the wording. Labels describe outright the purpose of interaction elements (e.g., start new simulation). In addition, the most important information for interaction outside the menu is highlighted and placed at the top of the network view (i.e., double-click on individuals to infect them).

The interactive prototype has full functionality and can thus be configured via the control elements and can perform and display simulations.

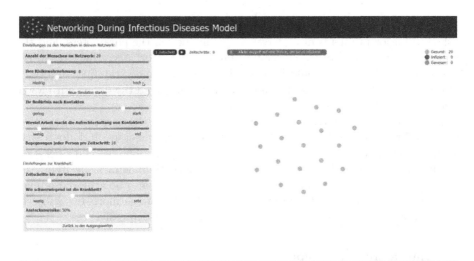

Fig. 4. Interactive prototype. The figure shows the interactive prototype of our user interface design. The design considers the most important feedback from the pre-liminary evaluation: more precise labeling of the parameters, a simple and structured layout, and where appropriate color codings to support the sliders' expressiveness. Since the prototype was designed for German-speaking users, the elements are labeled with German names: *Einstellungen zu den Menschen in deinem Netzwerk* = *settings for the individuals in your network*, *Anzahl der Menschen im Netzwerk* = *number of individuals in the network*, *Ihre Risikowahrnehmung* = *your risk perception*, *niedrig* = *low*, *hoch* = *high*, *Neue Simulation starten* = *start new simulation*, *Ihr Bedürfnis nach Kontakten* = *your desire for contacts*, *gering* = *low*, *stark* = *high*, *Wieviel Arbeit macht die Aufrechterhaltung von Kontakten?* = *how much effort is involved in maintaining contacts*, *wenig* = *not much*, *viel* = *much*, *Begegnungen jeder Person pro Zeitschritt* = *contacts per individual and time step*, *Einstellungen zur Krankheit* = *disease settings*, *Zeitschritte bis zur Genesung* = *time steps until recovery*, *Wie schwerwiegend ist die Krankheit?* = *how severe is the disease?*, *wenig* = *not very*, *sehr* = *very*, *Ansteckungsrisiko* = *risk of infection*, *Zurück zu den Ausgangswerten* = *reset to initial values*, *Zeitschritt* = *time step*, *Klicke doppelt auf eine Person, um die infizieren* = *double-click on individuals to infect them*, *Gesund* = *susceptible*, *Infiziert* = *infected*, *Genesen* = *recovered*.

5   Conclusion

In this paper, we have presented our approach to designing an interactive sim-ulation for the complex co-evolution of social networks and infectious diseases. One of our goals is to receive valuable feedback on the method of our approach. That is, we started with sketches to identify the most important elements for an interactive simulation. We then created two static designs for user interfaces and performed formative usability testing using semi-structured interviews. Although we had only three subjects, we received important feedback. Most notably, the participants considered the prototypes and the model too complex to understand without further explanation or some other form of guidance. Based on the findings from the interviews, we designed a fully functional interactive prototype.

The other goal of our work is to lay the foundation for enhancing the intuitive understanding of the efficacy of self-protective behavior and distancing measures following the outbreak of COVID-19. Although we believe the foundation was successfully laid, further work needs to be done before our simulation can be an effective tool for science communication. The next step in our work involves technically refining the prototype to facilitate surveying of a larger sample. This will enable the development of a two-pronged approach. Firstly, we will evaluate the scientific and technical validity of the simulation. Secondly, evaluating with individuals from the general population will inform us whether people can comprehend the spread of infectious diseases on social networks when playing with such a model. This investigation could be used to explore various phenomena of network theoretical infection epidemiology, such as clustering, which could aid in curbing the spread. To accomplish this, an evaluation concept must be created and coordinated with the domain experts and the simulation must be transformed to enable summative evaluation with end-users.

Acknowledgements. We would like to thank the participants in our research for their valuable input. This work has partly been funded by the federal ministry of research and education in Germany in the infoXpand project. https://www.overleaf.com/project/63a58ccd6d9b3e7c9e1e3e91.

References

1. Badham, J., Stocker, R.: The impact of network clustering and assortativity on epidemic behaviour. Theoret. Population Biol. **77**(1), 71–75 (2010). https://doi.org/10.1016/j.tpb.2009.11.003
2. Bedson, J., et al.: A review and agenda for integrated disease models including social and behavioural factors. Nat. Human Behav. **5**(7), 834–846 (2021). https://doi.org/10.1038/s41562-021-01136-2
3. Bezanson, J., Edelman, A., Karpinski, S., Shah, V.B.: Julia: a fresh approach to numerical computing. SIAM Rev. **59**(1), 65–98 (2017). https://doi.org/10.1137/141000671
4. Bubela, T., et al.: Science communication reconsidered. Nat. Biotechnol. **27**(6), 514–518 (2009). https://doi.org/10.1038/nbt0609-514
5. Evagorou, M., Korfiatis, K., Nicolaou, C., Constantinou, C.: An investigation of the potential of interactive simulations for developing system thinking skills in elementary school: a case study with fifth–graders and sixth–graders. Int. J. Sci. Educ. **31**(5), 655–674 (2009). https://doi.org/10.1080/09500690701749313
6. Fischhoff, B.: The sciences of science communication. Proceed. Nat. Acad. Sci. **110**(supplement_3), 14033–14039 (2013). https://doi.org/10.1073/pnas.121327311
7. Green, M., Brock, T.: The role of transportation in the persuasiveness of public narrative. J. Personal. Soc. Psychol. **79**, 701–21 (2000). https://doi.org/10.1037/0022-3514.79.5.701
8. Greenberg, S., Carpendale, S., Marquardt, N., Buxton, B.: Sketching user experiences: the workbook. Elsevier (2011)

9. Kappel, K., Holmen, S.J.: Why science communication, and does it work? a taxonomy of science communication aims and a survey of the empirical evidence. Front. Commun. **4**, 55 (2019). https://doi.org/10.3389/fcomm.2019.00055

10. Keeling, M.J.: The effects of local spatial structure on epidemiological invasions. Proceed. Royal Soc. London. Ser. B: Biol. Sci. **266**(1421), 859–867 (1999). https://doi.org/10.1098/rspb.1999.0716

11. Kosslyn, S.M.: Understanding charts and graphs. Appl. Cogn. Psychol. **3**(3), 185–225 (1989). https://doi.org/10.1002/acp.2350030302

12. Lewis, C.: Using the "thinking-aloud" method in cognitive interface design. IBM TJ Watson Research Center Yorktown Heights, NY (1982)

13. Mayer, R., Gallini, J.: When is an illustration worth ten thousand words? J. Educ. Psychol. **82**, 715–726 (1990). https://doi.org/10.1037/0022-0663.82.4.715

14. Miller, J.C.: Percolation and epidemics in random clustered networks. Phys. Rev. E **80**(2), 020901 (2009). https://doi.org/10.1103/PhysRevE.80.020901

15. Nisbet, M.C., Scheufele, D.A.: What's next for science communication? promising directions and lingering distractions. Am. J. Bot. **96**(10), 1767–1778 (2009)

16. Nunner, H., Buskens, V., Kretzschmar, M.: A model for the co-evolution of dynamic social networks and infectious disease dynamics. Comput. Soc. Netw. **8**(1), 19 (2021). https://doi.org/10.1186/s40649-021-00098-9

17. Nunner, H., Buskens, V., Teslya, A., Kretzschmar, M.: Health behavior homophily can mitigate the spread of infectious diseases in small-world networks. Soc. Sci. Med. **312**, 115350 (2022). https://doi.org/10.1016/j.socscimed.2022.115350

18. Tversky, B., Morrison, J.B., Betrancourt, M.: Animation: can it facilitate? Int. J. Hum.-Comput. Stud. **57**(4), 247–262 (2002). https://doi.org/10.1006/ijhc.2002.1017

19. Verelst, F., Willem, L., Beutels, P.: Behavioural change models for infectious disease transmission: a systematic review (2010–2015). J. Royal Soc. Interface **13**(125), 20160820 (2016). https://doi.org/10.1098/rsif.2016.0820

20. Watts, D.J., Strogatz, S.H.: Collective dynamics of 'small-world' networks. Nature **393**(6684), 440–442 (1998). https://doi.org/10.1038/30918. Number: 6684, Publisher: Nature Publishing Group

21. Willem, L., Verelst, F., Bilcke, J., Hens, N., Beutels, P.: Lessons from a decade of individual-based models for infectious disease transmission: a systematic review (2006–2015). BMC Infect. Diseases **17**(1), 612 (2017). https://doi.org/10.1186/s12879-017-2699-8

22. Zacharia, Z.C.: The impact of interactive computer simulations on the nature and quality of postgraduate science teachers' explanations in physics. Int. J. Sci. Educ. **27**(14), 1741–1767 (2005). https://doi.org/10.1080/09500690500239664

A Scale to Evaluate the Post-pandemic Tourist Experience in Valparaíso

Virginica Rusu[1]([✉])(iD), Cristian Rusu[2](iD), and Marisol Castro[1]

[1] Universidad de Playa Ancha, Av. Playa Ancha 850, 2340000 Valparaíso, Chile
{virginica.rusu,marisol.castro}@upla.cl
[2] Pontificia Universidad Católica de Valparaíso, Av. Brasil 2241, 2340000 Valparaíso, Chile
cristian.rusu@pucv.cl

Abstract. Tourist eXperience (TX) is hard to evaluate due to its complexity, and the highly personal and subjective nature of experiences. TX can be considered as a particular case of Customer eXperience (CX), which is an extension of User eXperience (UX). Tourism was dramatically affected by the COVID-19 pandemic, and TX evaluation should explicitly consider the post-pandemic context. We developed a scale to evaluate the post-pandemic TX in Valparaíso, Chile. The scale was refined based on experts' opinion, was validated through a pilot test, and was later applied in a survey with 316 participants. Statistical validation indicate that the scale is reliable. It includes 56 items grouped in 8 dimensions: emotions, local culture, authenticity of the place, entertainment, services, post-pandemic experience, loyalty, and general perception. Survey's results confirm the importance of evaluating TX pandemic-related issues. They emphasize the potential of Valparaíso as destination, but also indicate some major issues that should be addressed: safety, cleanliness, sustainability, and inclusiveness.

Keywords: Tourist Experience · Customer Experience · Tourist Experience Evaluation · Scale · Post-pandemic

1 Introduction

The concepts of Tourist eXperience (TX) and Customer eXperience (CX) have been extensively discussed. It is hard to agree on their definitions, because experiences are personal and subjective, and TX and CX are complex and multidimensional. Laming and Mason highlight that CX includes all physical and emotional responses that a customer experiences before, during and after coming into contact, directly or indirectly, with a brand/company, during his/her whole "journey", including the post consumption stage [1]. Customer-company interactions occur through products, systems and services that the company offers. Tourists are specific types of costumers, that are using tourism-related services, products and systems. CX can be seen as a natural extension of User eXperience (UX), a well-known and highly explored topic in Human-Computer Interaction (HCI) [2–4]. It focuses on a person's interaction with all services, systems and products that a company/organization/brand offers, instead of focusing on the interaction with a single product, system or service [4].

A. Coman and S. Vasilache (Eds.): HCII 2023, LNCS 14026, pp. 371–388, 2023.
https://doi.org/10.1007/978-3-031-35927-9_26

Many scales have been proposed to evaluate TX. Tourism was dramatically affected by the COVID-19 pandemic, and TX scales should explicitly consider the post-pandemic context. We developed a scale to evaluate the post-pandemic TX in Valparaíso, Chile, in a process that included 4 steps: (1) developing the scale based on literature, (2) refining the scale based on experts' opinion, (3) validating the scale through a pilot test, and (4) applying the scale in a survey with over 300 participants and statistically validated it. The first and the second steps of the process were analyzed in previous work [5, 6]. This paper documents the whole process of developing the scale, comparing its preliminary and final versions, and discussing the results of the pilot test and of the survey. Section 2 briefly analyzes the concepts that fundaments our study. Section 3 describes the scale's development, and analyze the results of the survey. Finally, Sect. 4 highlights conclusions and proposes future work.

2 Experiences and Tourism

2.1 User eXperience

UX is one of the main topics in HCI research and practice. As the ISO 9241-210 standard indicates, UX includes "the perceptions and responses of the person resulting from the use and/or anticipated use of a product, system or service" [7]. So, UX does not limit to the interaction with interactive software systems, it refers to a person interaction with any kind of product, system or service.

UX with tourism-related digital products is one of our main research topics. We focused on UX evaluations, proposing specific heuristics and evaluation methodologies. Among others, we studied online travel agencies [8–10], virtual museums [11–13], and national parks [14]. We intend to further explore the potential of new, specific heuristics, when evaluating the tourist experience with tourism-related services [15, 16].

2.2 Costumer eXperience

The CX concept was initially proposed in marketing. Almost a decade ago, Lewis highlighted its relevance in HCI, and pointed out that CX is the link between HCI and Service Science [2]. In our view, CX is a natural extension of UX, that examine a person's interactions with all products, systems and services that a company offers [3, 4]. Experience with one company's artifact will most probably affect the perception of other artifacts of the same company, and the overall person's experience.

For some years, we examined TX as a particular case of CX, examining quantitative data available at online travel agencies websites [17–19]. We are currently developing TX evaluation tools; our study proposes a scale to evaluate the post-pandemic TX in Valparaíso, Chile [5, 6].

2.3 Tourism eXperience

Several TX definitions were proposed. Godovykh and Tasci offer a comprehensive review of CX in tourism [20]. In their view, experience is "the totality of cognitive, affective, sensory, and conative responses, on a spectrum of negative to positive, evoked by all stimuli encountered in pre, during, and post phases of consumption affected by situational and brand-related factors filtered through personal differences of consumers, eventually resulting in differential outcomes related to consumers and brands". Even if their definition refers to experiences in tourism, it does not limit to TX, and may apply to experiences in other fields.

Several scholars are using the concept of "memorable" TX [21–27]. Tung and Ritchie identify four dimensions of memorable TX: affect, expectations, consequentiality, and recollection [21].

2.4 Evaluating the Post-pandemic Tourism eXperience

Scales are common tools to evaluate TX. Many scales have been proposed. Many studies are proposing new TX scales, and are validating the underlying models that fundament those scales. Some scales are more general, others are focusing on specific tourism sectors, or specific destinations.

As tourism was dramatically affected by the COVID-19 pandemic, we think that TX scales should explicitly consider the post-pandemic context. As we did not find a proper scale to evaluate TX in Valparaíso, considering the pandemic restrictions, we developed a new scale. Our scale is based on 12 scales proposed by other authors [22–33]. It includes items adapted from other scales, as well as new items, related to the post-pandemic context, and to Valparaíso specificity as destination.

2.5 Developing a Scale for Tourist Experience Evaluation in Valparaíso

We created the new scale in several iterations:

1. We developed a preliminary version of the scale, based on literature [5]. The scale was reviewed by two UX/CX experts, and was refined based on their feedback.
2. The scale was evaluated by 30 experts, academics, and tourism students, and was refined based on their feedback [6].
3. The scale was validated through a pilot test, that involved 20 participants. Scale's reliability was evaluated.
4. The scale was applied to 316 tourists, and was statistically validated.

The process of constructing the scale is described below.

2.6 The Preliminary Scale

We created the first version of the scale based on literature review [5]. The scale included 56 items, grouped in 8 TX dimensions: emotions (8 items), local culture (8 items), authenticity of the place (13 items), entertainment (8 items), services (11 items), post-pandemic experience (4 items), loyalty (2 items), and general perception (2 items). The scale was reviewed by two UX/CX experts, with computer science and psychology background, and items were refined based on their feedback.

The preliminary scale included 43 adapted and 13 original items. Most of the original items are related to Valparaíso particularity (8 items), or are COVID-19 pandemic-related

(4 items); 1 new item is rather general (medical and health services availability). The preliminary scale's dimensions and items are shown in Table 2.

2.7 Refining the Scale Based on Experts' Feedback

The scale was quantitatively and qualitatively examined, in late 2021 – early 2022, by:

- 11 tourism experts, that work in governmental and private tourism sector in Valparaíso area;
- 10 academics from Chile, Spain and Argentina;
- 9 tourism undergraduate students, from Universidad de Playa Ancha, Valparaíso, Chile.

The 30 participants were asked to evaluate each of the 56 items, using a 5-point Likert scale, where 1 is not appropriate at all, and 5 is very appropriate. They were also asked to make comments on dimensions, on items, and on the whole scale [6].

Table 1. Overall opinions on the preliminary scale.

	Min	Max	Average	Std. Dev.
Experts (11)	2.89	5.00	4.45	0.38
Academics (10)	3.20	5.00	4.38	0.38
Tourism students (9)	3.33	4.89	4.52	0.32

Table 1 synthetizes the quantitative evaluations of the scale. All groups of participants have a positive opinion, with averages from 4.38 to 4.52. Opinions are rather homogeneous, with low standard deviations. Table 2 details the quantitative evaluation of the preliminary scale. It also indicates actions that were performed on scale's items.

The items with highest approval were "*I would like to visit Valparaíso again in the future*" (Loyalty), "*The experience met my expectations*", and "*I was satisfied with the experience*" (General Perception). The three items scored an average of 4.90. The item with lowest approval was "*It was a liberating experience*" (Emotions), that scored 3.33. Many participants indicated that the term "liberating" may be confusing; the item was eliminated. Items "*I will remember the emotions and sensations that I felt*", and "*I felt positive emotions in general*" (Emotions), had good approval; however, they were consider rather general, possibly confusing, and difficult to evaluate, and were therefore eliminated. (Perceived) safety was considered an emotion-related issue, and was moved from dimension "Services" to dimension "Emotions".

Items "*I participated in activities organized by local communities*", and "*The local community organizes activities open to visitors*" (Local Culture), were considered subjective, difficult to evaluate, and were removed. A tourist lack of participation in certain activities does not necessary mean that those activities are inexistent. A destination identity is not always fully related to its culture, that is why the item "*The identity of Valparaíso is remarkable*" was also eliminated.

Table 2. Quantitative evaluation of the preliminary scale.

Dimensions	Items	Averages	Std. Dev	Actions
Emotions	It was a liberating experience	3.33	1.32	Eliminate
	It was a unique experience	4.63	0.89	Keep
	It was a revitalizing experience, that took me out of monotony	4.35	0.80	Adapt
	I had fun	4.55	0.72	Keep
	I will remember the emotions and sensations that I felt	4.41	1.07	Eliminate
	I felt positive emotions in general	4.54	0.68	Eliminate
	I enjoyed the overall experience	4.63	0.61	Keep
	I will always remember this experience	3.94	1.20	Keep
Emotions (8 items)		*4.30*	*0.53*	
Local Culture	The relationship with the local community was nice	4.43	0.82	Adapt
	I experienced local traditions and customs	4.77	0.57	Keep
	I participated in activities organized by local communities	4.66	0.76	Eliminate
	The local community organizes activities open to visitors	4.03	1.38	Eliminate
	I got a good impression of the local community	4.57	0.77	Keep
	The local community is unique, and different from my own community	4.17	1.18	Adapt
	The local community was ready to help and provide information on Valparaíso	4.59	0.97	Keep
	The identity of Valparaíso is remarkable	4.51	0.97	Eliminate

(*continued*)

Table 2. (*continued*)

Dimensions	Items	Averages	Std. Dev	Actions
Local Culture (8 items)		*4.47*	*0.60*	
Authenticity of the Place	I learned new things	4.59	0.72	Adapt
	I appreciated the historic richness of Valparaíso	4.73	0.64	Adapt
	I appreciated the uniqueness of the funiculars ("elevators")	4.48	0.82	Adapt
	I appreciated the uniqueness of the trolleys	4.55	0.77	Adapt
	I appreciated the uniqueness and importance of the stairs for Valparaíso	4.50	0.82	Keep
	I appreciated the historical case of Valparaiso, as world heritage	4.72	0.58	Keep
	I appreciated the Valparaíso harbor and its commercial relevance	4.48	0.97	Adapt
	I appreciated the coast, the sea, and the associated services	4.34	0.80	Keep
	I appreciated the gastronomy of Valparaíso	4.51	0.77	Keep
	I appreciated Valparaíso's architecture	4.72	0.52	Keep
	I appreciated the variety of touristic attractions	4.47	0.94	Keep
	Valparaíso offers a significant cultural diversity	4.37	1.00	Keep
	Valparaíso's climate is pleasant	3.85	1.31	Keep
Authenticity of the Place (13 items)		*4.48*	*0.56*	
Entertainment	Guided tours are available	4.31	1.09	Adapt
	Cultural activities are freely available	4.50	0.90	Adapt

(*continued*)

Table 2. (*continued*)

Dimensions	Items	Averages	Std. Dev	Actions
	Valparaíso offers cultural attractions (e.g. galleries, cultural centers, museums)	4.57	0.86	Keep
	Valparaíso offers activities concerning its history	4.03	0.93	Eliminate
	I enjoyed participating in activities that Valparaíso offers	4.53	0.82	Keep
	I performed activities that I have never done before	4.23	1.01	Keep
	Valparaíso offers night entertainment attractions	4.07	1.17	Keep
	I enjoyed carnivals and/or festivals specific to Valparaíso	4.30	0.99	Eliminate
Entertainment (8 items)		*4.32*	*0.63*	
Services	Valparaíso offers diverse options of accommodations	4.41	1.02	Adapt
	Valparaíso offers diverse restaurants/places to eat	4.52	0.95	Adapt
	Valparaíso offers diverse leisure and relaxation services	4.34	1.01	Keep
	Public restrooms are available	3.93	1.44	Eliminate
	Medical and health services are available	4.38	1.05	Eliminate
	Valparaíso has public security services	4.31	1.11	Eliminate
	Valparaíso offers accessible tourist information services	4.41	1.02	Keep
	Tourist agents were friendly	4.41	1.02	Adapt
	Tourism service quality was as promised	4.48	1.02	Adapt
	Valparaíso has appropriate signaling for emergency procedures, as for tsunamis and earthquakes	4.48	1.02	Adapt

(*continued*)

Table 2. (*continued*)

Dimensions	Items	Averages	Std. Dev	Actions
	Secure areas for tsunamis and earthquakes are clearly indicated	4.45	1.09	Eliminate
Services (11 items)		*4.38*	*0.90*	
Post-pandemic Experience	I felt safe, without fear of COVID-19 contagion	4.73	0.83	Keep
	I felt that social distance measures where appropriate	4.67	0.92	Keep
	COVID-19 related safety measures where appropriately informed	4.57	1.01	Adapt
	COVID-19 related safety measures did not impede that my experience was enjoyable	4.60	0.97	Keep
Post-pandemic Experience (4 items)		*4.64*	*0.83*	
Loyalty	I would recommend Valparaíso as destination to other tourists	4.87	0.51	Keep
	I would like to visit Valparaíso again in the future	4.90	0.40	Keep
Loyalty (2 items)		*4.88*	*0.41*	
General Perception	The experience met my expectations	4.90	0.40	Keep
	I was satisfied with the experience	4.90	0.40	Keep
General Perception (2 items)		*4.90*	*0.40*	

All items of the dimension Authenticity of the Place were kept, some with slightly changed definitions. One new item was included: "*I discovered a mix of colors, sounds, smells and flavors typical for Valparaíso*", as suggested by participants.

Items "*Valparaíso offers activities concerning its history*", and "*I enjoyed carnivals and/or festivals specific to Valparaíso*" (Entertainment), were eliminated. Firstly, participants objected that history-related activities should be considered "entertainment". Secondly, carnivals/festivals can only be experienced in very specific seasons, and cannot be evaluated by all tourists. "*Valparaíso offers water sports*" was included as new item; nautical tourism has a great potential in Valparaíso, due to its location on the Pacific coast.

Dimension Services was subject to major changes. Several of its initial items were removed for being too general, or redundant: "*Public restrooms are available*", "*Medical and health services are available*", "*Valparaíso has public security services*", "*Secure areas for tsunamis and earthquakes are clearly indicated*". Participants suggested several new items instead, related to sustainability, inclusiveness, transportation, internet connection, among others.

Based on participants' comments, several items were adapted, clarifying their meaning and/or better focusing. All items of the dimensions Post-pandemic Experience, Loyalty, and General Perception had good approval rates, and were considered pertinent. The refined version of the scale has the same number of items as the initial one (56), but only 29 items were kept unchanged. Table 3 highlights the most important changes, synthetizing the eliminated and the new items. The full new version of the scale is presented in Table 5.

Table 3. Scale's refinement based on experts' opinion.

Dimensions	Eliminated items	New items
Emotions	It was a liberating experience I will remember the emotions and sensations that I felt I felt positive emotions in general	I felt safe
Local Culture	I participated in activities organized by local communities The local community organizes activities open to visitors The identity of Valparaíso is remarkable	None
Authenticity of the Place	None	I discovered a mix of colors, sounds, smells and flavors typical for Valparaíso
Entertainment	Valparaíso offers activities concerning its history I enjoyed carnivals and/or festivals specific to Valparaíso	Valparaíso offers water sports

(*continued*)

Table 3. (*continued*)

Dimensions	Eliminated items	New items
Services	Public restrooms are available Medical and health services are available Valparaíso has public security services Secure areas for tsunamis and earthquakes are clearly indicated	Valparaíso offers appropriate transportation Valparaíso offers good internet connection Digital information on Valparaíso and its attractions is available Valparaíso has appropriate touristic signaling Valparaíso is clean and well maintained Valparaíso is a sustainable destination Valparaíso is an inclusive destination I perceived professionalism and competence of the tourist staff I perceived a good value for money
Post-pandemic Experience	None	None
Loyalty	None	None
General Perception	None	None

2.8   Validating the Scale Through a Pilot Test

In order to check scale's reliability, we performed a pilot test that involved 20 participants, in early 2022. They were all tourist in Valparaíso. Participants were asked to evaluate all scale's items using a 7-point Likert scale (from 1 – strongly disagree, to 7 – strongly agree). All participants agreed that items are clearly stated, and easy to understand.

We used Cronbach's α test to check scale's reliability. Results are presented in Table 4. The scale has a good reliability (0.913), superior to the acceptable level of 0.700.

The highest α values were obtained for dimensions Post-pandemic Experience, and General Perception. The lowest values were obtained for Loyalty. Excepting Loyalty, all the others dimensions have Cronbach's α values higher than 0.700. When eliminating items, α values for dimensions does not improve significantly. In some cases, α values get slightly higher; however, differences are minors (in most cases less than 0.050), and the items are considered relevant, so they were kept unchanged: "*I felt safe*" (Emotions), "*I learned about the history of Valparaíso*", "*I appreciated Valparaíso's architecture*", "*Valparaíso's climate is pleasant*" (Authenticity of the Place), "*Valparaíso offers appropriate transportation*" (Services), and "*COVID-19 related safety measures did not impede that my experience was enjoyable*" (Post-pandemic Experience). On the contrary, when the following items are eliminated, Cronbach's α values for the associated

Table 4. Cronbach's α test for data collected in the pilot test.

Dimensions	Cronbach's α
Emotions	0.759
Local Culture	0.723
Authenticity of the Place	0.852
Entertainment	0.840
Services	0.732
Post-pandemic Experience	0.869
Loyalty	0.683
General Perception	0.906
Scale	*0.913*

dimensions get lower, and this is a validation that the items are relevant and have to be maintained: "*I enjoyed the overall experience*" (Emotions), "*The local community is unique*" (Local Culture), "*I appreciated the historical case of Valparaiso, as world heritage*" (Authenticity of the Place), "*I enjoyed participating in activities that Valparaíso offers*" (Entertainment), "*Digital information on Valparaíso and its attractions is available*" (Services), and "*I felt safe, without fear of COVID-19 contagion*" (Post-pandemic Experience).

Based on the result of the pilot test, we did not consider necessary to make new changes to the scale. The only change that we made was how the scale is applied in practice. Many participants in the pilot test indicates that evaluating items on a 7-point scale is quite difficult, so we decided to use a 5-point scale instead.

2.9 Applying the Scale: A Survey

The scale was used in a survey with 316 participants, all of them tourist that experienced Valparaíso as destination. We used the convenience sampling, and we collected data in April – May 2022. Most of the participants were Chileans (312 participants, 98.73%); only 4 were foreigners (1.27%). Gender balance was somehow more equilibrated: 198 participants were females (62.66%), 114 participants were males (36.07%); 1 participant indicates "other" as gender (0.32%), and 3 preferred to not discharge the information (0.95%).

Most of the participants belonged to the age group from 21 to 30 y/o, but all age groups were reasonably covered:

- Under 20: 41 participants (12.97%),
- From 21 to 30: 90 participants (28.48%),
- From 31 to 40: 65 participants (20.57%),
- From 41 to 50: 48 participants (15.19%),
- From 51 to 60: 46 participants (14.56%),

- From 61 or over: 26 participants (8.23%).

Most of the participants were employed (170 participants, 53.80%); 94 were students (29.75%), 26 were in charge of the domestic work (8.23%), 14 were retired (4.43), 5 were unemployed (1.58%), and 7 choose the option "other" when asked for their employment status (2.21%). 24 participants got a PhD or MSc degree (7.59%), 145 were college graduated or students (45.89%), and 147 did not possess a college degree (46.52%). It is significant that most of the participants (260, 82.28%) were visiting Valparaíso for the very first time.

Confirmatory factor analysis (CFA) was used to validate the scale, in order to (1) check the underlaying model, and (2) check if significant changes are necessary [34, 35]. We used the maximum likelihood for missing data, as some of the 316 observations were incomplete, and we processed data with STATA 17. The model has 8 factors (scale's dimensions) and 56 variables (scale's items).

All factorial loads are statistically significant at p-value = 0.000; all items are significant for their associated dimensions. Covariances between factors are all significant. The likelihood ratio Chi-Squared (χ^2) is 4040.283, which is significant (p-value = 0.000). The root mean squared error of approximation (RMSEA) is 0.075, which is considered acceptable. The incremental fit indices are lower than 0.900 (and lower than 0.950, as recommended lately): the comparative fit index (CFI) is 0.860, and the non-normed fit index (NNFI) is 0.868. Therefore, our model can still be improved.

Averages and standard deviations for all items are presented in Table 5.

Table 5. The scale for evaluating the post-pandemic tourist experience in Valparaíso, Chile.

Dimensions	Items	Average	Std. Dev
Emotions	It was a unique experience	3.64	1.14
	It was a revitalizing experience	3.62	1.20
	I had fun	3.96	1.15
	I felt safe	2.60	1.17
	I enjoyed the overall experience	3.82	1.14
	I will remember this experience	3.93	1.14
Emotions (6 items)		*3.59*	*1.00*
Local Culture	The local community was welcoming	3.58	1.13
	I learned local traditions and customs	3.38	1.24
	The local community is unique	3.50	1.16
	The local community was ready to help and provide information on Valparaíso	3.59	1.19
	I got a good impression on the local community	3.54	1.18

(continued)

Table 5. (*continued*)

Dimensions	Items	Average	Std. Dev
Local Culture (5 items)		*3.52*	*1.04*
Authenticity of the Place	I learned new things on Valparaíso	3.54	1.23
	I learned about the history of Valparaíso	3.45	1.30
	I appreciated the funiculars ("elevators") of Valparaíso	3.74	1.34
	I appreciated the trolleys of Valparaíso	3.74	1.37
	I appreciated the uniqueness and importance of the stairs for Valparaíso	3.82	1.27
	I appreciated the historical case of Valparaiso, as world heritage	3.79	1.28
	I appreciated the Valparaíso harbor and its relevance	3.89	1.23
	I appreciated the coast, the sea, and the associated services	3.92	1.25
	I appreciated the gastronomy of Valparaíso	3.77	1.26
	I discovered a mix of colors, sounds, smells and flavors typical for Valparaíso	3.85	1.24
	I appreciated Valparaíso's architecture	4.01	1.21
	Valparaiso offers a variety of touristic attractions	3.89	1.19
	Valparaíso offers a significant cultural diversity	3.90	1.22
	Valparaíso's climate is pleasant	3.87	1.17
Authenticity of the Place (14 items)		*3.81*	*1.06*
Entertainment	Good quality guided tours are available	3.04	1.21
	Various activities are freely available	3.60	1.22
	Valparaíso offers cultural attractions (e.g. galleries, cultural centers, museums)	3.77	1.21

(*continued*)

Table 5. (*continued*)

Dimensions	Items	Average	Std. Dev
	I enjoyed participating in activities that Valparaíso offers	3.59	1.23
	I performed activities that I have never done before	3.35	1.33
	Valparaíso offers water sports	3.04	1.32
	Valparaíso offers night entertainment attractions	3.67	1.30
Entertainment (7 items)		*3.49*	*1.11*
Services	I found accommodation that suits me	3.60	1.24
	I was surprised by the diversity of restaurants/places to eat	3.68	1.22
	Valparaíso offers appropriate transportation	3.47	1.21
	Valparaíso offers diverse leisure and relaxation services	3.50	1.25
	Valparaíso offers accessible tourist information services	3.15	1.27
	Valparaíso offers good internet connection	3.52	1.27
	Digital information on Valparaíso and its attractions is available	3.49	1.29
	Valparaíso has appropriate touristic signaling	3.28	1.25
	Valparaíso has appropriate signaling for tsunamis and earthquakes emergencies	3.55	1.28
	Valparaíso is clean and well maintained	2.25	1.31
	Valparaíso is a sustainable destination	2.91	1.32
	Valparaíso is an inclusive destination	2.85	1.36
	I perceived professionalism and competence of the tourist staff	3.26	1.30
	I perceived that the tourist staff was friendly	3.38	1.26
	Tourism service quality was as expected	3.39	1.25

(*continued*)

Table 5. (*continued*)

Dimensions	Items	Average	Std. Dev
	I perceived a good value for money	3.42	1.24
Services (16 items)		*3.30*	*1.01*
Post-pandemic Experience	I felt safe, without fear of COVID-19 contagion	2.91	1.26
	I felt that social distance measures where appropriate	2.83	1.23
	COVID-19 related safety measures where appropriate	3.12	1.25
	COVID-19 related safety measures did not impede that my experience was enjoyable	3.39	1.29
Post-pandemic Experience (4 items)		*3.07*	*1.13*
Loyalty	I would recommend Valparaíso as destination to other tourists	3.81	1.22
	I would like to visit Valparaíso again in the future	3.96	1.21
Loyalty (2 items)		*3.88*	*1.19*
General Perception	The experience met my expectations	3.70	1.18
	I was satisfied with the experience	3.74	1.18
General Perception (2 items)		*3.72*	*1.16*

Dimension Post-pandemic Experience scored lowest (3.07), almost identical to the central point of the scale. Two of its items got low scores: "*I felt that social distance measures where appropriate*" (2.83), and "*I felt safe, without fear of COVID-19 contagion*" (2.91). This confirms the importance of evaluating pandemic-related issues. Three items of the dimension Services got low scores: "*Valparaíso is clean and well maintained*" (2.25), "*Valparaíso is an inclusive destination*" (2.85), and "*Valparaíso is a sustainable destination*" (2.91). All three highlight important issues to be attended by Valparaíso's authorities, as well as safety, which also got one of the lowest scores: "*I felt safe*" scored only 2.60.

It is remarkable that dimension Authenticity of the Place got the highest score (3.81). This stresses the potential of Valparaíso as destination. Almost all dimension's items got scores higher than 3.70. Items that stand out are: "*I appreciated Valparaíso's architecture*" (4.01), "*I appreciated the coast, the sea, and the associated services*" (3.92), "*Valparaíso offers a significant cultural diversity*" (3.90) "*I appreciated the Valparaíso harbor and its relevance*" (3.89), and "*Valparaíso offers a variety of touristic attractions*" (3.89). Overall, emotions were positive: "*I had fun*" (3.96), and "*I will remember this experience*" (3.93). Dimension Loyalty scored 3.88, and item "*I would like to visit*"

Valparaíso again in the future" got a remarkably high score (3.96). Dimension General Perception also got a favorable score (3.72).

3 Conclusions and Future Work

TX evaluation is challenging as TX is multidimensional, subjective, and highly personal. One of the most common TX evaluation artifacts are scales. We developed a scale to evaluate TX in Valparaíso, Chile. It includes 56 items, grouped in 8 dimensions: emotions (6 items), local culture (5 items), authenticity of the place (14 items), entertainment (7 items), services (16 items), post-pandemic experience (4 items), loyalty (2 items), and general perception (2 items). Our scale attends general TX factors, Valparaíso's specificity as destination, and also the post-pandemic context.

The scale was initially developed based on literature. It was then evaluated by 30 tourism experts/scholars/professional, and was refined based on their feedback; 12 items have been replaced, 16 items were adapted, and 28 items were kept unchanged. Scale's reliability was checked in a pilot study involving 20 participants.

The scale was later used in a survey that included 316 participants. Confirmatory factor analysis showed that all items are significant for their associated dimensions, and covariances between factors are all significant. However, the incremental fit indices indicate that the underlying model of our scale can be further improved.

Survey's results highlight the importance of pandemic-related issues. They indicate the potential of Valparaíso as destination, especially based on its architecture, coast, harbor, cultural diversity, and the variety of touristic attractions. They also point out major issues that should be addressed in order to improve TX in Valparaíso: safety, cleanliness, sustainability, and inclusiveness.

As future work, we will check the underlaying model of our scale, based on structural equation modeling. We intend to use the scale in future surveys.

Acknowledgments. This project was financed by Dirección General de Investigación of Universidad de Playa Ancha, Chile (Concurso Regular 2020, code HUM 04-2122). We appreciate the help of Leslie Márquez and Patricia González, which collected data as part of their duties as technical staff in the above-mentioned project. They also used data in their undergraduate thesis, under the supervision of Dr. Virginica Rusu. Data have not been published previously, and their thesis is only available at Universidad de Playa Ancha, Valparaíso, Chile.

References

1. Laming, C., Mason, K.: Customer experience - an analysis of the concept and its performance in airline brands. Res. Transp. Bus. Manag. **10**, 15–25 (2014)
2. Lewis, J.R.: Usability: lessons learned... and yet to be learned. Int. J. Hum.-Comput. Interact. **30**(9), 663–684 (2014)
3. Rusu, V., Rusu, C., Botella, F., Quiñones, D.: Customer experience: is this the ultimate experience? In: Interacción 2018, Proceedings of the XIX International Conference on Human Computer Interaction. ACM (2018)

4. Rusu, V., Rusu, C., Botella, F., Quiñones, D., Bascur, C., Rusu, V.Z.: Customer experience: a bridge between service science and human-computer interaction. In: Ahram, T., Karwowski, W., Pickl, S., Taiar, R. (eds.) IHSED 2019. AISC, vol. 1026, pp. 385–390. Springer, Cham (2020). https://doi.org/10.1007/978-3-030-27928-8_59

5. Rusu, V., Márquez, L., Gonzalez, P., Rusu, C.: Evaluating the post-pandemic tourist experience: a scale for tourist experience in Valparaíso, Chile. In: Meiselwitz, G. (ed.) SCSM 2022. LNCS, vol. 13316, pp. 331–342. Springer, Cham (2022). https://doi.org/10.1007/978-3-031-05064-0_25

6. Rusu, V., Márquez, L., González, P., Rusu, C.: Desarrollo de una escala de evaluación de la experiencia del turista post-pandemia en Valparaíso: validación de la escala en base al juicio de expertos. In: IX Congreso Latinoamericano de investigación turística, Libro de resúmenes extendidos, pp. 10–14. CLAIT, Valdivia, Chile (2022)

7. ISO 9241-210. Ergonomics of Human-system Interaction—Part 210: Human-centered Design for Interactive Systems. International Organization for Standardization (2010)

8. Rusu, C., Rusu, V., Quiñones, D., Roncagliolo, S., Rusu, V.Z.: Evaluating online travel agencies' usability: what heuristics should we use? In: Meiselwitz, G. (ed.) SCSM 2018. LNCS, vol. 10913, pp. 121–130. Springer, Cham (2018). https://doi.org/10.1007/978-3-319-91521-0_10

9. Rusu, V., Rusu, C., Quiñones, D., Botella, F., Roncagliolo, S., Rusu, V.Z.: On-line travel agencies' usability: evaluator experience. In: Meiselwitz, G. (ed.) SCSM 2019. LNCS, vol. 11579, pp. 452–463. Springer, Cham (2019). https://doi.org/10.1007/978-3-030-21905-5_35

10. Díaz, J., et al.: Website transformation of a Latin American airline: effects of cultural aspects and user experience on business performance. IEEE LA Trans. **17**(5), 766–774 (2019)

11. Rusu, C., Rusu, V.Z., Muñoz, P., Rusu, V., Roncagliolo, S., Quiñones, D.: On user experience in virtual museums. In: Meiselwitz, G. (ed.) SCSM 2017. LNCS, vol. 10282, pp. 127–136. Springer, Cham (2017). https://doi.org/10.1007/978-3-319-58559-8_12

12. Rusu, V.Z., Quiñones, D., Rusu, C., Cáceres, P., Rusu, V., Roncagliolo, S.: Approaches on user experience assessment: user tests, communicability and psychometrics. In: Meiselwitz, G. (ed.) SCSM 2018, LNCS, vol. 10913, pp. 97–111. Springer, Cham (2018). https://doi.org/10.1007/978-3-319-91521-0_8

13. Rusu, V.Z., Rusu, C., Cáceres, P., Rusu, V., Quiñones, D., Muñoz, P.: On user experience evaluation: combining user tests and psychometrics. In: Karwowski, W., Ahram T. (eds.) IHSI 2018. AISC, vol. 722, pp. 626–632, Springer, Cham (2018). https://doi.org/10.1007/978-3-319-73888-8_97

14. Delgado, D., Zamora, D., Quiñones, D., Rusu, C., Roncagliolo, S., Rusu, V.: User experience heuristics for national park websites. In: Meiselwitz, G. (ed.) SCSM 2020. LNCS, vol. 12195, pp. 194–204. Springer, Cham (2020). https://doi.org/10.1007/978-3-030-49576-3_14

15. Quiñones, D., Rusu, C., Rusu, V.: A methodology to develop usability/user experience heuristics. Comput. Stand. Interfaces **59**, 109–129 (2018)

16. Quiñones, D., Rusu, C.: Applying a methodology to develop user experience heuristics. Comput. Stand. Interfaces **66**, 103345 (2019)

17. Rusu, V., et al.: Assessing the customer experience based on quantitative data: virtual travel agencies. In: Marcus, A. (ed.) DUXU 2016. LNCS, vol. 9746, pp. 499–508. Springer, Cham (2016). https://doi.org/10.1007/978-3-319-40409-7_47

18. Rusu, V., Rusu, C., Guzmán, D., Roncagliolo, S., Quiñones, D.: Online travel agencies as social media: analyzing customers' opinions. In: Meiselwitz, G. (ed.) SCSM 2017. LNCS, vol. 10282, pp. 200–209. Springer, Cham (2017). https://doi.org/10.1007/978-3-319-58559-8_17

19. Rusu, V., Rusu, C., Quiñones, D., Roncagliolo, S., Carvajal, V., Muñoz, M.: Customer experience in Valparaiso hostels: analyzing tourists' opinions. In: Meiselwitz, G. (ed.) SCSM 2020.

LNCS, vol. 12195, pp. 226–235. Springer, Cham (2020). https://doi.org/10.1007/978-3-030-49576-3_17

20. Godovykh, M., Tasci, A.: Customer experience in tourism: a review of definitions, components, and measurements. Tour. Manag. Pers. **35**, 100694 (2020)

21. Tung, V., Ritchie, J.R: Exploring the essence of memorable tourism experiences. Ann. of Tour. Res. **38**(4), 1367–1386 (2011)

22. Kim, J., Ritchie, J., McCormick, B.: Development of a scale to measure memorable tourism experiences. J. of Trav. Res. **51**(1), 12–25 (2010)

23. Ali, F., Hussain, K., Ragavan, N.: Memorable customer experience: examining the effects of customers experience on memories and loyalty in Malaysian resort hotels. Proc. – Soc. and Beh. Sci. **144**, 273–279 (2014)

24. Kim, J.: The antecedents of memorable tourism experiences: the development of a scale to measure the destination attributes associated with memorable experiences. Tour. Manag. **44**, 34–45 (2014)

25. Chen, H., Rahman, I.: Cultural tourism: an analysis of engagement, cultural contact, memorable tourism experience and destination loyalty. Tour. Manag. Persp. **26**, 153–163 (2018)

26. Coelho, M., Gosling, M.: Memorable tourism experience (MTE): scale proposal and test. Tour. Manag. Stud. **14**(4), 15–24 (2018)

27. Lončarić, D., Dlačić, J., Perišić, M.: What makes summer vacation experience memorable? An empirical study from Croatia. Zbornik Veleučilišta u Rijeci. **6**(1), 67–80 (2018)

28. Gallarza, M., Gil, I.: La investigación conceptual sobre valor percibido en la experiencia turística. Propuesta de un Modelo Verbal Gráfico. Estudios turísticos. **174**, 7–32 (2007)

29. Martín-Ruiz, D., Castellanos-Verdugo, M., Oviedo-García, M.: A visitors' evaluation index for a visit to an archaeological site. Tour. Manag. **31**, 590–596 (2010)

30. Lu, L., Chi, C., Liu, Y.: Authenticity, involvement, and image: evaluating tourist experiences at historic districts. Tour. Manag. **50**, 85–96 (2015)

31. Sarra, A., Di Zio, S., Cappucci, M.: A quantitative valuation of tourist experience in Lisbon. Ann. of Tour. Res. **53**, 1–16 (2015)

32. Saayman, M., Li, G., Uysal, M., Song, H.: Tourist satisfaction and subjective well-being: an index approach. Int. J. Tourism Res. **20**, 388–399 (2018)

33. Torres, P., Baez, S.: Tourist experience measurement in Quito city. Rev. Bras. Pesq. Tur. São Paulo **12**(1), 133–156 (2018)

34. Steenkamp, J.B., van Trijp, H.: The use of LISREL in validating marketing construct. Int. J. Res. Mark. **8**(4), 283–299 (1991)

35. Hair, J., Anderson, R., Tatham, R., Black, W.: Análisis Multivariante, 5th edn. Prentice Hall Iberia, Madrid (1999)

Making Assumptions Transparent: Iterative Exploratory Modeling as a Stepping Stone for Agent-Based Model Development

Leonard Stellbrink$^{(\boxtimes)}$ (ID), Lilian Kojan (ID), and André Calero Valdez (ID)

University of Lübeck, Institute for Multimedia and Interactive Systems,
Ratzeburger Allee 160, Lübeck, Germany
{leonard.stellbrink,lilian.kojan,andre.calerovaldez}@uni-luebeck.de
https://www.imis.uni-luebeck.de/en

Abstract. In the case of infectious diseases, the interaction between human behavior and disease dynamics can greatly influence the resulting outbreak size and characteristics. People behave differently depending on the information available, so the influence of local and global information about a virus outbreak is studied. Agent-based modeling provides a tool for representing individual behavioral differences, but its calibration is complex. Several factors influence model results, such as the network structure representing social relationships. Using an exploratory methodology called "Iterative Exploratory Modeling", the assumptions used for a particular agent-based model are tested and verified, demonstrating the benefits of said approach. While genuine disease dynamics can be achieved with the used graph based on the Barabási-Albert model, the specific graph attributes have a much larger impact on the results than the local and global information. This emphasizes the need for testing assumptions at a fundamental level, which "Iterative Exploratory Modeling" can provide.

Keywords: Information · Dynamics · Simulation · Agent-Based Modeling · Multi-Agent Simulation · Epidemiology · Social Networks · Graphs · Network Aspects · Social Influence · Local vs. Global Information

1 Introduction

The impact of pandemics on human life has become apparent in recent years. In particular, the interdependence of human behavior and disease dynamics has become a research focus. Sometimes referred to as "coupled contagion" [12], individual protective behavior is a function of risk perception and thus influences the spread of disease over time. In addition, the state of the disease spread also influences risk perception, creating a feedback loop. This effect is often abstracted in traditional modeling, especially compartmental modeling, leading to an incomplete representation of some driving forces behind disease spread.

Agent-based modeling is useful for this coupling of behavior and disease spread. The heterogeneity of the agents in a model allows behavioral changes to occur based on the effect of receiving information. This paper uses an exploratory approach called "*Iterative Exploratory Modeling (IEM)*" to understand the underlying assumptions that generate different model results. Therefore, *IEM* aims to test the assumptions' validity, especially regarding the graph used to represent the social network. *IEM* makes the assumptions transparent, showing eventual dependencies on the model results. The goal is to transform the process of agent-based modeling into a method that is easier to understand.

2   Preliminaries

One of the best analogies to the principle of agent-based modeling comes from biology, from the field of swarm intelligence. Here the basic insight is as follows:

> "Complex collective behavior can emerge from individuals following simple rules. [5, p. 110]"

This paper uses the terms *agent-based modeling*, and *agent-based model*, *ABM* is used as a shorthand for both terms. An *agent-based modeling* is a simulation involving many agents' interactions. Simulation, in this case, refers to the concrete execution of the code in which the modeling is implemented, while modeling refers to the conceptual level. This interaction follows defined rules; the agents and the space they interact in have defined properties. The goal of the simulation is to study the outcome of the interaction of the agents based on these defined rules and constraints.

2.1   Use Cases of *ABM*

ABM can be used to pursue entirely different goals. The purpose of modeling is not always to predict phenomena or values; *ABM* can also describe these phenomena or explain their mechanisms. Wilensky and Rand define eight different use cases for *ABM*:

> say(1) description, (2) explanation, (3) experimentation, (4) providing sources of analogy, (5) communication/education, (6) providing focal objects or centerpieces for scientific dialogue, (7) as thought experiments, and (8) prediction [20, p. 28].

An experimental approach can facilitate the understanding of a complex system. If the model is built according to the known properties, new parameters and rules can be easily inserted, whose influence can be successively determined by analyzing the simulation results [20]. Thus, one of the conclusions from the previous paragraphs is that even very simple models can yield surprising results. Especially in the social sciences, the goal of an *ABM* is often an understanding of the system's interrelationships and the parameters' effects. Therefore a reality-based representation is less important [6,13].

2.2   Epidemiological Basics

The theoretical foundations of epidemiology are highly relevant to modeling the spread of an epidemic. The importance of this area of research has become apparent to the general public in recent years, as the COVID-19 pandemic has caused drastic changes in many areas of personal and public life.

Epidemiology and social sciences are usually considered separately, but it is crucial to consider and use findings from both fields when studying pandemics. The example of the COVID-19 pandemic shows the substantial impact on social science issues such as individual protective behavior or social solidarity. Even before that, infectious diseases such as HIV have always had and continue to have a major impact on global sociopolitical issues [11]. Demographic parameters also play an essential role, as the risk of contracting the disease may depend not only on genetic factors but also, for example, on age [17].

This paper uses a basic Susceptible-Infected-Recovered (*SIR*) model. The key indicators that are discussed in this paper are incidence and prevalence. The maxima of the respective numbers of persons who can be assigned to a specific condition according to the *SIR* model are suitable as other critical figures for investigating the spread of an epidemic. That is, the maximum of infected persons and the maximum incidence are apparent values to classify the epidemic. Furthermore, the duration of the infection period in the case of a temporally limited spread of infectious disease and the proportion of persons who were never infected after the end of the epidemic are meaningful [18].

2.3   Social Networks

The social network, i.e., the network of interpersonal relationships of a human being, can be represented by graphs. Typical approaches include random networks produced by generative models such as the Erdős-Rényi model and so-called *small world* networks generated by the Watts-Strogatz model. Scale-free networks can be built using the Barabási-Albert model, and the resulting graphs are referred to in this paper as *BA* graphs. The latter has been established for mapping *Social Networks* in the context of epidemiology because they resemble many real-world networks. An example is the study of the number of sexual partners, where Liljeros represents the mechanism of a scale-free network [2,9,15,16]. However, mapping a *social network* by a *BA* graph is also criticized because some assumptions are too simple. Moreover, Jin and Yu also note that most networks are weighted in reality, which is not valid for any of the presented graphs [14,19]. With *IEM*, I aim to make the influence of these assumptions more apparent.

These networks are created iteratively in the case of the *BA* graph, following a principle of *preferential attachment* that is often described as "the rich get richer" [16]. Thus, the graph starts with a certain number of nodes with connections (edges) between them, to which new nodes are added. The existing node with the most edges has the highest probability of forming edges with the newly added nodes. The result is a graph in which a few nodes have a very high number of edges, but most nodes have very few edges. Thus, a scale-free network also exhibits the property that defines *small world* networks, namely a small number of steps required to move from node to node, starting from a starting node to any other node.

In epidemiology, this means that scale-free networks such as the *BA* graph show a very rapid spread of infectious diseases - but this also makes them more sensitive to isolating the few nodes that cause many infections. These nodes thus correspond to the "super-spreaders" that were also a problem during the COVID-19 pandemic [3,15,16].

2.4   Research Question and Assumptions

The concept of *Iterative Exploratory Modeling*, introduced in the next chapter, does not involve traditional research questions from which I derive testable hypotheses. Instead, I subsume the focus of the investigation under this more open research question:

> How do behavior changes due to information gain affect the overall epidemiological picture?

The focus here is on the impact of modeled parameters on infection incidence. Specifically, information about the epidemic situation should induce a change in agents' behavior, and I will examine the extent of different levels of risk reduction. This information can be at the global level (equivalent to information from official sources such as government agencies or the media) or at the local level (through information exchange with other agents or using a contact tracing app). Moreover, the impact of vaccination effectiveness and isolation will be analyzed.

As described above, the formulation of assumptions instead of hypotheses could be more useful. Therefore, I will test two basic assumptions.

The first of these is

> *An increase in the number of infections leads to a behavior of minimizing the risk of individual people.*

The second reads:

> *Risk minimization of individual agents reduces the spread of the epidemic and decreases its ultimate magnitude.*

3   Iterative Exploratory Modeling

I follow an unconventional and open approach called *Iterative Exploratory Modeling* in this paper. Wilensky and Rand define *Exploratory Modeling* as the second overarching category of modeling [20]. This method is an advantage of agent-based modeling because it allows a model to be built to explain observed phenomena. I create a model from initially chosen parameters, the results of this model are analyzed, and I progressively approximate the model to the observed phenomenon.

I explicitly extend this concept by an iterative approach called *Iterative Exploratory Modeling*. It represents a partially cyclical process in which I make basic assumptions, which are not changed, and from which I generate a model. This model then produces results through simulation, which are analyzed to discover emergent phenomena. I extend the model progressively and then re-examine the results (see Fig. 1). I do not change the original assumptions, but the model and the parameters used can be modified. Parameters may also be added or removed. This process continues, ideally, until emergent behavior is discovered.

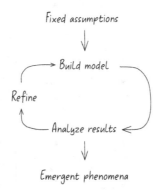

Fig. 1. Iterative Exploratory Modeling

3.1 Model

I will now demonstrate the Iterative Exploratory Modeling approach using the model I introduced in the previous chapter. Fixed assumptions are:

- Individual agents
- Graph as space
- *SIR* model of certain complexity

These three main assumptions establish the following details: Agents represent individuals with specific attributes that may vary from person to person. These agents are located in a graph representing the *social network* of individuals. Through a *SIR* model described in Sect. 2.2, I model the infection event where there are at least three states *Susceptible, Infected,* and *Recovered.* An agent can only be in one of these states at a time. The agents can interact with each other and behave dynamically.

The basis for the agent-based model is the framework *Agents.jl*, available for the programming language Julia [4,8]. For this work, I use Julia v1.5.4 and Agents.jl v4.5.6. The advantage of this framework is the ease of use, but the high performance compared to other frameworks is also highlighted [1].

There are also three components to the basic structure of *ABM*. The concrete model has properties that partly determine the model's functioning or are used to collect the results. The agents, which are part of the model and are located in the space, also have properties, but these only affect the individual agent. Finally, the space has properties that define the type of space and its concrete nature. The Fig. 2 overviews the relationships between the components and their properties.

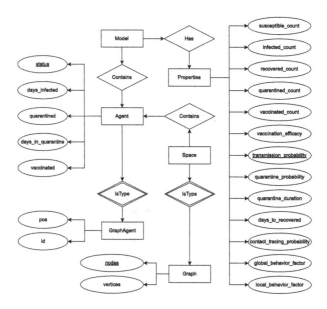

Fig. 2. Entity relationship diagram of the model used. It shows the components of the model and their properties, as well as the relationships among them.

In the *ABM* presented here, the configuration defines the fixed properties of the model and the default parameters. These are the total number of agents (which corresponds to the number of nodes in the graph), a parameter defining the *Preferential Attachment* used to create the *BA* graph, the number of steps (days) for which the model should be simulated, and the default parameters.

I use these default values unless other values or ranges are defined in the list of parameters. They are partly based on the chosen maximum values for the parameter ranges investigated in this work and partly on a realistic assumption. For example, I assume an isolation period of seven days and an infection period of 14 days can be assumed. The transmission probability, on the other hand, is chosen intuitively and then adjusted to a realistic spread by approximating the *SIR* model. To reiterate, the focus of this paper is to demonstrate the use of *Iterative Exploratory Modeling*, meaning that realistic parameter values are not always needed. Instead, the idea is to test the validity of these intuitive assumptions.

I approximate vaccine effectiveness to be 80% based on the average effectiveness of all COVID-19 vaccines relative to the delta variant. The probability of contact tracing is also adjusted to a realistic number based on the number of devices on which the application is installed. The values for the local and global behavioral factors are based on the assumption that infecting all people within a person's radius will cause them to change their behavior, ultimately halving the risk of infection. The global behavioral factor assumes that even if the entire population is infected, the risk of infection is reduced by no more than 25%. I make this assumption intuitively and discuss the implications of this assumption in Sect. 4.1.

The values for these are:

- Total number of agents (number of nodes): 1000
- Number of connected nodes and new connections a newly added node has: 3
- Number of steps (days): 150
- Isolation duration: 7 days
- Vaccine effectiveness: 80%.
- Transmission probability: 20%.
- Probability of contact tracing: 50%.
- Isolation probability: 0%.
- Duration of infection/number of days until transition to *Recovered*: 14
- Local Behavioral Factor: 0.5
- Global Behavioral Factor: 0.25

I define the effectiveness of the vaccination by *vaccination_efficacy*, which can take values between 0 and 100 (%). This corresponds to a reduction of the probability of transmission by this percentage. I define the transmission probability of the infectious disease by *transmission_probability*. This value can range from 0 to 1 and is the factor used to model the risk of infection. The *quarantine_probability* property defines the probability that an infected agent will be quarantined and can range from 0 to 100 (%). Due to a terminology error, I defined this parameter as quarantine. The correct value is "isolation". I perform the check to see if an agent goes into isolation each day the agent is infected. This increases the probability of an agent going into isolation from day to day. I intend this modeling to reflect that infection is usually not detected immediately but may be detected several days after the initial infection. In some instances may never be detected. Thus, assuming a defined isolation probability of 10%, the total probability of an agent going into isolation is calculated to be approximately 80% for an infection period of 14 days. *quarantine_duration* denotes the duration of isolation, *days_to_recovered* the duration of infection or the number of days after which an agent changes from *infected* to *recovered*.

To represent behavioral changes, two factors represent the reduction in risk of infection due to increased hygiene measures or social distancing. These factors can take values between 0 and 1, with 1 representing a complete reduction in the risk of infection. Specifically, the global behavioral factor refers to the mechanism by which increasing numbers of infections among the total number of agents leads to behavior that minimizes the risk of individual agents. I define the number of infections among the total number of agents as global information intended to represent, for example, media reports or notifications by authorities. The local information, which influences the local behavior factor, is defined as the number of infections in the agent's neighborhood. Here, the agent's neighborhood denotes all neighbors, i.e., directly connected nodes, that the agent has according to the *social network* modeled with a *BA* graph. However, to represent that an individual agent is unaware of every infection of its neighbors, I define a probability called *Contact Tracing Probability*. This determines the fraction of infections in its neighborhood the agent is informed about. Conceptually, I model this approach using a contact tracing app, such as the "Corona-Warn-App". The probability that the agent's neighbors use this app results in a fraction of neighbors whose infection the agent is informed about. Thus, this parameter directly affects the Local Behavioral Factor and can also be considered a factor for the strength of the effect of local information. Therefore, if a local behavior factor of 0.5 would mean a halving of the risk of infection for a *Contact Tracing Probability* of 100%, this would only mean a 25% reduction in risk for a *Contact Tracing Probability* of 50%.

The parameter ranges studied in this paper are as follows:

- Vaccination Efficacy: 70%, 80%, and 90%.
- Isolation Probability: 0 to 10% in 2.5% increments.
- Contact Tracing Probability: 0 to 100% in 10% increments.
- Local Behavior Factor: 0 to 0.5 in increments of 0.1
- Global Behavior Factor: 0 to 0.25 in 0.05 increments

After defining the parameters to be simulated, I initialize the model with the specified configuration and the chosen parameters. Here the graph representing the *social network* is created, where an agent is assigned to each node in a second step, leading to the nodes representing the agents. Exactly one agent with the state *Infected* is always inserted into the graph at the node with the highest node degree. This node has the most connections to other nodes, leading to a fast infection spread. I also chose this step to guarantee the spread of the infectious disease since if the number of neighbors is low or the agents have no neighbors, the spread may die after a very short time or never spread. The nodes with no neighbors represent individuals who live in complete isolation and, therefore, can never be affected by the infection.

4 Summary of Results and Discussion

With the default parameters, a reasonable representation of an epidemic is achieved by the implemented *SIR* model; the trajectory of infection numbers corresponds to the typical trajectories given in the literature. Adding vaccination to the *SIR* model increases the sophistication of the model, but the effect of different levels of vaccination effectiveness is small. Adding isolation adds a parameter to the model with a substantial impact on infection spread.

Certain key figures and parameters are abbreviated as follows:

- *Susceptible Fraction Remaining (SFR)*: Proportion of agents with *Susceptible* status at the endpoint of the simulation, equal to the proportion of agents never infected.
- *First to Last Infected (FTLI)*: Number of time steps between the first and last time an agent exhibited the *Infected* status, this maps the'width' of the infection curve.
- *Day of maximum Incidence (DomInc)*: Time step with the highest incidence
- *Day of maximum Infected (DomInf)*: Time step with maximum number of agents with *Infected* status.

The effect of isolation probability is most evident in the number of maximum infected agents and the proportion of agents that were never infected at the end of the simulation (*SFR*). Increasing the isolation probability results in a large decrease in these metrics. Increasing the *Contact Tracing Probability* leads to a reduction in the size of the epidemic in the form of a reduction in the maximum number of infected or an increase in the proportion of agents never infected at the end of the simulation. This effect is evident when considered without isolation, but it is a weaker reduction than for isolation probability. A higher *Contact Tracing Probability* at the maximum local behavior factor leads to a significant decrease in the maximum number of infected at low isolation probabilities. However, as the isolation probability increases, this effect diminishes because it is masked by the significant influence of the isolation probability. The local behavioral factor leads to a weak reduction in the size of the epidemic as a function of the *Contact Tracing Probability*, which is not as strongly influenced by the isolation probability. The global behavioral factor leads to a very weak reduction even without isolation. The effect of all parameters on the metrics *FTLI*, as well as *DomInf* and *DomInc* is very small or non-existent. These results are discussed in the next section.

4.1 Discussion

In this section, I will first discuss the issues arising from the specific model I implemented. I will then discuss how these issues relate to the Iterative Exploratory Modeling approach.

One of the issues found in retrospect is that an insufficient implementation of vaccination leads to low immunization influence on the model results. There is a fixed probability that agents can enter the *Vaccinated* state at each time step. This results in a linear trend for the time period presented here. At the time of maximum infection, the proportion vaccinated is approximately equal to the proportion infected. At this time, only about a quarter of the agents are protected by vaccination, which explains the weak effect. *IEM* has two benefits here: For one, the model in its current state demonstrates the considerable influence of the protection granted by vaccination on disease transmission which is in itself a key result. If I take the IEM approach further, I could adjust the vaccination implementation and compare model results to the previous state.

Another key finding of this exploratory approach is the strong influence of the graph used to represent the social network. One of the implications of this finding is that isolation strongly influences the model results. The argument is that due to the small number of highly connected nodes, it is sufficient for one or more of these nodes to become isolated and significantly hinder the spread of the disease. Due to the high variation between runs as a result of the different graphs, this emphasizes the need for calibration and batch runs. Another possibility would be to keep the graph used for simulation fixed.

An additional problem with scale-free graphs is the lack of homophily, which can significantly affect network clustering and the disease dynamics. Another problem is that static networks cannot represent the dynamic processes in human relationships, such as forming and terminating connections [15,18]. Therefore, the *IEM* approach allowed me to discover an influence on model mechanics that was also discussed by [15,18].

The type of graph used to map the social network significantly impacts the spread of the virus. *FTLI* represents the number of steps between the first and the last infected agent, so it also describes the "duration" of the spread. The spread of the virus in the concrete *BA* graph may always be very uniform. That is, the maximum number of infected and therefore *SFR* is independent of the 'duration' of the infection period. Even if more agents are infected, the virus does not spread 'faster' than if only a few agents are infected. This may be due to the *small world* properties of the *BA* graph. Also, the small size of the graph used may have unintended consequences. With a relatively small number of agents (1000) and a relatively small average path length, propagation within the chart might be very uniform, regardless of the number of infected agents. This effect could be further analyzed by increasing the number of agents or by examining the properties of the graph more closely.

Because of its implementation, the *Contact Tracing Probability* is, in fact, only a reinforcement factor for the local behavioral factor. With a *Contact Tracing Probability* of 0%, the local behavior factor does not affect reducing the transmission probability; with a *Contact Tracing Probability* of 100%, it has a significant effect. This explains the dependence of the two values. The influence on the number of infections can be explained by the fact that the local behavior factor of 0.5 is less limited upwards than, e.g., the global behavior factor of 0.25. In addition, the local behavior factor is related to infections near the agent. There, the entire perimeter can be infected proportionally faster. The global behavior factor, associated with the number of infected people in the total number of agents, is usually lower. The strong influence of these two effects on the metric shown is due to their interaction.

The small effect of the global behavior factor can be explained by analogy with the strong impact of the local behavior factor. On the one hand, the maximum value of the global behavior factor is limited to 0.25, i.e., it can only reduce the risk of infection by 25%. In addition, this effect still depends on the proportion of infected people, which rarely exceeds 50%. In the best case, the transmission probability is reduced by 12.5%. Since the ratio of infected persons is typically closer to 25%, the small effect due to the definition is obvious.

4.2 Benefits of Simple Models

ABM are also suitable as an introduction to a complex topic because of their explicit modeling of parameters. One perspective on this model, not only because of the approach of *Iterative Exploratory Modeling* (defined in Sect. 3, is to see it as a starting point for the investigation of a phenomenon. Therefore, if discovered, inconsistencies or methodological errors are always an opportunity to improve the existing model. This is especially true in the iterative context of Iterative Exploratory Modeling, where this work can be a valuable starting point for further investigation. Another insight from Sect. 2 is that even simple models can produce interesting results. Thus, increasing the complexity of the model is no guarantee that the results will be more relevant. Therefore, it should be mentioned here that "simple" is not necessarily "bad".

In this sense, the requirement that an *ABM* should always add value for application in the real world is fulfilled [7]. At least if this added value, as according to Epstein and Bruch&Atwell, also lies in reviewing the assumptions and simplifications underlying a model, raising new questions, working out ambiguities, and highlighting advantages and disadvantages of these aspects [6,10].

4.3 Verification of Assumptions

The basic assumptions of the model concern the representation of *Social Networks* as *BA* graphs, the simplification of behavioral changes as a direct reduction of the transmission probability, and the representation of agents as nodes, as well as the restriction of the *SIR* model to a very simple implementation.

The model's representation of typical *SIR* curves, described in Sect. 4, confirms the first assumption. Thus, *BA* graphs are suitable for representing *Social Networks* in the context of an *ABM* model integrated with an *SIR* model. However, it should be emphasized that the properties of the graph significantly impact the results of the *ABM*. Therefore, one of the most important findings of this work is the importance of studying the influence of the graph used on the *ABM*. The precise definition of the properties of the graph contributes significantly to the results of the *ABM*. The second assumption that the effect of behavioral changes can be directly implemented as a reduction in transmission probability must be viewed critically. Although it was found that the second assumption was confirmed, the influence of the psychological process in the background is not represented in this way. Perhaps a better representation of human behavior by a simple behavioral model is needed here. The representation of agents as nodes and that of the simple *SIR* model, at least to achieve a qualitative similarity of *SIR* numbers to observed data, can be interpreted as permissible based on the results.

5 Outlook and Further Work

Further iteration steps, which are conceivable in the context of *Iterative Exploratory Modeling*, but which I could not implement in this work, are presented here.

5.1   Further Iteration Steps

Additional attributes could be added to the agents to achieve more realistic heterogeneity. So far, this is only represented by probabilistic behavior, which has drawbacks. An age-dependent transmission probability could be introduced, or similar to Kitchovitch and Liò, a perception of perceived risk [15]. This could be a good guideline for implementing more complex behavior. This behavior could also be made dependent on the individual characteristics of the agent, which would allow a complete mapping of a behavioral change. This behavior could be adapted and influenced by interaction with other agents. The interaction could be modeled by building a perceptual model that stores an interaction history and uses it to adjust the properties of the agents. This perceptual model would also be a step towards implementing deterministic behavior. Another iterative step could be to implement a spatial model that better represents specific effects of infection risk and daily life. A spatial model would also expand the possibilities for interaction between agents. In addition, simulation steps could be defined on a smaller scale to allow for more dynamic processes. Finally, an adaptation of the *SIRV* model could be considered to accurately model the willingness to vaccinate, which increases with an increasing number of infections or certain behaviors. Finally, the possibility of re-infection with the virus could be included.

5.2   Outlook

The main result of this work is to highlight the validity of the assumptions made in the modeling process. This includes the verification of the mapping of *Social Networks* by a *BA* graph, a reduction of the behavioral model to a direct influence on the transmission probability, and the use of a simple *SIR* model. Using a *BA* graph in combination with the *SIR* model is valid for studying the spread of an epidemic. Reducing the behavioral model is helpful for a basic understanding, but I recommend an extension with a simple behavioral model. Incorporating risk perception could make the behavior deterministic and thus reduce the randomness of the model.

Understanding complex systems is relevant in many fields, and the interaction of epidemiology and human behavior is complicated. Using an unconventional and open-ended approach called *Iterative Exploratory Modeling*, the goal is to understand and explain the underlying mechanisms of a model. I based this modeling on a combination of the approaches of *Agent Based Modeling* and a *SIR* model. The latter is suitable for creating a sufficiently accurate abstraction of the processes under investigation, which I used to test various assumptions. This way, an understanding model can be built iteratively, covering different levels of complexity. This process results in a model that can be a starting point for further research. The conditions for a more comprehensive view of the phenomena are justified by testing the critical assumptions of the model. The contribution to the understanding of epidemics and human behavior made in this work should therefore contribute to reducing the risk and magnitude of future epidemics.

References

1. Agents.jl: ABM Framework Comparison (2022). https://juliadynamics.github.io/ Agents.jl/stable/comparison/#ABM-Framework-Comparison-1
2. Alizadeh, M., Cioffi-Revilla, C., Crooks, A.: Generating and analyzing spatial social networks. Comput. Math. Organ. Theory **23**(3), 362–390 (2016). https://doi.org/ 10.1007/s10588-016-9232-2
3. Barabási, A.L., Albert, R.: Emergence of scaling in random networks. Science **286**(5439), 509–512 (1999). https://doi.org/10.1126/science.286.5439.509
4. Bezanson, J., Edelman, A., Karpinski, S., Shah, V.B.: Julia: a fresh approach to numerical computing. SIAM Rev. **59**(1), 65–98 (2017). https://doi.org/10.1137/ 141000671
5. Bonabeau, E., Meyer, C.: Swarm intelligence: a whole new way to think about business. Harv. Bus. Rev. 106–114 (2001). https://pubmed.ncbi.nlm.nih. gov/11345907/. https://hbr.org/2001/05/swarm-intelligence-a-whole-new-way-to-think-about-business
6. Bruch, E., Atwell, J.: Agent-based models in empirical social research. Sociol. Methods Res. **44**(2), 186–221 (2015). https://doi.org/10.1177/0049124113506405
7. Calero Valdez, A., Ziefle, M.: Human factors in the age of algorithms. Understanding the human-in-the-loop using agent-based modeling. In: Meiselwitz, G. (ed.) SCSM 2018. LNCS, vol. 10914, pp. 357–371. Springer, Cham (2018). https://doi. org/10.1007/978-3-319-91485-5_27
8. Datseris, G., Vahdati, A.R., DuBois, T.C.: Agents.jl: a performant and feature-full agent-based modeling software of minimal code complexity. SIMULATION 003754972110688 (2022). https://doi.org/10.1177/00375497211068820
9. Edmonds, B.: How are physical and social spaces related? – Cognitive Agents as the Necessary "Glue", pp. 195–214. Physica-Verlag HD, Heidelberg (2006). https:// doi.org/10.1007/3-7908-1721-X_10
10. Epstein, J.M.: Why model? J. Artif. Soc. Soc. Simul. **11**(4), 12 (2008). https:// www.jasss.org/11/4/12.html
11. Epstein, J.M., Axtell, R.: Growing Artificial Societies: Social Science from the Bottom Up. Brookings Institution Press (1996)
12. Epstein, J.M., Parker, J., Cummings, D., Hammond, R.A.: Coupled contagion dynamics of fear and disease: mathematical and computational explorations. PLoS ONE **3**(12), e3955 (2008). https://doi.org/10.1371/journal.pone.0003955
13. Gilbert, N., Terna, P.: How to build and use agent-based models in social science. Mind Soc. **1**(1), 57–72 (2000). https://doi.org/10.1007/BF02512229
14. Jin, K., Yu, U.: Reference to global state and social contagion dynamics. Front. Phys. **9**(May), 1–9 (2021). https://doi.org/10.3389/fphy.2021.684223
15. Kitchovitch, S., Liò, P.: Risk perception and disease spread on social networks. Procedia Comput. Sci. **1**(1), 2345–2354 (2010). https://doi.org/10.1016/j.procs. 2010.04.264
16. Liljeros, F.: The web of human sexual contacts. Struct. Dyn. Netw. 227–228 (2017). https://doi.org/10.1515/9781400841356.227
17. May, R.M., Anderson, R.M.: Spatial heterogeneity and the design of immunization programs. Math. Biosci. **72**(1), 83–111 (1984). https://doi.org/10.1016/0025-5564(84)90063-4
18. Nunner, H., Buskens, V., Kretzschmar, M.: A model for the co-evolution of dynamic social networks and infectious disease dynamics. Comput. Soc. Netw. **8**(1), 1–33 (2021). https://doi.org/10.1186/s40649-021-00098-9

19. Wang, T., Krim, H., Viniotis, Y.: Analysis and control of beliefs in social networks. IEEE Trans. Sig. Process. **62**(21), 5552–5564 (2014). https://doi.org/10.1109/TSP. 2014.2352591
20. Wilensky, U., Rand, W.: An Introduction to Agent-Based Modeling: Modeling Natural, Social, and Engineered Complex Systems with NetLogo. The MIT Press, Cambridge (2015). http://www.jstor.org/stable/j.ctt17kk851

Characterizing Users' Propensity to Misinformation Engagement During COVID-19 Based on the Five Factor Model of Personality

Xiao Wang[1] , Sijing Chen[2]([✉]) , Yu Yang[1] , and Didi Dong[1]

[1] School of Information Management, Central China Normal University, Wuhan 430079, China
[2] National Engineering Research Center for Educational Big Data, Central China Normal University, Wuhan 430079, China
csj16912@163.com

Abstract. Characterizing the vulnerable people to misinformation engagement is important for combating misinformation. This study has examined the main effects and interaction effects of personality traits on misinformation engagement through multinomial logistic regression based on digital-traces data of 1,398 social media users. Some interesting findings were revealed, for instance, people high in neuroticism were likely to engage in misinformation. Additionally, higher neuroticism increased the likelihood that conscientious people would comment on misinformation. Main contributions of this study are the construction of a personality trait scale based on digital-trace indicators and the disclosure of relationship between users' personality traits and their misinformation engagement behaviors. The findings of this research can provide insights on the understanding of factors behind the misinformation engagement behaviors and support the detection of users who are vulnerable to misinformation on social media.

Keywords: Personality · Misinformation Engagement · Digital Trace · Social Media

1 Introduction

In the past few years, the sharing of misinformation on social media platforms has become more and more prevalent, especially in the current COVID-19 pandemic. Existing researches have investigated the factors driving the emergency-relevant mis-information dissemination from perspectives of misinformation content, misinformation publisher, misinformation receiver, etc. [1–3]. It is undeniable that the information receiver plays a critical role in the process of misinformation propagation, and the behavior of information receivers on social media can be affected by their personality traits [4]. When probing the relationship between personality traits and misinformation engagement behavior, prior studies mainly use self-reported data and focus on misinformation forwarding behavior [5, 6]. Few studies have subdivided misinformation engagement behavior and explored the relationship between personality traits and different engagement behaviors. Hence, this study aims to analyze the influence of personality traits on misinformation engagement behaviors, namely, misinformation forwarding, commenting and liking, based on the data of users' digital traces on social media. The findings of this research can shed lights on the driving factors behind misinformation engagement behaviour and support the automatic detection of people who are susceptible to emergency-related misinformation.

2   Literature Review

2.1   Factors Contributing to Users' Misinformation Engagement Behavior

The rapid proliferation of misinformation can cause unnecessary confusion and anxiety among the public [7]. Various studies have explored the factors that contribute to the spread of misinformation. Through the literature survey, we summarized the influencing factors affecting users' misinformation engagement from the perspective of information receivers.

Firstly, how people perceive and process the misinformation would affect their engagement with it. Comparing to positive and neutral information, people pay more attention to negative information, which is called the negativity bias [8]. Meanwhile, information sharing on social media is a social sharing of emotions [9]. Hence, when users browse online, they are more likely to forward misinformation that conveys emotions such as nervousness, anxiety and fear [10]. Secondly, motivation also plays an important role in users' information behavior on online social networks [11]. Though the classification of motivation varies, findings reveal that users may share misinformation for entertainment purposes and the act of sharing makes them feel satisfied [12] without considering the possible consequences of the act [13]. Moreover, self-disclosure, trust, and, fear of missing out (FOMO) are influential factors that contribute to misinformation sharing. To be specific, prior studies suggest that individuals' forwarding of misinformation may be a result of constructing or enhancing social connection [14–16]. Social support and willingness to take risk result from a relatively high level of trust may encourage people to share misinformation [17, 18]. And the FOMO, born out of rejection by social or peer group, may compel users to engage in misinformation to fit into group behavioral pattern [19, 20].

2.2   Personality and Users' Information Behavior on Social Media

In addition to the aforementioned receivers' factors, an increasing attention has been paid on the role of personality traits of receivers in the spread of misinformation. Personality is a relatively stable internal factors that is shaped by an individual's psychological processes [21] and reflects the individual's consistent behavioral patterns, experiential characteristics, and stable intrinsic motivations [21]. As regarded as the most widely accepted personality trait model [22], the Five Factor Model (FFM) describes individual personality traits from five dimensions (i.e., extraversion, agreeableness, responsibility, neuroticism and openness to experience), which has been proved to be universal across cultures [23, 24]. Traditional measurement requires participants to fill a questionnaire to assess their personality and behaviors, which are time-consuming and expensive [25, 26]. Comparing to this, online digital traces are more accurate predictors [27, 28] and can objectively record users' behaviors in a non-experimental environment.

Studies of influence of personality traits on online information behaviors are mainly conducted with data from platforms such as Facebook [11, 29, 30], LinkedIn [31], SNS [32, 33], Instagram [34] and Sina Weibo [35, 36]. It is found that different personality traits have different impacts on users' information processing styles [37], self-disclosure behavior [38, 39], Internet addiction [33, 40, 41], and etc. Regarding the misinformation-related behaviors, personality traits were found to have significant main effects on sharing [6, 42, 43] and spreading [44]. Moreover, negative impacts on society stability and individuals' psychology caused by the spread of misinformation on social media will be magnified under the emergency context. Previous research has investigated the impact of personality traits on misinformation dissemination during the Boston Marathon bombing [45], the Hurricane Maria [46], and COVID-19 pandemic [47, 48].

In general, the inadequacies of existing studies are as follows. First, previous research has not explored the effect of personality traits on other types of misinformation engagement, e.g., comment, and like. Second, the interaction effect of personality traits on misinformation engagement has not been investigated yet. Third, although studies on digital trace measurement of personality traits is abundant, their application in Chinese context needs to be improved. Thus, in the present study, we utilize the data collected from Sina Weibo to measure users' personality traits and examine the main effects and interaction effects of personality traits on different types of misinformation engagement.

3   Theoretical Analysis and Research Hypotheses

We propose a theoretical model describing factors affecting misinformation engagement during COVID-19 from two aspects, i.e., the personality traits of misinformation receivers and social characteristics of both misinformation publishers and receivers. Additionally, we also concern the interaction effects between personality traits on misinformation engagement. In this study, misinformation engagement is theoretically divided into forwards, comments, and likes according to common inter-actions on social media.

3.1   Personality Traits of Information Receivers and Their Misinformation Engagement on Social Media

Previous studies have demonstrated the impacts of personality traits on information behaviors [11, 49]and misinformation sharing [5, 50]. Therefore, we hypothesize:

H1: Personality traits of the receiver have significant effects on the forwarding/commenting/liking of misinformation.

Extraversion and Misinformation Engagement. Extraversion indicates the intensity of interpersonal interaction, the need for stimulation, and the ability to obtain pleasure. Past research on social media has shown that extraverts have more social connections than others [30] and are more active on social media [33]. Additionally, studies have shown that extroverts tend to share information in the first place regardless of the authenticity of such information [51]. Therefore, we speculate that when major emergencies like COVID-19 occur, users who score high in extroversion are more likely to engage in the misinformation.

H1a: People higher in extraversion would be more likely to forward/comment/like the misinformation post.

Agreeableness and Misinformation Engagement. Agreeableness is a sign of compassion, kindness, and tolerance. Previous studies have shown that agreeable users are more likely to express positive emotions in their posts on social media [52, 53]. Additionally, because of courtesy and concerning for others, agreeable people will refuse to deliver negative comments [6] and share controversial news on social media platforms [54], while they are more likely to share news that has been officially con-firmed. Thus, in the context of COVID-19, we hypothesize:

H1b: People higher in agreeableness would be less likely to forward/comment/like the misinformation post.

Conscientiousness and Misinformation Engagement. Conscientiousness tends to be organized, reliable, and pursue long-term goals [32]. Previous studies have shown that conscientious users tend to carefully manage their image by expressing fewer likes [55] and participating in fewer activities [56] on social media. In other words, conscientious users tend to be more cautious and self-control in the current era of digital transparency. Besides, conscientious users usually spend more time on aca-demic activities than leisures when surfing the Internet. In that case, they may prefer to spend time on looking up information known to be reliable [57, 58] and be responsible for the consequences of their information behaviors [59]. Therefore, we hypothesize:

H1c: People higher in conscientiousness would be less likely to for-ward/comment/like the misinformation post.

Neuroticism and Misinformation Engagement. Neurotic users tend to be emotionally unstable and are more likely to experience negative emotions, such as anger, anxiety, stress, and depression [47]. Studies have shown that neurotic users are more likely to share information online and use more negative words in their posts because they regard media news as non-threatening [52, 60]. Additionally, users higher in neuroticism were more likely to believe in misinformation [6], interact with it, and seek emotional support [61, 62]. Besides, neurotic users tend to spend more time on social media and keep in touch with others [11]. Therefore, to maintain connections with others, neurotic users are more likely to respond to posts of hot topics like COVID-19, regardless of whether the information is reliable.

H1d: People higher in neuroticism would be less likely to forward/comment/like the misinformation post.

Openness and Misinformation Engagement. Openness is often used to describe a person's cognitive style. Users higher in openness usually have larger social networks, both online and offline [29]. They also tend to strengthen and expand their social networks by liking and sharing messages on social media [63]. Additionally, they tend to share information in the first place on social media [48] even before the information has been officially reported [11, 64]. And their engagement is more likely to be motivated by skepticism and criticism than acceptance and belief [58].

H1e: People higher in openness would be less likely to forward/comment/like the misinformation post.

3.2 Users' Social Characteristics and Their Misinformation Engagement on Social Media

The account authentication granted to publishers by the platform may increase the trust of ordinary users in them and the information they publish. Hence, result in a higher probability of users to engage in misinformation [18] published or disseminated by these verified publishers. The number of followers reflects the source popularity of a misinformation post, which may affect the of misinformation [65]. Therefore, we propose the following hypotheses:

H2: Social characteristics of the publisher have a positive effect on the forwarding/commenting/liking of misinformation.

H2a: The certification status of the publisher has a positive effect on the forwarding/commenting/liking of misinformation.

H2b: The number of followers of the publisher has a positive effect on the forwarding/commenting/liking of misinformation.

Besides, social characteristics of misinformation receivers, e.g., number of history posts and number of followers/followings, may also correlate with misinformation engagement behaviors. Specifically, the number of posts and the number of followings reflects the active level of a user on the social media platform. The more active the user is on the social media platform, and the more likely the user is to engage in the misinformation before confirming its veracity. The number of followers, reflecting the breadth of one's social network. Forwarding, commenting, or liking a misinformation post can be a way for socializing [66] or fact finding [67]. Thus, we propose the following hypotheses:

H3: Social characteristics of the information receiver have a significant effect on the forwarding/commenting/liking of misinformation.

H3a: The number of receiver's history posts is positively related with the forwarding/commenting/liking of misinformation.

H3b: The number of receiver's followings is positively related with the forwarding/commenting/liking of misinformation.

H3c: The number of receiver's followers is negatively related with the forwarding/commenting/liking of misinformation.

3.3   Interaction Effects of Personality Traits on Misinformation Engagement

Personality traits of a person are complex. The FFM divides it into five basic dimensions, and there is a certain correlation between the five dimensions [25, 47]. Existing studies on the interaction between personality traits cover the contexts of competitive sports, workplace and academic performance, etc. [68–71]. Regarding the influence of personality traits on users' misinformation engagement, most research focuses on the main effect, and only a few studies concern the interaction effects. For instance, Li et al. [47] argue that high conscientiousness may result in misinformation sharing when interact with high extraversion due to the influence of fear. To fill this research gap, we propose the following hypotheses:

H4: Interaction between personality traits of the receiver has a significant effect on the forwarding/commenting/liking of misinformation.

H4a: Individuals with high extraversion and high neuroticism are more likely to forward/comment/like misinformation.

H4b: Individuals with high extraversion and high conscientiousness are more likely to forward/comment/like misinformation.

H4c: Individuals with low agreeableness and low conscientiousness are more likely to forward/comment/like misinformation.

4   Methods

Before this investigation, the research plan was ethically reviewed by the College's Academic Committee. The misinformation posts, user's account information, and history posts involved in the research are publicly visible on Sina Weibo platform. Users' nicknames were replaced by numbers to remain anonymous in the follow-up data processing and analysis.

4.1   Data Collection

To gather the verified misinformation cases on social media platform, the Weibo Community Management Center was used for its professional screening mechanism (Chen et al., 2021). On 1st December 2021, we crawled all the COVID-19 related misinformation cases from Weibo Community Management Center which were generated since 1st August 2020. In total, there were 11 misinformation posts regarding COVID-19. Then we crawled the account information and history posts of users, who engaged in misinformation by forwarding, or commenting or liking the misinformation posts. In addition, we also crawled data of users who followed the misinformation publisher as the control group as they may have been exposed to the 11 mis-information posts but not engaged in them. For history posts, we took the publication time of each misinformation post as the starting point, retrospectively crawled the six-months history posts of users who engaged in the misinformation post. The dataset of history posts contains user's original posts, forwarded posts, comments add-ed when forwarding, etc. During the collection process, some user homepages cannot be accessed due to platform security policies or voluntary application for closure. Besides, some users may have deleted their history posts or not published/forwarded posts. Finally, we collected the account information and history posts of 1,398 users.

4.2 Measurements

Misinformation Engagement. The dependent variable is misinformation engagement, which is categorical and contains five classes, namely, following (U1), forwarding (U2), commenting (U3), liking (U4) and the multi-type engagement (U5). Users who followed the publisher of misinformation but did not interact with the misinformation (U1), are regarded as the reference group in the regression analysis. Users with multi-type engagement (U5) refers to those who engaged in the misinformation posts through more than one way. Of the 1,398 users in the study, 556 (39.77%) forwarded the misinformation, 274 (19.60%) commented the misinformation, 256 (18.31%) liked the misinformation, 105 (7.51%) had multi-type engagement, and 207 (14.81%) did not engage in the misinformation.

Personality Traits. To describe one's personality traits, we apply the Five Factor Model (McCrae & Costa, 1987), which contains five dimensions: extraversion, agreeableness, conscientiousness, neuroticism, and openness to experience. Questionnaires and interviews need to arouse participants' memory or ask for their opinions, and thus are likely to be affected by their current emotions and motivations. The social activity and linguistic expression recorded in social media are users' performance in non-experimental environments, therefore are traceable and objective [72]. For the accuracy and scientific nature of the digital trace data in measuring individuals' personality, we surveyed a large body of literature [11, 23, 33, 43, 49, 52, 53, 57, 61–64, 73–77]. Considering indicator intelligibility and data availability, we construct a scale to measure users' personality traits via digital traces (as shown in Table 1).

In Table 1, the sign of "±" represents the positive or negative relationship between indicators and personality traits, for instance, the greater the number of followers a user has, the more likely he/she is extraverted. "1" means that if the user provided a profile, the person is more likely to be extroverted. The data completeness of personal information is measured according to the item weight set by Sina Weibo platform. We divide the history posts into two categories: one contains all the user-generated content, including original posts and comments added when forwarding, named as "user posts"; the other consists of all the reposts, named as "forwarded posts", which reflects one's interests rather opinions. Different types of words in linguistic indicators are obtained from LIWC-SC (2015). After processing and normalizing the indicator-related data, the entropy method is used to determine the weight of digital trace index in different personality traits and calculate the score of each user on five personality dimensions.

Social Characteristics. Social characteristics of misinformation publisher and receiver are regarded as independent variables in this research. The number of receivers' posts/followings/followers and the number of publishers' followers were convert-ed into categorical variables with two levels (i.e., low or high) according to the median to weaken outliers. "Publisher verified" is a binary variable, which signs whether the account of misinformation publisher is verified by the platform.

Table 1. Measurements of Personality Traits

Category	Indicators	Extraversion	Agreeableness	Conscientiousness	Neuroticism	Openness
Indicators from personal information	Num. of followers	+			-	+
	Data completeness of personal information	+		-	-	+
	Filled in "profile" in personal information	1				1
	Word count of the "profile" in the personal information				+	
	Num. of "tags" in personal information		+			
Statistical indicators from history posts	Num. of history posts	+	-			+
	Median of the weekly post frequency	+		-	+	
	Ratio between original posts and reposts		+			
	Number of total words in user posts		+			+
	Ratio of English words to the total words in user posts	-				
	Num. of "@" used in user posts	+		+		
	Num. of users who was "@" in user posts	+		+		
	Num. of pictures in user posts	+			-	+
	Num. of videos in user posts					+
	Num. of links in user posts					+
	Num. of '!' in user posts	+				
	Num. of ';' in user posts			+		
	Num. of '?' in user posts					+
Linguistic indicators from history posts	Num. of work-related words in history posts			+	-	

(*continued*)

Table 1. (*continued*)

Category	Indicators	Extraversion	Agreeableness	Conscientiousness	Neuroticism	Openness
	Num. of achieve-related words in history posts			+		
	Num. of leisure-related words in history posts	+		-		
	Num. of function words in user posts	-				
	Num. of personal pronouns in user posts	+		-		
	Num. of first-person singular pronouns in user posts				+	+
	Num. of first-person plural pronouns in user posts		+			
	Num. of second-personal pronouns in user posts					-
	Num. of second-person plural pronouns in user posts	+				
Linguistic indicators from history posts	Num. of third-person singular pronouns in user posts				+	+
	Num. of third-person plural pronouns in user posts					+
	Num. of impersonal pronouns in user posts	-				
	Num. of prepositional words in user posts					+
	Num. of adverbs in user posts					-

(*continued*)

Table 1. (*continued*)

Category	Indicators	Extraversion	Agreeableness	Conscientiousness	Neuroticism	Openness
	Num. of connectives in user posts	-				
	Num. of negative words in user posts	-	-	+	+	
	Num. of quantitative unit words in user posts					-
	Num. of specific words in user posts					-
	Num. of question words in user posts					+
	Num. of affective words in user posts					-
	Num. of positive emotion words in user posts	+	+			-
	Num. of negative emotion words in user posts				+	
	Num. of anxiety words in user posts				+	+
	Num. of social words in user posts	+				
	Num. of discrepancy words in user posts				+	
	Num. of tentative words in user posts				+	
	Num. of differentiation words in user posts				+	
	Num. of relativity words in user posts		+			
	Num. of motion words in user posts					+
	Num. of space words in user posts		+			
	Num. of time words in user posts		+	+		
	Num. of swear words in user posts	-				-
	Num. of assent words in user posts	+				-
	Num. of non-fluency words in user posts					-

Control Variables. To eliminate the interference of the misinformation content and receiver's gender in the results, the two factors are set as control variables in the study. Both of them are categorical variables. Misinformation content is represented by labels which was manually coded by three annotators independently, and then discussed to obtain consensus results. Other factors, such as age, location, registration time and etc., provided by less than half of the users, are excluded in this research.

4.3 Data Analysis

We calculate means, standard deviations, and Pearson correlations to give a preliminary overview of our research variables. Multicollinearity was checked by the VIF of the linear regression analysis. Multinomial logistic regression is used to examine the relationship between the dependent variable (misinformation engagement) and independent variables (receiver's personality traits, social characteristics of publisher and receiver) because of the categorical feature of dependent variable [78]. All the interaction items are modeled separately.

5 Results

5.1 Descriptive Statistics

Means, standard deviation (SD), correlation coefficients, and VIF of variables in the research are shown in Table 2. The VIF of Extraversion (16.982) and the VIF of Openness (17.286) were both greater than 10, indicating a serious collinearity problem. To address the collinearity, we delete the variable with the highest VIF from the model. After removing the variable "Openness", all variables' VIF are less than 10, indicating the absence of multicollinearity.

5.2 Main Effects of Social Characteristics and Personality on Misinformation Engagement

Subsequently, the remaining variables were analyzed through the multinomial logistic regression with the group of non-engaged (U1) as the reference group. Results are shown in Table 3. Values in parentheses are odds ratios presented with their 95% confidence intervals.

Comparing R2, AIC, and BIC of the baseline model (0.168, 3903.249, 3966.162), model 1 (0.49, 3312.992, 3480.762), and model 2 (0.546, 3199.748, 3451.402), we find that personality traits are more effective in predicting misinformation engagement than the control variables and social characteristics. Specifically, by adding the social characteristics and personality traits, model 2 can explain 54.6% of the reasons for the change of users' engagement in misinformation.

In terms of social characteristics, RPN, RFIN, and PFEN, show significant impacts on misinformation engagement. To be specific, the more posts a receiver has posted, the more likely he/she is to engage in misinformation (H3a is supported); the more social media accounts a receiver has followed, the less likely he/she is to engage in misinformation (H3b is not supported); the more followers a misinformation publisher has, the less likely its receivers are to engage in misinformation (H2b is not supported). Additionally, the verified status of misinformation publisher (PV) positively affects users' misinformation engagement, except for misinformation commenting (H2a is partly supported). However, we found no significant relationship between receivers' number of followers and receivers' misinformation engagement behaviors (H3c is not supported).

Table 2. Descriptive statistics and correlation coefficients of research variables

	1	2	3	4	5	6	7	8	9	10	11	12	13
1. Gender	—												
2. RPN	-0.070**	—											
3. RFIN	0.039	0.252**	—										
4. RFEN	-0.041	0.376**	0.343**	—									
5. MT	-0.315**	0.137**	-0.056*	0.004	—								
6. PV	-0.159**	0.091**	-0.090**	0.035	0.390**	—							
7. PFEN	0.143**	-0.135**	0.059*	-0.016	-0.390**	0.062*	—						
8. E	0.006	0.375**	0.192**	0.289**	-0.039	-0.01	0.016	—					
9. A	-0.025	0.181**	0.073**	0.195**	-0.053*	-0	0.111**	0.514**	—				
10. C	-0.021	0.358**	0.098**	0.150**	0.031	0.044	-0.024	0.679**	0.509**	—			
11. N	0.006	0.361**	0.125**	0.168**	0.028	0.003	-0.029	0.714**	0.476**	0.898**	—		
12. O	0.01	0.378**	0.177**	0.296**	-0.007	-0.02	-0.008	0.964**	0.510**	0.646**	0.722**	—	
13. ME	-0.008	-0.092**	-0.110**	-0.003	-0.003	-0.02	-0.172**	-0.032	-0.061*	-0.051	-0.041	-0.047	—
VIF	1.125	1.411	1.203	1.332	1.605	1.302	1.309	16.982	1.524	6.273	6.751	17.286	—
Mean	—	—	—	—	—	—	—	0.068	0.091	0.037	0.041	0.065	—
SD	—	—	—	—	—	—	—	0.047	0.09	0.056	0.056	0.046	—
Range	1-2	1-2	1-2	1-2	1-2	1-2	1-2	0-0.691	0-0.597	0-0.888	0-0.659	0-0.497	1-5

N = 1398

**p<0.01, *p<0.05

RPN number of receiver's posts, RFIN number of receiver's followings, RFEN number of receiver's followers, MT misinfo tag, PV publisher verified, PFEN number of publisher's followers, E extraversion, A agreeableness, C conscientiousness, N neuroticism, O openness to experience, ME misinformation engagement

Table 3. Multinomial logistic regression analysis predicting misinformation engagement from social characteristics and personality traits

Misinformation Engagement	Variables	Baseline Model	Model 1	Model 2
Forwarding vs. Non-engaged	Gender	-0.445*	-0.344	-0.422
		(0.2)	(0.241)	(0.251)
	MT	2.561***	0.786*	0.634
		(0.283)	(0.365)	(0.387)
	RPN		3.118***	2.672***
			(0.258)	(0.285)
	RFIN		-1.816***	-1.978***
			(0.244)	(0.252)
	RFEN		-0.075	0.034
			(0.238)	(0.25)
	PV		1.318***	1.415***
			(0.26)	(0.273)
	PFEN		-2.841***	-2.782***
			(0.279)	(0.289)
	E			-1.449
				(2.665)
	A			-3.821***
				(0.836)
	C			5.129
				(5.649)
	N			13.477*
				(5.698)
Commenting vs. Non-engaged	Gender	-0.652**	-0.569*	-0.575*
		(0.24)	(0.266)	(0.271)
	MT	3.659***	2.902***	2.992***
		(0.603)	(0.642)	(0.647)
	RPN		0.861**	1.236***
			(0.265)	(0.298)
	RFIN		-1.388***	-1.458***
			(0.251)	(0.255)
	RFEN		0.207	0.234
			(0.246)	(0.256)
	PV		-0.183	-0.168
			(0.251)	(0.257)
	PFEN		-3.14***	-3.18***
			(0.381)	(0.383)
	E			0.559
				(2.896)
	A			-2.035*
				(0.853)
	C			-30.444**
				(10.325)

(*continued*)

Table 3. (*continued*)

Misinformation Engagement	Variables	Baseline Model	Model 1	Model 2
	N			6.33 (7.424)
Liking vs. Non-engaged	Gender	0.15(0.206)	0.211 (0.228)	0.156 (0.234)
	MT	0.364 (0.215)	-0.988** (0.3)	-1.069** (0.313)
	RPN		0.684** (0.261)	0.747* (0.291)
	RFIN		-1.597*** (0.24)	-1.676*** (0.244)
	RFEN		0.325 (0.239)	0.422 (0.248)
	PV		1.17*** (0.268)	1.279*** (0.277)
	PFEN		-2.125*** (0.254)	-2.099*** (0.256)
	E			-3.37 (2.754)
	A			-2.611** (0.824)
	C			-22.821* (8.826)
	N			19.569** (6.489)
Multi-engaged vs. Non-engaged	Gender	-0.832** (0.315)	-0.751* (0.335)	-0.784* (0.343)
	MT	0.976** (0.336)	-0.47 (0.432)	-0.533 (0.455)
	RPN		1.961*** (0.314)	1.494*** (0.344)
	RFIN		-1.415*** (0.302)	-1.585*** (0.31)
	RFEN		0.417 (0.304)	0.477 (0.316)
	PV		1.186** (0.343)	1.255*** (0.351)
	PFEN		-2.319*** (0.364)	-2.345*** (0.379)
	E			0.056 (3.186)
	A			-3.157** (1.036)
	C			3.443 (5.982)
	N			13.156* (5.874)
R-squared		0.168	0.49	0.546
AIC		3903.249	3312.992	3199.748
BIC		3966.162	3480.762	3451.402

N = 1398

***p<0.001,**p<0.01, *p<0.05

RPN number of receiver's posts, RFIN number of receiver's followings, RFEN number of receiver's followers, MT misinfo tag, PV publisher verified, PFEN number of publisher's followers, E extraversion, A agreeableness, C conscientiousness, N neuroticism, O openness to experience, ME misinformation engagement

Regarding the relationship between receivers' personality traits and their misinformation engagement, H1b is supported, H1c is partly supported, H1a and H1d are not supported. Specifically, receivers lower in agreeableness (Coef. = -3.821, p < 0.001) or higher in neuroticism (Coef. = 13.477, p < 0.05) are more likely to forward misinformation. Receivers lower in agreeableness (Coef. = −2.035, p < 0.05) or conscientiousness (Coef. = −30.444, p < 0.01) are more likely to comment misinformation. Receivers higher in neuroticism (Coef. = 19.569, p < 0.01) tend to like misinformation and receivers higher in agreeableness (Coef. = −2.611, p < 0.01) or conscientiousness (Coef. = −22.821, p < 0.05) are less likely to do so. Additionally, receivers lower in agreeableness (Coef. = −3.157, p < 0.01) or higher in neuroticism (Coef. = 13.156, p < 0.05) are more likely to engage in misinformation through multiple ways.

5.3 Interaction Effects of Personality on Misinformation Engagement

Apart from the main effects, we modeled six two-way interaction items respectively to analyze the interaction effects of personality traits on the misinformation engagement. Table of the regression results is not presented because of the length limitation. Comparing the R2, AIC, and BIC of main effect models (Model 1 and 2) and the R2, AIC, and BIC of interaction effect models (Model 3 to 8), we find that the addition of interaction items can improve the prediction ability of the model in most cases, except for model 4 with E#C interaction items (0.499, 3331.398, 3604.024). Specifically, E#A (Coef. = −20.920) and A#C (Coef. = −59.875) show a significant two-way interaction on misinformation forwarding. It means that introverts lower in agreeableness tend to forward misinformation. Users lower in agreeableness and conscientiousness are more likely to forward misinformation. E#N (Coef. = 102.356), A#C (Coef. = 69.42) and C#N (Coef. = 44.525) show a significant two-way interaction effect on misinformation commenting. It suggests that, for extraverted or conscientious users, higher levels of neuroticism would prompt them to comment on misinformation, and if users exhibited high agreeableness, their conscientiousness would further push them to comment on misinformation.

6 Discussion and Conclusion

By collecting digital traces of users on Sina Weibo, we measured users' personality traits and examined the main and interaction effects of personality traits on different ways of misinformation engagement. The findings of this research can offer insights into the efforts to automatically detect people who are vulnerable to misinformation and prevent the crisis of public opinion.

Results of this study suggest that users higher in agreeableness are less likely to engage in misinformation, which is in line with the findings of Lee et al. [6], Wehli [54], and Buchanan and Benson [43]. That is, users who score high in agreeableness would refuse to publish negative comments or share misinformation regarding controversial issues. Results also indicate that users with high conscientiousness scores are less likely to comment and like the misinformation. This may due to the cautious behavioral pattern of conscientiousness, which leads to the less participation in social media activities [56] and less demand for gaining attention [62]. However, it should be noted that the relationship between conscientiousness and misinformation engagement may be mediated by receivers' fear emotion [47]. We also find that users who score high in neuroticism are more likely to engage in misinformation. As prior research has revealed, neuroticisms tend to perceive their information behavior on social media as low risk [60], so they are more likely to indulge in social media interactions and seek emotional support online [61, 62]. Neuroticisms care more about the feeling of information sharing and the connection with others rather than the content they share on social media. As a result, these people are more likely to believe online misinformation [6] and tend to forward, like or engage in misinformation through multiple ways.

Apart from the main effects mentioned above, four two-way interaction effects of personality traits have been discovered in this research. Firstly, in line with Buchan-an [50], we found that lower conscientiousness increases the likelihood that users with low agreeableness would forward misinformation and decreases the likelihood that users with low agreeableness would comment on misinformation. Secondly, we found that higher neuroticism increased the possibility that extraverts would comment on misinformation, which is consistent with findings of Buchanan [50] and Correa et al. [37]. It means that users who are more active, more willing to build relationship with others, and spend more time on social media are more likely to comment on misinformation. Thirdly, it was found that a higher level of agreeableness decreased the probability that extraverts would forward misinformation. Previous research suggest-ed that people who score high on extraversion, agreeableness, and neuroticism tend to process information in an empirical manner and are therefore more susceptible to misinformation [79]. However, our research suggests that users with high extraversion and agreeableness are less likely to engage in misinformation when the influence of neuroticism is excluded. Finally, we also found that users who were both conscientious and neurotic were more likely to comment on misinformation. We speculate that conscientious but emotional unstable people are likely to comment on false information because of their demand for emotional support online.

There are some limitations in the present study. First, personality trait estimation is a challenging task so we will further verify the applicability of existing digital trace indicators in Chinese social media platforms. And the automatic estimation of personality traits based on machine learning algorithms is planned to be conducted in our future research. Second, the quantitative limitation and uneven distribution of the research sample may affect the analysis results to some extent. In further research, we will increase the sample size from one or multiple platforms and horizontally compare the influence of personality traits on misinformation participation among different platforms.

Acknowledgment. This study was funded by the National Social Science Funds of China (NSSFC) Grant Nos. 21CTQ014.

References

1. Seah, S., Weimann, G.: What influences the willingness of Chinese WeChat users to forward food-safety rumors? Int. J. Commun. **14**, 2186–2207 (2020)

2. Nadarevic, L., Reber, R., Helmecke, A.J., Köse, D.: Perceived truth of statements and simulated social media postings: an experimental investigation of source credibility, repeated exposure, and presentation format. Cogn. Res. Principles Implications **5**(1), 1–16 (2020). https://doi.org/10.1186/s41235-020-00251-4

3. Ahmed, S., Tan, H.W.: Personality and perspicacity: role of personality traits and cognitive ability in political misinformation discernment and sharing behavior. Personal. Individ. Differ. **196**, 111747 (2022)

4. Indu, V., Thampi, S.M.: A systematic review on the influence of user personality in rumor and misinformation propagation through social networks. In: Thampi, S.M., Krishnan, S., Hegde, R.M., Ciuonzo, D., Hanne, T., Kannan R., J. (eds.) SIRS 2020. CCIS, vol. 1365, pp. 216–242. Springer, Singapore (2021). https://doi.org/10.1007/978-981-16-0425-6_17

5. Lynn, T., Muzellec, L., Caemmerer, B., Turley, D.: Social network sites: early adopters' personality and influence. JPBM **26**(1), 42–51 (2017)

6. Lai, K., Xiong, X., Jiang, X., Sun, M., He, L.: Who falls for rumor? Influence of personality traits on false rumor belief. Personal. Individ. Differ. **152**, 109520 (2020)

7. Budak, C., Agrawal, D., El Abbadi, A.: Limiting the spread of misinformation in social networks. In: Proceedings of the 20th International Conference on World Wide Web, pp. 665–674. ACM, Hyderabad, India (2011)

8. Baumeister, R.F., Bratslavsky, E., Finkenauer, C., Vohs, K.D.: Bad is stronger than good. Rev. Gen. Psychol. **5**(4), 323–370 (2001)

9. Wetzer, I.M., Zeelenberg, M., Pieters, R.: "Never eat in that restaurant, I did!": Exploring why people engage in negative word-of-mouth communication. Psychol. Mark **24**(8), 661–680 (2007)

10. Zhang, H., Qu, C.: Emotional, especially negative microblogs are more popular on the web: evidence from an fMRI study. Brain Imaging Behav. **14**(5), 1328–1338 (2018). https://doi.org/10.1007/s11682-018-9998-6

11. Moore, K., McElroy, J.C.: The influence of personality on Facebook usage, wall postings, and regret. Comput. Hum. Behav. **28**(1), 267–274 (2012)

12. Shao, G.: Understanding the appeal of user-generated media: a uses and gratification perspective. Internet Res. **19**(1), 7–25 (2009)

13. Nov, O., Naaman, M., Ye, C.: Analysis of participation in an online photo-sharing community: a multidimensional perspective. J. Am. Soc. Inf. Sci. **61**(3), 555–566 (2009)

14. Whitty, M.T., Joinson, A.: Truth, Lies and Trust on the Internet. Routledge, London (2008)

15. Winter, S., et al.: Another brick in the Facebook wall – how personality traits relate to the content of status updates. Comput. Hum. Behav. **34**, 194–202 (2014)

16. Buglass, S.L., Binder, J.F., Betts, L.R., Underwood, J.D.M.: Motivators of online vulnerability: the impact of social network site use and FOMO. Comput. Hum. Behav. **66**, 248–255 (2017)

17. Krasnova, H., Spiekermann, S., Koroleva, K., Hildebrand, T.: Online social networks: why we disclose. J. Inf. Technol. **25**(2), 109–125 (2010)

18. Lin, S.-W., Liu, Y.-C.: The effects of motivations, trust, and privacy concern in social networking. Serv. Bus. **6**(4), 411–424 (2012)

19. Oulasvirta, A., Rattenbury, T., Ma, L., Raita, E.: Habits make smartphone use more pervasive. Pers. Ubiquit. Comput. **16**(1), 105–114 (2012)

20. Baumeister, R.F., Tice, D.M.: Point-counterpoints: anxiety and social exclusion. J. Soc. Clin. Psychol. **9**(2), 165–195 (1990)

21. Kazdin, A.E. (ed.): Encyclopedia of Psychology. American Psychological Association; Oxford University Press, Washington, D.C (2000)

22. Boyle, G.J., Matthews, G., Saklofske, D.H. (eds.): The SAGE Handbook of Personality Theory and Assessment. SAGE Publications, Los Angeles, CA (2008)

23. Qiu, L., Lu, J., Ramsay, J., Yang, S., Qu, W., Zhu, T.: Personality expression in Chinese language use: PERSONALITY AND CHINESE LANGUAGE USE. Int. J. Psychol. **52**(6), 463–472 (2017)

24. Schmitt, D.P., Allik, J., McCrae, R.R., Benet-Martínez, V.: The geographic distribution of big five personality traits: patterns and profiles of human self-description across 56 nations. J. Cross Cult. Psychol. **38**(2), 173–212 (2007)

25. Costa, P.T., McCrae, R.R.: The revised NEO personality inventory (NEO-PI-R). In: The SAGE Handbook of Personality Theory and Assessment: Volume 2—Personality Measurement and Testing, pp. 179–198. SAGE Publications Ltd. (2008)

26. Farr, J.L.: Handbook of Employee Selection. Routledge London (2013)

27. Skowron, M., Tkalčič, M., Ferwerda, B., Schedl, M.: Fusing social media cues: personality prediction from Twitter and Instagram. In: Proceedings of the 25th International Conference Companion on World Wide Web - WWW '16 Companion, pp. 107–108. ACM Press, Canada (2016)

28. Youyou, W., Kosinski, M., Stillwell, D.: Computer-based personality judgments are more accurate than those made by humans. Proc. Natl. Acad. Sci. U.S.A. **112**(4), 1036–1040 (2015)

29. Quercia, D., Lambiotte, R., Stillwell, D., Kosinski, M., Crowcroft, J.: The personality of popular Facebook users. In: Proceedings of the ACM 2012 Conference on Computer Supported Cooperative Work, pp. 955–964. ACM, Seattle, Washington, USA (2012)

30. Gosling, S.D., Augustine, A.A., Vazire, S., Holtzman, N., Gaddis, S.: Manifestations of personality in online social networks: self-reported Facebook-related behaviors and observable profile information. Cyberpsychol. Behav. Soc. Netw. **14**(9), 483–488 (2011)

31. Fernandez, S., Stöcklin, M., Terrier, L., Kim, S.: Using available signals on LinkedIn for personality assessment. J. Res. Pers. **93**, 104122 (2021)

32. Chen, X., Pan, Y., Guo, B.: The influence of personality traits and social networks on the self-disclosure behavior of social network site users. Internet Res. **26**(3), 566–586 (2016)

33. Kuss, D.J., Griffiths, M.D.: Online social networking and addiction—a review of the psychological literature. IJERPH **8**(9), 3528–3552 (2011)

34. Kircaburun, K., Griffiths, M.D.: Instagram addiction and the Big Five of personality: the mediating role of self-liking. J. Behav. Addict. **7**(1), 158–170 (2018)

35. Wang, Y., Zhao, N.: Prediction model of interaction anxiousness based on Weibo data. Front. Publ. Health **10** (2022)

36. Xue, D., et al.: Personality recognition on social media with label distribution learning. IEEE Access **5**, 13478–13488 (2017)

37. Correa, T., Hinsley, A.W., de Zúñiga, H.G.: Who interacts on the web?: The intersection of users' personality and social media use. Comput. Hum. Behav. **26**(2), 247–253 (2010)

38. Schrammel, J., köffel, c., tscheligi, m.: personality traits, usage patterns and information disclosure in online communities. In: People and Computers XXIII Celebrating People and Technology (2009)

39. Zywica, J., Danowski, J.: The faces of Facebookers: investigating social enhancement and social compensation hypotheses; predicting FacebookTM and offline popularity from sociability and self-esteem, and mapping the meanings of popularity with semantic networks. J. Comput.-Mediat. Commun. **14**(1), 1–34 (2008)

40. Ryan, T., Xenos, S.: Who uses Facebook? An investigation into the relationship between the Big Five, shyness, narcissism, loneliness, and Facebook usage. Comput. Hum. Behav. **27**(5), 1658–1664 (2011)

41. Andreassen, C.S., Griffiths, M.D., Gjertsen, S.R., Krossbakken, E., Kvam, S., Pallesen, S.: The relationships between behavioral addictions and the five-factor model of personality. J. Behav. Addict. **2**(2), 90–99 (2013)

42. Golkar Amnieh, I., Kaedi, M.: Using estimated personality of social network members for finding influential nodes in viral marketing. Cybern. Syst. **46**(5), 355–378 (2015)

43. Buchanan, T., Benson, V.: Spreading disinformation on Facebook: do trust in message source, risk propensity, or personality affect the organic reach of "Fake News"? Soc. Media Soc. **5**(4), 205630511988865 (2019)

44. Muris, P., Roelofs, J., Rassin, E., Franken, I., Mayer, B.: Mediating effects of rumination and worry on the links between neuroticism, anxiety and depression. Personal. Individ. Differ. **39**(6), 1105–1111 (2005)

45. Starbird, K., Maddock, J.: Rumors, false flags, and digital vigilantes: misinformation on Twitter after the 2013 Boston Marathon bombing. In: iConference 2014 Proceedings. iSchools (2014)

46. Liu, C., Tian, Q., Chen, M.: Distinguishing personality recognition and quantification of emotional features based on users' information behavior in social media. J. Database Manag. **32**(2), 76–91 (2021)

47. Li, K., Li, J., Zhou, F.: The effects of personality traits on online rumor sharing: the mediating role of fear of COVID-19. IJERPH **19**(10), 6157 (2022)

48. Sampat, B., Raj, S.: Fake or real news? Understanding the gratifications and personality traits of individuals sharing fake news on social media platforms. AJIM **74**(5), 840–876 (2022)

49. Azucar, D., Marengo, D., Settanni, M.: Predicting the Big 5 personality traits from digital footprints on social media: a meta-analysis. Personal. Individ. Differ. **124**, 150–159 (2018)

50. Buchanan, T.: Why do people spread false information online? The effects of message and viewer characteristics on self-reported likelihood of sharing social media disinformation. PLoS ONE **15**(10), e0239666 (2020)

51. Sindermann, C., Schmitt, H.S., Rozgonjuk, D., Elhai, J.D., Montag, C.: The evaluation of fake and true news: on the role of intelligence, personality, interpersonal trust, ideological attitudes, and news consumption. Heliyon **7**(3), e06503 (2021)

52. Schwartz, H.A., et al.: Personality, gender, and age in the language of social media: the open-vocabulary approach. PLoS ONE **8**(9), e73791 (2013)

53. Liu, L., Preotiuc-Pietro, D., Riahi Samani, Z., Moghaddam, M. E., Ungar, L.: Analyzing personality through social media profile picture choice. ICWSM **10**(1), 211–220 (2021)

54. Wehrli, S.: Personality on social network sites: an application of the five factor model. In: ETH Zurich Sociology Working Paper, vol. 7, pp. 1–17 (2008)

55. Amichai-Hamburger, Y., Vinitzky, G.: Social network use and personality. Comput. Hum. Behav. **26**(6), 1289–1295 (2010)

56. Kosinski, M., Bachrach, Y., Kohli, P., Stillwell, D., Graepel, T.: Manifestations of user personality in website choice and behaviour on online social networks. Mach. Learn. **95**(3), 357–380 (2014)

57. McElroy, H.: Townsend, DeMarie: dispositional factors in internet use: personality versus cognitive style. MIS Q. **31**(4), 809 (2007)

58. Heinström, J.: Five personality dimensions and their influence on information behaviour. Inf. Res. **9**(1), 165 (2003)

59. Meng, K.S., Leung, L.: Factors influencing TikTok engagement behaviors in China: an examination of gratifications sought, narcissism, and the Big Five personality traits. Telecommun. Policy **45**(7), 102172 (2021)

60. Amichai-Hamburger, Y., Kaplan, H., Dorpatcheon, N.: Click to the past: the impact of extroversion by users of nostalgic websites on the use of Internet social services. Comput. Hum. Behav. **24**(5), 1907–1912 (2008)

61. Hughes, D.J., Rowe, M., Batey, M., Lee, A.: A tale of two sites: Twitter vs. Facebook and the personality predictors of social media usage. Comput. Hum. Behav. **28**(2), 561–569 (2012)

62. Seidman, G.: Self-presentation and belonging on Facebook: how personality influences social media use and motivations. Personal. Individ. Differ. **54**(3), 402–407 (2013)

63. Bachrach, Y., Kosinski, M., Graepel, T., Kohli, P., Stillwell, D.: Personality and patterns of Facebook usage. In: Contractor, N., Uzzi, B. (eds.) WebSci '12: Proceedings of the 4th Annual ACM Web Science Conference, pp. 24–32. ACM, N.Y. (2012)

64. Ross, C., Orr, E.S., Sisic, M., Arseneault, J.M., Simmering, M.G., Orr, R.R.: Personality and motivations associated with Facebook use. Comput. Hum. Behav. **25**(2), 578–586 (2009)

65. Chen, S., Xiao, L., Kumar, A.: Spread of misinformation on social media: what contributes to it and how to combat it. Comput. Hum. Behav. **141**, 107643 (2023)

66. Apuke, O.D., Omar, B.: Fake news and COVID-19: modelling the predictors of fake news sharing among social media users. Telematics Inform. **56**, 101475 (2021)

67. Shen, Y.-C., Lee, C.T., Pan, L.-Y., Lee, C.-Y.: Why people spread rumors on social media: developing and validating a multi-attribute model of online rumor dissemination. OIR **45**(7), 1227–1246 (2021)

68. Kaiseler, M., Levy, A., Nicholls, A.R., Madigan, D.J.: The independent and interactive effects of the Big-Five personality dimensions upon dispositional coping and coping effectiveness in sport. Int. J. Sport Exercise Psychol. **17**(4), 410–426 (2019)

69. Silvia, P.J., Nusbaum, E.C., Berg, C., Martin, C., O'Connor, A.: Openness to experience, plasticity, and creativity: exploring lower-order, high-order, and interactive effects. J. Res. Pers. **43**(6), 1087–1090 (2009)

70. Grant, S., Langan-Fox, J.: Occupational stress, coping and strain: the combined/interactive effect of the Big Five traits. Personal. Individ. Differ. **41**(4), 719–732 (2006)

71. Zhou, M.: Moderating effect of self-determination in the relationship between Big Five personality and academic performance. Personal. Individ. Differ. **86**, 385–389 (2015)

72. Wu, P., et al.: Exploring the psychological effects of COVID-19 home confinement in China: a psycho-linguistic analysis on Weibo data pool. Front. Psychol **12**, 587308 (2021)

73. Hinds, J., Joinson, A.: Human and computer personality prediction from digital footprints. Curr. Dir. Psychol. Sci. **28**(2), 204–211 (2019)

74. Hamburger, Y.A., Ben-Artzi, E.: The relationship between extraversion and neuroticism and the different uses of the Internet. Comput. Hum. Behav. **16**(4), 441–449 (2000)

75. Yarkoni, T.: Personality in 100,000 words: a large-scale analysis of personality and word use among bloggers. J. Res. Pers. **44**(3), 363–373 (2010)

76. Golbeck, J., Robles, C., Turner, K.: Predicting personality with social media. In: CHI '11 extended Abstracts on Human Factors in Computing Systems, pp. 253–262. ACM, Vancouver BC, Canada (2011)

77. Farnadi, G., et al.: Computational personality recognition in social media. User Model. User-Adap. Inter. **26**(2–3), 109–142 (2016). https://doi.org/10.1007/s11257-016-9171-0

78. Lan, X., Sun, Q.: Exploring psychosocial adjustment profiles in Chinese adolescents from divorced families: the interplay of parental attachment and adolescent's gender. Curr. Psychol. **41**, 1–17 (2020). https://doi.org/10.1007/s12144-020-01097-1

79. Pacini, R., Epstein, S.: The relation of rational and experiential information processing styles to personality, basic beliefs, and the ratio-bias phenomenon. J. Pers. Soc. Psychol. **76**(6), 972–987 (1999)

Advancements in the Design and Evaluation of Social Computing Platforms

Evaluating a Spoken Argumentative Dialogue System

Annalena Aicher[1]([⊠])[iD], Stefan Hillmann[2][iD], Thilo Michael[2][iD],
Sebastian Möller[2][iD], Wolfgang Minker[1][iD], and Stefan Ultes[3][iD]

[1] Institute of Communications Engineering, Ulm University, Albert-Einstein-Allee
43, 89081 Ulm, Germany
{annalena.aicher,wolfgang.minker}@uni-ulm.de
[2] Quality and Usability Lab, TU Berlin, Ernst-Reuter-Platz 7, 10587 Berlin,
Germany
{stefan.hillmann,thilo.michael,sebastian.moller}@tu-berlin.de
[3] Language Generation and Dialogue Systems, University of Bamberg,
An der Weberei 5, 96047 Bamberg, Germany
stefan.ultes@uni-bamberg.de

Abstract. A natural way for humans to build an opinion on a topic is
through the gathering and exchange of new arguments. Speech interfaces
for argumentative dialogue systems (ADS) are rather scarce and quite
complex. To provide a more natural and intuitive interface, we include an
adaption of a recently introduced natural language understanding (NLU)
framework tailored to argumentative tasks into a complete end-to-end
ADS. Within this paper we investigate the influence of two different
input/output modalities (speech/speech and drop-down menu/text) and
discuss issues and problems we encountered in a user study with 202
participants using our ADS.

Keywords: Preference Modeling · Interest Modeling ·
Human-Computer Interaction · Spoken Dialogue Systems ·
Cooperative Argumentative Dialogue Systems

1 Introduction

Conversations display a natural way for humans to resolve different points of
view and build an opinion. Most popular virtual agents are trained to handle simple conversations, e.g. travel inquiries, still they are inept to demanding
conversations [17]. Especially, dialogue systems that exchange arguments and
can converse with humans via natural language display a big challenge in artificial intelligence. Such complex tasks demand for a flexible natural language
understanding (NLU), an argumentative dialogue structure, and the integration
of commonsense knowledge. The speech-driven argumentative dialogue system

This work has been funded by the DFG within the project "BEA - Building Engaging Argumentation", Grant no. 313723125, as part of the Priority Program "Robust
Argumentation Machines (RATIO)" (SPP-1999).

(ADS) we introduce in this paper combines these components and enables the user to scrutinize arguments on both sides of a controversial topic. To the best of our knowledge it is the first ADS which tries to cooperatively engage the user to explore arguments in natural language in order to support an unbiased and critically reflected opinion building process. We evaluate this spoken interaction in comparison to a robust baseline (menu input via mouse click), especially in terms of naturalness and usability aspects in a user study with 202 participants.

The remainder of the paper is as follows: Sect. 2 gives an overview of related work and Sect. 3 describes the ADS architecture. Section 4 explains the experimental study setting and Sect. 5 discusses the evaluation results. We close with a brief conclusion and outlook on future work in Sect. 6.

2   Related Work

Unlike most approaches to human-machine argumentation, we pursue a cooperative exchange of arguments. In contrast, Slonim et al. [18] use a classical debating setting. Their IBM Debater is an autonomous debating system that can engage in a competitive debate with humans via natural language. Another speech-based approach was introduced by Rosenfeld et al. [16] presenting a system based on weighted Bipolar Argumentation Frameworks. Arguing chatbots such as Debbie [15] and Dave [11] interact via text with the user. A menu-based framework that incorporates the beliefs and concerns of the opponent was also presented Hadoux et al. [10]. In the same line, Chalaguine et al. [7] used a previously crowd-sourced argument graph and considered the concerns of the user to persuade them. A persuasive prototype chatbot is introduced by [6] to convince users to vaccinate against COVID-19 using computational models of argument. Furthermore, Fazzinga et al. [9] discuss an approach toward a dialogue system architecture using argumentative concepts to perform reasoning. In contrast to all aforementioned ADS we aim for a system that cooperatively engages the users to explore arguments and state their preferences in natural language. Therefore we modified our previously introduced menu-based argumentative dialogue system [2] and extended it for our purpose. It served as a suitable basis as it also engages in a deliberative dialogue with a human user by providing all the con and pro aspects to a given argument.

3   Architecture of ADS

In the following, the architecture of our ADS and its components are outlined. An overview over the whole system's architecture is given in Fig. 1.

3.1   Dialogue Framework and Model

In order to be able to combine the presented system with existing argument mining approaches to ensure the flexibility of the system in view of discussed topics, we follow the argument annotation scheme introduced by Stab et al. [19]. It distinguishes three different types of components (Major Claim, Claim, Premise),

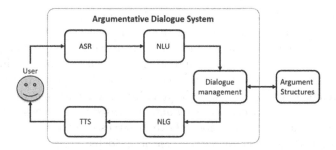

Fig. 1. Architecture of our ADS. After the user's spoken input is processed by the Automatic Speech Recognition module (ASR), it is passed to the Natural Language Understanding unit, which extracts the respective information. This abstractly represented information can be processed by the dialogue management, which decides a suitable corresponding system response by interacting with an argument structure. Once an appropriate response is selected it is processed by a Natural Language Generation (NLG) module which formulates its textual representation and finally presented it to the user in natural language through the Text-to-Speech (TTS) module. In the case of the menu system, the ASR and TTS modules were omitted.

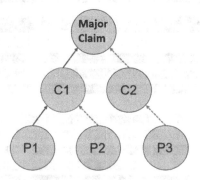

Fig. 2. Visualization of the argument tree structure. The major claim is the root node, which is supported by claim C2 (denoted by a green arrow) and attacked by claim C1 (denoted by a red arrow). The respective leaf nodes are the premises P1, P2 and P3. (Color figure online)

which are structured in the form of bipolar argumentation trees as depicted in Fig. 2. The overall topic of the debate is formulated as the *Major Claim* representing the root node in the graph. *Claims* (C1 and C2 in Fig. 2) on the other hand are assertions that formulate a certain opinion targeting the *Major Claim* but still need to be justified by further arguments, *premises* (P1 and P2) respectively. We consider two relations between these argument components (nodes), *support* (green arrows), or *attack* (red arrows). Each component apart from the Major Claim (which has no relation) has exactly one unique relation to another component. This leads to a non-cyclic tree structure, where each parent-node (C1 and C2) is supported or attacked by its child-nodes. If no child-nodes exist, the node is a leaf (e.g. P1, P2, and P3) and marks the end of a branch.

The interaction between the system and the user is separated in turns, consisting of a user action and corresponding answer of the system. In general, we distinguish three main types of moves(actions), the user can choose from: preference moves, information seeking moves, and others (navigation moves, help requests, status quo, exit). We use explicit user feedback (*prefer,reject*) to estimate the (overall) preference considering wBAGs [3,4]. In the herein presented study, a sample debate on the topic *Marriage is an outdated institution* is chosen [14], which suits the argument scheme described above. It serves as a knowledge base for the arguments and is taken from the *Debatabase* of the idebate.org[1] website. It consists of a total of 72 argument components (1 Major Claim, 10 Claims, and 61 Premises) and their corresponding relations are encoded in an OWL ontology [5] for further use. Due to the generality of the annotation scheme, the system is not restricted to the herein considered data. In general, every argument structure that can be mapped into the applied scheme can be processed by the system.

3.2   Interface and NLU Framework

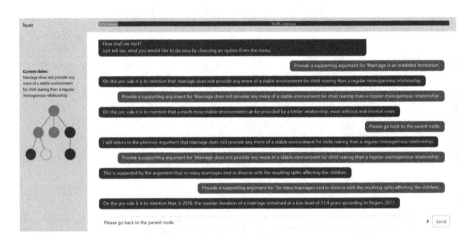

Fig. 3. GUI of the menu system with folded drop-down menu. Above the drop-down menu, the dialogue history is shown. On the left side, the sub-graph of the current branch is visible.

The system's graphical user interface (GUI) is illustrated in Fig. 3. The interface can either provide a drop-down menu or speech input as needed. In the drop-down system, users can choose their action by clicking, whereas in the speech system, an NLU framework based upon the one introduced by Abro et al. [1] processes the

---

spoken user utterance. This input is captured with a browser-based audio recording that is further processed by the `Python` library `SpeechRecognition`[2] using the Google Speech Recognition API. Its intent classifier uses the BERT Transformer Encoder presented by Devlin et al. [8] and a bidirectional LSTM classifier. The system-specific intents are trained with a set of sample utterances of a previous user study. After a user intent is recognized, the spoken system response is presented using the speech synthesis provided by Google Web Speech API.

In the speech-based system, instead of the drop-down menu displayed in Fig. 3, a button with the label "Start Talking" is shown. The button is pressed to start and stop the speech recording. Except for this difference, both systems share the same architecture. The visualization of the dialogue history shows the system's responses left-aligned and corresponding user moves right-aligned (see Fig. 3). A progress bar above the dialogue history shows the number of arguments that were already discussed and how many are still unknown to the user at each stage of the interaction. Furthermore, on the left side, the subgraph of the bipolar argument tree structure (with the displayed claim as root) is shown. The current position (i.e., argument) is displayed with a white node outlined with a green line. Already heard arguments are shown in green and skipped arguments are in red. Nodes shown in grey are still unheard.

The natural language generation is based on the original textual representation of the argument components. The annotated sentences are slightly modified to form a stand-alone utterance serving as a template for the respective system response. Additionally, a list of natural language representations for each type of system move was defined. During the generation of the utterances, the explicit formulation and introductory phrase are randomly chosen from this list.

4   User Study Setting

The study was conducted online via the crowdsourcing platform "Crowdee" (https://www.crowdee.com/, 12–29th November 2021) with participants from the UK, US, and Australia. All 292 participants (140 female, 152 male) were non-experts without a topic-specific background. After an introduction to the system (short text and demo video), the users had to listen to enough arguments to build a well-founded opinion (at least ten). The first 139 participants interacted with our ADS via drop-down menu input, and the other 153 via speech. The end of the interaction could be chosen freely as soon as at least ten arguments were heard.

After the conversation, the participants had to rate 40 statements on a five-point Likert scale (1 = totally disagree, 5 = totally agree) concerning the interaction. They were taken from a questionnaire according to ITU-T Recommendation P.851[3] [13].

Analyzing the questionnaire answers and feedback, 90 participants seemed to have issues, or their data showed anomalies. Their data were excluded according to previously defined exclusion criteria: Contradictory answers in control questions in the questionnaire, taking less than 30 s to read through the introduction

---

[2] https://pypi.org/project/SpeechRecognition/, last accessed 19.09.2022.
[3] Such questionnaires can be used to evaluate the quality of speech-based services.

and watch the introduction videos, taking less than 120 s to answer 40+15 questions in the final questionnaire. This leads to a total number of 202 data records: menu: 104 (50 female, 54 male, and speech: 98 (39 female, 59 male), which were used for the following evaluation.

5   Results and Discussion

In the following, we discuss the results of the previously described user study and scrutinize the used evaluation method.

On average the participants interacted with the ADS for 31:45 (menu: 27.57 speech: 35.34) minutes. This significant difference can be explained by the fact that the spoken interaction (speaking and hearing) inherently takes longer than clicking on an option in a drop-down menu and reading the response. Another significant difference between the speech and menu system is observable in the number of how many arguments that have been heard (average menu/speech: 22/15). Even though the average time the users of the menu system interacted with the ADS is lower, the number of provided arguments is significantly higher compared to the speech system. 9.6%/17.3% of the menu/speech system participants quit the conversation after hearing the minimum number of arguments (in total: 13.4%). Most of the participants heard between 20–30 arguments out of 72 available arguments. Whereas some participants in the menu system listened to even more arguments only one participant in the speech system did so. Additional to the six categories of the ITU-T Rec. P.851 (see Sect. 4) we added the category "Argumentation" as it is of special interest considering the purpose of the system. The respective results are shown in Table 1. The mean M and standard deviation SD are determined for each question and system. To determine whether the difference between the two systems means Δ_M is significant, we used the non-parametric Mann-Whitney U test [12] for two independent samples with no specific distribution.

The category "Overall Quality" ("What is your overall impression of the system?") is not included in Table 1 as it is rated on a different 5-point Likert scale ($5 = $ Excellent, $4 = $ Good, $3 = $ Fair, $2 = $ Poor, $1 = $ Bad). We perceive a highly significant ($\alpha < 0.01$) difference between both systems, as the menu system with a rating of 3.49 outperformed the speech system rated with 2.66 ($r = 0.394$).

Regarding all aspects, the speech system is outperformed significantly. In more detail, the biggest differences occurred in ratings whether the system provided the expected information (IPS 1) or errors which occurred (SB 4). Clearly, this points to a lack of processing the user utterances (errors in the ASR or NLU module). By checking the dialogue logs of the interactions with users in the speech system, we found that about 15% of all speech utterances were processed erroneously. Even though the NLU module matched about a third of these erroneously recognized utterances to the right move, the impact is still significant. Furthermore, we noticed inconsistencies in the user behavior, as users repeated their request multiple times, without reacting to the system's answer to choose another move. In contrast to the menu system where the users were always only displayed the possible actions, the speech users had to figure out what actions

Table 1. Means and standard deviations of the questionnaire items grouped by the following aspects: information provided by the system (IPS), communication with the system (COM), system behaviour (SB), dialogue (DI), user's impression of the system (UIS), acceptability (ACC), and argumentation (ARG). $|\Delta_M|$ denotes the absolute difference between the two mean values with * indicating its significance with $\alpha < 0.05$.

Asp.	Question	Menu		Speech		
		M	SD	M	SD	$|\Delta_M|$
IPS	The system has provided you the desired information	**3.56**	0.98	2.48	1.14	1.08*
	The system's answers and proposed solutions were clear	**4.1**	0.83	3.64	1.04	0.46*
	You would rate the provided information as true	**3.77**	0.87	3.45	0.92	0.32*
	The information provided by the system was complete	**3.53**	1.08	2.53	1.10	1.0*
COM	The system always understood you well	**3.51**	0.92	2.81	1.10	0.70*
	You had to concentrate in order to understand what the system expected from you	**3.58**	0.93	2.92	1.07	0.66*
	The system's responses were well understandable	**3.8**	0.77	3.53	0.81	0.27*
	You were able to interact efficiently with the system	**3.48**	0.99	2.93	1.07	0.55*
SB	You knew at each point of the interaction what the system expected from you.	**3.45**	1.03	2.49	1.13	0.98*
	In your opinion, the system processed your responses(specifications) correctly	**3.84**	0.81	2.86	1.12	0.98*
	The system's behavior was always as expected	**3.52**	0.91	2.86	1.06	0.66*
	The system often failed to understand you	2.38	0.88	**3.47**	1.07	1.09*
	The system reacted naturally	**3.13**	1.08	2.76	1.03	0.37*
	The system reacted flexibly	**3.14**	1.01	2.66	1.09	0.48*
	You were able to control the interaction in the desired way	**3.3**	1.07	2.49	1.15	0.81*
	The system reacted too slowly	3.18	1.22	**3.86**	1.10	0.68*
	The system reacted politely	**4.11**	0.68	4.06	0.66	0.05*
	The system's responses were too long	2.37	0.95	**2.67**	0.92	0.3*
DI	You perceived the dialogue as natural	**3.13**	1.02	2.44	1.06	0.69*
	It was easy to follow the flow of the dialogue	**3.49**	0.98	2.77	1.19	0.72*
	The dialogue was too long	2.43	0.90	**2.74**	0.97	0.31*
	The course of the dialogue was smooth	**3.39**	0.98	2.86	1.06	0.53*
	You and the system could clear misunderstandings easily	**3.34**	0.88	2.65	1.09	0.69*
	You would have expected more help from the system	2.95	0.94	**3.6**	0.94	0.65*
UIS	Overall, you were satisfied with the dialogue	**3.69**	0.89	3.18	1.01	0.51*
	The dialogue with the system was useful	**3.11**	1.17	2.56	1.23	0.55*
	It was easy for you to obtain the information you wanted	**3.73**	0.86	3.34	0.94	0.39*
	You have perceived the dialogue as pleasant	**3.65**	0.97	2.77	1.07	0.88*
	You felt relaxed during the dialogue	**3.25**	1.21	2.65	1.24	0.60*
	Using the system was fun	**3.43**	1.05	2.71	1.15	0.72*
ACC	In the future, you would use the system again	**3.55**	1.01	2.97	1.08	0.58*
	You would would recommend the system to a friend	**3.39**	1.07	2.61	1.05	0.78*
ARG	I felt motivated by the system to discuss the topic	**3.44**	0.97	2.72	1.18	0.72*
	I would rather use this system than read the arguments in an article	**3.1**	1.28	2.23	1.25	0.87*
	The possible options to respond to the system were sufficient	**3.38**	0.98	2.87	1.10	0.51*
	The arguments the system presented are conclusive	**3.16**	1.07	2.79	1.09	0.37*
	I felt engaged in the conversation with the system	**3.51**	1.05	2.7	1.17	0.81*
	The interaction with the system was confusing	2.82	1.16	**3.62**	1.11	0.80*
	I do not like that the arguments are provided incrementally	3.01	1.05	**3.42**	0.97	0.41*

they can perform and formulate them. Even though the speech system's design incorporated a "Help" button, as well as the "available" options move, it seems quite a lot of users did not use them. But only 35% of the users spend enough time on the introduction website to read through the explanation and watch the according video properly. This is further underpinned by feedback, stating that "It was not possible to do what I wanted to do. I repeated myself many times"/"I was stuck in the argument and could not get back"/"The idea is cool, still sometimes things got messy when I could not proceed to the argument I wanted to go to.". Therefore, in the future, the study setting should be double-staged, which ensures that all participants passing the first stage have well understood how to interact with our ADS. Another option is a study in the lab, where the participants can be supervised and the environmental conditions are controlled.

The results show that the I/O modalities and respective difficulties/problems decrease the rating of the general impression of the system, even in aspects that have no relation to the former. For example, the incremental approach to present arguments (ARG 7), the sufficiency of different options (ARG 3), or the conclusiveness of arguments (ARG 4) which are content- but not modality-dependent are rated significantly worse than in the menu system. Therefore, it is crucial to solve the identified issues.

Even though the introduced speech system does not outperform the menu baseline, we could show that the menu system provides a robust baseline and tends to be rated positively in almost every question. Thus, it will serve as a baseline to which enhanced versions of the spoken ADS will be compared to.

6   Conclusion and Future Work

In this work, we discussed an evaluation of the argumentative dialogue system BEA in two different I/O modalities by conducting a crowd-sourcing study. Due to an erroneous ASR module and issues in understanding how to communicate with our ADS via speech, we observed that the speech-based interaction was rated significantly lower than our well-performing menu baseline. Still, the general argument exploration behaviour shows strong parallels when disregarding isolated outliers in the baseline system. In future work, we will enhance the system's ASR and robustness of the NLU by training on larger datasets and including fallback such as a request for repetition in case the intent recognition accuracy falls below a threshold value. Furthermore, by incorporating the implicit detection of the user interest, the system will be able to proactively suggest new arguments and engage the users to express themselves more naturally. Finally, we will evaluate these extensions of the speech-based system in a broad combined crowd-sourcing and laboratory study, incorporating a double-staged setup and proactively uttered assistance, and investigate if we can improve user satisfaction and motivation to engage in an argumentative discussion.

References

1. Abro, W.A., Aicher, A., Rach, N., Ultes, S., Minker, W., Qi, G.: Natural language understanding for argumentative dialogue systems in the opinion building domain. Knowl.-Based Syst. **242**, 108318 (2022), ISSN 0950–7051. https://www.sciencedirect.com/science/article/pii/S0950705122001149
2. Aicher, A., Rach, N., Minker, W., Ultes, S.: Opinion building based on the argumentative dialogue system BEA. In: Marchi, E., Siniscalchi, S.M., Cumani, S., Salerno, V.M., Li, H. (eds.) Increasing Naturalness and Flexibility in Spoken Dialogue Interaction. LNEE, vol. 714, pp. 307–318. Springer, Singapore (2021). https://doi.org/10.1007/978-981-15-9323-9_27
3. Amgoud, L., Ben-Naim, J.: Evaluation of arguments from support relations: axioms and semantics. In: Proceedings of the 25th International Joint Conference on Artificial Intelligence, IJCAI-16, pp. 900–906 (2016). https://www.ijcai.org/Proceedings/16/Papers/132.pdf
4. Amgoud, L., Ben-Naim, J.: Weighted bipolar argumentation graphs: axioms and semantics. In: Proceedings of the Twenty-Seventh International Joint Conference on Artificial Intelligence, IJCAI-18, pp. 5194–5198 (2018)
5. Bechhofer, S.: Owl: Web ontology language. In: Encyclopedia of Database Systems, pp. 2008–2009, Springer, Boston (2009). https://doi.org/10.1007/978-0-387-39940-9_1073
6. Chalaguine, L., Hunter, A.: Addressing popular concerns regarding COVID-19 vaccination with natural language argumentation dialogues. In: Vejnarová, J., Wilson, N. (eds.) ECSQARU 2021. LNCS (LNAI), vol. 12897, pp. 59–73. Springer, Cham (2021). https://doi.org/10.1007/978-3-030-86772-0_5
7. Chalaguine, L.A., Hunter, A.: A persuasive chatbot using a crowd-sourced argument graph and concerns. In: COMMA (2020)
8. Devlin, J., Chang, M.-W., Lee, K., Toutanova, K.: BERT: pre-training of deep bidirectional transformers for language understanding. In: Proceedings of the 2019 Conference of the North American Chapter of the Association for Computational Linguistics: Human Language Technologies, vol. 1 (Long and Short Papers), pp. 4171–4186. Association for Computational Linguistics, Minneapolis (2019)
9. Fazzinga, B., Galassi, A., Torroni, P.: An argumentative dialogue system for COVID-19 vaccine information. In: Baroni, P., Benzmüller, C., Wáng, Y.N. (eds.) CLAR 2021. LNCS (LNAI), vol. 13040, pp. 477–485. Springer, Cham (2021). https://doi.org/10.1007/978-3-030-89391-0_27
10. Hadoux, E., Hunter, A., Polberg, S.: Strategic argumentation dialogues for persuasion: framework and experiments based on modelling the beliefs and concerns of the persuadee. Argum. Comput. **14**, 1–53 (2022). https://doi.org/10.3233/AAC-210005
11. Le, D.T., Nguyen, C.T., Nguyen, K.A.: Dave the debater: a retrieval-based and generative argumentative dialogue agent. In: Proceedings of the 5th Workshop on Argument Mining, pp. 121–130 (2018). https://www.aclweb.org/anthology/W18-5215
12. McKnight, P.E., Najab, J.: Mann-Whitney U Test, pp. 1–1. American Cancer Society (2010). ISBN 9780470479216
13. P.851, I.T.R.: Subjective quality evaluation of telephone services based on spoken dialogue systems (11/2003). International Telecommunication Union (Nov 2003)
14. Rach, N., Langhammer, S., Minker, W., Ultes, S.: Utilizing argument mining techniques for argumentative dialogue systems. In: Proceedings of the 9th International Workshop On Spoken Dialogue Systems (IWSDS) (May 2018)

15. Rakshit, G., Bowden, K.K., Reed, L., Misra, A., Walker, M.A.: Debbie, the debate bot of the future. In: Advanced Social Interaction with Agents - 8th International Workshop on Spoken Dialog Systems, pp. 45–52 (2017)
16. Rosenfeld, A., Kraus, S.: Strategical argumentative agent for human persuasion. In: ECAI'16, pp. 320–328 (2016)
17. Saha, T., Saha, S., Bhattacharyya, P.: Towards sentiment-aware multi-modal dialogue policy learning. Cogn. Comput, pp. 1–15 (11 2020)
18. Slonim, N., et al.: An autonomous debating system. Nature **591**(7850), 379–384 (2021)
19. Stab, C., Gurevych, I.: Annotating argument components and relations in persuasive essays. In: COLING, pp. 1501–1510 (2014)

Development of New Moral Foundation Vignettes for Unethical Behavior Against Whistleblowers

Stefan Becker[1]([✉]) and Christian W. Scheiner[2,3]

[1] Universität zu Lübeck, Lübeck, Germany
stefan.becker@uni-luebeck.de
[2] Universität zu Lübeck, Lübeck, Germany
christian.scheiner@uni-luebeck.de
[3] Christian-Albrechts-Universität zu Kiel, Kiel, Germany

Abstract. Within the last years, whistleblowing has received considerable attention, as calls for ethical behavior in the workplace have grown louder. Despite this fact, research has shown that individuals who blow the whistle are often frowned upon and treated poorly. Previous research already tried to explain unethical behavior on social media by linking moral receptors with moral disengagement in the context of unethical behavior. For an explanation on the origins and variations in human reasoning typically Moral Foundations Theory and its 'gold-standard' measurement scale—the Moral Foundation Questionnaire—are used. The scale has been used extensively in a range of empirical projects. However, recent research also raises criticisms from both theoretical and empirical perspectives. In this paper, a comprehensive set of Moral Foundations vignettes is developed to address some of the issues raised with the current questionnaire. Each vignette depicts a behavior violating a particular moral foundation. The validity of the developed vignettes is demonstrated through exploratory and confirmatory factor analysis. The resulting set of Moral Foundation Vignettes consists of 41 scenarios categorized in eight different factors, where Care foundation is subdivided into three different factors.

Keywords: Moral Receptors · Moral Foundations · Moral Foundation Theory · Moral Foundation Vignettes · Unethical Behavior · Whistleblower

1 Introduction

Within the last years, calls for ethical behavior in the workplace have grown louder and more forceful [45]. As a result, whistleblowing has received considerable attention. But, instead of being applauded for exposing illegal actions, whistleblowers are far too often castigated for trying to challenge and overturn the status quo [1, 13, 34, 37, 39, 44]. At this, organizations and its members use different forms of retaliation, ranging from more formal undesirable actions (such as

A. Coman and S. Vasilache (Eds.): HCII 2023, LNCS 14026, pp. 435–449, 2023.
https://doi.org/10.1007/978-3-031-35927-9_30

termination, demotion, involuntary transfer, assignment of unmanageable tasks, and professional blacklisting) to more informal ones (e.g., social ostracism, and bullying).

Although much research has been conducted on the individual as well as the contextual determinants of reporting illicit behavior, little work has been done examining the specific factors for when and why retaliation occurs. Previous research has already identified the role of moral disengagement as a possible explanation, why decent people conduct malign behavior [2,3,35,40,41]. As a result, researchers gained important insights into the mechanisms that allow people to detach from their own moral standards without feeling pain or regret. Additionally, Scheiner [40] proposed to use moral receptors as a starting point to trigger unethical behavior discussing that there is also a link between moral receptors and moral disengagement. Building upon this idea, we argued that this framework is also capable in describing the boundary conditions and mechanisms for when and why retaliation against whistleblowers occurs [4].

Typically, to explain the origins of and variation in human moral reasoning, Moral Foundations Theory (MFT) is used. According to MFT, there are six, innate but modifiable moral foundations (Care, Fairness, Loyalty, Authority, Sanctity, and Liberty) [19,20,22,26], which guide peoples' moral judgments and emotions. These foundations allow us to be very sensitive to certain social stimuli (e.g., injustice) and to immediately respond to them intuitively, often mediating this response through specific emotions (e.g., anger).

The established measure of these foundations – the Moral Foundations Questionnaire (MFQ) – has been used extensively in a range of empirical projects [5,7,12,15,26,42]. While the MFQ has been widely validated [17], the scale has recently also come in for criticism [8,9,24,25,36]. In this paper, we aim to address the problems of MFQ by introducing and validating a new set of Moral Foundations Vignettes (MFVs) used for explaining the unethical behavior against whistleblowers.

2   Theoretical Background

2.1   Moral Foundation Theory

According to the social intuitionism model [18], moral judgment is an intuitive process, characterized by automatic, affective reactions to stimuli. MFT categorizes these moral intuitions into different "foundations" [20–22] explaining why individuals and groups differ in what they see as moral or immoral. Each foundation represents a set of intuitions that have evolved to solve certain social challenges throughout evolutionary history. The current and most widely accepted draft of the theory posits six foundations [19,26]:

1. Harm/Care (Harming, Hurting, Caring, Kindness) – This foundation includes concerns about caring, protecting, and nurturing vulnerable individuals or animals from harm.

2. Fairness/Reciprocity (Justice, Fairness, Reciprocity) – This foundation includes reciprocal relationship among people as well as aspects concerning justice, fairness, and equality.
3. In-group/Loyalty (Group membership, Loyalty, Patriotism, Self-sacrifice) – This foundation relates to our formation of groups in society and the different obligations of group membership.
4. Authority/Respect (Obedience, Deference) – This foundation is based on our tendency to create hierarchically structured societies of dominance and subordination. It includes aspects centered on respect for authority, and leadership.
5. Purity/Sanctity (Temperance, Chastity, Piety) – This foundation roots from our ancestors' instinct to avoid diseases. It underlies the widespread idea that the body is a temple which can be desecrated by immoral activities and contaminants.
6. Liberty/Autonomy (Freedom, Oppression, Subjugation) – This foundation includes acts restricting the freedom of others, particularly actions by those in a position of power over another person.

Research on moral foundations has relied on the Moral Foundations Questionnaire, characterized by two sets of questions: the first asks respondents to make abstract moral judgments, the second asks to report on the relevance of each foundation to their moral decision-making [17]. The questionnaire has proved to be particularly useful for the evaluation of variations in moral judgment. At this, moral foundations theory has had a large impact in psychology and a variety of other disciplines. In political science, researchers gained explanations for different political attitudes, shifts in attitudes and ideologies [11,15,19], examined differences in donation behavior [48], and tried to understand how the public evaluates politicians' character [6]. In other disciplines, Moral Foundation Theory has been used, for instance, to examine the effects of general religiosity on moral foundations [28,38], to understand the role of moral salience and its mediating effects in the context of decision making in video games [27,32,47], to examine cross-cultural differences [19], and to quantify moral foundations from various topics in everyday conversations on social media [29].

2.2   Moral Foundation Questionnaire: Introduction, Extensions, and Criticism

As a measurement instrument investigating the inter-individual variability, the Moral Foundation Questionnaire allows for examining whether and to what extent individuals' moral judgments relate to the five originally postulated moral foundations (Harm/Care, Fairness/Reciprocity, In-group/Loyalty, Authority/Respect, Purity/Sanctity) [19]. The MFQ consists of 30 items - divided into a relevance and judgment section - plus 2 'catch' items used to filter out inattentive participants. The relevance section asks respondents to rate the relevance of fifteen considerations to questions of right and wrong on a 6-point rating scale (e.g., "When you decide whether something is right or wrong, to what extent do you consider whether or not someone was cruel?" for harm). In addition to this, the second section consists of fifteen agree/disagree items (e.g., "Respect for authority is something all children need to learn." for authority). At this, the relevance scale investigates the explicit theories people have about what is morally relevant to them, while the judgment scale examines the extent to which the five moral foundations are used concretely in the expression of judgments and evaluations. In total, there are six items for each of the five foundations and scoring occurs by averaging the responses to each of the six items per moral foundation. In order to include the sixth foundation, the desire of people for autonomy and freedom, the original MFQ can be accompanied by Iyer et al.'s [26] nine items for measuring endorsement of the liberty foundation.

Although the MFQ has been shown to be reliable and valid [17], the scale has also come in for criticism both on theoretical as well as empirical ground. In terms of predicting political orientation, several meta-analyses examining the relationship between moral foundations and political orientation, researchers found that correlations between the five foundations and political orientation is close to zero in Black samples [10,31]. By manipulating the goals of moral behavior, Voelkel and Brandt also illustrated the shifting relationship between some moral foundations and political ideology [46].

Further, recent confirmatory factor analyses have found only reasonable levels of model fit when using the default five-foundation model [9,25,30,36,43]. In a large-scale analysis of measurement invariance of the 5-factor structure of the MFQ in 27 countries, Iurino and Saucier [25] concluded that there was little support for a five-, but rather for a two-factor model related to harm and social order. Including the liberty items introduced by Iyer et al. [26], Harper and Rhodes [24] re-examined the dimensionality of the full MFQ in combination with the liberty scale. Instead of giving support for a 6-factor solution, in two concurrent studies only three meaningful clusters emerged, namely traditionalism, compassion, and liberty. Similar issues with fit have also been reported at the level of individual foundations. Among studies that have not explicitly tested the fit of the 5-factor model of the MFQ, the internal consistency of each of the moral foundations has produced poor coefficients with Cronbach's alpha coefficients between 0.24 to 0.69 [15–17,23].

A final point regarding the scale is that its structure also limits the types of questions for which it can be used. Here, an important point is that the MFQ relies largely on respondents' evaluations of abstract principles rather than judgment of concrete scenarios. At this, measuring the relevance of various moral issues does not necessarily correspond to the actual moral judgment that people make [15]. Even if someone views respect as highly relevant to morality, this person may refrain from making harsh judgments about others' disrespectful behavior. Also, several items contain an indefinite and ambiguous reference point. Responses to the item "Whether or not someone showed a lack of respect for authority" might differ depending on the interpretation of the authority to which someone is showing disrespect [14].

3   Method

In this paper, we aim to address some of the problems discussed before by developing and validating a large set of moral foundations vignettes that would satisfy the following criteria: a) measure judgment of concrete moral violations of third-parties, and b) contain subsets mapping onto the moral foundations.

Following the approach of Clifford et al. [8], we started by writing a large number of scenarios representing valid violations of specific moral foundations, adapting previous stimuli whenever possible. Each vignette shows a behavior that violates a particular moral foundation. As we are interested especially in discovering which moral emotions can trigger or prevent unethical behavior against whistleblowers, we focus the content of our scenarios on events that could plausibly occur within the scope of organizations and whistleblowing. By varying the content of the scenarios within a given foundation, we try to reduce redundancy, avoid memory interactions, and ensure complete conceptual coverage of the foundations. We also tried to avoid overtly political content as well as scenarios that might require temporally or culturally bounded knowledge.

To encourage respondents to visualize themselves as witnesses of third-party violations, all of our scenarios start with the phrase "You see someone...". For example, a Fairness violation reads: "You see someone using company funds to enrich himself." Using this structure ensures that respondents imagine a third party committing the violation and that any induced emotions are the result of imagining witnessing the violation. Next, we describe how the individual items for the different moral foundations were constructed.

For the *Care* foundations, we focused on scenarios triggering compassion for a person who is suffering (e.g., "You see someone being bullied by others"), or eliciting anger against the person causing the distress (e.g., "You see someone physically attacking others"). In order to avoid confounds with other foundations, we avoided scenarios invoking a social hierarchy (Authority, Liberty), and focus on scenarios involving strangers (Loyalty).

Fairness is triggered by situations involving cheating, dishonesty, unfair behavior, or a lack of gratitude. Similar to the Care vignettes, we tried to avoid scenarios in which loyalty (group behavior) or authority (disobedience towards executives) concerns might arise.

Loyalty violations consist of individuals putting their own interests ahead of their group (i.e., colleagues, or company).

Authority violations consist primarily of disobedience or disrespect to traditional authority figures (e.g., managers, supervisors, leaders).

Violations of *Sanctity* include behaviors that are considered degrading (getting excessively drunk) or raise concerns about contamination (urinating in the corner of the office, not washing hands after going to the toilet). Haidt also suggested that certain symbols, such as a church, cross, or flag, can also become sacralized [19]. Therefore, we also tested vignettes that involved violating corporate symbols (corporate logo or flag).

Liberty vignettes consist of behaviors in which people use coercion or restrict freedom of choice, especially actions by people who hold a position of power over another person (e.g., someone who prevents others from voicing their concerns).

In total, we ended up with 69 scenarios plus 6 'catch' items; the latter containing morally acceptable behavior and serving as a check on participant attention (see Table 1). To further narrow down the number of items for a final version, two surveys were conducted, which will be briefly presented.

Setting. Both surveys were performed over a period of approximately six weeks in January and February 2023. They were designed as online surveys used to get as many responses as possible in a short amount of time. Invitation to the first survey was sent by e-mail to all students at the University of Lübeck, explaining the reason for the survey and asking the recipients to participate and to share the survey. The invitation was also included within a newsletter published by the author's institute. Anonymity was guaranteed. No incentives were provided to this group. Additionally, we published the link to our second online survey on Prolific. Here, participants received a monetary incentive completing the survey.

Sample. In total, 269 respondents (Study 1: 165 participants, Study 2: 104 participants) were recruited. 31 participants did not start the survey (Study 1: 27 participants, Study 2: 4 participants, exploitation rate: 88.4 %). We also applied further quality controls to remove participants who gave incomplete answers or who provided responses that were suggestive of biased or inauthentic answers (e.g., always rating items as 1, 3 or 5, including those that were reverse-coded). At this, another 59 respondents have to be excluded (Study 1: 55 participants, Study 2: 4 participants). With a value of 66.5 %, an excellent completion rate was achieved. While the participants of the first study were of German nationality, the demographics of the 100 respondents participating in the second survey suggest cross-cultural origins from a total of 19 different countries. The top 5 nationalities were as follows: South African (44), Polish (12), Portuguese (11), Greek (6), and Italian (5).

Instruments. While the first study was conducted in German, for the second study all items were carefully translated into English respecting the original content and magnitude of moral violation, and ensuring that the English version is still clear and objective. The items were randomly assigned within the questionnaire to avoid showing of a pattern of the mechanisms by grouping items of the same process. Respondents were asked to rate how morally wrong the behavior is on a 5-point scale labeled morally wrong, rather wrong, neutral, rather correct, morally correct.

4   Results

To find out about the properties of the 75 moral foundation items as a basis for item selection, descriptive statistics and item statistics were calculated. In addition, exploratory and confirmatory factor analysis as well as reliability analysis were calculated for the 75 items developed.

The average rating as well as standard deviations for each item are shown in Table 1 (left). Item means range between 1.07 ("You see someone bulling others." and "You see someone physically attacking others.", respectively) and 4.86 ("You see someone making sure that everyone should be treated equally."), standard deviations of the 75 items range between 0.25 ("You see someone bulling others." and "You see someone physically attacking others.", respectively) and 1.04 ("You see someone intervening in a fight.").

Exploratory Factor Analysis. Although MFT proposes a six factor structure, we started with an exploratory factor analysis to examine the extent to which individual scenarios load cleanly onto the expected factors, and not on others. Respondents' wrongness ratings for all moral scenarios, with the exception of the 'catch' items, were entered as manifest variables in a maximum likelihood exploratory factor analysis resulting into 19 factors with an eigenvalue greater than 1. Next, a parallel analysis was conducted, which indicated that eight factors should be retained. Based on the results of the parallel analysis, a second exploratory factor analysis (using maximum likelihood extraction with Varimax rotation) was run with the instruction to extract eight factors. The Kaiser-Meyer-Olkin measure of sampling adequacy (0.80) and Bartlett's test for sphericity ($\chi^2(2346) = 6199.86, p < 0.001$) suggested that the data was suitable for testing dimensionality. The resulting rotated factor loadings are shown in Table 1 (right) with factor loadings greater than or equal to .5 in bold and factor loadings less than .4 in gray. The eight factors explain a total of 41.69 % of the variances.

In the first factor, 7 out of 14 Authority scenarios have factor loadings greater than 0.5 (loadings from 0.52 to 0.63), and three others have at least a factor loading of greater than 0.4 ("interrupting an executive in front of everyone at a project meeting.": 0.47, "trying to undermine all the leader's ideas in front of the others.": 0.48 with a weak cross-load onto Liberty (0.37), and "not respecting the general rules of conduct.": 0.44 with a weak cross-load on Sanctity (0.32)). However, two Sanctity scenarios also have loadings greater than 0.5 on Authority. Both scenarios involving the violation against corporate symbols ("publicly spitting on the company's logo.": 0.64, and "trampling on the corporate flag.": 0.70).

9 of the 17 Sanctity scenarios load onto the second factor with loadings greater than 0.4 (8 greater than 0.5and loadings from 0.53 to 0.64). As described before, both scenarios involving violations of corporate symbols have high loadings on Authority, and almost negligible loadings on Sanctity, 0.18 and 0.06, respectively.

Turning to the third factor, 5 of the 8 Liberty scenarios have factor loadings greater than 0.5 (loadings from 0.54 to 0.70), while no other scenarios load moderate onto this factor. Of the remaining three Liberty scenarios, one loads solely but weakly on Liberty (0.31), one loads on both Liberty and Authority (0.36 and 0.35, respectively), and the last loads negatively but weakly on Authority (−0.30).

Of the 13 Fairness scenarios, only 5 load onto the fourth factor with loadings greater than 0.5. A sixth Fairness scenario only shows a weak factor loading ("lying about the amount of hours they've worked overtime.": 0.32).

Regarding the fifth factor, 6 of the 7 Loyalty scenarios have factor loadings greater than 0.4 (5 greater than 0.5 and loadings from 0.53 to 0.89). Overall, there is a clear separation between the Authority and Loyalty foundations within the data.

Finally, instead of loading completely on one factor, 9 of 10 Care scenarios form three distinct factors. Within the first Care factor, the detrimental act of the oppressor is emphasized, which might correspond to an expression of anger towards the person causing the suffering. The three scenarios have factor loadings of 0.57, 0.77 and 0.91, respectively. The second Care factor concerns scenarios involving compassion for the person being oppressed. All three scenarios have factor loadings between 0.57 and 0.83. The last factor corresponds to acts of gloating with scenarios having factor loadings of 0.68, 0.70 and 0.78, respectively. The last Care scenario has only a weak loading onto Liberty ("taking advantage of the weakness of others for their own purposes.": 0.39).

In summary, our findings from the exploratory factor analysis show strong support for the expected divisions within the moral domains. We uncovered factors associated with each of the moral foundations. We also found evidence of a division within the Care foundation depending on whether the oppressor or the person being oppressed is emphasized, or as an reaction to gloating.

Confirmatory Factor Analysis. Previous research on Moral Foundation Theory provides strong predictions about the factor structure of moral judgment, suggesting a two-, five-, or six-factor model (the latter results from adding Liberty) [16,25,26,36]. A confirmatory factor analysis was run on our data using the lavaan SPSS package. We used an eight-factor model consisting of Care – Oppression, Care – Compassion, Care – Gloating, Fairness, Liberty, Authority, Loyalty, and Sanctity as default model resulting in a good fit ($\chi^2(2182) = 3443.31$; RMSEA $= 0.057$, see Table 2). We also ran a confirmatory analysis on two simpler models (a two- as well as a six-factor model) to replicate the findings of other authors [25,36]. Results are illustrated in Table 2 showing that these models provided a worse fit to the data as indicated by degradations in the RMSEA and AIC.

Recommended set of vignettes. The results of the exploratory factor analysis as well as the confirmatory factor analysis already illustrate a good fit for an eight-factor model. As shown in Table 1, a number of vignettes either did not load strongly on the predicted factor (loading greater than 0.4), or cross-loaded onto another factors. Thus, these vignettes may not be good measures of the intended concepts. At this, vignettes are retained only if they demonstrated factor loadings greater than 0.5 on the predicted factor, and did not have cross-loading differences between the intended and another factor greater than 0.2. Both vignettes involving the violation against corporate symbols were included into the final set of vignettes, but were reassigned to Authority instead of Sanctity. The resulting set of 41 vignettes contains 3 to 9 vignettes per foundation. Removing weak loading scenarios also improve model fit statistics for all models (see Table 2). Again, the eight-factor model best describes the data

Table 1. First draft of moral foundation vignettes. *Wrongness* presenting the average rating as well as the standard deviation of moral wrongness on a 5-point scale. Vignettes with an ∗, represent 'catch' items of morally acceptable behaviors. Additionally, results of the exploratory factor analysis of moral judgments are given. Factor loadings ≥ 0.5 are shown in bold. Factor loadings ≤ 0.4 are shown in gray.

Foundation	Scenario	Mean	SD				Factors				
Authority	You see someone interrupting an executive in front of everyone at a project meeting.	2.38	0.89	0.47	0.25	-0.08	0.16	0.16	0.05	-0.06	0.14
Authority	You see someone secretly surfing the Internet on his or her smartphone during a project meeting.	2.48	0.91	**0.59**	0.16	0.18	0.12	0.09	-0.02	-0.13	0.12
Authority	You see someone talking loudly to others at a project meeting.	1.98	0.76	0.34	0.21	0.17	0.04	0.05	0.12	0.12	-0.09
Authority	You see someone turn and walk away while a manager asks about that person's work.	1.77	0.74	**0.52**	0.23	0.18	-0.02	0.05	0.02	0.19	0.04
Authority	You see someone proclaiming that an executive is a bad person.	2.36	0.88	**0.60**	0.06	-0.02	0.15	-0.01	0.01	0.19	0.13
Authority	You see someone not following a leader's instructions.	2.28	0.79	**0.63**	0.20	-0.03	0.05	0.18	0.07	0.06	0.19
Authority	You see someone refusing to welcome people from the management.	2.15	0.77	**0.60**	0.07	0.04	0.11	0.29	0.06	0.09	-0.07
Authority	You see someone trying to undermine all the leader's ideas in front of the others.	1.80	0.74	0.48	0.21	0.37	0.12	0.15	-0.04	0.08	-0.01
Authority	You see someone disrespecting another person's expertise.	1.73	0.65	0.30	0.32	0.31	0.12	0.07	0.03	0.18	0.12
Authority	You see someone not respecting the general rules of conduct.	1.69	0.62	0.44	0.32	0.14	0.05	0.02	0.13	0.12	0.04
Authority	You see someone not following the company's guidelines.	2.06	0.72	**0.58**	0.32	-0.05	0.09	0.24	0.05	0.10	0.02
Authority	You see someone deliberately disregarding a directive from an executive.	2.18	0.84	**0.54**	0.34	-0.05	0.11	0.10	0.14	0.04	0.17
Authority	You see someone speaking badly about the person celebrating the birthday at a company.	1.74	0.68	0.32	0.21	0.19	-0.02	0.26	-0.06	0.06	0.13
Authority	You see someone disrespecting specialist knowledge of others.	1.78	0.66	0.33	0.27	0.29	0.10	0.05	0.19	0.09	-0.04
Authority	You see someone following the instructions of the supervisor.∗	4.17	0.76	-	-	-	-	-	-	-	-
Sanctity	You see someone spitting on the ground.	1.84	0.79	0.09	0.33	0.13	0.04	0.06	0.07	0.17	0.04
Sanctity	You see someone wipe his or her own nose on his or her top.	2.38	0.88	0.24	**0.59**	-0.03	0.14	0.05	-0.01	-0.03	0.09
Sanctity	You see someone doing something disgusting.	1.89	0.76	0.04	**0.58**	0.16	0.14	0.16	-0.07	0.04	-0.04
Sanctity	You see someone urinating in the corner of the office.	1.08	0.39	0.01	0.09	**0.60**	-0.06	-0.06	0.03	0.14	-0.18
Sanctity	You see someone showing up to work unwashed and unkempt.	2.12	0.86	0.38	**0.64**	-0.04	0.10	0.11	-0.07	0.00	0.14
Sanctity	You see someone showing up to work drunk and vomiting.	1.32	0.56	0.30	**0.61**	-0.04	-0.08	0.04	-0.04	-0.12	-0.03
Sanctity	You see someone not washing their hands after going to the toilet.	1.83	0.76	0.07	**0.53**	0.18	0.14	0.12	0.17	0.08	0.60
Sanctity	You see someone publicly spitting on the company's logo.	1.70	0.85	0.18	0.06	0.03	0.20	-0.05	0.00	0.15	
Sanctity	You see someone trampling on the corporate flag.	2.02	0.93	0.06	0.08	**0.69**	0.07	0.00	-0.04	0.03	
Sanctity	You see someone coming into the office with a contagious disease.	1.50	0.72	0.06	0.32	0.26	0.26	0.15	0.28	**0.60**	0.01
Sanctity	You see someone coming to the office with unwashed clothes for several days.	2.22	0.95	0.18	**0.58**	-0.11	0.17	0.11	-0.05	-0.02	0.29
Sanctity	You see someone getting excessively drunk at a company party.	2.20	0.98	0.31	**0.55**	0.18	0.12	0.11	0.04	-0.08	-0.06
Sanctity	You see someone eating everything away at a company party.	2.44	0.79	0.20	0.29	0.04	0.26	0.01	-0.03	-0.07	-0.03
Sanctity	You see someone not flushing after going to the toilet.	1.58	0.68	0.07	**0.60**	0.02	0.05	0.11	0.11	0.11	-0.10
Sanctity	You see someone leaving a toilet heavily soiled.	1.44	0.63	0.25	0.49	0.20	0.21	0.06	0.14	0.11	-0.18
Sanctity	You see someone not cleaning up after the he or she has made something dirty.	1.79	0.76	0.12	0.35	0.34	0.08	0.06	0.11	0.03	0.04
Sanctity	You see someone rinsing glasses with just water and not soap and then putting them back on the shelf.	2.32	0.98	0.09	0.30	0.10	0.25	0.05	-0.04	0.17	0.16
Sanctity	You see someone showing up to work well-groomed.∗	4.42	0.76	-	-	-	-	-	-	-	-
Liberty	You see someone imposing his or her values on others.	1.46	0.55	0.07	0.01	**0.55**	0.11	0.10	0.08	0.01	-0.02
Liberty	You see someone preventing others from freely expressing their opinions.	1.42	0.54	0.06	-0.05	**0.70**	0.11	0.10	0.14	0.15	0.05
Liberty	You see someone preventing others from voicing their concerns.	1.43	0.53	0.06	0.19	**0.62**	0.26	0.10	0.01	0.10	0.06
Liberty	You see someone forcing others to act unethically.	1.17	0.39	-0.02	0.03	**0.57**	0.13	-0.05	0.03	0.03	0.20
Liberty	You see someone preventing others from expressing their opinion publicly.	1.49	0.55	-0.03	0.03	**0.54**	0.08	0.17	0.03	0.19	0.14
Liberty	You see someone not wanting to take the responsibility for a mistake of his or her own.	1.45	0.54	0.35	0.13	0.36	0.10	0.16	0.05	0.10	-0.04
Liberty	You see someone blaming someone else for his or her own mistake.	1.19	0.50	-0.02	0.05	0.31	0.14	0.03	0.04	0.21	-0.07
Liberty	You see someone completely submissive to the executives.	2.68	1.01	-0.20	0.08	0.01	-0.01	-0.05	-0.17	0.07	-0.17
Liberty	You see someone encouraging others to express their opinions freely.∗	4.62	0.73	-	-	-	-	-	-	-	-
Fairness	You see someone claiming someone else's results for his or her own.	1.19	0.46	0.09	0.04	0.33	0.12	0.11	0.26	0.19	0.60
Fairness	You see someone using company funds to enrich him or herself.	1.46	0.61	0.14	0.18	0.28	0.13	0.08	0.02	0.24	0.08
Fairness	You see someone not reporting the misconduct of others.	1.89	0.88	0.17	0.20	0.24	0.25	-0.08	-0.01	0.02	0.10
Fairness	You see someone being unjustifiably evaluated worse than the others.	1.49	0.60	0.11	0.09	0.24	**0.53**	0.04	0.05	0.24	0.09
Fairness	You see someone being unjustifiably assigned worse tasks.	1.64	0.68	0.06	0.08	0.25	**0.58**	0.11	0.03	0.10	0.05
Fairness	You see someone being unjustifiably favored in career opportunities.	1.68	0.66	0.16	0.20	0.22	**0.64**	0.01	-0.01	0.19	-0.05
Fairness	You see someone being unjustifiably left out of career opportunities.	1.61	0.66	0.15	0.12	0.14	**0.85**	0.05	0.01	0.15	0.05
Fairness	You see someone being treated unfairly.	1.59	0.66	0.13	0.11	0.02	**0.79**	0.02	-0.02	0.21	-0.01
Fairness	You see someone not returning a favor.	2.29	0.95	0.09	0.26	0.21	0.29	0.18	0.07	-0.13	0.01
Fairness	You see someone sweet-talking an executive to be considered for the next career opportunity.	1.97	0.91	0.05	0.14	0.24	0.26	0.05	0.04	-0.06	-0.07
Fairness	You see someone lying about the amount of hours they've worked overtime.	1.60	0.74	0.17	0.17	0.20	0.32	0.05	-0.05	-0.04	0.11
Fairness	You see someone getting hired only because that person knows the manager personally.	1.86	0.85	0.23	0.27	0.28	0.19	0.00	-0.12	-0.15	0.16
Fairness	You see someone getting a good rating for team performance without having contributed anything to the team result.	1.70	0.67	0.21	0.11	0.26	0.30	0.22	-0.15	-0.03	0.09
Fairness	You see someone making sure that everyone should be treated equally.∗	4.86	0.42	-	-	-	-	-	-	-	-
Loyalty	You see someone telling others how bad his or her own company is.	1.91	0.63	0.17	0.18	0.05	0.12	**0.89**	0.11	0.01	0.07
Loyalty	You see someone discussing company internals with outsiders.	1.76	0.57	0.32	0.18	0.06	0.06	**0.53**	0.06	-0.04	0.11
Loyalty	You see someone making professional secrets of colleagues public.	1.53	0.61	0.28	0.03	0.09	-0.01	**0.60**	0.12	0.10	0.06
Loyalty	You see someone telling others that the competitor company is better than his or her own.	1.97	0.62	0.06	0.12	0.15	0.07	**0.54**	0.12		
Loyalty	You see someone leaving the company to work for the competing company.	3.10	0.95	0.06	0.13	-0.11	0.68	0.02	0.00	-0.02	0.17
Loyalty	You see someone behaving submissively to colleagues.	1.63	0.58	0.22	0.21	0.24	0.02	**0.59**	0.14	0.17	0.03
Loyalty	You see someone speaking out against their own company.	1.75	0.57	0.22	0.14	0.18	0.10	0.45	0.14	0.07	0.23
Loyalty	You see someone stay loyal to the company.∗	3.93	0.86	-	-	-	-	-	-	-	-
Care	You see someone bullying others.	1.07	0.25	0.00	-0.02	0.16	0.03	0.12	**0.91**	-0.08	-0.02
Care	You see someone offending others.	1.17	0.38	0.07	0.12	0.14	-0.02	0.13	**0.57**	0.10	-0.11
Care	You see someone physically attacking others.	1.07	0.25	0.13	0.08	0.11	-0.08	0.15	**0.77**	0.03	0.09
Care	You see someone being bullied by others.	1.31	0.55	0.04	0.11	0.10	0.22	0.15	0.14	**0.67**	0.08
Care	You see someone being offended by others.	1.46	0.57	-0.01	0.03	0.17	0.16	0.05	-0.02	**0.83**	0.03
Care	You see someone being beaten by others.	1.26	0.51	0.05	-0.05	0.16	0.18	0.03	-0.01	**0.57**	-0.01
Care	You see someone taking advantage of the weakness of others for their own purposes.	1.41	0.67	0.16	0.04	0.39	0.18	0.21	0.13	-0.10	0.20
Care	You see someone excited about someone losing his or her job.	1.63	0.81	0.24	0.01	0.18	0.02	0.15	0.00	0.02	**0.70**
Care	You see someone excited about someone losing his or her privileges.	1.79	0.79	0.27	0.04	0.31	0.04	0.01	0.12	-0.07	**0.68**
Care	You see someone excited about someone losing his or her reputation within the company.	1.69	0.75	0.31	0.02	0.26	0.04	0.05	-0.06	0.15	**0.78**
Care	You see someone intervening in a fight.∗	4.09	1.04	-	-	-	-	-	-	-	-

Table 2. Confirmatory factor analysis of wrongness ratings.

# of Factors	Description	χ^2	df	χ^2/df	RMSEA	90 % C.I.	AIC
2	Individualization and binding	4376.26	2078	2.11	0.079	0.075,0.082	21832.97
6	Original MFT, plus Liberty	3991.89	2262	1.76	0.065	0.062,0.069	22149.76
8	Division of Oppression, Compassion, and Gloating	3443.31	2182	1.58	0.057	0.053,0.060	21432.40
Model fit statistics for recommended set of vignettes							
2	Individualization and binding	2246.70	778	2.89	0.103	0.098,0.108	12823.69
6	Original MFT, plus Liberty	1506.96	764	1.97	0.074	0.068,0.079	12111.95
8	Improved model with Division of Oppression, Compassion, and Gloating	1104.39	751	1.47	0.051	0.045,0.058	11735.39

($\chi^2(751) = 1104.39$; RMSEA $= 0.051$), with good coefficients for internal consistency (Cronbach's alpha) between 0.79 and 0.87 (Care – Oppression $= 0.79$; Care – Compassion $= 0.79$; Care – Gloating $= 0.86$; Fairness $= 0.86$; Liberty $= 0.79$; Authority $= 0.87$; Loyalty $= 0.81$; and Sanctity $= 0.84$).

5   Discussion and Conclusion

In this paper, we aimed to address the criticism about the unreliable factor structure [25,36] and poor internal consistency of the MFQ [15–17,23] by introducing a new scale for the measurement of Moral Foundation Theory, a concept introduced by Jonathan Haidt to explain the origins of and variation in human moral reasoning [20]. Our developed set of Moral Foundations Vignettes (MFVs) provide a set of scenarios that represent concrete moral violations that could plausibly occur within the scope of organizations and whistleblowing. The MFVs have been carefully controlled with respect to the content of the scenarios to reduce redundancy, avoid interactions with memory, and ensure complete conceptual coverage of the foundations. Finally, including vignettes with overtly political content as well as scenarios that might require temporally or culturally bounded knowledge was avoided. In total, sixty-nine plus six 'catch' items were developed and tested in two first studies.

In spite of the traditional six-factor structure of MFT, parallel analysis indicated an eight-factor model better describing the data in our sample. Here, Care foundation was subdivided by three factors emphasizing the oppressor's detrimental act (Oppression), compassion for the person being oppressed (Compassion), and acts of gloating (Gloating). Exploratory factor analysis showed that several vignettes loaded poorly onto their intended foundation, leading to their removal from the final set of MFV. It should also be noted that two vignettes involving violations of corporate symbols did not load on sanctity, as the authors expected, but rather on authority. This initially contradictory result may be explained by the fact that while certain symbols, such as churches, crosses, or flags, can be sacralized, this does not necessarily apply to corporate symbols (e.g., trampling on the corporate flag or spitting on the corporate logo). At this, this morally reprehensible act is more likely to be attributed to a violation towards an authority figure (Authority) instead of a violation of Sanctity by the respondents. In total, the final item set consists of 41 vignettes with 3 to 9 items for each factor. In confirmatory factor analysis, the resultant scale demonstrated broadly acceptable model fit indices in relation to RMSEA and AIC, and good internal consistency. Further, the eight-factor model also fit the data better than the two- or six-factor structure proposed by other authors [25, 26, 36].

Despite these remarkable results, the MFV presented here should be considered as preliminary or temporary solution. Further studies are necessary to demonstrate the criterion validity of our new scale by comparing it to the existing measurement of the moral foundations—the MFQ. Our results also raise new questions about the moral domain. For instance, we find evidence that the Care foundation consists of at least three separate aspects (Oppression, Compassion, and Gloating). Other studies suggests a differentiation between physical and emotional harm, sometimes further subdivided into physical harm against humans or animals [8, 24], where our result could not reproduce this classification. In this context, further research is needed to clarify the various aspects of different foundations, particularly the Care Foundation, and to determine whether the subdivision found in our study represents an artifact of item formulation or is based on truly separable subclasses of Care.

Given the popularity and widespread use of MFT, a comprehensive study may also be necessary systematically testing a larger pool of potential MFV items, particularly for those factors currently represented by only a few items (e.g., the three Care factors). The eight-factor structure itself may be questioned due to the limited set of vignettes used to develop it. Thus, it could be that these items themselves introduced bias into the measures. A larger pool of potentially morally relevant items will provide researchers with a sufficiently large and diverse set of stimuli for testing their hypotheses, but also could yield a different factor structure. Thus, we currently do not endorse the developed MFVs as the final form for investigating triggers for unethical behavior. Rather, it offers a measurement for MFT with a better internal consistency of each moral foundation than the current 'gold-standard', i.e. MFQ.

At the end, the present work should be viewed as exploratory in nature and as such does require confirmation in large, independent, and cross-cultural samples. Using Prolific to acquire survey participants already resulted in a small sample of 100 cross-cultural respondents. A very first analysis of the survey data already indicates that there might be cross-cultural differences in judging scenarios of moral conduct differently, a behavior that other authors have also been able to show [25, 33]. Therefore, further studies are necessary to better understand the cultural differences in how the various moral foundations are characterized.

References

1. Andon, P., Free, C., Jidin, R., Monroe, G.S., Turner, M.J.: The impact of financial incentives and perceptions of seriousness on whistleblowing intention. J. Bus.
Ethics **151**(1), 165–178 (2016). https://doi.org/10.1007/s10551-016-3215-6
2. Bandura, A.: Impeding ecological sustainability through selective moral disengagement. Int. J. Innov. Sustain. Dev. **2**(1), 8 (2007). https://doi.org/10.1504/IJISD.
2007.016056, http://www.inderscience.com/link.php?id=16056
3. Baron, R.A., Zhao, H., Miao, Q.: Personal motives, moral disengagement, and
unethical decisions by entrepreneurs: cognitive mechanisms on the "Slippery
Slope". J. Bus. Ethics **128**(1), 107–118 (2015). https://doi.org/10.1007/s10551-
014-2078-y, http://link.springer.com/10.1007/s10551-014-2078-y
4. Becker, S., Scheiner, C.W.: The role of moral receptors and moral disengagement
in the conduct of unethical behaviors against whistleblowers on social media. In:
Meiselwitz, G. (ed.) Social Computing and Social Media: Design, User Experience
and Impact, Lecture Notes in Computer Science, vol. 13315, pp. 449–467. Springer
International Publishing, Cham (2022). https://doi.org/10.1007/978-3-031-05061-
9_32
5. Christie, N.C., et al.: The moral foundations of needle exchange attitudes. Soc.
Cogn. **37**(3), 229–246 (2019). https://doi.org/10.1521/soco.2019.37.3.229, https://
guilfordjournals.com/doi/10.1521/soco.2019.37.3.229
6. Clifford, S.: Linking issue stances and trait inferences: a theory of moral
exemplification. J. Politics **76**(3), 698–710 (2014). https://doi.org/10.
1017/S0022381614000176, https://www.journals.uchicago.edu/doi/10.1017/
S0022381614000176
7. Clifford, S.: Individual differences in group loyalty predict partisan strength. Polit.
Behav. **39**(3), 531–552 (2017). https://doi.org/10.1007/s11109-016-9367-3, http://
link.springer.com/10.1007/s11109-016-9367-3
8. Clifford, S., Iyengar, V., Cabeza, R., Sinnott-Armstrong, W.: Moral foundations
vignettes: a standardized stimulus database of scenarios based on moral foundations theory. Behav. Res. Methods **47**(4), 1178–1198 (2015). https://doi.org/10.
3758/s13428-014-0551-2
9. Curry, O.S., Jones Chesters, M., Van Lissa, C.J.: Mapping morality with a compass: testing the theory of 'morality-as-cooperation' with a new questionnaire. J.
Res. Pers. **78**, 106–124 (2019). https://doi.org/10.1016/j.jrp.2018.10.008, https://
linkinghub.elsevier.com/retrieve/pii/S0092656618303568
10. Davis, D.E., et al.: The Moral Foundations Hypothesis does not Replicate well in
Black Samples. J. Pers. Soc. Psychol. **110**(4), e23–e30 (2016). https://doi.org/10.
1037/pspp0000056, http://doi.apa.org/getdoi.cfm?doi=10.1037/pspp0000056
11. Day, M.V., Fiske, S.T., Downing, E.L., Trail, T.E.: Shifting liberal and conservative
attitudes using moral foundations theory. Pers. Soc. Psychol. Bull. **40**(12), 1559–
1573 (2014). https://doi.org/10.1177/0146167214551152, http://journals.sagepub.
com/doi/10.1177/0146167214551152
12. Egorov, M., Kalshoven, K., Pircher Verdorfer, A., Peus, C.: It's a Match: moral-
ization and the effects of moral foundations congruence on ethical and unethical
leadership perception. J. Bus. Ethics **167**(4), 707–723 (2020). https://doi.org/10.
1007/s10551-019-04178-9, http://link.springer.com/10.1007/s10551-019-04178-9
13. Francis, R.: Freedom to speak up - a review of whistleblowing in the NHS. Tech.
Rep., London (2015). iSSN: 0029–6570

14. Frimer, J.A., Biesanz, J.C., Walker, L.J., MacKinlay, C.W.: Liberals and conservatives rely on common moral foundations when making moral judgments about influential people. J. Pers. Soc. Psychol. 104(6), 1040–1059 (2013).https://doi.org/10.1037/a0032277, http://doi.apa.org/getdoi.cfm?doi=10.1037/a0032277

15. Graham, J., Haidt, J., Nosek, B.A.: Liberals and conservatives rely on different sets of moral foundations. J. Pers. Soc. Psychol. **96**(5), 1029–1046 (2009). https://doi.org/10.1037/a0015141, http://doi.apa.org/getdoi.cfm?doi=10.1037/a0015141

16. Graham, J., Nosek, B.A., Haidt, J.: The moral stereotypes of liberals and conservatives: exaggeration of differences across the political spectrum. PLoS ONE **7**(12), e50092 (2012). https://doi.org/10.1371/journal.pone.0050092, https://dx.plos.org/10.1371/journal.pone.0050092

17. Graham, J., Nosek, B.A., Haidt, J., Iyer, R., Koleva, S., Ditto, P.H.: Mapping the moral domain. J. Pers. Soc. Psychol. **101**(2), 366–385 (2011). https://doi.org/10.1037/a0021847, http://doi.apa.org/getdoi.cfm?doi=10.1037/a0021847

18. Haidt, J.: The Emotional Dog and its Rational Tail: a social intuitionist approach to moral judgment. Psychol. Rev. **108**(4), 814–834 (2001). https://doi.org/10.1037/0033-295X.108.4.814, http://doi.apa.org/getdoi.cfm?doi=10.1037/0033-295X.108.4.814

19. Haidt, J.: The Righteous Mind: why good people are divided by politics and religion. Penguin (2013)

20. Haidt, J., Graham, J.: When Morality Opposes Justice: conservatives have moral intuitions that Liberals may not Recognize. Soc. Justice Res. **20**(1), 98–116 (2007). https://doi.org/10.1007/s11211-007-0034-z, http://link.springer.com/10.1007/s11211-007-0034-z

21. Haidt, J., Joseph, C.: Intuitive Ethics: how innately prepared intuitions generate culturally variable virtues. Daedalus **133**(4), 55–66 (2004). https://doi.org/10.1162/0011526042365555, https://direct.mit.edu/daed/article/133/4/55-66/27470

22. Haidt, J., Joseph, C.: The Moral Mind: how five sets of innate intuitions guide the development of many culture-specific virtues, and perhaps even modules. In: Carruthers, P., Laurence, S. (eds.) The Innate Mind, Volume 3, vol. 15, pp. 367–392. Oxford University PressNew York, 1 edn. (2008). https://doi.org/10.1093/acprof:oso/9780195332834.003.0019, https://academic.oup.com/book/10254/chapter/157962014, iSSN: 18255167

23. Harper, C.A., Hogue, T.E.: The role of intuitive moral foundations in Britain's vote on EU membership. J. Commun. Appl. Soc. Psychol. **29**(2), 90–103 (2019). https://doi.org/10.1002/casp.2386, https://onlinelibrary.wiley.com/doi/10.1002/casp.2386

24. Harper, C.A., Rhodes, D.: Reanalysing the factor structure of the moral foundations questionnaire. British J. Soc. Psychol. **60**(4), 1303–1329 (2021). https://doi.org/10.1111/bjso.12452, https://onlinelibrary.wiley.com/doi/10.1111/bjso.12452

25. Iurino, K., Saucier, G.: Testing measurement invariance of the moral foundations questionnaire across 27 countries. Assessment **27**(2), 365–372 (2020). https://doi.org/10.1177/1073191118817916, http://journals.sagepub.com/doi/10.1177/1073191118817916

26. Iyer, R., Koleva, S., Graham, J., Ditto, P., Haidt, J.: Understanding libertarian morality: the psychological dispositions of self-identified libertarians. PLoS ONE **7**(8), e42366 (2012). https://doi.org/10.1371/journal.pone.0042366

27. Joeckel, S., Bowman, N.D., Dogruel, L.: Gut or Game? The influence of moral intuitions on decisions in video games. Media Psychol. **15**(4), 460–485 (2012). https://doi.org/10.1080/15213269.2012.727218, http://www.tandfonline.com/doi/abs/10.1080/15213269.2012.727218

28. Johnson, K.A., et al.: Moral foundation priorities reflect U.S. christians' individual differences in religiosity. Pers. Indiv. Diff. **100**, 56–61 (2016). https://doi.org/10.1016/j.paid.2015.12.037, https://linkinghub.elsevier.com/retrieve/pii/S0191886915301185

29. Kaur, R., Sasahara, K.: Quantifying moral foundations from various topics on twitter conversations. In: 2016 IEEE International Conference on Big Data (Big Data), pp. 2505–2512. IEEE, Washington DC, USA (2016). https://doi.org/10.1109/BigData.2016.7840889, http://ieeexplore.ieee.org/document/7840889/

30. Kim, K.R., Kang, J.S., Yun, S.: Moral intuitions and political orientation: similarities and differences between South Korea and the United States. Psychol. Rep. **111**(1), 173–185 (2012). https://doi.org/10.2466/17.09.21.PR0.111.4.173-185, http://journals.sagepub.com/doi/10.2466/17.09.21.PR0.111.4.173-185

31. Kivikangas, J.M., Fernández-Castilla, B., Järvelä, S., Ravaja, N., Lönnqvist, J.E.: Moral foundations and political orientation: systematic review and meta-analysis. Psychol. Bull. **147**(1), 55–94 (2021). https://doi.org/10.1037/bul0000308, http://doi.apa.org/getdoi.cfm?doi=10.1037/bul0000308

32. Krcmar, M., Cingel, D.P.: Moral foundations theory and moral reasoning in video game play: using real-life morality in a game context. J. Broadcasting Electron. Media **60**(1), 87–103 (2016). https://doi.org/10.1080/08838151.2015.1127246, http://www.tandfonline.com/doi/full/10.1080/08838151.2015.1127246

33. Marques, L.M., et al.: Translation and validation of the moral foundations vignettes (MFVs) for the Portuguese language in a Brazilian sample. Judgment Decis. Making **15**(1), 149–158 (2020). https://doi.org/10.1017/S1930297500006963, https://www.cambridge.org/core/product/identifier/S1930297500006963/type/journal_article

34. Mesmer-Magnus, J.R., Viswesvaran, C.: Whistleblowing in organizations: an examination of correlates of whistleblowing intentions, actions, and retaliation. J. Bus. Ethics **62**(3), 277–297 (2005). https://doi.org/10.1007/s10551-005-0849-1, http://link.springer.com/10.1007/s10551-005-0849-1, iSBN: 0551005084

35. Moore, C., Detert, J.R., Treviño, L.K., Baker, V.L., Mayer, D.M.: Why employees do bad things: moral disengagement and unethical organizational behavior. Pers. Psychol. **65**(1), 1–48 (2012). https://doi.org/10.1111/j.1744-6570.2011.01237.x

36. Nilsson, A., Erlandsson, A.: The Moral foundations taxonomy: structural validity and relation to political ideology in Sweden. Pers. Indiv. Differ. **76**, 28–32 (2015). https://doi.org/10.1016/j.paid.2014.11.049, https://linkinghub.elsevier.com/retrieve/pii/S0191886914006989

37. Park, H., Bjørkelo, B., Blenkinsopp, J.: External whistleblowers' experiences of workplace bullying by superiors and colleagues. J. Bus. Ethics **161**(3), 591–601 (2020). https://doi.org/10.1007/s10551-018-3936-9, http://link.springer.com/10.1007/s10551-018-3936-9, iSBN: 0123456789

38. Piazza, J., Sousa, P.: Religiosity, political orientation, and consequentialist moral thinking. Soc. Psychol. Pers. Sci. **5**(3), 334–342 (2014). https://doi.org/10.1177/1948550613492826, http://journals.sagepub.com/doi/10.1177/1948550613492826

39. Rothschild, J., Miethe, T.D.: Whistle-blower disclosures and management retaliation. Work Occupations **26**(1), 107–128 (1999). https://doi.org/10.1177/0730888499026001006

40. Scheiner, C.W.: The role of moral receptors and moral disengagement in the conduct of unethical behaviors on social media. In: Lecture Notes in Computer Science (including subseries Lecture Notes in Artificial Intelligence and Lecture Notes in Bioinformatics), vol. 12194 LNCS, pp. 335–348 (2020). https://doi.org/10.1007/978-3-030-49570-1_23, http://link.springer.com/10.1007/978-3-030-49570-1_23, iSSN: 16113349

41. Scheiner, C.W., Krämer, K., Baccarella, C.V.: Cruel Intentions? – The role of moral awareness, moral disengagement, and regulatory focus in the unethical use of social media by entrepreneurs. In: Meiselwitz, G. (ed.) SCSM 2016. LNCS, vol. 9742, pp. 437–448. Springer, Cham (2016). https://doi.org/10.1007/978-3-319-39910-2_41

42. Silver, J.R., Silver, E.: Why are conservatives more punitive than liberals? A moral foundations approach. Law Hum. Behav. 41(3), 258–272 (2017). https://doi.org/10.1037/lhb0000232, http://doi.apa.org/getdoi.cfm?doi=10.1037/lhb0000232

43. Smith, K.B., Alford, J.R., Hibbing, J.R., Martin, N.G., Hatemi, P.K.: Intuitive ethics and political orientations: testing moral foundations as a theory of political ideology. Am. J. Polit. Sci. 61(2), 424–437 (2017). https://doi.org/10.1111/ajps.12255, https://onlinelibrary.wiley.com/doi/10.1111/ajps.12255

44. Torre, J., Verducci, T.: The Yankee Years. Doubleday, New York, NY (2009)

45. Treviño, L.K., Weaver, G.R., Reynolds, S.J.: Behavioral ethics in organizations: a review. J. Manage. 32(6), 951–990 (2006). https://doi.org/10.1177/0149206306294258, http://journals.sagepub.com/doi/10.1177/0149206306294258, iSBN: 8148637261

46. Voelkel, J.G., Brandt, M.J.: The effect of ideological identification on the endorsement of moral values depends on the target group. Pers. Soc. Psychol. Bull. 45(6), 851–863 (2019). https://doi.org/10.1177/0146167218798822, http://journals.sagepub.com/doi/10.1177/0146167218798822

47. Weaver, A.J., Lewis, N.: Mirrored morality: an exploration of moral choice in video games. Cyberpsychol. Behav. Soc. Netw. 15(11), 610–614 (2012). https://doi.org/10.1089/cyber.2012.0235, http://www.liebertpub.com/doi/10.1089/cyber.2012.0235

48. Winterich, K.P., Zhang, Y., Mittal, V.: How political identity and charity positioning increase donations: insights from moral foundations theory. Int. J. Res. Market. 29(4), 346–354 (2012). https://doi.org/10.1016/j.ijresmar.2012.05.002, https://linkinghub.elsevier.com/retrieve/pii/S0167811612000638

Usability Evaluation Techniques for Virtual Environments: An Exploratory Study

John W. Castro[1(✉)], Gianina Madrigal[1], and Luis A. Rojas[2]

[1] Departamento de Ingeniería Informática Y Ciencias de La Computación, Universidad de Atacama, Copiapó, Chile
john.castro@uda.cl, gianina.madrigal.17@alumnos.uda.cl
[2] Departamento de Ciencias de La Computación Y Tecnologías de La Información, Universidad del Bío-Bío, Chillan, Chile
lurojas@ubiobio.cl

Abstract. Virtual reality is a concept of specialized hardware that generates an experience with different levels of intensity and interactivity within environments in which users feel immersed in an apparently real world and is defined based on the technology. Currently, several fields, such as education and health, use virtual reality. Due to the wide range of users (children, youth, adults, and even older adults) who can interact with virtual environments, it is essential to consider the usability of this type of software system. The evaluation of usability is carried out through usability tests. Research on evaluating virtual environments' usability is scattered in several scientific databases. To the best of our knowledge, no research work compiles and reports globally on which techniques are used to evaluate the usability of such software systems. We conducted a systematic mapping study to assess the general panorama of techniques related to usability evaluation that are being used in virtual environments. We identified a total of 30 primary studies. The main techniques for usability evaluation are interviews, heuristic evaluation, surveys, usability experiments and expert evaluation. Some of these techniques are being used together. In addition, we have identified some works that propose frameworks or methodologies for evaluating the usability of virtual reality systems.

Keywords: Usability Evaluation · Virtual Environments · Exploratory Study

1 Introduction

Virtual reality (VR) is a concept of specialized hardware that generates an experience with different levels of intensity and interactivity within environments in which users feel immersed in an apparently real world and is defined based on the technology [1, 2]. Currently, several fields, such as education [3], health [4], and seismic safety [5], use virtual reality. Due to the wide range of users (children, youth, adults, and even older adults) who can interact with virtual environments, it is essential to consider the usability of this type of software system, which increases efficiency and user satisfaction, also improving their productivity [6].

© The Author(s), under exclusive license to Springer Nature Switzerland AG 2023
A. Coman and S. Vasilache (Eds.): HCII 2023, LNCS 14026, pp. 450–465, 2023.
https://doi.org/10.1007/978-3-031-35927-9_31

Usability is one of the most critical indicators in determining the quality of a software product [7–9]. It corresponds to how a group of users can use a software system to achieve specific objectives with effectiveness, efficiency, and satisfaction [6]. The evaluation of usability is carried out through usability tests since, despite the efforts of software developers, the first designs tend to be flawed since they can, for example, [6]: (i) Assume knowledge that users do not possess, (ii) use confusing or highly technical vocabulary, and (iii) impose excessive mental workload on users. To avoid these situations, it is necessary to evaluate usability so that the user will not feel dissatisfied with the final product [6]. Research on evaluating virtual environments' usability is scattered in several scientific databases.

To the best of our knowledge, no research work compiles and reports globally on which techniques are used to evaluate the usability of such software systems. Therefore, professionals and researchers who need this information will have to: (i) Spend much time searching and finding relevant sources of knowledge, (ii) review the resources obtained according to specific criteria, (iii) extract information from multiple sources, and, finally, (iv) conclude from the information found. This problem becomes more acute when it is considered that the scientific community periodically contributes new bibliographic resources.

This research seeks to assess the general panorama of techniques related to usability evaluation that are being used in virtual environments. For this, we conducted a systematic mapping study (SMS). The databases used are Scopus, IEEE Xplore, and Web of Science (WoS). We identified a total of 30 primary studies. The main techniques for usability evaluation are interviews, heuristic evaluation, surveys, usability experiments and expert evaluation. Some of these techniques are being used together. In addition, we have identified some works that propose frameworks or methodologies for evaluating the usability of virtual reality systems [10, 11].

This paper is organized as follows. In Sect. 2, we present the related work. Section 3 describes the research method (i.e., SMS). In Sect. 4, we discuss the results of the SMS. Section 5 presents possible threats to validity, and finally, the conclusions are presented in Sect. 6.

2 Related Work

As a result of our pilot search, we found three studies [12–14] related to our research. Karre et al. [12] report usability studies carried out in the industry when developing VR products. Karre et al. [12] focused on those studies that design VR scenes precisely and develop a simple protocol to perform or set up a setup for the usability evaluation of those scenes. This study aims to contribute when choosing a usability evaluation method for future VR products at an industrial level. Although this study is complete, it is outdated since it was carried out from 2000 to 2018.

The second work [13] reports specific usability evaluation techniques in augmented reality (AR) systems, specifically in education. Sheikh et al. [13] state that some critical challenges must be considered to implement RA, especially in the educational area. In this area, the users may require a greater demand for motor skills due to the interaction with 3D projections. In this work, the authors report a miscellany of usability techniques that are pretty efficient when evaluating AR systems for education. While this could be extended to other areas that use such technology, it does not focus on all applicable areas of AR technology.

In the latest study, Zanatta et al. [14] report works that evaluate the usability of VR systems and robotic devices applied to neuromotor rehabilitation. The authors focus on a variety of essential areas to be able to implement a VR system in the area of rehabilitation, among which usability is mentioned. In addition, this research addresses the usability techniques that were visualized in the primary studies identified in their research. Although the study by Zanatta et al. [14] provides updated and complete information and provides some recommendations, it is not generic enough since it focuses on one of the many areas in which VR is applied.

After carrying out an analysis of the studies mentioned above, it is possible to point out that the present research paper differs from the last two (i.e., [13] and [14]). On the one hand, this research is not limited to particular areas, and not only VR is considered, but also AR and mixed reality (MR) to obtain a broader vision of how the usability of systems is being evaluated that use these technologies. On the other hand, our work differs from the first study described (i.e., [12]) since we carried out an updated investigation (from 2018 to September 2022), and the focus of the research questions is different. Therefore, this research work is necessary since VR, AR, and MR technologies are constantly growing, and knowing which techniques are used to evaluate their usability correctly is necessary.

3   Research Method

Software engineering considers usability as one of the key attributes of software [7, 8]. *Usability* is a measure that can be used in any product without being exclusive to computer systems. The secondary study reported in this work has been developed following the guidelines established by Kitchenham et al. [15] for carrying out an SMS. Following these guidelines, the following activities were carried out: (i) formulation of the research questions; (ii) definition of the search strategy; (iii) selection of primary studies, (iv) extraction; (v) and synthesis of the extracted data.

3.1   Research Questions

The information extracted from the primary studies aims to answer the following research questions (RQ): (RQ1) What are the usability techniques used to evaluate virtual environments? (RQ2) What are the main problems and challenges in applying techniques to evaluate the usability of virtual environments? (RQ3) What are the extended reality environments currently being evaluated?

3.2   Define the Search Strategy

The SMS begins with identifying the keywords, so it is necessary to identify a Control Group (CG). The CG is defined as a set of studies specifically related to the area of interest. In addition, the studies belonging to the CG must represent the research as accurately as possible and answer the research questions formulated [16]. The CG arises from the need for objectivity in selecting the search string.

A manual search of studies related to the research context is performed to form the CG. Likewise, these studies should answer the research questions. As a result of the search, five primary studies were identified [17–21]. Before building the search string, it is verified that the CG studies are in the Scopus database since it has the most significant number of studies. As a result of this verification, all the CG studies are found in Scopus, which is why it is the best option for research.

To obtain the keywords that will make up the search string, the Atlas.ti program (version 22) is used. Based on the above, a table was generated with the frequency of all the words and combinations that appeared in the CG articles. Only those words that were directly related to the research questions and that were present in a significant percentage of the articles belonging to the CG were chosen (we call this percentage coverage). Subsequently, each word obtained was assigned a value from 0 to 1, determined by its frequency of use, so that the most repeated word in the CG studies had the value 1. Table 1 shows a fragment of the list of words obtained due to this selection process. It shows the words, their coverage, frequency of use, and assigned weight (calculated based on coverage and frequency of use – see Eq. 1).

$$Weight = ((Word\ coverage)/(Maximum\ coverage) +$$
$$(Word\ frequency)/(Maximum\ frequency))/2 \qquad (1)$$

Table 1. Fragment of the list of words obtained from the selection process.

Words	Coverage (%)	Frequency	Weight
Usability	100	222	1
Evaluation	100	123	0.7770
VR	100	101	0.7275
Virtual reality	100	90	0.7027
Study	100	59	0.6329
Evaluations	60	38	0.3856
Test	100	34	0.5766
Studies	80	28	0.4631
Assessment	60	19	0.3428

3.3 Formation of the Search String

After obtaining the keywords, several search strings were built, for which three components related to the context of the investigation were considered (i.e., to identify the current panorama of how the usability evaluation of virtual environments is carried out).

454   J. W. Castro et al.

The defined components were the following: (i) evaluation, (ii) usability, and (iii) virtual environments. The logical operator AND was used to join each of the components and OR to include synonyms of the terms of the same component. Six strings were built to search for CG studies in the Scopus database. Table 2 shows the number of studies found, and the number of CG studies found for each string tested.

Table 2. Search strings.

ID	Search string	Studies found	GC found	Ratio X	Ratio Y	Average
1	(study OR evaluation OR studies OR assessment OR evaluations OR test) AND usability AND (VR OR "virtual reality" OR "virtual environment" OR immersive)	1955	5	1	0.00256	0.50128
2	(study OR evaluation OR assessment OR test) AND usability AND (VR OR "virtual reality" OR "virtual environment" OR immersive)	1801	5	1	0.00278	0.50139
3	(study OR evaluation OR assessment OR test) AND usability AND (VR OR "virtual reality" OR "virtual environment")	1833	5	1	0.00273	0.50136
4	(study OR evaluation OR assessment) AND (usability) AND (VR OR "virtual reality" OR immersive)	1777	5	1	0.00281	0.50141
5	(study OR evaluation OR assessment) AND (usability) AND (VR OR "virtual reality")	1666	4	0.8	0.00300	0.40150
6	(study OR evaluation OR studies OR assessment OR evaluations OR test) AND usability AND (VR OR "virtual reality")	1764	5	1	0.00284	0.50142

As seen in Table 2, five of the six search strings found all five CG studies, making it necessary to search for a method to select one of the strings. This method consists of calculating the proportions X (see Eq. 2) and Y (see Eq. 3) and the average between them (see Eq. 4).

$$X\ Ratio = \frac{(No.\ of\ articles\ found\ in\ the\ control\ group)}{(Total\ of\ articles\ in\ the\ control\ group)} \qquad (2)$$

$$Y\ Ratio = \frac{(No.\ of\ articles\ found\ from\ the\ control\ group)}{(Total\ of\ articles\ found\ per\ search\ string)} \qquad (3)$$

$$Average = \frac{(XRatio + YRatio)}{2} \qquad (4)$$

As observed in Table 2, the X proportion varies only once since only one of the strings did not find all the CG studies in Scopus. However, proportion Y shows specific differences since it is based on calculating the proportion of the CG studies found in the total results obtained by each string. To ensure that the selected string is the ideal one for our investigation, the mean between the X and Y ratio is calculated. Table 2 shows that string 6 has the highest mean, so it is selected as the most suitable string. Table 3 shows the structure of the final search string.

Table 3. Final search string.

Keywords				
study OR evaluation OR studies OR assessment OR evaluations OR test	AND	usability	AND	VR OR "virtual reality"

Although the tests of the strings were carried out in the Scopus database, a search was still carried out in IEEE Xplore and WoS with the final selected string to find more results. This search considered studies from 2018 to June 14, 2022. The databases were analyzed sequentially using the search fields shown in Table 4. The search fields used were determined by the options provided by each database due to the different query syntaxes [22–24]. If a duplicate appeared, the first result was kept.

Table 4. Search field per database.

Database	Search fields	Number of results
Scopus	"Title OR Abstract OR Keywords"	1425
IEEE Xplore	"Abstract"	198
Web of Science	"Title OR Abstract OR Keywords"	1035

3.4 Inclusion and Exclusion Criteria

This section presents the inclusion and exclusion criteria for selecting the primary studies. The inclusion criteria are the following:

- The study indicates the techniques used during the usability evaluation; AND

- The study reports in detail the usability evaluation or a usability study; OR
- The study reports in detail a method/technique/tool proposal to evaluate the usability of virtual reality systems.

Regarding the exclusion criteria, they are the following:

- The study only uses a survey or questionnaire to evaluate the usability.
- The study does not mention the usability evaluation technique used in the abstract.
- The study reports pilot or preliminary usability tests.
- The study is written in a language other than English.

It should be considered that it is sufficient for a study to meet one of the exclusion criteria in order not to be considered.

3.5 Select the Studies

A total of 2658 studies were found in the three databases used. After excluding duplicate studies, the number was reduced to 1781. Subsequently, a selection of studies was made by applying the inclusion and exclusion criteria to the title and abstract of each non-duplicate study, reducing the number to 289 pre-selected. Finally, the selection criteria were strictly applied to the full text of the pre-selected studies. Figure 1 shows the entire

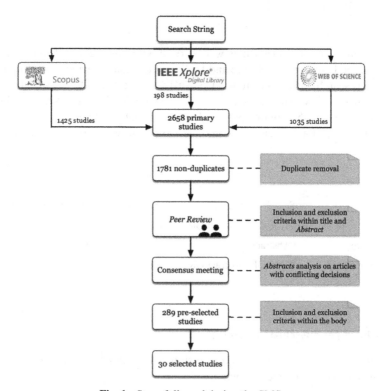

Fig. 1. Steps followed during the SMS.

filtering and analysis process with the inclusion and exclusion criteria used to select 30 primary studies. The complete list of the primary studies can be found in Annex A. The results of applying the different filters during the selection process for each database can be seen in Table 5.

Table 5. Number of remaining studies after filtering the database results.

Database	Studies found	Duplicate-free	Pre-selected studies	Primary studies
Scopus	1425	1418	244	25
IEEE Xplore	198	26	8	0
Web of Science	1035	337	37	5
Total	**2658**	**1781**	**289**	**30**

4 Results and Discussion

This section presents the results obtained in the SMS, divided into two parts: An overview of the primary studies and the answers to the research questions.

The first part is summarized in Fig. 2, which presents a synthetic view of the identified primary studies. In this figure, the results have been segmented into two areas. The first (left side) consists of two XY scatterplots (top and bottom) with bubbles at the intersections of the categories type-year of publication (left side - top) and type of publication-techniques/frameworks for evaluation usability (left side - bottom). The publication types are journals, book chapters, conferences, and workshops. The size of each bubble is determined by the number of primary studies classified as belonging to each category. The second area (right side - top) of Fig. 2 presents the number of primary studies by year of publication. As can be seen, interest in evaluating the usability of virtual environments decreased in 2019 and 2020. Subsequently, interest increased in 2021 and only decreased slightly in 2022, although for this year, studies up to September.

The second part of this section presents the synthesis of the analysis of the primary studies from which the research questions were answered.

4.1 Usability Evaluation Techniques

In this section, the research question *What are the usability techniques used to evaluate virtual environments?* is answered. From the analysis of the primary studies, 15 usability evaluation techniques were identified that are applied (see Table 6). In Table 6, the usability evaluation techniques are ordered from the most to the least used.

In addition to the techniques used for usability evaluation, some framework proposals [PS1, PS4, PS5, PS12, PS15, PS20, PS23] were identified to carry out such activity. The proposed frameworks are different in each of the primary studies. For example, the study by Harms [PS12] describes an automated VR usability evaluation method. It is important to note that this method has been applied before in desktop applications

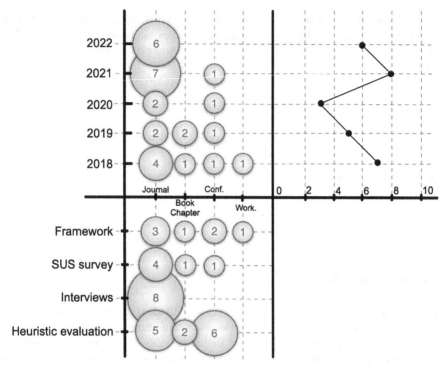

Fig. 2. Mapping for primary study distribution between usability evaluation techniques along with publication type.

and websites; that is, this method has been adapted. The approach is based on three steps. In the last step, usability smells are detected from the generated task trees. Harms [PS12] consider usability smells to be certain user behaviors that indicate an underlying usability problem. Some usability smells are Missing User Guidance, High GUI Element Distance, and Required Inefficient Actions.

4.2 Problems and Challenges in Applying Usability Evaluation Techniques

This section answers the second research question *What are the main problems and challenges in applying techniques to evaluate the usability of virtual environments?* Upon exhaustive inspection, it was found that only seven of the primary studies [PS3, PS5, PS8, PS13, PS15, PS16, PS28] report the results (i.e., whether the application of the technique was successful or, on the contrary, there were problems) or challenges to apply the usability techniques or frameworks proposed by the authors.

It is essential to mention usability problems related to the sample size [PS5] and the type of sampling performed [PS8]. In the first case, the samples can be small. In the second case, sampling is done for convenience, a non-probabilistic or random method, where the researcher chooses the sample by proximity and without considering whether it is representative. Another problem, indicated in the study by Verkuyl et al. [PS8], is related to the number of rounds executed in the usability evaluations. However, this is

Table 6. Usability Evaluation Techniques.

Usability Techniques	Primary studies
Interviews	[PS2][PS7][PS9][PS19][PS22][PS24][PS26][PS29]
Heuristic evaluation	[PS6][PS8][PS10][PS13][PS14][PS25][PS30]
SUS survey	[PS2][PS10][PS11][PS19][PS22][PS24]
Adapted survey	[PS8][PS16][PS17][PS21]
Usability experiment	[PS9][PS10][PS17]
Expert evaluation	[PS3][PS11][PS19]
Cognitive walkthrough	[PS6][PS13]
User feedback	[PS7][PS27]
Thinking aloud	[PS8][PS27]
Usability test recording	[PS26][PS27]
Questionnaires	[PS26][PS27]
Group-based usability testing	[PS15][PS16]
Persons	[PS6]
Eye Tracking	[PS27]
Usability metrics	[PS28]

linked to the budget and time of the projects. Likewise, another challenge related to the sample is identifying the representative subjects necessary for developing VR software [PS15].

Likewise, problems and challenges are directly related to the application of usability evaluation techniques [PS3, PS13, PS16, PS26]. In the case of the expert evaluation technique [PS3], the main problem lies in the subjectivity of said evaluation since it is still an opinion, where the experts give their impressions over a well-founded opinion.

The first challenge is found when applying the technique of "group-based usability testing" [PS16]. This corresponds to the organization of the scenarios/environments and the high dropout rates of the participants. An additional limitation in the usability evaluation reported in the study is that the authors carried out a pretest to collect the participants' demographic data, which could cause some preparation in the sample of participants, making the results unreliable.

Also, we find usability metrics as an evaluation technique. The application formula of this technique is carried out through direct or indirect questionnaires for data collection. This generates a drawback related to subjectivity since the answers tend to be related to the participants' impressions rather than actual experiences. In addition, the questionnaires are carried out post-test, which tends to distort the answers, since when answering them after carrying out the tests with the software for a while, the experiences become blurred and are not entirely true [PS28].

Finally, the problems associated with evaluating usability through hybrid methods are related to the increase in the overall cost of usability evaluation and the complexity of applying them [PS13].

4.3 Evaluated Extended Reality Environments

This section answers the third research question *What are the extended reality environments currently being evaluated?* After conducting an analysis of the primary studies, three types of extended reality environments were identified: VR, AR and MR.

A total of 25 primary studies report the usability evaluation of VR software systems [PS1-PS8, PS10-PS13, PS15-PS20, PS23-PS26, PS28-PS30]. VR is defined as a reality in which the participants are fully immersed in a fictional world and can interact with that reality. That world can simulate the properties of specific real-world environments, whether existing or fictional. In addition, to be able to immerse yourself in this virtual reality, display devices are necessary, which function as barriers to keeping the user within this virtual world [25, 26].

Only three primary studies [PS9, PS14, PS21] report usability evaluation of AR software systems. AR is a variation of VR, and AR is a technology that unites real space and objects with computer-generated (virtual) objects, which are superimposed on the real world in real-time. The main difference between VR and AR is that AR does not fully replace the real world [26, 27].

Concerning MR, only two primary studies [PS22, PS27] report the usability evaluation of software systems with this technology. The MR unites objects of the virtual type with other objects in the real world. The main difference between MR and AR is that, in the case of the latter, virtual objects are not only superimposed on the real world but can also be interacted with. MR digital objects are tied to real space. For example, a hologram can be seen superimposed on a specific object. On the contrary, in AR, a hologram of a specific object can be placed on any flat surface [27].

5   Validity Threats

In our SMS we identified three threats to validity. First, the validity of the SMS is threatened by only including studies written in English. Second, although the terms used (derived from a CG) in the search string were the most commonly used in other studies in the research area, other terms used to describe relevant work may have been overlooked.

Third, the authors of an SMS may make judgmental errors when selecting the studies. We define inclusion and exclusion criteria directly related to the objective and research questions to counteract this threat. In addition, to verify the concordance in the selection of the studies, meetings were held between the investigators to check the discarded preselected studies.

Another aspect related to the study selection process is the declared scope of our research since only papers published between 2018 and 2022 were considered. Some studies directly related to the objective of our research have likely been discarded, considering only this period. In addition, only the scientific databases Scopus, IEEE Xplore, and WoS were considered. Despite having found many results, more usability evaluations could have been reported.

6 Conclusions

This research paper describes the SMS carried out to identify the state of the art of techniques that are being used to evaluate the usability of virtual environments. From 2018 to 2022, we found 30 primary studies published mainly in journals and conferences. Interest in evaluating the usability of virtual environments has increased since 2020. Below we report the conclusions based on the research questions posed above.

RQ1: What are the usability techniques used to evaluate virtual environments?

According to the results of the SMS, it was possible to know the general panorama of the usability evaluation techniques used in developing virtual environments. The most commonly used techniques for evaluating the usability of this type of software system are: interviews, heuristic evaluation, and surveys (SUS survey and adapted survey). Also noteworthy are usability experiments and expert evaluation. In addition to usability evaluation techniques, we identified some framework proposals, reflecting that traditional techniques seem insufficient in some cases.

RQ2: What are the main problems and challenges in applying techniques to evaluate the usability of virtual environments?

Only seven primary studies report challenges or whether the application of the technique was successful. The problems identified correspond to the sample size, the sampling type, and the application of usability evaluation techniques. The techniques that presented problems in their application were usability metrics and hybrid methods.

RQ3: What are the extended reality environments currently being evaluated?

We identified three types of extended reality environments: VR, AR, and MR. Most of the primary studies (close to 80%) identified in the SMS report usability evaluation of VR software systems.

As future work, we consider including more databases (e.g., SpringerLink and ScienceDirect). In addition, we will analyze if the techniques have been applied as prescribed by the Human Computer-Interaction area or if, on the contrary, they have been adapted. In the case of finding adapted usability evaluation techniques, we will identify which adaptations were made and what reasons motivated such adaptations.

Acknowledgment. This work was supported in part by the ANID FONDECYT-Iniciación project under Grant 11230496 and in part by the Universidad de Atacama.

Appendix A: Primary Studies

This appendix lists the references of the primary studies used for the SMS described in this paper.

[PS1] He, L., Li, H., Xue, T., Sun, D., Zhu, S., Ding, G.: Am I in the theater? Usability study of live performance based virtual reality. In: ACM Symposium on Virtual Reality Software and Technology (VRST'18), pp. 1–11, Tokyo, Japan (2018).

[PS2] Pedroli, E., Greci, L., Colombo, D., Serino, S., Cipresso, P., Arlati, S., Mondellini, M., Boilini, L., Giussani, V., Goulene, K., Agostoni, M., Sacco, M., Stramba-Badiale, M., Riva, G., Gaggioli, A.: Characteristics, usability, and users experience of a system combining cognitive and physical therapy in a virtual environment: Positive bike. Sensors, 18(7), 2343 (2018).

[PS3] Kabassi, K., Maravelakis, E., Konstantaras, A.: Heuristics and fuzzy multicriteria decision making for evaluating museum virtual tours. International Journal of the Inclusive Museum, 11(3), 1–21 (2018).

[PS4] Barricelli, B. R., De Bonis, A., Di Gaetano, S., Valtolina, S.: Semiotic framework for virtual reality usability and ux evaluation: A pilot study. In: 2nd Workshop on Games-Human Interaction (GHItaly'18), pp.1–6, Castiglione della Pescaia, Grosseto, Italy (2018).

[PS5] Liu, Y., Yang, N., Li, A., Paterson, J., McPherson, D., Cheng, T., Yang, A. Y.: Usability Evaluation for Drone Mission Planning in Virtual Reality. In: Chen, J. and Fragomeni, G. (eds.). Virtual, Augmented and Mixed Reality: Applications in Health, Cultural Heritage, and Industry. VAMR 2018. Lecture Notes in Computer Science, vol 10910, pp. 313–330. Springer, Cham (2018).

[PS6] Tromp, J. G., Wolff, A., Torres, J. C., My, H. T.: Usability evaluation of the interactive 3D virtual cultural heritage museum display: Fountain of the lions software application. International Journal of Engineering and Technology, 7(2.28), 95–99 (2018).

[PS7] Birnie, K. A., Kulandaivelu, Y., Jibb, L., Hroch, P., Positano, K., Robertson, S., Campbell, F., Abla, O., Stinson, J.: Usability testing of an interactive virtual reality distraction intervention to reduce procedural pain in children and adolescents with cancer. Journal of Pediatric Oncology Nursing, 35(6), 406–416 (2018).

[PS8] Verkuyl, M., Romaniuk, D., Mastrilli, P.: Virtual gaming simulation of a mental health assessment: A usability study. Nurse Education in Practice, 31, 83–87 (2018).

[PS9] Rohrbach, N., Gulde, P., Armstrong, A. R., Hartig, L., Abdelrazeq, A., Schröder, S., Neuse, J., Grimmer, T., Diehl-Schmid, J., Hermsdörfer, J.: An augmented reality approach for ADL support in Alzheimer's disease: A crossover trial. Journal of Neuro Engineering and Rehabilitation, 16, 1–16, article 66 (2019).

[PS10] Li, Z., Wang, J., Yan, Z., Wang, X., Anwar, M. S.: An interactive virtual training system for assembly and disassembly based on precedence constraints. In: Gavrilova, M., Chang, J., Thalmann, N., Hitzer, E., Ishikawa, H. (eds) Advances in Computer Graphics. CGI 2019. Lecture Notes in Computer Science, vol 11542, pp. 81–93. Springer, Cham (2019).

[PS11] De Melo, M. S. P., Da Sílva Neto, J. G., Da Sílva, P. J. L., Teixeira, J. M. X. N., Teichrieb, V.: Analysis and comparison of robotics 3D simulators. In: 21st Symposium on Virtual and Augmented Reality (SVR'19), 242–251, Rio de Janeiro, Brazil (2019).

[PS12] Harms, P.: Automated usability evaluation of virtual reality applications. ACM Transactions on Computer-Human Interaction, 26(3), article 14 (2019).

[PS13] Doumanis, I., Economou, D.: Using cognitive walkthrough and hybrid prototyping to gather user requirements in early design virtual reality prototypes. In: Beck, D., Peña-Rios, A., Ogle, T., Economou, D., Mentzelopoulos, M., et al. (eds.) Immersive Learning Research Network. iLRN 2019. Communications in Computer and Information Science, vol 1044, pp. 234–246. Springer, Cham (2019).

[PS14] Dantes, G. R., Suputra, P. H., Sudarma, I. K., Suwastini, N. K. A., Dantes, K. R.: Evaluating and redesigning virtual reality 'underwater tourism' application based on heuristic method. International Journal of Business Information Systems, 35(2), 225–238 (2020).

[PS15] Granić, A., Nakić, J., Marangunić, N.: Scenario-based group usability testing as a mixed methods approach to the evaluation of three-dimensional virtual learning environments. Journal of Educational Computing Research, 58(3), 1–24 (2020).

[PS16] Delamarre, A., Lisetti, C., Buche, C.: A cross-platform classroom training simulator: Interaction design and evaluation. In: International Conference on Cyberworlds (CW'20), 86–93, Caen, France (2020).

[PS17] Birt, J., Vasilevski, N.: Comparison of single and multiuser immersive mobile virtual reality usability in construction education. Educational Technology & Society, 24(2), 93–106 (2021).

[PS18] Besoain, F., Jego, L., Gallardo, I.: Developing a virtual museum: Experience from the design and creation process. Information, 12(6), 244 (2021).

[PS19] Schmidt, M., Schmidt, C., Glaser, N., Beck, D., Lim, M., Palmer, H.: Evaluation of a spherical video-based virtual reality intervention designed to teach adaptive skills for adults with autism: a preliminary report. Interactive Learning Environments, 29(3), 345–364 (2021).

[PS20] Jangid, V., Kongsilp, S.: FishTank sandbox: A software framework for collaborative usability testing of fish tank virtual reality interaction techniques. In: 27th ACM Symposium on Virtual Reality Software and Technology (VRST'21), pp. 1–3, article 70, Osaka, Japan (2021).

[PS21] Strada, F., Bottino, A., Lamberti, F., Mormando, G., Ingrassia, P. L.: Holo-BLSD - A holographic tool for self-training and self-evaluation of emergency response skills. IEEE Transactions on Emerging Topics in Computing, 9(3), 1581–1595 (2021).

[PS22] Rzeszewski, M., Orylski, M.: Usability of webxr visualizations in urban planning. ISPRS International Journal of Geo-Information, 10, 721 (2021).

[PS23] Thalmann, M., Ringli, L., Adcock, M., Swinnen, N., de Jong, J., Dumoulin, C., Guimarães, V., de Bruin, E. D.: Usability study of a multicomponent exergame training for older adults with mobility limitations. International Journal of Environmental Research and Public Health, 18, 13422 (2021).

[PS24] Hassandra, M., Galanis, E., Hatzigeorgiadis, A., Goudas, M.; Mouzakidis, C., Karathanasi, E. M., Petridou, N., Tsolaki, M.; Zikas, P.; Evangelou, G., Papagiannakis, G., Bellis, G., Kokkotis, C., Panagiotopoulos, S. R., Giakas, G., Theodorakis, Y.: A virtual reality app for physical and cognitive training of older people with mild cognitive impairment: Mixed methods feasibility study. JMIR Serious Games, 9(1), 1–21, article e24170 (2021).

[PS25] Fajar, M., Udjaja, Y., David, Chowanda, A., Juarto, B., Yulianto: A comparative investigation of usability issues toward virtual reality implementation in a state-owned shipping service enterprise. ICIC Express Letters, Part B: Applications, 13(5), 545–552 (2022).

[PS26] Kamińska, D., Zwoliński, G., Laska-Leśniewicz, A.: Usability testing of virtual reality applications—The pilot study. Sensors, 22, 1342 (2022).

[PS27] Ogunseiju, O. R.; Gonsalves, N.; Akanmu, A. A.; Bairaktarova, D.; Bowman, D. A.; Jazizadeh, F.: Mixed reality environment for learning sensing technology applications in Construction: A usability study. Advanced Engineering Informatics, 53, article 101637 (2022).

[PS28] Alpala, L. O.; Quiroga-Parra, D. J.; Torres, J. C.; Peluffo-Ordonez, D. H.: Smart factory using virtual reality and online multi-user: Towards a metaverse for experimental frameworks. Applied Sciences, 12, 6258 (2022).

[PS29] Cheng, K. H.: Teachers' perceptions of exploiting immersive virtual field trips for learning in primary education. Journal of Research on Technology in Education, 54(3), 438–455 (2022).

[PS30] Mitre-Ortiz, A., Munoz-Arteaga, J., Cardona-Reyes, H.: Developing a model to evaluate and improve user experience with hand motions in virtual reality environments. Universal Access in the Information Society, 1–15 (2022).

References

1. Tham, J., Duin, A.H., Gee, L., Ernst, N., Abdelqader, B., McGrath, M.: Understanding virtual reality: presence, embodiment, and professional practice. IEEE Trans. Prof. Commun. **61**(2), 178–195 (2018)
2. Kardong-Edgren, S.S., Farra, S.L., Alinier, G., Young, H.M.: A call to unify definitions of virtual reality. Clin. Simul. Nurs. **31**, 28–34 (2019)
3. Hickman, L., Akdere, M.: Exploring virtual reality for developing soft-skills in stem education. In: 2017 7th World Engineering Education Forum (WEEF'17), pp. 461–465, Kuala Lumpur, Malaysia (2017)
4. Heiyanthuduwa, T.A., Amarapala, K.W.N.U., Gunathilaka, K.D.V.B., Ravindu, K.S., Wickramarathne, J., Kasthurirathna, D.: VirtualPT: virtual reality based home care physiotherapy rehabilitation for elderly. In: 2020 2nd International Conference on Advancements in Computing (ICAC'20), pp. 311–316, Malabe, Sri Lanka (2020)
5. Li, C., Liang, W., Quigley, C., Zhao, Y., Yu, L.F.: Earthquake safety training through virtual drills. IEEE Trans. Visual Comput. Graphics **23**(4), 1275–1284 (2017)
6. Hertzum, M.: Usability testing: A practitioner's guide to evaluating the user experience. Synthesis Lectures on Human-Centered Informatics, Morgan & Claypool Publishers (2020)
7. Castro, J.W., Garnica, I., Rojas, L.: Automated tools for usability evaluation: a systematic mapping study. In: Meiselwitz, G. (eds.) Social Computing and Social Media: Design, User Experience and Impact. HCII 2022. Lecture Notes in Computer Science, 13315, pp. 28–46. Springer, Cham (2022). https://doi.org/10.1007/978-3-031-05061-9_3
8. Losana, P., Castro, J.W., Ferre, X., Villalba-Mora, E., Acuña, S.T.: A systematic mapping study on integration proposals of the personas technique in agile methodologies. Sensors **21**(18), article 6298, Special Issue Recent Advances in Human-Computer Interaction (2021)
9. Ren, R., Zapata, M., Castro, J.W., Dieste, O., Acuña, S.T.: Experimentation for chatbot usability evaluation: a secondary study. IEEE Access **10**, 12430–12464 (2022)
10. Barricelli, B.R., De Bonis, A., Di Gaetano, S.: Semiotic framework for virtual reality usability and UX evaluation: a pilot study. In: 2nd Workshop on Games-Human Interaction (GHItaly'18), pp. 1–6, Castiglione della Pescaia, Grosseto, Italy (2018)
11. Moore, A.G., Hu, X., Eubanks, J.C., Aiyaz, A.A., McMahan, R.P.: A formative evaluation methodology for VR training simulations. In: 2020 IEEE Conference on Virtual Reality and 3D User Interfaces Abstracts and Workshops (VRW'20), pp. 125–132, Atlanta, GA, USA (2020)

12. Karre, S.A., Mathur, N., Reddy, Y.R.: Understanding usability evaluation setup for VR products in industry: a review study. ACM SIGAPP Appl. Comput. Rev. **19**(4), 17–27 (2020)
13. Sheikh, S., Heyat, M.B.B., AlShorman, O., Masadeh, M., Alkahatni, F.: A review of usability evaluation techniques for augmented reality systems in education. In: 2021 Innovation and New Trends in Engineering, Science and Technology Education Conference (IETSEC'21), pp. 1–6 (2021)
14. Zanatta, F., Giardini, A., Pierobon, A., D'Addario, M., Steca, P.: A systematic review on the usability of robotic and virtual reality devices in neuromotor rehabilitation: patients' and healthcare professionals' perspective. BMC Health Serv. Res. **22**(1), 1–16 (2022)
15. Kitchenham, B.A., Budgen, D., Brereton, O.P.: Using mapping studies as the basis for further research–a participant-observer case study. Inf. Softw. Technol. **53**(6), 638–651 (2011)
16. Zhang, H., Babar, M.A., Tell, P.: Identifying relevant studies in software engineering. Inf. Softw. Technol. **53**(6), 625–637 (2011)
17. Özdinç, F., Tüzün, H., Ergün, E., Bayrak, F., Kula, A.: Usability testing of a three-dimensional library orientation game. In: Games User Research: A Case Study Approach, Publisher: CRC Press, pp. 77–95 (2016)
18. Pedroli, E., et al.: Characteristics, usability, and users experience of a system combining cognitive and physical therapy in a virtual environment: positive bike. Sensors (Basel) **18**(7), 2343 (2018)
19. Oliveira, E., Simões, F.P., Correia, W.F.: Heuristics evaluation and improvements for low-cost virtual reality. In: 2017 19th Symposium on Virtual and Augmented Reality (SVR'17), pp. 178–187, Curitiba, Brazil (2017)
20. Naranjo, J.E., Urrutia, F.U., Garcia, M.V., Gallardo-Cárdenas, F., Franklin, T.O., Lozada-Martínez, E.: User experience evaluation of an interactive virtual reality-based system for upper limb rehabilitation. In: 2019 Sixth International Conference on eDemocracy & eGovernment (ICEDEG'19), pp. 328–333, Quito, Ecuador (2019)
21. Besoain, F., Jego, L., Arenas-Salinas, M.: Implementation of a gamified puzzle based on pro-origami protein structure cartoons: an experience in virtual reality. In: 2018 IEEE Biennial Congress of Argentina (ARGENCON'18), pp. 1–7, San Miguel de Tucuman, Argentina (2018)
22. Castro, J.W., Acuña, S.T.: Comparativa de selección de estudios primarios en una revisión sistemática. In XVI Jornadas de Ingeniería del Software y Bases de Datos (JISBD'11), pp. 319–332, A Coruña, España (2011)
23. Magües, D., Castro, J.W., Acuña, S.T.: Usability in agile development: a systematic mapping study. In XLII Conferencia Latinoamericana de Informática (CLEI'16), pp. 677–684, Valpariso, Chile (2016)
24. Ren, R., Castro, J.W., Acuña, S.T., De Lara, J.: Evaluation techniques for chatbot usability: a systematic mapping study. Int. J. Softw. Eng. Knowl. Eng. **29** (11n12), 1673–1702 (2019)
25. Milgram, P., Kishino, F.: A taxonomy of mixed reality visual displays. IEICE Trans. Inf. Syst. **77**(12), 1321–1329 (1994)
26. Çöltekin, A., et al.: Extended reality in spatial sciences: a review of research challenges and future directions. ISPRS Int. J. Geo Inf. **9**(7), 439 (2020)
27. Rzeszewski, M., Orylski, M.: Usability of WebXR visualizations in urban planning. ISPRS Int. J. Geo Inf. **10**(11), 721 (2021)

"I Love You, My Dear Friend": Analyzing the Role of Emotions in the Building of Friendships in Online Fanfiction Communities

Sourojit Ghosh$^{(\boxtimes)}$ (iD), Niamh Froelich, and Cecilia Aragon (iD)

University of Washington, Seattle, USA
{ghosh100,niamhf,aragon}@uw.edu

Abstract. As people continue to develop friendships over the Internet in greater numbers than in-person, the complex factors behind them become important to study. One such factor is emotional expression, and we are motivated to better understand how it plays a role in both continuing existing and building new friendships. In this study, we examined the role of emotions in the formation of different degrees of bonds between members on Fanfiction.net, an online community where members post fanfiction and receive reviews from readers. We developed an emotional taxonomy and used it to qualitatively code 11,292 reviews from Fanfiction.net. We introduce a novel metric of counting characters in reviews, an adjusted character count (ACC). We found that both positive and negative reviews have implications on friendship building, such as through in-depth mentorship and co-creation. Through a mixed-methods analysis of different degrees of emotional expression and review length, we observe users going from shallow connections based on short reviews with low emotional expression to stronger relationships through repeated demonstrations of high emotional investment to tight friendships which transcend the fictional content being exchanged.

Keywords: distributed mentoring · friendship-building · fanfiction

1 Introduction

Participation in online communities has become an almost unavoidable part of our daily lives, participation which is defined by creating and consuming content. Such engagement with content often involves emotional expression, both publicly in the form of comments/reactions, and privately to people in users' networks through exchanging content. However, while the benefits of participation in online communities for mental health [34], informal learning [22] and community building are well-known, insufficient attention has been given to the importance of emotional expression as a means of building community in online communities. Specifically, there is a need to understand the role of the nature or strengths of these emotions in such community building processes.

In this study, we address this gap through an examination of one of the largest online text-based communities: Fanfiction.net. When an author uploads a new story or a chapter of an existing story on Fanfiction.net, they may receive comments, or "reviews", which is the platform's primary affordance of communication. These reviews are impactful on writers, with greater numbers of reviews received being correlated with an improvement in writing [18] and with the creation of more content [6]. Researchers have found that authors and reviewers may develop bonds by exchanging reviews [6,10,15]. However, reviews are not just important for *what* they say; it also matters *how* they convey their intent, since the emotions expressed in a review may completely alter its impact. As a community as rife with emotional expression, Fanfiction.net is perfect to study for our purpose.

We build on prior work [10] which highlighted the presence of multiple layers of user networks on Fanfiction.net, in accordance to social network theory [12]. We study the importance of nature and degrees of emotional expression in user traversal across such layers in social networks. By manually qualitatively coding reviews for emotions using a taxonomy developed through a grounded-theory approach combined with a quantitative analysis of review lengths and volumes, we contribute to a growing understanding of interaction patterns and emotional expression in online fanfiction communities, and beyond.

We offer three contributions to the field with this work: (1) detailing the characteristics of bonds between users in online Fanfiction communities, (2) providing a rigorously developed and tested taxonomy of emotions expressed by members in online Fanfiction communities, and (3) contributing to a body of work that expressing negative emotions can also lead to community formation in online communities, if they are considered in context.

2   Related Work

2.1   Emotional Expression in Online Communities

Emotions are an inseparable part of social media, to the point where there is a demonstrable "online disinhibition effect" [41] with people preferring to express more emotions online than in-person. Emotional expression from a few users encourages others to be more emotive [23], and expressive participation and recognizing others with similar emotional reactions is also a powerful tool for extending and receiving social support [33] as it serves to both bring together users with shared successes [26] and unite members sharing similar difficulties or losses [11]. Expressing emotions helps construct generalized shared realities [37] between users, a key factor in both the initial formation and the continued progress of their interpersonal relationships.

The nature of emotions – whether positive or negative – expressed also plays an important role in their formation of user connections. Sharing positive emotions leads to finding social support [20,26], while sharing negative emotions or talking about difficult periods in their lives has resulted in members not being able to find supportive communities [11]. Therefore, the majority opinion about online communities is that expressing positive emotions generates more positivity and in turn leads to building communities, while expressing negative emotions might not be as effective for community building.

However, we believe that if negative emotions are considered *in context*, they might also be important factors in forming communities of positive support. While mutual anger or negativity can bring together trolls and create destructive communities of misinformation and hate speech [40], expressing negative emotions such as sadness by being vulnerable can bring members together in mutual solidarity. Typically, work along these lines exist in the context of online health communities [27] or conversations about mental health/depression in online spaces [11], where members bond through sharing their struggles and difficulties in similar situations. Our work proposes another such example, considering online fanfiction communities, and argues that it can be extended to other text-based online communities.

2.2   Identifying Emotional Expression in Online Communities

In text-based online communities, a common way of identifying and studying emotional expression is through *sentiment analysis*: "a computational treatment of opinion, sentiment, and subjectivity in text" [32]. Such processes typically involve training machine-learning algorithms on a list of sentiment-classified texts, and then applying the trained model to a list of unclassified texts.

While this approach has been arguably successful with large corpora of texts, there are disadvantages. Such algorithms, if trained on low-quality or biased data, generate unideal outputs [21]. Most algorithmic sentiment analysis also ranges between different degrees of Positive and Negative emotions and are thus unable to recognize many parts of the emotion spectrum [21], though some algorithms do accommodate different emotions like Love, Joy, and Frustration [44]. Finally, algorithmic detection of emotions, especially by large social media spaces algorithms that use such detection to personalize content recommendation, has been viewed by users as invasive and discomforting [2].

An alternative to using algorithmic sentiment analysis is human-encoding text. These approaches combine elements of grounded theory [7] and thematic analysis [3] with techniques such as keyword-spotting [24] and contextual analysis [20]. Manual coding of emotions might be more time-consuming but has several advantages over algorithmic sentiment analysis, such as higher reliability of coded data [21]. We thus adopt a manual approach to emotion detection.

2.3   User Participation in Online Fanfiction Communities

Thomas [43] defines fanfiction as "stories produced by fans based on plotlines and characters from either a single source text or else a canon of work". Fanfiction allows fans to actively engage with their favorite storylines and actively "seek out fellow-fans to gush over their object of affection" [47].

One of the primary reasons that members participate in online fanfiction communities is because of the different forms of social support abundant within such communities. In such communities, a majority of members identify as women or

LGBTQ [30], making them potential safe spaces that are welcoming and positive. Genderqueer individuals who participate in online fanfiction communities leverage this social support and feel more confident to safely self-explore with lesser fear of backlash, as compared to other online communities such as Facebook where such self-exploration can beget high volumes of negativity [14]. Members here also find support through difficult periods of their lives, as participation provides reduced isolation during personally challenging moments in members' lives as they share their stories with other community members and lean on each other to get through their difficulties [39].

To understand the types of bonds and networks formed between members in online fanfiction communities, Campbell et al. [6] proposed the theory of *distributed mentoring*: a form of mentorship in member-networks spanning the globe where everyone has something to contribute to and learn from each other. They note how members find both content-based and social support from the community as they experience personal growth and, in turn, mentor others. This notion of paying it forward is an important aspect of sustaining longer and more meaningful bonds as they jumping to each other's defense when someone receives negative comments while also forming giving and receiving positive, actionable feedback through targeted reviews and rich discussions [18].

Davis et al. [10] applied social network theory [12] to online fanfiction communities, defining 2–3 layers of user networks with the number of users decreasing and the strength of bonds increasing towards the center of the network. We extend this work by studying the effect of emotional expression in the traversal of such networks, using the *Affect* aspect of the distributed mentoring framework.

3   Methods

3.1   Defining Levels of Engagement in Fanfiction Communities

Since Davis et al. [10] do not provide definitions for the aforementioned layers, we begin by providing some terminology for them. Hereafter in this section, we refer to two users: users A and B. We do so because labeling them as 'author' and 'reviewer' would not do justice to the fact that members on Fanfiction.net frequently exist as both [6,18].

When they directly interact with each other for the first time, users A and B establish a **connection**. At this point, they are simply the newest nodes on each other's social networks, and likely have no information about each other beyond the first set of content exchanged. These connections are weak and, if interactions end here or continue briefly and in shallow terms, they likely will exist at the periphery of each other's social networks and the connection will soon fizzle out. Connections are also most likely to be unidirectional, since a single short interaction might not have much effect on each other.

If the connected users A and B continue to communicate, they may start to form a **relationship**. Such relationships are built on and sustained by large volumes of content exchanged and each other's responsiveness, as well as the evolution of the nature of content into more thoughtful conversations, as demonstrated by previous work both outside of online fanfiction communities (e.g. [42]) and within them (e.g. [6,19]). These works demonstrate that these relationships are founded and maintained by reciprocal exchanges of high volumes of content at moderate to speedy rates of response.

For the relationship between users A and B to evolve into a *friendship*, the nature of the content exchanged plays the most important role, more than the volume and frequency of conversations. The users must have a sense of 'Shared Life' [45] and develop a meaningful connection beyond the content of the stories/reviews exchanged.

Therefore, we label Davis et al.'s [10] layers as *connections*, *relationships* and *friendships*, starting from the outermost and moving inwards to the central user. In our analysis, we examine how members on Fanfiction.net exist in these layers for each other, and how they traverse them.

3.2   Data Collection

We worked with data gathered by Yin et al. [48], which consists of 28 million chapters from 6.5 million stories by 1.5 million authors, and over 176 million reviews from 8.5 million users stretching across 16 years (since 2000) on Fanfiction.net. This dataset is available at http://research.fru1t.me. For our analysis, we first randomly selected 10,000 reviews from this dataset. After coding these 10,000 reviews for emotions (Sect. 3.3), we identified the stories/chapters which were the most represented in our dataset. We then acquired the rest of the reviews for those chapters from the master dataset, randomly shuffled them to reorder them, and coded those with the intention of fully covering the reviews for those stories/chapters. For these stories, we also read the authors' notes in the chapters (if present) to obtain a sense of the authors' communication with reviewers. We also obtained associated metadata, such as authors' notes (A/N), timestamps, reviewer's history of reviewing an author's work, and author's history of reviewing this stories the reviewer might have authored.

Since we conducted manual qualitative coding, we did not want to exceed 12,000 reviews for this analysis and thus restricted this extension to stories with more than 15 reviews per chapter in our original selection of 10,000 reviews. In sum, we coded a total of 11,292 reviews across 6,992 unique stories spanning 9,313 chapters from 1,014 unique authors.

3.3   Forming the Taxonomy of Emotion Codes

We begin our analysis by first determining our taxonomies of qualitative coding. For topics, we adopted Evans et. al's [15] taxonomy of 13 topics of reviews on Fanfiction.net (Shallow Positive, Targeted Positive, Targeted corrective/constructive, Targeted positive and corrective/constructive, Non-constructive Negative, Discussion about the story, Discussion not about the story, One-sided connection, Two-sided connection, Fandom Remarks, Update encouragement, Review fishing, and Miscellaneous), since it is well established within fanfiction literature [10,18]. We then determine the taxonomy of emotions, to be consistent in our decision to pre-determine taxonomies of codes before beginning to code.

We began with the 8 primary emotions from Plutchik's Wheel of Emotions [35] (i.e. Joy, Sadness, Acceptance, Disgust, Fear, Anger, Surprise, and Anticipation), and adapted it for our purposes, pursuant to recommendations by Saldana [38]. We randomly selected a test-set of 500 reviews from Yin et al.'s [48] dataset (and not our subset of 11,292 reviews) and began individually coding each review with this taxonomy. A team of five coders conducted this process: two undergraduate, two Masters and one PhD student. During this process, we looked for cases where at least one of the 8 emotions applied perfectly either to the entire review or some of its parts, or when none of these emotions were applicable. Alongside the Wheel, we allowed ourselves to introduce our own codes wherever we felt appropriate, or where we observed in vivo emotion codes (i.e. emotions directly mentioned) [9].

After our individual encoding, we began to compare our usages of the 8 emotions and external/in vivo codes. We first observed that across the five of us, there were no applications of "Acceptance" and "Fear" in the 500 test reviews, so we decided to exclude them from our taxonomy. We each found ample usage of "Sadness" and "Surprise", so we decided to keep them unaltered. We found a majority of us using "Disgust" on its own but also in conjunction with some form of "Disturbed" e.g. for reviews where members described being 'creeped out', so we amended "Disgust" to "Disturbed/Disgust". All of us used "Anger", but also in conjunction with the external code "Frustration" e.g. for reviews where members were angry at the author for not publishing an update soon enough, so we amended "Anger" to "Anger/Frustration". For similar reasons of co-occurrence, "Anticipation" was amended to "Anticipation/Hope" and "Joy" was amended to "Joy/Happiness". However, with "Joy/Happiness", all coders observed there to be over 150 reviews each where we coded "Joy" or something similarly unsure. We therefore determined the need for a milder form of "Joy/Happiness", and therefore introduced the code "Like", following [25].

Further, "Dislike" and "Confused" were introduced because they occurred most frequently in the consolidated list of in vivo codes. "No Emotion" was introduced to avoid situations where we would have to force ourselves to assign an emotion where we could not confidently apply at least one emotion. Finally, we added "Unknown" for non-English reviews to avoid misunderstanding or losing linguistic context in the process of translating these reviews [16,46].

We thus established a taxonomy of 11 emotions, depicted in Table 1 with definitions and examples. Having arrived at this list, we selected another test-set of 500 reviews, and repeated the above process. The second round of coding did not yield any new emotions, nor did it question the validity of any of the 11 emotions, and the taxonomy was thus formalized.

For our analysis, we divided our taxonomy into Positive, Negative, and Unclassified emotions as also depicted in Table 1. We classified 'Surprise' as a Positive emotion following the lead of Robinson [36], and based on our observations from the test-sets where expressions of surprise are almost always determined to be positive ones, such as "omg I did NOT see that coming, good twist". For similar reasons, we assigned 'Confused' as a Negative emotion.

Table 1. The taxonomy of emotion codes, along with definitions, examples and type of emotion (Positive, Negative, Unclassified). Note that all examples are snippets from reviews in our dataset.

Emotion Code	Definition	Example	Emotion Type
Like	The reviewer expresses generic or slightly positive emotions, without going into too much depth	Wow, I really like this chapter	Positive
Joy/Happiness	The reviewer has more than just a slightly positive reaction to the story and has taken time to adequately express this	I LOVE this story! Excellent work!	Positive
Anticipation/Hope	The reviewer is expressing their hope of seeing upcoming work	Good job I'll be waiting for more	Positive
Surprise	The reviewer is surprised, either pleasantly or otherwise	Whoa I did not see that coming	Positive
Dislike	The reviewer expresses generic or slightly negative emotions, without going into too much depth	I was a little disappointed	Negative
Disturbed/Disgust	The reviewer expresses discomfort with the content of the story, either with some specific parts or the general tone	Ugh Snape makes me want to crawl out of my skin	Negative
Anger/Frustration	The reviewer expresses an extreme negative reaction either to the story or the lack of updates	This is absolutely garbage	Negative
Sadness	The reviewer expresses sadness, either mildly or through tears	Broke my heart :,(I cried a bit	Negative
Confused	The reviewer expresses confusion, as most often indicated by one or more questions	Why would Harry do that??	Negative
Unknown	The text is either indecipherable or is in a language other than English	me encanta!	Unclassified
No emotion	Any emotion cannot be reliably assigned to the text	I'm a Boy	Unclassified

We allocated a list of ordinal (and not discrete) scores to our Positive and Negative (and not Unclassified) emotions because we had a rationale for keeping degrees of emotions different in our taxonomy without quantifiably comparing differences, as mentioned above e.g. with 'Like' and 'Joy/Happiness'. We define 'Joy/Happiness' to be stronger than 'Like' in Table 1, so 'Joy/Happiness' is classified as Strong Positive. 'Like', 'Anticipation/Hope' and 'Surprise' are all Mild Positives. Similarly for Negative emotions, we classify 'Anger/Frustration' and 'Disturbed/Disgust' as Strong Negatives, while 'Dislike', 'Confused' and 'Sadness' are all Mild Negatives. We only combine emotions when they are either entirely Positive or Negative, as explained in Table 2, and not in instances where reviews are coded with a mixture of Positive and Negative emotions. We make no claims about the overall Positive/Negative effect of a combination of Positive and Negative emotions, since we do not classify any emotions as perfectly complementary to one other e.g. we cannot say that 'Like' indicates the *same* amount of positivity as the amount of negativity captured by 'Dislike'.

Table 2. Classification of scores obtained as a combination of emotions

Combination of emotions	Resultant scores obtained
1 Mild emotion	Mild
≥ 2 Mild emotions and 0 Strong emotions	Moderate
≤ 1 Mild emotions and 1 Strong emotion	Strong
≥ 2 Mild emotions and ≥ 1 Strong emotions	Very Strong
≥ 0 Mild emotions and ≥ 2 Strong emotions	Very Strong

3.4   Applying the Taxonomy of Codes to the Data

After formalizing the taxonomy of emotion codes, we began coding our dataset of 11,292 reviews with emotions and topics. We coded the data in batches of 500 reviews (292 for the last batch), with each batch being coded by three independent coders. Reviews could be coded for any non-zero number of emotions and topics, since no emotions or topics were defined as mutually exclusive.

Like during our test encodings, we continued to take advantage of affect labels (wherever present) that corresponded to emotions in our taxonomy, either directly or as a synonym. We also used seed words [1] where certain words/phrases immediately correlated to certain emotions, e.g. phrases like "update soon!" and "I can't wait" were determined to be seed phrases for "Anticipation/Hope."

Further, we incorporated Liu et al.'s [28] suggestion of leveraging real-world knowledge and our understandings of what emotions are evoked by real-world events, e.g. a review containing "My mother is sick" was coded 'Sadness' because we felt that in most cases of the mother's illness, the child experiences sadness. With a fully formed taxonomy, we deemed it a powerful contextual attribute to add to our qualitative coding process. However, we still avoided using personal preferences or knowledge regarding fandoms during coding.

At the end of each batch of 500 reviews, the coders met to discuss disagreements. For each disagreement, each coder laid out their rationale for their encoding and the group voted by simple majority on an agreed-upon encoding. All reviews were first consolidated before progressing to the next batch, to hopefully observe progressively fewer disagreements in future encodings as a result of these consolidation conversations. The observed disagreement rate (percentage of 500 reviews where disagreements needed to be resolved) decreased from 19% in the first session to under 4% in the last session. To measure inter-rater reliability

(IRR), we use the Generalized Cohen's Kappa [17], because of its robustness over Cohen's Kappa [8] (the most-used IRR metric) in being able to handle a mixture of mutually and non-mutually exclusive categories.

3.5 Adjusted Character Count (ACC)

Our metric of length was an adjusted character count (ACC) as opposed to word count, because we observed reviews in our dataset containing different intentional (mis)spellings of words such that counting them as words would lead to a loss of emotional strength. For example, reviews such as "I love it!" and "I LOOOOOOOVE IT!!" are both three words, but the latter expresses a far stronger emotion through the use of capitalization or repetition of characters [4].

We counted emojis through their individual characters, instead of as one, since they provide stronger expressions of emotions than words [29] and therefore we counted them as more than just a single character. For a similar reason [5], we count capitalization as an extra character. We were careful to not make this extra addition for grammatical capitalizations such as at the start of sentences, in "I", at the start of proper nouns or for acronyms. Table 3 provides a detailed explanation of the metric of the ACC.

Table 3. Illustrative examples of adjusted character count

Review	ACC	Explanation
I love this!	10	I = 1 + love = 4 + this = 4 + ! = 1 => 10
I LOVE THIS :)	20	I = 1 + love = 4 + this = 4 + :) = 2 => 11 + 10 (capitalizations) - 1 (adjusting I) = 20
I love Harry!	11	I = 1+ love = 4 + Harry = 5 + ! = 1 => 11 + 2 (capitalizations) - 2 (adjusting I and H) = 11

4   Findings

Table 4 contains percentages and counts of each emotion in our qualitative coding process, accompanied by agreement scores. The numbers sum up to exceed the total number of reviews coded since emotions were not mutually exclusive.

We excluded 1,022 reviews that were coded as Unknown, and 253 reviews coded as No emotion from our analysis. Based on our classification of emotions as Positive or Negative, we categorized the reviews as Positive or Negative if they had *exclusively* Positive or Negative emotions expressed, respectively. If reviews contained both Positive and Negative emotions, we classified them as Mixed.

We identified 1,014 unique authors and 6,586 unique reviewers. We classify reviewers into two groups: those who only leave a single review on an author's work (hereafter referred to as *single-reviewers*), and those who write multiple reviews on the same author's work (hereafter referred to as *repeat-reviewers*). We

Table 4. Percentages of emotions in reviews, with agreement scores.

Emotion	Percentage of Reviews	Agreement scores
Like	29.01% (N = 3,275)	0.579
Joy/Happiness	40.75% (N = 4,602)	0.588
Anticipation/Hope	38.16% (N = 4.309)	0.739
Dislike	1.65% (N = 186)	0.881
Disturbed/Disgust	2.90% (N = 327)	0.903
Anger/Frustration	3.44% (N = 368)	0.862
Sadness	7.93% (N = 896)	0.860
Surprise	2.52% (N = 285)	0.876
Confused	2.51% (N = 284)	0.823
Unknown	9.06% (N = 1,022)	0.997
No emotion	1.73% (N = 253)	0.622

identified 3,674 single-reviewers and 2,912 repeat-reviewers in our coded data. It is important to mention that before labeling a user as a single-reviewer of a story, we examine within Yin et al.'s [48] larger dataset whether they are indeed single-reviewers, accounting for the fact that our sample selected reviews at random and could easily mischaracterize members as single-reviewers just because they are represented only once in our selection.

We now define, based on our observations over a combination of qualitative analysis of review texts and quantitative analysis of review counts and lengths, the characteristics of *connections*, *relationships*, and *friendships* in the following sections. All quotes presented in this section are obfuscated to protect the anonymity of members who wrote them, in accordance with best practices for protecting their privacies.

4.1 Defining Connections

We defined *connections* to be shallow, mostly one-time interactions between members. We also imagine that this layer of the social network will contain the largest number of members.

We first observe that there are more single-reviewers (N = 3,674) than repeat-reviewers (N = 2,912). There is a correlation present between being a single-reviewer and writing 'Shallow Positive' reviews with Mild Positive emotions, reviews requiring the least effort and investment from the reviewer [18]. Single-reviewers write Shallow Positive reviews with Mild Positive emotions (N = 1,398; mean ACC = 133.67 characters) with a significantly (Mann-Whitney U test, p = 0.002) higher mean ACC than repeat-reviewers (N = 548; mean ACC = 119.52 characters). Finally, we observe that there are a few repeat-reviewers (N = 89) who only write Mild Shallow Positive reviews (mean ACC = 78.07 characters). Most of these repeat-reviewers leave 2 reviews (74%) on an author's work, and some write 3 (26%). Some illustrative examples of Mild

Shallow Positive reviews, either from single or repeat-reviewers, are:

"Good."
"I like your writing."
"Keep it up."

Therefore, we characterize such single-reviewers who write Mild Shallow Positive reviews and repeat-reviewers who write 2–3 Mild Shallow Positive reviews as having *connections* with the author.

4.2   Defining Relationships

We defined *relationships* to be based on repeated interactions with high volumes of content exchanged, and the nature of the content being more thoughtful than shallow connections. For this analysis, we focus only on repeat-reviewers since, by definition, single-reviewers do not exchange content repeatedly. This is motivated by our observations that Positive reviews from repeat-reviewers ($N = 2{,}258$; mean $ACC = 168.50$ characters) are significantly longer (Mann-Whitney U test, $p = 0.043$) than those from single-reviewers ($N = 3{,}107$; mean $ACC = 163.19$ characters). The same is true for Negative reviews (Mann-Whitney U test, $p = 0.036$), as Negative reviews from repeat-reviewers ($N = 265$; mean $ACC = 161.89$ characters) are significantly longer than those from single-reviewers ($N = 284$; mean $ACC = 154.10$ characters), though no such statistically significant difference was observed for Mixed reviews (Mann-Whitney U test, $p = 0.052$) from single or repeat reviewers. These results lead us to infer that repeat-reviewers are more engaged with an author's work than single-reviewers. The summarized data for the reviews from single and repeat-reviewers is shown in Table 5.

Table 5. Summary of type of reviews from single and repeat-reviewers

Type of Reviewer	Type of Review	N	Mean ACC
Single	Positive	3107	163.19
Single	Negative	284	154.10
Single	Mixed	281	247.91
Repeat	Positive	2258	168.50
Repeat	Negative	265	161.89
Repeat	Mixed	523	312.76

We further note most (61%) repeat-reviewers moving from writing Mild Shallow Positive reviews (mostly Positive, but also some Negative) to more expressive (i.e. Moderate and beyond) reviews coded with a variety of topics. While this does not mean that they do not ever again write Mild Shallow Positive reviews after their first Moderate or stronger review, the progression from Mild Shallow Positive reviews into more expressive ones indicates an increasing degree of thoughtfulness. We also observe that repeat-reviewers express Strong Positive emotions ($N = 346$; mean ACC $= 188.37$ characters) with a significantly (Mann-Whitney U test, $p = 0.029$) higher mean ACC than single-reviewers ($N = 427$; mean ACC $= 160.99$ characters). The same is true for Very Strong Positive emotions (Mann-Whitney U test, $p = 0.021$) i.e. repeat-reviewers express Very Strong Positive emotions ($N = 67$; mean ACC $= 284.45$ characters) with higher mean ACCs than single-reviewers ($N = 212$; mean ACC $= 153.67$ characters). These results further strengthen our finding that as a member keeps reviewing an author's work, they get more invested and write more emotive reviews.

A case study is presented below as qualitative evidence. All quotes are presented from repeat reviewers in the order in which they were submitted, though quotes presented after each other do not imply that they are consecutive.

Case Study 1

Exciting first chapter! Can't wait for more! - coded as Like + Anticipation/Hope + Shallow Positive + Update encouragement (this is this reviewer's first review for any story by this author, and is on the first chapter of this story).

You captured it all. Everything from <quote from story> to <character name1> and <character name2>'s reaction. I especially enjoyed the <quote from story> line. - coded with Joy/Happiness + Targeted Positive.

Thanks, <reviewer> for your consistent reviews and support! (author, in A/N of a chapter).

You are so goddamn talented! Your writing style is incredible...I am sorry for not reviewing every chapter, I keep hitting next as soon as I finish!!...Keep 'em coming! - coded Joy/Happiness + Anticipation/Hope + Targeted Positive + Discussion about the story (this is an excerpt from a longer review, the entire review has an ACC of 456 characters).

Thank you to all my lovely fans ... <reviewer>, your reviews were very helpful to me... (author in A/N in last chapter of story).

This was a wonderful journey ... I am so happy to have been a part of this... - coded as Joy/Happiness + Shallow Positive (this is an excerpt from a longer review with ACC 684 characters, on the last chapter of this story).

In this example, the reviewer began with Moderate Positive emotions which were more than just Shallow Positive and continued being expressive with Moderate/Strong Positive emotions, leading to a bidirectional conversation with the author outside of the context of the story.

While we have thus far considered Positive emotions in the context of relationship-building, our data shows evidence that Negative emotions too can lead to relationship formation, if they are considered in the contexts in which they were written. We present one such example of a short interaction between an author and a reviewer where the reviewer expresses mostly Negative emotions, but they still develop a relationship.

Case Study 2

Noooo! That is so sad... damn cliffie! - coded as Sadness + Anger/Frustration + Update encouragement + Discussion about the story (this is this reviewer's first review for any story by this author, and is an excerpt from the longer review which has a total ACC of 291 characters)
UGH WHY DO YOU ALWAYS LEAVE AT SUCH A CLIFFIE - coded as Anger/Frustration + Update encouragement
Special s/o to <reviewer name> for your reviews (author, in A/N of a chapter).
I'm SO ANNOYED rn when is the next chapter coming?? - coded as Anticipation/Hope + Anger/Frustration + Update encouragement
Thank you for the reviews, <reviewer name>. Your continued hatred towards <character name> told me that I was writing him well (author in A/N in last chapter of story).
What a beautiful ending, I'm still crying ... thank you for writing this - coded as Sadness + Joy / Happiness + Shallow Positive (this is an excerpt from a longer review with ACC of 551 characters, on the last chapter of this story).

Thus, we characterize reviewers who leave thoughtful and expressive reviews over the course of the author's work, sometimes even leading to a conversation from the author's side, as having formed relationships with the authors.

4.3   Defining Friendships

We defined friendships as the strongest form of user bonds, where members must demonstrate some sense of 'Shared Life' [45] through meaningful conversations beyond the content of the story. We imagine such bonds to the strongest, and the fewest in number. Through our findings, we demonstrate one such set of interactions between an author and a reviewer. Some excerpts of the conversation are illustrated below.

Loving it so far! Keep it up - coded as Like + Anticipation/Hope + Shallow Positive + Update encouragement (this review is on the first chapter of this story, this reviewer has reviewed other work by this author before).
Pretty good overall. You have a remarkably interesting story... <making suggestions for improvement>... DM me if u want to talk more! - coded as Like + Discussion about the story + Targeted positive and corrective/constructive.
Thank you so much for your help with this story! I'm off to review yours! (author, in A/N of a chapter).
Your writing has helped me so much, you have no idea. - coded as Like + Discussion not about the story.
Take care of yourself! The updates can wait, most important is ur health. - coded as Like + Discussion not about the story (in response to the author in the previous A/N talking about going through a difficult personal situation and not being able to write as frequently).

Thank you <reviewer> for your lovely messages, they help me in my tough time (author, in A/N of next chapter).

It has been a privilege to come on this journey with you, looking forward to what you do next! - coded as Joy/Happiness + Anticipation/Hope + Discussion about the story + Update encouragement (this review is on the last chapter of the story).

We observe an author and a reviewer starting out with low interaction and gradually growing into friends. They provide each other behind-the-scenes support, both with their writing and as a supportive individual during times of difficulty, and publicly uplift each other. We characterize such bonds as friendships.

5 Discussion

5.1 Traversing Across Connections, Relationships and Friendships

We define the three forms of bonds that members can form in online fanfiction communities as connections, relationships and friendships. In this section, we explore the processes by which such bonds form and strengthen over time.

We observe that the formation of the initial *connection* is the result of the first interaction, which can be short and surface-level. If the members do not communicate further after this, or if they only exchange stories and Shallow Positive reviews a few more times, the bond does not grow any stronger.

Section 4.2 narrates an interaction which began as two members not having previously had bidirectional interaction growing into a *relationship* based on sustained reviews which become more emotive and demonstrate the reviewer's deep investment into the author's work. This investment is publicly appreciated by the author, and by the end of the conversation, it is apparent that the two share a bond stronger than a peripheral connection.

Finally, Sect. 4.3 captures a brief excerpt of a conversation where two members developed a strong bond through the course of long, sustained interactions. We cannot speculate whether they had a relationship prior to the first review on this story, but since the reviewer had written at least one review on this author's prior work, we can state that there was at least a unidirectional connection. However, through their interactions, they definitely pass through the relationship stage through their bidirectional interaction and reviewing each others' work. They grow into a *friendship* stage where the author acknowledges the reviewer as an important source of support through difficulties in their personal life. Such support is indicative of a stronger bond beyond the fictional content exchanged, and likely to be sustained beyond the conclusion of the story.

5.2 Building Connections, Relationships and Friendships

Connections. In Sect. 4.1, we observe the abundance of single-reviewers who leave short reviews with Mild emotional expression on an author's work, or repeat-reviewers who write 2–3 similarly short and Mildly emotive reviews.

Though connections are the outermost layer of the three-tiered social network and contain the weakest bonds [12], they form an important part of a member's community experience. Our finding that members in the connection layer write short, Shallow Positive reviews with Mildly Positive emotions contributes towards the established understanding of online fanfiction communities being largely supportive spaces, a major reason behind which are such single-reviewers. Their short but positive reviews might not individually have an impact on the author, but together they aggregate to form an abundance [6] of positive reviews that create an environment which uplifts the author and may deter trolls.

Relationships. Section 4.2 indicates that repeat-reviewers move from writing Mild Shallow Positive reviews to expressing stronger emotions in more depth and higher levels of engagement with the author's work, sometimes even leading to a bidirectional conversation. Within Davis et al.'s [10] three-tiered structure, such relationships would fall in the second layer. Members in this layer are important for the author because the accretion of commentary [6] and the continued threads of conversation where the same familiar names show up in the reviews of every chapter creates a strong sense of community for the author. In some cases, as in Sect. 4.2, this leads to the authors having a small conversation with the reviewer and building a relationship. Like on other online communities where exchanging support and positive messaging leads to relationship formation [31], repeat-reviewers and authors on Fanfiction.net form bidirectional relationships through positive feedback loops of updates and reviews, creating mutually positive feelings among all parties and leave them eager for more.

Friendships. In Sect. 4.3, we explore the formation of a friendship between users, going above and beyond the relationship stage with the nature of their back-and-forth conversations. Within Davis et al.'s [10] three-tiered structure, this would be the innermost layer where the bonds are the strongest. Since this layer is expected to contain the least number of members, it perhaps explains why we were able to find only one concrete example to illustrate this. The members described show a sense of 'Shared Life' [45] beyond the exchange of fanfiction content and reviews. The authors foster each others' development as writers through bidirectional exchanges of feedback, and stand by each other during periods of personal difficulty in their lives. We see the friendship grow from the initial reviews, which start from being simply complimentary and then grow into providing more thoughtful feedback, as they then indicate a having a growing impact on each others' lives.

We thus establish the importance of different types and degrees of bonds between members in online fanfiction communities that contribute to improving their experiences and participation. Each degree plays an important and irreplaceable part, and create a positive and supportive community that makes everyone feel valued.

5.3   Contextual Importance of Negative Emotions

While we observe the importance of expressing Positive emotions to various degrees affect the formation of connections, relationships and friendships among members of Fanfiction.net, we also observe that, when they are considered in context, some Negative emotional expression too can be a factor in those processes. In Sect. 4.2, a majority of emotions expressed by the reviewer are Negative, but upon considering them contextually, we observe how they contribute to the formation and sustenance of a relationship between the author and the reviewer. The reviewer expresses Sadness as a result of a deep immersion within the story and the plight of the characters, and their Anger/Frustration at the many cliffhangers reflects the author's success at hooking them to the story. Their investment and emotive reviews are helpful to the author, as they acknowledge, and contributes towards the author's future chapters [18]. Considering such expressions of Anger/Frustration as negative or hateful does not do justice to this investment and would fail to notice the impact of such expectations in the formation of the relationship. Thus, the Negative emotions expressed by the reviewer are not indicative of hatred, but rather signs of a strong engagement. Through this example, we demonstrate how, in some cases, even expressing Negative emotions can lead to the formation and sustenance of relationships in online communities, if the content of such text be considered in the contexts in which they were written.

5.4   Accounting for Unequal Bond Strengths Between Members

We also believe that it is important to account for potentially unequal bond strengths between members on Fanfiction.net, especially between authors and reviewers. For instance, while an author might only have a weak *connection* with a reviewer by virtue of receiving a single or a few short reviews, the reviewer might actually have a lot stronger unidirectional feeling towards the author's work. For instance, the reviewer might really like every chapter update posted by the author, and the work might speak to them beyond the content of the fanfiction, but they might not leave long reviews or any reviews at all. Silently reading, or lurking, is a common practice on Fanfiction.net [13], which makes it difficult to definitively study whether connections, relationships and friendships are always equally reciprocated between members. While we believe that the relationships and friendships presented in Sects. 4.2 to 4.3 are equally reciprocated, it is also important to acknowledge that some bonds in online fanfiction communities might not be equally strong on both sides. This might be especially true for connections and relationships, though friendships as we define them require a sense of strong reciprocity.

5.5   Implications for Distributed Mentoring

Our findings have implications for the furthering the theory of distributed mentoring [6]. Our biggest contribution is on the *Affect* attribute of the framework which was previously only defined to encompass feelings of positivity to moderate the effect of negative comment. Our investigation shows the importance of emotive expression towards building a strong sense of community. We also found that Positive emotions extend beyond just counteracting negative comments to a whole spectrum of excitement and encouragement where reviewers seem to ride the characters' successes, celebrate the authors' enthusiasm and extend comfort to authors experiencing personal struggles. We believe that *Affect* in distributed mentoring is so much more than just providing emotional support – it is a way to understand the importance of emotionally charged reviews on an author's personal and professional development.

6   Conclusion

In this study, we observe different types of user engagement on Fanfiction.net, and the importance of emotional expression in the formation of relationships and friendships between members. We find evidence of users forming connections, relationships and friendships based on emotional expression, both Positive and Negative. We observe the formation of connections as a result of a single interaction between authors and reviewers, relationships based on the exchange of long and frequent bidirectional communication with strong emotional expression, and friendships founded and sustained on deep and meaningful emotionally-charged conversations extending beyond the fictional content of stories.

Our mixed-method analysis deepens our understanding of *Affect* in distributed mentoring and underscores the role of both positive and negative emotions in friendship and learning, implying that the success of an online community may depend on the presence of an environment where members feel encouraged to express their emotions and connect with others over similar ones.

Acknowledgements. We are grateful to the students that helped us in our qualitative coding process: Isabella Nguyen, Arthur Liu, and Miaoxin Wang. We are also grateful for the feedback and support from Ruoxi (Anna) Shang, Andrea Figueroa, Jenna Frens and John Fowler. Finally, we are thankful for our reviewers for their insightful feedback that undoubtedly improved the quality of this work.

References

1. Aman, S., Szpakowicz, S.: Identifying expressions of emotion in text. In: Matoušek, V., Mautner, P. (eds.) TSD 2007. LNCS (LNAI), vol. 4629, pp. 196–205. Springer, Heidelberg (2007). https://doi.org/10.1007/978-3-540-74628-7_27
2. Andalibi, N., Buss, J.: The human in emotion recognition on social media: attitudes, outcomes, risks. In: Proceedings of the 2020 CHI Conference on Human Factors in Computing Systems, pp. 1–16 (2020)
3. Braun, V., Clarke, V.: Using thematic analysis in psychology. Qual. Res. Psychol. **3**(2), 77–101 (2006)
4. Brooks, M., et al.: Statistical affect detection in collaborative chat. In: Proceedings of the 2013 Conference on Computer Supported Cooperative Work, pp. 317–328 (2013)

5. Butterick, M.: Butterick's Practical Typography. Matthew Butterick (2013)

6. Campbell, J., Aragon, C., Davis, K., Evans, S., Evans, A., Randall, D.: Thousands of positive reviews: distributed mentoring in online fan communities. In: Proceedings of the 19th ACM Conference on Computer-Supported Cooperative Work and Social Computing, pp. 691–704 (2016)

7. Charmaz, K.: Constructing Grounded Theory: A Practical Guide Through Qualitative Analysis. Sage, Thousand Oaks (2006)

8. Cohen, J.: A coefficient of agreement for nominal scales. Educ. Psychol. Measur. **20**(1), 37–46 (1960)

9. Corbin, J., Strauss, A.: Basics of Qualitative Research: Techniques and Procedures for Developing Grounded Theory. Sage Publications, Thousand Oaks (2014)

10. Davis, R., Frens, J., Sharma, N., Muralikumar, M.D., Aragon, C., Evans, S.: Mentorship network structure: how relationships emerge online and what they mean for amateur creators. In: Proceedings of the Connected Learning Summit (2020)

11. De Choudhury, M., Counts, S., Horvitz, E.J., Hoff, A.: Characterizing and predicting postpartum depression from shared Facebook data. In: Proceedings of the 17th ACM Conference on Computer Supported Cooperative Work and Social Computing, pp. 626–638 (2014)

12. Dunbar, R.I., Arnaboldi, V., Conti, M., Passarella, A.: The structure of online social networks mirrors those in the offline world. Soc. Netw. **43**, 39–47 (2015)

13. Dym, B., Brubaker, J.R., Fiesler, C., Semaan, B.: "Coming out okay" community narratives for LGBTQ identity recovery work. Proc. ACM Hum.-Comput. Interact. **3**(CSCW), 1–28 (2019)

14. Dym, B., Fiesler, C.: Social norm vulnerability and its consequences for privacy and safety in an online community. Proc. ACM Hum.-Comput. Interact. **4**(CSCW2), 1–24 (2020)

15. Evans, S., et al.: More than peer production: fanfiction communities as sites of distributed mentoring. In: Proceedings of the 2017 ACM Conference on Computer Supported Cooperative Work and Social Computing, pp. 259–272 (2017)

16. Farquhar, S., Fitzsimons, P.: Lost in translation: the power of language. Educ. Philos. Theory **43**(6), 652–662 (2011)

17. Figueroa, A., Ghosh, S., Aragon, C.: Generalized Cohen's kappa: a novel interrater reliability metric for non-mutually exclusive categories. In: Proceedings of the Human Interface and the Management of Information Thematic Area in the Context of the 25th International Conference on Human-Computer Interaction (HCI International). Springer, Cham (2023)

18. Frens, J., Davis, R., Lee, J., Zhang, D., Aragon, C.: Reviews matter: how distributed mentoring predicts lexical diversity on fanfiction. net. In: Proceedings of the Connected Learning Summit (2018)

19. Froelich, N., et al.: Reciprocity in reviewing on fanfiction.net. In: Stephanidis, C., Antona, M., Ntoa, S. (eds.) HCII 2021. CCIS, vol. 1421, pp. 39–44. Springer, Cham (2021). https://doi.org/10.1007/978-3-030-78645-8_5

20. Garas, A., Garcia, D., Skowron, M., Schweitzer, F.: Emotional persistence in online chatting communities. Sci. Rep. **2**(1), 1–8 (2012)

21. Ghosh, S., et al.: "do we like this, or do we like like this?": Reflections on a human-centered machine learning approach to sentiment analysis. In: Proceedings of the 4th International Conference on Artificial Intelligence in HCI in the Context of the 25th International Conference on Human-Computer Interaction (HCI International). Springer, Cham (2023)

22. Ghosh, S., Figueroa, A.: Establishing tiktok as a platform for informal learning: evidence from mixed-methods analysis of creators and viewers. In: Proceedings of the 56th Hawaii International Conference on System Sciences, pp. 2431–2440 (2023)

23. Guillory, J., Spiegel, J., Drislane, M., Weiss, B., Donner, W., Hancock, J.: Upset now? Emotion contagion in distributed groups. In: Proceedings of the SIGCHI Conference on Human Factors in Computing Systems, pp. 745–748 (2011)

24. Hancock, J.T., Landrigan, C., Silver, C.: Expressing emotion in text-based communication. In: Proceedings of the SIGCHI Conference on Human Factors in Computing Systems, pp. 929–932 (2007)

25. Keltner, D., Cowen, A.: A taxonomy of positive emotions. Curr. Opin. Behav. Sci. **39**, 216–221 (2021)

26. Kivran-Swaine, F., Brody, S., Diakopoulos, N., Naaman, M.: Of joy and gender: emotional expression in online social networks. In: The ACM Conference on Computer Supported Cooperative Work Companion, pp. 139–142 (2012)

27. Levonian, Z., et al.: Patterns of patient and caregiver mutual support connections in an online health community. Proc. ACM Hum.-Comput. Interact. **4**(CSCW3), 1–46 (2021)

28. Liu, H., Lieberman, H., Selker, T.: A model of textual affect sensing using real-world knowledge. In: Proceedings of the 8th International Conference on Intelligent User Interfaces, pp. 125–132 (2003)

29. Lo, S.K.: The nonverbal communication functions of emoticons in computer-mediated communication. Cyberpsychol. Behav. **11**(5), 595–597 (2008)

30. Lulu: The slow dance of the infinite stars (2013)

31. Ma, H., et al.: Write for life: persisting in online health communities through expressive writing and social support. Proc. ACM Hum.-Comput. Interact. **1**(CSCW), 1–24 (2017)

32. Pang, B., Lee, L., et al.: Opinion mining and sentiment analysis. Found. Trends® Inf. Retrieval **2**(1–2), 1–135 (2008)

33. Papoutsaki, A., So, S., Kenderova, G., Shapiro, B., Epstein, D.A.: Understanding delivery of collectively built protocols in an online health community for discontinuation of psychiatric drugs. Proc. ACM Hum.-Comput. Interact. **5**(CSCW2), 1–29 (2021)

34. Pennebaker, J.W., Zech, E., Rimé, B.: Disclosing and sharing emotion: psychological, social, and health consequences (2001)

35. Plutchik, R.: The nature of emotions: human emotions have deep evolutionary roots, a fact that may explain their complexity and provide tools for clinical practice. Am. Sci. **89**(4), 344–350 (2001)

36. Robinson, D.L.: Brain function, emotional experience and personality. Neth. J. Psychol. **64**(4), 152–168 (2008)

37. Rossignac-Milon, M., Bolger, N., Zee, K.S., Boothby, E.J., Higgins, E.T.: Merged minds: generalized shared reality in dyadic relationships. J. Pers. Soc. Psychol. **120**(4), 882 (2021)

38. Saldaña, J.: The Coding Manual for Qualitative Researchers. Sage, Thousand Oaks (2021)

39. Sereda, A.: 'dirty stories saved my life': Fanfiction as a source of emotional support (2019)

40. Starbird, K., Arif, A., Wilson, T.: Disinformation as collaborative work: surfacing the participatory nature of strategic information operations. Proc. ACM Hum.-Comput. Interact. **3**(CSCW), 1–26 (2019)

41. Suler, J.: The online disinhibition effect. Cyberpsychol. Behav. **7**(3), 321–326 (2004)
42. Takhteyev, Y., Gruzd, A., Wellman, B.: Geography of twitter networks. Soc. Netw. **34**(1), 73–81 (2012)
43. Thomas, B.: What is fanfiction and why are people saying such nice things about it?? Storyworlds: J. Narrat. Stud. **3**, 1–24 (2011)
44. Tian, F., Zheng, Q., Zhao, R., Chen, T., Jia, X.: Can e-learner's emotion be recognized from interactive Chinese texts? In: 2009 13th International Conference on Computer Supported Cooperative Work in Design, pp. 546–551. IEEE (2009)
45. Vallor, S.: Flourishing on Facebook: virtue friendship & new social media. Ethics Inf. Technol. **14**(3), 185–199 (2012)
46. Van Nes, F., Abma, T., Jonsson, H., Deeg, D.: Language differences in qualitative research: is meaning lost in translation? Eur. J. Ageing **7**(4), 313–316 (2010)
47. Van Steenhuyse, V.: The writing and reading of fan fiction and transformation theory. CLCWeb: Comp. Lit. Cult. **13**(4), 4 (2011)
48. Yin, K., Aragon, C., Evans, S., Davis, K.: Where no one has gone before: a metadataset of the world's largest fanfiction repository. In: Proceedings of the 2017 CHI Conference on Human Factors in Computing Systems, pp. 6106–6110 (2017)

Reducing Stress Through Formative Assessments: A Case of the Digital Platform

Ajrina Hysaj[1] (ID), Georgina Farouqa[2](✉) (ID), Sara Azeem Khan[3](✉) (ID),
and Laith Hiasat[4](✉) (ID)

[1] University of Wollongong in Dubai, Dubai, United Arab Emirates
ajrinahysaj@uowdubai.ac.ae
[2] University of Walden, Minneapolis, USA
georginafarouqa@yahoo.com
[3] University of Wollongong in Dubai, Dubai, United Arab Emirates
sara.azeem.13@gmail.com
[4] Rochester Institute of Technology – Dubai, Dubai, United Arab Emirates
laithhiasat@gmail.com

Abstract. Educators worldwide are interested in understanding factors that contribute in a successful learning experience for undergraduate students in the online platform. To explain such interest scholars have focused their attention on exploring ways of supporting students learning process utilizing the digital technology. In our study we aimed to explore the perceptions of multicultural undergraduate students on ways that they prefer to be assessed in the digital learning platform. The sample size was 90 undergraduate students enrolled in a variety of universities in the UAE. For this study, the researchers used a mixed method approach using a structure questionnaire to collect the data. The 15 items of the questionnaire were formulated to gauge undergraduates perceived levels of stress, knowledge and willingness to use online sources for conducting research. Participants were selected through purposeful random sampling. The selection of participants was based on the inclusion criteria that helped in understanding the problem. Finally, the findings were described and recommendations for future research were presented.

Keywords: Multicultural Students · Formative Assessments · Digital Platform · Reducing Stress · Plagiarism

1 Introduction

For many undergraduate students, higher education is their first step towards an adult life guided by responsibilities and hard-work, and for many others higher education is the path towards a successful learning experience that may lead to a successful career and improved life-study and living standards [49]. Therefore, higher education serves for many as a gate towards a better life for oneself, loved ones and the society as a whole. Higher education in most countries is viewed as the bridge between higher school and professional life and universities worldwide being those private or federal universities, are considered as the cradle of the theoretical base of knowledge necessary for the practical knowledge which extensively takes part during professional life [19, 38]. The theoretical part of academic knowledge is the base for the practical knowledge and its successful application depends on the understanding of its importance and functions. However, it is a well-known fact that students worldwide, despite been eager to receive a university degree, are not always ready to be effective recipients of this kind of knowledge [11, 14]. The reasons for reluctance or hesitation may vary from the inability to comprehend profoundly the matter being taught to realizing that the degree that they have chosen is not the one they are any longer passionate about. While educators in tertiary level cannot do much with regard to the latter issue, since it is a personal choice, they can definitely have a greater say in supporting students understanding of the matter being taught which may as well have a correlation with the desire of students to study for the degree of their choice and subsequently support student retention [32, 33].

During tertiary education undergraduate students are faced with many academic and personal challenges that may impact greatly their understanding of the academic surrounding and impact their career choices later in life [8, 41, 44]. Furthermore, higher education is a multifaceted reality whose responsibility is to empower students with academic knowledge but also to inform them about themselves; the extent of their strength and the possible degree of their limitations [1, 40]. Therefore, the knowledge that undergraduates acquire informs their academic and personal growth. A fulfilling learning experience in university may lead to a successful career and to happy individuals which understandably have the possibility of creating a better society [43, 48]. Nevertheless, the application of knowledge acquired during university years requires continues nurturing to allow errors that may occur along the way and to support non-bias growth of undergraduates [9, 12, 45].

One of the many ways that undergraduates can be supported by educational institutions in their learning and overall experience in the university is through the provision of formative feedback [29]. Formative feedback becomes even more crucial for multicultural students whose first language is not English because their linguistic capacities may hinder their understanding if the matter being taught and result in loss of interest to participate in classroom activities, submit assignments or even drop out from subjects considered as very challenging and to a certain degree incomprehensible [2, 29, 34]. Another major issue in tertiary education is the high degree of occurrence of plagiarism. According to Buckley and Cowap [7], Tindall and Curtis [42], Fatima et al. [15], Hysaj and Elkhouly [21] and Kratovil [31], one of the reasons that may influence multicultural undergraduate students to plagiarise especially in academic writing tasks, is the lack of academic knowledge in English language. Another factor that may influence undergraduates' decision to involve in academic misconduct is the pressure from family and universities to perform at the best of their capacity [20, 22, 31, 42]. Although from an outsiders' perspective this seems not only fair but even the most logical expectation that families, universities and societies at large, may have, it yet does not support undergraduates learning experience and it may influence in undue stress that can hinder even further the learning process [15, 31, 42]. Issues that may lead students to commit academic misconduct are many, however from an educator perspective it is valuable to explore the possible connection that may exist between the undue stress from tests or assignments and the occurrence of academic misconduct, therefore, this study aims to look into stress as one of the components that may lead to academic misconduct.

2 Literature Review

2.1 Digital Technology from the Lenses of Multicultural Undergraduate Students

Educators and researchers in higher education have been looking into teaching and learning from a holistic perspective that considers students as the most important stakeholder in the equation of a successful learning experience, hence considering students improved academic performance as not only possible but also expected to be achieved [9, 45]. Placing students' needs in the centre of teaching and learning allows educators to focus on students' needs and it supports teaching and learning process since these needs are taken into consideration when designing curriculums or when assessing students and more importantly when delivering, applying and constructing knowledge. Knowledge construction and its appropriate application by the students are the ultimate goal of educators [23]. The spread of ICT has been incorporated into this goal and it has therefore become necessarily to explore its impact in teaching and learning [18]. Naturally, such impact became even more evident during the outbreak of COVID 19, showing that the relation between higher education and ICT was stronger than previously thought. The outbreak of COVID 19 created the necessity to look into the digitalization of education and especially higher education not only from a holistic perspective but even from a more inclusive perspective considering all the parties involved in teaching and learning process [3, 17].

Due to the wide spread of digital information and the easy access to its use, digital technology has become a focal point of higher education and educators and researchers are constantly trying to navigate its uses, benefits and its drawbacks [2, 3, 19]. Therefore, it is safe to say that despite being it challenging to be analysed and understood, digital technology is exciting to explore and offers a wide range of possibilities to support students' learning experience [37]. Furthermore, since the digital technology is highly incorporated into teaching and learning process, it becomes valuable to analyse how it affects the cognitive, affective and behavioural attitude of undergraduate students [5]. Studies that have aimed at exploring the use of digital technology in teaching and learning, have taken place in a variety of countries worldwide which highlights the necessity to consider ways of utilization of digital technology. Furthermore, many studies have aimed at exploring the corpus of research of digital technology in relation to teaching and learning, nevertheless most of these studies have addressed issues related to the use of digital technology but not necessarily to the impact the technology has on students or even the perceptions that students have about digital technology in general from a personal and academic perspective [5, 44, 48]. This approach can support not only teaching and learning process but most importantly it can allow educators to view the use of digital technology from a more holistic and inclusive platform.

Many studies have analysed the use of digital platform in higher education by employing a quantitative or mixed method approach and fewer studies have looked at it from a qualitative approach. Moreover, even fewer studies have ventured to explore it from a theoretical approach or looked at it from a student-cantered approach [24, 25, 46, 47].

Considering that students are by far the most important stakeholders in teaching and learning it is valuable to explore and understand ways they perceive the successful use of digital technology in higher education. These ways and approaches should include all the aspects of teaching and learning starting with the knowledge transferred from educators to students in the digital platform and including in it the formative feedback offered during the learning process and finally the variety of assessments used to gauge the accumulated knowledge. Finally, a very important factor yet not enough explored is the tendency of students to engage in plagiarism instances while using the digital technology [13, 14, 28].

2.2 Digitalizing Assessments in Higher Education

The outbreak of COVID-19 imposed the use of remote learning in schools and universities worldwide. The degree and depth of use that remote learning experienced in different parts of the world was conditioned by economic, technological and educative factors [17–20, 37]. Most universities around the globe were able to adapt their teaching and learning from face-to-face to a digital platform in a relatively short period of time, considering the necessity imposed due to the sudden outbreak. Nevertheless, not many of them had the adequate tools or the necessarily knowledge to ensure a smooth adaptation and an adequate utilization of the digital platform [46, 47, 50]. Although, many educators tried employing relatively successful ways of teaching and learning, the sudden switch from face-to-face to the online platform did not give enough time to consider carefully one of the most important factors of teaching and learning, the way students get assessed [19, 37].

Assessments are by far crucial to the teaching and learning process as they measure the degree of knowledge accumulated by students at any given time and in any given subject [6]. Moreover, assessment allow students to understand their strengths and weaknesses and train them on a variety of soft skills starting from time management, stress management and even collaboration and communication [16]. Therefore, the purpose of the assessments needs to include many personal and academic factors related to students personal and academic growth. Assessments utilizing the digital technology require to be considered even more carefully as they employ digital tools which can improve teaching and learning and make it possible for students to enjoy the process and subsequently perform better academically [39, 50]. Furthermore, while aiming to explore the perceptions of undergraduate students on assessments using the digital technology it is beneficial to understand the types of assessments that encourage the improvement in cognitive, behavioural and affective attitude of undergraduate students. Therefore, considering assessments as supportive tools more than assessing tools of accumulated knowledge in higher education can encourage improved academic performance in undergraduate students [39, 50].

Although the main role of assessments is to assess the accumulated knowledge against a given marking criteria, it is as well necessary and useful to consider the impact these assessments have on undergraduate students' desire to learn [6, 16, 39].The desire to learn is highly connected with the desire to get engaged in the learning process, which can be translated to improved student satisfaction and subsequent enhanced academic performance. From an academic perspective it could be very beneficial if such role is played by summative assessments, however, as theoretical and practical research has shown, such role is generally played by formative assessment more than it is played by summative assessment [6, 39, 50].The reasons for such occurrence could be related to stress, anxiety and the low levels of self-confidence experienced in undergraduate students mainly due to outside factors like peer or family pressure as well as the necessity to maintain a certain expected status. Therefore, exploring formative assessments could support the process of engaging students with the learning process as much as it could support their knowledge acquisition and their empowerment through deep learning and sharpening of soft skills much required in the work environment.

2.3   Reducing Multicultural Students Stress Through Formative Assessments

Formative feedback is by far a very important and powerful tool in supporting students' learning experience and improving their academic performance, and yet, it is not researched extensively [27, 36]. Ways that formative feedback can facilitate learning are integral to the types that this form of assessment can be provided to achieve the main goal of education which is to encourage active and deep learning. Formative feedback could be offered in a variety of forms such as process-writing through the provision of draft and final versions of the same assessment, more than one attempt exams as well as peer or reflective assessment to name a few [6, 15]. A common goal that all types of formative assessments have is to improve students' learning process by encouraging their pro-active engagement with the learning process. Another very valuable aspect of the provision of formative feedback is the effect it may have in reduction of stress levels in undergraduates since, it does not focus on the achieved grade but instead on the process of learning and its many unexplored and unpolished angles [27, 39].

This matters especially for multicultural students who have not studied English and may be new to tertiary study in English speaking countries or students whose first language is not English [18]. Understandably, the effective formative feedback is seen as a way to equip these students with the required knowledge without increasing the stress levels that at most times is present during higher education [20, 35]. One of the ways that formative assessment may be offered in academic writing classes is through process-oriented writing. According to McGarrell and Verbeem [26], Hysaj and Hamam [20] and Mahapatra [35], process- oriented writing can facilitate the reduction of stress because it values the process of reflecting on errors and correcting those without being pressured to perform for receiving a mark between-draft revision. Draft compositions are utilized to explore students' understanding of a given topic in a broad perspective as well as to gauge their ability to look for relevant details based on the respective assessment marking criteria. Therefore, process-oriented writing serves to measure students acquired knowledge on the topic as well as their critical and analytical thinking ability to analyse the adequate information appropriately. Furthermore, academic writing requires an adequate use of all the writing mechanics related to vocabulary, grammar and referencing skills which take time to develop and require continuous practice [35]. Therefore, process-oriented writing can support the exploration of students' assumptions on a specific piece of academic writing and on academic writing in general. Moreover, it can encourage active engagement of students with academic writing and facilitate the understanding of students with regard to refining their communicative intentions [26].

For instance, the study by Bader et al. [4] that analysed the perceptions of students upon receiving formative feedback on assignments emphasized a very important factor related to student successful experience in higher education and that is the praise that students received from their teachers. Not only did students feel that their opinion mattered but most importantly they formalized their understanding of the assignments through the opportunities they received but also, they established an improved degree of self-awareness of material, data and feedback interpretation that subsequently improved their degree of self-respect and self-worthiness. Therefore, not only their levels of stress got reduced but most importantly they acquired a transferable knowledge at a deep level and enjoyed the process as a whole [4].

A large number of undergraduate students whose first language is not English involve in plagiarism related instances due to the lack of information on what constitutes plagiarism as well as the shortage of informative tools that facilitate learning of academic writing skills [33–35, 41]. For example, according to Casado [9] many undergraduates are eager in speaking about their perspectives in the tertiary level and yet, they are not given the chance to do so. Furthermore, many multicultural students are unaware of appropriate ways of paraphrasing texts and do not possess any theoretical or practical understanding of the mechanics of paraphrasing and referencing skills [26, 34, 45]. For this very large category of learners, formative feedback is the best way to go as it not only supports their understanding of the techniques of academic writing but it also develops their level of knowledge of academic language in English language while effecting positively their self-esteem and self-worthiness [4, 15, 17]. More importantly during the process of receiving formative feedback undergraduates improve their level of engagement and feel part of the process of knowledge acquisition [24, 25].

Students engagement with the learning process has two sides, one that reflects the degree to which students engage with the process of learning, in other words their individual effort and the other one that reflects the extent to which the educational institutes engage with students to understand their learning needs [4]. Understandably both these components are highly interconnected and equally valuable. Furthermore, if utilized appropriately they jointly have the power to substantially improve students' learning experience by encouraging active engagement in their studies that can lead to successful experiences with the learning process which translates to students' success [33, 35, 37, 41]. The degree of success that students experience due to active engagement with the learning process is very closely related to improved students' retention. According to Bader et al. [4] and Hysaj [24], the range of related terms that are linked to student engagement and retention is quite broad and it includes not only personal and academic factors but also institutional and societal ones. Nevertheless, formative assessments are unquestionably one of the factors that may influence students' level of engagement with the learning process [43, 45].

More generally, formative assessment supports the tendency of educational institutes to create a diverse and inclusive environment that encourages critical thinking through reflective learning. Students as main stakeholders in the education system play a crucial role in the success or failure of it, yet their perspectives are not always given careful consideration when planning lessons or designing curricula [20]. For instance, the study by Bader et al. [4] that analysed the perceptions of students upon receiving formative feedback on assignments emphasized a very important factor related to student successful experience in higher education and that is the praise that students received from their teachers. Not only did students feel that their opinion mattered but most importantly they formalized their understanding of the assignments through the opportunities they received but also, they established an improved degree of self-awareness of material, data and feedback interpretation that subsequently improved their degree of self-respect and self-worthiness. Therefore, not only their levels of stress got reduced but most importantly they acquired a transferable knowledge at a deep level and enjoyed the process as a whole [4, 26–28, 32].

Another very pressing matter in higher education is the degree of plagiarism reported in higher education. According to Tindall and Curtis [42], Khan et al. [30], Kratovil [31], a large number of undergraduate students whose first language is not English involve in plagiarism related instances due to the lack of information on what constitutes plagiarism as well as the shortage of informative tools that facilitate learning of academic writing skills. Furthermore, many multicultural students are unaware of appropriate ways of paraphrasing texts and do not possess any theoretical or practical understanding of the mechanics of paraphrasing and referencing skills [29, 30, 32, 42]. For this very large category of learners, formative feedback is the best way to go as it not only supports their understanding of the techniques of academic writing but it also develops their level of knowledge of academic language in English language while effecting positively their self-esteem and self-worthiness. More importantly during the process of receiving formative feedback undergraduates improve their level of engagement and feel part of the process of knowledge acquisition [21, 22, 26].

3   Methodology

For this study, we utilized a mixed method approach using a structured questionnaire to collect data relevant to the levels of stress, knowledge, and encouragement to use online sources from four years university students in UAE. The sample group consisted of university undergraduate students. Participants were selected through purposeful random sampling. The selection of participants was based on the inclusion criteria that helped in understanding the problem. This allowed for participants to provide insight from first year to senior students at universities. The questionnaire was made available to participants in an online format and sent by email or /and (SNS). The questionnaire was created using Google forms. It consisted of 15 questions aimed at understanding students' perception about stress, knowledge, and use of online sources. The questionnaire emphasized the identification of types of assessments that influence knowledge and stress level of students. Participants were provided a selection of four pre-determined response options and one open ended response option. In total, 90 questionnaires were completed. Responses were thematically analyzed using QDA Miner Lite 2.0.7, qualitative and mixed method analysis software.

4 Results

The first objective of the study was to better understand the stress level of students undergo when they complete different kinds of assessments like exams, research papers and projects. The results are displayed in Table 1.

Table 1. Stress level of students during assessments

Cover and included terms	Occurrence Frequency	Percentage of comments
1. Before an exam		
1.1 Very Stressed	33	36.70%
1.2 Stressed	31	34.40%
1.3 Moderately Stressed	21	23.30%
1.4 Not Stressed	5	5.60%
2. During an exam		
2.1 Very Stressed	27	30%
2.2 Stressed	20	22.20%
2.3 Moderately Stressed	36	40%
2.4 Not Stressed	6	6.70%
3. Exams replaced with research papers or projects		**28.90%**
3.1 Very Stressed	11	12.20%
3.2 Stressed	15	16.70%
3.3 Moderately Stressed	35	38.90%
3.4 Not Stressed	29	32.20%
4. Writing a research paper		
4.1 Very Stressed	9	10%
4.2 Stressed	17	18.90%
4.3 Moderately Stressed	41	45.60%
4.4 Not Stressed	23	25%
5. Completing a project		
5.1 Very Stressed	8	8.90%
5.2 Stressed	14	15.60%
4.3 Moderately Stressed	37	41.10%
4.4 Not Stressed	30	33.30%

Approximately 70% of participants felt stressed before exams and 52% felt stressed during exams. Through a lens focused on students' perception of stress, this outcome inevitably affects the concentration level of students that might influence their academic performance. According to data collected through the questionnaire 24% of participants felt stressed while completing a project. Other 29% felt stressed when writing a research paper. Similarly, 29% felt stressed when they did not need to complete an exam, alternatively they we required to write a research paper or complete a project. The second objective of the study was to better understand whether students felt stressed while using online sources to complete their assessments. Results are presented in Table 2.

Table 2.   Stress level of students during using online sources

Cover and included terms	Occurrence Frequency	Percentage of comments
1. Online exams		
1.1 Very Stressed	6	6.70%
1.2 Stressed	25	27.80%
1.3 Moderately Stressed	37	41.10%
1.4 Not Stressed	21	23.30%
2. Online exams with multiple attempts		
2.1 Very Stressed	0	0%
2.2 Stressed	4	4.40%
2.3 Moderately Stressed	18	20%
2.4 Not Stressed	68	75.60%
3. Writing a research paper		
3.1 Very Stressed	3	3.40%
3.2 Stressed	10	11.20%
3.3 Moderately Stressed	35	39%
3.4 Not Stressed	39	43%
4. Completing a project		
4.1 Very Stressed	0	0%
4.2 Stressed	7	7.80%
4.3 Moderately Stressed	34	37.80%
4.4 Not Stressed	47	52.20%

In the questionnaire, (34.50%) of the participants felt stressed when they were required to complete an online exam. A few (4%) felt stressed when they knew that they have multiple attempts to complete the online exam. Some (15%) felt stressed when they are writing a research paper while (8%) felt stressed when they completed a project. It was important to understand how encouraged students were to use online sources to complete their assessments, whether they were working on research paper, completing a project or an online assessment. Results are shown in Table 3.

The majority of questionnaire participants (80%) informed that they were encouraged to use online sources to complete a project. Similarly (78%) were encouraged to use online sources to write a research paper. Almost half of participants (53%) indicated

Table 3. Students' level of encouragement to use online sources

Cover and included terms	Occurrence Frequency	Percentage of comments
1. Online assessments		
1.1 Very encouraged	17	18.90%
1.2 Encouraged	31	34.40%
1.3 Moderately encouraged	32	35.60%
1.4 Not encouraged	10	11.10%
2. Writing research papers		
2.1 Very encouraged	45	50%
2.2 Encouraged	25	27.80%
2.3 Moderately encouraged	18	20%
2.4 Not encouraged	2	2.20%
3. Completing projects		
3.1 Very encouraged	44	48.90%
3.2 Encouraged	28	31.10%
3.3 Moderately encouraged	17	18.90%
3.4 Not encouraged	1	1%

that they would use online sources to complete assessments. These high rates of online sources preference among students indicate the importance of utilizing technology in higher education. In this study it was also important to further understand the level of knowledge that students achieved after they completed exams, writing research, or completing a project. Results are shown in Table 4.

Most of the participants (91%) achieved deep learning after they completed a project. Similarly, (85%) achieved knowledge when writing a research paper. More than half of participants (58%) achieved deep learning and knowledge when completing an exam. Very few (2%) felt that they gain no knowledge when writing a research paper or completing a project. Few (17%) indicated that they achieved low level of knowledge when writing research or completing a project. One third of participants identified their level of knowledge as low when taking exams. Few participants answered the questions in an open-ended format that we provided in the study.

Example of participants' responses to open ended response option:

1. Stress during exams: "If I don't know the answer, I start getting stressed".
2. Stress while working on a project: "I haven't worked on one in university yet, but as far as I know, if I have all the information available, I wouldn't be stressed".
3. Stress level using online sources to complete a research paper: "As long as I find appropriate and easily interpretable sources, I wouldn't be stressed" "I would enjoy the process rather than be stressed".
4. Level of knowledge gained from writing a research paper: "Depends, if I am interested in the topic or not".

Table 4. Achievement of deep learning

Cover and included terms	Occurrence Frequency	Percentage of comments
1. Exams		
1.1 High level of knowledge	14	15.60%
1.2 Average level of knowledge	38	42.20%
1.3 Low level of knowledge	33	36.70%
1.4 No knowledge	5	5.60%
2. Writing research papers		
2.1 High level of knowledge	37	41.10%
2.2 Average level of knowledge	43	43.80%
2.3 Low level of knowledge	9	10%
2.4 No knowledge	0	0%
3. Completing projects		
3.1 High level of knowledge	48	53.90%
3.2 Average level of knowledge	33	37.10%
3.3 Low level of knowledge	6	6.70%
3.4 No knowledge	2	2.20%

5 Discussion

Unfortunately, despite the crucial role that undergraduates play in education in general and especially in formative assessment practices their input is not always explored and in most cases is under-researched, hence this study aimed at addressing this issue. Furthermore, the transference of knowledge that may occur due to the provision of formative feedback is another factor that requires exploration for the benefit of undergraduates and higher education at large. According to the survey data, a large percentage of students felt stressed before and during exams. Stress that students undergo can have a negative effect on the learning process and can lead to academic misconduct [15, 31, 42]. Stress percentage significantly dropped when exams were replaced by research papers or projects. The goal of formative assessments is to encourage students to be actively engaged in their learning rather than being stressed focusing on their grades [27, 39]. To address the level of knowledge gained by assessments, data suggested that students felt that they gain better knowledge when they write research papers or work on project compared to the knowledge they gain when they sit for exams. Complementary to the prioritization of achieving deep learning, it was also imperative to understand students' perception of deep learning achieved by different assessments. The percentage of deep learning achieved through projects was the highest while students expressed that they achieved less deep learning after taking an exam. Furthermore, improving current assessment approaches to reduce stress and enhance knowledge, many factors are considered. These include further expanding and improving the use of online sources, strategies used by faculty to promote student engagement in their studies through research papers and projects. This aligns with literature related to assessments as a tool to measure knowledge in addition to time and stress management as well as collaborative and communication skills that they develop when completing formative assessments [16]. Concurrently, using online sources contributed to the decrease of stress level percentage. The majority of students felt no stress when while using online sources to complete exams or write research papers or projects. Students' stress level significantly dropped when they completed online exams that allows multiple attempts. Directly responding to the results, formative assessment and use of online sources are preferred by the majority of students. Further identification of which type of assessments of which assessment enhance knowledge and the stress that student experience assisted in achieving long lasting deep learning that students can benefit from and use in their future career that will contribute in their success in the challenging work environment. Similarly, the conditions of students when they complete assessment can influence their level of knowledge significantly. Constructive knowledge using technology can enhance students learning and achieve the goal of educators that seek proper delivery and application of knowledge [26]. Moreover, using digital tools can assist students in improving learning and improve their academic achievement [39, 50]. As students' perception of their learning experience and their preferred assessment tools is not fully explored, this study aimed at exploring the level of stress students felt when completing assessments as well as the level of knowledge and deep learning that they achieved. It was also important to better understand students views of utilizing technology to enhance their learning. Based on the results of the study, it would be advantageous to sharpen the higher education leadership lens and plan additional significant assessments that would support students learning and place them at the centre of the learning process. Further research is needed to explore faculty's assessment preference as well as challenges that faculty members might face in providing students with deep significant learning experience. In addition to utilizing technology and modern strategies to help students achieve and use knowledge gained in the studies in their future careers.

6 Conclusion and Recommendations

This paper aimed at exploring the perceptions of undergraduate students of formative assessment and the role it plays in learning process and specifically its relation to stress and deep learning. As such, this paper aimed at contributing to bridging the gap between research in the use of digital technology and practice of formative assessments in the digital platform. The survey findings amplified the students voice about the ways they prefer to be assessed, the stress they suffer from, and their enthusiasm to use technology in their learning. Students are the focal point in the learning process, yet their needs and preferences are not taken into consideration when planning assessment. Students feel stressed when they complete exams as they focus on the grade rather than knowledge. Alternatively, they enjoy and acquire more knowledge when completing formative assessments especially using online sources. The role of educators is also crucial in achieving the best learning outcome by students. However, further exploration is needed to better understand their perception. Higher education institutions need to consider the needs of students and provide them with modern technologies to get them ready to face the challenges of their future professional life.

References

1. Adeokun, C.O., Opoko, A.P.: Exploring the Link between motivation for course-choice and retention in the architectural profession: students' perspectives. Mediterranean J. Soc. Sci. **6**(6 S1), p.191 (2015)
2. Altmann, M., Langesee, L.M., Misterek, J.: Designing formative feedback guidelines in virtual group work from a student's perspective. In: Edulearn21 Proceedings (pp. 8698–8706). IATED (2021)
3. Anthony Jnr, B., Abbas Petersen, S.: Examining the digitalisation of virtual enterprises amidst the COVID-19 pandemic: a systematic and meta-analysis. Enterprise Inf. Syst. **15**(5), pp.617–650 (2021)
4. Bader, M., Burner, T., Iversen, S.H., Varga, Z.: Student perspectives on formative feedback as part of writing portfolios. Assess. Eval. Higher Educ. (2019)
5. Bond, M.: Facilitating student engagement through the flipped learning approach in K-12: a systematic review. Comput. Educ. **151**, 103819 (2020)
6. Bryan, C., Clegg, K. (eds.): Innovative assessment in higher education: a handbook for academic practitioners. Routledge (2019)
7. Buckley, E., Cowap, L.: An evaluation of the use of Turnitin for electronic submission and marking and as a formative feedback tool from an educator's perspective. Br. J. Edu. Technol. **44**(4), 562–570 (2013)
8. Calkins, L.N., Welki, A.: Factors that influence choice of major: why some students never consider economics. Int. J. Soc. Econ. (2006)
9. Casado, M.: Teaching methods in higher education: a student perspective. J. Hosp. Tour. Educ. **12**(2), 65–70 (2000)
10. Díaz-Méndez, M., Paredes, M.R., Saren, M.: Improving society by improving education through service-dominant logic: reframing the role of students in higher education. Sustainability **11**(19), 5292 (2019)
11. Dicker, R., Garcia, M., Kelly, A., Mulrooney, H.: What does 'quality'in higher education mean? Perceptions of staff, students and employers. Stud. High. Educ. **44**(8), 1425–1441 (2019)
12. Dziewanowska, K.: Value types in higher education–students' perspective. J. High. Educ. Policy Manag. **39**(3), 235–246 (2017)
13. Eaton, S.E., Lock, J.V., Schroeder, M.: Canadian Symposium on Academic Integrity: Program and Abstracts (2019)
14. Eaton, C., Howell, S.T., Yannelis, C.: When investor incentives and consumer interests diverge: private equity in higher education. Rev. Financ. Stud. **33**(9), 4024–4060 (2020)
15. Fatima, A., Abbas, A., Ming, W., Hosseini, S., Zhu, D.: Internal and external factors of plagiarism: evidence from Chinese public sector universities. Account. Res. **26**(1), 1–16 (2019)
16. Gao, X., Li, P., Shen, J., Sun, H.: Reviewing assessment of student learning in interdisciplinary STEM education. Int. J. STEM Educ. **7**(1), 1–14 (2020). https://doi.org/10.1186/s40594-020-00225-4
17. Hamam, D., Hysaj, A.: Technological pedagogical and content knowledge (TPACK): Higher education teachers' perspectives on the use of TPACK in online academic writing classes. In: Stephanidis, C., Antona, M., Ntoa, S. (eds.) HCII 2021. CCIS, vol. 1421, pp. 51–58. Springer, Cham (2021). https://doi.org/10.1007/978-3-030-78645-8_7

18. Hamam, D., Hysaj, A.: The aftermath of COVID 19: future insights for teachers' professional development in higher education. J. Asia TEFL **19**(1), 303 (2022)
19. Horgan, D., et al.: Digitalisation and COVID-19: the perfect storm. Biomedicine Hub **5**(3), 1–23 (2020)
20. Hysaj, A., Hamam, D.: Academic writing skills in the online platform-A success, a failure or something in between? A study on perceptions of higher education students and teachers in the UAE. In: 2020 IEEE International Conference on Teaching, Assessment, and Learning for Engineering (TALE) (pp. 668–673). IEEE (2020)
21. Hysaj, A., Elkhouly, A.: Why do students plagiarize? The case of multicultural students in an Australian university in the United Arab Emirates. In: ENAI Conference (2020)
22. Hysaj, A., Suleymanova, S.: Safeguarding academic integrity in crisis induced environment: a case study of emirati engineering and IT students in a private university in the UAE. In: Meiselwitz, G. (ed.) HCII 2021. LNCS, vol. 12775, pp. 236–245. Springer, Cham (2021). https://doi.org/10.1007/978-3-030-77685-5_19
23. Hysaj, A., Hamam, D.: The Journal of Asia TEFL (2021)
24. Hysaj, A.: Group reports in the online platform: a puzzle, a ride in the park or a steep slope: a case study of multicultural undergraduate students in the United Arab Emirates. In: 2021 IEEE International Conference on Engineering, Technology & Education (TALE) (pp. 745–750). IEEE (2021)
25. Hysaj, A.: COVID-19 pandemic and online teaching from the lenses of K-12 STEM teachers in Albania. In: 2021 IEEE International Conference on Engineering, Technology & Education (TALE) (pp. 01–07). IEEE (2021)
26. Hysaj, A., Hamam, D.: Dimensions of Formative Feedback During the COVID-19 Pandemic: Evaluating the Perceptions of Undergraduates in Multicultural EAP Classrooms. In: Meiselwitz, G. (ed.) Social Computing and Social Media: Applications in Education and Commerce: 14th International Conference, SCSM 2022, Held as Part of the 24th HCI International Conference, HCII 2022, Virtual Event, June 26 – July 1, 2022, Proceedings, Part II, pp. 103–114. Springer International Publishing, Cham (2022). https://doi.org/10.1007/978-3-031-05064-0_8
27. Hysaj, A., Haroon, H.A.: Online Formative Assessment and Feedback: A Focus Group Discussion Among Language Teachers. In: Meiselwitz, G. (ed.) Social Computing and Social Media: Applications in Education and Commerce: 14th International Conference, SCSM 2022, Held as Part of the 24th HCI International Conference, HCII 2022, Virtual Event, June 26 – July 1, 2022, Proceedings, Part II, pp. 115–126. Springer International Publishing, Cham (2022). https://doi.org/10.1007/978-3-031-05064-0_9
28. Jereb, E., et al.: Factors influencing plagiarism in higher education: a comparison of German and Slovene students. PLoS ONE **13**(8), e0202252 (2018)
29. Juwah, C., Macfarlane-Dick, D., Matthew, B., Nicol, D., Ross, D., Smith, B.: Enhancing student learning through effective formative feedback. Higher Educ. Acad. **140**, 1–40 (2004)
30. Khan, Z.R., Hysaj, A., John, S.R. and Khan, S.: Gateway to preparing K-12 students for higher education–reflections on organizing an academic integrity camp. In: European Conference on Academic Integrity and Plagiarism, p. 65 (2021)
31. Kratovil, A.: Plagiarism in the graduate nursing program: occupation stress or lack of knowledge? Nurs. Sci. Q. **34**(4), 374–377 (2021)
32. Layali, K., Al-Shlowiy, A.: Students' perceptions of e-learning for ESL/EFL in Saudi universities at time of coronavirus: a literature review. Indonesian EFL Journal **6**(2), 97–108 (2020)
33. Li, M.: Multimodal pedagogy in TESOL teacher education: students' perspectives. System **94**, 102337 (2020)
34. Ludvigsen, K., Krumsvik, R., Furnes, B.: Creating formative feedback spaces in large lectures. Comput. Educ. **88**, 48–63 (2015)

35. Mahapatra, S.K.: Online formative assessment and feedback practices of ESL teachers in India, Bangladesh and Nepal: a multiple case study. Asia Pac. Educ. Res. **30**(6), 519–530 (2021)

36. McGarrell, H., Verbeem, J.: Motivating revision of drafts through formative feedback. ELT J. **61**(3), 228–236 (2007)

37. Mohd Arif, M.F.B., Choo Ta, G.: COVID-19 Pandemic management: a review of the digitalisation leap in Malaysia. Sustainability **14**(11), 6805 (2022)

38. Parker, K.: The growing partisan divide in views of higher education. Pew Res. Center, **19** (2019)

39. Schwinning, N., Striewe, M., Massing, T., Hanck, C., Goedicke, M.: Towards digitalisation of summative and formative assessments in academic teaching of statistics. arXiv preprint arXiv:1811.02391 (2018)

40. Segers, M., Dochy, F.: New assessment forms in problem-based learning: the value-added of the students' perspective. Stud. High. Educ. **26**(3), 327–343 (2001)

41. Sujarwo, S., Sukmawati, S., Akhiruddin, A., Ridwan, R., Siradjuddin, S.S.S.: An analysis of university students' perspective on online learning in the midst of covid-19 pandemic. Jurnal Pendidikan Dan Pengajaran **53**(2), 125–137 (2020)

42. Tindall, I.K., Curtis, G.J.: Negative emotionality predicts attitudes toward plagiarism. Journal of Academic Ethics **18**(1), 89–102 (2020)

43. Trautwein, C., Bosse, E.: The first year in higher education—critical requirements from the student perspective. High. Educ. **73**(3), 371–387 (2017)

44. Tymon, A.: The student perspective on employability. Stud. High. Educ. **38**(6), 841–856 (2013)

45. Vickerman, P.: Student perspectives on formative peer assessment: an attempt to deepen learning? Assess. Eval. High. Educ. **34**(2), 221–230 (2009)

46. Webb, A., McQuaid, R.W. and Webster, C.W.R.: Moving learning online and the COVID-19 pandemic: a university response. World Journal of Science, Technology and Sustainable Development (2021)

47. Wilkens, L., Haage, A., Lüttmann, F., Bühler, C.R.: Digital teaching, inclusion and students' needs: Student perspectives on participation and access in higher education. Social Inclusion **9**(3), 117–129 (2021)

48. Wong, A.C.K.: Considering reflection from the student perspective in higher education. SAGE Open **6**(1), 2158244016638706 (2016)

49. Woodall, T., Hiller, A., Resnick, S.: Making sense of higher education: students as consumers and the value of the university experience. Stud. High. Educ. **39**(1), 48–67 (2014)

50. Zitzmann, N.U., Matthisson, L., Ohla, H., Joda, T.: Digital undergraduate education in dentistry: a systematic review. Int. J. Environ. Res. Public Health **17**(9), 3269 (2020)

Examining the Effectiveness of a Robotic-Human-Machine-Interface on Sleepiness During Highway Automated Driving

Nihan Karatas[1](✉)[ORCID], Yuki Yoshihara[1][ORCID], Hiroko Tanabe[1][ORCID], Takahiro Tanaka[1][ORCID], Kazuhiro Fujikake[2][ORCID], Shuhei Takeuchi[3][ORCID], Kenji Iwata[3][ORCID], Makoto Harazawa[3][ORCID], and Naoki Kamiya[3][ORCID]

[1] Institute of Innovation for Future Society, Nagoya University, Aichi, Japan
karatas@mirai.nagoya-u.ac.jp
[2] School of Psychology, Chukyo University, Aichi, Japan
[3] Tokai Rika Co. Ltd., Aichi, Japan

Abstract. The automation of vehicles is increasing and is expected to become a part of our daily lives in the near future. Furthermore, the progress in automated driving operations will change the driver's role to that of a passive monitor. However, a lack of active involvement in driving situations and monotonous driving environments increase driver sleepiness. Considering the low automation levels in vehicles (i.e., Levels 2 and 3), drivers' arousal levels and ability to monitor the road environment are critical. In this study, we examined the effectiveness of a robotic-human-machine-interface (RHMI) in alleviating the sleepiness level of drivers through random news information presentation. We conducted a within-subject experiment with 12 participants in a driving simulator environment and compared three conditions: no information was provided (the control condition); information was provided through a voice-only interface; and information was provided through an RHMI prototype. The qualitative and quantitative results of this experiment revealed that the information provision interfaces (voice-only and RHMI) had the potential to alleviate the sleepiness level in Level 2 highway automated driving. In addition, the RHMI prototype alleviated sleepiness and improved the arousal of drivers more than in the voice-only and no-information provision conditions.

Keywords: robotic-human-machine interface · sleepiness · automated driving

1 Introduction

Sleepiness occurs because of an interruption in the circadian rhythm and a lack of rest [7]. It affects the ability to perform daily tasks and driving performance, which can ultimately cause fatal traffic accidents [21]. Because fully automated vehicles are regarded as the future of transportation, they are expected to operate without driver involvement to reduce human error and provide more energy-efficient, comfortable, and convenient methods of transportation [10]. This level of automation provides drivers with opportunities to relax or focus on other non-driving-related tasks [13]. However, depending on the automation level of the vehicle, the extent of sleepiness of the driver is important. Particularly, when the automated system controls the vehicle, certain environmental conditions or road characteristics can trigger takeover requests at automation levels 2 and 3, where drivers are expected to monitor the road and take over control if the quality of the sensors degrades and safe transportation can no longer be guaranteed [10]. Moreover, owing to the lack of active involvement in driving situations and monotonous driving environments, drivers may become fatigued faster than when they are manually driving the vehicle [5,14].

Taking drivers out of an automated system's operational loop reduces vigilance and situational awareness [2,8,12]. Therefore, using highly automated driving functions for extended periods may leave drivers in a state where they are immediately unable to perform smoothly and safely. Studies have been conducted to decrease the level of sleepiness and keep drivers awake. Gershon et al. [6] developed an interactive cognitive task to improve driver performance and mental state while driving. The report revealed that using a cell phone helps maintain alertness while driving for long periods [1]. According to [15], drivers showed better lane keeping and higher EEG-related alertness levels when engaged in a secondary verbal task. Despite the well-documented dangers of cell phone use [16], such usage may be effective as a motivating secondary task when experiencing boredom or fatigue. [22] used a human-machine interface device that comfortably wakes the driver from sleep. However, drivers require a safer, more seamless, familiar and intuitive interface that maintains their wakefulness and is feasible for long periods of driving.

Intelligent agents that help users perform particular tasks have been widely used as voice assistants in daily lives [11]. Driving is one of the promising usage domains that considerably benefits from these agents. In-vehicle intelligent agents are expected to proactively engage in driving tasks over a wider spectrum to secure road safety and support drivers in both driving- and non-driving-related activities [20]. Furthermore, they are expected to provide versatile information on vehicle status and road events. However, these agents must be constructed carefully to reduce distraction, improve vigilance and prevent unintended consequences, such as overreliance, particularly when driver intervention is still required in conditional automation [20].

Previous research has shown that a robotic-human-machine interface (RHMI) is a more noticeable, familiar, and acceptable medium as a driving support compared to voice-only and animated driving agents [17]. Moreover, it is effective in improving safe driving skills (i.e., reducing the speed of the car and increasing the frequency of checking left and right when approaching intersections) in driving simulation environments [19] and in real-world driving situations [18]. Therefore, in this study, we examined whether a RHMI was capable of alleviating driver sleepiness through random news information presentation. This study aimed to understand whether the physicality of an RHMI is effective in alleviating driver sleepiness.

2 Method

We focused on understanding whether an RHMI reduces the sleepiness level of drivers during highway driving at automated level 2. We conducted an experiment with no information provided as the base condition and compared it with the voice-only and RHMI prototype conditions. For the voice-only condition, we used text-to-speech software, AI Talk ([1]), used the voice "Nozomi," and placed a mini Bluetooth speaker that was not visible from the driving seat. Furthermore, we used an RHMI prototype for the RHMI conditions (Fig. 1). In both voice-only and RHMI conditions, news reports were announced in a timely manner. As the time interval. In the voice-only condition, just before starting to announce the news, a "pon" sound was applied as a cue for drivers to prepare themselves for an upcoming information announcement [17]. As shown in Table 1, news from different topics were announced four times. One of the topics was used for the voice-only condition, whereas the other was used for the RHMI condition.

Fig. 1. Robotic human-machine interface (RHMI) prototype consisted of a lid, body and pedestal. Its LED eyes are shown under the lid. The figure also shows the experimental environment. The RHMI was oriented from participants toward the driving environment.

---

[1] https://www.ai-j.jp/.

2.1   RHMI Prototype

The RHMI prototype consists of three parts: body, lid, and pedestal (Fig. 1). The body of the robot was 40 mm when the lid was closed and 54 mm when the lid was opened by 20° (max). The width of the body was 70 mm. The height and width of the pedestal were 62 mm and 150 mm, respectively. The pedestal was connected to a computer via a USB cable. The robot was positioned on the left side of the driver (the driver's seat was on the right side). It was oriented away from the driver. We designed expressions for the RHMI Prototype using eye and lid colors and body motions. The RHMI prototype has two LED eyes and a lid with a ring. The small body and lid have one degree of freedom. The head inside the body can turn left and right, whereas the lid can move up and down. The colors of the eyes and ring LED, the speed of the body and lid, and the angle of the lid and body movements were adjustable. Furthermore, we used the same voice as in the voice-only condition of AI Talk for the robot's voice. The default behavior of the robot was set to watch the road by turning its head to the right and left at a degree of 135° and a speed of 5 rpm. In addition, the lid angle was set to 5°. When the robot started announcing the news, just before starting its speech, the lid of the robot's opening angle increased from 5° to 12° in 1 s as an equivalence of the "pon" sound in the voice-only condition.

The behavior and speech lines of the robot were arranged using the Wizard of Oz design settings. We created a graphical user interface (GUI) composed of buttons to trigger the movements for each RHMI behavior. The GUI was automated with a time-based script using the PyAutoGUI library[2]. Furthermore, the mouse and keyboard can perform automated interactions with other applications by using this library in a Python script.

2.2   Participants

The participants in this study were recruited from a human resources service company. Twelve participants (six females) aged 32 to 51 years (M = 45.916, SD = 6.855) with regular driving licenses participated in the experiment. The experiment was conducted as a within-subject study in a driving simulator environment where a 35-km-long highway simulation road was run by an automated level 2 for 15 min.

2.3   Experimental Protocol

A consent form, demographic questionnaire, and driving-style questionnaire were required at the beginning of the experiment. Furthermore, during the experimental sessions, the eye-gaze data of the participants was collected using Tobii Pro Glasses (Tobii Co., Ltd.), and driving simulator log data was collected.

After completing each experimental condition, the participants were asked to fill out an acceptance questionnaire. The acceptance questionnaire items were

---

[2] https://pyautogui.readthedocs.io.

Table 1. The topics and the content of the news that was announced within three minutes intervals. The first and second contents were randomly chosen for the voice-only and RHMI conditions.

Topic	Content
1. Weather	1.1 While record-breaking heat continues in Europe, the maximum temperature exceeded 40 °C for the first time in recorded history in various parts of the United Kingdom, and transportation was disrupted. The civic life was greatly disturbed. 1.2 The World Meteorological Organization (WMO) said at a recent meeting that heatwaves across Europe are likely to peak at the end of this month, but temperatures are expected to continue until the middle of next week. It may continue to exceed the average year.
2. Stock price	2.1 On the Tokyo stock market, the Nikkei stock average continued to rise sharply, closing the first session at 27,599.52 yen, up 637.84 yen (2.37%) from the previous day rice field. 2.2 In the stock market for emerging companies, the Tokyo Stock Exchange Mothers Index continued to rise today. The previous closing was 12.54 points (1.83%) higher than 696.11, the previous day.
3. Politics	3.1 At the press conference the day before, the Biden administration in the United States gave Ukraine approximately $ 270 million yen Japan announced that they will provide additional military assistance of more than 36.7 billion yen. 3.2 The fourth round of the election for the leadership of the British ruling party and the Conservative Party was held on the 19th, and the votes were counted on the same day. Former Finance Minister Rishi Sunak received 118 votes to maintain his top spot for the previous polls.
4. Technology	4. 1 Netflix, a major American video distribution company, announced that the number of paying subscribers worldwide at the end of last June was about 220.67 million. Compared to the end of March, the number of members decreased by 970,000. 4. 2 Twitter Inc. filed a lawsuit against Elon Musk, a major electric vehicle company, to fulfill the purchase agreement. A court in eastern Delaware today ordered a five-day trial promptly

formed internally in our laboratory, and their reliability was verified in previous experiments [3,4]. In addition, we used a user experience questionnaire [9] to compare the valence, pragmatic quality, and hedonic aspects of the system under three conditions. Finally, we used a sleepiness questionnaire to evaluate participants' sleepiness levels before and after each experimental condition. Each participant took approximately 1.5 h to complete the experiment.

We took the necessary precautions against the possibility of COVID-19 during the experiments.

This study was approved by the Institutional Review Board of the Institute of Innovation for Future Society at Nagoya University.

3   Results

We analyzed the results from questionnaires that were completed after the experimental conditions and from the eye-gaze tracker used during the experimental sessions.

3.1   Qualitative Results

We analyzed the acceptability questionnaire, user experience quality, and subjective sleepiness check for a subjective assessment of the experimental results. All statistical analyses were performed using IBM SPSS Statistics (version 27).

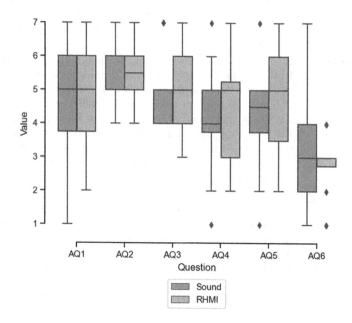

Fig. 2. Figure shows the box plot for the acceptance questionnaire results.

Acceptability. The acceptability questionnaire consisted of six 7-point Likert scale questions: (1) Strongly Disagree, (2) disagree, (3) somewhat disagree, (4) neither agree nor disagree, (5) somewhat agree, (6) agree, and (7) strongly agree. The questionnaire items were as follows: AQ1, I think this interface is preferable; AQ2, I think this interface is reliable; AQ3, I think this interface makes it easy to understand the operation mode; AQ4, I would like to use this interface; AQ5, This interface gives a sense of security; AQ6, I find this interface confusing. For this set of questionnaires, a paired t-test was used to compare the voice-only and RHMI conditions. The results showed no significant difference in any of the questionnaire items at α =.05 level. However, RHMI showed a tendency toward slightly higher acceptance rates regarding system reliability, willingness to use it, and sense of security (Fig. 2).

User Experience Quality (UEX). The UEX questionnaire consisted of 7-point Likert scale with 26 adjective pairs. A paired t-test was used to compare the voice-only and RHMI conditions. The results showed a significant difference on the efficiency factor (t(11) = -2.049, p = .032), and novelty factor (t(11) = 4.117, p = .000) at α =.05 level. According to these results, the voice-only condition was more efficient (M = 4.687, SD = 1.201) than the RHMI condition (M = 4.229, SD = 1.125). In contrast, the RHMI condition was more novel (M = 4.687, SD = 1.163) than the voice-only condition (M = 3.77, SD = 1.12) (Fig. 3).

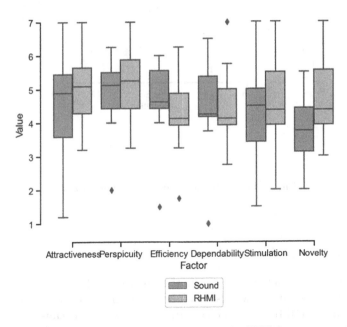

Fig. 3. Figure shows the results for the UEX factors.

Subjective Sleepiness Check. The sleepiness check consisted of 6-point Likert scale items: (0) not sleepy at all, (1) feeling a little sleepy, (2) feeling sleepy, (3) sleeping, (4) very sleepy, and (5) extremely sleepy. Participants were asked to rate their sleepiness levels before and after each experimental session. To analyze the subjective effect of each condition on the participants' sleepiness levels, we substituted the sleepiness level of the participants before and after the experimental sessions *(difference_sleepiness = sleepiness_after - sleepiness_before)* and conducted a one-way repeated ANOVA at α =.05. The results showed no significant difference between conditions, $F(2,33) = 1.028$, $p = .374$. However, the voice-only and RHMI conditions tended to alleviate the perceived sleepiness of the participants compared with the no information provision condition (Fig. 4).

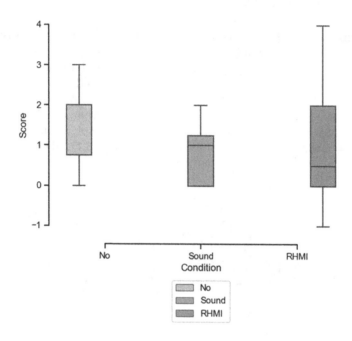

Fig. 4. Perceived sleepiness of the participants.

3.2 Quantitative Results

We used eye-gaze data recorded during the experimental sessions for quantitative assessment. Furthermore, we also used 36 recordings from 12 participants (one recording from RHMI prototype condition was omitted because of a recording problem that occurred during the session). We analyzed the left and right pupil sizes and eye eccentricities of the participants during each experimental session.

Pupil Size. To objectively analyze the sleepiness level of the participants, we examined both the left and right pupil size data of the participants during each experimental session. We performed a one-way repeated ANOVA to analyze the eccentricity during the three experimental conditions. The results showed no significant difference between the conditions for either pupil size (left: (F(2,33) = 0.082, p = .921), right: (F(2,33) = 0.482, p = .623)) (Fig. 5).

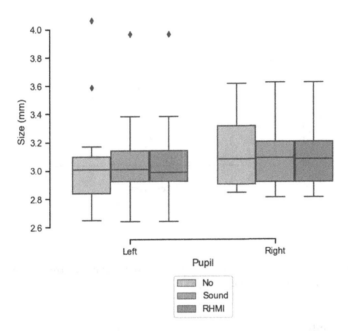

Fig. 5. The graph depicts the mean of the left and right pupil size of the participants during each experimental condition.

Eye Eccentricity. We define *eccentricity* as the variance in the combined angle of the horizontal and vertical fixation points of the gaze data. The combined angle is the square root of the sum of the squared vertical and horizontal points (Pythagoras theorem), and thus there is a one-dimensional angle between the zero intercept and gaze point. We used the SD of the gaze-shifting angles to understand the awakening levels of the participants. If the variance is high within a specific time, the driver is awake and their sleepiness level is low. We expected that in the experimental conditions with RHMI, the participants' awareness would be higher owing to the robots' behaviors that would nudge them to be alerted, compared to the other two conditions.

We performed a one-way repeated ANOVA to analyze the eccentricity during the three experimental conditions. There was no significant difference between the conditions (F(2,36) = 1.524, p = .238). From these results, it was not clear whether there was an effect for RHMI that could be effective in alleviating the sleepiness of participants. However, the RHMI showed a tendency toward a higher rate of increased eccentricity in the participants compared with the other two conditions (Fig. 6).

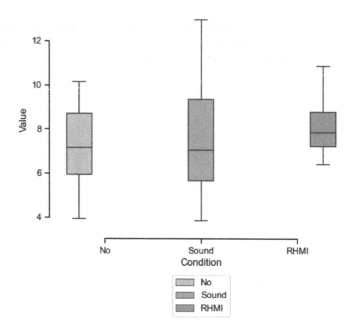

Fig. 6. The box plot depicts the mean of standard deviations of gaze eccentricity during the three experimental conditions.

4   Discussion

In this study, we aim to understand the effectiveness of an RHMI prototype on driver sleepiness while driving on a highway using automated driving. We therefore conducted a within-subject study with no information provision, voice-only information provision, and an RHMI prototype. Subjective and objective data were collected using questionnaires and eye-gaze data trackers.

Regarding the objective evaluation of this study, the pupil size and gaze eccentricity of the participants showed no significant differences between the conditions. Therefore, it was unclear whether the RHMI prototype had a clear effect on decreasing the sleepiness levels of the participants. However, the slightly higher gaze eccentricity of the participants during the RHMI condition (Fig. 6) revealed that the RHMI prototype tended to alleviate the sleepiness of the participants.

Regarding the subjective evaluation of this study, the acceptance question-naire showed that the RHMI prototype tended to be perceived as more reliable and wanted to be used and secured compared with the other two conditions (Fig. 2). In addition, the voice-only condition was perceived to be significantly more efficient than the RHMI prototype. The reason for this result may point to the workload of the drivers, where an element in the peripheral vision increases the visual demand of the driver. On the other hand, the RHMI prototype was perceived as significantly more novel (Fig. 3). This result indicates that using a robotic agent on the dashboard of a car evokes interest from drivers.

Finally, the results of the sleepiness check analysis showed no statistically significant differences between conditions. Therefore, it is unclear whether the RHMI is an effective method for alleviating sleepiness. However, the results showed a tendency of the voice-only and RHMI prototype conditions to alleviate the sleepiness of the participants compared with using no information provision.

4.1 Limitations and Future Work

Twelve participants participated in the experiment. This may explain the lack of significant results. In addition, the news we chose for this experiment was neither exciting nor interesting to most participants. Moreover, information was announced periodically. The periodic announcement of news information may have created a carryover effect for the remaining experimental conditions. Furthermore, sleepiness levels were measured within a relatively short period. This may have created a floor effect on the results. In the future, we aim to collect more participants, extend the experimental sessions, and use personalized news content and interaction methods between drivers and RHMIs to evaluate the reduction in sleepiness levels in a familiar and seamless manner.

5 Conclusion

In this study, we examined the effectiveness of a robotic agent in alleviating the sleepiness of drivers while driving on a highway with automated driving. The results of this experiment revealed that information provision interfaces (sound only and RHMI) have the potential to alleviate the sleepiness level in highway automated driving at Level 2. Moreover, the RHMI, owing to its physicality, holds the potential to be perceived as safer, easier to use, and more novel. Therefore, a robotic interface can be considered an information provision that can help alleviate driver sleepiness.

References

1. Atchley, P., Chan, M., Gregersen, S.: A strategically timed verbal task improves performance and neurophysiological alertness during fatiguing drives. Hum. Factors **56**(3), 453–462 (2014)
2. Endsley, M.R., Kiris, E.O.: The out-of-the-loop performance problem and level of control in automation. Hum. Factors **37**(2), 381–394 (1995)
3. Fujikake, K., Tanaka, T., Yamagishi, M., Yonekawa, T., Inagami, M., Kinoshita, F., et al.: Comparison of subjective evaluation of different forms of driving agents by elderly people. Jap. J. Ergonomics **53**, 214–224 (2017)
4. Fujikake, K., et al.: Effect of driving behavior improvement by driving-support and feedback-support of driver-agent. Trans. Soc. Autom. Eng. Japan **50**(1), 134 (2019)

5. Gasser, T.M., Westhoff, D.: Bast-study: Definitions of automation and legal issues in germany. In: Proceedings of the 2012 Road Vehicle Automation Workshop. Automation Workshop (2012)
6. Gershon, R.R., Barocas, B., Canton, A.N., Li, X., Vlahov, D.: Mental, physical, and behavioral outcomes associated with perceived work stress in police officers. Crim. Justice Behav. **36**(3), 275–289 (2009)
7. Goel, N., Basner, M., Rao, H., Dinges, D.F.: Circadian rhythms, sleep deprivation, and human performance. Prog. Mol. Biol. Transl. Sci. **119**, 155–190 (2013)
8. Kaber, D.B., Perry, C.M., Segall, N., McClernon, C.K., Prinzel, L.J., III.: Situation awareness implications of adaptive automation for information processing in an air traffic control-related task. Int. J. Ind. Ergon. **36**(5), 447–462 (2006)
9. Laugwitz, B., Held, T., Schrepp, M.: Construction and evaluation of a user experience questionnaire. In: Holzinger, A. (ed.) USAB 2008. LNCS, vol. 5298, pp. 63–76. Springer, Heidelberg (2008). https://doi.org/10.1007/978-3-540-89350-9_6
10. NHTSA: National Highway Traffic Safety Administration Preliminary statement of policy concerning automated vehicles. Washington DC **1**, 14 (2013)
11. Padgham, L., Winikoff, M.: Developing intelligent agent systems: a practical guide. John Wiley & Sons (2005)
12. Parasuraman, R., Davies, D.: A taxonomic analysis of vigilance performance. Vigilance: Theory, operational performance, and physiological correlates, pp. 559–574 (1977)
13. Pfleging, B., Rang, M., Broy, N.: Investigating user needs for non-driving-related activities during automated driving. In: Proceedings of the 15th International Conference on Mobile and Ubiquitous Multimedia, pp. 91–99 (2016)
14. Schömig, N., Hargutt, V., Neukum, A., Petermann-Stock, I., Othersen, I.: The interaction between highly automated driving and the development of drowsiness. Procedia Manufact. **3**, 6652–6659 (2015)
15. Shi, J., Xiao, Y., Atchley, P.: Analysis of factors affecting drivers' choice to engage with a mobile phone while driving in Beijing. Transport. Res. F: Traffic Psychol. Behav. **37**, 1–9 (2016)
16. Strayer, D.L., Johnston, W.A.: Driven to distraction: dual-task studies of simulated driving and conversing on a cellular telephone. Psychol. Sci. **12**(6), 462–466 (2001)
17. Tanaka, T., et al.: Driver agent for encouraging safe driving behavior for the elderly. In: Proceedings of the 5th International Conference on Human Agent Interaction, pp. 71–79 (2017)
18. Tanaka, T., Fujikake, K., Yoshihara, Y., Karatas, N., Aoki, H., Kanamori, H., et al.: Preliminary study for feasibility of driver agent in actual car environment-driver agent for encouraging safe driving behavior (3). J. Transport. Technol. **10**(02), 128 (2020)
19. Tanaka, T., et al.: Driving behavior improvement through driving support and review support from driver agent. In: Proceedings of the 6th International Conference on Human-Agent Interaction, pp. 36–44 (2018)
20. Wang, M., Hock, P., Lee, S.C., Baumann, M., Jeon, M.: Genie vs. Jarvis: characteristics and design considerations of in-vehicle intelligent agents. In: 13th International Conference on Automotive User Interfaces and Interactive Vehicular Applications, pp. 197–199 (2021)
21. Williamson, A., Friswell, R., Olivier, J., Grzebieta, R.: Are drivers aware of sleepiness and increasing crash risk while driving? Accident Anal. Prevent. **70**, 225–234 (2014)

22. Yamabe, S., Kawaguchi, S., Anakubo, M.: Comfortable awakening method for sleeping driver during autonomous driving. Int. J. Intell. Transp. Syst. Res. **20**(1), 266–278 (2022)

Negotiating on Social Media – Creating and Claiming Value While Establishing a Valuable Relationship

Christian W. Scheiner[1,2(✉)]

[1] Institute for Entrepreneurship & Business Development, Universität zu Lübeck, Lübeck, Germany
christian.scheiner@uni-luebeck.de
[2] Christian-Albrechts-Universität zu Kiel, Kiel, Germany

Abstract. The course and evaluation of negotiations is determined to a great extent by perceived subjective value. Negotiators want to feel respected, accepted, and valued by the other negotiator (feelings about the self). The relationship should be valued during the negotiation (feelings about the relationship) and the negotiation process should be conducted in such a way that the process-related interests are taken into account (feelings about the process). At the same time, economic interests need to be met (feelings about the instrumental outcomes). Only when the elements of subjective value are taken into account in negotiations, value can be created and claimed. Within this paper, a model of negotiation is developed which incorporates the specifics and characteristics of social media as form of computer-mediated negotiation. Afterwards, Taylor Swift's negotiations with Spotify and Apple will be used as case studies to highlight the potentials and pitfalls of social media negotiations and to draw conclusions and recommendations for future negotiations.

Keywords: Negotiation · Negotiating · Subjective value · Interests · Social media · Claiming value · Value creation · Creating value · Managing relationships · Interpersonal relationship · Case study · Taylor Swift · Apple · Spotify · Music streaming · Apple Music

1 Introduction

Negotiations occur more and more on social media as a form of computer-mediated negotiation. Reasons for this development, can be found in the decision of organizations to use this communication channel actively to negotiate with e.g. customers or the public, or in the fact that Social Media has become a dominant communication tool in general.

Previous research could show that social media communication is for instance a means to attract public attention, to increase brand evaluations, to influence sales, to foster brand loyalty or to leverage brand communities [e.g. 1–7]. Luo, Zhang & Duan [8] even show that social media-based metrics are an important indicator for firm equity value.

© The Author(s), under exclusive license to Springer Nature Switzerland AG 2023
A. Coman and S. Vasilache (Eds.): HCII 2023, LNCS 14026, pp. 514–528, 2023.
https://doi.org/10.1007/978-3-031-35927-9_35

With social media, a new playground has been added to negotiations which is characterized by a high potential but also by imminent risks. Research on social media negotiations is, however, a nascent and developing field. For that reason, a theoretical negotiation model is developed in this paper incorporating the specifics and characteristics of social media as means for negotiating.

Afterwards, Taylor Swift's negotiations with the two music streaming services, Spotify and Apple Music, will be used as case studies to highlight the potentials and pitfalls of social media negotiations and to draw conclusions and recommendations for future negotiations.

2 Theoretical Background

2.1 Negotiation

Negotiation is a decision-making process in form of a social interaction. Two or more parties try to allocate scarce resources and resolve perceived incompatible, interdependent interests [9].

Negotiations take place in all areas of life from the professional to the private. Hence, whenever people cannot achieve a goal without the cooperation of others, they are in a negotiation [10]. Walton and McKersie [11] distinguish between two fundamental negotiation categories: distributive and integrative bargaining.

Distributive bargaining is characterized by a complete a "fixed-sum, variable-share payoff. [...] It describes a situation in which there is some fixed value available to the parties but in which they may influence shares which go to each. As such there is a fundamental and complete conflict of interests" ([11], p. 13). The subject matter of distributive negotiations is defined by Walton and McKersie [11] as issues in form of a fixed total objective value.

In absence of a fixed-sum or zero-sum condition, where maximum results are available through joint problem solving, Walton and McKersie [11] speak of integrative bargaining. Instead of issues, problems are the subject matter of this negotiation category. "Problems [...] are agenda items which contain possibilities for greater or lesser amounts of value which can be made available to" (p. 127) the negotiating parties. A "problem in its purest form would be an agenda item for which the parties would assign the same preference ordering to all possible outcomes and about which the two parties would be equally concerned" (p. 127). A welfare orientation is guiding the behavior of negotiators in the process [11]. The negotiator is not "concerned about the payoff available for him [/her], his [/her] primary concern is to increase the total sum" (p. 17). The process of integrative bargaining contains three steps: (1) Identifying the problem, (2) searching for alternate solutions and their consequences, and (3) ordering the preferences of solutions and selecting a course of action [11].

Based on the work of Brett [12], Brett and Thompson [13] propose a general negotiation model (see Fig. 1). The core elements of the model are the interests and priorities of negotiators which set the framework for the outcome potential, and the chosen strategy by negotiators by which the degree of value capturing is determined. While motives, concerns, and given position comprise the given interests, priorities stand for the underlying value hierarchy of negotiators. Strategy can be understood as goal-directed, guidelines for negotiators' behavior.

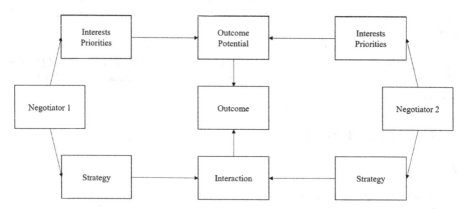

Fig. 1. A model of negotiated outcomes. (Brett & Thompson [13] based on Brett [12])

2.2 Subjective Value in Negotiations

A common, initial assumption is that economic outcomes are the sole purpose and characteristic of successful negotiations [14]. Hence, rationality and optimality are seen as the most important characteristics for negotiators' performance [14–16]. Descriptive negotiation research literature draws, however, attention to the phenomenon that negotiators do not behave fully rational, and in game-theoretic, optimal way [10]. The economic outcome is, as a consequence, only one element determining the success of and the satisfaction with the negotiation outcome.

Next to economic elements, satisfaction is also influenced by the perceived and felt negotiation experience as affective states serve as an important source of information for negotiators [17]. Curhan et al. [17] argue that affect can provide a robust and long-lasting "gut-check" about a negotiation experience. This idea is based on the mood-as-information theory by Schwarz and Clore [18]. The theory states that affect plays a role in information processing in at least three ways. First, affective states have an informational function. People may use their momentary affective state to make different kinds of judgement, Second, affective states have a directional function. They direct one's attention to specific pieces of information in order to gain an understanding of the causes for present affective state. Third, affective states may foster the availability of mood-congruent thoughts or information.

Given a large body of research incorporating subjective, social psychological factors as well as negotiator satisfaction, Curhan, Elfenbein, and Xu [19] conducted a large-scale investigation to provide a comprehensive framework of subjective outcomes in negotiations. Based on their findings, they introduced the umbrella construct of subjective value which consists of four dimensions (see Fig. 2). The first dimension is "feelings about the instrumental outcomes" and comprises elements such as the belief of having achieved a strong objective settlement, being satisfied with the negotiation outcome, or believing to have won. The second dimension is "feelings about the self ". It concerns issues such as the feeling of being respectfully treated by the other party, feeling competent during the negotiation, or doing "right thing". The third dimension "feelings about the relationship" focuses on whether a negotiator feels that own needs have been recognized by the other party, conflict has been avoided, and/or the relationship is valued and not damaged by the negotiation. The fourth dimension is "feelings about the negotiation process". Here issues such as fairness, being heard, brainstorming options together, or showing a positive attitude play a vital role. Feelings about the relationship and about the process appeared in the study of Curhan et al. [19] to be elements of a larger dimension of rapport.

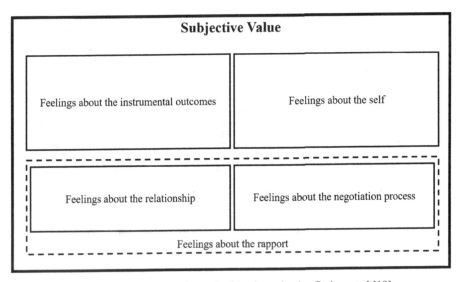

Fig. 2. The four dimensions of subjective value by Curhan et al.[19]

The value of subjective value in negotiations can be threefold [19]. First, subjective value can serve as a good in itself. The quality of the relationship can be more valuable than the issues in the current negotiation. As a consequence, negotiators may limit or neglect instrumental, economic interests to protect or strengthen relationships. Even in cases where the other person is unknown to negotiators, participants in ultimatum games made financial trade-offs to serve their feelings of fairness to others. Lax and Sebenius [20] trace this back to the "almost universal quest for social approval or the simple pleasure one derives from being treated with respect, even in a one-time encounter" (p. 74). Second, negotiators use their intuition about the objective outcome to assess their negotiation performance [19]. In most cases, an objective evaluation is aggravated or impeded by imperfect information. Imperfect information can result from the lack of adequate economic measures, the lack of reliable information, the poor-quality data basis or incomplete information. As a result, negotiators turn to their gut feeling or intuition in order to evaluate their performance. The intuitive evaluation can be in line with the objective performance, but does not necessarily have to be. In any way, the felt performance is shaping future behavior, intentions as well as the possibility to improve of negotiation skills. Third, subjective value can be a predictor for future economic value [19]. Positive feelings about a previous negotiation can influence subsequent negotiations with the same counterpart positively. Given past experiences, negotiators can be more willing to share information, be more empathetic or be more willing to consider the perspective of the other side. Curhan et al.[19] argue for that reason that "a positive subjective experience in negotiation may be considered a kind of asset that improves the tangible quality of working relationships" (p. 525).

In light of the importance of subjective value the negotiation model of Brett and Thompson [13] is adjusted by incorporating subjective value and by specifying the element of outcome (see Fig. 3).

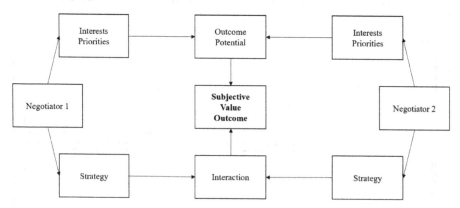

Fig. 3. Adjusted model of negotiated outcomes based on Brett and Thompson [13].

2.3   Computer-Mediated and Social Media Negotiation

Research on negotiation bears typically the assumption that negotiations are conducted in a face-to-face setting, when all negotiators are in the same place at the same time [21]. The influence of the type of communication media used in negotiations is, therefore, often not considered.

However, this general assumption cannot be sustained in social media negotiations as they are in principle not face-to-face negotiations. Social media negotiations are a form of computer-mediated communication and negotiation. The distinction between face-to-face negotiations and computer-mediated and social media communication needs to be made as indirectness becomes a central factor [22]. This indirectness of interaction causes important limitations and disadvantages. In most cases, usual visual and social cues are deprived from the interaction in computer-mediated negotiations as the negotiators are not in the same room at the same time. Thus, they cannot perceive and draw conclusions from the other person's posture, gestures, and/or facial expressions [21]. Even if a video-based communication media is used (e.g. Zoom, Microsoft Teams, Webex), the perception is limited to a fraction of the whole situation and the surroundings. If a text-based communication is chosen for the negotiation (e.g. e-mail), negotiators lack the opportunity to gather cues from speech-related elements such as intonation or timing. Estimating the level of agreement, understanding or importance is, therefore, impeded and needs to be clarified by other means.

Weisband and Atwater [23] emphasize, in addition, that text-based communication affects the perception of the other negotiator in way that the person is perceived less individualized and known compared to face-to-face negotiations. The other negotiator becomes more abstract. This in turn increases the perceived difference from the other person. Hence, people are less likely to believe that the other person shares similar traits to them. This is known as the "identifiable other" effect [21] and exerts an influence also on the behavior of negotiators. The findings of Griffith and Northcraft [24] suggest for instance that the chosen negotiation strategy is influenced by the level of identifiability. In cases, where the other counterpart is anonymous, negotiators are more likely to choose a distributive strategy.

Kiesler, Zubrow, Moses, and Geller [25] add another important facet to the difference between communication behavior on text-based communication and face-to-face communication by showing that people seem to be more disinhibited in text-based communication. Study participants tended to use more impolite and offending as well as (extremely) positive comments. They also found that conversation partners via a computer-mediated technology were rated more negative than those in face-to-face conversations.

Computer-mediated negotiation affects, in addition, the perception of message content. In absence of peripheral factors given in face-to-face communication, people pay closer attention to quality and content of messages in computer-mediated negotiations [21, 26]. With the focus on the message, the sensitivity increases towards perceived negative cues. Two factors lead to this increased sensitivity. First, when receiving an e-mail, people assume that the message content is written deliberately and thoughtfully. Embedding negative elements into the message must have been, therefore, intentionally which in turn can elevate anger. Second, when receiving a message with negative or negatively interpreted content, recipient have more time to think about the content which can further boost negative emotions.

Besides the effects that have their origin in the computer-mediated nature of social media, social media-specific characteristics need to be considered in negotiations. Carr and Hayes [27] define social media in general as "Internet-based channels that allow users to opportunistically interact and selectively self-present, either in real-time or asynchronously, with both broad and narrow audiences who derive value from user-generated content and the perception of interaction with user" (p. 50).

Following this definition, multidirectionality is a core element of social media. Messages "can flow from user to user, user to audience, audience, to user, or audience to audience". Hence, communication can be interpersonal and mass-oriented at the same time, which needs to be reflected in the messages during the negotiation.

Having a broad audience observing a negotiation, implies that additional stakeholders can participate in the negotiation, can gain insights into the (ongoing) negotiation, and may exert influence on the negotiation process and outcome directly or indirectly.

Ashbrook and Zalba [28] examined for instance the influence of social media on two diplomatic negotiations. They found that social media had a disruptive and unantici-pated influence on the Transatlantic Trade and Investment Partnership and a German Constitutional Court's ruling on the European Central Bank's Public Debt Purchasing Program.

Another important influence is the foundational characteristic of channel disentrain-ment or asynchrony. Users can decide if, whether, and how they participate. Simultaneous interaction can be part of the participation, but does not necessarily need to be given. The "channel is persistently available whether a user is active or not" [27, p. 50]. Discussion about the negotiation issues can continue without the presence of the negotiation parties shaping the room for possible negotiation outcomes.

Car and Hayes [27] emphasize, in addition, that social interaction on social media is already given if users think that an interaction took place, independently whether this perception is artificially designed or is based on true human interaction. This adds to the problem of indirectness of computer-mediated negotiations as the element of social resides in the perception of a user and not in the existence of an actual person.

In summary, negotiations on social media are influenced by general computer-mediated as well as social media specific factors. These factors can complicate the negotiation process and can affect the negotiation outcome negatively as the interaction between the negotiating parties are completely mediated by social media (see Fig. 4).

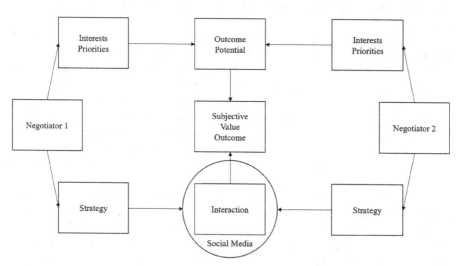

Fig. 4. Adjusted model of negotiations on social media based on Brett and Thompson [13].

3 Taylor Swift vs. Music Streaming Services

To apply the developed model of negotiation on social media, the negotiation of Taylor Swift with Apple as well as Spotify will be examined in the following. The negotiation started in 2014 and concerned the usage of Taylor Swift's music on Spotify and Apple Music.

3.1 Taylor Swift's Standpoint or the Framework for Negotiations

The general framework of the negotiations was laid by an op-ed of Taylor Swift for The Wall Street Journal in 2014 where she shared her view and thoughts on the future of the music industry. Contrary to other opinions, Taylor Swift strongly believed in a promising and prosper future of the music industry [29]. It would be, however, important to be aware of the value of music; not just as a music listener but also as an artist.

"In recent years, you've probably read the articles about major recording artists who have decided to practically give their music away, for this promotion or that exclusive deal. My hope for the future, not just in the music industry, but in every young girl I meet...is that they all realize their worth and ask for it.

Music is art, and art is important and rare. Important, rare things are valuable. Valuable things should be paid for. It's my opinion that music should not be free, and my prediction is that individual artists and their labels will someday decide what an album's price point is. I hope they don't underestimate themselves or undervalue their art" [29].

She also highlighted that file sharing and music streaming services had significantly impacted the album sales negatively. She even stated that "every artist has handled this blow" to emphasize the financial magnitude and emotional quality of those developments.

3.2 Taylor Swift vs. Spotify

On November 2014, Taylor Swift decided to remove her entire catalogue from Spotify without explaining it publicly at that exact moment. A spokesman of Spotify confirmed two days later in an email to CNET that "Taylor and her management team asked us to remove her content from Spotify so it was all removed this morning" [30]. In a blog post Spotify tried to reach out to Taylor Swift in a masspersonal message saying that.

"[w]e hope she'll change her mind and join us in building a new music economy that works for everyone. [...] We believe fans should be able to listen to music wherever and whenever they want, and that artists have an absolute right to be paid for their work and protected from piracy. [...] Now there's 40 million of us who want you to stay, stay, stay. It's a love story, baby, just say, yes" [30].

With this blog post, Spotify tried to address three elements of the subjective value of Taylor Swift which were in line with elements of Spotify's subjective value. It acknowledged the feelings about the instrumental outcome, by pointing to a fair compensation for artists and the protection from piracy. With respect to the feelings about the relationship, Spotify placed emphasis on the highly valued relationship with Taylor Swift not only by Spotify itself but also representative for all its 40 million users. Feelings about the self were also addressed as Spotify acknowledges that Taylor Swift is doing the right thing in demanding a fair compensation, and expresses, furthermore, its respect towards her personally and as an artist.

On November 6, Taylor Swift, gave an interview explaining her decision. Asked whether her new album would have been sold less if it would have been available also on streaming services, she replied that.

"[i]f I had streamed the new album, it's impossible to try to speculate what would have happened. But all I can say is that music is changing so quickly, and the landscape of the music industry itself is changing so quickly, that everything new, like Spotify, all feels to me a bit like a grand experiment. And I'm not willing to contribute my life's work to an experiment that I don't feel fairly compensates the writers, producers, artists, and creators of this music. And I just don't agree with perpetuating the perception that music has no value and should be free. [...] I try to stay really open-minded about things, because I do think it's important to be a part of progress. But I think it's really still up for debate whether this is actual progress, or whether this is taking the word "music" out of the music industry. Also, a lot of people were suggesting to me that I try putting new music on Spotify with "Shake It Off," and so I was open-minded about it. I thought, "I will try this; I'll see how it feels." It didn't feel right to me. I felt like I was saying to my fans, "If you create music someday, if you create a painting someday, someone can just walk into a museum, take it off the wall, rip off a corner off it, and it's theirs now and they don't have to pay for it." I didn't like the perception that it was putting forth. And so I decided to change the way I was doing things." [31]

Her answer revealed that her main concern seemed to be on the instrumental outcome. Yet, she emphasized that companies such as Spotify did not respect her as an artist which – in light of her article on The Wall Street Journal – seemed to be a central element of her identify (feeling about the self). She perceived no valuable relationship with streaming services as everything was reduced to pure business (feelings about the relationship). This type of business was in her opinion, additionally, not even on a serious level but rather an ongoing experiment (feelings about the self). In stating these things, Taylor Swift consciously neglected Spotify's subjective value outcome with respect to feelings about the instrumental outcome, feelings about the self, and feelings about the relationship.

A few days later, Daniel Ek, CEO and founder of Spotify, reacted and responded himself in a blog post. Ek wrote:

"We started Spotify because we love music and piracy was killing it. So all the talk swirling around lately about how Spotify is making money on the backs of artists upsets me big time. [...] When I hear stories about artists and songwriters who say they've seen little or no money from streaming and are naturally angry and frustrated, I'm really frustrated too. The music industry is changing – and we're proud of our part in that change – but lots of problems that have plagued the industry since its inception continue to exist. [...] Here's the thing I really want artists to understand: Our interests are totally aligned with yours. Even if you don't believe that's our goal, look at our business. Our whole business is to maximize the value of your music. We don't use music to drive sales of hardware or software. We use music to get people to pay for music. We're getting fans to pay for music again. We're connecting artists to fans they would never have otherwise found, and we're paying them for every single listen. We're not just streaming, we're mainstream." [32]

The focus of his response was on the feelings of the instrumental outcome by explaining how Spotify was serving the interest of artists. At the same time, his reaction seems to show that he felt unfairly treated and wrongly accused of malign behavior. This view resented in his opinion on a poor information base. He also expressed frustration that artists did not adequately value Spotify's performance and thus the relationship with Spotify.

At this point, the negotiation reached a level where a beneficial outcome and a return of Taylor Swift's music to Spotify's catalogue was completely impossible. Instead of using the elements of subjective value to create and claim mutual value, the negotiation became confrontational, highly emotional-laden and distributive. The relationship had suffered a damage.

It took three years, till Taylor Swift's returned with her music to Spotify in 2017. Looking back at the time, Daniel Ek said on "CBS This Morning" in 2018:

"I should've done a much better job communicating this, so I take full ownership for that. [...] I went to Nashville many, many times to talk to [Swift's] team, spent more time explaining the model, why streaming mattered. And the great news is I think she saw how streaming was growing." [33]

3.3 Taylor Swift vs. Apple

A few months after the negotiation with Spotify, on June 8 2015, Spotify's competitor Apple announced its new product Apple Music. Apple described Apple Music as "a revolutionary streaming music service. [...] Apple Music is really going to move the needle for fans and artists [...] Online music has become a complicated mess of apps, services and websites. Apple Music brings the best features together for an experience every music lover will appreciate" [34]. The product would be launched on June 30 and would start with a 3-month free-membership. Compensation of artists would start after those three months.

Three weeks later, on June 21, Taylor Swift published an open letter to Apple on her TUMBLR blog with the title "To Apple, Love Taylor". In her masspersonal letter, she outlined her concerns and reasons not to support Apple's new streaming service. Here is the text in full:

"To Apple, Love Taylor

I write this to explain why I'll be holding back my album, 1989, from the new streaming service, Apple Music. I feel this deserves an explanation because Apple has been and will continue to be one of my best partners in selling music and creating ways for me to connect with my fans. I respect the company and the truly ingenious minds that have created a legacy based on innovation and pushing the right boundaries.

I'm sure you are aware that Apple Music will be offering a free 3 month trial to anyone who signs up for the service. I'm not sure you know that Apple Music will not be paying writers, producers, or artists for those three months. I find it to be shocking, disappointing, and completely unlike this historically progressive and generous company.

This is not about me. Thankfully I am on my fifth album and can support myself, my band, crew, and entire management team by playing live shows. This is about the new artist or band that has just released their first single and will not be paid for its success. This is about the young songwriter who just got his or her first cut and thought that the royalties from that would get them out of debt. This is about the producer who works tirelessly to innovate and create, just like the innovators and creators at Apple are pioneering in their field...but will not get paid for a quarter of a year's worth of plays on his or her songs.

These are not the complaints of a spoiled, petulant child. These are the echoed sentiments of every artist, writer and producer in my social circles who are afraid to speak up publicly because we admire and respect Apple so much. We simply do not respect this particular call.

I realize that Apple is working towards a goal of paid streaming. I think that is beautiful progress. We know how astronomically successful Apple has been and we know that this incredible company has the money to pay artists, writers and producers for the 3 month trial period... even if it is free for the fans trying it out.

Three months is a long time to go unpaid, and it is unfair to ask anyone to work for nothing. I say this with love, reverence, and admiration for everything else Apple has done. I hope that soon I can join them in the progression towards a streaming model that seems fair to those who create this music. I think this could be the platform that gets it right.

But I say to Apple with all due respect, it's not too late to change this policy and change the minds of those in the music industry who will be deeply and gravely affected by this. We don't ask you for free iPhones. Please don't ask us to provide you with our music for no compensation.

Taylor" [35]

With Apple, Taylor Swift chose a completely different approach to negotiate. First, she decided to address Apple directly. Second, in contrast to Spotify she chose a more friendly and respectful tone. She begins by emphasizing the value of the existing relationship (feeling about the relationship), before expressing her admiration for Apple's trackrecord of innovations (feeling about the self). She refers, in addition, at various points within her open letter to the respect she has for Apple in general (feelings about the self). In light of this respect, she was surprised of Apple's decision not to compensate artists during the first three months (feelings about the self). Contrary to the negotiation with Spotify, she withdrew herself from the negotiation to some extent and stated that she wants to give a voice to those artists who will be affected most by Apple's ideas. In doing so, she protected once more the existing relationship with Apple.

Taylor Swift also acknowledged the legitimacy of Apple's instrumental interest in establishing a streaming service (feelings about the instrumental outcomes) but reminded

Apple that art possesses a certain value. Taylor Swift went even so far to put Apple's products on par with music and therewith with her own art.

Another important difference to her approach with Spotify concerns the subjective value element "feelings about the process". She reminded Apple that the compensation policy can be still changed for the better. The process was, from her point of view, ongoing and the result not yet found. There was also no external form of deadline in her letter to respond or reach a decision.

However, Taylor Swift and the public audience did not have to wait long for Apple's answer. Only a few hours later, Senior Vice President of Internet Software and Services, Eddy Cue, responded with the following tweet: "#AppleMusic will pay artist for streaming, even during customer's free trial period" [36]. To Rolling Stone, he explained: "When I woke up and read Taylor's note, it solidified quickly that we needed a change. […] Music is a big part of our DNA and we always strive to make sure artists are paid for their work" [37]. The decision to change the compensation policy, was not solely based on Taylor Swift's letter, but he acknowledged in a Vanity Fair article that it accelerated the process [38]. It was also important to him to talk to Taylor Swift before any response was released to the public (feelings about the self and the relationship). For he saw her as an equal partner and was aware of the implications of her actions for herself [38].

In conclusion, Taylor Swift was able to influence Apple's compensation policy. She protected and strengthened her relationship with Apple and became a trailblazer and important advocate for the interests of artists in the public eye as well as for her fellow artists.

Apple was able to prevent a damage to its image. I also boosted public attention for its product. Apple profited, in addition, from what Philip Elmer-Dewitt called the Taylor Swift effect. Music groups dropped their resistance and added their catalogue to Apple Music. Apple Music would, hence, have the biggest library of available songs from the start [39].

4 Conclusion

The course and evaluation of negotiations is determined less by rationality than by the perception of the subjective value. It is important for negotiators to feel respected, accepted, and valued by the other negotiator (feelings about the self). The relationship should be perceived as being valuable (feelings about the relationship) and the negotiation process should be conducted in such a way that the process-related interests are taken into account (feelings about the process). At the same time, the negotiation should lead to an outcome where economic interests are seen to be met. When the subjective value is not properly considered, negotiations can easily become emotional-laden and turn to conflicts. This leads either to the failure of negotiations or to inferior, unsatisfactory results.

When negotiations are conducted not face-to-face but on social media, negotiations become more challenging due to the systemic risks arising from computer-mediated negotiation characteristics in general as well as social media negotiation characteristics in specific.

Taylor Swift's negotiations with music streaming services on social media, are an interesting case to illustrate the potential and risk at the same time. While the negotiations with Spotify escalated fast and easily, the negotiations with Apple led incredible fast to a win-win-win result for all stakeholders.

When asked what made the difference, Taylor Swift told Vanity Fair "Apple treated me like I was a voice of a creative community that they actually cared about. [...] And I found it really ironic that the multi-billion-dollar company reacted to criticism with humility, and the start-up with no cash flow reacted to criticism like a corporate machine" [38]. It took time and several trips of Daniel Ek to Taylor Swift and her team to establish a relationship based on mutual trust. Only then was an agreement possible.

Learning from the Taylor Swift case, negotiators should consider carefully whether to conduct negotiations on social media or not. In most cases, the risk of escalation is high. For that reason, negotiators should be aware of the pitfalls of social media as negotiation medium and begin the negotiation with an appropriate strategy and toolbox in place. Only then, they can create and claim value in negotiations while establishing a valuable relationship.

References

1. Schau, H., Muñiz, A., Arnould, E.: How brand community practices create value. J. Mark. **73**(5), 30–51 (2009)
2. Kumar, A., Bezawada, R., Rishika, R., Janakiraman, R., Kannan, P.K.: From social to sale: the effects of firm generated content in social media on customer behavior. J. Mark. **80**(1), 7–25 (2016)
3. Wagner, T., Baccarella, C., Voigt, K.-I.: Framing social media communication: investigating the effects of brand post appeals on user interaction. Eur. Manag. J. **35**(5), 606–616 (2017)
4. Baccarella, C., Scheiner, C., Diehlmann F.: The devil on the entrepreneur's shoulder: analyzing the relationship between moral disengagement, founders' motives, and unethical behavior of entrepreneurs on social media. In: Schjoedt L., Brännback M., Carsrud A. (ed.): Understanding Social Media and Entrepreneurship. Exploring Diversity in Entrepreneurship, Springer, Cham, 2020, pp. 171–192 (2020). https://doi.org/10.1007/978-3-030-43453-3_9
5. Dewan, S., Ramaprasad, J.: Social media, traditional media, and music sales. MIS Q. **38**(1), 101–121 (2014)
6. Laroche, M., Habibi, M., Richard, M.-O.: To be or not to be in social media: how brand loyalty is affected by social media? Int. J. Inf. Manage. **33**(1), 76–82 (2013)
7. Naylor, R., Lamberton, C., West, P.: Beyond the "like" button: the impact of mere virtual presence on brand evaluations and purchase intentions in social media settings. J. Mark. **76**(6), 105–120 (2012)
8. Lou, X., Zhang, J., Duan, W.: Social media and firm equity value. Inf. Syst. Res. **24**(1), 146–163 (2013)
9. Pruitt, D.G.: Achieving integrative agreements. In: Bazerman, M.H., Lewicki, R.J. (eds.) Negotiating in organizations, pp. 35–49. Sage, Beverly Hills, CA (1983)
10. Thompson, L., Wang, J., Gunia, B.: Negotiation. Annu. Rev. Psychol. **61**(1), 491–515 (2010)
11. Walton, R., McKersie, R.: A Behavioral Theory of Labor Negotiations: An Analysis of a Social Interaction System. McGraw-Hill, New York (1965)
12. Brett, J.M.: Culture and negotiation. Int. J. Psychol. **35**(2), 97–104 (2000)
13. Brett, J., Thompson, L.: Negotiation. Organ. Behav. Hum. Decis. Process. **136**, 68–79 (2016)
14. Curhan, J.R., Elfenbein, H.A., Eisenkraft, N.: The objective value of subjective value: a multi-round negotiation study. J. Appl. Soc. Psychol. **40**(3), 690–709 (2010)

15. Neale, M.A., Bazerman, M.H.: Cognition and rationality in negotiation. Free Press, New York (1991)

16. Bazerman, M.H., Curhan, J.R., Moore, D.A.: The death and rebirth of the social psychology of negotiation. In: Fletcher, G.J.O., Clark, M.S. (eds.) Blackwell handbook of social psychology: Interpersonal processes, pp. 196–228. Blackwell, Oxford, England (2001)

17. Curhan, J., Elfenbein, H., Kilduff, G.: Getting off on the right foot: subjective value versus economic value in predicting longitudinal job outcomes from job offer negotiations. J. Appl. Psychol. **94**(2), 524–534 (2009)

18. Schwarz, N., Clore, G.L.: Mood, misattribution and judgments of well-being: informative and directive functions of affective states. J. Pers. Soc. Psychol. **45**(3), 513–523 (1983)

19. Curhan, J., Elfenbein, H., Xu, H.: What do people value when they negotiate? Mapping the domain of subjective value in negotiation. J. Pers. Soc. Psychol. **91**(3), 493–512 (2006)

20. Lax, D.A., Sebenius, J.K.: Interests: the measure of negotiation. Negot. J. **2**(1), 73–92 (1986). https://doi.org/10.1007/BF00998936

21. Nadler, J., Shestowsky, D.: Negotiation, Information Technology, and the Problem of the Faceless Other. In: Thompson, L.L. (ed.) Negotiation theory and research, pp. 145–172. Psychosocial Press (2006)

22. Spears, R., Lea, M.: Panacea or panopticon? The hidden power in computermediated communication. Commun. Res. **21**(4), 427–459 (1994)

23. Weisband, S., Atwater, L.: Evaluating self and others in electronic and face-to-face groups. J. Appl. Psychol. **84**(4), 632–639 (1999)

24. Griffith, T.L., Northcraft, G.B.: Distinguishing between the forest and the trees: media, features, and methodology in electronic communication research. Organ. Sci. **5**(2), 272–285 (1994)

25. Kiesler, S., Zubrow, D., Moses, A.M., Geller, V.: Affect in computer-mediated communication: an experiment in synchronous terminal-to-terminal discussion. Hum. Comput. Interact. **1**(1), 77–107 (1985)

26. Matheson, K., Zanna, M.P.: Persuasion as a function of self-awareness in computer-mediated communication. Soc. Behav. **4**(2), 99–111 (1989)

27. Carr, C., Hayes, R.: Social media: defining, developing, and divining. Atlantic J. Commun. **23**(1), 46–65 (2015)

28. Ashbrook, C., Zalba, A.: Social Media Influence on diplomatic negotiations: shifting the shape of the table. Negot. J. **37**(1), 83–96 (2021)

29. Swift, T.: For Taylor Swift, the future of music is a love story. The Wall Street J. (2014). https://www.wsj.com/articles/for-taylor-swift-the-future-of-music-is-a-love-story-1404763219. Retrieved on February 6, 2023

30. Reisinger, D.: Spotify to Taylor Swift: please 'stay stay stay'. CNET (2014). https://www.cnet.com/tech/services-and-software/taylor-swift-wont-let-the-players-play-on-spotify/. Retrieved on February 3, 2023

31. Willman, C.: Exclusive: Taylor Swift on being pop's instantly platinum wonder... and why she's paddling against the streams (2014). Yahoo!. https://www.yahoo.com/entertainment/blogs/music-news/exclusive--taylor-swift-on-being-pop-s-instantly-platinum-wonder----and-why-she-s-paddling-against-the-streams-085041907.html, retrieved on January 20, 2023

32. Dredge, S.: Spotify CEO speaks out on Taylor Swift albums removal: 'I'm really frustrated'. The Guardian (2014). https://www.theguardian.com/technology/2014/nov/11/spotify-ceo-taylor-swift-albums-daniel-ek. Retrieved on February 4, 2023

33. Britton, L.: Spotify boss explains how he convinced Taylor Swift to return to the streaming service. NME (2018). https://www.nme.com/news/music/spotify-boss-daniel-ek-talks-taylor-swift-streaming-return-2280169. Retrieved on February 6, 2023

34. Apple. Introducing Apple Music — All The Ways You Love Music. All in One Place. Press Release. Apple (2015). https://www.apple.com/newsroom/2015/06/08Introducing-Apple-Music-All-The-Ways-You-Love-Music-All-in-One-Place-/. Retrieved on December 6, 2022
35. Swift, T.: To Apple, Love Taylor. TUMBLR (2015). https://taylorswift.tumblr.com/post/122071902085/to-apple-love-taylor. Retrieved on June 30, 2015
36. Cue, E.: Twitter (2015). https://twitter.com/cue/status/612824775220555776. Retrieved on February 1, 2023
37. Knopper, S.: Apple Exec Eddy Cue: why taylor swift was right. RollingStone (2015). https://www.rollingstone.com/music/music-features/apple-exec-eddy-cue-why-taylor-swift-was-right-39608/. Retrieved on January 12, 2023
38. Duboff, J.: Taylor Swift: Apple Crusader, #GirlSquad Captain, and the Most Influential 25-Year-Old in America. Vanity Fair (2015). https://www.vanityfair.com/style/2015/08/taylor-swift-cover-mario-testino-apple-music. Retrieved on December 20, 2022
39. Bajarin, T.: How Taylor Swift Saved Apple Music. Time (2015). https://time.com/3940500/apple-music-taylor-swift-release/. Retrieved on February 1, 2023

'They're Not Risky' vs 'It Can Ruin Your Whole Life': How Parent-Child Dyads Differ in their Understandings of Online Risk

Olivia Williams[1]([envelope]) [ORCID], Kerrianne Buchanan[2] [ORCID], and Yee-Yin Choong[2] [ORCID]

[1] University of Maryland, College Park, MD, USA
OMurphy1@umd.edu
[2] National Institute of Standards and Technology, Gaithersburg, MD, USA
{kerrianne.buchanan,yee-yin.choong}@nist.gov

Abstract. Encountering or engaging in risky online behavior is an inherent aspect of being an online user. In particular, youth are vulnerable to such risky behavior, making it important to know how they understand and think about this risk-taking behavior. Similarly, with parents being some of the first and most prominent influencers on youth's online knowledge and behavior, it is important to know about parents' understanding and how they attempt to protect and influence their children's knowledge and behavior. In this qualitative study, we conducted semi-structured interviews with 40 youth/parent dyads with youth in 3rd-12th grades in the United States. The purpose of this study was to understand more about how youth think about and engage in online risk and risk-taking behavior, and how their parents view and attempt to influence this knowledge. We found that youth of all ages have nuanced ideas about online risk—including viewing online risk as a source of resilience development, growth and learning—and that these ideas are often in contrast to how their parents view the same concept. Youth are more likely than their parents to view online risk as context-dependent and agentive but are less likely than their parents to think about or understand the consequences of online risky behavior. We use these findings to discuss implications for parents, youth, education and tool providers, and future research.

Keywords: Online Risk · Risky Online Behavior · Cybersecurity · Youth · Parents · Dyads

1 Introduction

Engaging in risky behavior is part of the human experience, and the rate at which youth participate in risky behavior steadily increases in frequency as youth grow from childhood, through adolescence, and into young adulthood [33]. Although youth risk-taking is popularly thought of as impulsive and negative behavior, investigations of

This material is based on work supported by the UMD and NIST Professional Research Experience Program (PREP) under Award Number 70NANB18H165.

risk-taking suggest that it is often planned and exploratory in nature, and that learning how to navigate risk is an important part of learning [7, 26]. In other words, youth's relationship with "risky behavior" is complex, and deserving of attention. As "being online" has become a simple fact of existence for US youth, and their repertoire of online activities only increases as they get older [2], it is important to explore how the complexities of youth risk-taking behavior extend into the online space.

We know that youth participate in a variety of risky behaviors online (e.g. [19]), and also that the very act of being online carries the inherent risk of exposure to inappropriate content [12]. We also know that parents are worried about their children's online use, and more than nine-in-ten parents feel responsible for protecting their children from inappropriate and risky online content [4]. The studies that help generate the above understandings are often specific in scope, focusing, for example, on narrow age groups (e.g. [21]), specific categories of risk like sexual exposure (e.g. [20]), or parents' concerns and risk-mediation efforts (e.g. [36]). While these specific investigations are valuable, what is missing from the conversation is a broader understanding of how youth and parents conceptualize youth online risk-taking behavior, how these conceptualizations compare in youth/parent pairs, and how they can help inform youth education from a family perspective.

To contribute to these broader understandings, we interviewed 40 youth/parent dyads with youth in 3rd-12th grades to answer the following research questions:

1. How do youth define and understand online risk?
2. How do parents understand youth online risk-taking?
3. What is the alignment between youth and parent understandings of youth online risk-taking?
4. What is the perceived role of parents in youth online risk-taking knowledge and behavior?

2 Related Research

2.1 Youth Online Risk-Taking

Research suggests that there are two distinct differences in the internet use and risk-taking behavior of younger children and their teenage counterparts. First, though most young children and pre-teens have internet access, their access tends to be more limited and monitored than their older counterparts [28]. Second, reports of risk-taking behavior, understandings of risk, and the types of danger and risks encountered all increase for older youth [11].

Children and Pre-Teens. For the most part, younger children take fewer and less extreme online risks, likely due in part to their frequently more restricted access and use [11, 17]. However, it does not mean that younger children are immune from unsafe experiences or taking more dangerous risks; in a study of 1700 primary school students in 4th-6th grades, 40% of participants had experienced and felt shocked by inappropriate content, and 7.5% of study participants reported meeting a stranger from online in real life with 21% of that group doing so alone [30]. Encouragingly, multiple studies show that even young children tend to be aware that risks exist, which is important because awareness is the first step in taking action [2]. However, this awareness of risk is sometimes met with an incomplete understanding of what online risks are, more specifically, or a lack of understanding of how to respond [2]. In a study of pre-teen online practices and risk-taking in New Zealand, the 39 nine- to 12-year-old participants reported few options responding to experienced risks, and the responses were usually reactionary (i.e. closing inappropriate pages) versus preventative [22]. Additionally, participants viewed some risk-laden encounters like cyberbullying as inevitable and equally likely to happen to everyone regardless of behavior.

Unlike these youth's assessment of risk as being inevitable and equal, the literature suggests that exposure to risk is not randomized and equal across subpopulations. Rather, there are characteristics that create unequal risk exposure and risk-taking behavior even in younger youth. Across the board, younger children are at a higher risk of cyber scams [11], and those with vulnerable off-line circumstances like family challenges, low self-esteem, special education needs, physical disabilities, and communication disabilities are more likely to engage in risky online behavior [11, 13]. Socio-economic status may also influence the availability of risk-taking opportunities. In a study that examined online risk alongside socioeconomic factors, students from the lowest-economically ranked participating school were more likely to talk about social networking and things like "Facebook popularity" despite only being nine and 10 years old [22]. Additionally, although these students comprised only one fifth of the study's sample, they reported being online the most—which increases the amount of time available to encounter or take risks—and represented 83% of reported Facebook contact risks, 70% of unknown friend request reports, and two thirds of cyberbullying comments [22]. Finally, some studies suggest that gender influences younger youth's risk-taking exposure and behavior; multiple studies suggest that even though girls are heavier users of social media, boys display more risky behavior and girls are more inclined to practice better security behavior [6, 11].

Teenagers. Teen risk-taking behavior looks slightly different and is more prolific than that of younger children. In a study of 68 teens' weekly online risk behavior and encounters, 82% reported experiencing at least one risk event, and participants averaged three total risk events over the course of the two-month study. Encouragingly, 87% of the risks recorded were low to medium[1] in nature—like a friend posting an unflattering photo online—meaning they posed zero or minimal long term consequences and elicited little to no emotional response from the teen. Of these low to medium level risks, 84% were encountered by the youth but not sought [35]. Research also indicates that teenagers are generally aware of what risky behaviors are, particularly when it comes to social media [37], but also tend to downplay the severity of online risks or become desensitized to them [35].

Unsurprisingly, teens who are categorized as "high risk" offline also tend to be more high-risk online in terms of risk-taking and risk exposure. Interviews with 8 foster families found that foster teens—whose life experiences often leave them prone to attention- and affection-seeking behavior—partake in risky online behaviors like meeting up with strangers in real life and sexually explicit exchanges [5]. Similarly, teens who have low self-esteem or self-image can sometimes encounter more risk online if they use internet connections as a means of escape [7]. For example, if a student has fewer friends at

---

[1] Risk level metrics/measures mentioned in this literature review reflect the language of cited articles and are not defined by the National Institute of Standards and Technology.

school and low self-esteem, the internet offers a space to "reinvent" oneself, which can be a positive thing, but can also lead to risk-taking behaviors like meeting strangers online to make new friends. Alternately, students who have positive social relationships with parents, teachers and friends tend to carry those positive relationships online where they engage with friends and peers and are less prone to encountering or taking risks [7, 29]. Other forms of "high risk" behavior can be created and perpetuated by online experiences themselves: experiencing a negative or dangerous event—particularly on social media—can lead to PTSD symptoms, which in turn makes children vulnerable to engaging in more risk as a coping mechanism [23].

Finally, teenagers experience internet addiction more than their younger counterparts, which creates more exposure to encountering or taking online risks. Specifically, teenage boys are more likely to display addictive tendencies than girls [14], with those addictive tendencies often revolving around high-risk activities like sexual exchanges and violent games that increase in frequency with age [25]. While resilience has been found to help protect teens and plays a moderating role between both online risk exposure and negative impacts and addiction and risk exposure [34], resilience is deeply intertwined with efficacy, and youth need guidance and knowledge about cybersecurity and safety in order to develop and benefit from resilience.

2.2 The Developmental Role of Risk

Adolescent development theories have been increasingly rejecting negative stereotypes of "impulsive" youth risk-taking, instead pointing out the developmental importance of exploratory risk-taking behavior that results in learning and resilience [26]. Research is beginning to make its way into examinations of youth's online risk-taking behavior as well [32]. Wiseniewski and colleagues [34] applied adolescent risk theory—an approach traditionally used to examine offline adolescent risk choices like substance abuse and sexual promiscuity—in a survey of 75 teenagers' responses to online risk exposure. The study found that the more resilient teenagers in their study were able to encounter "higher levels of online risk without incurring serious, psychological harm," and suggested that allowing teens more freedom to explore online was an important way to develop the resilience needed to navigate future encountered risk [34]. Other studies have similar conclusions, finding that resilience helps create a balance between the numerous benefits of online opportunities and the potential exposure to risky content or behavior that inevitably arises alongside these opportunities [31], and that learning how to actively cope with risky online situations enhances resilience and lessens the long-term effects of experiencing online stressors [23].

Studies that examine youth's responses to experiencing online risk also show that such responses to risk exposure are nuanced and do often reflect resilience in the face of encountered risk. For example, a large-scale survey of 25,101 European children aged 9–16 found that few youth who reported encountering risky content or interactions online—for example, sexting or communicating with a stranger—reported that the experience was harmful, negative or troubling [28]. Further, when those youth did encounter an online risk, many of the youth had a range of strategies including blocking suspicious strangers and reporting the incident online, and a majority reported knowing what to do in the face of undesirable interactions on the internet [28].

Finally, when thinking about resilience it is important to consider the level of risk that leads to the promotion of resilience and agency. From a developmental perspective, resilience is most likely to be built through the process of learning to navigating low to medium-level risks, and is more difficult to develop in the face of repeated exposure to extreme risk [23, 26]. Fortunately, studies suggest that a vast majority of the risks that youth tend to encounter carry a low to medium level of risk [35], suggesting that being free to experience and learn how to navigate online risks is actually an important part of youth's participation as strong and safe online users. Indeed, in these low to medium level risk scenarios, youth reactions to encountered risk included ignoring the situation, taking active measures to confront the situation, removing themselves from the risky scenario, fixing the problem, and asking for help [35]. Through this process of choosing appropriate reactions to lower-level risky scenarios, teens are able to build positive online social skills and risk resilience which in turn equip them with the skills needed to navigate future potentially risky scenarios.

2.3   The Role of Parents in Youth Online Behavior

Despite a resilience approach to youth online risk-taking suggesting the importance of experiencing risk to learn and grow, youth should not be alone in their efforts. For all youth, social relationships including friends and teachers but especially parents provide a source of support and bear weight on risk-taking awareness and behavior [28]. Youth of all ages report parents as an important resource in understanding and mitigating exposure to online risk [28]. In general, younger youth tend to experience more supervision than their teenage counterparts, and that supervision has been shown to have the potential to positively impact youth's online risk-taking behaviors. In a study of 1700 4th–6th grade students' internet use and supervision, those who reported some level of parental oversight were more likely to know everyone they interacted with online (versus interacting with strangers), and less likely to pass personal details and photos to unknown people than students who reported no parental oversight at all [30]. Similarly, in a study of the risks that 68 teenagers took over the course of eight weeks, only eight reported incidents involved high-risk situations, and parents were actively involved in mediating these high-risk incidents [35].

Finally, when it comes to parental risk mediation, the way parents choose to approach mediation and the relationships fostered by those approaches are important. In general, strong parent relationships have been shown to be risk-protective [10], while a lack of strong parent relationships can increase youth's exposure to risk and decrease their resilience in the face of online risks [16]. Further, mediation technique matters: more restrictive and suppressive forms of mediation (e.g. monitoring apps, access restriction) resulting in youth being less likely to disclose their online behaviors to their parents [18], and also being less able to learn how to develop resilience in the face of risk [34]. Alternately, "enabling mediation" [15] and other active mediation techniques—including interactions like asking questions, discussing, or modeling practices—have positive and resilience-building impacts on youth [24].

3 Methods

To understand how youth and parents define and understand youth online risk-taking, we conducted semi-structured interviews with 40 youth/parent dyads in spring 2021.

3.1 Recruitment and Participants

This study was approved by the Institutional Review Board (IRB) of (blinded for review). A contracting research firm recruited 40 youth/parent dyads using a preexisting user database. These dyads included four youth from each grade from 3rd through 12th and one of their parents. The youth participants ranged in age from eight to 18, with 21 identifying as male and 19 identifying as female. The parent participants ranged in age from 31 to 59, with 35 identifying as female and five identifying as male. For the purposes of data collection and analysis, dyads were sorted by youth grade into three categories: elementary school (ES; 3rd through 5th grades), middle school (MS; 6th through 8th grades), and high school (HS; 9th through 12th grades). In total, there were 12 ES dyads, 12 MS dyads, and 16 HS dyads.

3.2 Instruments

Data were collected using a pre-interview questionnaire and a semi-structured interview. The two instruments were designed to be mutually inclusive. The questionnaire collected demographic data, basic definitions, and positions about risky online behaviors and served as a pre-thinking exercise for participants for the interview. The interviews were curated to allow participants to expand upon and discuss their answers from the questionnaire.

The questionnaires were scaffolded to appropriately suit participants' age and role, resulting in three versions: one for youth participants in grades 3–5, one for youth participants in grades 6–12, and one for parent participants. The two youth questionnaires were identical in question number and content, with the only differences being the re-phrasing of questions and response options in age-appropriate language. The youth questionnaires included questions about demographic information; general technology use; and online risk. The parent questionnaire consisted of the same topics but was longer because parents were asked about both themselves and their children.

The semi-structured interview protocols were similarly scaffolded to appropriately suit participants' ages and roles. A semi-structured interview format was chosen for this study because of the afforded ability to both predictably discuss common topics with each participant, while also acknowledging that the variety of participants' knowledges and experiences surrounding online privacy, security, and risk would require some flexibility in the nature of follow-up questions and discussion 1. The two youth interview protocols were identical in scope, sequence, and content, with the only differences being attributable to adjustments for age-appropriate language or question phrasing. Youth participants were asked anchor questions about their knowledge of and behavior surrounding online risk, and parent participants were asked anchor questions about both their own knowledge of online risk as well as how they view their child's knowledge and behavior surrounding online risk.

Two members of the research team—one quantitative expert and one qualitative expert—created an initial draft of the questionnaires and semi-structured interview protocol tools using the research questions and extant literature as a guide. From there, the content and quality of both data collection tools were refined over the course of an iterative four step process. First, a survey expert evaluated the questionnaire tool and provided feedback on the formation of the questions, clarity, and response options. Second, research colleagues and four K-12 teachers evaluated the content of both tools and provided feedback on the phrasing of questions in both tools considering the audiences, as well as the alignment of the questions with the research questions. Third, two members of the research team used a talk-aloud protocol to conduct cognitive interviews of both tools with three youth (one elementary schooler, one middle schooler, and one high schooler). Finally, the tools and data collection procedure were piloted with three youth/parent dyads 8. After each iteration of review, both the questionnaire and interview tools were revised by the researchers based on comments, feedback, and youth responses/behavior during the cognitive interviews and pilots.

3.3 Procedure

All data collection occurred remotely over Zoom[2] and was audio-recorded for transcription. The youth/parent dyads signed informed consent and assent forms (for youth older than 12) and were briefed about the study together. After the briefing, the parents and youth completed the pre-interview questionnaires and interview process separately to reduce the chances of influencing each other's responses. We requested that parents complete the interview process first followed by the youth second to reduce any youth impression that we may be talking with their parents about their (youth's) interview responses. All dyads agreed to this structure except two, who swapped due to time obligations. Each of the 40 data collection Zoom calls were scheduled for 90 min, and the first author conducted all 80 interviews for consistency. Participants were compensated for their time with cash gift cards: parents received $75 and youth received $25. All data were collected anonymously, and the data collection process yielded 80 complete questionnaires and 546 pages of single-spaced interview transcripts.

3.4 Data Analysis

The qualitative data analysis for this study proceeded across two cycles and contained both inductive and deductive coding [27]. Cycle one began with the creation of a code deck by all three researchers using the research questions, extant literature, pilot interview data, and researcher memos from the interviews, and resulted in 84 first-cycle codes. This initial code deck was used by the first and third author to code a random selection of nine full dyad transcripts (three from each grade band) using NVivo coding software. As this coding took place, the two researchers also used inductive codes to label findings not

---

[2] Any mention of commercial products or reference to commercial organizations is for information only; it does not imply recommendation or endorsement by the National Institute of Standards and Technology nor does it imply that the products mentioned are necessarily the best available for the purpose.

otherwise covered in the deductive code book. The full research team then met to discuss the results of the initial coding cycle, resolve any coding discrepancies, and refine the code deck. This process was repeated two more times with different samples of three dyad transcripts to fully refine the code deck. Once this process was complete, the first and third author coded all 40 dyad transcripts.

After first-round coding was complete, the research team met to discuss patterns and themes using the research questions to frame the conversations. To fully capitalize on the analytic possibilities of our dyadic structure, we chose a progressive analysis strategy that involved four steps: (1) examining participants at the individual level, (2) comparing participants *within* the same peer groups (youth within each grade band, then all youth, then all parents), (3) comparing participants *across* peer groups (comparing all grade bands, then all grade bands with their respective parents, then all youth with all parents), (4) comparing pairs at the dyad level (individual youths with their parents), and finally, (5) comparing all dyads.

4   Results

The results of this study are evidenced with direct quotes from participants and cited with an alphanumeric identifier. In the identifiers, the "Y" or "P" indicates "youth" or "parent," the number is the dyad code, and the ES/MS/HS indicates whether the youth participant of that dyad was an elementary (3rd–5th), middle (6th–8th), or high school (9th–12th) student. For example, P04MS would be the parent of dyad number 4, whose child is in middle school.

4.1   How Do Youth Define and Understand Online Risk?

Youth Definitions of Online Risk. Our youth participants primarily defined online risk through the use of example. These examples included both taken (i.e., choice-based) and encountered (i.e., external forces finding them) risks. Their risk examples fell into 7 main categories: gaming, going to suspicious websites, being hacked, interacting with strangers, being targeted by strangers to reveal information, sharing sensitive information with others, and social media. Youth's provided risk examples showed no consistent patterns across ages or grade bands with the exception of social media, which was more frequently cited by middle and high schoolers. The range of these categories suggests that youth feel like being online, in general, poses some inherent risks, and that an online user is accepting some level of risk by engaging in common activities like gaming, web-browsing, and using social media.

How Youth Understand Online Risk. The range of youth's definitions and the way they talked about risky activities revealed that youth understandings of online risk are nuanced. Youth recognized that risk-taking is not monolithic, and that some risks are riskier than others. For example, when asked about whether he makes risky choices online, Y07ES explained that "I usually don't, really. Maybe rarely, just once in a while, but it's usually not that big of a risk. Like maybe…my friend will just send [a Zoom link] in Gmail or something and I could press the link…they're not risky [risks]." Y30HS similarly discussed the idea that online risks are varied in nature and added the element of individual context, explaining that online risk and its consequences "depends on what kind of person you are. If you're a school kid, then yes [there are consequences to certain risks], but if you're an adult just trying to make money, that's a different thing." For these youth, the idea of "online risk" was context-dependent and varied across situations and people. In these ways, youth saw themselves as having agency in the risk-taking process by deciding which risks were low-impact or worth the potential benefit, and generally felt positively about their ability to make sound risk assessments and choices.

There were two notable factors that influenced how youth understood the "riskiness" of different risks, and how they determined which risks were worth taking. The first factor was the availability of risk mitigation strategies. Youth participants named a variety of risk mitigation strategies, including exiting suspicious-looking websites, not responding to messages from strangers, getting help from their parents, and only posting or providing certain amounts of personal information (e.g., only using a first name). Most of these mitigation strategies were described as being reactive versus proactive in nature. For example, Y20MS did a virus scan after accidentally clicking on a link that took him to a website full of "not so good stuff" to "make sure that there's nothing on my computer." Y33MS explained that "once I've seen that it says 'insecure' at the top, I've gone immediately out of it…once it says insecure I'm out of there." When youth felt like they were aware of a mitigation strategy to counteract certain risks, these risks were deemed more acceptable or less risky. This was demonstrated by Y04HS, who admitted that "I use pirate movie sites because some of the movies I want to watch are like $40 and I don't want to pay $40…I know it's risky, but I've been doing it for years, and I know I've learned how to avoid the pop-ups by quickly closing it and [using a monitoring app]." Youth across grade bands cited risk-taking rationales, with middle and high school youth being more likely than their elementary counterparts to offer a risk-taking rationale or mitigation strategy for the risks they described.

The second factor influencing youth's thinking about risk was their understanding of trust and who can and cannot be trusted online. Trust emerged as an important component of youth's assessment of how risky certain risks are—or if certain activities were risky at all—and their decisions about whether to make certain potentially risky choices. For example, Y12ES clarified that "no one really that you don't trust should know your private information," and Y26ES noted that "some websites you can't trust at all."

In terms of risk-taking reasoning, while some youth attributed risky behavior to ignorance or stupidity, youth across ages and grade bands explained that risks were often taken for some sort of benefit that justified the risk. These risk-taking reasons included social benefits like making new friends and getting followers on social media, as well as non-social benefits like receiving a reward or accessing content, or satiating a curiosity. For example, Y21MS explained a TikTok trend that she participated in in which "there would be like 30 people inside of a group chat," and the 30 people would make different group chats so everyone could "just like each other's posts and stuff to get more likes and followers." Y21MS noted that while such groups "could get overwhelming" and that joining group texts with strangers was risky, she chose to participate "for the beginning so I got the follow and the like." Similarly, Y16ES described making a risky choice in an online game to share an in-game reward with a stranger. She acknowledged that "I knew it was risky because they might just leave the game…but I thought maybe they could be telling the truth."

The youth in this study downplayed the consequences of risky online behavior, articulating that many consequences either did not apply to them or could be mitigated through a variety of strategies. This understanding often led the youth to conclude that they were not making risky online choices. For example, when asked if they make any risky choices online, Y11HS concluded "No. I always asked to download things...I probably haven't done any risky things on the computer." Similarly, Y24HS noted that "I try not to [take risks] just because I know the consequences, and if I'm ever involved in one, I would just try to remove myself from it." Some youth also implied that the potential reward of some risks made the risk worth it, and couple of youth even went so far as to point out that some risks have positive outcomes like meeting "a nice person" (Y18ES) and "providing moments of failure in order to learn" (Y22HS). This idea of positive risk-taking was eloquently summed up by Y02MS, who explained that "there's not just bad people on the internet, so maybe you could make a friend. Which might be a risk, but it might be a good one to take if you ever meet that friend and they turn out to be who they say they are and they're nice."

Finally, some of youth's understandings about consequences seemed attributable to experience bias, with many of the youth who reported making risky choices online noting that these risky choices either did not have consequences, or had very minor consequences that were able to be mitigated. These consequence-less risks included everything from clicking on a presumed safe meme website from a friend that turned out to be an inauthentic link (Y20MS), to sharing a full name and home address in a math game chat room (Y35HS). Regardless of the reason, the youth's comments about the consequences of risky online behavior collectively demonstrated understandings that *either* risk is not an overly worrisome threat because "nothing probably will happen because nothing happened to me" (Y03MS), *or* that online risk-taking is something that other kids do, but that "I stay pretty safe" (Y06ES).

Youth Risk-Taking Behavior. When asked if they could remember taking any risks online or engaging in any risky behavior, the youth participants' responses were mixed and held no patterns based on grade range. There was a near-even split between youth who admitted taking a risk and youth who felt like they did not take risks, and there were no patterns in risk admissions or denials across ages or grade bands. Among youth who described making a risky choice, a majority of the described risks were in the past and made when the youth were younger. Examples include Y02MS who named a risk that happened when she was in third grade, and Y35HS whose risk story began with "when I was a small child..." All of the described risks were related to games or online entertainment, social media, sharing personal information within games or social media, or web browsing. Several youth spoke of their risks reflectively as points of growth. Y39HS described the risky choice of clicking on a "fishy" link before concluding that "I did have to click on it and learn from my mistake." Y02MS faced no consequences from her risky choice of secretly opening a Pinterest account in third grade, but described the incident as "not the best choice and it made me think more about it."

The rationales of the youth who felt that they did *not* take risks online varied, but, when provided, were all connected to some sort of preventative risk mitigation strategy that the youth had in place. These mitigation strategies included, in order of frequency: knowing to remove themselves from a potentially risky situation or website before any damage could be done; getting parental permission; staying on a few known sites; and using false information to protect personal information.

With a couple of notable exceptions—like Y35HS who shared their full name and address online—youth participants' defining examples, personal examples, and understandings about risky online behavior and its consequences were low-impact, and none carried serious consequences. The youth in this study overwhelmingly viewed online risk-taking behavior to be a nuanced and multi-faceted aspect of existing in the online world. This led to the youth being risk-tolerant of the risks that they could identify, and undeterred from participating in the online space, even when aspects of that space may contain risk.

4.2 How Do Parents Understand Youth Online Risk-Taking, and What is the Alignment Between Youth and Parent Understandings?

The parents in this study believed that youth their kids' age took the following risks online: interacting with strangers, over-sharing personal information, making poor security choices, viewing inappropriate content, and using social media and games. While this list topically overlaps the youth's risk definitions, there was less alignment of stated risks at the dyad level than at the full group level (i.e., individual youth/parent pairs were not frequently naming the same youth risks). For example, when asked what kinds of risks youth her daughter's age take online, P32MS named the choice-based risk of "downloading random things." While this was a response echoed amongst youth participants, it was not reflected by P32MS's daughter, who envisioned online risk as being interactive, and defined risky online behavior as "people you don't know very well asking for personal information."

Parents of younger youth tended to be more worried about their kids viewing inappropriate content and interacting with strangers. P06ES worries that youth her son's age are at risk of "giving up too much information, telling a person they don't know where they live because they assume it's a kid [and] a person can lure them." P26ES worried about her son talking to strangers on games and apps. In contrast, parents of older youth were generally more worried about poor security choices and the long-term consequences of over sharing on social media. For example, P11HS worried about her son "just doing something stupid and then it's on the internet forever and it can ruin your whole life...when I think of risky behavior, that's what I think of. I think of him doing something stupid and it's going to haunt him when he's an adult."

Across the board parents agreed that most youth online risk-taking was attributed to one of four things: "not knowing what they're clicking on [or] knowing what exactly they're doing" (P10ES), "a lapse of judgement" (P36HS), "the peer pressure...the friends" (P19MS), or "their desires and things they want" (P16ES). These understandings of risk-taking reasoning varied by the age of the children, with parents of elementary school youth attributing risk-taking reasoning to ignorance, middle school parents being the most worried about peer pressure, and high school parents finding the primary reasons for risk-taking to be social positioning and lapses of judgement or foresight. Middle and high school parents were also the most likely to conclude that "they (youth) are at the age of risky behavior, right?" (P02MS), suggesting that encountering risk online is an expected outcome of being a young online user. Unlike youth participants, no parents suggested that risk-taking might be beneficial or named any positive risk-taking reasonings.

Like the youth, there was an even split between parents who believed that their kids did *not* take risks online, and those that were sure that their kids *did* take risks online. Also like the youth participants, parents who believed that their child took online risks most commonly cited low-impact risks with only mild potential consequences like "going to different sites…[or] getting onto Discord on different server groups (P19MS), posting "weird pictures or little TikTok dances" (P10ES), and "befriend[ing] people who she's met online" (P21MS).

Though both parent and youth participant groups *as a whole* were evenly split on whether or not the youth in this study were risk-takers online, this alignment did not exist at the dyad level. Of the 19 youth who said they did not take risks online, six had a parent that specifically named a risk their child had taken, and another two parents were sure but did not provide examples. Similarly, 14 parents were sure their children were taking risks online, but only seven of these children agreed. Dyad 33 was an interesting example of this potential disconnect in action. When asked if he had made any risky choices online, Y33MS responded in the overall negative, explaining that he has "gone on risky websites, but then once I've seen that it says insecure on the top, I've gone immediately out of it." In comparison, P33MS felt sure that her son had made unmitigated risky choices online, describing an incident in which he and some friends were talking about another boy in their class in a way that "could eventually lead to something that is bullying" and that such behavior might be "use[d] against [him]" in the future. This example illustrates discrepancies born of different ideas about what risky online behavior is: P33MS saw risk in the possibility of future reputational damage and the shared idea across parents in this study that "once you put it on the internet, it is there forever," whereas Y33MS was conceptualizing risk as something that can be avoided with a set of mitigation strategies.

4.3   What is the Perceived Role of Parents in Youth Online Risk-Taking Knowledge and Behavior?

Ten parents and 10 youth *overall* named parents as a resource for support with risky online choices and their consequences. However, only three dyads were aligned on this point. Specifically, the parents of elementary schoolers who felt like their children were not risk takers also frequently described themselves as risk-mitigators, though there was little alignment in terms of what their youth were actually doing or little impact on their or their child's awareness of risk. For example, P22HS explained that various kids Y22HS's age make risky choices including things like sending "garbage texts," but that "I know he doesn't…[because] I check his phone." Y22HS, however, commented that "I know I've done something stupid in terms of social media" and described giving his number to a bot in a "click to win something" site that proceeded to send him lots of spam texts. In this example, P22HS was attempting to mitigate through device—and specifically text—monitoring, and felt secure about her son's online risk-taking because of that monitoring. In reality, however, there was evidence of risky behavior in the very texts that she was checking, and she either did not notice it, did not check at the right time, or did not flag the risk.

Further, youth and parents talked about parents-as-mitigators slightly differently. The youth who cited their parents as a risk resource noted things like "[they] (parents) just said that I could tell them if anything happened that made me feel uncomfortable or scared or unsafe...and were telling me if I needed a username for something what it should be or what it should look like" (Y02MS) and "plus I have my mom, who can also fix things for me" (Y04HS). For these and other youth who mentioned parents as a mitigating support, parents emerged as a trustworthy place to troubleshoot outcomes of risky choices that youth were not able to fully deal with on their own. One parent reflected a similar sentiment, explaining that "completely shutting them off...I just don't think that's a solution either. Because then, I'm just afraid that she will stop sharing things with me...the channel of communication would be completely cut off' (P18ES). Many other parents, however, imagined themselves as risk supports through the mitigating work of limiting access to spaces and opportunities to take risks. For example, P33MS noted that her son "is just not going to be allowed to join social media for some time," and P22HS checks her son's phone to see if he is engaging in risky behaviors. Despite these monitoring efforts, however, parental monitoring was not related to whether youth reported making risky choices, with youth of high-monitoring parents still reporting making risky online choices at similar rates to their non- or less-monitored peers.

Of the 15 parents who did not think their children took risks online, five were elementary school parents. Of these five, all but one positioned themselves and their role as mitigators or gatekeepers of safety as a rationale for their response. By contrast, the 10 middle and high school parents who felt that their children were not risk takers cited either personality-based reasons or did not provide a rationale for their response.

Similarly, of the parents who felt like their children were risk-takers, the parents of elementary and middle school youth referenced themselves and their roles as mitigators in their understandings of their children's risk-taking.

Finally, in both youth and parent understandings of parents-as-mitigators of youth online risk-taking, the primary mitigation strategies included conversations and device monitoring. In particular, conversations about risky choices and their consequences had the most directly observable impact on youth's understanding of risk and online risk-taking. For example, P24HS described sexting as a particularly risky choice for youth her son's age and reported that "he and I have definitely talked about that...I told him about [an] incident and how serious it was, and how this kid's future is pretty much ruined just for a stupid mistake." This conversation was seemingly echoed when Y24HS gave "sending inappropriate things to others...[and] sharing private pictures" as examples of risky online choices that should be avoided. Additionally, a few youth described their parents as "fixers" who were available in the case of emergency, like Y07ES who noted that "my dad had to once again get rid of the virus [and] put in a new security thing" when his online gaming led to a computer virus.

5   Discussion

Previous studies have suggested that youth do not perceive many online risks as being particularly harmful or negative and do not frequently encounter high-risk scenarios in their online lives [28, 35], and that youth of all ages are prepared with strategies to combat online risk when they do encounter it [28, 23]. Our study supported these previous findings with 40 youth in the United States through a unique, dyadic lens that examined broad understandings of youth risk-taking understandings from the family perspective.

The youth participants in our study primarily named mild risks and displayed a confidence in their conversations of risky online situations that—even if it was at times misplaced—created a sense of empowerment surrounding online risk. While it is possible that the youth's naming of few and mild risks could have been attributable to the context of the study (i.e., youth may be uninclined to admit to engaging in risky behavior to a relative stranger over Zoom), their named risks in general, lack of concern about consequences, and reported use of mitigation strategies collectively point to other possibilities about how youth envision online risk. The youth displayed a real and active understanding of risk mitigation that suggested a prevailing view of online risk-taking as navigable, part of the process of being online, and occasionally even beneficial. Collectively, these understandings suggest that youth—albeit subconsciously—approach online risk-taking from a resilience perspective and are prepared to capitalize on risk as an opportunity for learning and growth [26]. This holds important implications for how we think about teaching youth about online risk, and points to the importance of including resilience building, understandings of trust, and mitigation strategies into conversations about youth's online behavior. Common across all of these learning points is the necessity of reflection and intentional action. This necessity also points to the importance of helping youth recognize and weigh the outcomes of different responses to encountered risks, as well as the consequences of different risky choices so they can make informed decisions surrounding how to respond to risky online situations.

The parents in this study were not aligned with their youth in terms of their understandings of risky online behavior and were more likely than their children to view risk more simplistically as something that needs to be prevented to protect their youth from negative consequences. This was reflected in the number of parents who used restrictive monitoring techniques to help prevent certain risks from happening, particularly with their younger children. Because of this disconnect, youth were most likely to learn from their parents (if at all) when risk outcomes were negative but did not experience opportunities to learn from their parents how to do risk cost/benefit analysis, or what to do when the benefits of taking a risk might outweigh the costs. This is particularly problematic given the youth's views of risky choices as being agentive and, when viewed alongside the fact that a high number of parents did not believe that their children were taking online risks, revealed some challenges.

As a few youth and parents in this study confirmed, parents can be a valuable resource for helping youth learn how to navigate encountering online risks [10]. This is especially true when parents practice "enabling mediation" [15] and talk with their children about online risk, responses options, and how to navigate encountering risk online. However, the combination of restrictive monitoring approaches—which did not demonstrably impact youth's risky encounters in this study and which can negatively impact youth's willingness to seek their parents out as supports [18]—with the amount of parents who do not recognize or want to admit that their children actually take risks hampers the degree to which parents are able to serve as a guide in building their child's risk resilience.

This creates a situation where parents are well-positioned to help empower their children to be more resilient and conscientious risk-takers but are unable to do so due to an incomplete understanding of the importance of informed youth risk-taking and reflection. This points to the importance of working with parents to be more risk-tolerant, to shift their understanding of risk to being growth-mindset in nature, and to recognize their own potential in proactively helping their children become more risk resilient and risk reflective as online users.

5.1 Implications

This study has implications for parents, those designing tools and education for youth and parents, and future research. First, our study and others like it [28] show not only that youth understand online risk as a concept, but also that they are interested in thinking about how to mitigate it and be resilient [26] to keep themselves, their accounts, and their devices safe online. This study also suggests, however, that youth may not always be the best at recognizing some of their own risk-taking behavior or its consequences and need the most support and feedback in these areas. This requires that parents adopt the same understandings—that risk is an inevitable and even important part of youth's online lives, and that youth need support with navigating the potential consequences of their choices—and approach working with their youth as risk supports. To do this, parents might choose to re-frame online risk as a growth opportunity instead of as something that youth will "get in trouble" for doing, and work to clearly establish themselves as a support and conversation partner instead of a rule enforcer. Parents might also choose to replace or supplement their device monitoring (e.g., checking cell phones and setting use limits) with conversations and proactive feedback about different online actions, the consequences of those actions, and what steps youth might take to mitigate or avoid those consequences. Tool providers and those who create educational and support tools for parents should also keep these goals in mind, and design parent and family supports that encourage conversations about risky online behavior and give feedback about different risky choices and risk responses. Further, tool and content providers that cater to youth could also integrate opportunities to help youth recognize, reflect on, and choose appropriate mitigation strategies in response to various online risks into their tools and platforms.

This study also leaves room for important future research in the online youth risk-taking space. Our study captured youth and parent perceptions about youth online risk-taking at a single moment in time, but also revealed that both parent and youth understandings about youth online risk-taking may change as youth age from young children into young adults. This presents opportunities for meaningful longitudinal projects to track risk understandings and self-reported behavior of dyads over time to investigate how perceptions and youth/parent interactions about online risk develop over time, and how these changing interactions impact youth knowledge and behavior. Additionally, as we know that parents want and need more support in terms of helping their children be safe online users, research examining the effectiveness of different parent and youth education tools could provide valuable insight into how to best help parents and youth work to support youth's online risk understandings and behaviors.

6 Limitations

This study had several limitations related to its methodology and procedure. First, because of the COVID-19 pandemic, interviews for this study happened via video platform. This meant that, although we requested that individual participants complete the interview privately, there was a nonzero chance of youth/parent participants overhearing and influencing each other's responses or responding with the possibility of being overheard by others. Further, we asked participants to self-report taken risks online—a potentially uncomfortable or sensitive topic to discuss with a researcher via video—which likely influenced the responses or the degree of description in the responses that we received. Collectively, these limitations mean that it is possible that risky choices and encountered risks were underreported. Data for this study also belong to a broader investigation of youth and parent understandings about youth's online privacy, security and risk knowledge. In this greater study, the conversations about risk featured in this paper came after conversations about online privacy and security, which could have led to potential order effects impacting participant responses.

Second, to be eligible for this study, participants had to have access to video-capable technology, have a parent in the home with time to participate, and be interested in participating in a youth/parent dyadic study. By design, these sampling criteria excluded dyadic pairs with parents who were working or otherwise busy during data collection hours (4–9 pm) or who did not have the technological tools to participate, and included pairs with a parent who was drawn to participate in such a study, possibly impacting the results.

Finally, our study was limited by its cross-sectional design focusing only on parents and youth at one point in time. This study was not longitudinal, meaning we could compare dyads within and across age groups, but could not examine the progression of parental influence and youth knowledge of the same dyads over time. Further, our theoretical approach requires an understanding that youth knowledge is impacted by a variety of factors including things like school and peers, but we only examined the influence of parents. Each of these design limitations offer important potential directions for future research focusing on longitudinal data and/or more holistic approaches to understanding how a variety of factors are influencing youth at different ages.

7 Conclusion

The 40 parent-child dyad pairs in this qualitative study demonstrated a misalignment across their understandings of risk, risk-taking behavior, and the consequences of risky behavior online. The 3rd-12th grade youth were more likely than their parents to view risk flexibly, agentively, and as a context-dependent concept, but demonstrated little awareness of the consequences of online risk and were not always able to recognize risky situations or choices they have engaged in online. Conversely, the parents were more conscious of the consequences of youth online risk-taking behavior but were less likely than their children to view risk as nuanced or as an opportunity for learning or growth. In short, neither group on their own had a complete understanding of risky online behavior and have much to learn from each other.

Ongoing efforts to support families with nuanced understandings about risk and risk mitigation strategies are an important next step in thinking about how to prepare youth to be confident, resilient online users. With taking and encountering risks being an inevitable aspect of being an online user, youth should continue to view risk-taking as an agentive concept, but also incorporate realistic understandings about the possible consequences of risky behavior so that they can learn to mitigate potential harmful effects of such risky behavior. Similarly, because parents play such an active and important role in youth online learning, parents should move towards understanding most online risk as a learning opportunity for growth rather than something "bad" that needs to be avoided. Overall, the more that we can help prepare parents to hold these more flexible ideas and to have constructive conversations with their children surrounding online risk and mitigating the consequences of risky online behavior, the more resilient youth online users can become.

References

1. Ayres, L.: Semi-structured interview. SAGE Encyclopedia Qual. Res. Meth. **1**, 810–811 (2008). https://doi.org/10.4135/9781412963909.n172
2. Annansingh, F., Veli, T.: An investigation into risks awareness and e-safety needs of children on the internet: a study of Devon UK. Interact. Technol. Smart Educ. **13**(2), 147–165 (2016). https://doi.org/10.1108/ITSE-09-2015-0029
3. Auxier, B., Anderson, M., Perrin, A., Turner, E.: Children's engagement with digital devices, screen time. Pew Research Center (2020). https://www.pewresearch.org/internet/2020/07/28/childrens-engagement-with-digital-devices-screen-time/
4. Auxier, B., Anderson, M., Perrin, A., Turner, E.: Parenting approaches and concerns related to digital devices. Pew Research Center (2020). https://www.pewresearch.org/internet/2020/07/28/parenting-approaches-and-concerns-related-to-digital-devices/
5. Badillo-Urquiola, K.A., Ghosh, A.K., Wisniewski, P.: Understanding the unique online challenges faced by teens in the foster care system. In: Companion of the 2017 ACM Conference on Computer Supported Cooperative Work and Social Computing, pp. 139–142, February 2017. https://doi.org/10.1145/3022198.3026314
6. Chai, S., BagchiSen, S., Morrell, C., Rao, H.R., Upadhyaya, S.J.: Internet and online information privacy: an exploratory study of preteens and early teens. IEEE Trans. Prof. Commun. **52**(2), 167–182 (2009). https://doi.org/10.1109/TPC.2009.2017985
7. Ciranka, S., van den Bos, W.: Adolescent risk-taking in the context of exploration and social influence. Dev. Rev. **61**, 100979 (2021). https://doi.org/10.1016/j.dr.2021.100979
8. Desimone, L.M., Le Floch, K.C.: Are we asking the right questions? Using cognitive interviews to improve surveys in education research. Educ. Eval. Policy Anal. **26**(1), 1–22 (2004). https://doi.org/10.3102/01623737026001001
9. Davis, K.: Young people's digital lives: the impact of interpersonal relationships and digital media use on adolescents' sense of identity. Comput. Hum. Behav. **29**(6), 2281–2293 (2013). https://doi.org/10.1016/j.chb.2013.05.022
10. Davis, K., Koepke, L.: Risk and protective factors associated with cyberbullying: are relationships or rules more protective? Learn. Media Technol. **41**(4), 521–545 (2016). https://doi.org/10.1080/17439884.2014.994219
11. El Asam, A., Katz, A.: Vulnerable young people and their experience of online risks. Hum.-Comput. Interact. **33**(4), 281–304 (2018). https://doi.org/10.1080/07370024.2018.1437544

12. Harriman, N., Shortland, N., Su, M., Cote, T., Testa, M.A., Savoia, E.: Youth exposure to hate in the online space: an exploratory analysis. Int. J. Environ. Res. Public Health **17**(22), 8531 (2020). https://doi.org/10.3390/ijerph17228531

13. Helsper, E.J.: Digital inequalities amongst digital natives. In: The Routledge Companion to Digital Media and Children, pp. 435–448. Routledge (2020). https://doi.org/10.4324/978135 1004107

14. Kalibova, P., Milkova, E.: Internet addictive behaviour of adolescents. Int. J. Educ. Inf. Technol. **10**, 139–143 (2016)

15. Kuldas, S., Sargioti, A., Milosevic, T., Norman, J.O.H.: A review and content validation of 10 measurement scales for parental mediation of children's Internet use. Int. J. Commun. **15**, 23 (2021). https://ijoc.org/index.php/ijoc/article/view/17265

16. Larraaga, E., Yubero, S., Ovejero, A., Navarro, R.: Loneliness, parent-child communication and cyberbullying victimization among Spanish youths. Comput. Hum. Beh. **65**(C), 1–8 (2016). https://doi.org/10.1016/j.chb.2016.08.015

17. Livingstone, S., Mascheroni, G., Staksrud, E.: European research on children's internet use: assessing the past and anticipating the future. New Media Soc. **20**(3), 1103–1122 (2018). https://doi.org/10.1177/1461444816685930

18. Lo Cricchio, M.G., Palladino, B.E., Eleftheriou, A., Nocentini, A., Menesini, E.: Parental mediation strategies and their role on youth's online privacy disclosure and protection: a systematic review. Eur. Psychol. **27**(2), 116–130 (2022). https://doi.org/10.1027/1016-9040/a000450

19. Longobardi, C., Fabris, M.A., Prino, L.E., Settanni, M.: Online sexual victimization among middle school students: prevalence and association with online risk behaviors. Int. J. Dev. Sustain. **15**(1–2), 39–46 (2021). https://doi.org/10.3233/DEV-200300

20. Madigan, S., et al.: The prevalence of unwanted online sexual exposure and solicitation among youth: A meta-analysis. J. Adolesc. Health **63**(2), 133–141 (2018). https://doi.org/10.1016/j.jadohealth.2018.03.012

21. Maqsood, S., Biddle, R., Maqsood, S., Chiasson, S.: An exploratory study of children's online password behaviours. In: Proceedings of the 17th ACM Conference on Interaction Design and Children, pp. 539–544, June 2018. https://doi.org/10.1145/3202185.3210772

22. McDonald-Brown, C., Laxman, K., Hope, J.: An exploration of the contexts, challenges and competencies of pre-teenage children on the internet. Int. J. Technol. Enhan. Learn. **8**(1), 1–25 (2016)

23. McHugh, B.C., Wisniewski, P.J., Rosson, M.B., Carroll, J.M.: When social media traumatizes teens: The roles of online risk exposure, coping, and post-traumatic stress. Internet Res. **28**(5), 1169–1188 (2018). https://doi.org/10.1108/IntR-02-2017-0077

24. Rega, V., Gioia, F., Boursier, V.: Parental mediation and cyberbullying: a narrative literature review. Marr. Family Rev. 1–37 (2022). https://doi.org/10.1080/01494929.2022.2069199

25. Reiner, I., Tibubos, A.N., Hardt, J., Müller, K., Wölfling, K., Beutel, M.E.: Peer attachment, specific patterns of internet use and problematic internet use in male and female adolescents. Eur. Child Adolesc. Psychiatry **26**(10), 1257–1268 (2017). https://doi.org/10.1007/s00787-017-0984-0

26. Romer, D., Reyna, V.F., Satterthwaite, T.D.: Beyond stereotypes of adolescent risk-taking: placing the adolescent brain in developmental context. Dev. Cogn. Neurosci. **27**, 19–34 (2017). https://doi.org/10.1016/j.dcn.2017.07.007

27. Saldaña, J.: The Coding Manual for Qualitative Researchers. The Coding Manual for Qualitative Researchers, 3rd Ed. pp.1–440 (2021). http://digital.casalini.it/9781529755992

28. Smahèl, D., et al.: EU Kids Online 2020: Survey results from 19 countries (2020). https://www.eukidsonline.ch/files/Eu-kids-online-2020-international-report.pdf

29. Strong, C., Lee, C.T., Chao, L.H., Lin, C.Y., Tsai, M.C.: Adolescent Internet use, social integration, and depressive symptoms: analysis from a longitudinal cohort survey. J. Dev. Behav. Pediatr. **39**(4), 318–324 (2018). https://doi.org/10.1097/DBP.0000000000000553

30. Valcke, M., Schellens, T., Van Keer, H., Gerarts, M.: Primary school children's safe and unsafe use of the Internet at home and at school: An exploratory study. Comput. Hum. Behav. **23**(6), 2838–2850 (2007). https://doi.org/10.1016/j.chb.2006.05.008

31. Vissenberg, J., d'Haenens, L.: Protecting youth's wellbeing online: Studying the associations between opportunities, risks, and resilience. Media Commun. **8**(2), 175–184 (2020). https://doi.org/10.17645/mac.v8i2.2774

32. Vissenberg, J., d'Haenens, L., Livingstone, S.: Digital literacy and online resilience as facilitators of young people's well-being? A Systematic review? Eur. Psychol. **27**(2), 76–85 (2022). https://doi.org/10.1027/1016-9040/a000478

33. Willoughby, T., Heffer, T., Good, M., Magnacca, C.: Is adolescence a time of heightened risk-taking? An overview of types of risk-taking behaviors across age groups. Dev. Rev. **61**, 100980 (2021). https://doi.org/10.1016/j.dr.2021.100980

34. Wisniewski, P., Jia, H., Wang, N., Zheng, S., Xu, H., Rosson, M.B., Carroll, J.M.: Resilience mitigates the negative effects of adolescent internet addiction and online risk exposure. In Proceedings of the 33rd Annual ACM Conference on Human Factors in Computing Systems, pp. 4029–4038, April 2015. https://doi.org/10.1145/2702123.2702240

35. Wisniewski, P., Xu, H., Rosson, M.B., Perkins, D.F., Carroll, J.M.: Dear diary: Teens reflect on their weekly online risk experiences. In: Proceedings of the 2016 CHI Conference on Human Factors in Computing Systems, pp. 3919–3930, May 2016. https://doi.org/10.1145/2858036.2858317

36. Wisniewski, P., Ghosh, A.K., Xu, H., Rosson, M.B. and Carroll, J.M.: Parental control vs. teen self-regulation: Is there a middle ground for mobile online safety?. In: Proceedings of the 2017 ACM Conference on Computer Supported Cooperative Work and Social Computing, pp. 51–69, February 2017. https://doi.org/10.1145/2998181.2998352

37. Yılmaz, R., Gizem, K.Y.F., Tuğba, Ö.H., Tuğra, K.: Examining secondary school students' safe computer and internet usage awareness: an example from Bartın province. Pegem Eğitim Ve Öğretim Dergisi **7**(1), 83–114 (2017). https://doi.org/10.14527/pegegog.2017.004

Verification of the Effects of Voice and Personalized Disaster Information from an Agent on Awareness that Disaster is Relevant to Oneself

Tomoki Yano[✉], Masayuki Ando, Kouyou Otsu, and Tomoko Izumi

Ritsumeikan University, 1-1-1, Noji-Higashi, Kusatsu, Shiga, Japan
is0478kf@ed.ritsumei.ac.jp, {mandou,k-otsu,
izumi-t}@fc.ritsumei.ac.jp

Abstract. Evacuation alert services that send disaster information to personal mobile devices (i.e., smartphones) are generally used during disasters. This study addresses the expression of alerts that foster disaster awareness among individuals. In this study, we consider the content and delivery method of disaster information to improve awareness and ensure that users perceive it as directly said to them. For the text content, we use the user's operational information on the smartphone as behavioral information to make them feel its relevance. We focus on the efficacy of providing text through a humanoid agent and its spoken voice as the delivery method. Three patterns are proposed each for the text content and delivery method. A comparative verification experiment was conducted to verify the proposed evacuation alert's effectiveness. Verification indicates that including participants' app browsing information in the alert and delivering the information via a humanoid agent and voice tend to increase the perceived message's directness and awareness of the disaster to each person.

Keywords: Disaster prevention · Personalized alert · Disaster information · Humanoid agents

1 Introduction

Delayed evacuation can exacerbate human losses in a disaster. The most effective approach to urge evacuation is to contact each of the evacuees directly, such as calling them, because it raises awareness that the disaster is relevant to them. However, calling each person during a disaster situation is difficult. One method of direct message delivery to each individual is via their mobile devices. That is, instead of calling, we consider information provided to mobile devices of evacuees to ensure that they perceive it as if it were being said to them directly.

In this study, we focus on evacuation alert services that send disaster information to personal mobile devices (i.e., smartphones) and consider the information expressions of alerts that generate awareness of personal disaster relevancy. Given the ubiquity of smartphones, we anticipate being able to issue personalized alerts utilizing the data stored on

A. Coman and S. Vasilache (Eds.): HCII 2023, LNCS 14026, pp. 548–557, 2023.
https://doi.org/10.1007/978-3-031-35927-9_37

individuals' devices. Studies have examined how textual expressions improve evacuation awareness. For example, Tanaka et al. [1] showed that using unfamiliar adverbs in relatively concise Japanese textual expressions encouraged rapid evacuation. In another study, textual expressions considering psychological factors were proposed, and the effects of enhancing evacuation awareness were compared [2]. The psychological factors considered in their study were fear-arousing communication [3], majority synching bias [4], and impatience. The studies above disregard the textual expression such that the evacuees perceive it as if it were directly said to them.

If an alert containing text addressing the individual user is received, the users should feel as if it were directed to them. Therefore, in this study, we consider the disaster information delivery method, which identifies each individual user. We discuss the information-providing of alerts in terms of what content should be included and how to provide such content. As for the content, we focus on the disaster information, including the user's operational information on the smartphone. This information in evacuation alerts may make people feel that the alert is relevant. In addition, the delivery method of the message to the user is also an important factor in generating awareness of the disaster. In this study, we examine the effect of providing the above contents through a humanoid agent with a voice, compared to providing them as text messages. Previous studies have demonstrated that the impression given to the message receiver is affected by the presence of humanoid agents. For example, the study on product recommendation in online shopping showed that presenting a humanoid agent increases familiarity, intelligence, and willingness to purchase products, compared to text-message guidance [5]. Introducing agents as a means of information guidance may alter users' perceptions and behavior when providing disaster information.

Thus, we propose providing evacuation alerts, including users' operational information on smartphones as behavioral information via a voice of a humanoid agent. To verify the effect of our proposal, we set three patterns, each for a behavioral information and information delivery method, and set nine patterns of alerts by combining them. This study shows the results of a comparative verification experiment for the nine alert patterns.

2   Information Expressions of Evacuation Alerts

2.1   Assumed Disaster Situation and Our Previous Study

In this study, we assume a situation in which heavy rainfall may cause rivers to overflow and flood. This situation is one in which the possibility of a disaster can be predicted, and there is time to evacuate before the disaster occurs.

In our previous study, we considered the information expression in an area mail, including the description of the user's state using location and behavioral information to identify each individual user [6]. The verification experiment results indicated that location information encourages a sense of urgency regarding a disaster, but behavioral information does not. The reason behavioral information is ineffective is that increasing the specificity of the expression of the receiver's state is difficult via area mail. Thus, in this study, we assume that a user receives disaster information from an application installed on their smartphone and consider the information expressions of alerts that generate awareness of disaster relevancy utilizing the user's behavioral information.

2.2 Text Content of Evacuation Alerts

In our previous study, as the behavioral information, we presented "this message is for you, who are reading it" and "this message is for you, who are reading it holding your phone". These expressions seem to specify the user's state, but they represent the natural behaviors of the user reading the message. This behavioral information was not perceived as indicative of the user. In the previous study, since we assumed the user received the information via the area mail, we could not include more personalized information in the evacuation alerts. Therefore, in this study, we assume the user receives evacuation alerts from an application installed on their smartphone, which obtains information regarding smartphone usage. As a concrete representation of the user's state, we focus on the user's operational information on the smartphone. Concretely, we use the browsing information on the video viewing application (e.g., YouTube), which is one of the most widely used applications. The contents of the texts in this study are in the following three patterns (Table 1):

- **A) No information condition**: The message does not contain information about the user's behavior.
- **B) Reception status condition:** The message gives reception status, "This message is for you, who received it."
- **C) Browsing information condition:** The message shows the user's browsing information. One example is "This message is for you, who are watching <u>music</u> videos on YouTube."

In the browsing information condition, the underlined words are the category names on the videos, such as sports, animals, cooking, and music. Because we aim to examine the influence of the specificity of the behavioral information about the user, the texts shown in Table 1 are simple expressions without including words that intensify the degree of danger or urgency.

Table 1. Contents provided by the application

Condition	Text Content
No information	A heavy rain warning is issued for Kusatsu city. The area near Kusatsu River is dangerous. Please evacuate
Reception status	**This message is for you, who received it.** A heavy rain warning is issued for Kusatsu city. The area near Kusatsu River is dangerous. Please evacuate
Browsing information	**This message is for you, who are watching <u>music videos</u> on YouTube.** A heavy rain warning is issued for Kusatsu city. The area near Kusatsu River is dangerous. Please evacuate

2.3 Information-Delivery Method

Next, we consider the delivery method of the text contents above. The behavioral information described in the previous session that directly points to the state of a user, such as browsing information, may change the user's perceptions and behavior when presented as if a person directly said it. From this motivation, we examine the effect of providing alerts via a humanoid agent with a voice, compared to providing alerts as text messages, which was motivated by the fact that the presence of humanoid agents affects the impression given to the receiver of the message [5]. Therefore, introducing agents as a means of information guidance when delivering disaster information may change receivers' perceptions and behavior. To verify the presence of a humanoid agent and the effect of an agent's voice, the following three information-delivery methods are considered:

- **i) Text message condition:** The text-based message is shown in a callout.
- **ii) Text-speaking agent condition:** A humanoid agent is shown, and the message appears in a callout.
- **iii) Voice-speaking agent condition:** A humanoid agent and message in a callout are shown with a voice reading the text.

3   Content of Experiment

We examine the effect of the specificity of the behavioral information described in Sect. 2.2 and the information presented by a humanoid agent described in Sect. 2.3 on the effect of generating awareness that disaster is relevant to oneself. There are three conditions for the behavioral information and three conditions for the delivery method. Therefore, we set nine patterns of providing disaster information by combining the behavioral information (A–C) and the presence of a humanoid agent and voice (i–iii). The pattern of information including the behavioral information B presented with the method i is denoted as [i-B].

3.1 Experiment Outline

In this experiment, participants were isolated in a room with a rain soundscape to complete the assigned daily task. The participants watched YouTube videos as a task. They were allowed to watch only videos designated by the experimenter from four genres: sports, animals, cooking, and music videos. The designated videos were selected because they do not include current weather conditions or information regarding the disaster. Therefore, they were considered to have no impact on the awareness of the disaster. The participant received an evacuation alert while watching videos and saw the content of the alert. After the participant confirmed it, they answered the questionnaire.

Twenty-seven university students from the authors' university participated in this experiment. We set the participant in nine groups and assigned five patterns to each group. Figure 1 shows the patterns evaluated by each group. Group 1 is used as an example to explain the assignment. The row including [i-A], [ii-A], and [iii-A] has fixed behavioral information and varied delivery methods of information. The column including [i-A], [i-B], and [i-C] has a fixed delivery method of information and varied behavioral information. Thus, each of the nine patterns was assigned to the five groups. Each group contained three participants to ensure that each pattern was evaluated by 15 participants. The order of patterns applied for a participant was randomly determined.

3.2 Evacuation Alert System Used in the Experiment

In the experiment, we used an experimental application designed for Android devices. The application allows an experimenter to send notifications and specified evacuation alerts to the participant's smartphone. When a participant tapes the alert notification shown in Fig. 2, disaster information is presented on the device. Figure 3 shows the information displayed on the evacuation alert application. The left of Fig. 3 is one example of the text message condition, in which only text appears in callouts. The right of Fig. 3 is one example of text-speaking and voice-speaking agent conditions. In the voice-speaking condition, voice speech is also an output.

For the humanoid agent, we imitated a person in the Japan Meteorological Agency or disaster announcers, generally recognized as people who convey disaster information in Japan. In this study, we set a male human-like agent with a suit as a model. The voice used in the voice-speaking agent condition was recorded by a voice actor imitating an announcer speaking in a calm tone.

The experimenter instructed the participants to answer the questionnaire immediately after confirming the disaster information. When the participants pressed the confirmation button on the screen shown in Fig. 3, a screen requesting responses to the questionnaire was displayed.

Group 1

[i-A]	[ii-A]	[iii-A]
[i-B]		
[i-C]		

Group 4

[i-A]		
[i-B]	[ii-B]	[iii-B]
[i-C]		

Group 7

[i-A]		
[i-B]		
[i-C]	[ii-C]	[iii-C]

Group 2

[i-A]	[ii-A]	[iii-A]
	[ii-B]	
	[ii-C]	

Group 5

	[ii-A]	
[i-B]	[ii-B]	[iii-B]
	[ii-C]	

Group 8

	[ii-A]	
	[ii-B]	
[i-C]	[ii-C]	[iii-C]

Group 3

[i-A]	[ii-A]	[iii-A]
		[iii-B]
		[iii-C]

Group 6

		[iii-A]
[i-B]	[ii-B]	[iii-B]
		[iii-C]

Group 9

		[iii-A]
		[iii-B]
[i-C]	[ii-C]	[iii-C]

Fig. 1. Patterns of the evacuation alerts evaluated by each group

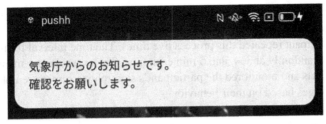

Fig. 2. Example of the notification (The notification is written in Japanese, saying, "Announcement from the Japan Meteorological Agency. Please check it.")

Fig. 3. Left figure shows one example of the text message condition, and the right is the text-speaking and voice-speaking agent conditions. In the callouts, some of the information defined in Table 1 are shown. In the voice-speaking condition, voice speech is also output. What is spoken is the same as the text in the callout.

3.3 Experimental Procedure

We first explained the flow and content of the experiment to the participant and obtained their consent to participate in the experiment. The experimenter left the room after explaining the experiment and confirming the start time, leaving only the participant in the room. However, the experimenter informed the participant that they were waiting outside the room and explained that the experiment could be interrupted at any time. Subsequently, the participants performed the specified daily task, watching YouTube videos, independently in a room with a rain soundscape. While the participant was watching the videos, they received one of the evacuation alerts on their phone. The participant confirmed it and then completed the questionnaire. After completing the questionnaire, they restarted watching videos.

Each participant repeated this process five times. The time interval for receiving the alerts was set randomly at 3, 4, and 5 min each time. The experimenter manually issued evacuation alerts and monitored the participant's smartphone screens remotely, sending tailored messages based on their behavior.

4 Results of the Experiment

4.1 Questionnaire Results

In this section, we present the questionnaire results and the analysis. We had 27 participants, and each alert pattern was evaluated by 15 participants. In the questionnaire, we asked the following questions in Table 2. The participants answered each question on a seven-point scale (1 = strongly disagree, 7 = strongly agree). Tables 3, 4, 5, 6 present the average scores for Q1–Q4, respectively. Two-way ANOVA was conducted for the text content and method of presentation. Table 7 shows the p-values obtained from the analysis.

Comparing the differences in delivery methods from Table 2 in Q1, which asked whether the message was directed to the participant, more positive answers were received in the text-speaking agent condition (ii) and the voice-speaking agent condition (iii). Even in the text message condition (i) and the text-speaking agent condition (ii), the browsing information condition (C), in which the behavioral information includes the category of the watched video, had positive answers that exceeded 5. Providing more specific behavioral information by a humanoid agent and voice enhanced the likelihood of positive responses to Q1. The results for Q2, which asked whether the message was relevant to the participant, were similar to Q1 and had more positive answers in the voice-speaking agent condition (iii). Patterns [iii-A] and [ii-C] had the same score of 5.27; the scores were high when specific behavioral information was presented, even without providing the information through a humanoid agent. The results of a two-way ANOVA for Q1 and Q2 in Table 7 showed significant differences in both delivery method and text content factors.

Table 2. Questionnaire items

	Questions
Q1	Did you think this message was directed at you?
Q2	Did you think the message was relevant to you?
Q3	Did you think that the disaster was happening close to you?
Q4	Did you think you would suffer from the disaster?

Table 3. Questionnaire results for Q1

		Method of presentation			Average
		[i]	[ii]	[iii]	
Text content	[A]	3.20	3.73	5.33	4.09
	[B]	3.73	4.53	5.67	4.64
	[C]	5.40	5.13	6.20	5.58
	Average	4.11	4.47	5.73	4.78

Table 4. Questionnaire results for Q2

		Method of presentation			Average
		[i]	[ii]	[iii]	
Text content	[A]	3.40	3.73	5.27	4.13
	[B]	3.60	4.40	5.60	4.53
	[C]	4.93	5.27	6.13	5.44
	Average	3.98	4.47	5.67	4.70

Table 5. Questionnaire results for Q3

		Method of presentation			Average
		[i]	[ii]	[iii]	
Text content	[A]	3.47	3.93	4.93	4.11
	[B]	3.20	3.67	5.13	4.00
	[C]	3.93	4.13	5.13	4.40
	Average	3.53	3.91	5.07	4.17

Table 6. Questionnaire results for Q4

		Method of presentation			Average
		[i]	[ii]	[iii]	
Text content	[A]	2.73	3.40	4.33	3.49
	[B]	2.73	3.13	4.53	3.47
	[C]	3.67	3.73	4.60	4.00
	Average	3.04	3.42	4.49	3.65

However, some results for Q3, which asked whether the disaster was happening close to the participant, had scores of 4 or less. However, the voice-speaking agent condition (iii) with the reception status condition (B) or browsing information condition (C) scored higher than 5. The analysis in Table 7 showed that while no significant differences in the text content factor were found, significant differences in the delivery method factor existed. The results for Q4, which asked whether the participant would suffer from the disaster, showed similar trends to the results for Q3, namely higher scores for the voice-speaking agent condition (iii) and the browsing information condition (C). However, the overall scores for Q4 were lower than those of other questions. The results of two-way ANOVA for Q4 showed significant differences in the text content and delivery method factors.

Table 7. Results of a two-way ANOVA

	Q1	Q2	Q3	Q4
Text content	0.000**	0.000**	0.256	0.034*
Method of presentation	0.000**	0.000**	0.000**	0.000**
Text content * Method of presentation	0.114	0.487	0.794	0.521

*:$p < 0.05$, **:$p < 0.01$t

4.2   Discussion

In the factor of the delivery method, the text-speaking agent condition and the voice-speaking agent condition achieved high scores for all questions from Q1 to Q4. These results suggest that providing a humanoid agent and voice information in evacuation alerts may effectively generate awareness of the disaster's relevancy to oneself. Notably, the voice information increased the scores significantly. Therefore, providing auditory information about evacuation alerts may strongly generate awareness of relevant disasters.

However, in the factor of text content, the scores for Q1 and Q2 tended to increase as the concreteness of the behavioral information increased. Still, the scores for Q3 and Q4 did not change even when the concreteness of information increased. However, expressions using browsing information, such as "This message is for you, who are watching music videos on YouTube," consistently had high scores. Alternatively, expressions that identified individuals effectively generated awareness of the disaster's relevancy to oneself.

However, the scores tended to be lower for Q3 and Q4, which asked whether the disaster was happening close to the participant or whether they would suffer from the disaster, compared to Q1 and Q2, which wondered whether this message was directed at the participant. Though the evacuation alert patterns in this study appear to indicate that the information is directed at the participants, their perception of the potential damage to their surroundings did not significantly increase.

5   Conclusion

In this study, we focused on evacuation alert services sending disaster information to personal mobile devices (i.e., smartphones) and considered the information expressions of alerts that generate awareness of the disaster's relevancy to oneself. As alert patterns, we considered the text content and delivery method of the alert. Concretely, the user's operational information on the smartphone was applied as the behavioral information. We also considered the effect of providing the text via a humanoid agent with voice. We conducted a comparative verification experiment on the nine patterns of evacuation alerts combining the text contents and delivery methods. For the delivery method, the results showed that the humanoid agent and voice information effectively generated awareness of the disaster's relevancy. The text contents showed that including participants' app browsing information in the text tended to increase the user's awareness of the disaster's relevancy.

Acknowledgement. This study was supported in part by JSPS KAKENHI (grant number JP20K11911).

References

1. Tanaka, K., Kato, T.: Perceived danger can be influenced by how the emergency information is expressed. Japanese J. Cogn. Psychol. **9**(1), 1–7 (2011)
2. Yasui, T., Kitamura, T., Izumi, T., Nakatani, Y.: A validation of textual expression about disaster information to induce evacuation. In: Proceedings of the 22th International Conference on Human-Computer Interaction (HCI'20), pp.289–301 (2020)
3. Janis, I.L., Feshbach, S.: Effects of fear-arousing communication. J. Ab-normal Soc. Psychol. **48**(1), 78–92 (1953)
4. Takayama, Y., Hirosaki, M.: Quick evacuation method for evacuation navigation system in poor communication environment at the time of disaster. In: Proceedings of the 2014 International Conference on Intelligent Networking and Collaborative Systems, pp.415–429 (2014)
5. Jing, L., Yamada, S., Terada, K.: Effects of agents' appearance on customer's buying motivations at online shopping site. Trans. Hum. Interface Soc. **17**(3), 307–316 (2015) (in Japanese)
6. Yano, T., Otsu, K., Izumi, T.: Verification of the effects of personalized evacuation alerts using behavioral or location information with the sense of urgency in a disaster. In: Proceedings of the 13th International Conference on Applied Human Factors and Ergonomics (AHFE 2022), Usability and User Experience, vol.39, pp.140–145 (2022)

Author Index

© The Editor(s) (if applicable) and The Author(s), under exclusive license
to Springer Nature Switzerland AG 2023
A. Coman and S. Vasilache (Eds.): HCII 2023, LNCS 14026, pp. 559–561, 2023.
https://doi.org/10.1007/978-3-031-35927-9

Printed in the United States
Baker & Taylor Publisher Services